Lecture Notes in Computer Science 4609

Commenced Publication in 1973
Founding and Former Series Editors:
Gerhard Goos, Juris Hartmanis, and Jan van Leeuwen

Erik Ernst (Ed.)

ECOOP 2007 – Object-Oriented Programming

21st European Conference
Berlin, Germany, July 30 - August 3, 2007
Proceedings

 Springer

Volume Editor

Erik Ernst
Department of Computer Science
University of Aarhus
Denmark
E-mail: eernst@daimi.au.dk

Library of Congress Control Number: 2007931196

CR Subject Classification (1998): D.1, D.2, D.3, F.3, C.2, K.4, J.1

LNCS Sublibrary: SL 2 – Programming and Software Engineering

ISSN   0302-9743
ISBN-10   3-540-73588-7 Springer Berlin Heidelberg New York
ISBN-13   978-3-540-73588-5 Springer Berlin Heidelberg New York

Springer is a part of Springer Science+Business Media

springer.com

© Springer-Verlag Berlin Heidelberg 2007
Printed in Germany

Typesetting: Camera-ready by author, data conversion by Scientific Publishing Services, Chennai, India
Printed on acid-free paper   SPIN: 12089611   06/3180   5 4 3 2 1 0

Preface

The 21st European Conference on Object-Oriented Programming, ECOOP 2007, was held in Berlin, Germany, on July 30 to August 3, 2007. ECOOP is the most important and inspiring forum in Europe and beyond for researchers, practitioners, and students working in that smorgasbord of topics and approaches known as object orientation. This topic area was explored and challenged by excellent invited speakers—two of which were the winners of this year's Dahl-Nygaard award—in the carefully refereed and selected technical papers, on posters, via demonstrations, and in tutorials. Each of the many workshops complemented this with a very interactive and dynamic treatment of more specific topics. Finally, panels allowed for loud and lively disagreement. Yet, it is one of ECOOP's special qualities that this plethora of activities add up to a coherent and exciting whole, rather than deteriorating into chaos.

The Program Committee received 161 submissions this year. Only 135 of them were carried through the full review process, because of a number of retractions and a number of submissions of abstracts that were never followed by a full paper. However, the remaining papers were of very high quality and we accepted 25 of them for publication. Helping very good papers to be published is more useful than having an impressively low acceptance rate. The papers were selected according to four groups of criteria, whose priority depended on the paper: relevance; originality and significance; precision and correctness; and presentation and clarity. Each paper had three, four, or five reviews, depending on how controversial it was. As a new thing this year we let the authors read their reviews before the Program Committee meeting, and solicited a short response from the authors; this seemed to be helpful in several ways. The discussions at the Program Committee meeting, February 1–2 2007, were often long and agitated, but at the end we were happy with the result.

The success of ECOOP 2007 was only possible because of the dedication, inspiration, and plain hard work of many people. I would like to thank the authors for submitting so many high-quality papers. I would also like to thank the Program Committee for writing the more than 500 reviews and participating very actively in the Program Committee meeting; the Organizing Chair Stephan Herrmann for helping with numerous problems along the way; the AITO Executive board and especially Dave Thomas for their good advice on several occasions; Richard van de Stadt who was in charge of the submission Web site and its software, for his impressively quick response times, high quality of work, and generally friendly nature; and finally Karen Kjær Møller, who helped us all very much with administrative and similar tasks during the Program Committee meeting.

May 2007   Erik Ernst

Organization

ECOOP 2007 was organized by the Institute for Communication and Software Technology at the Technical University of Berlin, under the auspices of AITO (Association Internationale pour les Technologies Objets) and in cooperation with ACM SIGPLAN and SIGSOFT.

Executive Committee

Conference Chairs
  Stefan Jähnichen (Technical University of Berlin, Germany)
  Peter Fritzson (University of Linköping, Sweden)
Program Chair
  Erik Ernst (University of Aarhus, Denmark)
Organizing Chairs
  Stephan Herrmann (Technical University of Berlin, Germany)
  Uwe Aßmann (Dresden University of Technology, Germany)

Organizing Committee

Demonstration and Poster Chairs
  Sabine Glesner (Technical University of Berlin, Germany)
  Christoph Meinel (Hasso Plattner Institute, Potsdam, Germany)
Doctoral Symposium Chair
  Danny Dig (University of Illinois at Urbana-Champaign, USA)
Exhibition Chairs
  Dirk Seifert (Technical University of Berlin, Germany)
  Peter Möckel (Deutsche Telekom Laboratories, Germany)
Panel Chairs
  Bernd Mahr (Technical University of Berlin, Germany)
  Judith Bishop (University of Pretoria, South Africa)
Tutorial Chairs
  Thomas Santen (Technical University of Berlin, Germany)
  Klaus Grimm (DaimlerChrysler AG, Germany)
Workshop Chairs
  Peter Pepper (Technical University of Berlin, Germany)
  Arnd Poetzsch-Heffter (Technical University of Kaiserslautern, Germany)

Workshop Committee
  Uwe Aßmann (Dresden University of Technology, Germany)
  Lodewijk Bergmans (University of Twente, The Netherlands)
  Nick Mitchell (IBM T.J. Watson Research Center, USA)
  Mario Südholt (Ecole des Mines, Nantes-INRIA, France)
  Jan Vitek (Purdue University, USA)

Sponsoring Organizations

Gold

Silver

Bronze

Program Committee

Mehmet Aksit (University of Twente, The Netherlands)
Jonathan Aldrich (Carnegie Mellon University, USA)
Gabriela Arévalo (Universidad Nacional de La Plata, Argentina)
Uwe Aßmann (Dresden University of Technology, Germany)
Andrew P. Black (Portland State University, USA)
Gilad Bracha (Cadence Design Systems, USA)
Shigeru Chiba (Tokyo Institute of Technology, Japan)
Yvonne Coady (University of Victoria, Canada)
Krzysztof Czarnecki (University of Waterloo, Canada)
Wolfgang De Meuter (Vrije Universiteit Brussel, Belgium)
Theo D'Hondt (Vrije Universiteit Brussel, Belgium)
Stéphane Ducasse (Université de Savoie, France)

Erik Ernst (University of Aarhus, Denmark)
Yossi Gil (The Technion, Israel)
Görel Hedin (Lund University, Sweden)
Urs Hölzle (Google Inc., USA)
Eric Jul (University of Copenhagen, Denmark)
Gerti Kappel (Vienna University of Technology, Austria)
Gregor Kiczales (University of British Columbia, Canada)
Karl Lieberherr (Northeastern University, USA)
Luigi Liquori (INRIA Sophia Antipolis, France)
David H. Lorenz (University of Virginia, USA)
Sean McDirmid (École Polytechnique Fédérale de Lausanne, Switzerland)
Erik Meijer (Microsoft, USA)
Birger Møller-Pedersen (University of Oslo, Norway)
James Noble (University of Wellington, New Zealand)
Klaus Ostermann (Darmstadt University of Technology, Germany)
Awais Rashid (Lancaster University, UK)
Nathanael Schärli (Google Inc., Switzerland)
Ulrik Pagh Schultz (University of Southern Denmark, Denmark)
Olin Shivers (Northeastern University, USA)
Mario Südholt (École des Mines de Nantes, France)
Clemens Szyperski (Microsoft, USA)
Peri Tarr (IBM T.J. Watson Research Center, USA)
Frank Tip (IBM T.J. Watson Research Center, USA)
Mads Torgersen (Microsoft, USA)
Mirko Viroli (Alma Mater Studiorum - Università di Bologna, Italy)
Jan Vitek (Purdue University, USA)
Roel Wuyts (Université Libre de Bruxelles, Belgium)
Elena Zucca (University of Genova, Italy)

Referees

Ahmed Abdelmeged	Nels Beckman	Maurizio Cimadamore
Marwan Abi-Antoun	Alexandre Bergel	Charles Consel
Jonathan Aldrich	Lodewijk Bergmans	Pascal Costanza
Ilham Alloui	Klaas van den Berg	Tom Van Cutsem
Tristan O.R. Allwood	Robert Bialek	Olivier Danvy
Vander Alves	Kevin Bierhoff	Jessie Dedecker
Davide Ancona	Christoph Bockisch	Birgit Demuth
Michal Antkiewicz	Elisa Gonzalez Boix	Marcus Denker
Leandro Antonelli	Viviana Bono	Brecht Desmet
Ivica Aracic	John Boyland	Dirk van Deun
Federico Balaguer	Pim van den Broek	Christophe Dony
Jennifer Baldwin	Walter Cazzola	Sophia Drossopoulou
Andreas Bartho	Bryan Chadwick	Andrew D. Eisenberg
Thiago Bartolomei	Ciera Christopher	Torbjörn Ekman

Sonia Fagorzi
Cormac Flanagan
Manuel Fähndrich
Alessandro Garcia
Alejandra Garrido
Vaidas Gasiunas
Sofie Goderis
Ryan M. Golbeck
Aaron Greenhouse
Giovanna Guerrini
Gurcan Gulesir
Kris Gybels
Christine Hang
Wilke Havinga
Florian Heidenreich
Charlotte Herzeel
Anders Hesselund
Robert Hirschfeld
Christian Hofer
Christian Hofmann
Terry Hon
Tony Hosking
Marianne Huchard
Christian Huemer
Jendrik Johannes
Andy Kellens
Tim Klinger
Sergei Kojarski
Gerhard Kramler

Stein Krogdahl
Adrian Kuhn
Ivan Kurtev
Giovanni Lagorio
Katja Lehmann
Keren Lenz
Ondřej Lhoták
Adrian Lienhard
Chuan-kai Lin
Ralf Lämmel
Michael Maher
Donna Malayeri
Itay Maman
Chris Matthews
Weiquin Ma
Stephan Merz
Isabel Michiels
Sam Michiels
Stijn Mostinckx
Emerson Murphy-Hill
Clémentine Nebut
Oscar Nierstrasz
David Notkin
Nathaniel Nystrom
Martin Odersky
Ellen Van Paesschen
Ebraert Peter
Damien Pollet
Claudia Pons

Jean Privat
Coen De Roover
Alexandru D. Salcianu
Corina Sas
Ilie Savga
Thorsten Schäfer
Mirko Seifert
Damien Sereni
Arjun Singh
Therapon Skotiniotis
Yuiri Solodkyy
Hasan Sozer
Tom Staijen
Bjarne Stroustrup
Stan Sutton
Bedir Tekinerdogan
Stijn Timbermont
Christelle Urtado
Dale Vaillancourt
Jorge Vallejos
Sylvain Vauttier
Andrzej Wasowski
Nathan Weston
John Whaley
Manuel Wimmer
Tobias Wrigstad
Arturo Zambrano

Table of Contents

Programs and Predicates

Language Design

Inheritance and Derivation

Dahl-Nygaard Prize Invited Talk

Aspects

Language About Language

Erlang – Software for a Concurrent World

Joe Armstrong

Ericsson AB
joe.armstrong@ericsson.com

Abstract. This talk is about Erlang and Concurrency Oriented Programming. We start with a short history of Erlang and of shared state and message passing concurrency. We argue that it is impossible to make fault-tolerant systems using mutable shared state concurrency models. We explain the thinking behind what has become known as "Erlang style concurrency" and show the relation to Concurrency Oriented Programming. We take a brief detour and talk about the commercial spread of Erlang, highlighting some of the more successful products and companies based on Erlang. We talk about the general problem of programming multicore computers and show how the goal of achieving factor N speedups on N-core processors with no change to the code, is being realised.

E. Ernst (Ed.): ECOOP 2007, LNAI 4609, p. 1, 2007.

Gradual Typing for Objects

Jeremy Siek[1] and Walid Taha[2]

[1] University of Colorado, Boulder, CO 80309, USA
and LogicBlox Inc., Atlanta, GA 30309, USA
jeremy.siek@colorado.edu
[2] Rice University, Houston, TX 77005, USA
taha@rice.edu

Abstract. Static and dynamic type systems have well-known strengths and weaknesses. In previous work we developed a *gradual type system* for a functional calculus named $\lambda_{\rightarrow}^{?}$. Gradual typing provides the benefits of both static and dynamic checking in a single language by allowing the programmer to control whether a portion of the program is type checked at compile-time or run-time by adding or removing type annotations on variables. Several object-oriented scripting languages are preparing to add static checking. To support that work this paper develops $\mathbf{Ob}_{<:}^{?}$, a gradual type system for object-based languages, extending the $\mathbf{Ob}_{<:}$ calculus of Abadi and Cardelli. Our primary contribution is to show that gradual typing and subtyping are orthogonal and can be combined in a principled fashion. We also develop a small-step semantics, provide a machine-checked proof of type safety, and improve the space efficiency of higher-order casts.

1   Introduction

Static and dynamic typing have complementary strengths, making them better for different tasks and stages of development. Static typing provides full-coverage error detection, efficient execution, and machine-checked documentation whereas dynamic typing enables rapid development and fast adaptation to changing requirements. *Gradual typing* allows a programmer to mix static and dynamic checking in a program and provides a convenient way to control which parts of a program are statically checked. The goals for gradual typing are:

- Programmers may omit type annotations on parameters and immediately run the program; run-time type checks are performed to preserve type safety.
- Programmers may add type annotations to increase static checking. When all parameters are annotated, *all* type errors are caught at compile-time.[1]
- The type system and semantics should minimize the implementation burden on language implementors.

In previous work we introduced gradual typing in the context of a functional calculus named $\lambda_{\rightarrow}^{?}$ [47]. This calculus extends the simply typed lambda calculus

---

[1] The language under study does not include arrays so the claim that we catch all type errors does not include the static detection of out-of-bound errors.

E. Ernst (Ed.): ECOOP 2007, LNAI 4609, pp. 2–27, 2007.

with a statically unknown (dynamic) type ? and replaces type equality with type consistency to allow for implicit coercions that add and remove ?s.

Developers of the object-oriented scripting languages Perl 6 [49] and JavaScript 4 [27] expressed interest in our work on gradual typing. In response, this paper develops the type theoretic foundation for gradual typing in object-oriented languages. Our work is based on the $\mathbf{Ob}^{<:}$ calculus of Abadi and Cardelli, a statically-typed object calculus with structural subtyping. We develop an extended calculus, named $\mathbf{Ob}^{?}_{<:}$, that adds the type ? and replaces the use of subtyping with a relation that integrates subtyping with type consistency.

The boundary between static and dynamic typing is a fertile area of research and the literature addresses many goals that are closely related to those we outline above. Section 8 describes the related work in detail.

The paper starts with a programmer's and an implementor's tour of gradual typing (Sections 2 and 3 respectively) before proceeding with the technical development of the new results in Sections 4, through 7.

Technical Contributions. This paper includes the following original contributions:

1. The primary contribution of this paper shows that type consistency and subtyping are orthogonal and can be naturally superimposed (Section 4).
2. We develop a syntax-directed type system for $\mathbf{Ob}^{?}_{<:}$ (Section 5).
3. We define a semantics for $\mathbf{Ob}^{?}_{<:}$ via a translation to the intermediate language with explicit casts $\mathbf{Ob}^{\langle\cdot\rangle}_{<:}$ for which we define a small-step operational semantics (Section 6).
4. We improve the space efficiency of the operational semantics for higher-order casts by applying casts in a lazy fashion to objects (Section 6).
5. We prove that $\mathbf{Ob}^{?}_{<:}$ is type safe (Section 7). The proof is a streamlined variant of Wright and Felleisen's syntactic approach to type soundness [5, 53]. The formalization and proof are based on a proof of type safety for $\mathbf{FOb}^{?}_{<:}$ (a superset of $\mathbf{Ob}^{?}_{<:}$ that also includes functions) we wrote in the Isar proof language [52] and checked using the Isabelle proof assistant [39]. The formalization for $\mathbf{FOb}^{?}_{<:}$ is available in a technical report [46].
6. We prove that $\mathbf{Ob}^{?}_{<:}$ is statically type safe for fully annotated programs (Section 7), that is, we show that neither cast exceptions nor type errors may occur during program execution.

2   A Programmer's View of Gradual Typing

We give a description of gradual typing from a programmer's point of view, showing examples in hypothetical variant of the ECMAScript (aka JavaScript) programming language [15] that provides gradual typing. The following Point class definition has no type annotations on the data member x or the dx parameter. The gradual type system therefore delays checks concerning x and dx inside the move method until run-time, as would a dynamically typed language.

```
class Point {
    var x = 0
    function move(dx) { this.x = this.x + dx }
}
var a : int = 1
var p = new Point
p.move(a)
```

More precisely, because the types of the variables x and dx are statically un-known the gradual type system gives them the "dynamic" type, written ? for short. The reader may wonder why we do not infer the type of x from its ini-tializer 0. We discuss the relation between gradual typing and type inference in Section 8. Now suppose the + operator expects arguments of type **int**. The gradual type system allows an *implicit coercion* from type ? to **int**. This kind of coercion could fail (like a down cast) and therefore must be dynamically checked. In statically-typed object-oriented languages, such as Java and C#, implicit up-casts are allowed (they never fail) but not implicit down-casts. Allowing implicit coercions that may fail is *the* distinguishing feature of gradual typing and is what allows gradual typing to support dynamic typing.

To enable the gradual migration of code from dynamic to static checking, gradual typing allows for a mixture of the two and provides seamless interaction between them. In the example above, we define a variable a of type **int**, and invoke the dynamically typed move method. Here the gradual type system allows an implicit coercion from **int** to ?. This is a safe coercion—it can never fail at run-time—however the run-time system needs to remember the type of the value so that it can check the type when it casts back to **int** inside of move.

Gradual typing also allows implicit coercions among more complicated types, such as object types. An object type is similar to a Java-style interface in that it contains a list of member signatures, however object types are compared struc-turally instead of by name. In the following example, the equal method has a parameter o annotated with the object type [x:**int**].

```
class Point {
    var x = 0
    function bool equal(o : [x:int]) { return this.x == o.x }
}
var p = new Point
var q = new Point
p.equal(q)
```

The method invocation p.equal(q) is allowed by the gradual type system. The type of parameter o is [x:**int**] whereas the type of the argument q is [x:?,equal:[x:**int**]→**bool**]. We compare the two types structurally, one member at a time. For x we have a coercion from ? to **int**, so that is allowed. Now consider the equal member. Because this is an object-oriented language with subtyping, we can use an object with more methods in a place that is expecting an object with fewer methods.

Next we look at a fully annotated program, that is, a program where all the variables are annotated with types. In this case the gradual type system acts like a static type system and catches *all* type errors during compilation. In the example below, the invocation of the annotated move method with a string argument is flagged as a static type error.

```
class Point {
    var x : int = 0
    function Point move(dx : int) { this.x = this.x + dx }
}
var p = new Point
p.move("hi") // static type error
```

3   An Implementor's View of Gradual Typing

Next we give an overview of gradual typing from a language implementor's point of view, describing the type system and semantics. The main idea of the type system is that we replace the use of type equality with type consistency, written $\sim$. The intuition behind type consistency is to check whether the two types are equal in the parts where both types are known. The following are a few examples. The notation $[l_1 : s_1, \ldots, l_n : s_n]$ is an object type where $l : s$ is the name l and signature s of a method. A signature has the form $\tau \to \tau'$, where τ is the parameter type and τ' is the return type of the method.

$$\text{int} \sim \text{int} \qquad \text{int} \not\sim \text{bool} \qquad ? \sim \text{int} \qquad \text{int} \sim ?$$

$$[x : \text{int} \to ?, y : ? \to \text{bool}] \sim [y : \text{bool} \to ?, x : ? \to \text{int}]$$

$$[x : \text{int} \to \text{int}, y : ? \to \text{bool}] \not\sim [x : \text{bool} \to \text{int}, y :? \to \text{bool}]$$

$$[x : \text{int} \to \text{int}, y : ? \to ?] \not\sim [x : \text{int} \to \text{int}]$$

To express the "where both types are known" part of the type consistency relation, we define a restriction operator, written $\sigma|_\tau$. This operator "masks off" the parts of type σ that are unknown in type τ. For example,

$$\text{int}|_? = ? \qquad \text{int}|_{\text{bool}} = \text{int}$$

$$[x : \text{int} \to \text{int}, y : \text{int} \to \text{int}]|_{[x: ? \to ?, y:\text{int} \to \text{int}]} = [x : ? \to ?, y : \text{int} \to \text{int}]$$

The restriction operator is defined as follows.

$$
\begin{aligned}
\sigma|_\tau = \ &\textbf{case } (\sigma, \tau) \textbf{ of} \\
&\quad (-, ?) \Rightarrow ? \\
&\ | \ ([l_1 : s_1, \ldots, l_n : s_n], [l_1 : t_1, \ldots, l_n : t_n]) \Rightarrow \\
&\qquad [l_1 : s_1|_{t_1}, \ldots, l_n : s_n|_{t_n}] \\
&\ | \ (-, -) \Rightarrow \sigma
\end{aligned}
$$

$$(\sigma_1 \to \sigma_2)|_{(\tau_1 \to \tau_2)} = (\sigma_1|_{\tau_1}) \to (\sigma_2|_{\tau_2})$$

Definition 1. *Two types σ and τ are* **consistent,** *written $\sigma \sim \tau$, iff $\sigma|_\tau = \tau|_\sigma$, that is, when the types are equal where they are both known.*[2]

Proposition 1. *(Basic Properties of $\sim$)*

1. $\sim$ *is reflexive.*
2. $\sim$ *is symmetric.*
3. $\sim$ *is not transitive. For example,* bool $\sim$? *and* ? $\sim$ int *but* bool $\not\sim$ int.
4. $\tau \sim \tau|_\sigma$.
5. *If neither σ nor τ contain* ?, *then $\sigma \sim \tau$ iff $\sigma = \tau$.*

A gradual type system uses type consistency where a simple type system uses type equality. For example, in the following hypothetical rule for method invocation, the argument and parameter types must be consistent.

$$\frac{\Gamma \vdash e_1 : [\ldots, l : \sigma \to \tau, \ldots] \quad \Gamma \vdash e_2 : \sigma' \quad \sigma' \sim \sigma}{\Gamma \vdash e_1.l(e_2) : \tau}$$

Gradual typing corresponds to static typing when no ? appear in the program (either explicitly or implicitly) because when neither σ nor τ contain ?, we have $\sigma \sim \tau$ if and only if $\sigma = \tau$, as stated in Proposition 1.

Broadly speaking, there are two ways to implement the run-time behavior of a gradually typed language. One option is to erase the type annotations and interpret the program as if it were dynamically typed. This is an easy way to extend a dynamically typed language with gradual typing. The disadvantages of this approach is that unnecessary run-time type checks are performed and some errors become manifest later in the execution of the program. We do not describe this approach here as it is straightforward to implement.

The second approach performs run-time type checks at the boundaries of dynamically and statically typed code. The advantage is that statically typed code performs no run-time type checks. But there is an extra cost in that run-time tags contain complete types so that objects may be completely checked at boundaries. There are observable differences between the two approaches. The following example runs to completion with the first approach but produces an error with the second approach.

```
function unit foo(dx : int) { }
var x : ? = false; foo(x)
```

In this paper we give a high-level description of the second approach by defining a cast-inserting translation from $\mathbf{Ob}^?_{<:}$ to an intermediate language with explicit casts named $\mathbf{Ob}^{\langle\cdot\rangle}_{<:}$. The explicit casts have the form $\langle \tau \Leftarrow \sigma \rangle e$, where σ is the type of the expression e and τ is the target type. As an example of cast-insertion, consider the translation of the unannotated move method.

---

[2] We chose the name "consistency" because it is analogous to the consistency of partial functions. This analogy can be made precise by viewing types as trees and then using the standard encoding of trees as partial functions from tree-paths to labels [41]. The ?s are interpreted as places where the partial function is undefined.

```
function move(dx) { this.x = this.x + dx }
⤳ function ? move(dx : ?) { this.x = ⟨?⇐ int⟩(⟨int⇐ ?⟩this.x + ⟨int⇐ ?⟩dx) }
```

We define the run-time behavior of $\mathbf{Ob}^{\langle\cdot\rangle}_{<:}$ with a small-step operational semantics in Section 6. The operational semantics defines rewrite rules that simplify an expression until it is either a value or until it gets stuck (no rewrite rules apply). A stuck expression corresponds to an error. We distinguish between two kinds of errors: *cast errors* and *type errors*. A cast error occurs when the run-time type of a value is not consistent with the target type of the cast. Cast errors can be thought of as triggering exceptions, though for simplicity we do not model exceptions here. We categorize all other stuck expressions as type errors.

Definition 2. *A program is* **statically type safe** *when neither cast nor type errors can occur during execution. A program is* **type safe** *when no type errors can occur during execution.*

In Section 7 we show that any $\mathbf{Ob}^{?}_{<:}$ program is *type safe* and that any $\mathbf{Ob}^{?}_{<:}$ program that is fully annotated is *statically type safe*.

4 Combining Gradual Typing and Subtyping

In previous work we discovered that approaches to gradual typing based on subtyping and ? as "top" do not achieve *static type safety* for fully annotated terms [47]. The problem is that if you allow an implicit down-cast from "top" to any type (? <: S), then you can use the normal up-cast rule R <: ? and transitivity to deduce R <: S for *any* two types R and S. The resulting type system therefore accepts all programs and does not reject programs that have static type errors. This discovery led us to the type consistency relation which formed the basis for our gradual type system for functional languages. However, subtyping is a central feature of object-oriented languages, so the question is how can we add subtyping to gradual type system while maintaining static type safety for fully annotated terms? It turns out to be as simple as adding subsumption:

$$\frac{\Gamma \vdash e : \sigma \quad \sigma <: \tau}{\Gamma \vdash e : \tau}$$

We do not treat ? as the top of the subtype hierarchy, but instead treat ? as neutral to subtyping, with only ? <: ?. The following defines subtyping.[3]

$$\text{int} <: \text{int} \quad \text{float} <: \text{float} \quad \text{bool} <: \text{bool} \quad ? <: ?$$

$$\text{int} <: \text{float} \quad [l_i : s_i{}^{i \in 1...n+m}] <: [l_i : s_i{}^{i \in 1...n}]$$

---

[3] The calculus $\mathbf{Ob}^{?}_{<:}$ does not include functions, so no subtyping rules for function types are provided here. The calculus $\mathbf{FOb}^{?}_{<:}$ in the technical report [46] includes function types.

While the type system is straightforward to define, more care is needed to define 1) a type checking *algorithm* and 2) an operational semantics that takes subtyping into account. In this section we discuss the difficulties in defining a type checking algorithm and present a solution.

It is well known that a type checking algorithm cannot use the subsumption rule because it is inherently non-deterministic. (The algorithm would need to guess when to apply the rule and what target type to use.) Instead of using subsumption, the standard approach is to use the subtype relation in the other typing rules where necessary [41]. The following is the result of applying this transformation to our gradually typed method invocation rule.

$$\frac{\Gamma \vdash e_1 : [\ldots, l : \sigma \to \tau, \ldots] \quad \Gamma \vdash e_2 : \sigma' \quad \sigma' <: \sigma'' \quad \sigma'' \sim \sigma}{\Gamma \vdash e_1.l(e_2) : \tau}$$

This rule still contains some non-determinacy because of the type σ''. We need a combined relation that directly compares σ' and σ.

Fortunately there is a natural way to define a relation that takes both type consistency and subtyping into account. To review, two types are consistent when they are equal where both are known, i.e., $\sigma \sim \tau$ iff $\sigma|_\tau = \tau|_\sigma$. To combine type consistency with subtyping, we replace type equality with subtyping.

Definition 3 (Consistent-Subtyping). $\sigma \lesssim \tau \equiv \sigma|_\tau <: \tau|_\sigma$

Here we apply the restriction operator to types σ and τ that may differ according to the subtype relationship, so we must update the definition of restriction to allow for objects of differing widths, as shown below.

$$\sigma|_\tau = \textbf{case } (\sigma, \tau) \textbf{ of}$$
$$(-, ?) \Rightarrow ?$$
$$| \ ([l_1 : s_1, \ldots, l_n : s_n], [l_1 : t_1, \ldots, l_m : t_m]) \textbf{ where } n \leq m \Rightarrow$$
$$[l_1 : s_1|_{t_1}, \ldots, l_n : s_n|_{t_n}]$$
$$| \ ([l_1 : s_1, \ldots, l_n : s_n], [l_1 : t_1, \ldots, l_m : t_m]) \textbf{ where } n > m \Rightarrow$$
$$[l_1 : s_1|_{t_1}, \ldots, l_m : s_m|_{t_m}, l_{m+1} : s_{m+1}, \ldots, l_n : s_n]$$
$$| \ (-, -) \Rightarrow \sigma$$

$$(\sigma_1 \to \sigma_2)|_{(\tau_1 \to \tau_2)} = (\sigma_1|_{\tau_1}) \to (\sigma_2|_{\tau_2})$$

The following proposition allows us to replace the conjunction $\sigma' <: \sigma''$ and $\sigma'' \sim \sigma$ with $\sigma' \lesssim \sigma$ in the gradual method invocation rule.

Proposition 2 (Properties of Consistent-Subtyping). *The following are equivalent:*

1. $\sigma \lesssim \tau$,
2. $\sigma <: \sigma'$ *and* $\sigma' \sim \tau$ *for some* σ'*, and*
3. $\sigma \sim \sigma''$ *and* $\sigma'' <: \tau$ *for some* σ''*.*

The method invocation rule can now be formulated in a syntax-directed fashion using the consistent-subtyping relation.

$$\frac{\Gamma \vdash e_1 : [\ldots, l : \sigma \to \tau, \ldots] \quad \Gamma \vdash e_2 : \sigma' \quad \sigma' \lesssim \sigma}{\Gamma \vdash e_1.l(e_2) : \tau}$$

It is helpful to think of the type consistency and subtyping relation as allowing types to differ along two different axes, with $\sim$ along the x-axis and $<:$ along the y-axis. With this intuition, the following informal diagram represents Proposition 2.

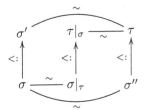

The following is an example of the above diagram for a particular choice of types.

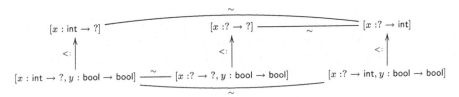

5   A Gradually Typed Object Calculus

We define a gradually typed object calculus named $\mathbf{Ob}^{?}_{<:}$ by extending Abadi and Cardelli's $\mathbf{Ob}_{<:}$ [1] with the unknown type ?. For purposes of exposition, we add one parameter (in addition to self) to methods. The syntax of $\mathbf{Ob}^{?}_{<:}$ includes three constructs for working with objects. The form $[l_i = \tau_i \, \varsigma(x_i : \sigma_i)e_i \ ^{i \in 1 \ldots n}]$ creates an object containing a set of methods. Each method has a name l_i, a parameter x_i with type annotation σ_i, a body e_i, and a return type τ_i. The ς symbol just means "method" and is reminiscent of the λ used in functional calculi. The self parameter is implicit. Omitting a type annotation is short-hand for annotating with type ?. Multi-parameter methods can be encoded using single-parameter methods [1]. The form $e_1.l(e_2)$ is a method invocation, where e_1 is the receiver object, l is the method to invoke, and e_2 is the argument. The form $e_1.l := \tau \, \varsigma(x:\sigma)e_2$ is a method update. The result is a copy of e_1 except that its method l is replaced by the right-hand side. Abadi and Cardelli chose not to represent fields in the core calculus but instead encode fields as methods. The following is an example of a point object in $\mathbf{Ob}^{?}_{<:}$:

[equal=**bool** ς(p:[x:**int**]) self.x.eq(p.x), x=zero].

Variables	$x \in \mathbb{X}$	$\supseteq$ {self}	
Method labels	$l \in \mathbb{L}$		
Ground Types	$\gamma \in \mathbb{G}$	$\supseteq$ {bool, int, float, unit}	
Constants	$c \in \mathbb{C}$	$\supseteq$ {true, false, zero, 0.0, ()}	
Types	ρ, σ, τ	$::= \gamma \mid [l_i : s_i{}^{i \in 1 \ldots n}]$	
Method Sig.	s, t	$::= \tau \rightarrow \tau$	
Expressions	e	$::= x \mid c \mid [l_i{=}_{\tau_i}\, \varsigma(x_i{:}\sigma_i)\, e_i{}^{i \in 1 \ldots n}] \mid$	

$e \in \mathbf{Ob}_{<:}$

$$e.l(e) \mid e.l{:=}_\tau\, \varsigma(x{:}\sigma)e$$

Syntactic Sugar	$l{=}e : \tau$	$\equiv\; l{=}_\tau\, \varsigma(x{:}\mathsf{unit})e$	$(x \notin e)$
	$e.l$	$\equiv\; e.l(())$	
	$e_1.l{:=}e_2 : \tau$	$\equiv\; e_1.l{:=}_\tau\, \varsigma(x{:}\mathsf{unit})e_2$	$(x \notin e)$

Types	ρ, σ, τ	$\mathrel{+}= ?$	

$e \in \mathbf{Ob}_{<:}^{?} \supset \mathbf{Ob}_{<:}$

Syntactic Sugar	$\varsigma(x)e$	$\equiv\; ?\, \varsigma(x{:}?)e$
	$l{=}e$	$\equiv\; l{=}e : ?$
	$e_1.l{:=}e_2$	$\equiv\; e_1.l{:=}e_2 : ?$

The gradual type system for $\mathbf{Ob}_{<:}^{?}$ is shown in Figure 1. (For reference, the type system for $\mathbf{Ob}_{<:}$ is in the Appendix, Fig. 4.) We use the symbol Γ for environments, which are finite partial functions from variables to types. The type system is parameterized on a *TypeOf* function that maps constants to types.

There are two rules for each elimination form. The first rule handles the case when the type of the receiver is unknown and the second rule handles when the type of the receiver is known. In the (GIVK1) rule for method invocation, the type of the receiver e_1 is unknown and the type of the argument e_2 is unconstrained. The rule (GIVK2) is described in Section 4, and is where we use the consistent-subtyping relation $\lesssim$. The rule (GUPD1) for method update handles the case when the type of the receiver e_1 is unknown. The new method body is type checked in an environment where self is bound to ? and the parameter x is bound to its declared type σ. The result type for this expression is $[l : \sigma \rightarrow \tau]$. [4] The rule (GUPD2) handles the case for method update when the type of the receiver is an object type ρ. The new method body is type checked in an environment where self is bound to ρ and x is bound to its declared type σ. The constraints $\sigma_k \lesssim \sigma$ and $\tau \lesssim \tau_k$ make sure that the new method can be coerced to the type of the old method.

---

[4] The result type for (GUPD1) is somewhat unsatisfactory because a method $l' \neq l$ can be invoked on e but not on the updated version of e. This can be easily resolved by extending the type system to include open object types in addition to closed object types, as is done in OCaml. If an object has an open object type you may invoke methods that are not listed in its type.

$$\boxed{\Gamma \vdash_G e : \tau}$$

$$(\text{GVAR}) \qquad \frac{\Gamma(x) = \tau}{\Gamma \vdash_G x : \tau}$$

$$(\text{GCONST}) \qquad \Gamma \vdash_G c : \mathit{TypeOf}(c)$$

$$(\text{GOBJ}) \qquad \frac{\Gamma, \mathsf{self} : \rho, x_i : \sigma_i \vdash_G e_i : \tau_i \quad \forall i \in 1 \ldots n}{\Gamma \vdash_G [l_i =_{\tau_i} \varsigma(x_i : \sigma_i) e_i{}^{i \in 1 \ldots n}] : \rho}$$
$$(\text{where } \rho \equiv [l_i : \sigma_i \to \tau_i{}^{i \in 1 \ldots n}])$$

$$(\text{GIVK1}) \qquad \frac{\Gamma \vdash_G e_1 : ? \quad \Gamma \vdash_G e_2 : \tau}{\Gamma \vdash_G e_1.l(e_2) : ?}$$

$$(\text{GIVK2}) \qquad \frac{\Gamma \vdash_G e_1 : [\ldots, l : \sigma \to \tau, \ldots] \quad \Gamma \vdash_G e_2 : \sigma' \quad \sigma' \lesssim \sigma}{\Gamma \vdash_G e_1.l(e_2) : \tau}$$

$$(\text{GUPD1}) \qquad \frac{\Gamma \vdash_G e : ? \quad \Gamma, \mathsf{self} : ?, x : \sigma \vdash e' : \tau}{\Gamma \vdash_G e.l :=_\tau \varsigma(x : \sigma) e' : [l : \sigma \to \tau]}$$

$$(\text{GUPD2}) \qquad \frac{\Gamma \vdash_G e_1 : \rho \quad \Gamma, \mathsf{self} : \rho, x : \sigma \vdash_G e_2 : \tau \quad \sigma_k \lesssim \sigma \quad \tau \lesssim \tau_k}{\Gamma \vdash_G e_1.l_k :=_\tau \varsigma(x : \sigma) e_2 : \rho}$$
$$(\text{where } \rho \equiv [l_i : \sigma_i \to \tau_i{}^{i \in 1 \ldots n}] \text{ and } k \in 1 \ldots n)$$

Fig. 1. A Gradual Type System for Objects

6 A Semantics for $\mathbf{Ob}^{?}_{<:}$

In this section we define a semantics for $\mathbf{Ob}^{?}_{<:}$ by defining a cast-inserting translation to the intermediate language $\mathbf{Ob}^{\langle \cdot \rangle}_{<:}$ and by defining an operational semantics for $\mathbf{Ob}^{\langle \cdot \rangle}_{<:}$. The syntax and typing rules for the intermediate language are those of $\mathbf{Ob}_{<:}$ [1] (Fig. 4 of the Appendix) extended with an explicit cast. The syntax and typing rule for the explicit cast are shown below.

Intermediate Language

$$\text{Expressions} \quad e \quad += \langle \tau \Leftarrow \tau \rangle e \qquad\qquad \boxed{e \in \mathbf{Ob}^{\langle \cdot \rangle}_{<:} \supset \mathbf{Ob}_{<:}}$$

$$\cdots \qquad \frac{\Gamma \vdash e : \sigma \quad \sigma \sim \tau \quad \sigma \neq \tau}{\Gamma \vdash \langle \tau \Leftarrow \sigma \rangle e : \tau} \qquad\qquad \boxed{\Gamma \vdash e : \tau}$$

Most run-time systems for dynamic languages associate a "type tag" with each value so that run-time type checks can be performed efficiently. In this paper we use a term-rewriting semantics that works directly on the syntax, without auxiliary structures. Instead of type tags, the cast expressions themselves are used to support run-time type checking. The cast includes both the source and target type because both pieces of information are needed at run-time to apply casts to objects.

We do not allow "no-op" casts in the intermediate language to simplify the canonical forms of values, e.g., a value of type **int** is an integer, and not an integer cast to **int**. The typing rule for casts requires the source and target type to be consistent, so the explicit cast may only add or remove ?'s from the type. Implicit up-casts due to subtyping remain implicit using a subsumption rule, as such casts are safe and there is no need for run-time checking.

6.1   The Cast Insertion Translation

The cast insertion translation is guided by the gradual type system, inserting casts wherever the type of a subexpression differs from the expected type. For example, recall the rule for method invocation.

$$(\text{GIVK2}) \frac{\Gamma \vdash_G e_1 : [\dots, l : \tau \to \tau', \dots] \quad \Gamma \vdash_G e_2 : \sigma \quad \sigma \lesssim \tau}{\Gamma \vdash_G e_1.l(e_2) : \tau'}$$

The type σ of e_2 may differ from the method's parameter type τ. We need to translate the invocation to a well typed term of $\mathbf{Ob}_{<:}^{\langle\cdot\rangle}$, where the argument type must be a subtype of the parameter type. We know that $\sigma \lesssim \tau$, so σ can differ from τ along both the type consistency relation $\sim$ and the subtype relation $<:$. So we have the diagram on the left:

A cast can move us along the x-axis, and the subsumption rule can move us along the y-axis. So a solution to the problem, shown above on the right, is to cast e_2 from σ to some type ρ where $\rho <: \tau$. (We could just as well move up along the y-axis via subsumption before casting along the x-axis; it makes no difference.) The following example shows how we can choose ρ for a particular situation and gives some intuition for how we can choose it in general.

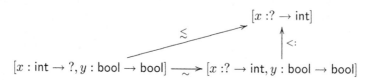

The type ρ must be the same width (have the same methods) as σ, and it must have a ? in all the locations that correspond to ?s in τ (and not have ?s where τ does not). In general, we can construct ρ with the merge operator, written $\sigma \leftharpoonup \tau$, defined below.

$$\sigma \leftharpoonup \tau \equiv \textbf{case } (\sigma, \tau) \text{ of}$$
$$(?, -) \Rightarrow \tau$$
$$\mid (-, ?) \Rightarrow ?$$
$$\mid ([l_1 : s_1, \ldots, l_n : s_n], [l_1 : t_1, \ldots, l_m : t_m]) \text{ where } n \leq m \Rightarrow$$
$$[l_1 : s_1 \leftharpoonup t_1, \ldots, l_n : s_n \leftharpoonup t_n]$$
$$\mid ([l_1 : s_1, \ldots, l_n : s_n], [l_1 : t_1, \ldots, l_m : t_m]) \text{ where } n > m \Rightarrow$$
$$[l_1 : s_1 \leftharpoonup t_1, \ldots, l_m : s_m \leftharpoonup t_m, l_{m+1} : s_{m+1}, \ldots, l_n : s_n]$$
$$\mid (-, -) \Rightarrow \sigma$$

$$(\sigma_1 \rightarrow \sigma_2) \leftharpoonup (\tau_1 \rightarrow \tau_2) = (\sigma_1 \leftharpoonup \tau_1) \rightarrow (\sigma_2 \leftharpoonup \tau_2)$$

With the merge operator, we have the following diagram:

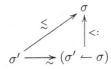

Proposition 3 (Basic Properties of $\leftharpoonup$)

1. $(\sigma \leftharpoonup \sigma) = \sigma$
2. $\sigma \sim (\sigma \leftharpoonup \tau)$
3. If $\sigma \lesssim \tau$ then $(\sigma \leftharpoonup \tau) <: \tau$.

The cast insertion judgment $\Gamma \vdash e \rightsquigarrow e' : \tau$ translates an expression e in the environment Γ to e' and determines that its type is τ. The cast insertion rule for method invocation (on known object types) is defined as follows using $\sigma' \leftharpoonup \sigma$ as the target of the cast on e_2.

$$(\text{CIVK2}) \frac{\Gamma \vdash e_1 \rightsquigarrow e_1' : [\ldots, l : \sigma \rightarrow \tau, \ldots] \quad \Gamma \vdash e_2 \rightsquigarrow e_2' : \sigma' \quad \sigma' \lesssim \sigma}{\Gamma \vdash e_1.l(e_2) \rightsquigarrow e_1'.l(\langle\!\langle\!\langle (\sigma' \leftharpoonup \sigma) \Leftarrow \sigma' \rangle\!\rangle e_2') : \tau}$$

In the case when $\sigma' = \sigma$, we do not insert a cast, which is why we use the following helper function.

$$\langle\!\langle \tau \Leftarrow \sigma \rangle\!\rangle e \equiv \text{if } \sigma = \tau \text{ then } e \text{ else } \langle \tau \Leftarrow \sigma \rangle e$$

The rest of the translation rules are straightforward. Fig. 2 gives the full definition of the cast insertion translation.

The cast-insertion judgment subsumes the gradual type system and additionally specifies how to produce the translation. In particular, a cast-insertion derivation can be created for precisely those terms accepted by the type system.

Proposition 4 (Cast Insertion and Gradual Typing)
$\Gamma \vdash_G e : \tau$ *iff* $\exists e'. \Gamma \vdash e \rightsquigarrow e' : \tau$.

When there is a cast insertion translation for term e, the resulting term e' is guaranteed to be a well-typed term of the intermediate language. Lemma 1 is used directly in the type safety theorem.

$$\boxed{\Gamma \vdash e \rightsquigarrow e' : \tau}$$

(CVar)
$$\frac{\Gamma(x) = \tau}{\Gamma \vdash x \rightsquigarrow x : \tau}$$

(GConst)
$$\Gamma \vdash c \rightsquigarrow c : \mathit{TypeOf}(c)$$

(CObj)
$$\frac{\Gamma, self : \rho, x_i : \sigma_i \vdash e_i \rightsquigarrow e_i' : \tau_i \quad \forall i \in 1 \ldots n}{\Gamma \vdash [l_i {=} \tau_i \, \varsigma(x_i : \sigma_i) e_i \ ^{i \in 1 \ldots n}] \rightsquigarrow [l_i {=} \tau_i \, \varsigma(x_i : \sigma_i) e_i' \ ^{i \in 1 \ldots n}] : \rho}$$
$$(\text{where } \rho \equiv [l_i : \sigma_i \to \tau_i \ ^{i \in 1 \ldots n}])$$

(CIvk1)
$$\frac{\Gamma \vdash e_1 \rightsquigarrow e_1' : ? \quad \Gamma \vdash e_2 \rightsquigarrow e_2' : \tau}{\Gamma \vdash_G e_1.l(e_2) \rightsquigarrow (\langle\!\langle [l : \tau \to ?] \Leftarrow ? \rangle\!\rangle e_1').l(e_2') : ?}$$

(CIvk2)
$$\frac{\Gamma \vdash e_1 \rightsquigarrow e_1' : [\ldots, l : \sigma \to \tau, \ldots] \quad \Gamma \vdash e_2 \rightsquigarrow e_2' : \sigma' \quad \sigma' \lesssim \sigma}{\Gamma \vdash e_1.l(e_2) \rightsquigarrow e_1'.l(\langle\!\langle (\sigma' \leftarrow \sigma) \Leftarrow \sigma' \rangle\!\rangle e_2') : \tau}$$

(CUpd1)
$$\frac{\Gamma \vdash e_1 \rightsquigarrow e_1' : ? \quad \Gamma, self : ?, x : \sigma \vdash e_2 \rightsquigarrow e_2' : \tau}{\Gamma \vdash e_1.l {:=} \tau \, \varsigma(x{:}\sigma) e_2 \rightsquigarrow (\langle\!\langle [l : \sigma \to \tau] \Leftarrow ? \rangle\!\rangle e_1').l {:=} \tau \, \varsigma(x{:}\sigma) e_2' : [l : \sigma \to \tau]}$$

(CUpd2)
$$\frac{\Gamma \vdash e_1 \rightsquigarrow e_1' : \rho \quad \Gamma, self : \rho, x{:}\sigma \vdash e_2 \rightsquigarrow e_2' : \tau}{\sigma_k \lesssim \sigma \quad \tau \lesssim \tau_k \quad e_3 \equiv \langle\!\langle \tau_k \Leftarrow \tau \rangle\!\rangle [x \mapsto \langle\!\langle \sigma \Leftarrow \sigma_k \rangle\!\rangle y] e_2'}{\Gamma \vdash e_1.l_k {:=} \tau \, \varsigma(x{:}\sigma) e_2 \rightsquigarrow e_1'.l_k {:=} \tau_k \, \varsigma(y{:}\sigma_k) e_3 : \rho}$$
$$(\text{where } \rho \equiv [l_i : \sigma_i \to \tau_i \ ^{i \in 1 \ldots n}] \text{ and } k \in 1 \ldots n)$$

Fig. 2. Cast Insertion

Lemma 1 (Cast Insertion is Sound)
If $\Gamma \vdash e \rightsquigarrow e' : \tau$ then $\Gamma \vdash e' : \tau$.

Proof. The proof is by induction on the cast insertion derivation. □

The next lemma is needed to prove *static type safety*, that is, a fully annotated term is guaranteed to produce neither cast nor type errors. The set of fully annotated terms of $\mathbf{Ob}_{<:}^{?}$ is exactly the $\mathbf{Ob}_{<:}$ subset of $\mathbf{Ob}_{<:}^{?}$. The function FV returns the set of variables that occur free in an expression.

Lemma 2 (Cast Insertion is the Identity for $\mathbf{Ob}_{<:}$)
If $\Gamma \vdash e \rightsquigarrow e' : \tau$ and $e \in \mathbf{Ob}_{<:}$ and $\forall x \in \mathrm{FV}(e) \cap \mathrm{dom}(\Gamma). \ \Gamma(x) \in \mathbf{Ob}_{<:}$ then $\Gamma \vdash e : \tau$ and $\tau \in \mathbf{Ob}_{<:}$ and $e = e'$.

Proof. The proof is by induction on the cast insertion derivation. □

Lemma 2 is also interesting for performance reasons. It shows that for fully annotated terms, no casts are inserted so there is no run-time type checking overhead.

6.2   Operational Semantics of $\mathbf{Ob}^{\langle \cdot \rangle}_{<:}$

In this section we define a small-step, evaluation context semantics [17, 18, 53] for $\mathbf{Ob}^{\langle \cdot \rangle}_{<:}$. Evaluation reduces expressions to values.

Definition 4 (Values and Contexts). *Simple values are constants, variables, and objects. Values are simple values or a simple value enclosed in a single cast. An evaluation context is an expression with a hole in it (written $[]$) to mark where rewriting (reduction) may take place.*

$$
\begin{array}{lll}
\textit{Simple Values} & \xi ::= c \mid x \mid [l_i{=}\tau_i \, \varsigma(x_i{:}\sigma_i)e_i \ ^{i\in 1...n}] \\
\textit{Values} & v ::= \xi \mid \langle \tau \Leftarrow \tau \rangle \xi \\
\textit{Contexts} & E ::= [] \mid E.l(e) \mid v.l(E) \mid E{:=}\tau \, \varsigma(x{:}\tau)e \mid \langle \tau \Leftarrow \tau \rangle E
\end{array}
$$

The reduction rules are specified in Fig. 3. When a reduction rule applies to an expression, the expression is called a redex:

Definition 5 (Redex). *redex* $e \equiv \exists e'. \, e \longrightarrow e'$

The semantics is parameterized on a δ-function that defines the behavior of the primitive methods attached to the constants. The rule for method invocation (IVK) looks up the body of the appropriate method and substitutes the argument for the parameter. The primitive method invocation rule (DELTA) simply evaluates to the result of applying δ. In both the (IVK) and (DELTA) rules, the argument is required to be a value as indicated by the use of meta-variable v. Method update (UPD) creates a new object in which the specified method has been replaced.

The traditional approach to evaluating casts is to apply them in an eager fashion. For example, casting at function types creates a wrapper function with the appropriate casts on the input and output [19, 20, 21, 48].

$$
\langle (\rho \to \nu) \Leftarrow (\sigma \to \tau) \rangle v \longrightarrow (\lambda x{:}\rho. \, \langle \nu \Leftarrow \tau \rangle(v \, (\langle \sigma \Leftarrow \rho \rangle x)))
$$

The problem with this approach is that the wrapper functions can build up, one on top of another, using memory in proportion to the number of cast applications. The solution we use here is to delay the application of casts, and to collapse sequences of casts into a single cast. When a cast is applied to a value that is already wrapped in a cast, either the (MERGE) or (REMOVE) rule applies, or else the cast is a "bad cast".

Definition 6 (Bad Cast)

$$
\begin{array}{l}
\textit{badcast } e \equiv \exists v \, \rho \, \sigma \, \sigma' \, \tau. \, e = \langle \tau \Leftarrow \sigma' \rangle \langle \sigma \Leftarrow \rho \rangle v \land \rho \not\lesssim \tau \\
\textit{BadCast } e \equiv \exists E \, e'. \, e = E[e'] \land \textit{badcast } e'
\end{array}
$$

The (MERGE) rule collapses two casts into a single cast, and is guarded by a type check. The target type of the resulting cast must be consistent with the inner source type ρ and it must be a subtype of the outer target type τ. We

(IVK)
$$o.l_j(v) \longrightarrow [\text{self} \mapsto o, x_j \mapsto v]e_j$$
$$(\text{where } o \equiv [l_i{=}\tau_i \, \varsigma(x_i{:}\sigma_i)e_i{}^{i \in 1 \ldots n}]) \quad (1 \leq j \leq n) \qquad \boxed{e \longrightarrow e}$$

(DELTA)
$$c.l(v) \longrightarrow \delta(c, l, v)$$

(UPD)
$$[l_i{=}\tau_i \, \varsigma(x_i{:}\sigma_i)e_i{}^{i \in 1 \ldots n}].l_j{:=}_\tau \, \varsigma(x{:}\sigma)e$$
$$\longrightarrow [l_i{=}\tau_i \, \varsigma(x_i{:}\sigma_i)e_i{}^{i \in \{1 \ldots n\} - \{j\}}, l_j{=}_\tau \, \varsigma(x{:}\sigma)e] \quad (1 \leq j \leq n)$$

(MERGE)
$$\frac{\rho \lesssim \tau \qquad \rho \neq \tau}{\langle \tau \Leftarrow \sigma' \rangle \langle \sigma \Leftarrow \rho \rangle v \longrightarrow \langle\!\langle (\rho \leftharpoonup \tau) \Leftarrow \rho \rangle\!\rangle v}$$

(REMOVE)
$$\frac{\rho = \tau}{\langle \tau \Leftarrow \sigma' \rangle \langle \sigma \Leftarrow \rho \rangle v \longrightarrow v}$$

(IVKCST)
$$(\langle \tau \Leftarrow \sigma \rangle v_1).l_j(v_2) \longrightarrow \langle \tau_2 \Leftarrow \sigma_2 \rangle (v_1.l_j(\langle \sigma_1 \Leftarrow \tau_1 \rangle v_2))$$
$$(\text{where } \sigma \equiv [\ldots, l_j : \sigma_1 \to \sigma_2, \ldots] \text{ and } \tau \equiv [\ldots, l_j : \tau_1 \to \tau_2, \ldots])$$

(UPDCST)
$$(\langle \tau \Leftarrow \sigma \rangle v).l_j :=_{\tau_2} \varsigma(x{:}\tau_1)e$$
$$\longrightarrow \langle \tau \Leftarrow \sigma \rangle (v.l_j :=_{\sigma_2} \varsigma(z{:}\sigma_1) \langle\!\langle \sigma_2 \Leftarrow \tau_2 \rangle\!\rangle [x \mapsto \langle\!\langle \tau_1 \Leftarrow \sigma_1 \rangle\!\rangle z]e)$$
$$(\text{where } \sigma \equiv [\ldots, l_j : \sigma_1 \to \sigma_2, \ldots] \text{ and } \tau \equiv [\ldots, l_j : \tau_1 \to \tau_2, \ldots])$$

(STEP)
$$\frac{e \longrightarrow e'}{E[e] \longmapsto E[e']} \qquad \boxed{e \longmapsto e}$$

(REFL)
$$e \longmapsto^* e \qquad \boxed{e \longmapsto^* e}$$

(TRANS)
$$\frac{e_1 \longmapsto^* e_2 \qquad e_2 \longmapsto e_3}{e_1 \longmapsto^* e_3}$$

Fig. 3. Reduction

therefore use the $\leftharpoonup$ operator and cast from ρ to $\rho \leftharpoonup \tau$. The (REMOVE) rule applies when the inner source and the outer target types are equal, and removes both casts.

The delayed action of casts on objects is "forced" when a method is invoked or updated. The rules (IVKCST) and (UPDCST) handle these cases.

7   Type Safety of $\mathbf{Ob}^?_{<:}$

The bulk of this section is dedicated to proving that the intermediate language $\mathbf{Ob}^{\langle \cdot \rangle}_{<:}$ is type safe. The type safety of our source language $\mathbf{Ob}^?_{<:}$ is a consequence of the soundness of cast insertion and the type safety of the intermediate language. The type safety proof for the intermediate language has its origins in the syntactic type soundness approach of Wright and Felleisen[53], but is substantially reorganized using some folklore.[5] We begin with a top-down overview of the proof and then list the lemmas and theorems in the standard bottom-up fashion.

The goal is to show that if a term e_s is well-typed ($\vdash e_s : \tau$) and reduces in zero or more steps to e_f ($e_s \longmapsto^* e_f$), then $\vdash e_f : \tau$ and e_f is either a value or contains a bad cast or e_f can be further reduced. Note that the statement "e_f is either a value or contains a bad cast or e_f can be further reduced" is equivalent to saying that e_f is not a *type error* as defined in Section 3. The proof of type safety is by induction on the reduction sequence. A reduction sequence (defined in Fig. 3) is either a zero-length sequence (so $e_s = e_f$), or a reduction sequence $e_s \longmapsto^* e_i$ to an intermediate term e_i followed by a reduction step $e_i \longmapsto e_f$. In the zero-length case, where $e_s = e_f$, we need to show that if e_s is well-typed then it is not a type error. This is shown in the Progress Lemma. In the second case, the induction hypothesis tells us that e_i is well-typed. We then need to show that if e_i is well-typed and $e_i \longmapsto e_f$ then e_f is well-typed. This is shown in the Preservation Lemma. Once we have a well-typed e_f, we can use the Progress Lemma to show that e_f is not a type error.

Progress Lemma. Suppose that e is well-typed and not a value and does not contain a bad cast. We need to show that e can make progress, i.e., there is some e' such that $e \longmapsto e'$. Therefore we need to show that e can be decomposed into an evaluation context E filled with a redex e_1 ($\exists e_2.\ e_1 \longrightarrow e_2$) so that we can apply rule (STEP) to get $E[e_1] \longmapsto E[e_2]$. The existence of such a decomposition is given by the Decomposition Lemma.[6] In general, when the Progress Lemma fails for some language, it is because there is a mistake in the definition of evaluation contexts (which defines where evaluation should take place) or there is a mistake in the reduction rules, perhaps because a reduction rule is missing.

Preservation Lemma. We need to show that if $\vdash e : \tau$ and $e \longmapsto e'$ then $\vdash e' : \tau$. Because $e \longmapsto e'$, we know there exists an E, e_1, and e_2 such that $e = E[e_1]$, $e' = E[e_2]$, and $e_1 \longrightarrow e_2$. The proof consists of three parts, each of which is proved as a separate lemma.

---

[5] The original proof of Wright and Felleisen requires the definition of faulty expressions which is more complicated than necessary because it relies on a proof by contradiction. Later type soundness proofs, such as [28, 38, 43], take a more direct approach. We use a proof organization similar to [5].

[6] Our Decomposition Lemma differs from the usual Unique Decomposition Lemma (but is similar to Lemma A.15 in [5]) in that we include the premise that the expression is well-typed and conclude with a stronger statement than usual, that the hole is filled with a redex. The usual approach is to conclude with a hole filled with something, let us call it a *pre-redex*, that turns out to be either a redex or an ill-typed term. We do not prove uniqueness here because it is not necessary in the proof of type safety. Nevertheless, decompositions are unique for $\mathbf{Ob}^{\langle\cdot\rangle}_{<:}$.

1. From $\vdash E[e_1] : \tau$ we know that e_1 is well-typed ($\vdash e_1 : \sigma$) and the context E is well-typed. The typing judgment for contexts (defined the Appendix, Fig. 5) assigns the context an input and output type, such as $\vdash E : \sigma \Rightarrow \tau$. (Subterm Typing)
2. Because e_1 is well-typed and $e_1 \longrightarrow e_2$, e_2 is well-typed with the same type as e_1. (Subject Reduction)
3. Filling E with e_2 produces an expression of type τ. More precisely, if $\vdash E : \sigma \Rightarrow \tau$ and $\vdash e_2 : \sigma$ then $\vdash E[e_2] : \tau$. (Replacement)

In general, Subterm Typing and Replacement hold for a language so long as evaluation contexts are properly defined. Subject Reduction, on the other hand, is highly dependent on the reduction rules of the language and is the crux of the type safety proof.

We now state the lemmas and theorems in the traditional bottom-up order, but without further commentary due to lack of space. We start with some basic properties of objects.

Proposition 5 (Properties of Objects)

1. *If $\Gamma \vdash [l_i = \tau_i \varsigma(x_i : \sigma_i)e_i{}^{i\in 1...n}] : \rho$ where $\rho \equiv [l_i : \sigma_i \rightarrow \tau_i{}^{i\in 1...n}]$ and $j \in 1...n$ and $\Gamma, \mathsf{self} : \rho, x_j : \sigma_j \vdash e' : \tau_j$*
   then $\Gamma \vdash [l_i = \tau_i \varsigma(x_i : \sigma_i)e_i{}^{i\in\{1...n\}-\{j\}}, l_j = \tau_j \varsigma(x_j : \sigma_j)e'] : \rho$.
2. *If $[l_i : \sigma_i \rightarrow \tau_i{}^{i\in 1...n}] <: [l_j : \rho_j \rightarrow \nu_j{}^{j\in 1...m}]$ and $k \in 1...m$ then $\rho_k = \sigma_k$ and $\nu_k = \tau_k$.*

7.1   Progress

Towards proving the Progress Lemma, we show that values of certain types have canonical forms.

Lemma 3 (Canonical Forms)

1. *If $\vdash v : \gamma$ then $\exists c \in \mathbb{C}. \, v = c$.*
2. *If $\vdash v : \rho$ where $\rho \equiv [l_i : \sigma_i \rightarrow \tau_i{}^{i\in 1...n}]$*
   then $\exists \overline{x} \, \overline{e}. \, v = [l_i = \tau_i \varsigma(x_i : \sigma_i)e_i{}^{i\in 1...n}]$
   or $\exists \overline{x} \, \overline{e} \, \sigma. \, v = \langle \sigma \Leftarrow \rho \rangle [l_i = \tau_i \varsigma(x_i : \sigma_i)e_i{}^{i\in 1...n}]$.
3. *$\nvdash \xi : ?$ (simple values do not have type ?)*

The main work in proving Progress is proving the Decomposition Lemma.

Lemma 4 (Decomposition). *If $\vdash e : \tau$ then $e \in Values$ or $\exists \sigma \, E \, e'. \, e = E[e'] \wedge (redex \, e' \vee badcast \, e')$.*

Proof. By induction on the typing derivation using the Canonical Forms Lemma and Proposition 5.   □

Lemma 5 (Progress). *If $\vdash e : \tau$ then $e \in Values$ or $\exists e'. e \longmapsto e'$ or $BadCast \, e$.*

Proof. Immediate from the Decomposition Lemma.   □

7.2   Preservation

Next we prove the Preservation Lemma and the three lemmas on which it relies: Subterm Typing, Subject Reduction, and Replacement.

Lemma 6 (Subterm Typing). *If* $\vdash E[e] : \tau$ *then* $\exists \sigma. \vdash E : \sigma \Rightarrow \tau$ *and* $\vdash e : \sigma$.

Proof. A straightforward induction on the typing derivation.   □

We assume that the δ function for evaluating primitives is sound.

Assumption 1 (δ-typability)
If $TypeOf(c) = [\dots, l : \sigma \to \tau, \dots]$ *and* $\vdash v : \sigma$ *then* $\vdash \delta(c, l, v) : \tau$.

Towards proving the Subject Reduction lemma, for the function application case we need the standard Substitution Lemma which in turn requires an Environment Weakening Lemma.

Definition 7. $\Gamma \subseteq \Gamma' \equiv \forall x \tau. \; \Gamma(x) = \tau \; implies \; \Gamma'(x) = \tau$

Lemma 7 (Environment Weakening)
If $\Gamma \vdash e : \tau$ *and* $\Gamma \subseteq \Gamma'$ *then* $\Gamma' \vdash e : \tau$.

Proof. A straightforward induction on the typing derivation.   □

Definition 8. *We write* $\Gamma \backslash \{x\}$ *for* Γ *restricted to have domain* $\mathrm{dom}(\Gamma) \backslash \{x\}$.

Lemma 8 (Substitution)
If $\Gamma \vdash e_1 : \tau$ *and* $\Gamma(x) = \sigma$ *and* $\Gamma \backslash \{x\} \subseteq \Gamma'$ *and* $\Gamma' \vdash e_2 : \sigma$
then $\Gamma' \vdash [x \mapsto e_2]e_1 : \tau$.

Proof. By induction on the typing derivation. All cases are straightforward except for (OBJ) and (UPD) for which we use Environment Weakening.   □

Lemma 9 (Inversions on Typing Rules)

1. *If* $\Gamma \vdash c : \sigma \to \tau$ *then there exists* σ' *and* τ' *such that* $TypeOf(c) = \sigma' \to \tau'$ *and* $\sigma <: \sigma'$ *and* $\tau' <: \tau$.
2. *If* $\Gamma \vdash \langle \tau' \Leftarrow \sigma \rangle e : \tau$ *then* $\tau' <: \tau$ *and* $\sigma \sim \tau'$ *and* $\sigma \neq \tau'$ *and* $\Gamma \vdash e : \sigma$.
3. *Suppose* $\Gamma \vdash [l_i = \tau_i \; \varsigma(x_i : \sigma_i)e_i \;^{i \in 1 \dots n}] : \tau$ *and let* $\rho \equiv [l_i : \sigma_i \to \tau_i \;^{i \in 1 \dots n}]$. *Then* $\rho <: \tau$ *and for any* $j \in 1 \dots n$ *we have* $\Gamma, \mathsf{self} : \rho, x_j : \sigma_j \vdash e_j : \tau_j$.

Proof. The proofs are by induction on the typing derivation.   □

Lemma 10 (Subject Reduction). *If* $\vdash e : \tau$ *and* $e \longrightarrow e'$ *then* $\vdash e' : \tau$.

Proof. The proof is by induction on the typing derivation, followed by case analysis on the reduction.

(Ivk) Use the Substitution and Inversion Lemmas and Proposition 5.
(Delta) Use δ-typability and the Inversion Lemma.
(Upd) Use Proposition 5 and the Inversion Lemma.

(**Merge**) Use Proposition 3 and the Inversion Lemma.
(**Remove, InvCst, UpdCst**) Use the Inversion Lemma.   □

Lemma 11 (Replacement). *If $E : \sigma \Rightarrow \tau$ and $\vdash e : \sigma$ then $\vdash E[e] : \tau$.*

Proof. A straightforward induction on the context typing derivation.   □

Lemma 12 (Preservation). *If $e \longmapsto e'$ and $\vdash e : \tau$ then $\vdash e' : \tau$.*

Proof. Apply Subterm Typing to get a well-typed evaluation context and redex. Then apply Subject Reduction and Replacement.   □

7.3   Type Safety

Lemma 13 (Type Safety of $Ob_{<:}^{\langle \cdot \rangle}$). *If $\vdash e : \tau$ and $e \longmapsto^* e'$ then $\vdash e' : \tau$ and $e' \in Values$ or $BadCast\ e'$ or $\exists e''.\ e' \longmapsto e''$.*

Proof. By induction on the evaluation steps. For the base case, where $e = e'$, we use Progress to show that e is either a value, a bad cast, or can make progress. For the case where $e_1 \longmapsto^* e_2$ and $e_2 \longmapsto e_3$, e_2 is well-typed by the induction hypothesis and therefore e_3 is well-typed by Preservation. Applying Progress to e_3 brings us to the conclusion.   □

Theorem 1 (Type Safety of $Ob_{<:}^?$). *If $\vdash e_1 \rightsquigarrow e_2 : \tau$ and $e_2 \longmapsto^* e_3$ then $\vdash e_3 : \tau$ and $e_3 \in Values$ or $BadCast\ e_3$ or $\exists e_4.\ e_3 \longmapsto e_4$.*

Proof. The expression e_2 is well-typed because cast insertion is sound (Lemma 1). We then apply Lemma 13.   □

Theorem 2 (Static Type Safety of $Ob_{<:}^?$). *If $e_1 \in Ob_{<:}$ and $\vdash e_1 \rightsquigarrow e_2 : \tau$ and $e_2 \longmapsto^* e_3$ then $\vdash e_3 : \tau$ and $e_3 \in Values$ or $\exists e_4.\ e_3 \longmapsto e_4$.*

Proof. By Lemma 2 we have $e_1 = e_2$, so e_2 does not contain any casts. By Lemma 13 we know that either e_3 is a value or a bad cast or can make progress. However, since e_2 did not contain any casts, there can be none in e_3.   □

8   Related Work

Type Annotations for Dynamic Languages. Several dynamic programming languages allow explicit type annotations, such as Common LISP [33], Dylan [16, 45], Cecil [10], Boo [13], extensions to Visual Basic.NET and C# proposed by Meijer and Drayton [36], the Bigloo [8, 44] dialect of Scheme [34], and the Strongtalk dialect of Smalltalk [6, 7]. In these languages, adding type annotations brings some static checking and/or improves performance, but the languages do not make the guarantee that annotating all parameters in the program prevents all type errors and type exceptions at run-time. This paper formalizes a type system that provides this stronger guarantee.

Soft Typing. Static checking can be added to dynamically typed languages using static analyses. Cartwright and Fagan [9], Flanagan and Felleisen [22], Aiken, Wimmers, and Lakshman [3], and Henglein and Rehof [29, 30] developed analyses that can be used, for example, to catch bugs in Scheme programs [23, 30]. These analyses provide warnings to the programmer while still allowing the programmer to execute their program immediately (even programs with errors), thereby preserving the benefits of dynamic typing. However, the programmer does not control which portions of a program are statically checked: these whole-program analyses have non-local interactions. Also, the static analyses bear a significant implementation burden on developers of the language. On the other hand, they can be used to reduce the amount of run-time type checking in dynamically typed programs (Chambers et al. [11, 14]) and therefore could also be used to improve the performance of gradually typed programs.

Dynamic Typing in Statically Typed Languages. Abadi et al. [2] extended a statically typed language with a Dynamic type and explicit injection (dynamic) and projection operations (typecase). Their approach does not satisfy our goals, as migrating code between dynamic and static checking not only requires changing type annotations on parameters, but also adding or removing injection and projection operations throughout the code. Our approach automates the latter.

Interoperability. Gray, Findler, and Flatt [25] consider the problem of interoperability between Java and Scheme and extended Java with a Dynamic type with implicit casts. They did not provide an account of the type system, but their work provided inspiration for our work on gradual typing. Matthews and Findler [35] define an operational semantics for multi-language programs but require programmers to insert explicit "boundary" markers between the two languages, reminiscent of the explicit injection and projections of Abadi et al.

Tobin-Hochstadt and Felleisen [51] developed a system that provides convenient inter-language migration between dynamic and static languages on a per-module basis. In contrast, our goal is to allow migration at finer levels of granularity and to allow for partially typed code. Tobin-Hochstadt and Felleisen build *blame tracking* into their system and show that errors may not originate from statically typed modules. Our gradual type system enjoys a similar property. If all parameters in a term are annotated then no casts are inserted into the term during compilation provided the types of the free variables in the term do not mention ? (Lemma 2). Thus, no cast errors can originate from such a term.

Hybrid typing. The Hybrid Type Checking of Flanagan et al. [21, 24] combines standard static typing with refinement types, where the refinements may express arbitrary predicates. The type system tries to satisfy the predicates using automated theorem proving, but when no conclusive answer is given, the system inserts run-time checks. This work is analogous to ours in that it combines a weaker and stronger type system, allowing implicit coercions between the two systems and inserting run-time checks. One notable difference between our system and Flanagan's is that his is based on subtyping whereas ours is based on type consistency.

Ou et al. [40] define a language that combines standard static typing with more powerful dependent typing. Implicit coercions are allowed to and from dependent types and run-time checks are inserted. This combination of a weaker and a stronger type system is again analogous to gradual typing.

Quasi-Static Typing. Thatte's Quasi-Static Typing [50] is close to our gradual type system but relies on subtyping and treats the unknown type as the top of the subtype hierarchy. In previous work [47] we showed that implicit down-casts combined with the transitivity of subtyping creates a fundamental problem that prevents the type system from catching all type errors even when all parameters in the program are annotated.

Riely and Hennessy [42] define a partial type system for Dπ, a distributed π-calculus. Their system allows some locations to be untyped and assigns such locations the type lbad. Their type system, like Quasi-Static Typing, relies on subtyping, however they treat lbad as "bottom", which allows objects of type lbad to be implicitly coercible to any other type.

Gradual Typing. The work of Anderson and Drossopoulou on BabyJ [4] is closest to our own. They develop a gradual type system for *nominal types* and their permissive type ∗ is analogous to our unknown type ?. Our work differs from theirs in that we address structural type systems.

Gronski, Knowles, Tomb, Freund, and Flanagan [26] provide gradual typing in the Sage language by including a Dynamic type and implicit down-casts. They use a modified form of subtyping to provide the implicit down-casts whereas we use the consistency relation. Their work does not include a result such as Theorem 2 of this paper which shows that all type errors are caught in programs with fully annotated parameters.

Herman alerted us to the space-efficiency problems in the traditional approach to higher-order casts. (We used the traditional approach in [47].) Concurrent to the work in this paper, Herman, Tomb, and Flanagan [31] proposed a solution a space-efficiency problem which, similar to our approach, delays the application of higher-order casts. However, the details of their approach are based on the coercion calculus from Henglein's Dynamic Typing framework [29]. The coercion calculus can be viewed as a way to *compile* the explicit casts of this paper, removing the interpretive overhead of traversing types at run-time.

Type inference. A language with gradual typing is syntactically similar to one with type inference [12, 32, 37]: both allow type annotations to be omitted. However, type inference does not provide the same benefits as dynamic typing (and therefore gradual typing). With type inference, programmers save the time it takes to write down the types but they must still go through the process of revising their program until the type inferencer accepts the program as well typed. As type systems are conservative in nature and of limited (though ever increasing) expressiveness, it may take some time to turn a program (even one without any real errors) into a program to which the type inferencer can assign a type. The advantage of dynamic typing (and therefore of gradual typing) is that programmers may begin executing and testing their programs right away.

9   Conclusion and Future Work

The debate between dynamic and static typing has continued for several decades, with good reason. There are convincing arguments for both sides. Dynamic typing is better suited for prototyping, scripting, and gluing components, whereas static typing is better suited for algorithms, data-structures, and systems programming. It is common practice for programmers to start developing a program in a dynamic language and then translate to a static language later on. However, static and dynamic languages are often radically different, making this translation difficult and error prone. Ideally, migrating between dynamic to static could take place gradually and within one language.

In this paper we present the formal definition of an object calculus $\mathbf{Ob}^?_{<:}$, including its type system and operational semantics. This language captures the key ingredients for implementing gradual typing in object-oriented languages, showing how the type consistency relation can be naturally combined with subtyping. The calculus $\mathbf{Ob}^?_{<:}$ provides the flexibility of dynamically typed languages when type annotations are omitted by the programmer and provides the benefits of static checking when all method parameters are annotated. The type system and run-time semantics of $\mathbf{Ob}^?_{<:}$ are relatively straightforward, so it is suitable for practical languages.

As future work, we intend to investigate the interaction between gradual typing and Hindley-Milner inference [12, 32, 37], and we intend to apply static analyses (such as Soft Typing [9] or Henglein's Dynamic Typing [29]) to reduce the number of run-time casts that must be inserted during compilation. There are a number of features we omitted from the formalization for the sake of keeping the presentation simple, such as recursive types and imperative update. We plan to add these features to our formalization in the near future. Finally, we intend to incorporate gradual typing into a mainstream dynamically typed programming language and perform studies to evaluate whether gradual typing can benefit programmer productivity.

Acknowledgments

We thank the anonymous reviewers for their suggestions. We thank Amer Diwan, Christoph Reichenbach, Ronald Garcia, Stephen Freund, David Herman, David Broman, and Cormac Flanagan for comments and feedback on drafts of this paper. This work was supported by NSF ITR-0113569 Putting Multi-Stage Annotations to Work, Texas ATP 003604-0032-2003 Advanced Languages Techniques for Device Drivers, and NSF SOD-0439017 Synthesizing Device Drivers.

References

[1] Abadi, M., Cardelli, L.: A Theory of Objects. Springer-Verlag New York, Inc. Secaucus, NJ, USA (1996)

[2] Abadi, M., Cardelli, L., Pierce, B., Plotkin, G.: Dynamic typing in a statically typed language. ACM Transactions on Programming Languages and Systems 13(2), 237–268 (1991)

[3] Aiken, A., Wimmers, E.L., Lakshman, T.K.: Soft typing with conditional types. In: POPL '94: Proceedings of the 21st ACM SIGPLAN-SIGACT symposium on Principles of programming languages, Portland, Oregon, United States, pp. 163–173. ACM Press, New York (1994)

[4] Anderson, C., Drossopoulou, S.: BabyJ - from object based to class based programming via types. In: WOOD '03, vol, vol. 82, Elsevier, Amsterdam (2003)

[5] Aydemir, B.E., Bohannon, A., Fairbairn, M., Foster, J.N., Pierce, B.C., Sewell, P., Vytiniotis, D., Weirich, G.W.S., Zdancewic, S.: Mechanized metatheory for the masses: The POPLmark challenge.(May 2005)

[6] Bracha, G.: Pluggable type systems. In: OOPSLA'04 Workshop on Revival of Dynamic Languages (2004)

[7] Bracha, G., Griswold, D.: Strongtalk: typechecking smalltalk in a production environment. In: OOPSLA '93: Proceedings of the eighth annual conference on Object-oriented programming systems, languages, and applications, pp. 215–230. ACM Press, New York, NY, USA (1993)

[8] Bres, Y., Serpette, B.P., Serrano, M.: Compiling scheme programs to.NET common intermediate language. In: 2nd International Workshop on.NET Technologies, Pilzen, Czech Republic (May 2004)

[9] Cartwright, R., Fagan, M.: Soft typing. In: PLDI '91: Proceedings of the ACM SIGPLAN 1991 conference on Programming language design and implementation, pp. 278–292. ACM Press, New York (1991)

[10] Chambers, C., et al.: The Cecil language: Specification and rationale. Technical report, Department of Computer Science and Engineering, University of Washington, Seattle, Washington (2004)

[11] Chambers, C., Ungar, D., Lee, E.: An efficient implementation of self a dynamically-typed object-oriented language based on prototypes. In: OOPSLA '89: Conference proceedings on Object-oriented programming systems, languages and applications, pp. 49–70. ACM Press, New York (1989)

[12] Damas, L., Milner, R.: Principal type-schemes for functional programs. In: POPL '82: Proceedings of the 9th ACM SIGPLAN-SIGACT symposium on Principles of programming languages, pp. 207–212. ACM Press, New York (1982)

[13] de Oliveira, R.B.: The Boo programming language (2005), http://boo.codehaus.org

[14] Dean, J., Chambers, C., Grove, D.: Selective specialization for object-oriented languages. In: PLDI '95: Proceedings of the ACM SIGPLAN 1995 conference on Programming language design and implementation, La Jolla, California, United States, pp. 93–102. ACM Press, New York (1995)

[15] ECMA Standard ECMA-262: ECMAScript Language Specification (1999)

[16] Feinberg, N., Keene, S.E., Mathews, R.O., Withington, P.T.: Dylan programming: an object-oriented and dynamic language. Addison Wesley Longman Publishing, Redwood City, CA (1997)

[17] Felleisen, M., Friedman, D.P.: Control operators, the SECD-machine and the lambda-calculus. pp. 193–217 (1986)

[18] Felleisen, M., Hieb, R.: The revised report on the syntactic theories of sequential control and state. Theoretical Computer Science 103(2), 235–271 (1992)

[19] Findler, R.B., Felleisen, M.: Contracts for higher-order functions. In: ACM International Conference on Functional Programming (October 2002)

[20] Findler, R.B., Flatt, M., Felleisen, M.: Semantic casts: Contracts and structural subtyping in a nominal world. In: European Conference on Object-Oriented Programming (2004)

[21] Flanagan, C.: Hybrid type checking. In: POPL 2006: The 33rd ACM SIGPLAN-SIGACT Symposium on Principles of Programming Languages, pp. 245–256. Charleston, South Carolina (2006)

[22] Flanagan, C., Felleisen, M.: Componential set-based analysis. ACM Trans. Program. Lang. Syst. 21(2), 370–416 (1999)

[23] Flanagan, C., Flatt, M., Krishnamurthi, S., Weirich, S., Felleisen, M.: Catching bugs in the web of program invariants. In: PLDI '96: Proceedings of the ACM SIGPLAN 1996 conference on Programming language design and implementation, Philadelphia, Pennsylvania, United States, pp. 23–32. ACM Press, New York (1996)

[24] Flanagan, C., Freund, S.N., Tomb, A.: Hybrid types, invariants, and refinements for imperative objects. In: FOOL/WOOD '06: International Workshop on Foundations and Developments of Object-Oriented Languages (2006)

[25] Gray, K.E., Findler, R.B., Flatt, M.: Fine-grained interoperability through mirrors and contracts. In: OOPSLA '05: Proceedings of the 20th annual ACM SIGPLAN conference on Object oriented programming systems languages and applications, pp. 231–245. ACM Press, New York, NY, USA (2005)

[26] Gronski, J., Knowles, K., Tomb, A., Freund, S.N., Flanagan, C.: Sage: Hybrid checking for flexible specifications. Technical report, University of California, Santa Cruz (2006)

[27] Group, E.T.W.: Ecmascript 4 netscape proposal

[28] Gunter, C.A., Remy, D., Riecke, J.G.: A generalization of exceptions and control in ml-like languages. In: FPCA '95: Proceedings of the seventh international conference on Functional programming languages and computer architecture, La Jolla, California, United States, pp. 12–23. ACM Press, New York (1995)

[29] Henglein, F.: Dynamic typing: syntax and proof theory. Science of Computer Programming 22(3), 197–230 (1994)

[30] Henglein, F., Rehof, J.: Safe polymorphic type inference for a dynamically typed language: Translating scheme to ml. In: FPCA '95, ACM SIGPLAN-SIGARCH Conference on Functional Programming Languages and Computer Architecture, La Jolla, California (June 1995)

[31] Herman, D., Tomb, A., Flanagan, C.: Space-efficient gradual typing. In: Trends in Functional Programming (TFP), April 2007 (2007)

[32] Hindley, R.: The principal type-scheme of an object in combinatory logic. Trans AMS 146, 29–60 (1969)

[33] G. L. S. Jr.: An overview of COMMON LISP. In: LFP '82: Proceedings of the, ACM symposium on LISP and functional programming, pp. 98–107, New York, NY, USA, 1982. ACM Press (1982)

[34] Kelsey, R., Clinger, W., J.R. (eds.) Revised[5] report on the algorithmic language scheme. Higher-Order and Symbolic Computation, 11(1), (August 1998)

[35] Matthews, J., Findler, R.B.: Operational semantics for multi-language programs. In: The 34th ACM SIGPLAN-SIGACT Symposium on Principles of Programming Languages, January 2007, ACM Press, New York (2007)

[36] Meijer, E., Drayton, P.: Static typing where possible, dynamic typing when needed: The end of the cold war between programming languages. In: OOPSLA'04 Workshop on Revival of Dynamic Languages (2004)

[37] Milner, R.: A theory of type polymorphism in programming. Journal of Computer and System Sciences 17(3), 348–375 (1978)

[38] Nanevski, A.: A modal calculus for exception handling. In: Intuitionistic Modal Logics and Applications Workshop (IMLA '05), Chicago, IL, June 2005 (2005)

[39] Nipkow, T., Paulson, L.C., Wenzel, M. (eds.): Isabelle/HOL. LNCS, vol. 2283. Springer, Heidelberg (2002)

[40] Ou, X., Tan, G., Mandelbaum, Y., Walker, D.: Dynamic typing with dependent types (extended abstract). In: 3rd IFIP International Conference on Theoretical Computer Science (August 2004)

[41] Pierce, B.C.: Types and programming languages. MIT Press, Cambridge, MA, USA (2002)

[42] Riely, J., Hennessy, M.: Trust and partial typing in open systems of mobile agents. In: POPL '99: Proceedings of the 26th ACM SIGPLAN-SIGACT symposium on Principles of programming languages, San Antonio, Texas, United States, pp. 93–104. ACM Press, New York, NY, USA (1999)

[43] Sabry, A.: Minml: Syntax, static semantics, dynamic semantics, and type safety. Course notes for b522 (February 2002)

[44] Serrano, M.: Bigloo: a practical Scheme compiler. Inria-Rocquencourt (April 2002)

[45] Shalit, A.: The Dylan reference manual: the definitive guide to the new object-oriented dynamic language. Addison Wesley Longman Publishing Co., Inc. Redwood City, CA, USA (1996)

[46] Siek, J., Taha, W.: Gradual typing for objects: Isabelle formaliztaion. Technical Report CU-CS-1021-06, University of Colorado, Boulder, CO (December 2006)

[47] Siek, J.G., Taha, W.: Gradual typing for functional languages. In: Scheme and Functional Programming Workshop (September 2006)

[48] Taha, W., Makholm, H., Hughes, J.: Tag elimination and jones-optimality. In: Danvy, O., Filinski, A. (eds.) PADO 2001. LNCS, vol. 2053, pp. 257–275. Springer, Heidelberg (2001)

[49] Tang, A.: Pugs blog

[50] Thatte, S.: Quasi-static typing. In: POPL '90: Proceedings of the 17th ACM SIGPLAN-SIGACT symposium on Principles of programming languages, pp. 367–381. ACM Press, New York, NY, USA (1990)

[51] Tobin-Hochstadt, S., Felleisen, M.: Interlanguage migration: From scripts to programs. In: Dynamic Languages Symposium (2006)

[52] Wenzel, M.: The Isabelle/Isar Reference Manual. TU München (April 2004)

[53] Wright, A.K., Felleisen, M.: A syntactic approach to type soundness. Information and Computation 115(1), 38–94 (1994)

Appendix

$$\boxed{\Gamma \vdash e : \tau}$$

(VAR) $\dfrac{\Gamma(x) = \tau}{\Gamma \vdash x : \tau}$

(CONST) $\Gamma \vdash c : \mathit{TypeOf}(c)$

(OBJ) $\dfrac{\Gamma, \mathsf{self} : \rho, x_i : \sigma_i \vdash e_i : \tau_i \quad \forall i \in 1 \ldots n}{\Gamma \vdash [l_i = \tau_i \, \varsigma(x_i : \sigma_i) e_i \,^{i \in 1 \ldots n}] : \rho}$
$(\text{where } \rho \equiv [l_i : \sigma_i \to \tau_i \,^{i \in 1 \ldots n}])$

(IVK) $\dfrac{\Gamma \vdash e_1 : [\ldots, l : \sigma \to \tau, \ldots] \quad \Gamma \vdash e_2 : \sigma}{\Gamma \vdash e_1.l(e_2) : \tau}$

(UPD) $\dfrac{\Gamma \vdash e_1 : \rho \quad \Gamma, \mathsf{self} : \rho, x : \sigma \vdash e_2 : \tau \quad \sigma_k <: \sigma \quad \tau <: \tau_k}{\Gamma \vdash e_1.l_k := \tau \, \varsigma(x : \sigma) e_2 : \rho}$
$(\text{where } \rho \equiv [l_i : \sigma_i \to \tau_i \,^{i \in 1 \ldots n}] \text{ and } k \in 1 \ldots n)$

(SUB) $\dfrac{\Gamma \vdash e : \sigma \quad \sigma <: \tau}{\Gamma \vdash e : \tau}$

Fig. 4. The type system for $\mathbf{Ob}_{<:}$

$$\boxed{\vdash E : \tau \Rightarrow \tau}$$

(CXHOLE) $\vdash [] : \tau \Rightarrow \tau$

(CXIVKL) $\dfrac{\vdash E : \sigma \Rightarrow [\ldots, l : \rho \to \tau, \ldots] \quad \vdash e : \rho}{\vdash E.l(e) : \sigma \Rightarrow \tau}$

(CXIVKR) $\dfrac{\vdash e : [\ldots, l : \rho \to \tau, \ldots] \quad \vdash E : \sigma \Rightarrow \rho}{\vdash e.l(E) : \sigma \Rightarrow \tau}$

(CXUPD) $\dfrac{\vdash E : \sigma' \Rightarrow \rho \quad \mathsf{self} : \rho, x : \sigma \vdash e : \tau \quad \sigma_k <: \sigma \quad \tau <: \tau_k}{\vdash E.l_k := \tau \, \varsigma(x : \sigma) e : \sigma' \Rightarrow \rho}$
$(\text{where } \rho \equiv [l_i : \sigma_i \to \tau_i \,^{i \in 1 \ldots n}] \text{ and } 1 \leq k \leq n)$

(CXSUB) $\dfrac{\vdash E : \sigma \Rightarrow \rho \quad \vdash \rho <: \rho'}{\vdash E : \sigma \Rightarrow \rho'}$

Fig. 5. Well-typed contexts

Generic Universe Types

Werner Dietl[1], Sophia Drossopoulou[2], and Peter Müller[1]

[1] ETH Zurich
{Werner.Dietl,Peter.Mueller}@inf.ethz.ch
[2] Imperial College London
S.Drossopoulou@imperial.ac.uk

Abstract. Ownership is a powerful concept to structure the object store and to control aliasing and modifications of objects. This paper presents an ownership type system for a Java-like programming language with generic types. Like our earlier Universe type system, Generic Universe Types enforce the owner-as-modifier discipline. This discipline does not restrict aliasing, but requires modifications of an object to be initiated by its owner. This allows owner objects to control state changes of owned objects, for instance, to maintain invariants. Generic Universe Types require a small annotation overhead and provide strong static guarantees. They are the first type system that combines the owner-as-modifier discipline with type genericity.

1 Introduction

The concept of object ownership allows programmers to structure the object store hierarchically and to control aliasing and access between objects. Ownership has been applied successfully to various problems, for instance, program verification [18,20,21], thread synchronization [5,15], memory management [2,6], and representation independence [3].

Existing ownership models share fundamental concepts: Each object has at most one owner object. The set of all objects with the same owner is called a *context*. The *root context* is the set of objects with no owner. The ownership relation is a tree order.

However, existing models differ in the restrictions they enforce. The original ownership types [9] and their descendants [4,7,8,24] restrict aliasing and enforce the *owner-as-dominator* discipline: All reference chains from an object in the root context to an object o in a different context go through o's owner. This severe restriction of aliasing is necessary for some of the applications of ownership, for instance, memory management and representation independence.

However, for applications such as program verification, restricting aliasing is not necessary. Instead, it suffices to enforce the *owner-as-modifier* discipline: An object o may be referenced by any other object, but reference chains that do not pass through o's owner must not be used to modify o. This allows owner objects to control state changes of owned objects and thus maintain invariants. The owner-as-modifier discipline has been inspired by Flexible Alias Protection [23]. It is enforced

E. Ernst (Ed.): ECOOP 2007, LNAI 4609, pp. 28–53, 2007.

by the Universe type system [12], in Spec#'s dynamic ownership model [18], and Effective Ownership Types [19]. The owner-as-modifier discipline imposes weaker restrictions than the owner-as-dominator discipline, which allows it to handle common implementations where objects are shared between objects, such as collections with iterators, shared buffers, or the Flyweight pattern [12,22]. Some implementations can be slightly adapted to satisfy the owner-as-modifier discipline, for example an iterator can delegate modifications to the corresponding collection which owns the internal representation.

Although ownership type systems have covered all features of Java-like languages (including for example exceptions, inner classes, and static class members) there are only three proposals of ownership type systems that support generic types. SafeJava [4] supports type parameters and ownership parameters independently, but does not integrate both forms of parametricity. This leads to significant annotation overhead. Ownership Domains [1] combine type parameters and domain parameters into a single parameter space and thereby reduce the annotation overhead. However, their formalization does not cover type parameters. Ownership Generic Java (OGJ) [24] allows programmers to attach ownership information through type parameters. For instance, a collection of Book objects can be typed as "my collection of library books", expressing that the collection object belongs to the current this object, whereas the Book objects in the collection belong to an object "library". OGJ enforces the owner-as-dominator discipline. It piggybacks ownership information on type parameters. In particular, each class C has a type parameter to encode the owner of a C object. This encoding allows OGJ to use a slight adaptation of the normal Java type rules to also check ownership, which makes the formalization very elegant.

However, OGJ cannot be easily adapted to enforce the owner-as-modifier discipline. For example, OGJ would forbid a reference from the iterator (object 6) in Fig. 1 to a node (object 5) of the map (object 3), because the reference bypasses the node's owner. However, such references are necessary, and are legal in the owner-as-modifier discipline. A type system can permit such references in two ways.

First, if the iterator contained a field theMap that references the associated map object, then path-dependent types [1,4] can express that the current field of the iterator points to a Node object that is owned by theMap. Unfortunately, path-dependent types require the fields on the path (here, theMap) to be final, which is too restrictive for many applications.

Second, one can loosen up the static ownership information by allowing certain references to point to objects in any context [12]. Subtyping allows values with specific ownership information to be assigned to "any" variables, and downcasts with runtime checks can be used to recover specific ownership information from such variables. In OGJ, this subtype relation between any-types and other types would require covariant subtyping, for instance, that Node<This> is a subtype of Node<Any>, which is not supported in Java (or C#). Therefore, piggybacking ownership on the standard Java type system is not possible in the presence of "any".

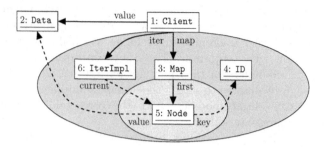

Fig. 1. Object structure of a map from ID to Data objects. The map is represented by Node objects. The iterator has a direct reference to a node. Objects, references, and contexts are depicted by rectangles, arrows, and ellipses, respectively. Owner objects sit atop the context of objects they own. Arrows are labeled with the name of the variable that stores the reference. Dashed arrows depict references that cross context boundaries without going through the owner. Such references must not be used to modify the state of the referenced objects.

In this paper, we present Generic Universe Types (GUT), an ownership type system for a programming language with generic types similar to Java 5 and C# 2.0. GUT enforces the owner-as-modifier discipline using an **any** ownership modifier (analogous to the **readonly** modifier in non-generic Universe types [12]). Our type system supports type parameters for classes and methods. The annotation overhead for programmers is as low as in OGJ, although the presence of **any** makes the type rules more involved. A particularly interesting aspect of our work is how generics and ownership can be combined in the presence of an **any** modifier, in particular, how a restricted form of ownership covariance can be permitted without runtime checks.

Outline. Sec. 2 illustrates the main concepts of GUT by an example. Secs. 3 and 4 present the type rules and the runtime model of GUT, respectively. Sec. 5 presents the type safety and the owner-as-modifier property theorems. Details and proofs can be found in the accompanying technical report [10].

2   Main Concepts

In this section, we explain the main concepts of GUT informally by an example. Class Map (Fig. 2) implements a generic map from keys to values. Key-value pairs are stored in singly-linked Node objects. Class Node extends the superclass MapNode (both Fig. 3), which is used by the iterator (classes Iter and IterImpl in Fig. 4). The **main** method of class Client (Fig. 5) builds up the map structure shown in Fig. 1. For simplicity, we omit access modifiers from all examples.

Ownership Modifiers. A type in GUT is either a type variable or consists of an ownership modifier, a class name, and possibly type arguments. The *ownership modifier* expresses object ownership relative to the current receiver object this[1]. Programs may contain the ownership modifiers peer, rep, and any. peer expresses that an object has the same owner as the this object, rep expresses that an object is owned by this, and any expresses that an object may have any owner. any types are supertypes of the rep and peer types with the same class and type arguments because they convey less specific ownership information.

The use of ownership modifiers is illustrated by class Map (Fig. 2). A Map object owns its Node objects since they form the internal representation of the map and should, therefore, be protected from unwanted modifications. This ownership relation is expressed by the rep modifier of Map's field first, which points to the first node of the map.

```
class Map<K, V> {
    rep Node<K, V> first;

    void put(K key, V value) {
        rep Node<K, V> newfirst = new rep Node<K, V>();
        newfirst.init(key, value, first);
        first = newfirst;
    }

    pure V get(K key) {
        peer Iter<K, V> i = iterator();
        while (i.hasNext()) {
            if (i.getKey().equals(key)) return i.getValue();
            i.next();
        }
        return null;
    }

    pure peer Iter<K, V> iterator() {
        peer IterImpl<K, V, rep Node<K, V> > res;
        res = new peer IterImpl<K, V, rep Node<K, V> >();
        res.setCurrent(first);
        return res;
    }

    pure peer IterImpl<K, V, rep Node<K, V> > altIterator() {
        /* same implementation as method iterator() above */
    }
}
```

Fig. 2. An implementation of a generic map. Map objects own their Node objects, as indicated by the rep modifier in all occurrences of class Node. Method altIterator is for illustration purposes only.

The owner-as-modifier discipline is enforced by disallowing modifications of objects through any references. That is, an expression of an any type may be

---

[1] We ignore static methods in this paper, but an extension is possible [20].

used as receiver of field reads and calls to side-effect free (*pure*) methods, but not of field updates or calls to non-pure methods. To check this property, we require side-effect free methods to be annotated with the keyword pure.

Viewpoint Adaptation. Since ownership modifiers express ownership relative to this, they have to be adapted when this "viewpoint" changes. Consider Node's inherited method init (Fig. 3). After substituting the type variable X, the third parameter has type peer Node<K,V>. The peer modifier expresses that the parameter object must have the same owner as the receiver of the method. On the other hand, Map's method put calls init on a rep Node receiver, that is, an object that is owned by this. Therefore, the third parameter of the call to init also has to be owned by this. This means that from this particular call's viewpoint, the third parameter needs a rep modifier, although it is declared with a peer modifier. In the type system, this *viewpoint adaptation* is done by combining the type of the receiver of a call (here, rep Node<K,V>) with the type of the formal parameter (here, peer Node<K,V>). This combination yields the argument type from the caller's point of view (here, rep Node<K,V>).

```
class MapNode<K, V, X extends peer MapNode<K, V, X> > {
    K key; V value; X next;

    void init(K k, V v, X n) { key = k; value = v; next = n; }
}

class Node<K, V> extends MapNode<K, V, peer Node<K, V> > {}
```

Fig. 3. Nodes form the internal representation of maps. Class MapNode implements nodes for singly-linked lists. Using a type variable for the type of next is useful to implement iterators. The subclass Node instantiates MapNode's type parameter X to implement a list of nodes with the same owner.

Viewpoint adaptation and the owner-as-modifier discipline provide encapsulation of internal representation objects. Assume that class Map by mistake leaked a reference to an internal node, for instance, by making first public or by providing a method that returns the node. By viewpoint adaptation of the node type, rep Node<K,V>, clients of the map can only obtain an any reference to the node and, thus, the owner-as-modifier discipline guarantees that clients cannot directly modify the node structure. This allows the map to maintain invariants over the node, for instance, that the node structure is acyclic.

Type Parameters. Ownership modifiers are also used in actual type arguments. For instance, Map's method iterator instantiates IterImpl with the type arguments K, V, and rep Node<K,V>. Thus, local variable res has type peer IterImpl<K,V,rep Node<K,V>>, which has two ownership modifiers. The *main modifier* peer expresses that the IterImpl object has the same owner as this, whereas the *argument modifier* rep expresses that the Node objects used by the iterator are owned by this. It is important to understand that this argument modifier again expresses ownership relative to the current this object (here, the Map object), and not relative to the instance of the generic class that contains the argument modifier (here, the IterImpl object res).

```
interface Iter<K, V> {
    pure K getKey();
    pure V getValue();
    pure boolean hasNext();
    void next();
}

class IterImpl<K, V, X extends any MapNode<K, V, X>>
implements Iter<K, V> {
    X current;

    void setCurrent(X c) { current = c; }
    pure K getKey() { return current.key; }
    pure V getValue() { return current.value; }
    pure boolean hasNext() { return current != null; }
    void next() { current = current.next; }
}
```

Fig. 4. Class IterImpl implements iterators over MapNode structures. The precise node type is passed as type parameter. The upper bound allows methods to access a node's fields. Interface Iter hides IterImpl's third type parameter from clients.

Type variables have upper bounds, which default to any Object. In a class C, the ownership modifiers of an upper bound express ownership relative to the C instance this. However, when C's type variables are instantiated, the modifiers of the actual type arguments are relative to the receiver of the method that contains the instantiation. Therefore, checking the conformance of a type argument to its upper bound requires a viewpoint adaptation. For instance, to check the instantiation peer IterImpl<K,V,rep Node<K,V>> in class Map, we adapt the upper bound of IterImpl's type variable X (any MapNode<K,V,X>) from viewpoint peer IterImpl<K,V,rep Node<K,V>> to the viewpoint this. With the appropriate substitutions, this adaptation yields any MapNode<K,V,rep Node<K,V>>. The actual type argument rep Node<K,V> is a subtype of the adapted upper bound. Therefore, the instantiation is correct. The rep modifier in the type argument and the adapted upper bound reflects correctly that the current node of this particular iterator is owned by this.

Type variables are not subject to the viewpoint adaptation that is performed for non-variable types. When type variables are used, for instance, in field declarations, the ownership information they carry stays implicit and does, therefore, not have to be adapted. The substitution of type variables by their actual type arguments happens in the scope in which the type variables were instantiated. Therefore, the viewpoint is the same as for the instantiation, and no viewpoint adaptation is re-quired. For instance, the call expression `iter.getKey()` in method `main` (Fig. 5) has type `rep ID`, because the result type of `getKey()` is the type variable K, which gets substituted by the first type argument of `iter`'s type, `rep ID`.

Thus, even though an `IterImpl` object does not know the owner of the keys and values (due to the implicit `any` upper bound for K and V), clients of the iterator can recover the exact ownership information from the type arguments. This illustrates that Generic Universe Types provide strong static guarantees similar to those of owner-parametric systems [9], even in the presence of `any` types. The corresponding implementation in non-generic Universe types requires a downcast from the `any` type to a `rep` type and the corresponding runtime check [12].

```
class ID { /* ... */ }
class Data { /* ... */ }

class Client {
    void main(any Data value) {
        rep Map<rep ID, any Data> map = new rep Map<rep ID, any Data>();
        map.put(new rep ID(), value);

        rep Iter<rep ID, any Data> iter = map.iterator();
        rep ID id = iter.getKey();
    }
}
```

Fig. 5. Main program for our example. The execution of method `main` creates the object structure in Fig. 1.

Limited Covariance and Viewpoint Adaptation of Type Arguments. Subtyping with covariant type arguments is in general not statically type safe. For instance, if `List<String>` were a subtype of `List<Object>`, then clients that view a string list through type `List<Object>` could store `Object` instances in the string list, which breaks type safety. The same problem occurs for the own-ership information encoded in types. If `peer IterImpl<K,V,rep Node<K,V>>` were a subtype of `peer IterImpl<K,V,any Node<K,V>>`, then clients that view the iterator through the latter type could use method `setCurrent` (Fig. 4) to set the iterator to a `Node` object with an arbitrary owner, even though the it-erator requires a specific owner. The covariance problem can be prevented by disallowing covariant type arguments (like in Java and C#), by runtime checks, or by elaborate syntactic support [13].

However, the owner-as-modifier discipline supports a limited form of covari-ance without any additional checks. Covariance is permitted if the main modifier of the supertype is `any`. For example, `peer IterImpl<K,V,rep Node<K,V>>` is an admissible subtype of `any IterImpl<K,V,any Node<K,V>>`. This is safe be-cause the owner-as-modifier discipline prevents mutations of objects referenced through **any** references. In particular, it is not possible to set the iterator to an any **Node** object, which prevents the unsoundness illustrated above.

Besides subtyping, GUT provides another way to view objects through different types, namely viewpoint adaptation. If the adaptation of a type argument yields an **any** type, the same unsoundness as through covariance could occur. Therefore, when a viewpoint adaptation changes an ownership modifier of a type argument to **any**, it also changes the main modifier to **any**.

This behavior is illustrated by method **main** of class **Client** in Fig. 5. Assume that **main** calls **altIterator()** instead of **iterator()**. As illustrated by Fig. 1, the most precise type for the call expression **map.altIterator()** would be **rep IterImpl<rep ID, any Data, any Node<rep ID, any Data>>** because the **IterImpl** object is owned by the **Client** object **this** (hence, the main modifier **rep**), but the nodes referenced by the iterator are neither owned by **this** nor peers of **this** (hence, **any Node**). However, this viewpoint adaptation would change an argument modifier of **altIterator**'s result type from **rep** to **any**. This would allow method **main** to use method **setCurrent** to set the iterator to an **any Node** object and is, thus, not type safe. The correct viewpoint adaptation yields **any IterImpl<rep ID, any Data, any Node<rep ID, any Data>>**. This type is safe, because it prevents the **main** method from mutating the iterator, in particular, from calling the non-pure method **setCurrent**.

Since **next** is also non-pure, **main** must not call **iter.next()** either, which renders **IterImpl** objects useless outside the associated **Map** object. To solve this issue, we provide interface **Iter**, which does not expose the type of internal nodes to clients. The call **map.iterator()** has type **rep Iter<rep ID, any Data>**, which does allow **main** to call **iter.next()**. Nevertheless, the type variable **X** for the type of **current** in class **IterImpl** is useful to improve static type safety. Since the current node is neither a **rep** nor a **peer** of the iterator, the only alternative to a type variable is an **any** type. However, an **any** type would not capture the relationship between an iterator and the associated list. In particular, it would allow clients to use **setCurrent** to set the iterator to a node of an arbitrary map. For a discussion of alternative designs see [10].

3   Static Checking

In this section, we formalize the compile time aspects of GUT. We define the syntax of the programming language, formalize viewpoint adaptation, define subtyping and well-formedness conditions, and present the type rules.

3.1   Programming Language

We formalize Generic Universe Types for a sequential subset of Java 5 and C# 2.0 including classes and inheritance, instance fields, dynamically-bound methods, and the usual operations on objects (allocation, field read, field update, casts). For simplicity, we omit several features of Java and C# such as interfaces, exceptions, constructors, static fields and methods, inner classes, primitive types and the corresponding expressions, and all statements for control flow. We do not expect that any of these features is difficult to handle (see for instance [4,11,20]). The language we use is similar to Featherweight Generic Java [14]. We added field updates because the treatment of side effects is essential for ownership type systems and especially the owner-as-modifier discipline.

Fig. 6 summarizes the syntax of our language and our naming conventions for variables. We assume that all identifiers of a program are globally unique except for this as well as method and parameter names of overridden methods. This can be achieved easily by preceding each identifier with the class or method name of its declaration (but we omit this prefix in our examples).

The superscript ^{s} distinguishes the sorts for static checking from corresponding sorts used to describe the runtime behavior, but is omitted whenever the context determines whether we refer to static or dynamic entities.

$\overline{\mathrm{T}}$ denotes a sequence of Ts. In such a sequence, we denote the i-th element by T_i. We sometimes use sequences of tuples $S = \overline{\mathrm{X}\,\mathrm{T}}$ as maps and use a function-like notation to access an element $S(\mathrm{X}_i) = \mathrm{T}_i$. A sequence $\overline{\mathrm{T}}$ can be empty. The empty sequence is denoted by ϵ.

A program (P $\in$ Program) consists of a sequence of classes, the identifier of a main class (C $\in$ ClassId), and a main expression (e $\in$ Expr). A program is executed by creating an instance o of C and then evaluating e with o as this object. We assume that we always have access to the current program P, and keep P implicit in the notations. Each class (Cls $\in$ Class) has a class identifier, type variables with upper bounds, a superclass with type arguments, a list of field declarations, and a list of method declarations. FieldId is the sort of field identifiers f. Like in Java, each class directly or transitively extends the predefined class Object.

A type (^{s}T $\in$ ^{s}Type) is either a non-variable type or a type variable identifier (X $\in$ TVarId). A non-variable type (^{s}N $\in$ ^{s}NType) consists of an ownership modifier, a class identifier, and a sequence of type arguments.

An ownership modifier (u $\in$ OM) can be $\mathtt{peer}_u$, $\mathtt{rep}_u$, or $\mathtt{any}_u$, as well as the modifier $\mathtt{this}_u$, which is used solely as main modifier for the type of this. The modifier $\mathtt{this}_u$ may not appear in programs, but is used by the type system to distinguish accesses through this from other accesses. We omit the subscript u if it is clear from context that we mean an ownership modifier.

A method (mt $\in$ Meth) consists of the method type variables with their upper bounds, the purity annotation, the return type, the method identifier (m $\in$ MethId), the formal method parameters (x $\in$ ParId) with their types, and an expression as body. The result of evaluating the expression is returned by the method. ParId includes the implicit method parameter this.

To be able to enforce the owner-as-modifier discipline, we have to distinguish statically between side-effect free (pure) methods and methods that potentially have side effects. Pure methods are marked by the keyword pure. In our syntax, we mark all other methods by nonpure, although we omit this keyword in our examples. To focus on the essentials of the type system, we do not include purity checks, but they can be added easily [20].

An expression (e ∈ Expr) can be the `null` literal, method parameter access, field read, field update, method call, object creation, and cast.

Type checking is performed in a type environment ($^s\Gamma \in {}^s\text{Env}$), which maps the type variables of the enclosing class and method to their upper bounds and method parameters to their types. Since the domains of these mappings are disjoint, we overload the notation, where $^s\Gamma(X)$ refers to the upper bound of type variable X, and $^s\Gamma(x)$ refers to the type of method parameter x.

$$
\begin{array}{lll}
\text{P} \in \text{Program} & ::= & \overline{\text{Cls}}\ \text{C}\ \text{e} \\
\text{Cls} \in \text{Class} & ::= & \text{class}\ \text{C}<\overline{\text{X}\ {}^s\text{N}}>\ \text{extends}\ \text{C}<\overline{{}^s\text{T}}>\ \{\ \overline{\text{f}\ {}^s\text{T}};\ \overline{\text{mt}}\ \} \\
{}^s\text{T} \in {}^s\text{Type} & ::= & {}^s\text{N}\ |\ \text{X} \\
{}^s\text{N} \in {}^s\text{NType} & ::= & \text{u}\ \text{C}<\overline{{}^s\text{T}}> \\
\text{u} \in \text{OM} & ::= & \text{peer}_u\ |\ \text{rep}_u\ |\ \text{any}_u\ |\ \text{this}_u \\
\text{mt} \in \text{Meth} & ::= & <\overline{\text{X}\ {}^s\text{N}}>\ \text{w}\ {}^s\text{T}\ \text{m}(\overline{\text{x}\ {}^s\text{T}})\ \{\ \text{return}\ \text{e}\ \} \\
\text{w} \in \text{Purity} & ::= & \text{pure}\ |\ \text{nonpure} \\
\text{e} \in \text{Expr} & ::= & \text{null}\ |\ \text{x}\ |\ \text{e.f}\ |\ \text{e.f=e}\ |\ \text{e.m}<\overline{{}^s\text{T}}>(\overline{\text{e}})\ |\ \text{new}\ {}^s\text{N}\ |\ ({}^s\text{T})\ \text{e} \\
{}^s\Gamma \in {}^s\text{Env} & ::= & \overline{\text{X}\ {}^s\text{N}};\ \overline{\text{x}\ {}^s\text{T}} \\
\end{array}
$$

Fig. 6. Syntax and type environments

3.2   Viewpoint Adaptation

Since ownership modifiers express ownership relative to an object, they have to be adapted whenever the viewpoint changes. In the type rules, we need to *adapt a type T from a viewpoint* that is described by another type T' *to the viewpoint* this. In the following, we omit the phrase "to the viewpoint this". To perform the viewpoint adaptation, we define an overloaded operator ▷ to: (1) Adapt an ownership modifier from a viewpoint that is described by another ownership modifier; (2) Adapt a type from a viewpoint that is described by an ownership modifier; (3) Adapt a type from a viewpoint that is described by another type.

Adapting an Ownership Modifier w.r.t. an Ownership Modifier. We explain viewpoint adaptation using a field access $e_1.f$. Analogous adaptations occur for method parameters and results as well as upper bounds of type parameters. Let u be the main modifier of e_1's type, which expresses ownership relative to this. Let u' be the main modifier of f's type, which expresses ownership relative to the object that contains f. Then relative to this, the type of the field access $e_1.f$ has main modifier u▷u'.

$$
\begin{array}{ll}
\text{▷} :: \text{OM} \times \text{OM} \to \text{OM} & \\
\text{this} \triangleright \text{u}' = \text{u}' & \text{u} \triangleright \text{this} = \text{u} \\
\text{peer} \triangleright \text{peer} = \text{peer} & \text{rep} \triangleright \text{peer} = \text{rep} \\
\text{u} \triangleright \text{u}' = \text{any} \quad \text{otherwise} & \\
\end{array}
$$

The field access $e_1.f$ illustrates the motivation for this definition: (1) Accesses through this (that is, e_1 is the variable this) do not require a viewpoint adaptation since the ownership modifier of the field is already relative to this.

(2) In the formalization of subtyping (see ST-1) we combine an ownership modifier u with $this_u$. Again, this does not require a viewpoint adaptation.

(3) If the main modifiers of both e_1 and f are peer, then the object referenced by e_1 has the same owner as this and the object referenced by $e_1.f$ has the same owner as e_1 and, thus, the same owner as this. Consequently, the main modifier of $e_1.f$ is also peer. (4) If the main modifier of e_1 is rep and the main modifier of f is peer, then the main modifier of $e_1.f$ is rep, because the object referenced by e_1 is owned by this and the object referenced by $e_1.f$ has the same owner as e_1, that is, this. (5) In all other cases, we cannot determine statically that the object referenced by $e_1.f$ has the same owner as this or is owned by this. Therefore, in these cases the main modifier of $e_1.f$ is any.

Adapting a Type w.r.t. an Ownership Modifier. As explained in Sec. 2, type variables are not subject to viewpoint adaptation. For non-variable types, we determine the adapted main modifier using the auxiliary function $\triangleright_m$ below and adapt the type arguments recursively:

$$\triangleright :: \text{OM} \times {}^s\text{Type} \rightarrow {}^s\text{Type}$$
$$u \triangleright X = X$$
$$u \triangleright N = (u \triangleright_m N) \ C\langle\overline{u \triangleright T}\rangle \qquad \text{where } N = u' \ C\langle\overline{T}\rangle$$

The adapted main modifier is determined by $u \triangleright u'$, except for unsafe (covariance-like) viewpoint adaptations, as described in Sec. 2, in which case it is any. Unsafe adaptations occur if at least one of N's type arguments contains the modifier rep, u' is peer, and u is rep or peer. This leads to the following definition:

$$\triangleright_m :: \text{OM} \times {}^s\text{NType} \rightarrow \text{OM}$$
$$u \triangleright_m u' \ C\langle\overline{T}\rangle = \begin{cases} \text{any} & \text{if } (u = \text{rep} \vee u = \text{peer}) \wedge u' = \text{peer} \wedge \text{rep} \in \overline{T} \\ u \triangleright u' & \text{otherwise} \end{cases}$$

The notation $u \in \overline{T}$ expresses that at least one type T_i or its (transitive) type arguments contain ownership modifier u.

Adapting a Type w.r.t. a Type. We adapt a type T from the viewpoint described by another type, $u \ C\langle\overline{T}\rangle$:

$$\triangleright :: {}^s\text{NType} \times {}^s\text{Type} \rightarrow {}^s\text{Type}$$
$$u \ C\langle\overline{T}\rangle \triangleright T = (u \triangleright T)[\overline{T/X}] \qquad \text{where } \overline{X} = \text{dom}(C)$$

The operator $\triangleright$ adapts the ownership modifiers of T and then substitutes the type arguments $\overline{T}$ for the type variables $\overline{X}$ of C. This substitution is denoted by $[\overline{T/X}]$. Since the type arguments already are relative to this, they are not subject to viewpoint adaptation. Therefore, the substitution of type variables happens after the viewpoint adaptation of T's ownership modifiers. For a declaration class $C\langle\overline{X}\rangle$ ..., dom(C) denotes C's type variables $\overline{X}$.

Note that the first parameter is a non-variable type, because concrete ownership information u is needed to adapt the viewpoint and the actual type arguments $\overline{T}$ are needed to substitute the type variables $\overline{X}$. In the type rules, subsumption will be used to replace type variables by their upper bounds and thereby obtain a concrete type as first argument of $\triangleright$.

Example. The hypothetical call `map.altIterator()` in `main` (Fig. 5) illustrates the most interesting viewpoint adaptation, which we discussed in Sec. 2. The type of this call is the adaptation of `peer IterImpl<K,V,rep Node<K,V>>` (the return type of `altIterator`) from `rep Map<rep ID,any Data>` (the type of the receiver expression). According to the above definition, we first adapt the return type from the viewpoint of the receiver type, `rep`, and then substitute type variables.

The type arguments of the adapted type are obtained by applying viewpoint adaptation recursively to the type arguments. The type variables K and V are not affected by the adaptation. For the third type argument, `rep ▷ rep Node<K,V>` yields `any Node<K,V>` because `rep ▷ rep=any`, and again because the type variables K and V are not subject to viewpoint adaptation. Note that here, an ownership modifier of a type argument is promoted from `rep` to `any`. Therefore, to avoid unsafe covariance-like adaptations, the main modifier of the adapted type must be `any`. This is, indeed, the case, as the main modifier is determined by `rep ▷_m peer IterImpl<K,V,rep Node<K,V>>`, which yields `any`.

So far, the adaptation yields `any IterImpl<K,V,any Node<K,V>>`. Now we substitute the type variables K and V by the instantiations given in the receiver type, `rep ID` and `any Data`, and obtain the type of the call:

```
any IterImpl<rep ID, any Data, any Node<rep ID,any Data>>
```

3.3   Subclassing and Subtyping

We use the term *subclassing* to refer to the relation on classes as declared in a program by the `extends` keyword, irrespective of main modifiers. *Subtyping* takes main modifiers into account.

Subclassing. The subclass relation ⊑ is defined on instantiated classes, which are denoted by C<T̄>. The subclass relation is the smallest relation satisfying the rules in Fig. 7. Each un-instantiated class is a subclass of the class it extends (SC-1). The form `class C<X̄ N̄>` extends C'<T̄'> { f̄ T̄; m̄ }, or a prefix thereof, expresses that the program contains such a class declaration. Subclassing is reflexive (SC-2) and transitive (SC-3). Subclassing is preserved by substitution of type arguments for type variables (SC-4). Note that such substitutions may lead to ill-formed types, for instance, when the upper bound of a substituted type variable is not respected. We prevent such types by well-formedness rules, presented in Fig. 9.

Subtyping. The subtype relation <: is defined on types. The judgment $\Gamma \vdash T <: T'$ expresses that type T is a subtype of type T' in type environment Γ. The environment is needed since types may contain type variables. The rules for this subtyping judgment are presented in Fig. 8. Two types with the same main modifier are subtypes if the corresponding classes are subclasses. Ownership modifiers in the `extends` clause (T̄') are relative to the instance of class C, whereas the modifiers in a type are relative to `this`. Therefore, T̄' has to be adapted from the viewpoint of the C instance to `this` (ST-1). Since both `this`_u and `peer`

$$\text{SC-1} \frac{\texttt{class } \texttt{C<}\overline{X}\texttt{> extends } \texttt{C'<}\overline{T'}\texttt{>}}{\texttt{C<}\overline{X}\texttt{>} \sqsubseteq \texttt{C'<}\overline{T'}\texttt{>}} \qquad \text{SC-2} \frac{}{\texttt{C<}\overline{T}\texttt{>} \sqsubseteq \texttt{C<}\overline{T}\texttt{>}}$$

$$\text{SC-3} \frac{\begin{array}{c}\texttt{C<}\overline{T}\texttt{>} \sqsubseteq \texttt{C''<}\overline{T''}\texttt{>} \\ \texttt{C''<}\overline{T''}\texttt{>} \sqsubseteq \texttt{C'<}\overline{T'}\texttt{>}\end{array}}{\texttt{C<}\overline{T}\texttt{>} \sqsubseteq \texttt{C'<}\overline{T'}\texttt{>}} \qquad \text{SC-4} \frac{\texttt{C<}\overline{T}\texttt{>} \sqsubseteq \texttt{C'<}\overline{T'}\texttt{>}}{\texttt{C<}\overline{T}\texttt{[}T''/X''\texttt{]>} \sqsubseteq \texttt{C'<}\overline{T'}\texttt{[}T''/X''\texttt{]>}}$$

Fig. 7. Rules for subclassing

express that an object has the same owner as `this`, a type with main modifier $\texttt{this}_u$ is a subtype of the corresponding type with main modifier `peer` (ST-2). This rule allows us to treat `this` as an object of a `peer` type. Subtyping is transitive (ST-3). A type variable is a subtype of its upper bound in the type environment (ST-4). Two types are subtypes, if they obey the limited covariance described in Sec. 2 (ST-5). Covariant subtyping is expressed by the relation $<:_a$. Covariant subtyping is reflexive (TA-1). A supertype may have more general type arguments than the subtype if the main modifier of the supertype is `any` (TA-2). Note that the sequences $\overline{T}$ and $\overline{T'}$ in rule TA-2 can be empty, which allows one to derive, for instance, `peer Object` $<:_a$ `any Object`. Reflexivity of $<:$ follows from TA-1 and ST-5.

$$\text{ST-1} \frac{\texttt{C<}\overline{T}\texttt{>} \sqsubseteq \texttt{C'<}\overline{T'}\texttt{>}}{\Gamma \vdash u\ \texttt{C<}\overline{T}\texttt{>} <: u \triangleright (\texttt{this}_u\ \texttt{C'<}\overline{T'}\texttt{>})} \qquad \text{ST-2} \frac{}{\Gamma \vdash \texttt{this}_u\ \texttt{C<}\overline{T}\texttt{>} <: \texttt{peer } \texttt{C<}\overline{T}\texttt{>}}$$

$$\text{ST-3} \frac{\begin{array}{c}\Gamma \vdash T <: T'' \\ \Gamma \vdash T'' <: T'\end{array}}{\Gamma \vdash T <: T'} \qquad \text{ST-4} \frac{}{\Gamma \vdash X <: \Gamma(X)} \qquad \text{ST-5} \frac{T <:_a T'}{\Gamma \vdash T <: T'}$$

$$\text{TA-1} \frac{}{T <:_a T} \qquad \text{TA-2} \frac{T <:_a T'}{u\ \texttt{C<}\overline{T}\texttt{>} <:_a \texttt{any } \texttt{C<}\overline{T'}\texttt{>}}$$

Fig. 8. Rules for subtyping and limited covariance

In our example, using rule TA-1 for K and V, and rule TA-2 we obtain `rep Node<K,V>` $<:_a$ `any Node<K,V>`. Rules TA-2 and ST-5 allow us to derive

    `peer IterImpl<K,V,rep Node<K,V>>` $<:$ `any IterImpl<K,V,any Node<K,V>>`,

which is an example for limited covariance. Note that it is not possible to derive

    `peer IterImpl<K,V,rep Node<K,V>>` $<:$ `peer IterImpl<K,V,any Node<K,V>>`;

that would be unsafe covariant subtyping as discussed in Sec. 2.

3.4 Lookup Functions

In this subsection, we define the functions to look up the type of a field or the signature of a method.

Field Lookup. The function $^sfType(\mathtt{C},\mathtt{f})$ yields the type of field $\mathtt{f}$ as declared in class $\mathtt{C}$. The result is undefined if $\mathtt{f}$ is not declared in $\mathtt{C}$. Since identifiers are assumed to be globally unique, there is only one declaration for each field identifier.

$$\text{SFT}\,\frac{\texttt{class C<\_> extends \_<\_> \{ \ldots T f\ldots; \_ \}}}{^sfType(\mathtt{C},\mathtt{f}) = \mathtt{T}}$$

Method Lookup. The function $mType(\mathtt{C},\mathtt{m})$ yields the signature of method $\mathtt{m}$ as declared in class $\mathtt{C}$. The result is undefined if $\mathtt{m}$ is not declared in $\mathtt{C}$. We do not allow overloading of methods; therefore, the method identifier is sufficient to uniquely identify a method.

$$\text{SMT}\,\frac{\texttt{class C<\_> extends \_<\_> \{ \_ ; } \ldots \texttt{<}\overline{\mathtt{X}_m\ \mathtt{N}_b}\texttt{> w } \mathtt{T}_r\ \mathtt{m}(\overline{\mathtt{x}\ \mathtt{T}_p}) \ldots\}}{mType(\mathtt{C},\mathtt{m}) = \texttt{<}\overline{\mathtt{X}_m\ \mathtt{N}_b}\texttt{> w } \mathtt{T}_r\ \mathtt{m}(\overline{\mathtt{x}\ \mathtt{T}_p})}$$

3.5 Well-Formedness

In this subsection, we define well-formedness of types, methods, classes, programs, and type environments. The well-formedness rules are summarized in Fig. 9 and explained in the following.

$$\text{WFT-1}\,\frac{\mathtt{X} \in \mathrm{dom}(\Gamma)}{\Gamma \vdash \mathtt{X}\ \mathtt{ok}} \qquad \text{WFT-2}\,\frac{\Gamma \vdash \overline{\mathtt{T}}\ \mathtt{ok} \qquad \begin{array}{c}\texttt{class C<\_ }\overline{\mathtt{N}}\texttt{> } \ldots \\ \Gamma \vdash \overline{\mathtt{T}} <: ((\mathtt{u}\ \mathtt{C}\texttt{<}\overline{\mathtt{T}}\texttt{>}) \triangleright \overline{\mathtt{N}})\end{array}}{\Gamma \vdash \mathtt{u}\ \mathtt{C}\texttt{<}\overline{\mathtt{T}}\texttt{>}\ \mathtt{ok}}$$

$$\text{WFM-1}\,\frac{\begin{array}{c}\Gamma = \overline{\mathtt{X}_m\ \mathtt{N}_b}, \overline{\mathtt{X}\ \mathtt{N}}; \mathtt{this}\ (\mathtt{this}_u\ \mathtt{C}\texttt{<}\overline{\mathtt{X}}\texttt{>}), \overline{\mathtt{x}\ \mathtt{T}_p} \\ \Gamma \vdash \mathtt{T}_r, \overline{\mathtt{N}_b}, \overline{\mathtt{T}_p}\ \mathtt{ok} \qquad \Gamma \vdash \mathtt{e} : \mathtt{T}_r \qquad override(\mathtt{C},\mathtt{m}) \\ \mathtt{w} = \mathtt{pure} \;\Rightarrow\; (\overline{\mathtt{T}_p} = \overline{\mathtt{any} \triangleright \mathtt{T}_p} \;\wedge\; \overline{\mathtt{N}_b} = \overline{\mathtt{any} \triangleright \mathtt{N}_b})\end{array}}{\texttt{<}\overline{\mathtt{X}_m\ \mathtt{N}_b}\texttt{> w } \mathtt{T}_r\ \mathtt{m}(\overline{\mathtt{x}\ \mathtt{T}_p})\ \{\ \mathtt{return\ e}\ \}\ \mathtt{ok\ in}\ \mathtt{C}\texttt{<}\overline{\mathtt{X}\ \mathtt{N}}\texttt{>}}$$

$$\text{WFM-2}\,\frac{\begin{array}{c}\forall\ \texttt{class C'<}\overline{\mathtt{X}'\ \mathtt{N}'}\texttt{>} : \quad \mathtt{C}\texttt{<}\overline{\mathtt{X}}\texttt{>} \sqsubseteq \mathtt{C}'\texttt{<}\overline{\mathtt{T}'}\texttt{>} \wedge \mathrm{dom}(\mathtt{C}) = \overline{\mathtt{X}} \Rightarrow \\ mType(\mathtt{C}',\mathtt{m})\ \text{is undefined}\ \vee\ mType(\mathtt{C},\mathtt{m}) = mType(\mathtt{C}',\mathtt{m})[\overline{\mathtt{T}'/\mathtt{X}'}]\end{array}}{override(\mathtt{C},\mathtt{m})}$$

$$\text{WFC}\,\frac{\begin{array}{c}\overline{\mathtt{X}\ \mathtt{N}}; \_ \vdash \overline{\mathtt{N}}, \overline{\mathtt{T}}, (\mathtt{this}_u\ \mathtt{C}'\texttt{<}\overline{\mathtt{T}'}\texttt{>})\ \mathtt{ok} \\ \overline{\mathtt{mt}}\ \mathtt{ok\ in}\ \mathtt{C}\texttt{<}\overline{\mathtt{X}\ \mathtt{N}}\texttt{>} \qquad \mathtt{rep} \notin \overline{\mathtt{N}}\end{array}}{\texttt{class C<}\overline{\mathtt{X}\ \mathtt{N}}\texttt{> extends C'<}\overline{\mathtt{T}'}\texttt{> \{ } \overline{\mathtt{f}\ \mathtt{T}}; \overline{\mathtt{mt}}\ \} \ \mathtt{ok}}$$

$$\text{WFP}\,\frac{\begin{array}{c}\overline{\mathtt{Cls}}\ \mathtt{ok} \\ \texttt{class C<>}\ldots \in \overline{\mathtt{Cls}} \\ \epsilon; \mathtt{this}\ (\mathtt{this}_u\ \mathtt{C}\texttt{<>}) \vdash \mathtt{e} : \mathtt{N}\end{array}}{\overline{\mathtt{Cls}}, \mathtt{C}, \mathtt{e}\ \mathtt{ok}} \qquad \text{SWFE}\,\frac{\begin{array}{c}\Gamma = \overline{\mathtt{X}\ \mathtt{N}}, \overline{\mathtt{X}'\ \mathtt{N}'}\ ; \\ \mathtt{this}\ (\mathtt{this}_u\ \mathtt{C}\texttt{<}\overline{\mathtt{X}}\texttt{>}), \overline{\mathtt{x}\ \mathtt{T}} \\ \texttt{class C<}\overline{\mathtt{X}\ \mathtt{N}}\texttt{> } \ldots \\ \Gamma \vdash \overline{\mathtt{N}}, \overline{\mathtt{N}'}, \overline{\mathtt{T}}\ \mathtt{ok}\end{array}}{\Gamma\ \mathtt{ok}}$$

Fig. 9. Well-formedness rules

Well-Formed Types. The judgment $\Gamma \vdash$ T ok expresses that type T is well-formed in type environment Γ. Type variables are well-formed, if they are contained in the type environment (WFT-1). A non-variable type u C<$\overline{\text{T}}$> is well-formed if its type arguments $\overline{\text{T}}$ are well-formed and for each type parameter the actual type argument is a subtype of the upper bound, adapted from the viewpoint u C<$\overline{\text{T}}$> (WFT-2). The viewpoint adaptation is necessary because the type arguments describe ownership relative to the this object where u C<$\overline{\text{T}}$> is used, whereas the upper bounds are relative to the object of type u C<$\overline{\text{T}}$>. Note that rule WFT-2 permits type variables of a class C to be used in upper bounds of C. For instance in class IterImpl (Fig. 4), type variable X is used in its own upper bound, any MapNode<K, V, X>.

Well-Formed Methods. The judgment mt ok in C<$\overline{\text{X}}\,\overline{\text{N}}$> expresses that method mt is well-formed in a class C with type parameters $\overline{\text{X}}\,\overline{\text{N}}$. According to rule WFM-1, mt is well-formed if: (1) the return type, the upper bounds of mt's type variables, and mt's parameter types are well-formed in the type environment that maps mt's and C's type variables to their upper bounds as well as this and the explicit method parameters to their types. The type of this is the enclosing class, C<$\overline{\text{X}}$>, with main modifier this$_u$; (2) the method body, expression e, is well-typed with mt's return type; (3) mt respects the rules for overriding, see below; (4) if mt is pure then the only ownership modifier that occurs in a parameter type or the upper bound of a method type variable is any. We will motivate the fourth requirement when we explain the type rule for method calls.

Method m respects the rules for overriding if it does not override a method or if all overridden methods have the identical signatures after substituting type variables of the superclasses by the instantiations given in the subclass (WFM-2). For simplicity, we require that overrides do not change the purity of a method, although overriding non-pure methods by pure methods would be safe.

Well-Formed Classes. The judgment Cls ok expresses that class declaration Cls is well-formed. According to rule WFC, this is the case if: (1) the upper bounds of Cls's type variables, the types of Cls's fields, and the instantiation of the superclass are well-formed in the type environment that maps Cls's type variables to their upper bounds; (2) Cls's methods are well-formed; (3) Cls's upper bounds do not contain the rep modifier.

Note that Cls's upper bounds express ownership relative to the current Cls instance. If such an upper bound contains a rep modifier, clients of Cls cannot instantiate Cls. The ownership modifiers of an actual type argument are relative to the client's viewpoint. From this viewpoint, none of the modifiers peer, rep, or any expresses that an object is owned by the Cls instance. Therefore, we forbid upper bounds with rep modifiers by Requirement (3).

Well-Formed Programs. The judgment P ok expresses that program P is well-formed. According to rule WFP, this holds if all classes in P are well-formed, the main class C is a non-generic class in P, and the main expression e is well-typed in an environment with this as an instance of C. We omit checks for valid appearances of the ownership modifier $this_u$. As explained earlier, $this_u$ must not occur in the program.

Well-Formed Type Environments. The judgment Γ ok expresses that type environment Γ is well-formed. According to rule SWFE, this is the case if all upper bounds of type variables and the types of method parameters are well-formed. Moreover, this must be mapped to a non-variable type with main modifier $this_u$ and an uninstantiated class.

3.6   Type Rules

We are now ready to present the type rules (Fig. 10). The judgment $\Gamma \vdash e : T$ expresses that expression e is well-typed with type T in environment Γ. Our type rules implicitly require types to be well-formed, that is, a type rule is applicable only if all types involved in the rule are well-formed in the respective environment.

$$\text{GT-Subs}\frac{\Gamma \vdash e : T \quad \Gamma \vdash T <: T'}{\Gamma \vdash e : T'} \quad \text{GT-Var}\frac{x \in \text{dom}(\Gamma)}{\Gamma \vdash x : \Gamma(x)} \quad \text{GT-Null}\frac{T \neq this_u \ \_<\_>}{\Gamma \vdash null : T}$$

$$\text{GT-New}\frac{N \neq any_u \ \_<\_>}{\Gamma \vdash new\ N : N} \quad \text{GT-Cast}\frac{\Gamma \vdash e_0 : T_0}{\Gamma \vdash (T)\ e_0 : T}$$

$$\text{GT-Read}\frac{\begin{array}{c}\Gamma \vdash e_0 : N_0 \\ N_0 = \_\ C_0<\_> \\ T_1 = fType(C_0, f)\end{array}}{\Gamma \vdash e_0.f : N_0 \triangleright T_1} \quad \text{GT-Upd}\frac{\begin{array}{c}\Gamma \vdash e_0 : N_0 \quad N_0 = u_0\ C_0<\_> \\ T_1 = fType(C_0, f) \\ \Gamma \vdash e_2 : N_0 \triangleright T_1 \\ u_0 \neq any \quad rp(u_0, T_1)\end{array}}{\Gamma \vdash e_0.f = e_2 : N_0 \triangleright T_1}$$

$$\text{GT-Invk}\frac{\begin{array}{c}\Gamma \vdash e_0 : N_0 \quad N_0 = u_0\ C_0<\_> \\ mType(C_0, m) = <\overline{X_m\ N_b}>\ w\ T_r\ m(\overline{x\ T_p}) \\ \Gamma \vdash \overline{T} <: (\overline{N_0 \triangleright N_b})[\overline{T/X_m}] \quad \Gamma \vdash \overline{e_2} : (\overline{N_0 \triangleright T_p})[\overline{T/X_m}] \\ (u_0 = any \Rightarrow w = pure) \quad rp(u_0, \overline{T_p} \circ \overline{N_b})\end{array}}{\Gamma \vdash e_0.m<\overline{T}>(\overline{e_2}) : (N_0 \triangleright T_r)[\overline{T/X_m}]}$$

Fig. 10. Type rules

An expression of type T can also be typed with T's supertypes (GT-Subs). The type of method parameters (including this) is determined by a lookup in the type environment (GT-Var). The null-reference can have any type other than a $this_u$ type (GT-Null). Objects must be created in a specific context. Therefore only non-variable types with an ownership modifier other than any_u are allowed for object creations (GT-New). The rule for casts (GT-Cast) is straightforward; it could be strengthened to prevent more cast errors statically, but we omit this check since it is not strictly needed.

As explained in detail in Sec. 3.2, the type of a field access is determined by adapting the declared type of the field from the viewpoint described by the type of the receiver (GT-Read). If this type is a type variable, subsumption is used to go to its upper bound because *fType* is defined on class identifiers. Subsumption is also used for inherited fields to ensure that f is actually declared in C_0. (Recall that $fType(C_0, f)$ is undefined otherwise.)

For a field update, the right-hand side expression must be typable as the viewpoint-adapted field type, which is also the type of the whole field update expression (GT-Upd). The rule is analogous to field read, but has two additional requirements. First, the main modifier u_0 of the type of the receiver expression must not be **any**. With the owner-as-modifier discipline, a method must not update fields of objects in arbitrary contexts. Second, the requirement $rp(u_0, T_1)$ enforces that f is updated through receiver **this** if its declared type T_1 contains a **rep** modifier. For all other receivers, the viewpoint adaptation $N_0 \triangleright T_1$ yields an **any** type, but it is obviously unsafe to update f with an object with an arbitrary owner. It is convenient to define *rp* for sequences of types. The definition uses the fact that the ownership modifier $\mathtt{this}_u$ is only used for the type of **this**:

$$rp :: \mathtt{OM} \times \overline{{}^s\mathtt{Type}} \to bool$$
$$rp(\mathtt{u}, \overline{\mathtt{T}}) = \mathtt{u} = \mathtt{this}_u \vee (\forall i : \mathtt{rep} \notin \mathtt{T}_i)$$

The rule for method calls (GT-Invk) is in many ways similar to field reads (for result passing) and updates (for argument passing). The method signature is determined using the receiver type N_0 and subsumption. The type of the invocation expression is determined by viewpoint adaptation of the return type T_r from the receiver type N_0. Modulo subsumption, the actual method arguments must have the formal parameter types, adapted from N_0 and with actual type arguments $\overline{T}$ substituted for the method's type variables X_m. For instance, in the call `first.init(key, value, first)` in method `put` (Fig. 2), the adapted third formal parameter type is `rep Node<K,V>` $\triangleright$ `peer Node<K,V>` (note that `Node` substitutes the type variable `X` by `peer Node<K,V>`). This adaptation yields `rep Node<K,V>`, which is also the type of the third actual method argument.

To enforce the owner-as-modifier discipline, only pure methods may be called on receivers with main modifier **any**. For a call on a receiver with main modifier **any**, the viewpoint-adapted formal parameter type contains only the modifier **any**. Consequently, arguments with arbitrary owners can be passed. For this to be type safe, pure methods must not expect arguments with specific owners. This is enforced by rule WFM-1 (Fig. 9). Finally, if the receiver is different from **this**, then neither the formal parameter types nor the upper bounds of the method's type variables must contain **rep**.

4   Runtime Model

In this section, we explain the runtime model of Generic Universe Types. We present the heap model, the runtime type information, well-formedness conditions, and an operational semantics.

4.1 Heap Model

Fig. 11 defines our model of the heap. The prefix ^{r} distinguishes sorts of the runtime model from their static counterparts.

$$
\begin{aligned}
\text{h} \in \text{Heap} \quad &= \quad \text{Addr} \rightarrow \text{Obj} \\
\iota \in \text{Addr} \quad &= \quad \text{Address} \mid \text{null}_a \\
\text{o} \in \text{Obj} \quad &= \quad {}^r\text{T}, \text{Fs} \\
{}^r\text{T} \in {}^r\text{Type} \quad &= \quad \iota_o \; \text{C<}\overline{{}^r\text{T}}\text{>} \\
\text{Fs} \in \text{Fields} \quad &= \quad \text{FieldId} \rightarrow \text{Addr} \\
\iota_o \in \text{OwnerAddr} \quad &= \quad \iota \mid \text{any}_a \\
{}^r\Gamma \in {}^r\text{Env} \quad &= \quad \overline{\text{X} \; {}^r\text{T}}; \; \overline{\text{x} \; \iota}
\end{aligned}
$$

Fig. 11. Definitions for the heap model

A heap ($\text{h} \in \text{Heap}$) maps addresses to objects. An address ($\iota \in \text{Addr}$) can be the special null-reference null_a. An object ($\text{o} \in \text{Obj}$) consist of its runtime type and a mapping from field identifiers to the addresses stored in the fields.

The runtime type (${}^r\text{T} \in {}^r\text{Type}$) of an object o consists of the address of o's owner object, of o's class, and of runtime types for the type arguments of this class. We store the runtime type arguments including the associated ownership information explicitly in the heap because this information is needed in the runtime checks for casts. In that respect, our runtime model is similar to that of the .NET CLR [16]. The owner address of objects in the root context is null_a. The special owner address any_a is used when the corresponding static type has the any_u modifier. Consider for instance an execution of method main (Fig. 5), where the address of this is 1. The runtime type of the object stored in map is $1 \; \text{Map<}1 \; \text{ID}, \text{any}_a \; \text{Data>}$. For simplicity we drop the subscript o from ι_o whenever it is clear from context whether we refer to an Addr or an OwnerAddr.

The first component of a runtime environment (${}^r\Gamma \in {}^r\text{Env}$) maps method type variables to their runtime types. The second component is the stack, which maps method parameters to the addresses they store.

Subtyping on Runtime Types. Judgment $\text{h}, \iota \vdash {}^r\text{T} <: {}^r\text{T}'$ expresses that the runtime type ${}^r\text{T}$ is a subtype of ${}^r\text{T}'$ from the viewpoint of address ι. The viewpoint, ι, is required in order to give meaning to the ownership modifier rep. Subtyping for runtime types is defined in Fig. 12. Subtyping is transitive (RT-3), and allows owner-invariant (RT-1) and covariant subtyping (RT-2).

Rule RTL introduces owner-invariant subtyping $<:_1$ and defines how subtyping follows subclassing if (1) the runtime types have the same owner address ι', (2) in the type arguments, the ownership modifiers this_u and peer are substituted by the owner address ι' of the runtime types (we use the same owner address for both modifiers since they both express ownership by the owner of this), (3) rep is substituted by the viewpoint address ι, (4) any_u is substituted by any_a, (5) the type variables $\overline{\text{X}}$ of the subclass C are substituted consistently by

$^{\overline{r}}$T, and (6) either the owner of ι is ι' or **rep** does not appear in the instantiation of the superclass. This ensures that the substitution of ι for **rep**-modifiers is meaningful. Note that in a well-formed program, **this**$_u$ never occurs in a type argument; nevertheless we include the substitution for consistency. Rule RTL gives the most concrete runtime type deducible from static subclassing.

$$RT\text{-}1\frac{\mathbf{h},\iota\vdash{}^r\mathbf{T}<:_1{}^r\mathbf{T}'}{\mathbf{h},\iota\vdash{}^r\mathbf{T}<:{}^r\mathbf{T}'} \qquad RT\text{-}2\frac{{}^r\mathbf{T}<:_a{}^r\mathbf{T}'}{\mathbf{h},\iota\vdash{}^r\mathbf{T}<:{}^r\mathbf{T}'} \qquad RT\text{-}3\frac{\mathbf{h},\iota\vdash{}^r\mathbf{T}<:{}^r\mathbf{T}''\quad \mathbf{h},\iota\vdash{}^r\mathbf{T}''<:{}^r\mathbf{T}'}{\mathbf{h},\iota\vdash{}^r\mathbf{T}<:{}^r\mathbf{T}'}$$

$$RTL\frac{\mathtt{C}<\overline{\mathtt{X}}>\sqsubseteq\mathtt{C}'<{}^{\overline{s}}\overline{\mathtt{T}}>\quad dom(\mathtt{C})=\overline{\mathtt{X}}\quad owner(\mathbf{h},\iota)=\iota'\;\vee\;\mathbf{rep}\notin{}^{\overline{s}}\overline{\mathtt{T}}}{\mathbf{h},\iota\vdash\iota'\;\mathtt{C}<{}^{\overline{r}}\overline{\mathtt{T}}><:_1\iota'\;\mathtt{C}'<{}^{\overline{s}}\overline{\mathtt{T}}[\iota'/\mathbf{this}_u,\iota'/\mathbf{peer},\iota/\mathbf{rep},\mathbf{any}_a/\mathbf{any}_u,{}^{\overline{r}}\overline{\mathtt{T}}/\overline{\mathtt{X}}]>}$$

$$RTA\text{-}1\frac{}{{}^r\mathbf{T}<:_a{}^r\mathbf{T}} \qquad RTA\text{-}2\frac{{}^{\overline{r}}\overline{\mathtt{T}}<:_a{}^{\overline{r}}\overline{\mathtt{T}}'}{\iota'\;\mathtt{C}<{}^{\overline{r}}\overline{\mathtt{T}}><:_a\mathbf{any}_a\;\mathtt{C}<{}^{\overline{r}}\overline{\mathtt{T}}'>} \qquad RTH\text{-}1\frac{h(\iota)={}^r\mathtt{T},\_\quad \mathbf{h},\iota\vdash{}^r\mathbf{T}<:{}^r\mathbf{T}'}{\mathbf{h}\vdash\iota:{}^r\mathbf{T}'}$$

$$RTH\text{-}2\frac{}{\mathbf{h}\vdash\mathbf{null}_a:{}^r\mathbf{T}'} \qquad RTS\frac{{}^s\mathtt{T}=\mathbf{this}_u\,\_<\_>\Rightarrow\iota={}^r\Gamma(\mathbf{this})}{\mathbf{h},{}^r\Gamma\vdash\iota:{}^s\mathtt{T}}$$

Fig. 12. Rules for subtyping on runtime types

As for subtyping for static types, we have limited covariance for runtime types. Covariant subtyping is expressed by the relation $<:_a$. The rules for limited covariance, RTA-1 and RTA-2, are analogous to the rules TA-1 and TA-2 for static types (Fig. 8). Reflexivity of $<:$ follows from RTA-1 and RT-2.

The judgment $\mathbf{h}\vdash\iota:{}^r\mathbf{T}'$ expresses that in heap $\mathbf{h}$, the address ι has type $^r\mathbf{T}'$. The type of ι is determined by the type of the object at ι and the subtype relation (RTH-1). The **null** reference can have any type (RTH-2).

Finally, the judgment $\mathbf{h},{}^r\Gamma\vdash\iota:{}^s\mathtt{T}$ expresses that in heap $\mathbf{h}$ and runtime environment $^r\Gamma$, the address ι has a runtime type that corresponds to the static type $^s\mathtt{T}$ (see below for the definition of dyn) and that the main modifier **this**$_u$ is used solely for the type of **this** (RTS).

From Static Types to Runtime Types. Static types and runtime types are related by the following *dynamization function*, which is defined by rule DYN:

$$dyn::{}^s\mathbf{Type}\times\mathbf{Heap}\times{}^r\mathbf{Env}\to{}^r\mathbf{Type}$$

$$DYN\frac{{}^r\Gamma=\overline{\mathtt{X}'\;{}^r\mathtt{T}'};\;\mathbf{this}\;\iota,\_\quad \mathbf{h},\iota\vdash h(\iota)\downarrow_1<:_1\iota'\;\mathtt{C}<{}^{\overline{r}}\overline{\mathtt{T}}>}{\mathrm{dom}(\mathtt{C})=\overline{\mathtt{X}}\qquad free({}^s\mathtt{T})\subseteq\overline{\mathtt{X}}\circ\overline{\mathtt{X}'}}{dyn({}^s\mathtt{T},\mathbf{h},{}^r\Gamma)={}^s\mathtt{T}[\iota'/\mathbf{this},\iota'/\mathbf{peer},\iota/\mathbf{rep},\mathbf{any}_a/\mathbf{any}_u,{}^{\overline{r}}\overline{\mathtt{T}}/\overline{\mathtt{X}},{}^{\overline{r}}\overline{\mathtt{T}'}/\overline{\mathtt{X}'}]}$$

This function maps a static type $^s\mathtt{T}$ to the corresponding runtime type. The viewpoint is described by a heap $\mathbf{h}$ and a runtime environment $^r\Gamma$. In $^s\mathtt{T}$, dyn

substitutes `rep` by the address of the `this` object (ι), `peer` and this_u by the owner of ι (ι'), and any_u by any_a. It also substitutes all type variables in ^sT by the instantiations given in ι' `C<`$\overline{^r T}$`>`, a supertype of ι's runtime type, or in the runtime environment. The substitutions performed by dyn are analogous to the ones in rule RTL (Fig. 12), which also involves mapping static types to runtime types. We do not use dyn in RTL to avoid that the definitions of $<:$ and dyn are mutually recursive. We use projection $\downarrow_i$ to select the i-th component of a tuple, for instance, the runtime type and field mapping of an object.

Note that the outcome of dyn depends on finding ι' `C<`$\overline{^r T}$`>`, an appropriate supertype of the runtime type of the `this` object ι, which contains substitutions for all type variables not mapped by the environment ($\text{free}(^s\text{T})$ yields the free type variables in ^sT). Thus, one may wonder whether there is more than one such appropriate superclass. However, because type variables are globally unique, if the free variables of ^sT are in the domain of a class then they are not in the domain of any other class. To obtain the most precise ownership information we use the owner-invariant runtime subtype relation $<:_1$ defined in rule RTL.

To illustrate dynamization, consider an execution of `put` (Fig. 2), in an environment $^r\Gamma$ whose `this` object has address 3 and a heap `h` where address 3 has runtime type 1 `Map<1 ID,`any_a `Data>` (see Fig. 1). We determine the runtime type of the object created by `new rep Node<K,V>`. The dynamization of the type of the new object w.r.t. `h` and $^r\Gamma$ is $dyn(\text{rep Node<K,V>}, \text{h}, {}^r\Gamma)$, which yields 3 `Node<1 ID,`$\text{any}_a$ `Data>`. This runtime type correctly reflects that the new object is owned by `this` (owner address 3) and has the same type arguments as the runtime type of `this`.

It is convenient to define the following overloaded version of dyn:

$$dyn(^s\text{T}, \text{h}, \iota) = dyn(^s\text{T}, \text{h}, (\epsilon; \text{this } \iota))$$

4.2   Lookup Functions

In this subsection, we define the functions to look up the runtime type of a field or the body of a method.

Field Lookup. The runtime type of a field `f` is essentially the dynamization of its static type. The function $^r fType(\text{h}, \iota, \text{f})$ yields the runtime type of `f` in an object at address ι in heap `h`. In its definition (RFT, in Fig. 13), `C` is the runtime class of ι, and C' is the superclass of `C` which contains the definition of `f`.

Method Lookup. The function $mBody(\text{C}, \text{m})$ yields a tuple consisting of `m`'s body expression as well as the identifiers of its formal parameters and type variables. This is trivial if `m` is declared in `C` (RMT-1, Fig. 13). Otherwise, `m` is looked up in `C`'s superclass C' (RMT-2).

4.3   Well-Formedness

In this subsection, we define well-formedness of runtime types, heaps, and runtime environments. The rules are presented in Fig. 13.

$$\text{RFT} \frac{\text{h}(\iota)\downarrow_1 = \_ \text{C<\_>} \quad \text{C<\_>} \sqsubseteq \text{C}'\text{<\_>}}{{}^r fType(\text{h}, \iota, \text{f}) = dyn({}^s fType(\text{C}', \text{f}), \text{h}, \iota)}$$

$$\text{RMT-1} \frac{\text{class C<\_> extends \_<\_> \{ \_ ; } ... \text{<}\overline{X}\text{\_> \_ \_ m}(\overline{x}\,\_) \text{ \{ return e \}} ... \text{ \}}}{mBody(\text{C}, \text{m}) = (\text{e}, \overline{x}, \overline{X})}$$

$$\text{RMT-2} \frac{\text{class C<\_> extends C}'\text{<\_> \{ no method m \}}}{mBody(\text{C}, \text{m}) = mBody(\text{C}', \text{m})}$$

$$\text{WFRT} \frac{\begin{array}{c}\iota' \in \text{dom}(\text{h}) \cup \{\text{null}_a, \text{any}_a\} \qquad \text{h}, \iota \vdash \overline{{}^r T} \text{ ok} \\ \text{class C<\_}\ \overline{{}^s N}\text{>} \ ... \qquad \text{h}, \iota \vdash \overline{{}^r T} <: dyn(\overline{{}^s N}, \text{h}, \iota)\end{array}}{\text{h}, \iota \vdash \iota' \text{ C<}\overline{{}^r T}\text{> ok}}$$

$$\text{WFH} \frac{\begin{array}{c}\text{null}_a \notin \text{dom}(\text{h}) \qquad \forall \iota: \ \text{h}, \iota \vdash \text{h}(\iota)\downarrow_1 \text{ ok} \ \wedge \ \text{null}_a \in owners(\text{h}, \iota) \\ \forall \iota, \text{f}: \ \text{h}(\iota)\downarrow_2 = \text{Fs} \ \wedge \ {}^r fType(\text{h}, \iota, \text{f}) = {}^r T \implies \text{h} \vdash \text{Fs}(\text{f}) : {}^r T\end{array}}{\text{h ok}}$$

$$\text{WFRE} \frac{\begin{array}{c}{}^r\Gamma = \overline{X \ {}^r T} \text{ ; this } \iota, \overline{x \ \iota'} \qquad {}^s\Gamma = \overline{X \ {}^s N}, \ \overline{X' \ \_} \text{ ; this } (\text{this}_u \text{ C<}\overline{X'}\text{>}), \overline{x \ {}^s T'} \\ \text{h ok} \quad {}^s\Gamma \text{ ok} \quad \iota \neq \text{null}_a \quad \text{h}, {}^r\Gamma \vdash \overline{{}^r T} \text{ ok} \quad \text{h}, {}^r\Gamma \vdash \overline{{}^r T} <: \overline{dyn({}^s N, \text{h}, {}^r\Gamma)} \\ \text{h}, {}^r\Gamma \vdash \iota : \text{this}_u \text{ C<}\overline{X'}\text{>} \qquad \qquad \text{h}, {}^r\Gamma \vdash \overline{\iota'} : \ \overline{{}^s T'}\end{array}}{\text{h} \vdash {}^r\Gamma : {}^s\Gamma}$$

Fig. 13. Rules for field and method lookup, and well-formedness

Well-Formed Runtime Types. The judgment $\text{h}, \iota \vdash \iota' \text{ C<}\overline{{}^r T}\text{>}$ ok expresses that runtime type $\iota' \text{ C<}\overline{{}^r T}\text{>}$ is well-formed for viewpoint address ι in heap h. According to rule WFRT, the owner address ι' must be the address of an object in the heap h or one of the special owners null_a and any_a. All type arguments must also be well-formed types. A runtime type must have a type argument for each type variable of its class. Each runtime type argument must be a subtype of the dynamization of the type variable's upper bound. We use $\text{h}, {}^r\Gamma \vdash {}^r T$ ok as shorthand for $\text{h}, {}^r\Gamma(\text{this}) \vdash {}^r T$ ok.

Well-Formed Heaps. A heap h is well-formed, denoted by h ok, if and only if the null_a address is not mapped to an object, the runtime types of all objects are well-formed, the root owner null_a is in the set of owners of all objects, and all addresses stored in fields are well-typed (WFH). By mandating that all objects are (transitively) owned by null_a and because each runtime type has one unique owner address, we ensure that ownership is a tree structure.

Well-Formed Runtime Environments. The judgment $\text{h} \vdash {}^r\Gamma : {}^s\Gamma$ expresses that runtime environment ${}^r\Gamma$ is well-formed w.r.t. a well-formed heap h and a well-formed static type environment ${}^s\Gamma$. According to rule WFRE, this is the case if and only if: (1) ${}^r\Gamma$ maps all method type variables $\overline{X}$ that are contained in ${}^s\Gamma$ to well-formed runtime types $\overline{{}^r T}$, which are subtypes of the dynamizations of the corresponding upper bounds $\overline{{}^s N}$; (2) ${}^r\Gamma$ maps this to an address ι. The object at address ι is well-typed with the static type of this, $\text{this}_u \text{ C<}\overline{X'}\text{>}$. (3) ${}^r\Gamma$ maps the formal parameters $\overline{\mathtt{x}}$ that are contained in $^s\Gamma$ to addresses $\overline{\iota'}$. The objects at addresses $\overline{\iota'}$ are well-typed with the static types of $\overline{\mathtt{x}}$, $^s\overline{\mathtt{T'}}$.

4.4 Operational Semantics

We describe program execution by a big-step operational semantics. The transition $\mathtt{h}, {}^r\Gamma, \mathtt{e} \rightsquigarrow \mathtt{h'}, \iota$ expresses that the evaluation of an expression $\mathtt{e}$ in heap $\mathtt{h}$ and runtime environment $^r\Gamma$ results in address ι and successor heap $\mathtt{h'}$. A program with main class $\mathtt{C}$ is executed by evaluating the main expression in a heap $\mathtt{h_0}$ that contains exactly one $\mathtt{C}$ instance in the root context where all fields $\overline{\mathtt{f}}$ are initialized to $\mathtt{null}_a$ ($\mathtt{h_0} = \{\iota \mapsto (\mathtt{null}_a\ \mathtt{C}<>, \overline{\mathtt{f}\ \mathtt{null}_a})\}$) and a runtime environment $^r\Gamma_0$ that maps this to this $\mathtt{C}$ instance ($^r\Gamma_0 = \epsilon; \mathtt{this}\ \iota$). The rules for evaluating expressions are presented in Fig. 14 and explained in the following.

$$\text{OS-Var} \frac{}{\mathtt{h}, {}^r\Gamma, \mathtt{x} \rightsquigarrow \mathtt{h}, {}^r\Gamma(\mathtt{x})} \qquad \text{OS-Null} \frac{}{\mathtt{h}, {}^r\Gamma, \mathtt{null} \rightsquigarrow \mathtt{h}, \mathtt{null}_a}$$

$$\text{OS-Cast} \frac{\begin{array}{c} \mathtt{h}, {}^r\Gamma, \mathtt{e_0} \rightsquigarrow \mathtt{h'}, \iota \\ \mathtt{h'}, {}^r\Gamma \vdash \iota : {}^s\mathtt{T} \end{array}}{\mathtt{h}, {}^r\Gamma, ({}^s\mathtt{T})\ \mathtt{e_0} \rightsquigarrow \mathtt{h'}, \iota} \qquad \text{OS-New} \frac{\begin{array}{c} \iota \notin dom(h) \qquad \iota \neq \mathtt{null}_a \\ {}^r\mathtt{T} = dyn({}^s\mathtt{N}, \mathtt{h}, {}^r\Gamma) = {}_{\_}\ \mathtt{C}<> \\ \mathit{Fs}(\mathit{fields}(\mathtt{C})) = \mathtt{null}_a \\ \mathtt{h'} = \mathtt{h}[\iota \mapsto ({}^r\mathtt{T}, \mathtt{Fs})] \end{array}}{\mathtt{h}, {}^r\Gamma, \mathtt{new}\ {}^s\mathtt{N} \rightsquigarrow \mathtt{h'}, \iota}$$

$$\text{OS-Read} \frac{\begin{array}{c} \mathtt{h}, {}^r\Gamma, \mathtt{e_0} \rightsquigarrow \mathtt{h_0}, \iota_0 \\ \iota_0 \neq \mathtt{null}_a \\ \iota = \mathtt{h'}(\iota_0) \downarrow_2 (\mathtt{f}) \end{array}}{\mathtt{h}, {}^r\Gamma, \mathtt{e_0}.\mathtt{f} \rightsquigarrow \mathtt{h'}, \iota} \qquad \text{OS-Upd} \frac{\begin{array}{c} \mathtt{h}, {}^r\Gamma, \mathtt{e_0} \rightsquigarrow \mathtt{h_0}, \iota_0 \\ \iota_0 \neq \mathtt{null}_a \\ \mathtt{h_0}, {}^r\Gamma, \mathtt{e_2} \rightsquigarrow \mathtt{h_2}, \iota \\ \mathtt{h'} = \mathtt{h_2}[\iota_0.\mathtt{f} := \iota] \end{array}}{\mathtt{h}, {}^r\Gamma, \mathtt{e_0}.\mathtt{f} = \mathtt{e_2} \rightsquigarrow \mathtt{h'}, \iota}$$

$$\text{OS-Invk} \frac{\begin{array}{c} \mathtt{h}, {}^r\Gamma, \mathtt{e_0} \rightsquigarrow \mathtt{h_0}, \iota_0 \qquad \iota_0 \neq \mathtt{null}_a \qquad \mathtt{h_0}, {}^r\Gamma, \overline{\mathtt{e_2}} \rightsquigarrow \mathtt{h_2}, \overline{\iota_2} \\ \mathtt{h_0}(\iota_0) \downarrow_1 = {}_{\_}\ \mathtt{C_0}<> \qquad \qquad mBody(\mathtt{C_0}, \mathtt{m}) = (\mathtt{e_1}, \overline{\mathtt{x}}, \overline{\mathtt{X}}) \\ {}^r\overline{\mathtt{T}} = dyn({}^s\overline{\mathtt{T}}, \mathtt{h}, {}^r\Gamma) \qquad {}^r\Gamma' = \overline{\mathtt{X}\ {}^r\mathtt{T}}; \mathtt{this}\ \iota_0, \overline{\mathtt{x}\ \iota_2} \qquad \mathtt{h_2}, {}^r\Gamma', \mathtt{e_1} \rightsquigarrow \mathtt{h'}, \iota \end{array}}{\mathtt{h}, {}^r\Gamma, \mathtt{e_0}.\mathtt{m}<{}^s\overline{\mathtt{T}}>(\overline{\mathtt{e_2}}) \rightsquigarrow \mathtt{h'}, \iota}$$

Fig. 14. Operational semantics

Parameters, including this, are evaluated by looking up the stored address in the stack, which is part of the runtime environment $^r\Gamma$ (OS-Var). The null expression always evaluates to the $\mathtt{null}_a$ address (OS-Null). For cast expressions, we evaluate the expression $\mathtt{e_0}$ and check that the resulting address is well-typed with the static type given in the cast expression w.r.t. the current environment (OS-Cast). Object creation picks a fresh address, allocates an object of the appropriate type, and initializes its fields to $\mathtt{null}_a$ (OS-New). $\mathit{fields}(\mathtt{C})$ yields all fields declared in or inherited by $\mathtt{C}$.

For field reads (OS-Read) we evaluate the receiver expression and then look up the field in the heap, provided that the receiver is non-null. For the update of a field f, we evaluate the receiver expression to address ι_0 and the right-hand side expression to address ι, and update the heap h_2, which is denoted by $h_2[\iota_0.f := \iota]$ (OS-Upd). Note that the limited covariance of Generic Universe Types does not require a runtime ownership check for field updates.

For method calls (OS-Invk) we evaluate the receiver expression and actual method arguments in the usual order. The class of the receiver object is used to look up the method body. Its expression is then evaluated in the runtime environment that maps m's type variables to actual type arguments as well as m's formal method parameters (including this) to the actual method arguments. The resulting heap and address are the result of the call. Note that method invocations do not need any runtime type checks or purity checks.

5 Properties

In this section, we present the theorems and proof sketches for type safety and the owner-as-modifier property as well as two important auxiliary lemmas.

Lemmas. The following lemma expresses that viewpoint adaptation from a viewpoint to this is correct. Consider the this object of a runtime environment $^r\Gamma$ and two objects o_1 and o_2. If from the viewpoint this, o_1 has the static type ^sN, and from viewpoint o_1, o_2 has the static type ^sT, then from the viewpoint this, o_2 has the static type ^sT adapted from ^sN, $^sN \triangleright {}^sT$. The following lemma expresses this property using the addresses ι_1 and ι_2 of the objects o_1 and o_2, respectively.

Lemma 1 (Adaptation from a Viewpoint)

$$\left. \begin{array}{l} h, {}^r\Gamma \vdash \iota_1 : {}^sN, \quad \iota_1 \neq \text{null}_a \\ h, {}^r\Gamma' \vdash \iota_2 : {}^sT \\ \mathit{free}({}^sT) \subseteq \mathit{dom}({}^sN) \circ \overline{X} \\ {}^r\Gamma' = \overline{X} \; \mathit{dyn}(\overline{{}^sT}, h, {}^r\Gamma); \; \text{this} \; \iota_{1,\_} \end{array} \right\} \implies h, {}^r\Gamma \vdash \iota_2 : ({}^sN \triangleright {}^sT)[\overline{{}^sT/X}]$$

This lemma justifies the type rule GT-Read. The proof runs by induction on the shape of static type ^sT. The base case deals with type variables and non-generic types. The induction step considers generic types, assuming that the lemma holds for the actual type arguments. Each of the cases is done by a case distinction on the main modifiers of ^sN and ^sT.

The following lemma is the converse of Lemma 1. It expresses that viewpoint adaptation from this to an object o_1 is correct. If from the viewpoint this, o_1 has the static type ^sN and o_2 has the static type $^sN \triangleright {}^sT$, then from viewpoint o_1, o_2 has the static type ^sT. The lemma requires that the adaptation of ^sT does not change ownership modifiers in ^sT from non-any to any, because the lost ownership information cannot be recovered. Such a change occurs if ^sN's main modifier is any or if ^sT contains rep and is not accessed through this (see definition of rp, Sec. 3.6).

Lemma 2 (Adaptation to a Viewpoint)

$$\left.\begin{array}{l} \mathbf{h},{}^{r}\Gamma \vdash \iota_1 : {}^{s}\mathbf{N}, \quad \iota_1 \neq \mathbf{null}_a \\ \mathbf{h},{}^{r}\Gamma \vdash \iota_2 : ({}^{s}\mathbf{N} \triangleright {}^{s}\mathbf{T})[\overline{{}^{s}\mathbf{T}/\mathbf{X}}] \\ {}^{s}\mathbf{N} = \mathbf{u}\ \_<\_>, \quad \mathbf{u} \neq \mathbf{any}, \quad rp(\mathbf{u}, {}^{s}\mathbf{T}) \\ free({}^{s}\mathbf{T}) \subseteq dom({}^{s}\mathbf{N}) \circ \overline{\mathbf{X}}, \quad {}^{s}\mathbf{T} \neq \mathbf{this}_u\ \_<\_> \\ {}^{r}\Gamma' = \overline{\mathbf{X}}\ dyn(\overline{{}^{s}\mathbf{T}}, \mathbf{h}, {}^{r}\Gamma); \ \mathbf{this}\ \iota_1, \_ \end{array}\right\} \implies \mathbf{h},{}^{r}\Gamma' \vdash \iota_2 : {}^{s}\mathbf{T}$$

This lemma justifies the type rule GT-Upd and the requirements for the types of the parameters in GT-Invk. The proof is analogous to the proof for Lemma 1.

Type Safety for Generic Universe Types is expressed by the following theorem. If a well-typed expression e is evaluated in a well-formed environment (including a well-formed heap), then the resulting environment is well-formed and the result of e's evaluation has the type that is the dynamization of e's static type.

Theorem 1 (Type Safety)

$$\left.\begin{array}{l} \mathbf{h} \vdash {}^{r}\Gamma : {}^{s}\Gamma \\ {}^{s}\Gamma \vdash \mathbf{e} : {}^{s}\mathbf{T} \\ \mathbf{h},{}^{r}\Gamma, \mathbf{e} \rightsquigarrow \mathbf{h}', \iota \end{array}\right\} \implies \left\{\begin{array}{l} \mathbf{h}' \vdash {}^{r}\Gamma : {}^{s}\Gamma \\ \mathbf{h}',{}^{r}\Gamma \vdash \iota : {}^{s}\mathbf{T} \end{array}\right.$$

The proof of Theorem 1 runs by rule induction on the operational semantics. Lemma 1 is used to prove field read and method results, whereas Lemma 2 is used to prove field updates and method parameter passing.

We omit a proof of progress since this property is not affected by adding ownership to a Java-like language. The basic proof can be adapted from FGJ [14] and extensions for field updates and casts. The new runtime ownership check in casts can be treated analogously to standard Java casts.

Owner-as-Modifier discipline enforcement is expressed by the following theorem. The evaluation of a well-typed expression e in a well-formed environment modifies only those objects that are (transitively) owned by the owner of this.

Theorem 2 (Owner-as-Modifier)

$$\left.\begin{array}{l} \mathbf{h} \vdash {}^{r}\Gamma : {}^{s}\Gamma \\ {}^{s}\Gamma \vdash \mathbf{e} : {}^{s}\mathbf{T} \\ \mathbf{h},{}^{r}\Gamma, \mathbf{e} \rightsquigarrow \mathbf{h}', \_ \end{array}\right\} \implies \left\{\begin{array}{l} \forall \iota \in dom(\mathbf{h}), \mathbf{f} : \\ \mathbf{h}(\iota){\downarrow_2}(\mathbf{f}) = \mathbf{h}'(\iota){\downarrow_2}(\mathbf{f}) \ \lor \\ owner(\mathbf{h}, {}^{r}\Gamma(\mathbf{this})) \in owners(\mathbf{h}, \iota) \end{array}\right.$$

where $owner(\mathbf{h}, \iota)$ denotes the direct owner of the object at address ι in heap $\mathbf{h}$, and $owners(\mathbf{h}, \iota)$ denotes the set of all (transitive) owners of this object.

The proof of Theorem 2 runs by rule induction on the operational semantics. The interesting cases are field update and calls of non-pure methods. In both cases, the type rules (Fig. 10) enforce that the receiver expression does not have the main modifier any. That is, the receiver object is owned by this or the owner of this. For the proof we assume that pure methods do not modify objects that exist in the prestate of the call. In this paper we do not describe how this is enforced in the program. A simple but conservative approach forbids all object creations, field updates, and calls of non-pure methods [20]. The above definition also allows weaker forms of purity that permit object creations [12] and also approaches that allow the modification of newly created objects [25].

6 Conclusion

We presented Generic Universe Types, an ownership type system for Java-like languages with generic types. Our type system permits arbitrary references through any types, but controls modifications of objects, that is, enforces the owner-as-modifier discipline. This allows us to handle interesting implementations beyond simple aggregate objects, for instance, shared buffers [12]. We show how any types and generics can be combined in a type safe way using limited covariance and viewpoint adaptation.

Generic Universe Types require little annotation overhead for programmers. As we have shown for non-generic Universe Types [12], this overhead can be further reduced by appropriate defaults. The default ownership modifier is generally peer, but the modifier of upper bounds, exceptions, and immutable types (such as String) defaults to any. These defaults make the conversion from Java 5 to Generic Universe Types simple.

The type checker and runtime support for Generic Universe Types are implemented in the JML tool suite [17].

As future work, we plan to use Generic Universe Types for program verification, extending our earlier work [20,21]. We are also working on path-dependent Universe Types to support more fine-grained information about object ownership, and to extend our inference tools for non-generic Universe Types to Generic Universe Types.

Acknowledgments. We are grateful to David Cunningham and to the anonymous ECOOP '07 and FOOL/WOOD '07 reviewers for their helpful comments. This work was funded in part by the Information Society Technologies program of the European Commission, Future and Emerging Technologies under the IST-2005-015905 MOBIUS project, and the EPSRC grant Practical Ownership Types for Objects and Aspect Programs, EP/D061644/1.

References

1. Aldrich, J., Chambers, C.: Ownership domains: Separating aliasing policy from mechanism. In: Odersky, M. (ed.) ECOOP 2004. LNCS, vol. 3086, pp. 1–25. Springer, Heidelberg (2004)
2. Andrea, C., Coady, Y., Gibbs, C., Noble, J., Vitek, J., Zhao, T.: Scoped types and aspects for real-time systems. In: Thomas, D. (ed.) ECOOP 2006. LNCS, vol. 4067, pp. 124–147. Springer, Heidelberg (2006)
3. Banerjee, A., Naumann, D.: Representation independence, confinement, and access control. In: Principles of Programming Languages (POPL), pp. 166–177. ACM Press, New York (2002)
4. Boyapati, C.: SafeJava: A Unified Type System for Safe Programming. PhD thesis, MIT (2004)
5. Boyapati, C., Lee, R., Rinard, M.: Ownership types for safe programming: Preventing data races and deadlocks. In: Object-Oriented Programming, Systems, Languages, and Applications (OOPSLA), pp. 211–230. ACM Press, New York (2002)

6. Boyapati, C., Salcianu Jr., A., Beebee, W., Rinard, M.: Ownership types for safe region-based memory management in real-time Java. In: Programming language design and implementation (PLDI), pp. 324–337. ACM Press, New York (2003)
7. Clarke, D.: Object Ownership and Containment. PhD thesis, University of New South Wales (2001)
8. Clarke, D., Drossopoulou, S.: Ownership, encapsulation and the disjointness of type and effect. In: Object-Oriented Programming, Systems, Languages, and Applications (OOPSLA), pp. 292–310. ACM Press, New York (2002)
9. Clarke, D.G., Potter, J.M., Noble, J.: Ownership types for flexible alias protection ACM SIGPLAN Notices. In: Object-Oriented Programming Systems, Languages, and Applications (OOPSLA), vol. 33(10) (1998)
10. Dietl, W., Drossopoulou, S., Müller, P.: Formalization of Generic Universe Types. Technical Report 532, ETH Zurich (2006), sct.inf.ethz.ch/publications
11. Dietl, W., Müller, P.: Exceptions in ownership type systems. In: Poll, E. (ed.) Formal Techniques for Java-like Programs, pp. 49–54 (2004)
12. Dietl, W., Müller, P.: Universes: Lightweight ownership for JML. Journal of Object Technology (JOT) 4(8) (2005)
13. Emir, B., Kennedy, A.J., Russo, C., Yu, D.: Variance and generalized constraints for C# generics. In: Thomas, D. (ed.) ECOOP 2006. LNCS, vol. 4067, pp. 279–303. Springer, Heidelberg (2006)
14. Igarashi, A., Pierce, B.C., Wadler, P.: Featherweight Java: a minimal core calculus for Java and GJ. ACM Transactions on Programming Languages and Systems (TOPLAS) 23(3), 396–450 (2001)
15. Jacobs, B., Piessens, F., Leino, K.R.M., Schulte, W.: Safe concurrency for aggregate objects with invariants. In: Software Engineering and Formal Methods (SEFM), pp. 137–147. IEEE Computer Society Press, Los Alamitos (2005)
16. Kennedy, A., Syme, D.: Design and Implementation of Generics for the.NET Common Language Runtime. In: Programming Language Design and Implementation (PLDI), pp. 1–12 (2001)
17. Leavens, G.T., Poll, E., Clifton, C., Cheon, Y., Ruby, C., Cok, D., Müller, P., Kiniry, J.: JML reference manual. Department of Computer Science, Iowa State University (2006), Available from www.jmlspecs.org
18. Leino, K.R.M., Müller, P.: Object invariants in dynamic contexts. In: Odersky, M. (ed.) ECOOP 2004. LNCS, vol. 3086, pp. 491–516. Springer, Heidelberg (2004)
19. Lu, Y., Potter, J.: Protecting representation with effect encapsulation. In: Principles of programming languages (POPL), pp. 359–371. ACM Press, New York (2006)
20. Müller, P. (ed.): Modular Specification and Verification of Object-Oriented Programs. LNCS, vol. 2262. Springer, Heidelberg (2002)
21. Müller, P., Poetzsch-Heffter, A., Leavens, G.T.: Modular invariants for layered object structures. Science of Computer Programming 62, 253–286 (2006)
22. Nägeli, S.: Ownership in design patterns. Master's thesis, ETH Zurich (2006), sct.inf.ethz.ch/projects/student_docs/Stefan_Naegeli
23. Noble, J., Vitek, J., Potter, J.M.: Flexible alias protection. In: Jul, E. (ed.) ECOOP 1998. LNCS, vol. 1445, Springer, Heidelberg (1998)
24. Potanin, A., Noble, J., Clarke, D., Biddle, R.: Generic ownership for generic Java. In: Object-Oriented Programming Systems, Languages, and Applications (OOPSLA), October 2006, pp. 311–324. ACM Press, New York (2006)
25. Salcianu, A., Rinard, M.C.: Purity and side effect analysis for Java programs. In: Cousot, R. (ed.) VMCAI 2005. LNCS, vol. 3385, pp. 199–215. Springer, Heidelberg (2005)

Declarative Object Identity Using Relation Types*

Mandana Vaziri, Frank Tip, Stephen Fink, and Julian Dolby

IBM T. J. Watson Research Center, P.O. Box 704, Yorktown Heights, NY 10598, USA
{mvaziri,ftip,sjfink,dolby}@us.ibm.com

Abstract. Object-oriented languages define the identity of an object to
be an address-based object identifier. The programmer may customize
the notion of object identity by overriding the `equals()` and `hashCode()`
methods following a specified contract. This customization often introduces latent errors, since the contract is unenforced and at times impossible to satisfy, and its implementation requires tedious and error-prone
boilerplate code. Relation types are a programming model in which object identity is defined declaratively, obviating the need for `equals()`
and `hashCode()` methods. This entails a stricter contract: identity never
changes during an execution. We formalize the model as an adaptation
of Featherweight Java, and implement it by extending Java with relation
types. Experiments on a set of Java programs show that the majority of
classes that override `equals()` can be refactored into relation types, and
that most of the remainder are buggy or fragile.

1   Introduction

IX: That every individual substance expresses the whole universe in its own
manner and that in its full concept is included all its experiences together with
all the attendant circumstances and the whole sequence of exterior events.
G. W. Leibniz, Discourse on Metaphysics (1686)

Object-oriented languages such as Java and C# support an address-based notion of identity for objects or reference types. By default, the language considers no two distinct object instances *equal*; Java's `java.lang.Object.equals()`
tests object identity by comparing addresses. Since programmers often intend
alternative notions of equality, classes may override the `equals()` method, implementing an arbitrary programmer-defined identity relation.

In order for standard library classes such as collections to function properly,
Java mandates that an `equals()` method satisfy an informal contract. First, it
must define an equivalence relation, meaning that `equals()` should encode a
reflexive, symmetric, and transitive relation. Second, the contract states that "it
must be consistent", i.e., two objects that are equal at some point in time must
remain equal, unless the state of one or both changes. Third, no object must be

---

* This work has been supported in part by the Defense Advanced Research Projects
Agency (DARPA) under contract No. NBCH30390004.

E. Ernst (Ed.): ECOOP 2007, LNAI 4609, pp. 54–78, 2007.

equal to **null**. Furthermore, when a programmer overrides **equals()**, he must also override **hashCode()** to ensure that equal objects have identical hash-codes.

Programmer customization of identity semantics causes problems for several reasons. First, creating an equivalence relation is often non-trivial and, in some cases, impossible [12] (for details, see Section 2). Second, the language has no mechanism to enforce the contract either statically or dynamically, leaving plenty of rope by which programmers routinely hang themselves. We found buggy or fragile **equals()** methods in nearly every Java application that we examined. Third, programmer identity tests often comprise repetitive and error-prone boiler-plate code, which must be updated manually as the code evolves. Even more boiler-plate code arises in patterns such as caching via hash-consing [18].

To alleviate these problems, we propose a programming model in which object identity is specified declaratively, without tedious and error-prone **equals()** and **hashCode()** methods. The model features a new language construct called a *relation type*. A relation type declares zero or more fields, and designates a (possibly empty) subset of these as immutable *key fields*, i.e. the field itself may not be mutated. An instance of a relation type is called a *tuple*. A tuple's identity is fully determined by its type and the identities of the instances referred to by its key fields. In other words, two tuples a and b are equal if and only if: (i) a and b are of the same type and, (ii) corresponding key fields in a and b are equal. Conceptually, our programming model provides a relational view of the heap, as a map from identities to their associated mutable state. One can think of tuples with the same identity as pointing to the same heap location, and our model permits efficient implementations (e.g., the use of space-efficient shared representations in combination with pointer-equality for fast comparisons).

Our model enforces a stricter contract than Java's since object identity *never* changes, and tuples of different types *must* have different identities. Several concepts arise as special cases of relation types: (i) a *class* of objects is one with an address as its only key field, (ii) a *value-type* [5,15] is one with *only* key fields, and (iii) a SINGLETON [17] is a type with *no* key fields.

We formalize our programming model as an adaptation of Featherweight Java, and prove that hash-consing identities preserves semantics. We implemented relation types in a small extension of Java called RJ, and created an RJ-to-Java compiler. We examined the classes that define **equals()** methods in several Java applications and refactored these classes to use relation types instead. We found that the majority of classes that define **equals()** can be refactored with minimal effort into relation types, and that most of the remainder are buggy or fragile.

To summarize, this paper makes the following contributions:

1. We present a programming model in which object identity is defined declaratively using a new language construct called relation types. By construction, relation types satisfy a strict contract that prevents several categories of bugs, and admits efficient implementations. Objects, value types, and singletons arise as special cases of the model.

2. We formalize the model using an adaptation of Featherweight Java, and prove that hash-consing is a safe optimization in this model.

3. We extended Java with relation types (RJ), and created an RJ-to-Java compiler. Experiments indicate that the majority of classes that define `equals()` in several Java applications can be refactored into relation types, and that most of the remainder are buggy or fragile.

2 Overview of RJ

This section examines Java's equality contract and illustrates several motivating problems. We then informally present our new approach based on relation types.

2.1 Java's Equality Contract

The contract for the `equals()` method in `java.lang.Object` [1] states that:

The `equals` method implements an equivalence relation on non-null object references:

(1) It is *reflexive*: for any non-null reference value x, x.equals(x) should return true.
(2) It is *symmetric*: for any non-null reference values x and y, x.equals(y) should return true if and only if y.equals(x) returns true.
(3) It is *transitive*: for any non-null reference values x, y, and z, if x.equals(y) returns true and y.equals(z) returns true, then x.equals(z) should return true.
(4) It is *consistent*: for any non-null reference values x and y, multiple invocations of x.equals(y) consistently return `true` or consistently return `false`, provided no information used in equals comparisons on the objects is modified.
(5) For any non-null reference value x, x.equals(null) should return false.

Furthermore, whenever one overrides `equals()`, one must also override `hashCode()`, to ensure that equal objects have identical hash-codes.

```
class Point {                              class ColorPoint extends Point{
    int x;                                     Color color;
    int y;                                     public boolean equals(Object o){
    public boolean equals(Object o){               if (!(o instanceof Point))
        if (!(o instanceof Point))                     return false;
            return false;                          if (!(o instanceof ColorPoint))
        return ((Point)o).x == x                       return o.equals(this);
        && ((Point)o).y == y;                      return super.equals(o) &&
    }                                              ((ColorPoint)o).color == color;
}                                              }
                                           }
```

Fig. 1. A class `Point` and its subclass `ColorPoint`

This contract has several problems. First, it is impossible to extend an instantiable class with a new field, and have the subclass be comparable to its superclass, while preserving the equivalence relation. Consider the example shown in Figure 1 (taken from [12]). Here, the `equals()` method of `ColorPoint` must be written as such to preserve symmetry. However, this violates transitivity as indicated in [12]. If one defines three points as follows:

```
ColorPoint p1 = new ColorPoint(1, 2, Color.RED);
Point p2 = new Point(1,2);
ColorPoint p3 = new ColorPoint(1, 2, Color.BLUE);
```

then `p1.equals(p2)` is true and so is `p2.equals(p3)`, but `p1.equals(p3)` is false since `color` is taken into account.

A second problem with the contract is that the consistency (non-)requirement allows the identity relation defined by the `equals()` method to change over time: `equals()` may refer to mutable state. If an object's identity relation changes while the object resides in a collection, the collection's operations (e.g. `add()` and `remove()`) will not function as intended.

Most importantly, neither the compiler nor the runtime system enforces the contract in any way. If the programmer mistakenly violates the contract, the problem can easily manifest as symptoms arbitrarily far from the bug source. A correct implementation involves nontrivial error-prone boilerplate code, and mistakes easily and commonly arise, as we shall see in Section 2.2.

Java's contract (but not C#'s) is also under-specified because it permits `equals()` and `hashCode()` to throw run-time exceptions that could be avoided.

2.2 Examples

We carefully examined several applications, and found many problems in implementations of `equals()` and `hashCode()` methods, such as:

(a) **Dependence on mutable state.** Figure 2(a) shows a fragile code fragment from `org.hsqldb.GroupedResult.ResultGroup` in *hsqldb*, where `equals()` and `hashCode()` refer to a mutable field `row` of type `Object[]`, which is updated elsewhere. If the program modifies a `row` while a `ResultGroup` is stored in a collection, then subsequent attempts to retrieve elements from that collection may fail or produce inconsistent results. While the `equals()` contract does not prohibit `equals()` and `hashCode()` from referring to mutable state, it "handles" these cases by declaring that "all bets are off" when the identity relation changes. The programmer must carefully maintain the non-local invariant that mutations do not overlap with relevant collection lifetimes, often resulting in buggy or hard-to-maintain code.

(b) **Asymmetry.** Figure 2(b) shows excerpts from two classes from *jfreechart*, one a superclass of the other. These `equals()` implementations are asymmetric: it is easy to construct a `NumberAxis a` and a `CyclicNumberAxis b` such that `a.equals(b)` but `!b.equals(a)`. This violates the contract and may produce inconsistent results if a heterogeneous collection contains both types of objects.

(c) **Contract for `equals()`/`hashCode()`.** In Figure 2(c), from *bcel*, `equals()` and `hashCode()` refer to different subsets of the state, so two equal objects may have different hashcodes. The developers apparently knew of this problem as is evident from the comment "If the user changes the name or type, problems with the targeter hashmap will occur".

(d) **Exceptions and null values.** Figure 2(d) shows an `equals()` method from *pmd*, which has two immediate problems. First, if the parameter `o` is `null`, the method throws a `NullPointerException` rather than return *false* as per the contract. Second, the code will throw a `ClassCastException` if the object is ever compared to one of an incompatible type.

```
class ResultGroup {
  Object[] row;
  int hashCode;
  private ResultGroup(Object[] row) {
    this.row = row;
    hashCode = 0;
    for (int i = groupBegin;
        i < groupEnd; i++) {
      if (row[i] != null) {
        hashCode += row[i].hashCode();
      }
    }
  }
  public int hashCode() { return hashCode; }
  public boolean equals(Object obj) {
    if (obj == this) { return true; }
    if (obj == null ||
        !(obj instanceof ResultGroup)) {
      return false;
    }
    ResultGroup group = (ResultGroup)obj;
    for (int i = groupBegin;
        i < groupEnd; i++) {
      if (!equals(row[i], group.row[i])) {
        return false;
      }
    }
    return true;
  }
  private boolean equals(Object o1,
      Object o2) {
    return (o1 == null) ? o2 == null
        : o1.equals(o2);
  }
}
```

(a) Program fragment taken from *hsqldb*

```
public class NumberAxis extends ValueAxis ... {
  private boolean autoRangeIncludesZero;
  public boolean equals(Object obj) {
    if (obj == this) { return true; }
    if (!(obj instanceof NumberAxis)) {
      return false;
    }
    if (!super.equals(obj)) { return false; }
    NumberAxis that = (NumberAxis) obj;
    if (this.autoRangeIncludesZero !=
        that.autoRangeIncludesZero) {
      return false; }
    ...
  }
}
public class CyclicNumberAxis
    extends NumberAxis {
  protected double period;
  public boolean equals(Object obj) {
    if (obj == this) { return true; }
    if (!(obj instanceof CyclicNumberAxis)) {
      return false;
    }
    ...
```

```
    ...
    if (!super.equals(obj)) { return false; }
    CyclicNumberAxis that =
        (CyclicNumberAxis) obj;
    if (this.period != that.period) {
      return false;
    }
    ...
  }
```

(b) Program fragment taken from *jfreechart*

```
public class LocalVariableGen implements ... {
  public int hashCode() {
    //If the user changes the name or type,
    //problems with the targeter hashmap
    //will occur
    int hc = index ^ name.hashCode()
        ^ type.hashCode();
    return hc;
  }
  public boolean equals( Object o ) {
    if (!(o instanceof LocalVariableGen)) {
      return false;
    }
    LocalVariableGen l = (LocalVariableGen) o;
    return (l.index == index)
        && (l.start == start)
        && (l.end == end);
  }
}
```

(c) Program fragment taken from *bcel*

```
public class MethodNameDeclaration
  public boolean equals(Object o) {
    MethodNameDeclaration other =
        (MethodNameDeclaration) o;
    if (!other.node.getImage().
        equals(node.getImage())) {
      return false;
    }
    ...
  }
```

(d) Program fragment taken from *pmd*

```
public class emit {
  protected static void emit_action_code( ... ){
    ...
    if (prod.action() != null &&
        prod.action().code_string() != null &&
        !prod.action().equals(""))
      out.println(prod.action().code_string());
    ...
  }
}
```

(e) Program fragment taken from *javacup*

Fig. 2. Problems with the equality contract encountered in practice

(e) Inadvertent test of incomparable types. Figure 2(e) shows a buggy
code fragment taken from method java_cup.emit.emit_action_code() in
javacup. Here, the last part of the condition, !prod.action().equals(""),

compares an object of type `java_cup.action_part` with an object of type
`String`. Such objects are never equal to each other, hence the condition trivially succeeds. This bug causes spurious blank lines in the parser that is generated by *javacup*. We confirmed with the developers [26] that they intended
to write `!prod.action().code_string().equals("")`. More generally, the
problem stems from the property that objects of arbitrary types may be
considered equal, precluding compile-time type-based feasibility checks.

2.3 Revised Equality Contract

We propose a model that forces programmers to define object identity declaratively by explicitly indicating the fields in a type that comprise its identity,
which automatically induces an equivalence relation $==_R$. Our programming
model enforces a new equality contract that differs from Java's as follows:

- It is *enforced*: The language implementation generates $==_R$ automatically
  and forbids the programmer from manipulating this relation explicitly.
- It is *more strict* than the original contract in item (4'); object identity cannot
  change throughout the execution.
- The problems with defining an equivalence relation in the presence of subclassing are resolved by making relation types and their subtypes incomparable: x $==_R$ y yields false if x and y are not of exactly the same type.

The revised contract, shown below, is consistent with Java's equality contract.
Note that items (1'), (2'),(3'), and (5') are essentially the same as before.

Revised Equality Contract for $==_R$ identity relation, on non-null references:

(1') $==_R$ is *reflexive*: For any non-null reference value x, x $==_R$ x must return true.
(2') $==_R$ is *symmetric*: For any non-null reference values x and y, x $==_R$ y returns true if and
only if y $==_R$ x returns true.
(3') $==_R$ is *transitive*: For any non-null reference values x, y, and z, if x $==_R$ y returns true and
y $==_R$ z returns true, then x $==_R$ z must return true.
(4') For any non-null reference values x and y, multiple tests x $==_R$ y consistently return true,
or consistently return false throughout the execution.
(5') For any non-null reference value x, x $==_R$ null must return false.

2.4 Relation Types

Our programming model introduces a new notion of class called a *relation type*.
We informally present the notion here; Section 3 defines the semantics formally.

A relation type resembles a class in Java, except a programmer may not
override the `equals()` and `hashCode()` methods. Instead, the programmer must
designate a (possibly empty) subset of instance fields as *key fields*, using the
keyword `key`. Key fields are implicitly `final` and `private`. We call an instance
of a relation type a *tuple*, and its identity is fully determined by its type and the
identities of the instances referred to by its key fields.

The programmer does not explicitly allocate a tuple using `new`; instead, he
calls a predefined `id()` method, whose formal parameters correspond exactly

to the types of the key fields (including all those declared in its supertypes). Informally, the id() method does an associative lookup to find the tuple with the same identity. If no such tuple is found, id() creates a new tuple.

```
relation Car {                          1.   public static void main(String[] args){
    key String model;                   2.       Person p1 = Person.id(123);
    key int year;                       3.       Person p2 = Person.id(123);
    key String plate;                   4.       Person p3 = Person.id(456);
}                                        5.       // p1 == p2
                                         6.       // p1 != p3
relation Person {                        7.       // p1.SSN = 789 --> compile error
    key int SSN;
    Name name;                           8.       Name n1 = Name.id("Alice","Jones");
}                                        9.       Name n2 = FullName.id("Alice","Jones","Leah");
                                        10.       p1.name = n1;
relation Name {                         11.       // n1 != n2
    key String first;                   12.       // n1 == ((FullName)n2).toName()
    key String last;                    13.       // p2.name.first == "Alice"
}                                       14.       // p2.name.last == "Jones"

relation FullName extends Name {        15.       Policy pol1 = new Policy();
    key String middle;                  16.       Policy pol2 = new Policy();
    String nickname;                    17.       // pol1 != pol2
}
                                        18.       Car c1 = Car.id("Chevy",2004,"DZN-6767");
class Policy { ... }                    19.       CarInsurance cins = CarInsurance.id(p1,c1);
                                        20.       cins.policy = pol1;
relation CarInsurance {                 21.       cins.computePremium();
    key Person person;
    key Car car;                        22.       PolicyMgr pm = PolicyMgr.id();
    Policy policy;                      23.       pm.add(pol1);
    int computePremium() { ... }        24.       pm.add(pol2);
}
                                        25.       Set<Person> people = new HashSet<Person>();
relation PolicyMgr {                    26.       people.add(p1);
    // no key fields                    27.       people.add(p3);
    public void addPolicy(Policy p){    28.       // people.contains(p2) is true
        policies.add(p);
    }                                   29.       p2.name = n2;
    List<Policy> policies =             30.       // ((FullName)p1.name).middle == "Leah";
        new ArrayList<Policy>();        31.       // people.contains(p2) is still true
}                                       32.   }
```

Fig. 3. Example of relation types

Figure 3 shows an example of pseudo-code with relation types. Relation type Car declares key fields model, year, and plate. This means that two cars with the same model, year and plate have the same identity and are indistinguishable. Since Car has no mutable state, it corresponds to a value type [5].

Relation types are more general than value types because tuples may contain mutable state. Consider relation type Person, which has a key field SSN and a mutable field Name. This means that there exists at most one Person tuple with a given SSN, and that assignments to SSN are forbidden. So on the right side of the example, variables p1 and p2 refer to the same tuple (they are aliased). Assignments to the non-key field name are allowed (see line 10).

Inheritance among relation types resembles single inheritance for classes: subtypes may add (but not remove) additional key fields as well as other instance fields and methods. A subtype inherits methods and fields declared in a relation supertype. A relation type and its subtype are incomparable; subtype tuples have different identities from supertype tuples. Should the programmer want to compare a tuple to the corresponding subtuple of a subtype, the language provides predefined *coercion methods* to convert subtypes to supertypes.

Consider the relation type `Name` and its subtype `FullName` in the figure. Tuples of these relations have different identities (see line 11), and the predefined coercion operator `toName()` must be used to compare the corresponding key fields of these relations (see line 12). The assertions shown on lines 13 and 14 follow from the fact that `p1` and `p2` refer to the same tuple.

Conceptually, Java classes (with address-based identity) correspond to relation types with an implicitly defined key field `address`, assigned a unique value by an object constructor. We use the `class` keyword to indicate a relation type with an implicit `address` field. For example, the tuples (objects) of type `Policy` created at lines 15 and 16 have different identities (see line 17). Note that classes may not explicitly declare `key` fields or inherit from relation types that do. Our `relation` keyword indicates the absence of an `address` key field.

The relation type `CarInsurance` illustrates how relation types provide a relational view of the heap. The `CarInsurance` type maps distinct identities to mutable state stored in the `policy` field. By analogy to relational databases, the `CarInsurance` type resembles a relational table with three columns, two of which are keys. The type also defines methods such as `computePremium()` that may refer to all of all state of a particular `CarInsurance` tuple.

If a relation type has no key fields, then it corresponds to the SINGLETON design pattern [17], since its identity consists solely of the type. Figure 3 shows a (singleton) relation type `PolicyMgr` that provides access to a globally accessible list of insurance policies. Lines 22–24 access this list.

Finally, lines 25–31 illustrate what happens when we insert tuples into collections. Here, we define a set `people` and add `p1` and `p3` to it. Since `p1` and `p2` are equal, the test `people.contains(p2)` returns true. Now if we modify `p2` by changing its `name` field (line 26), `p2` remains in the set as expected (line 28). The result of the test remains unchanged because the identity of `p2` did not depend on mutable state, and `p2` was not removed from the set.

2.5   Lifetime Management and Namespaces

Thus far, we assumed that each relation type provides a global namespace for tuples of a given type. Under this model, the program can support at most one tuple with a given identity. Now, consider the case where a tuple t has a non-key field that points to an object v. Normally, if t becomes garbage, and there are no other references to v, then v becomes garbage. However, if the program can reconstruct t's identity (which is the case if, e.g., all of t's key fields are of primitive types), then the implementation cannot know whether the program will try to retrieve v in the future. In such cases, t and v are immortal and cannot be garbage-collected, effectively causing a memory leak.

For a more flexible, practical model, the programmer can use *scopes* to provide separate namespaces for a type, and also to control tuple lifetime. Consider the pseudo-code of Figure 4(a). The code creates two `Persons`, each with the same identity (3), but which reside in different scopes. First, the program creates a namespace of type `Scope<Person>` via a call to a built-in method `Person.newScope()`. Type `Scope<Person>` provides an `id()` method with the same signature as that of `Person`. Then, rather than creating a tuple from global namespace via `Person.id()`, the program allocates a tuple from a particular named scope (e.g., `s1.id()`).

Regarding garbage collection: a tuple becomes garbage when the program holds no references to its containing scope (provided all of its key fields have become garbage). In the example code, if `foo` returns `jack`, then `jane` may be garbage-collected when `foo` returns, since there will be no live references to `jane` nor its scope `s2`.

```
Person foo() {                                  Person foo() {
  Scope<Person> s1 = Person.newScope();           Object s1 = new Object();
  Person jack = s1.id(3);                         Person jack = Person.id(3,s1);
  jack.setName(Name.id("Jack","Sprat"));          jack.setName(Name.id("Jack","Sprat"));
  Scope<Person> s2 = Person.newScope();           Object s2 = new Object();
  Person jane = s2.id(3);                         Person jane = Person.id(3,s2);
  jane.setName(Name.id("Jane","Sprat"));          jane.setName(Name.id("Jane","Sprat"));
  return (*) ? jack : jane;                       return (*) ? jack : jane;
}                                               }
              (a)                                             (b)
```

Fig. 4. Example of scopes

The base programming model can emulate programming with scopes by adding to each relation type an implicit key field called `scope`, whose type is an object. This will be discussed further in Section 4.1.

3   A Core Calculus for RJ

We formally define a core calculus for the RJ language as an adaptation of Featherweight Java [19] (FJ). For simplicity, we adopt the notation and structures of the model presented in [19]. RJ differs from Featherweight Java in that it has relation types instead of classes, and allows assignment.

3.1   Syntax

We use the notation $\bar{x}$ to denote a possibly empty sequence, indexed starting at 1, and • for the empty sequence. The size of the sequence is indicated by $\#\bar{x}$. We write $\bar{x} \in X$ to denote $x_1 \in X, \cdots, x_{\#\bar{x}} \in X$ (and similarly $\bar{x} \notin X$). For any partial function F, we write $Dom(F)$ for the domain of F. The notation $F(\bar{x})$ is short for the sequence $F(x_1), \cdots, F(x_n)$.

We use L to denote a relation type declaration, and M a method. We write R, S and T for relation type names; f, g and h for field names; x for variables; e and

c for expressions; l and a for memory locations, with subscripts as needed. The notation "$\bar{R}\ \bar{x}$" is shorthand for the sequence "$R_1\ x_1, \cdots, R_n\ x_n$" and similarly "$\bar{R}\ \bar{f};$" is shorthand for the sequence declarations "$R_1\ f_1; \cdots R_n\ f_n;$" for some n. The declaration "$\texttt{key}\ \bar{R}\ \bar{f};$" is similar with the annotation 'key' preceding every declaration in the sequence.

The syntax of the RJ language is shown below:

$L ::= \texttt{relation}\ R\ \texttt{extends}\ R\ \{\ \texttt{key}\ \bar{R}\ \bar{f};\ \bar{R}\ \bar{f};\ \bar{M}\ \}$

$M ::= R\ m(\bar{R}\ \bar{x})\ \{\ \texttt{return}\ e;\ \}$

$e ::= x \mid e.f \mid e.m(\bar{e}) \mid e\ \texttt{==}\ e \mid \texttt{if}\ e\ \texttt{then}\ e\ \texttt{else}\ e \mid e.f \leftarrow e \mid R.\texttt{id}(\bar{e}) \mid l$

A relation type is declared to be a subtype of another using the **extends** keyword and consists of series of field declarations and a series of method declarations. Some field declarations are marked with the keyword **key** and represent the *key fields* of the relation type. Key fields are immutable, and non-key fields may or may not be mutable. We assume that there is an uninstantiatable relation type **Relation** at the top of the type hierarchy with no fields and no methods. As in Featherweight Java, a subtype inherits fields and methods, field declarations are not allowed to shadow fields of supertypes, and methods may override other methods with the same signature. A method declaration specifies a method's return type, name, formal parameters, and body. The body consists of a single statement which returns an expression e, which may refer to formal parameters and the variable **this**. Note that relation types do not have constructors. Instead, a tuple is constructed using a method **id()** with predefined functionality.

An expression consists of a variable, a field access, a method call, an equality test, or an **if–then–else** construct. Other forms are an assignment $e.f \leftarrow e$, which assigns to $e.f$ and evaluates to the value being assigned, or a relation construction expression $R.\texttt{id}(\bar{e})$, which takes as many parameters as there are key fields in R and its supertypes (in the same order). Informally, $R.\texttt{id}(\bar{e})$ refers to the tuple of type R whose arguments are denoted by $\bar{e}$. If such a tuple already exists, then it is returned (with all existing non-key state), otherwise it is created with all non-key fields set to **null**. Finally, an expression may be a memory location l, which is used for defining semantics only and not by the programmer.

A relation table *RTable* is a mapping from a relation type name R to a declaration of the form "$\texttt{relation}\ R\ \dots$". *RTable* is assumed to contain an entry for every relation type except for the top level type **Relation**. The subtype relation (denoted $<:$) is obtained in a customary way [19]. An RJ program consists of a pair (*RTable*, e) of a relation table and an expression.

3.2 Semantics

Figure 5 shows some auxiliary functions needed to define the reduction rules of RJ. The function *keys*() returns the set of key fields of a relation type, while *nonKeys*() returns its non-key fields. Function *fields*() returns the sequence of all fields of a relation type. Partial function *mbody*(m, R) looks up the body of method named m for relation type R and returns a pair of formal parameters and the expression that constitutes its body, written as $\bar{x}.e$. The notation $m \notin \bar{M}$ means that there is no method declaration for a method named m in $\bar{M}$. We do not deal with method overloading as in Featherweight Java.

The *arity* of a relation type R is the number of key fields in R and all its supertypes, and is denoted by $|R|$.

Key lookup:

$$keys(\texttt{Relation}) = \bullet$$

$$\frac{\text{relation } R \text{ extends } S \ \{\texttt{key } \bar{T} \ \bar{g};\ \bar{R} \ \bar{f};\ \bar{M}\} \quad keys(S) = \bar{S} \ \bar{h}}{keys(R) = \bar{S} \ \bar{h},\ \bar{T} \ \bar{g}}$$

Non-Key lookup:

$$nonKeys(\texttt{Relation}) = \bullet$$

$$\frac{\text{relation } R \text{ extends } S \ \{\texttt{key } \bar{T} \ \bar{g};\ \bar{R} \ \bar{f};\ \bar{M}\} \quad nonKeys(S) = \bar{S} \ \bar{h}}{nonKeys(R) = \bar{S} \ \bar{h},\ \bar{R} \ \bar{f}}$$

Field lookup:

$$fields(R) = keys(R),\ nonKeys(R)$$

Method body lookup:

$$\frac{\text{relation } R \text{ extends } S \ \{\texttt{key } \bar{T} \ \bar{g};\ \bar{R} \ \bar{f};\ \bar{M}\} \quad T \ m(\bar{T} \ \bar{x})\{ \ \texttt{return } e;\ \} \in \bar{M}}{mbody(m,\ R) = \bar{x}.e}$$

$$\frac{\text{relation } R \text{ extends } S \ \{\texttt{key } \bar{T} \ \bar{g};\ \bar{R} \ \bar{f};\ \bar{M}\} \quad m \notin \bar{M}}{mbody(m,\ R) = mbody(m,\ S)}$$

Fig. 5. Auxiliary functions for RJ

Traditionally, a heap is defined as a map from memory locations and field names to memory locations. In our programming model, the identity of a tuple constitutes a high-level address for it. To reflect this, the heap in our model is comprised of two components: a map from locations to identities, and a map from identities and field names to locations. There is therefore a level of indirection to introduce these high-level addresses.

Let Locs be a set of memory locations, Ids a set of *identities*, and Fields the set of field names. We use k to denote an identity. Let a *heap* $\mathcal{H}$ be a partial function of type (Ids, Fields) $\rightarrow$ Locs, and a *heap index* $\mathcal{L}$ a partial function of type Locs $\rightarrow$ Ids. A heap index $\mathcal{L}$ *corresponds to* a heap $\mathcal{H}$ if and only if $\mathcal{L}$ is defined for every location in the range of $\mathcal{H}$ and every identity in the domain of $\mathcal{H}$ is in the range of $\mathcal{L}$. We use the notation $\mathcal{H}[(k, f) \rightarrow l]$ to denote the heap function identical to $\mathcal{H}$ except at (k, f), which is mapped to l. Similarly, $\mathcal{L}[l \rightarrow k]$ denotes heap index $\mathcal{L}$ with l mapped to k. We write $\mathcal{L}[\bar{l} \rightarrow \bar{k}]$ to denote $\mathcal{L}[l_1 \rightarrow k_1] \cdots [l_n \rightarrow k_n]$, where $\bar{l}$ and $\bar{k}$ have size n.

The function $alloc_n(\mathcal{L})$ allocates a sequence of n fresh locations not mapped by $\mathcal{L}$. We write $alloc(\mathcal{L})$ as a shorthand for $alloc_1(\mathcal{L})$.

Finally, we introduce a function $\mathcal{I}$ that computes the identity of a tuple, given its type and the identities of its key fields. Formally, $\mathcal{I}$ is a partial injective function $\mathcal{I}$ that maps a relation type and a sequence of identities to an identity in IDS. $\mathcal{I}(R, \bar{k})$ is defined when $\#\bar{k} = |R|$, and undefined otherwise. Note that the base case for constructing identities is to construct the identity for a relation type without key fields (i.e., a singleton).

The typing rules for RJ are straightforward adaptations of those for Feather-weight Java, and can be found in a forthcoming technical report [32].

Figure 6 shows reduction rules for RJ. A reduction step is of the form: $(\mathcal{L}, \mathcal{H}, e) \longrightarrow (\mathcal{L}', \mathcal{H}', e')$ and means that e reduces in one step to e' in the context of heap index $\mathcal{L}$ and heap $\mathcal{H}$, resulting in $\mathcal{L}'$ and $\mathcal{H}'$. We use the notation $\longrightarrow_{RJ}$ to denote one step of reduction in RJ, when it is not clear from context. We write $\longrightarrow_{RJ}^*$ to denote the reflexive, transitive closure of the $\longrightarrow_{RJ}$ relation.

Rule R-FIELD reduces expression $l.f_i$, where l is a location, by looking up the identity that l maps to in $\mathcal{L}$, and the location mapped to by this identity and field f_i in $\mathcal{H}$, i.e. $\mathcal{H}(\mathcal{L}(l), f_i)$.

Rule R-INVK deals with method invocation and applies only after the receiver and parameters have been reduced to locations. The expression $[\bar{a}/\bar{x}, l/\text{this}]e$ denotes e in which formal parameters $\bar{x}$ and this have been replaced with actual parameters $\bar{a}$ and receiver l, respectively.

Rules R-EQ-TRUE R-EQ-FALSE show how to reduce an equality between two memory locations l_1 and l_2. These are equal if they hold the same identity, i.e., $\mathcal{L}(l_1) = \mathcal{L}(l_2)$.

Rules R-IF-TRUE and R-IF-FALSE show the reduction for the if-then-else expression in the obvious way.

Rule R-ASSIGN shows how to reduce an assignment expression $l.f_i \leftarrow a$. Field f must be non-key, and l and a locations. The expression reduces to a and the heap $\mathcal{H}$ is replaced with one that is identical except at $(\mathcal{L}(l), f_i)$, which is now mapped to a.

Rule R-ID-NOKEY shows the reduction of a constructor expression for a relation type with no key fields $R.\text{id}()$. This expression is reduced to a fresh memory location l, which is mapped to the corresponding identity $k = \mathcal{I}(R)$ in the new heap index.

Rule R-ID-CREATE shows the reduction of a constructor expression $R.\text{id}(\bar{a})$ for the case where the identified tuple has not been created yet. For this rule to apply, the arguments must have been already reduced to locations $\bar{a}$. The identity k of the tuple is computed using $\mathcal{I}(R, \mathcal{L}(\bar{a}))$. The expression $l, \bar{l} = alloc_{\#\bar{a}+1}(\mathcal{L})$ allocates $\#\bar{a} + 1$ fresh memory locations from $\mathcal{L}$, one for the tuple itself, and $\#\bar{a}$ for each of its key fields. The constructor expression reduces to location l, which is mapped to k in the new heap index. The heap itself is also updated at (k,g) for each key field g in $\bar{g}$ of R to a fresh memory location. The notation $\mathcal{H}[(k, \bar{g}) \rightarrow \bar{l}]$ represents $\mathcal{H}[(k, g_1) \rightarrow l_1] \cdots [(k, g_n) \rightarrow l_n]$, where $\bar{g}$ and $\bar{l}$ have size n. The typing rules [32] guarantee that the constructor for R has as many arguments as its number of key fields, which means that sequences $\bar{a}$ and $\bar{g}$ have the same length. Rule R-ID-CREATE applies when $(k, \bar{g})$ is not in the domain of $\mathcal{H}$ and the tuple is therefore created.

$$\frac{fields(R) = \bar{R}\ \bar{f} \quad l \in \text{Locs} \quad l_i = \mathcal{H}(\mathcal{L}(l), f_i)}{(\mathcal{L},\ \mathcal{H},\ l.f_i) \ \longrightarrow \ (\mathcal{L},\ \mathcal{H},\ l_i)} \quad \text{(R-Field)}$$

$$\frac{mbody(m, R) = \bar{x}.e \quad l, \bar{a} \in \text{Locs}}{(\mathcal{L},\ \mathcal{H},\ l.m(\bar{a})) \ \longrightarrow \ (\mathcal{L},\ \mathcal{H},\ [\bar{a}/\bar{x},\ l/this]e)} \quad \text{(R-Invk)}$$

$$\frac{l_1, l_2 \in \text{Locs} \quad \mathcal{L}(l_1) = \mathcal{L}(l_2)}{(\mathcal{L},\ \mathcal{H},\ l_1 == l_2) \ \longrightarrow \ (\mathcal{L},\ \mathcal{H},\ true)} \quad \text{(R-Eq-True)}$$

$$\frac{l_1, l_2 \in \text{Locs} \quad \mathcal{L}(l_1) \neq \mathcal{L}(l_2)}{(\mathcal{L},\ \mathcal{H},\ l_1 == l_2) \ \longrightarrow \ (\mathcal{L},\ \mathcal{H},\ false)} \quad \text{(R-Eq-False)}$$

$$(\mathcal{L},\ \mathcal{H},\ \text{if } true \text{ then } e_T \text{ else } e_F) \ \longrightarrow \ (\mathcal{L},\ \mathcal{H},\ e_T) \quad \text{(R-If-True)}$$

$$(\mathcal{L},\ \mathcal{H},\ \text{if } false \text{ then } e_T \text{ else } e_F) \ \longrightarrow \ (\mathcal{L},\ \mathcal{H},\ e_F) \quad \text{(R-If-False)}$$

$$\frac{nonKeys(R) = \bar{R}\ \bar{f} \quad l, a \in \text{Locs}}{(\mathcal{L},\ \mathcal{H},\ l.f_i \leftarrow a) \ \longrightarrow \ (\mathcal{L},\ \mathcal{H}[(\mathcal{L}(l), f_i) \rightarrow a],\ a)} \quad \text{(R-Assign)}$$

$$\frac{k = \mathcal{I}(R) \quad l = alloc(\mathcal{L})}{(\mathcal{L},\ \mathcal{H},\ R.id()) \ \longrightarrow \ (\mathcal{L}[l \rightarrow k],\ \mathcal{H},\ l)} \quad \text{(R-Id-NoKey)}$$

$$\frac{\bar{a} \in \text{Locs} \quad k = \mathcal{I}(R, \mathcal{L}(\bar{a})) \quad keys(R) = \bar{R}\ \bar{g}}{(k, \bar{g}) \notin Dom(\mathcal{H}) \quad l, \bar{l} = alloc_{\#\bar{a}+1}(\mathcal{L})}{(\mathcal{L},\ \mathcal{H},\ R.id(\bar{a})) \ \longrightarrow \ (\mathcal{L}[l \rightarrow k][\bar{l} \rightarrow \mathcal{L}(\bar{a})],\ \mathcal{H}[(k,\bar{g}) \rightarrow \bar{l}],\ l)} \quad \text{(R-Id-Create)}$$

$$\frac{\bar{a} \in \text{Locs} \quad k = \mathcal{I}(R, \mathcal{L}(\bar{a})) \quad keys(R) = \bar{R}\ \bar{g}}{(k, \bar{g}) \in Dom(\mathcal{H}) \quad l = alloc(\mathcal{L})}{(\mathcal{L},\ \mathcal{H},\ R.id(\bar{a})) \ \longrightarrow \ (\mathcal{L}[l \rightarrow k][\bar{l} \rightarrow \mathcal{L}(\bar{a})],\ \mathcal{H},\ l)} \quad \text{(R-Id-Find)}$$

$$\frac{(\mathcal{L},\ \mathcal{H},\ e) \ \longrightarrow \ (\mathcal{L}',\ \mathcal{H}',\ e')}{(\mathcal{L},\ \mathcal{H},\ e.f) \ \longrightarrow \ (\mathcal{L}',\ \mathcal{H}',\ e'.f)} \quad \text{(RC-Field)}$$

$$\frac{(\mathcal{L},\ \mathcal{H},\ e) \ \longrightarrow \ (\mathcal{L}',\ \mathcal{H}',\ e')}{(\mathcal{L},\ \mathcal{H},\ e.m(\bar{c})) \ \longrightarrow \ (\mathcal{L}',\ \mathcal{H}',\ e'.m(\bar{c}))} \quad \text{(RC-Invk-Recv)}$$

$$\frac{(\mathcal{L},\ \mathcal{H},\ e) \ \longrightarrow \ (\mathcal{L}',\ \mathcal{H}',\ e') \quad l, \bar{a} \in \text{Locs}}{(\mathcal{L},\ \mathcal{H},\ l.m(\bar{a}, e, \bar{c})) \ \longrightarrow \ (\mathcal{L}',\ \mathcal{H}',\ l.m(\bar{a}, e', \bar{c}))} \quad \text{(RC-Invk-Arg)}$$

$$\frac{(\mathcal{L},\ \mathcal{H},\ e) \ \longrightarrow \ (\mathcal{L}',\ \mathcal{H}',\ e')}{(\mathcal{L},\ \mathcal{H},\ e == c) \ \longrightarrow \ (\mathcal{L}',\ \mathcal{H}',\ e' == c)} \quad \text{(RC-Eq-1)}$$

$$\frac{(\mathcal{L},\ \mathcal{H},\ e) \ \longrightarrow \ (\mathcal{L}',\ \mathcal{H}',\ e') \quad l \in \text{Locs}}{(\mathcal{L},\ \mathcal{H},\ l == e) \ \longrightarrow \ (\mathcal{L}',\ \mathcal{H}',\ l == e')} \quad \text{(RC-Eq-2)}$$

$$\frac{(\mathcal{L},\ \mathcal{H},\ e) \ \longrightarrow \ (\mathcal{L}',\ \mathcal{H}',\ e')}{(\mathcal{L},\ \mathcal{H},\ e.f \leftarrow c) \ \longrightarrow \ (\mathcal{L}',\ \mathcal{H}',\ e'.f \leftarrow c)} \quad \text{(RC-Assign-1)}$$

$$\frac{(\mathcal{L},\ \mathcal{H},\ e) \ \longrightarrow \ (\mathcal{L}',\ \mathcal{H}',\ e') \quad l \in \text{Locs}}{(\mathcal{L},\ \mathcal{H},\ l.f \leftarrow e) \ \longrightarrow \ (\mathcal{L}',\ \mathcal{H}',\ l.f \leftarrow e')} \quad \text{(RC-Assign-2)}$$

$$\frac{(\mathcal{L},\ \mathcal{H},\ e) \ \longrightarrow \ (\mathcal{L}',\ \mathcal{H}',\ e') \quad \bar{a} \in \text{Locs}}{(\mathcal{L},\ \mathcal{H},\ R.id(\bar{a}, e, \bar{c})) \ \longrightarrow \ (\mathcal{L}',\ \mathcal{H}',\ R.id(\bar{a}, e', \bar{c}))} \quad \text{(RC-Id-Arg)}$$

Fig. 6. Computation and Congruence Rules for RJ

Rule R-ID-FIND is similar, except that the tuple exists in the heap and it is therefore not updated. The constructor expression still reduces to a fresh memory location l, which is mapped to the identity k in the new heap index.

The rest of the reduction rules (Figure 6) ensure that an expression is reduced in a deterministic fixed order.

RJ's computation on a program $(RTable, e)$ starts in a state $(\mathcal{L},\ \mathcal{H},\ e)$, where $\mathcal{L}$ and $\mathcal{H}$ have empty domains, and consists of a sequence of states obtained by applying the reduction rules, until none applies.

3.3   The RJ-HC Language

In this section, we prove that the hash-consing optimization [18], which consists of storing equal values at the same memory location, preserves semantics for RJ. To this end, we present RJ-HC, a version of the core calculus of RJ with a hash-consing operational semantics.

RJ-HC has the same syntax and auxiliary functions as RJ, except for memory allocation, which performs hash-consing. The auxiliary function $alloc_{RJ\text{-}HC}(\mathcal{L},\ k)$ in RJ-HC returns a location l that maps to k in $\mathcal{L}$, if such a location exists, and a fresh location otherwise. We write $alloc_{RJ\text{-}HC}(\mathcal{L},\ \bar{k})$ to denote the sequence $alloc_{RJ\text{-}HC}(\mathcal{L},\ k_1),\ \cdots,\ alloc_{RJ\text{-}HC}(\mathcal{L},\ k_n)$, where n is the length of $\bar{k}$.

The reduction rules of RJ-HC are identical to RJ, except for R-ID-NOKEY, R-ID-CREATE, and R-ID-FIND. Figure 7 shows these new rules for RJ-HC. Rule R-ID-NOKEY-HC is similar to that in RJ, except that it uses the new allocation function. There is a single rule R-ID-HC for the constructor expression, which also uses the hash-consing allocation function. It always updates the heap $\mathcal{H}$, possibly rewriting it with existing values.

We use the notation $\longrightarrow_{RJ\text{-}HC}$ to denote one step of reduction in RJ-HC, when it is not clear from context. We write $\longrightarrow^*_{RJ\text{-}HC}$ to denote the reflexive, transitive closure of the $\longrightarrow_{RJ\text{-}HC}$ relation.

$$\frac{k = \mathcal{I}(R)\quad l = alloc_{RJ\text{-}HC}(\mathcal{L},\ k)}{(\mathcal{L},\ \mathcal{H},\ R.\mathrm{id}())\ \longrightarrow\ (\mathcal{L}[l \to k],\ \mathcal{H},\ l)} \quad\text{(R-ID-NOKEY-HC)}$$

$$\frac{\bar{a} \in \textsc{Locs}\quad k = \mathcal{I}(R, \mathcal{L}(\bar{a}))\quad keys(R) = \bar{R}\ \bar{g}}{l = alloc_{RJ\text{-}HC}(\mathcal{L},\ k)\quad \bar{l} = alloc_{RJ\text{-}HC}(\mathcal{L},\ \mathcal{L}(\bar{a}))}{(\mathcal{L},\ \mathcal{H},\ R.\mathrm{id}(\bar{a}))\ \longrightarrow\ (\mathcal{L}[l \to k][\bar{l} \to \mathcal{L}(\bar{a})],\ \mathcal{H}[(k,\bar{g}) \to \bar{l}]\ ,\ l)} \quad\text{(R-ID-HC)}$$

Fig. 7. New Computation Rules for RJ-HC

We now show that RJ and RJ-HC have the same behavior on the same program $(RTable, e)$. First, some definitions:

Definition 1 (Well-Formed State). *A state* $(\mathcal{L},\ \mathcal{H},\ e)$ *in a computation of RJ (RJ-HC) is* well-formed *if* $\mathcal{L}$ *corresponds to* $\mathcal{H}$ *and for every location* l *appearing in* e, $\mathcal{L}$ *is defined at* l.

It is easy to show that reduction preserves well-formedness both in RJ and RJ-HC.

Definition 2 (Structural Equivalence). *We say that two well-formed states* $(\mathcal{L},\ \mathcal{H},\ e)$ *and* $(\mathcal{L}',\ \mathcal{H}',\ e')$ *are structurally equivalent if:*

1. $\mathcal{H}$ *and* $\mathcal{H}'$ *have the same domain and for all* (k,f) *in that domain:* $\mathcal{L}(\mathcal{H}(k,f)) = \mathcal{L}'(\mathcal{H}'(k,f))$
2. $[\mathcal{L}(\bar{l})/\bar{l}]e = [\mathcal{L}'(\bar{l}')/\bar{l}']e'$, *where* $\bar{l}$ *and* $\bar{l}'$ *are sequences of locations appearing in* e *and* e', *respectively. To denote this condition we write* $e \equiv e'$ *when* $\mathcal{L}$ *and* $\mathcal{L}'$ *are clear from the context.*

In Definition 2, item 1 states that the heaps and heap indices must have the same structure. Item 2 states that expressions e and e' where all locations are substituted with their corresponding identities are syntactically identical.

Lemma 1. *Assume that* $(\mathcal{L}_o,\ \mathcal{H}_o,\ e_o)$ *and* $(\mathcal{L},\ \mathcal{H},\ e)$ *are structurally equivalent states resulting from the computation of RJ-HC and RJ, respectively, on the same program. If* $(\mathcal{L}_o,\ \mathcal{H}_o,\ e_o) \longrightarrow_{\text{RJ-HC}} (\mathcal{L}'_o,\ \mathcal{H}'_o,\ e'_o)$ *then there exists a state* $(\mathcal{L}',\ \mathcal{H}',\ e')$, *such that* $(\mathcal{L},\ \mathcal{H},\ e) \longrightarrow_{\text{RJ}} (\mathcal{L}',\ \mathcal{H}',\ e')$ *and* $(\mathcal{L}'_o,\ \mathcal{H}'_o,\ e'_o)$ *and* $(\mathcal{L}',\ \mathcal{H}',\ e')$ *are structurally equivalent.*

Proof. By induction on the derivation of $(\mathcal{L}_o,\ \mathcal{H}_o,\ e_o) \longrightarrow_{\text{RJ-HC}} (\mathcal{L}'_o,\ \mathcal{H}'_o,\ e'_o)$ with a case analysis on the last reduction rule used. The proof can be found in [32].

Theorem 1. *Assume that* $(\mathcal{L}_o,\ \mathcal{H}_o,\ e_o)$ *and* $(\mathcal{L},\ \mathcal{H},\ e)$ *are structurally equivalent states resulting from the computation of RJ-HC and RJ, respectively, on the same program. If* $(\mathcal{L}_o,\ \mathcal{H}_o,\ e_o) \longrightarrow^*_{\text{RJ-HC}} (\mathcal{L}'_o,\ \mathcal{H}'_o,\ e'_o)$ *then there exists a state* $(\mathcal{L}',\ \mathcal{H}',\ e')$, *such that* $(\mathcal{L},\ \mathcal{H},\ e) \longrightarrow^*_{\text{RJ}} (\mathcal{L}',\ \mathcal{H}',\ e')$ *and* $(\mathcal{L}'_o,\ \mathcal{H}'_o,\ e'_o)$ *and* $(\mathcal{L}',\ \mathcal{H}',\ e')$ *are structurally equivalent.*

Proof. By induction on the length n of reduction sequence $(\mathcal{L}_o,\ \mathcal{H}_o,\ e_o) \longrightarrow^*_{\text{RJ-HC}} (\mathcal{L}'_o,\ \mathcal{H}'_o,\ e'_o)$.

Case: $n = 0$. Trivial.

Case: $(\mathcal{L}_o,\ \mathcal{H}_o,\ e_o) \longrightarrow_{\text{RJ-HC}} (\mathcal{L}''_o,\ \mathcal{H}''_o,\ e''_o) \longrightarrow^*_{\text{RJ-HC}} (\mathcal{L}'_o,\ \mathcal{H}'_o,\ e'_o)$.
By Lemma 1, we know that there exists a state $(\mathcal{L}'',\ \mathcal{H}'',\ e'')$ such that $(\mathcal{L},\ \mathcal{H},\ e) \longrightarrow_{\text{RJ}} (\mathcal{L}'',\ \mathcal{H}'',\ e'')$ and $(\mathcal{L}''_o,\ \mathcal{H}''_o,\ e''_o)$ and $(\mathcal{L}'',\ \mathcal{H}'',\ e'')$ are structurally equivalent. By the induction hypothesis, there exists a state $(\mathcal{L}',\ \mathcal{H}',\ e')$ such that $(\mathcal{L}'',\ \mathcal{H}'',\ e'') \longrightarrow^*_{\text{RJ}} (\mathcal{L}',\ \mathcal{H}',\ e')$, and $(\mathcal{L}',\ \mathcal{H}',\ e')$ and $(\mathcal{L}'_o,\ \mathcal{H}'_o,\ e'_o)$ are structurally equivalent. $\qquad\square$

4   Implementation and Evaluation

To evaluate the utility of relation types, we extended Java with relation types and developed a compiler for translating programs written in the resulting RJ language to Java. We examined the classes that define `equals()` and `hashCode()` in a number of open-source Java applications. For each application, we determined if and how these classes could be rewritten with relation types.

4.1   Implementation

RJ adds a few minor extensions to Java syntax:

- The `relation` keyword indicates that a class or interface is a relation type.
- The `key` keyword indicates that a field in a relation type is a key field. A relation class may have zero or more key fields.
- Each relation class R implicitly defines an `id()` method with return type R and argument types corresponding to the key fields in R and its supertypes.

Conceptually, the hierarchy of relation types is completely distinct from the hierarchy of (non-relation) reference types. For pragmatic reasons, the implementation makes `java.lang.Object` the implicit supertype of a all relation types, but relation types cannot inherit explicitly from a reference type or vice versa.

We have implemented RJ using the Java 5.0 metadata facility. Embedding the RJ language in Java enabled us to leverage the Eclipse JDT refactoring framework as the basis for our compiler. Concretely, relation types are annotated with a `@Relation` annotation and key fields with a `@Key` annotation. Furthermore, we model the implicitly defined `id()` method as a constructor annotated with the `@Id` annotation[1]. Since our experiments target converting Java classes into relation types, our RJ implementation allows non-relation types and relations to co-exist. Specifically, we allow the declaration of `equals()` and `hashCode()` methods in non-relation Java classes.

We implemented a simple type checker for RJ that enforces the following constraints on relation types:

- Up-casts (implicit or explicit) from a relation type to `Object` are disallowed.
- Key fields must be `private` and `final`, but there is no restriction on the type of objects they point to.
- Declaring `equals()` and `hashCode()` in a relation type is disallowed.
- In order to avoid programmer errors, the application of the `==` and `!=` operators to one operand of a relation type and another operand of a reference type results in a type error.
- Calling `equals()` on an expression of a relation type is a type error.

The RJ compiler translates RJ to Java using the AST rewriting infrastructure in Eclipse. The translation involves the following steps: (i) generation of a nested `Key` class that contains the key fields declared in a relation type and that implements appropriate `equals()` and `hashCode()` methods, (ii) generation of a static map that contains the relation's tuples, (iii) generation of a constructor that initializes the key fields from corresponding formal parameters, (iv) generation of the `id()` method that returns a tuple with a given identity if it already

---

[1] In a full language implementation, the programmer would not need to declare an `id()` method; our prototype implementation requires the explicit constructor as an expedient way to interoperate with the Eclipse Java development tools.

exists, and creates such a tuple otherwise, and (v) updating the references to key fields (necessary because these fields are moved into the generated Key class). Figure 8 shows the annotated source and generated code for the Person class from Figure 3.

```
@Relation public class Person {
    @Key private final int SSN;
    @Key private final Name name;
    @Id private Person(int SSN, Name name) {
        this.SSN = SSN;
        this.name = name;
    }
}
```

```
public class Person {                              ...
  protected final Key key;                           this.name = name;
  protected Person(Key key) {                       }
    this.key = key;                                 public boolean equals(Object o) {
  }                                                   if (o = null &&
  public static Person id(int SSN, Name name) {         getClass().equals(o.getClass())) {
    Key k = new Key(SSN, name);                         Key other = (Key) o;
    Person c = m.get(k);                                return SSN == other.SSN &&
    if (c == null) {                                      (name == null) ? (other.name == null)
      c = new Person(k);                                  : name.equals(other.name);
      m.put(k, c);                                    }
    }                                                 return false;
    return c;                                       }
  }                                                 public int hashCode() {
  private static Map<Key, Person> m =                 return 6079 * SSN + 6089 *
    new HashMap<Key, Person>();                         ((name == null) ? 1 : name.hashCode());
                                                    }
  protected static class Key {                      private final int SSN;
    public Key(int SSN, Name name) {                private final Name name;
      this.SSN = SSN;                             }
      ... // continued on right column          }
```

Fig. 8. RJ source code implemented with Java annotations (top), and generated Java implementation (bottom)

In the basic implementation discussed so far, tuples are never garbage collected. Therefore we extended our implementation to use weak references, so tuples can be collected when their identity becomes unreachable, as discussed in Section 2.5. In this approach, key fields use WeakReferences as pointers, and relation types use the ReferenceQueue notification mechanism to remove a tuple when any of its weak referents becomes dead. Additionally, the canonicalized tuple objects are cached using SoftReferences. If none of the key fields of a relation type are of reference types, the scope mechanism discussed in Section 2.5 can be used. A scope is a reference, so when the scope dies, so do its tuples.

Our current prototype implementation maximizes the amount of sharing and follows one of many possible implementation strategies. This strategy was chosen in part because it results in significant changes to the aliasing patterns in our benchmarks, and hence makes a good test that our rewriting was done correctly. Note that while hash-consing is often regarded as an optimization, it is unlikely that our prototype implementation actually maximizes performance, since the benefits of hash-consing need to balanced against costs such as finding the hash-consed objects when needed. Furthermore, our implementation uses ordinary `java.util.HashMap` objects to implement hash-consing, which will hurt our performance since the standard hash tables employ a rather allocation-intensive mechanism for defining hash keys. For this reason, we do not present performance results for our current prototype.

Beyond the current prototype, there are many implementation tradeoffs to consider. We have considerable freedom to copy and move objects around in our model, and this may allow an implementation to base decisions about copying on the likely impact on locality; this could even be based on runtime feedback if sufficient support were included in a virtual machine. Our model also provides greater freedom to use aggressive optimizations such as object inlining [16] that involve re-arranging objects in memory. It remains as future work to evaluate optimized implementations to discover empirically what implementation tradeoffs work well in practice.

4.2   Case Study: *javacup*

We now describe in detail one case study, investigating how *javacup* (version 11a), an LALR parser generator written in Java, can be refactored to use relation types. We examined each class that overrides `equals()`, identified the intended key fields by examining the `equals()` and `hashCode()` implementations, and then manually rewrote the class into a relation type. We then compiled the resulting RJ version of *javacup* into Java, ran both the original version and this generated version on a grammar for Java 5 and ensured that the resulting generated parsers are identical.

In the course of this exercise, we needed to apply a number of refactorings that preserve the behavior of *javacup*, but that ease the introduction of relation types. The most significant of these refactorings consisted of:

- Key fields were made `private` and `final`. In a few cases, methods that initialize these fields were inlined into a calling constructor, or eliminated as dead code. In a few cases, some minor code restructuring was needed to eliminate "spurious mutability".
- Nontrivial constructors were replaced by a combination of (i) simple constructors that only initialize key fields, and (ii) factory methods [17] that contain the remaining initialization code for, e.g., initializing mutable fields.
- In a few cases, the code contained implicit up-casts to type `Object` because tuples were stored into collections. In such cases, we parameterized uses of collection types with parameters of the appropriate relation type in order to avoid the up-cast.

After performing these steps, we deleted the `equals()` and `hashCode()` methods, added `@Relation`, `@Key`, and `@Id` annotations, and ensured that the resulting code could be compiled and executed successfully.

Interestingly, we found that the resulting version of *javacup* produced a parser with significantly different source text than the parser produced by the original

Table 1. Summary of results for *javacup* case study

class	actions performed
java_cup.production_part	Converted into relation type: 1 key field, 0 non-key fields
java_cup.action_part	Converted into relation type: 1 key field, 0 non-key fields
java_cup.symbol_part	Converted into relation type: 1 key field, 0 non-key fields
java_cup.parse_action	Converted into singleton relation type (0 key fields, 0 non-key fields)
java_cup.nonassoc_action	Converted into singleton relation type (0 key fields, 0 non-key fields)
java_cup.shift_action	Converted into relation type: 1 key field and 0 non-key fields
java_cup.reduce_action	Converted into relation type: 1 key field, 0 non-key fields. Error in use of equals() previously discussed in Section 2.2.
java_cup.production	Converted into relation type: 1 key field, 14 non-key fields
java_cup.action_production	Converted into relation type: 0 key field, 2 non-key fields
java_cup.lr_item_core	This class and its subclass lalr_item were refactored into a combination of 2 classes without equals()/hashCode() and one relation type with 2 key fields and 0 non-key fields.
java_cup.lalr_item	See comments for java_cup.lr_item_core.
java_cup.lalr_state	Converted into relation type: 1 key field, 2 non-key fields
java_cup.symbol_set	Not converted because equals() refers to mutable state. Note: equals() is dead, so could simply be removed.
java_cup.terminal_set	Not converted because equals() refers to mutable state. Note: equals() is dead, so could simply be removed. Does not declare hashCode(), hence equals()/hashCode() contract violated.
java_cup.lalr_item_set	Not converted because equals() refers to mutable state.

javacup, but that these parsers *behave identically* when applied to a number of inputs. Further investigation revealed that the output of the original version depended on iterators whose order relied on hash-codes of the elements stored in hash-tables. The hashCode() methods in our generated code differ from those in the original *javacup*, which resulted in different (but equivalent) generated parsers. As a further experiment, we rewrote *javacup* to use LinkedHashMaps[2] instead of Hashtables, and repeated the entire experiment. The resulting *javacup* produced a parser that was syntactically identical to the original *javacup* output.

Table 1 shows, for each class in *javacup* with an application-defined equals() method, the outcome of this exercise. As the table shows, of 15 classes with application-defined equals() methods, 12 could be converted into relation types, and most of them with relatively little effort. Classes lr_item_core and lalr_item required a somewhat nontrivial transformation. The equals() methods in these classes do not reflect general object identity, but only apply within the context of an lalr_item_set. We therefore removed these equals() methods and rewrote lalr_item_set to appropriately manipulate these objects using a newly created relation type ItemKey. Another item of note was a bug in a use of reduce_action.equals() that we previously discussed in Section 2.2. Classes symbol_set, terminal_set and lalr_item_set could not be converted because their equals() methods refer to mutable collections. Interestingly, the equals() methods in symbol_set and terminal_set are dead, and could be removed.

---

[2] A LinkedHashMap is a hash-table for which the iteration order is determined by the order in which elements are inserted instead of depending on the hash-codes of the elements.

Furthermore, class `terminal_set` violates the `equals()`/`hashCode()`contract by not overriding `Object.hashCode()`.

4.3   Other Benchmarks

We repeated the methodology of the case study on a number of open-source Java applications.

The benchmarks *ant, hsqldb, jfreechart*[3], *lucene,* and *pmd* are open-source codes; we used the versions collected in the DaCapo benchmarks [11], version `dacapo-2006-10`. *Bcel* is the Apache Bytecode Engineering Library [4], version 5.2. *Shrike* is the `com.ibm.wala.shrike` project from the T. J. Watson Libraries for Analysis (WALA) [2], version 1.0. We use *shrike* regularly, and chose it for consideration based on prior knowledge that it would suit relation types. *Shrike* also has sophisticated, hand-rolled hash-consing, which is now generated automatically by the RJ compiler. The other benchmarks were chosen based on their having a reasonable number of `equals()` methods, and based on the availability of some drivers to test for correct behavior.

As described for *javacup* earlier, we transformed each code by hand where necessary to make fields `private` and `final`, remove unnecessary mutable state, and similar local changes. While we believe our transformations were correct (modulo erroneous existing behavior), we have no mechanical proof that the changes are semantics-preserving. We ran a number of dynamic tests for each code, including unit tests where available, the DaCapo drivers, and other drivers we created, and verified that for each test the RJ implementation behaves identically to the original implementation. This methodology gives us some confidence that the RJ versions are correct.

Table 2 summarizes our findings. The columns of the table show, for each benchmark, from left to right:

1. The number of `equals()` methods originally declared.
2. The number of `equals()` methods eliminated by conversion to relation types.
3. The percentage of eliminated `equals()` methods.
4. The total number of relation types introduced.
5. The number of relation types that correspond to value types (i.e., all fields are key fields).
6. The number of relation types that correspond to singletons.
7. The number of relation types that have non-key fields.
8. A summary of the bugs and issues that we encountered, as explained in the legend of the table.

As the table reflects, during this exercise we were able to convert the majority of candidate classes to relation types with little program modification. Most of these types actually represent values with no mutable state. As is well known,

---

[3] *jfreechart* has more than 200 `equals()` methods—a daunting number to study by hand. So we looked only at the first two packages in lexicographic order: `org.jfree.chart.annotations` and `org.jfree.chart.axis`.

Table 2. Summary of results

benchmark	#equals()			#relation types				bugs/issues
	orig.	removed	%	total	value	sing.	non-value	
ant	12	9	75.0	9	3	0	6	H,M
bcel	20	14	70.0	22	11	5	11	F,H,M
hsqldb	12	2	16.7	2	0	0	2	E,F,M,S
javacup	14	11	78.6	11	8	2	3	H,M,T
jfreechart	46	33	71.7	40	40	1	0	H,M,S
lucene	27	27	100.0	27	23	0	4	E,M
pmd	12	5	41.7	5	3	2	2	E,F,M,N,S
shrike	32	32	100.0	61	55	3	6	M

Explanation of codes used for Bugs/Issues:
  E `equals()` method throws exception if passed unanticipated argument
  F fragile (e.g., `equals()` defined in terms of `toString()`)
  H `equals()`/`hashCode()` contract violated
  M `equals()`/`hashCode()` depends on mutable state
  N violates contract for `equals(null)`
  S symmetry requirement in `equals()` contract violated
  T inadvertent test of incomparable types

programming in a functional style without mutation eliminates many classes of bugs and generally leads to more robust, maintainable code. Relation types fit well into such a programming style.

The last column of the table shows that we found violations of the contract and other problems in every code. This reinforces our claim that the current unenforced contract leads to fragile and error-prone code. Relation types encourage more robust code by enforcing a stricter contract and removing the need for tedious, error-prone boiler-plate code.

Of the types which we did not convert to relation types, most fall into one of two categories. The first category comprises types where the programmer had already manually applied hash-consing or other caching and pooling optimizations. In such cases, the program complexity exceeded our threshold for rewriting in these experiments. Relation types would obviate the need for such manual storage optimizations, since the compiler can implement hash-consing and related representation transformations automatically.

The other category comprises types where identity depends on mutable state. Many instances of mutable identity appear spurious, and could be eliminated with a slightly more functional design. We also found a fairly large number of cases we call *piecemeal initialization*. In these cases, the program incrementally builds up an object's state piecemeal; for example, the program parses an XML document and mutates an object to represent the state as it parses. However, the object becomes logically immutable after initialization. To support such patterns, we plan to extend RJ with a facility to "freeze" a mutable object into an immutable relation tuple. Note that, in our current model, it is not possible to construct two tuples t_1 and t_2 such that the identity of t_1 is determined by t_2 and vice versa. The proposed extension would remedy this limitation.

5   Related Work

Baker [6] studies issues related to object identity in Common Lisp and concludes that the existing functions for testing equality in that language are problematic for a number of reasons, chiefly the fact that successive calls to EQUAL may produce different answers if there is a dependence on mutable state. Although the languages under consideration are quite different, Baker's proposed solution is similar in spirit to ours in the sense that objects of different types are never equal, and that an object's identity should not rely on mutable state.

The C# language [24] supports both reference equality, i.e. equal object identifiers, and value equality. As in Java, C# `Equals()` supports reference equality by default for reference types. The C# programmer can override `Equals` and `==` to support structural or value equivalence as desired, raising the same issues as when overriding `equals()` in Java. C# also supports built-in structural equality for C# *value types*, but restricts value types to structs and enumerations, with no inheritance.

A relation type's *key* annotation enforces an immutability constraint on the annotated field. Several other works have addressed language designs that incorporate immutability concepts. Pechtchanski and Sarkar [25] propose a framework of immutability specification along three dimensions: lifetime, reachability, and context. Our *key* annotation indicates persistent and shallow immutability: The value of a key field never changes but there is no constraint on mutability of state reached from a key field (similar to "final" in Java). Of course, a key annotation conveys more information than immutability constraints by identifying the state that contributes to object identity.

Much other work defines analyses and languages for immutability constraints (see [10,13,20,28,29]). Javari [29] adds support for reference immutability to Java, and enforces specifications expressing transitive immutability constraints. Javari also allows for the declaration of read-only methods that cannot modify the state of the receiver object, and read-only classes for which all instance fields are implicitly read-only. Our programming model could be combined with language extensions such as those in Javari, to support immutability constraints on non-key fields which do not contribute to the identity relation.

In our model, a relation type that has only key fields is a value type. Value types [5,15,24,33] provide many benefits for the programmer. For example, they provide referential transparency: functions that manipulate only values have deterministic behavior. Since values are immutable, they eliminate aliasing issues and make code less error-prone. From an implementation viewpoint, value types simplify analyses that allow a number of aggressive compiler optimizations, such as unboxing [27], object inlining [16], memoization [23], data replication in distributed or cluster computing settings [15], and hash-consing [18].

Bacon's Kava language [5] is a variation on Java with a uniform object model that supports user-defined value types. Kava's notion of a value is that of an immutable object, with all fields pointing to other values. All value types are subclasses of a type `Value`, and they may inherit from other value types and from interfaces. In our experience, Java programs commonly include "value-like" classes that define equality and hashcode based on an immutable subset of instance fields, but that also have some mutable state associated with them. Our relation types allow for such classes, and unify values and objects by providing a generalization of both as relations that map key fields to some possibly mutable state. Furthermore, due to this uniformity, we need not segregate type hierarchies for values and non-values, and a relation type may inherit from a value.

Our value-types are also more general than Titanium's [33] immutable classes, and C#'s value types [24], which do not support inheritance for "value-like" classes. Fortress's value objects [3] also do not support "value-like" classes, but they do allow fields of values to be set in order to allow piecemeal initialization.

Tuples have been added to object-oriented languages in various work (for example [21,30,22]). Our tuples differ in that they have keys, similar to primary keys in a row of a relational database, and relation types implicitly define a map from keys to non-keys. A relation type does not contain two tuples with equal keys but different non-key parts.

Some languages integrate object and relational data models to facilitate communication with a database (see, e.g., [22,7]), or provide first-class language support for relationships (see, e.g., [9]). The focus of our programming model is to view the heap itself as a relational database, and use concepts from databases such as primary keys to express identity. In future work, we plan to investigate the application of relation types to support data access integration.

Linda's [14] data model introduced an associative memory called a *tuplespace* as a model for sharing data in parallel programming. Relation types could perhaps be applied in this setting, providing a strong coupling between the object-oriented language and the distributed tuplespace. Relation types would also facilitate optimizations for data replication, as mentioned previously.

We formalized relation types using an adaptation of Featherweight Java (FJ), a functional language. Other extensions of FJ introduce mutation [8], using a heap that maps memory locations to mutable state. Our model provides a level of indirection in the heap, augmenting values with mutable state, thus providing a uniform framework for the functional and non-functional language aspects.

6   Summary and Future Work

We presented a programming model that provides a relational view of the heap. In this model, object identity is specified declaratively using a new language construct called relation types and programmers are relieved from the burden of having to write error-prone `equals()` and `hashCode()` methods. We formalized the model as an extension of Featherweight Java and implemented it as an extension of Java. Our experiments indicate that the majority of classes that override `equals()` can be refactored into relation types, and that most of the remainder are buggy or fragile.

We plan to extend the model with other features that borrow from database concepts (e.g., atomic sets [31]), and raise the level of abstraction for navigating the heap. Some of our ideas include a query language on top of relation types and features for pattern matching. We also plan to support delayed initialization of key fields, and to experiment with optimized representations for relation types.

Acknowledgments. We are grateful to David Bacon, Michael Ernst, Doug Lea, Jan Vitek, Michael Weber, and the anonymous ECOOP reviewers for their constructive feedback. Bob Fuhrer's help with the implementation was invaluable.

References

1. http://java.sun.com/j2se/1.5.0/docs/api/java/lang/Object.html
2. T. J. Watson Libraries for Analysis(December 2006) http://wala.sourceforge.net
3. Allen, E., Chase, D., Hallett, J., Luchangco, V., Maessen, J.-W., Ryu, S., Steele, G., Tobin-Hochstadt, S.:The Fortress language specification, http://research.sun.com/projects/plrg/fortress.pdf
4. Apache Jakarta Project. BCEL (December 2006), http://jakarta.apache.org/bcel/
5. Bacon, D.F.: Kava: A Java dialect with a uniform object model for lightweight classes. Concurrency—Practice and Experience 15(3–5), 185–206 (2003)
6. Baker, H.G.: Equal rights for functional objects or, the more things change, the more they are the same. OOPS Messenger 4(4), 2–27 (1993)
7. Bierman, G., Meijer, E., Schulte, W.: The essence of data access in $C\omega$. In: Black, A.P. (ed.) ECOOP 2005. LNCS, vol. 3586, Springer, Heidelberg (2005)
8. Bierman, G., Parkinson, M.J., Pitts, A.M.MJ.: An imperative core calculus for Java and Java effects. Tech. Rep. 563, Computer Laboratory,University of Cambridge (April 2003)
9. Bierman, G.M., Wren, A.: First-class relationships in an object-oriented language. In: Black, A.P. (ed.) ECOOP 2005. LNCS, vol. 3586, pp. 262–286. Springer, Heidelberg (2005)
10. Birka, A., Ernst, M.D.: A practical type system and language for reference immutability. In: Proceedings of the 19th annual ACM SIGPLAN conference on Object-oriented programming, systems, languages, and applications (OOPSLA'04), pp. 35–49. ACM Press, New York (2004)
11. Blackburn, S.M., Garner, R., Hoffman, C., Khan, A.M., McKinley, K.S., Bentzur, R., Diwan, A., Feinberg, D., Frampton, D., Guyer, S.Z., Hirzel, M., Hosking, A., Jump, M., Lee, H., Moss, J.E.B., Phansalkar, A., Stefanović, D., VanDrunen, T., von Dincklage, D., Wiedermann, B.: The DaCapo benchmarks: Java benchmarking development and analysis. In: Proceedings of the 21st annual ACM SIGPLAN conference on Object-Oriented Programing, Systems, Languages, and Applications (OOPSLA'06), Portland, OR, USA, oct 2006, ACM Press, New York (2006)
12. Bloch, J.: Effective Java, Programming Language Guide. Addison-Wesley(2001)
13. Boyland, J., Noble, J., Retert, W.: Capabilities for sharing: A generalisation of uniqueness and read-only. In: Knudsen, J.L. (ed.) ECOOP 2001. LNCS, vol. 2072, pp. 2–27. Springer, Heidelberg (2001)

14. Carriero, N., Gelernter, D.: Linda in context. Commun. ACM 32(4), 444–458 (1989)
15. Charles, P., Grothoff, C., Saraswat, V., Donawa, C., Kielstra, A., Ebcioglu, K., von Praun, C., Sarkar, V.: X10: an object-oriented approach to non-uniform cluster computing. In: Proceedings of the 20th annual ACM SIGPLAN conference on Object oriented programming, systems, languages, and applications (OOPSLA'05), San Diego, CA, USA, pp. 519–538. ACM Press, New York (2005)
16. Dolby, J., Chien, A.: An automatic object inlining optimization and its evaluation. ACM SIGPLAN Notices 35(5), 345–357 (2000)
17. Gamma, E., Helm, R., Johnson, R., Vlissides, J.: Design Patterns, Elements of Reusable Object-Oriented Software. Addison-Wesley (1995)
18. Goto, E.: Monocopy and Associative Algorithms in an Extended Lisp. Tech. Rep. 74-03, Information Science Laboratory, University of Tokyo (1974)
19. Igarashi, A., Pierce, B.C, Wadler, P.: Featherweight Java: A minimal core calculus for Java and GJ. ACM Transactions on Programming Languages and Systems 23(3), 396–450 (2001)
20. Kniesel, G., Theisen, D.: Jac – access right based encapsulation for Java. Software: Practice and Experience 31(6), 555–576 (2001)
21. Krall, A., Vitek, J.: On extending Java. In: Mössenböck, H. (ed.) JMLC 1997. LNCS, vol. 1204, Springer, Heidelberg (1997)
22. Meijer, E., Shulte, W.: Unifying tables, objects and documents. In: DB-COOL (2003)
23. Michie, D.: Memo functions and machine learning. Nature, 218, 19–22
24. Microsoft. C# Language Specification. Microsoft Press (2001)
25. Pechtchanski, I., Sarkar, V.: Immutability specification and its applications. In: Java Grande, pp. 202–211 (2002)
26. PETTER, M.: personal communication (October 2006)
27. Peyton-Jones, S., Launchbury, J.: Unboxed values as first class citizens. In: Functional Programming Languages and Computer Architecture: 5th ACM Conference, Berlin, Germany, ACM Press, New York (1991)
28. Porat, S., Biberstein, M., Koved, L., Mendelson, B.: Automatic detection of immutable fields in Java. In: CASCON (2000)
29. Tschantz, M.S., Ernst, M.D.: Javari: adding reference immutability to Java. In: Proceedings of the 20th annual ACM SIGPLAN conference on Object oriented programming, systems, languages, and applications (OOPSLA'05), pp. 211–230. ACM Press, New York (2005)
30. van Reeuwijk, C., Sips, H J.: Adding tuples to Java: a study in lightweight data structures. In: JGI'02 (2002)
31. Vaziri, M., Tip, F., Dolby, J.: Associating synchronization constraints with data in an object-oriented language. In: POPL '06: Conference record of the 33rd ACM SIGPLAN-SIGACT symposium on Principles of programming languages, pp. 334–345. ACM Press, New York, NY, USA (2006)
32. Vaziri, M., Tip, F., Fink, S., Dolby, J.: Declarative object identity using relation types.Tech. rep.IBM Research (Forthcoming 2007)
33. Yelick, K., Semenzato, L., Pike, G., Miyamoto, C., Liblit, B.: abd Paul Hilfinger, A. K., Graham, S., Gay, D., Colella, P., and Aiken, A. Titanium: A high-performance Java dialect. Concurrency—Practice and Experience, Java Special Issue (1998)

Object-Relative Addressing:
Compressed Pointers in 64-Bit Java Virtual Machines

Kris Venstermans, Lieven Eeckhout, and Koen De Bosschere

ELIS Department, Ghent University, Belgium
{kvenster,leeckhou,kdb}@elis.UGent.be

Abstract. 64-bit address spaces come at the price of pointers requiring twice as much memory as 32-bit address spaces, resulting in increased memory usage.

This paper reduces the memory usage of 64-bit pointers in the context of Java virtual machines through pointer compression, called Object-Relative Addressing (ORA). The idea is to compress 64-bit raw pointers into 32-bit offsets relative to the referencing object's virtual address. Unlike previous work on the subject using a constant base address for compressed pointers, ORA allows for applying pointer compression to Java programs that allocate more than 4GB of memory.

Our experimental results using Jikes RVM and the SPECjbb and DaCapo benchmarks on an IBM POWER4 machine show that the overhead introduced by ORA is statistically insignificant on average compared to raw 64-bit pointer representation, while reducing the total memory usage by 10% on average and up to 14.5% for some applications.

1 Introduction

In our recent work [1], we reported that Java objects increase by 40% in size when comparing 64-bit against 32-bit Java virtual machines. About half of this increase comes from the increased header which doubles in size. The other half comes from increased object fields containing pointers or references.

Running 64-bit Java virtual machines can thus be costly in terms of memory usage. This is a serious concern on heavy-loaded systems with many simultaneously running programs that are memory-intensive. In fact, overall system performance can quickly deteriorate because of memory page swapping once physical memory gets exhausted. One way of dealing with the excessive memory usage on 64-bit systems is to have more physical memory in the machine as one would provide on a 32-bit system. However, this is costly as physical memory is a significant cost in today's computer systems.

This paper proposes to address the increased memory usage in 64-bit Java virtual machines through *Object-Relative Addressing (ORA)*. Object-relative addressing is a pointer compression technique that compresses pointers in object fields as 32-bit off-sets relative to the current object's address. The 64-bit virtual address of the referenced object is then obtained by adding the 32-bit offset to the 64-bit virtual address of the referencing object. In case the referenced object is further away than what can be represented by a 32-bit offset, object relative addressing interprets the 32-bit offset as an index in the *Long Address Table (LAT)* that translates the 32-bit offset into a 64-bit virtual address.

E. Ernst (Ed.): ECOOP 2007, LNAI 4609, pp. 79–100, 2007.

The advance of object-relative addressing over prior work on the subject by Adl-Tabatabai *et al.* [2], is that object-relative addressing is not limited to Java programs that consume less than 4GB of heap, or the 32-bit virtual address space. Object-relative addressing enables pointer compression to be applied to all Java programs, including Java programs that allocate more than 4GB of memory.

We envision that object-relative addressing is to be used in conjunction with a memory management strategy that strives at limiting the number of inter-object references that cross the 32-bit address range. Crossing the 32-bit address range incurs overhead because the LAT needs to be accessed for retrieving the 64-bit address corresponding to the 32-bit offset. Limiting the number of LAT accesses thus calls for a memory allocator and garbage collector that strives at allocating objects within a virtual memory region that is reachable through the (signed) 32-bit offset. Such memory allocators and garbage collectors can be built using techniques similar to object colocation [3], connectivity-based memory allocation and collection [4,5], region-based systems [6], *etc*.

The experimental results using the SPECjbb2000 and the DaCapo benchmarks and the Jikes RVM on an IBM POWER4 machine show that object-relative addressing does not incur a run time overhead. Some applications experience a performance improvement up to 4.0% while other applications experience a slowdown of at most 3.5%; on average though, no statistically significant performance impact is observed. The benefit of ORA comes in terms of memory usage: the amount of allocated memory reduces by 10% on average and for some applications up to 14.5%.

This paper is organized as follows. After having discussed prior work in object pointer compression in section 2, we will present object-relative addressing in section 3. Section 4 will then detail our experimental setup. The evaluation of ORA in terms of overall performance, memory hierarchy performance and memory usage will be presented in section 5. Finally, we will discuss related work in section 6 before concluding in section 7.

2   Object Pointer Compression: Prior Work

The prior work on the subject by Adl-Tabatabai *et al.* [2] propose a straightforward compression scheme for addressing the memory usage in 64-bit Java virtual machines. They represent 64-bit pointers as 32-bit offsets from a base address of a contiguous memory region. Dereferencing or decompressing a pointer then involves adding the 32-bit offset to a base address yielding a 64-bit virtual addess. Reverse, compressing a 64-bit virtual address into a 32-bit offset requires substracting the 64-bit address from the base address; the lower 32 bits are then stored. A similar approach was proposed by Lattner and Adve [7] for compressing pointers in linked data structures.

The fact that 64-bit virtual addresses are represented as 32-bit offsets from a base address implies that this pointer compression technique is limited to Java programs that consume less than 4GB of storage. If a Java program allocates more than 4GB of memory, the virtual machine has to revert to the 64-bit pointer representation. This could for example be done by setting the maximum heap size through a command line option: if the maximum heap size is larger than 4GB, uncompressed pointers are used; if smaller than 4GB, compressed pointers are used.

Adl-Tabatabai *et al.* apply their pointer compression method to both vtable pointers and pointers to other Java objects, so called object references. The 32-bit object references are then relative offsets to the heap's base address; the 32-bit vtable pointers are relative offsets to the vtable space's base address.

In this paper, we focus on compressing object references and do not address vtable pointer compression. The reason is that vtable pointers are not that big of an issue when it comes to pointer compression. The 32-bit vtable pointer offsets are highly likely to be sufficient even for programs that allocate very large amounts of memory; it is highly unlikely to require more than 4GB of memory for allocating vtables. In other words, the pointer compression method by Adl-Tabatabai *et al.* is likely to work properly when applied to vtable pointers. Moreover, recent work by Venstermans *et al.* [8] has proposed a technique that completely eliminates the vtable pointer from the object header through typed virtual addressing. We also refer to the related work section of this paper for a discussion on object header reduction techniques.

3   Object-Relative Addressing

Object-Relative Addressing (ORA) is a pointer compression technique for 64-bit Java virtual machines that does not suffer from the 4GB heap limitation in Adl-Tabatabai *et al.*'s method. The goal of ORA is to enable heap pointer compression for all Java programs, even for programs that allocate more than 4GB of memory.

3.1   Basic Idea

Figure 1 illustrates the basic idea of object-relative addressing (ORA) and compares ORA against the traditional way of referencing objects in 64-bit Java virtual machines. We call the referencing object the object that contains a pointer in its data fields. The object being referenced is called the referenced object. ORA references objects through 32-bit offsets. The 'fast' decompression path then adds this 32-bit offset to the referencing object's virtual address for obtaining the virtual address of the referenced object.

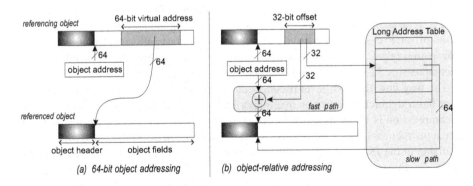

Fig. 1. Illustrating the basic idea of object-relative addressing (on the right) compared against the traditional 64-bit addressing (on the left)

```
read 32-bit object reference;
if (least significant bit of 32-bit reference is NOT set) {
    /* fast decompression path */
    add 32-bit object reference to 64-bit object
      virtual address to form 64-bit object address;
}
else {
    /* slow decompression path */
    index LAT for reading 64-bit object address;
}
```

Fig. 2. High-level pseudocode for decompressing 32-bit object references

This is the case when both the referencing object and the referenced object are close enough to each other so that a 32-bit offset is sufficiently large. In case both objects are further away from each other in memory than what can be addressed through a 32-bit offset, ORA follows the 'slow' decompression path. The 32-bit offset is then considered as an index into the *Long Address Table (LAT)* which holds 64-bit virtual addresses corresponding to 32-bit indexes.

The end result of object-relative addressing is that only 32 bits of storage are required for storing object references. This reduces the amount of memory consumed compared to the traditional way of storing object references which requires 64 bits of storage. We now go through the details of how ORA can be implemented. We discuss (i) how pointers are decompressed, (ii) how to compress pointers, (iii) how to deal with null pointer representation, (iv) how to manage the LAT, (v) what the implications are for garbage collection, (vi) how ORA compares to Adl-Tabatabai *et al.*'s method in terms of anticipated runtime overhead, and finally (vii) what the implications are for memory management.

3.2 Decompressing Pointers

Decompressing 32-bit object references requires determining whether the fast or slow path is to be taken. This is done at runtime by inspecting the least significant bit of the 32-bit offset; in case the least significant bit is zero, the fast path is taken; otherwise, the slow path is taken. This is illustrated in Figure 2 showing the high-level pseudocode for decompressing 32-bit object references into 64-bit virtual addresses.

The way how the high-level pseudocode is translated into native machine instructions has a significant impact on overall performance. And in addition, efficient pointer decompression is likely to result in different implementations on platforms with different instruction-set architectures (ISAs). For example, in case predicated execution is available in the ISA [9], a potential implementation could predicate the fast and slow paths. Or, in case a 'base plus index plus offset' addressing mode is available in the ISA, computing the address of an object field being accessed in the referenced object could be integrated into a single memory operation, *i.e.*, the decompression arithmetic could be combined with the field access. The referencing object's virtual address plus

```
                               ;; R4 contains the referencing
                               ;;    object's virtual address
        ld4  R1, [R4 + offset] ;; load 32-bit object offset and
                               ;;    sign-extend it into R1
                               ;; fast decompression path
        add  R2, R4, R1        ;; compute 64-bit address
        tst  R1, 1             ;; test least significant bit (LSB)
        bre  L2                ;; jump to L2 in case non-zero
L1:     ...                    ;; referenced object's virtual
                               ;;    address is in R2 here

        ...
L2:                            ;; slow decompression path
        mask R1                ;; compute LAT index by masking R1
        ld8  R2, [R5 + R1]     ;; load 64-bit address from LAT
                               ;; R5 contains LAT address and
                               ;;    R1 contains LAT index

        jmp  L1
```

Fig. 3. Low-level pseudocode for decompressing 32-bit object references: the if-then decompression approach

the 32-bit offset plus the offset of the object field in the referenced object could then be encoded in a single addressing mode.

In our experimental setup using a PowerPC setup, we were not able to implement these optimizations because the PowerPC ISA does not provide predication, nor does it support the 'base plus index plus offset' addressing mode. Instead, we consider two implementations to pointer decompression that are generally applicable across different ISAs. These two decompression implementations have different performance trade-offs which we discuss now and which we will experimentally evaluate in section 5.

If-then pointer decompression. The if-then implementation is shown in Figure 3. The assembler code generated for decompressing 32-bit object references optimizes the corresponding high-level pseudocode by optimizing for the most common case, namely the fast path. We (speculatively) compute the virtual address of the referenced object by adding the 32-bit offset with the referencing object's virtual address. In case the least significant bit of the 32-bit offset is zero, we then continue fetching and executing along the fall-through path. Only in case the least significant bit of the 32-bit offset is set, we jump to the slow path. The slow path selects a number of bits from the 32-bit offset that will serve as index into the LAT. The slow path then indexes the LAT which reads the 64-bit virtual address of the referenced object.

Patched pointer decompression. Patched pointer decompression optimizes the common case even further by assuming that the fast path is always taken. This results in the code shown in Figure 4. In other words, the 32-bit offset is added to the referencing object's virtual address to obtain the referenced object's virtual address. This avoids the conditional branch as needed in the if-then decompression implementation. In case the referenced object may not be reachable using a 32-bit offset, the decompression code

```
                                  ;; R4 contains the referencing
                                  ;;    object's virtual address
         ld4  R1, [R4 + offset]   ;; load 32-bit object offset and
                                  ;;    sign-extend it into R1
                                  ;; fast decompression path
         add  R2, R4, R1          ;; compute 64-bit address
L1:      ...                      ;; referenced object's virtual
                                  ;;    address is in R2 here
```

Fig. 4. Low-level pseudocode for decompressing 32-bit object references: the patched decompression approach before code patching is applied

```
                                  ;; R4 contains the referencing
                                  ;;    object's virtual address
         ld4   R1,  [R4 + offset] ;; load 32-bit object offset and
                                  ;;    sign-extend it into R1
         jmp L2


L1:      ...                      ;; referenced object's virtual
                                  ;;    address is in R2 here

         ...
L2:      add   R2, R4, R1         ;; compute 64-bit address
         tst   R1, 0              ;; test least significant bit (LSB)
         bre L1                   ;; jump to L1 in case zero
                                  ;; slow decompression path
         mask R1                  ;; compute LAT index by masking R1
         ld8   R2, [R5 + R1]      ;; load 64-bit address from LAT
                                  ;; R5 contains LAT address and
                                  ;;    R1 contains LAT index

         jmp  L1
```

Fig. 5. Low-level pseudocode for decompressing 32-bit object references: the patched decompression approach after code patching is applied

needs to be patched. Code patching is done at run time whenever pointer compression reveals that objects may no longer be reachable using compressed pointers, as will be discussed in the next section. The decompression code after patching is shown in Figure 5. Code patching replaces the addition (of the 32-bit offset with the referencing object's virtual address) with a jump to a piece of code that does the pointer decompression using the if-then approach. Since most object references will follow the fast path, the patched decompression approach (before patching is applied) will be substantially faster than the if-then decompression approach.

3.3 Compressing Pointers

Compressing 64-bit pointers to 32-bit offsets is done the other way around, see Figure 6. We first compute the difference between the 64-bit virtual addresses of the referenced

```
compute difference between 64-bit virtual addresses
   of the referenced object and the referencing object;
if (difference is smaller than 2GB) {
    /* fast compression path */
    store 32-bit offset;
}
else {
    /* slow compression path */
    allocate entry in LAT;
    store the referenced object's address in the
       LAT in allocated entry;
    store LAT index as a 32-bit value while setting
       the LSB of 32-bit value being stored;

    /* for the patched approach */
    patch pointer decompressions that need to;
}
```

Fig. 6. High-level pseudocode for compressing 64-bit object references

and referencing objects. If this difference is smaller than 2GB, *i.e.*, can be represented by a 32-bit offset, we then store the difference as a 32-bit offset in the referencing object's data fields. If on the other hand the difference is larger than 2GB, we allocate a LAT entry and store the referenced object's virtual address in the allocated LAT entry. The LAT entry's index is then stored in the referencing object's data fields while setting the LSB of the stored LAT index. In case of the patched decompression approach, all pointer decompressions that may read the 32-bit offset need to be patched. The patching itself is done as described in the previous section. This requires that the VM keeps track of the accesses to a given data field in an object of a given type.

3.4   Null Pointer Representation

An important issue when compressing references is how to deal with null pointers. The representation of a null value in native code is typically a 64-bit zero value. Compressing a 64-bit null value to a 32-bit representation under ORA is not trivial. A naive approach would represent the compressed null value as a 32-bit zero value. However, the 32-bit null value would then be decompressed to the this pointer, *i.e.*, the pointer to the object itself. This would make the null value indistinguishable from the this pointer.

For dealing with null pointer representation, we take the following approach. We first add the 32-bit compressed pointer to the referencing object's 64-bit virtual address. In case the least significant 32 bits of the resulting value are zero, we consider the 32-bit compressed pointer as the null value. This means we no longer have a single null value. As a result, a special treatment is required when comparing two pointers. In case both pointers represent the null value, a simple comparison may evaluate to not equal, for example, in case both compressed pointers come from different objects. As such, we need to capture this special case in the virtual machine's code generator when generating code that compares pointers. In addition, given that all memory addresses with the 32 least significant bits set to zero represent null values, we cannot allocate objects at these 4GB memory boundaries.

3.5 Managing the LAT

Another important issue to deal with is how to manage the Long Address Table (LAT). Allocating LAT entries is very straightforward by advancing the LAT head pointer. Managing LAT entries is done during garbage collection (GC). Let us first consider non-generational garbage collection. A SemiSpace garbage collector for example, which copies reachable objects from one space to the other upon a GC, requires that the LAT be recomputed, *i.e.*, a new LAT is built up during GC and the old LAT is discarded. A Mark-Sweep garbage collector that does not need to copy reachable objects, in theory, does not require recomputing the LAT. However, in order not to let the LAT explode because of entries pointing to dead objects, a good design choice is to also recompute the LAT upon a mark-sweep collection.

For generational garbage collectors, we recommend using two LATs, one associated with the nursery space and another one associated with the mature space. The nursery LAT contains references in and out of the nursery space; the mature LAT contains all other references. Upon a nursery GC, all reachable nursery objects are copied to the mature space; as such, the nursery LAT can be discarded and the mature LAT possibly needs to be updated for the newly copied objects. Upon a full GC, the same strategy can be used as under a non-generational GC, *i.e.*, the mature LAT needs to be rebuilt and in addition, the nursery LAT is discarded.

In case of the unlikely event of the LAT running full—the LAT can be chosen to be sufficiently large, and, in addition, a good object allocation strategy would strive at reducing the number of LAT entries allocated—a garbage collection could be triggered to reclaim unreachable memory. GC will rebuild the LAT, and as a result the LAT will likely shrink (or if needed, the LAT size could be increased). A data structure linking memory pages makes increasing the LAT relatively easy, *i.e.*, the LAT does not need to be copied.

3.6 Implications to Copying Garbage Collectors

Object-relative addressing raises the following issue to copying garbage collectors. Consider the case where object A has a reference to object B in its data fields. Assume object A is reachable; by consequence, object B is also reachable. The garbage collector has to assume both objects are live and a copying collector will thus have to copy both objects. Assume the copying collector first copies object A. The compressed pointer in A referencing to B then needs to be updated because object A was copied which changes the compressed pointer's base address. Upon copying object B, the compressed pointer in A referencing to B needs to be computed again because now B is moved. In other words, the compressed pointer in A needs to be recomputed twice under a copying garbage collector.

In order not to recompute the compressed pointer twice, we do the following. During garbage collection, we maintain both the original object A and a copied version of object A in the scan list, and we use the original object A to retrieve the virtual address of the referenced object B. As such, we need to recompute the compressed pointer only once, namely upon scanning object B.

3.7 Discussion

Note that pointer compression and decompression in ORA cannot be optimized as in the simple pointer compression technique proposed by Adl-Tabatabai et al. [2]. Adl-Tabatabai et al. report that it is "crucial to optimize the unnecessary compression and decompression in order to get net performance gains". This can be done by considering the phase ordering between code optimization and compression/decompression arithmetics to make sure the additional compression/decompression arithmetics get optimized whenever possible. The optimizations by the Adl-Tabatabai et al. approach include for example:

- *load-store forwarding*: If a loaded 32-bit offset is subsequently stored, the 32-bit offset does not need to be decompressed and subsequently compressed again; the 32-bit offset can be stored right away. This is not the case for ORA because the base address to which the 32-bit offset relates is the virtual address of the referencing object. And since the objects from which the 32-bit offset is loaded is likely to be different from the object to which the 32-bit offset needs to be stored, the 32-bit offset to be stored needs to be recomputed.
- *reference comparison*: Comparing objects' virtual addresses can be done easily by comparing the 32-bit offsets in the Adl-Tabatabai et al. approach. This is not the case for ORA; the 64-bit virtual addresses need to be decompressed from the 32-bit offsets before allowing for a comparison, the reason being that the base addresses are likely to be different for both 32-bit compressed pointers.
- *reassociation of address expressions*: Computing the address of an object field or array element involves two additions in Adl-Tabatabai et al.'s approach: the heap base needs to be added to the 32-bit offset plus the object field's offset. Under many circumstances, one addition can be pre-computed at compile time. For example, in case of an object field access, the heap base address and the object field's offset are both constants and can be pre-computed. Again, this is an optimization that cannot be applied to ORA because the base address is not constant. A related optimization is to apply common subexpression elimination. For example, if multiple fields of the same object are accessed, then the heap base address plus the 32-bit offset is a common subexpression that can be eliminated, *i.e.*, does not need to be recomputed over and over again. The latter optimization can also be applied under ORA.

In summary, the pointer compression approach by Adl-Tabatabai et al. allows for a number of optimizations that cannot be applied to ORA. Hence, it is to be expected that ORA will perform poorer than the pointer compression technique proposed by Adl-Tabatabai et al. However, ORA can apply pointer compression to Java programs that allocate more than 4GB of heap memory, which cannot be done using Adl-Tabatabatai et al.'s method.

It is interesting to note that, in case the 'base plus index plus offset' memory addressing mode would be available in the host ISA—again, which is not the case in our PowerPC setup—ORA would be able to apply an important optimization that would likely close (part of) the gap between ORA and Adl-Tabatabai *et al.*'s technique. Pointer decompression can then be combined with field offset computation into a single address expression. In that case, the optimization done by Adl-Tabatabai *et al.* to pre-compute constants would be subsumed by combining the pointer decompression with field offset computation.

3.8   Implications for Memory Management

As mentioned in the introduction, object-relative addressing is envisioned to be used in conjunction with a dedicated memory management approach for allocating objects in memory regions such that all inter-object references within a memory region can be represented by a 32-bit offset. To this end, ORA can rely on previously proposed memory management approaches that allocate connected objects into memory regions while minimizing the number of references across memory regions. Example memory management approaches that serve this need are object colocation [3], connectivity-based garbage collection [4,5] and region-based systems [6]. The smarter the memory management strategy, the smaller the number of LAT accesses, the smaller the compression/decompression overhead, and thus the higher overall performance.

In this context, it is also important to note that ORA is flexible in the sense that ORA can be activated and deactivated for particular object types; or, if needed, ORA can even be activated/deactivated for particular references between pairs of object types. It was this insight on ORA's flexibility that lead us to our compression/decompression scheme with patching. The slow decompression path is not called for at the beginning of the program execution as the heap is small enough—as such we always execute the fast path and thus eliminate executing the if-then statement. Once an inter-object reference is detected that cannot be represented by a 32-bit value, all the code that may possibly read the compressed pointer needs to be patched. ORA is flexible enough to handle such cases as a safety net in case the memory management strategy would fail to allocate objects so that all pointers can be represented as 32-bit offsets.

4   Experimental Setup

We now detail our experimental setup: the virtual machine, the benchmarks and the hardware platform on which we perform our measurements. We also detail how we performed our statistical analysis on the data we obtained.

4.1   Jikes RVM

The Jikes RVM is an open-source virtual machine developed by IBM Research [10]. We used the recent 64-bit AIX/PowerPC v2.3.5 port. We extended the 64-bit Jikes RVM in order to be able to support the full 64-bit virtual address range. In this paper, we use the GenMS garbage collector. GenMS is a generational collector that copies reachable

Table 1. The benchmarks used in this paper

suite	benchmark	description
SPECjbb2000	pseudojbb	models middle tier of a three-tier system
DaCapo	antlr	parses one or more grammar files and generates a parser and lexical analyzer for each
	bloat	performs a number of optimizations and analysis on Java bytecode files
	fop	takes an XSL-FO file, parses it and formats it, generating a PDF file
	hsqldb	executes a JDBCbench-like in-memory benchmark, executing a number of transactions against a model of a banking application
	jython	interprets the pybench Python benchmark
	pmd	analyzes a set of Java classes for a range of source code problems

objects from the nursery to the mature space upon a nursery space garbage collection. A full heap collection then collects the heaps using the mark-sweep strategy.

4.2 Benchmarks

The benchmarks that we use in this study come from the SPECjbb2000 and DaCapo benchmark suites, see Table 1. SPECjbb2000 is a server-side benchmark that models the middle tier (the business logic) of a three-tier system. Since SPECjbb2000 is a through-put benchmark that runs for a fixed amount of time, we use pseudojbb which runs for a fixed amount of work (35,000 transactions) and an increasing number of warehouses going from 1 up to 8 warehouses. The initial heap size is set to 256M and the maximum heap size is set to 512MB. The DaCapo benchmark suite [11] is a relatively new set of open-source, client-side Java benchmarks. The DaCapo benchmarks exhibits more complex code, richer object behaviors and more demanding memory system require-ments than the SPECjvm98 client-side benchmarks. We set the maximum heap size to 512MB with a 100MB initial heap size in all of our experiments. We use the DaCapo benchmarks under version beta-2006-08. Unfortunately, we were unable to run all Da-Capo benchmarks on Jikes RVM v2.3.5; we use the 6 DaCapo benchmarks mentioned in Table 1. For bloat and jython we use the small input—the large input failed to run. The other 4 DaCapo benchmarks are run with the large input.

4.3 Hardware Platform

The hardware platform on which we have done our measurements is the IBM POWER4 which is a 64-bit microprocessor that implements the PowerPC ISA. The POWER4 is an aggressive 8-wide issue superscalar out-of-order processor capable of processing over 200 in-flight instructions. The POWER4 is a dual-processor CMP with private L1 caches and a shared 1.4MB 8-way set-associative L2 cache. The L3 tags are stored on-chip; the L3 cache is a 32MB 8-way set-associative off-chip cache with 512 byte lines. The TLB in the POWER4 is a unified 4-way set-associative structure with 1K entries. The effective to real address translation tables (I-ERAT and D-ERAT) operate as caches for the TLB and are 128-entry 2-way set-associative arrays. The standard memory page size on the POWER4 is 4KB. Our 615 pSeries machine has one single POWER4 chip. The amount of RAM-memory equals 1GB.

In the evaluation section we will measure execution times on the IBM POWER4 using hardware performance counters. The AIX 5.1 operating system provides a library (pmapi) to access these hardware performance counters. This library automatically handles counter overflows and kernel thread context switches. The hardware performance counters measure both user and kernel activity.

4.4 Statistical Analysis

In the evaluation section, we want to measure the impact on performance of ORA. Since we measure on real hardware, non-determinism in these runs results in slight fluctuations in the number of execution cycles. In order to be able to take statistically valid conclusions from these runs, we employ statistics to determine 95% confidence intervals from 8 measurement runs. We use the unpaired or noncorresponding setup for comparing means, see [12] (pages 64–69).

5   Evaluation

In the evaluation section of this paper, we first measure the performance impact of ORA and subsequently focus on the reduction in memory usage and its impact on the memory subsystem.

5.1   Performance

For quantifying the performance impact of ORA applied to Java application objects, we consider five scenarios that we compare against the base case. Our base case is a 64-bit version of Jikes RVM which assumes 64-bit pointer representations in object data fields. Figure 7 shows the performance for each of the following five scenarios relative to the base case. Initially, we assume that all pointer compressions and decompressions occur through the fast path, *i.e.*, all inter-object references can be represented as 32-bit offsets. We then subsequently quantify the overhead of pointer compression and decompression through the slow path accessing the LAT.

Compressed pointers with zero heap base. The 'compressed pointer with zero heap base' is the scenario where all 64-bit pointers in object data fields are compressed to 32-bit pointers with the heap base address being zero. This means that loading the 32-bit compressed pointers (with zero extension) yields the virtual address of the referenced object; storing a compressed pointer is done by storing the four least significant bytes of the virtual address to memory. This scenario shows the best possible performance that can be achieved through compressed pointer representation: pointers are compressed and there is no compression/decompression overhead. The average performance gain is 5.0%, and up to 14.2% for hsqldb. This performance gain is a direct consequence of the memory savings through a reduced number of data cache misses and D-TLB misses.

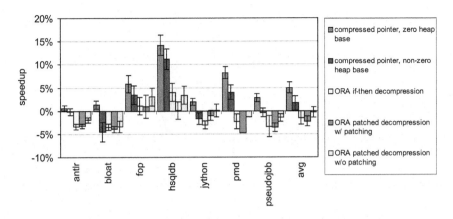

Fig. 7. Evaluating object-relative addressing in terms of performance

Compressed pointers with non-zero heap base. The 'compressed pointer with non-zero heap base' is similar to the previous scenario except that the heap base address is non-zero. In other words, decompressing a 32-bit pointer requires adding the 32-bit offset to the 64-bit heap base address. This scenario corresponds to Adl-Tabatabai *et al.*'s approach: it assumes that the heap space is no larger than 4GB, and assumes a fixed heap base address. The average performance gain for compressed pointers with a non-zero heap base drops to 1.7%; the maximum performance gain is observed for hsqldb (11.1%) and the largest slowdown is observed for bloat (-4.6%).

The 1.7% average performance gain over the base case is smaller than what is reported by Adl-Tabatabai *et al.* in [2]. The reason is that our results are for the PowerPC ISA using Jikes RVM whereas the results by Adl-Tabatabai *et al.* are for the Intel Itanium Processor Family (IPF) using ORP and StarJIT. As a result, not all optimizations implemented by Adl-Tabatabai *et al.* may be implemented in our system. Note however that the goal of this scenario is not to re-validate the approach proposed by Adl-Tabatabai *et al.*, but rather to quantify the overhead of pointer compression/decompression in our framework.

ORA with if-then decompression. The 'ORA if-then decompression' scenario implements object-relative addressing using the if-then decompression implementation. This scenario includes testing the LSB of the 32-bit compressed pointer for determining whether to take the fast or the slow path. This scenario incurs an average slowdown of 1.5%. The highest slowdown observed is 3.5% (bloat); the highest speedup observed is 4.0% (hsqldb).

ORA with patched decompression. There are two 'ORA patched decompression' scenarios. The first 'w/ patching' scenario assumes that all loads are patched, *i.e.*, all pointer decompressions are done by jumping to an if-then decompression scheme as shown in Figure 5. The second 'w/o patching' scenario assumes that none of the loads are patched, *i.e.*, all pointer decompressions are done by adding the 32-bit offset to the referencing object's virtual address as shown in Figure 4. As expected, the 'w/ patching'

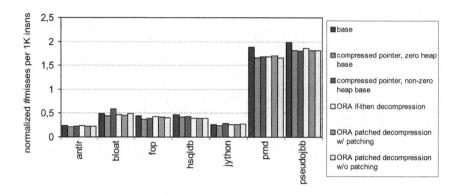

Fig. 8. The number of L2 misses per 1K instructions of the base run

scenario incurs a higher overhead than the 'if-then decompression' because of the jump instruction, however, this overhead is very small and not statistically significant. The 'w/o patching' scenario, which eliminates the jump instruction in the decompression scheme and which is the most realistic scenario in case an appropriate memory management strategy is available, results in a statistically insignificant average slowdown of 0.2%. The maximum slowdown observed is 3.4% (pmd) and the maximum speedup observed is 3.4% (hsqldb).

LAT access overhead. So far, we assumed that all decompressions occur along the fast path, *i.e.*, the slow decompression path is never taken. In order to quantify the overhead of going through the slow path we have set up a benchmarking experiment in which the nursery and mature space are located more than 4GB away from each other. This benchmarking experiment implies that all inter-generational pointers—from nursery objects to mature objects, and vice versa—have to pass through the LAT. In other words, a LAT entry is allocated for all inter-generational pointers, and the slow path is taken when compressing/decompressing inter-generational pointers. On average, 15.5% of all references go through the slow path, up to 23.6% (fop) and 36.6% (bloat). The average slowdown of this benchmarking experiment is 4.1% ± 1.3%. We want to emphasize that the sole purpose of this benchmarking experiment is to quantify the overhead due to taking the slow compression/decompression path; the goal of this experiment is not to present a use case scenario. In practice, when an appropriate memory management strategy is employed that limits the number of LAT accesses, even smaller slowdowns are to be expected.

5.2 Cache Hierarchy Performance

Figures 8 and 9 show the number of L2 and L3 misses per 1K instructions of the base run, respectively. In these graphs, we normalize the number of L2 and L3 misses for the various scenarios from above to the number of instructions in the base run. We clearly observe that the number of L2 misses and L3 misses (main memory accesses) reduces

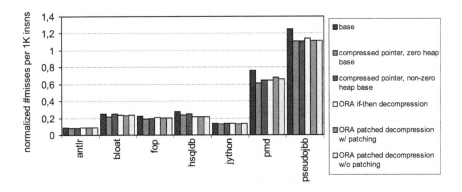

Fig. 9. The number of L3 misses per 1K instructions of the base run

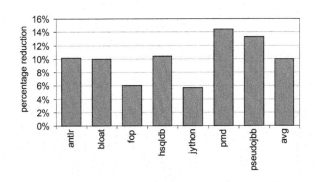

Fig. 10. Reduction in the number of allocated bytes through ORA

through ORA, up to 12.6% and 22.4% for pmd and hsqldb. In other words, ORA better utilizes the cache hierarchy reducing the pressure on main memory.

5.3   Memory Usage

We now analyze the impact of ORA on memory usage and quantify the impact of ORA on the number of bytes allocated and the number of memory pages touched.

Figure 10 shows the reduction in the number of allocated bytes through object-relative addressing. Compressing 64-bit object references reduce the number of allocated bytes by 10% on average and reductions up to 14.5% for pmd.

Figures 11 and 12 show the number of memory pages in use on the vertical axis as a function of time (measured in the number of allocations) on the horizontal axis for pseudojbb and hsqldb, respectively. Each figure shows two graphs, one for the base 64-bit pointer representation (top graph), and one for the compressed pointer representation through object-relative addressing (bottom graph). (We observed similar

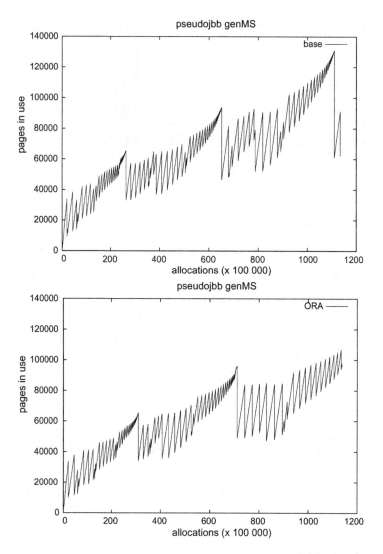

Fig. 11. Number of pages in use as a function of time for **pseudojbb**: the base 64-bit pointer representation (at the top) and the ORA compressed pointer representation (at the bottom)

curves for the other benchmarks.) The curves in these graphs increase as memory gets allocated until a garbage collection is triggered after which the number of used pages drops. The small drops correspond to nursery collections; the large drops correspond to mature collections collecting the full heap. The graph for hsqldb shows that the number of pages in use is substantially lower under ORA than under the base 64-bit pointer representation. The graph for **pseudojbb** shows that the reduced number of pages in use delays garbage collections, *i.e.*, it takes a longer time before a garbage collection is triggered.

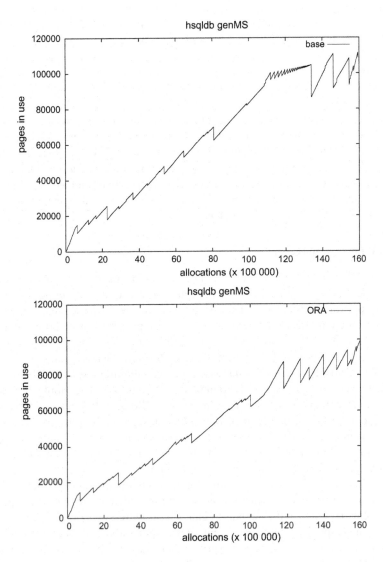

Fig. 12. Number of pages in use as a function of time for hsqldb: the base 64-bit pointer representation (at the top) and the ORA compressed pointer representation (at the bottom)

6   Related Work

6.1   Java Program Memory Characterization

Dieckmann and Hölzle [13] present a detailed characterization of the allocation behavior of SPECjvm98 benchmarks. Among the numerous aspects they evaluated, they also quantified object size and the impact of object alignment on the overall object size. This study was done on a 32-bit platform.

Venstermans *et al.* [1] compare the memory requirements for Java applications on a 64-bit virtual machine versus a 32-bit virtual machine. They concluded that objects are nearly 40% larger in a 64-bit VM compared to a 32-bit VM. There are two primary reasons for this. First, the header in 64-bit mode is twice as large as in 32-bit mode. This accounts for approximately half the object size increase. Second, a reference in 64-bit computing mode is twice the size as in 32-bit computing mode. This causes the data fields that contain references to increase; this accounts for roughly the other half of the total object size increase between 32-bit and 64-bit. Pointer compression as proposed in this paper addresses the size increase because of references in the object data fields.

A number of related research studies have been done on characterizing the memory behavior of Java applications, such as [14,15,16]. Other studies aimed at reducing the memory usage of Java applications, for example, using techniques such as heap compression [17], object compression [18], *etc.*

6.2   Pointer Compression

Mogul *et al.* [19] studied the impact of pointer size on overall performance on a Digital Alpha system using a collection of C programs. They compared the performance of the same application in both 64-bit and 32-bit mode. They concluded that while performance was often unaffected by larger pointers, some programs experienced significant performance degradations, primarily due to cache and memory page issues. The study done by Venstermans *et al.* [1] confirms these findings for Java programs.

Adl-Tabatabai [2] address the increased memory requirements of 64-bit Java implementations by compressing 64-bit pointers to 32-bit offsets. They apply their pointer compression technique to both the Type Information Block (TIB) pointer—or the vtable pointer—and the forwarding pointer in the object header and to pointers in the object itself. As mentioned before, the approach by Adl-Tabatabai *et al.* is limited to applications within a 32-bit address space. As such, applications that require more than 4GB of memory cannot benefit from pointer compression.

Lattner and Adve [7,20] apply a similar approach to compressing pointers in linked data structures. Linked data structures are placed in a memory region where pointers are represented relative to the memory region's base address.

Zhang and Gupta [21] compress 32-bit integer values and 32-bit pointer values into 15-bit entities, applied to 32-bit C programs. For integer values, in case the 18 most significant bits are identical, *i.e.*, all 1's or all 0's, the integer value can be compressed into a 15-bit entity by discarding the 17 most significant bits. A pointer in an object's field is compressed if the 17 most significant bits of the referencing object's virtual address is identical to the 17 most significant bits of the referenced object's virtual address; only the 15 least significant bits are then stored. This is similar to ORA at first sight, but there is a subtle but important difference. Whereas ORA allows for compressing pointers in case the referenced object is reachable with an n-bit offset from the referencing object, Zhang and Gupta's approach requires that both objects reside in the same 2^n-bit memory region. This may lead to the situation where two objects are close to each other, *i.e.*, the difference between both object's virtual addresses is smaller than what can be represented by an n-bit offset, yet the pointers cannot be compressed.

Pairs of compressed 15-bit entity compressed are packed together into a single 32-bit word. Accelerating compression/decompression is done through data compression extensions to the processor's ISA.

Kaehler and Krasner [22] describe the Large Object-Oriented Memory (LOOM) technique for accessing a 32-bit virtual address space on a 16-bit machine. Objects in secondary memory have 32-bit pointers to other objects. Primary (main) memory serves as a cache to secondary memory. Object pointers in main memory are represented as short 16-bit indices into an Object Table (OT). This OT contains the full 32-bit address of the object. Objects need to be moved to main memory before they can be referenced. Translation between 32-bit pointers and 16-bit indices is performed when moving objects to main memory.

6.3 Object Header Compression

A number of studies have been done on compressing object headers which we briefly discuss here.

Bacon *et al.* [23] present a number of header compression techniques for the Java object model on 32-bit machines. They propose three approaches for reducing the space requirements of the TIB pointer in the header: bit stealing, indirection and the implicit type method. Bit stealing and indirection still require a condensed form of a TIB pointer to be stored in the header. Implicit typing on the other hand, completely eliminates the TIB pointer. Various flavors of implicit typing have been proposed in the literature, such as Big Bag of Pages (BiBOP) approach by Steele [24] and Hanson [25], a hybrid BiBOP/bit-stealing approach by Dybvig *et al.* [26], and Selective Typed Virtual Addressing [8].

Shuf *et al.* [27] propose the notion of prolific types versus non-prolific types. A prolific type is defined as a type that has a sufficiently large number of instances allocated during a program execution. In practice, a type is called prolific if the fraction of objects allocated by the program of this type exceeds a given threshold. All remaining types are referred to as non-prolific. Shuf *et al.* found that only a limited number of types account for most of the objects allocated by the program. They then propose to exploit this notion by using short type pointers for prolific types. The idea is to use a few type bits in the status field to encode the types of the prolific objects. As such, the TIB pointer field can be eliminated from the object header. The prolific type can then be accessed through a type table. A special value of the type bits, for example all zeros, is then used for non-prolific object types. Non-prolific types still have a TIB pointer field in their object headers. A disadvantage of this approach is that the number of prolific types is limited by the number of available bits in the status field. In addition, computing the TIB pointer for prolific types requires an additional indirection. The advantage of the prolific approach is that the amount of memory fragmentation is limited since all objects are allocated in a single segment, much as in traditional VMs.

7 Conclusion

Pointers in 64-bit address spaces require twice as much memory as in 32-bit address spaces. This results in increased memory usage which degrades cache and TLB performance; in addition, physical memory gets exhausted quicker. This paper presented object-relative addressing (ORA) for implementation in 64-bit Java virtual machines. ORA compresses 64-bit pointers in object fields into 32-bit offsets relative to the referencing object's virtual address. The important benefit of ORA over prior work, which assumed 32-bit offsets relative to a fixed base address, is that ORA enables pointer compression for programs that allocate more than 4GB of memory. Our experimental results using Jikes RVM on an IBM POWER4 machine using SPECjbb and DaCapo benchmarks show that ORA incurs a statistically insignificant impact on overall performance compared to raw 64-bit pointer representation, while reducing the amount of memory allocated by 10% on average and up to 14.5% for some applications.

Acknowledgements

The authors would like to thank the anonymous reviewers for their valuable comments. Kris Venstermans is supported by a BOF grant from Ghent University. Lieven Eeckhout is a Postdoctoral Fellow with the Fund for Scientific Research—Flanders (Belgium) (FWO—Vlaanderen). This research is also partially supported by the IWT and HiPEAC.

References

1. Venstermans, K., Eeckhout, L., De Bosschere, K.: 64-bit versus 32-bit virtual machines for Java. Software—Practice and Experience 36(1), 1–26 (2006)
2. Adl-Tabatabai, A.R., Bharadwaj, J., Cierniak, M., Eng, M., Fang, J., Lewis, B.T., Murphy, B.R., Stichnoth, J.M.: Improving 64-bit Java IPF performance by compressing heap references. In: Proceedings of the International Symposium on Code Generation and Optimization (CGO), pp. 100–110. IEEE Computer Society Press, Los Alamitos (2004)
3. Guyer, S.Z., McKinley, K.S.: Finding your cronies: static analysis for dynamic object colocation. In: Proceedings of the 19th Annual ACM SIGPLAN Conference on Object-Oriented Programming, Systems, Languages, and Applications (OOPSLA), pp. 237–250. ACM Press, New York (2004)
4. Hirzel, M., Diwan, A., Hertz, M.: Connectivity-based garbage collection. In: Proceedings of the 18th ACM SIGPLAN Conference on Object-Oriented Programing, Systems, Languages, and Applications (OOPSLA), pp. 359–373. ACM Press, New York (2003)
5. Hirzel, M., Henkel, J., Diwan, A., Hind, M.: Understanding the connectivity of heap objects. In: Proceedings of the International Symposium on Memory Management (ISMM), pp. 36–39 (June 2002)
6. Cherem, S., Rugina, R.: Region analysis and transformation for Java programs. In: Proceedings of the 4th International Symposium on Memory Management (ISMM), pp. 85–96. ACM Press, New York (2004)
7. Lattner, C., Adve, V.: Transparent pointer compression for linked data structures. In: Proceedings of the Third 2005 ACM SIGPLAN Workshop on Memory Systems Performance (MSP), pp. 24–35. ACM Press, New York (2005)
8. Venstermans, K., Eeckhout, L., De Bosschere, K.: Space-efficient 64-bit Java objects through selective typed virtual addressing. In: Proceedings of the 4th Annual International Symposium on Code Generation and Optimization (CGO), pp. 76–86 (March 2006)

9. Mahlke, S.A., Hank, R.E., McCormick, J.E., August, D.I., Hwu, W.W.: A comparison of full and partial predicated execution support for ILP processors. In: Proceedings of the 22nd Annual International Symposium on Computer Architecture (ISCA), pp. 138–149 (June 1995)

10. Alpern, B., Attanasio, C.R., Barton, J.J., Burke, M.G., Cheng, P., Choi, J.D., Cocchi, A., Fink, S.J., Grove, D., Hind, M., Hummel, S.F., Lieber, D., Litvinov, V., Mergen, M.F., Ngo, T., Russell, J.R., Sarkar, V., Serrano, M.J., Shepherd, J.C., Smith, S.E., Sreedhar, V.C., Srinivasan, H., Whaley, J.: The Jalapeño Virtual Machine. IBM Systems Journal 39(1), 211–238 (2000)

11. Blackburn, S.M., Garner, R., Hoffman, C., Khan, A.M., McKinley, K.S., Bentzur, R., Diwan, A., Feinberg, D., Frampton, D., Guyer, S.Z., Hirzel, M., Hosking, A., Jump, M., Lee, H., Moss, J.E.B., Phansalkar, A., Stefanović, D., VanDrunen, T., von Dincklage, D., Wiedermann, B.: The DaCapo benchmarks: Java benchmarking development and analysis. In: Proceedings of the 21st Annual ACM SIGPLAN Conference on Object-Oriented Programming, Systems, Languages, and Applications (OOPSLA), pp. 169–190. ACM Press, New York (2006)

12. Lilja, D.J.: Measuring Computer Performance: A Practitioner's Guide. Cambridge University Press, Cambridge (2000)

13. Dieckmann, S., Hölzle, U.: A study of the allocation behavior of the specjvm98 Java benchmarks. In: Guerraoui, R. (ed.) ECOOP 1999. LNCS, vol. 1628, pp. 92–115. Springer, Heidelberg (1999)

14. Blackburn, S.M., Cheng, P., McKinley, K.S.: Myths and realities: the performance impact of garbage collection. In: Proceedings of the joint International Conference on Measurement and Modeling of Computer Systems (SIGMETRICS), pp. 25–36. ACM Press, New York (2004)

15. Kim, J.S., Hsu, Y.: Memory system behavior of Java programs: methodology and analysis. In: Proceedings of the International Conference on Measurement and Modeling of Computer Systems (SIGMETRICS), pp. 264–274. ACM Press, New York (2000)

16. Shuf, Y., Serrano, M.J., Gupta, M., Singh, J.P.: Characterizing the memory behavior of Java workloads: a structured view and opportunities for optimizations. In: Proceedings of the International Conference on Measurement and Modeling of Computer Systems (SIGMETRICS), pp. 194–205 (2001)

17. Chen, G., Kandemir, M., Vijaykrishnan, N., Irwin, M.J., Mathiske, B., Wolczko, M.: Heap compression for memory-constrained Java environments. In: Proceedings of the 18th ACM SIGPLAN Conference on Object-Oriented Programming, Systems, Languages, and Applications (OOPSLA), pp. 282–301. ACM Press, New York (2003)

18. Chen, G., Kandemir, M., Irwin, M.J.: Exploiting frequent field values in Java objects for reducing heap memory requirements. In: Proceedings of the 1st ACM/USENIX International Conference on Virtual Execution Environments (VEE), pp. 68–78. ACM Press, New York (2005)

19. Mogul, J.C., Bartlett, J.F., Mayo, R.N., Srivastava, A.: Performance implications of multiple pointer sizes. In: USENIX Winter, pp. 187–200 (1995)

20. Lattner, C., Adve, V.: Automatic pool allocation: improving performance by controlling data structure layout in the heap. In: Proceedings of the 2005 ACM SIGPLAN Conference on Programming Language Design and Implementation (PLDI), pp. 129–142. ACM Press, New York (2005)

21. Zhang, Y., Gupta, R.: Data compression transformations for dynamically allocated data structures. In: Computational Complexity, pp. 14–28 (2002)

22. Kaehler, T., Krasner, G.: LOOM: large object-oriented memory for Smalltalk-80 systems. In: Readings in object-oriented database systems, pp. 298–307. Morgan Kaufmann Publishers Inc. San Francisco (1990)

23. Bacon, D.F., Fink, S.J., Grove, D.: Space- and time-efficient implementation of the Java object model. In: Magnusson, B. (ed.) ECOOP 2002. LNCS, vol. 2374, pp. 111–132. Springer, Heidelberg (2002)
24. Steele, Jr., G.L.: Data representation in PDP-10 MACLISP. Technical Report AI Memo 420, Massachusetts Institute of Technology, Artificial Intelligence Laboratory (September 1997)
25. Hanson, D.R.: A portable storage management system for the Icon programming language. Software—Practice and Experience 10(6), 489–500 (1980)
26. Dybvig, R.K., Eby, D., Bruggeman, C.: Don't stop the BIBOP: Flexible and efficient storage management for dynamically-typed languages. Technical Report 400, Indiana University Computer Science Department (March 1994)
27. Shuf, Y., Gupta, M., Bordawekar, R., Singh, J.P.: Exploiting prolific types for memory management and optimizations. In: Proceedings of the 29th ACM SIGPLAN-SIGACT Symposium on Principles of Programming Languages (POPL), pp. 295–306. ACM Press, New York (2002)

Generational Real-Time Garbage Collection
A Three-Part Invention for Young Objects

Daniel Frampton[1], David F. Bacon[2], Perry Cheng[2], and David Grove[2]

[1] Australian National University,
Canberra ACT, Australia
Daniel.Frampton@anu.edu.au
[2] IBM T.J. Watson Research
19 Skyline Drive, Hawthorne, NY 10952, USA
bacon,perryche,groved@us.ibm.com

Abstract. While real-time garbage collection is now available in production virtual machines, the lack of generational capability means applications with high allocation rates are subject to reduced throughput and high space overheads.

Since frequent allocation is often correlated with a high-level, object-oriented style of programming, this can force builders of real-time systems to compromise on software engineering.

We have developed a fully incremental, real-time generational collector based on a *tri-partite nursery*, which partitions the nursery into regions that are being allocated, collected, and promoted. Nursery collections are incremental, and can occur within any phase of a mature collection.

We present the design, mathematical model, and implementation of our collector in IBM's production Real-time Java virtual machine, and show both analytically and experimentally that the collector achieves real-time bounds comparable to a non-generational Metronome-style collector, while cutting memory consumption and total execution times by as much as 44% and 24% respectively.

1 Introduction

With the advent of hard real-time garbage collection [1] and its incorporation into a production virtual machine [2], Java is finally making significant inroads into domains with hard real-time concerns such as audio processing, military command-and-control, telecommunications, and financial trading systems.

The engineering and product life-cycle advantages consequent from the simplicity of programming with garbage collection, coupled with reliable real-time performance, obviate the need for low-level, error-prone techniques such as object pooling and manual memory management with scoped regions [3]. Furthermore, programmers no longer need to code time-critical portions of the system in lower-level, less secure languages like C.

E. Ernst (Ed.): ECOOP 2007, LNAI 4609, pp. 101–125, 2007.

However, previous incremental and real-time collectors have generally not included generational collection. Generational collection takes advantage of the fact that most objects die quickly, and tends to increase throughput and decrease memory requirements.

Since frequent allocation is often correlated with a high-level, object-oriented style of programming, the lack of generational collection can force builders of real-time systems to compromise the software engineering of their systems by manually recoding to allocate fewer objects.

A few generational collectors with various levels of soft- or hard-real-time behavior have been built [4,5], but they collect the nursery synchronously. This either leads to long pauses (in the order of 50 ms) or a very limited nursery size. For example, if the target maximum pause time is 1 ms and the evacuation rate is 100 MB/s, then the nursery can be no larger than 100 KB. At such small sizes the survival rate is often too high to derive much benefit from generational collection.

In this paper, we present a fully generational version of the Metronome real-time garbage collector [1] in which both the nursery and mature collections are performed incrementally, and in which the scheduling of the two types of collections is only loosely coupled. This allows nursery collection to occur at any time, including in the middle of a full-heap collection.

This generational algorithm is more complex but yields one significant advantage: the ability to size the nursery independent of the real-time bounds of the application. This allows the collector to achieve very short pause times (nominally 500 μs) and reliable real-time behavior, while using a nursery large enough to achieve low survival rates.

The fundamental innovation in our work is the use of a *tri-partite nursery:* the nursery is split into three regions. There is an *allocation* nursery into which new objects are allocated. Meanwhile the previous nursery, then known as the *collect* nursery can be collected, with live objects copied out into the mature area. For algorithmic reasons, references may exist from the heap and collect nursery to objects in the previous nursery that were previously promoted. In order to forward these references we retain this previous nursery as the *promotion* nursery.

The contributions of this work are:

- An algorithm for a fully generational real-time garbage collection in which the nursery and major collections are both incremental and can be arbitrarily interleaved.
- A tri-partite nursery which allows a nursery evacuation while the application continues to allocate into a new nursery.
- An analysis of the space bounds and mutator utilization of a generational collector in which the nursery size is elastic. Furthermore, we derive the nursery size which optimizes utilization and memory consumption.
- Measurements of applications showing that our generational collector is able to achieve comparable real-time behavior to a non-generational Metronome system, while using significantly less memory and increasing throughput.

2   Metronome Overview

This section describes the Metronome algorithm and implementation, both for background on real-time collection and for the purpose of understanding the system against which we benchmark the generational collector in Section 5.

The original Metronome system [1] was implemented in Jikes RVM (12.4ms worst-case pause, 44% MMU at 22.2ms). The model and algorithm of a generational variant with a synchronous nursery – the syncopated Metronome – has been published [4]. There was no actual implementation of the generational collector – only arraylet pre-tenuring – and a measurement of the effective survival rates with and without pre-tenuring. The conclusion was that the synchronous nursery technique could work for small embedded benchmarks with low survival rates, but would not be suitable as a general-purpose solution.

A second-generation version of the original Metronome algorithm was implemented in IBM's J9 JVM (1ms worst-case pauses, 70% MMU at 10ms), and was released as a product by IBM in 2006 [2]. This product also includes a full implementation of RTSJ, The Real-Time Specification for Java [3]. The work described in this paper is a generational system built on the IBM J9 product, without the RTSJ features.

The Metronome algorithm is described in greater detail in [1], but there are some differences in the J9 implementation. We will describe the J9 implementation but point out the aspects which differ from the original Jikes RVM implementation. Among other things, the J9 version implements the complete Java semantics including finalizers and weak/soft/phantom references, which were not supported in the original version.

The Metronome is a hard real-time incremental collector. It uses a hybrid of non-copying mark-sweep collection (in the common case) and selective copying collection (when fragmentation occurs).

The virtual machine scheduler alternates between execution of application ("mutator") threads and garbage collector threads, using predictable quanta and predictable spacing between those quanta. The system runs on uni- or multiprocessors (the original system only ran on uniprocessors), but alternation between application and collector is synchronized across processors with a barrier synchronization.

2.1   Time Based Scheduling

A key contribution of the Metronome system is that it abandons a fine grained work-based approach – such as that of Baker [6] – in favor of a *time-based* approach. The fundamental observation here is that the race between collector and mutator occurs at a relatively coarse time granularity; namely that of a collection cycle. Bursty allocation behavior in small time windows can then be amortized over the relatively long period of a complete collection cycle. A time-based scheduler interleaves mutator and collector work in small quanta at a ratio determined by the model. This ensures that the collector keeps up, but does so in a predictable manner amenable to providing the required real-time guarantees on utilization levels.

Minimum Mutator Utilization (MMU). In order to achieve correct time-based behavior, Metronome uses the *minimum mutator utilization* or MMU metric introduced by Cheng and Blelloch [7]. MMU is a measure of the worst-case utilization by the application (mutator) over a particular time window. MMU is independent of the length of particular collector pauses, since multiple short pauses grouped closely together can be as disruptive as a single long pause.

The system by default runs at an MMU of 70% over a 10 ms time window (that is, the application always receives at least 7 ms out of every 10 ms of real time). Shorter time windows and/or higher MMUs are possible depending on the characteristics of the application.

The system uses *over-sampling* and instead of interrupting the application for a single 3 ms quantum every 10 ms, it instead uses quanta whose nominal length is 500 μs, with a worst-case quantum of less than 1 ms. Over-sampling both reduces variance and increases the robustness of the schedule.

The original Metronome collector did not use over-sampling and was able to run at an MMU of 60% in a 20 ms window, with a worst-case pause of 8 ms.

2.2 Collector Design

The collector is a snapshot-at-the-beginning algorithm that allocates objects black (marked). While it has been argued that such a collector can increase floating garbage, the worst-case performance is no different from other approaches and the termination condition is deterministic, which is a crucial property for real-time collection. As we will show subsequently, the introduction of generational collection greatly reduces the amount of floating garbage.

The key elements of the design and implementation of the Metronome collector are:

Time-based Scheduling. The Metronome collector achieves good minimum mutator utilization, or MMU, at high frequencies (1024 Hz) because it uses time-based rather than work-based scheduling. Time-based scheduling simply interleaves the collector and the mutator on a fixed schedule.

Guaranteed Real-time Bounds. Despite our use of time- rather than work-based scheduling, we are able to tightly bound memory utilization while still guaranteeing good MMU.

Incremental Mark-Sweep. Collection is a standard snapshot-at-the-beginning incremental mark-sweep algorithm [8] implemented with a weak tricolor invariant [9]. We extend traversal during marking so that it redirects any pointers pointing at from-space so they point at to-space. Therefore, at the end of a marking phase, the relocated objects of the previous collection can be freed.

Segregated Free Lists. Allocation is performed using segregated free lists. Memory is divided into fixed-sized pages, and each page is divided into blocks of a particular size. Objects are allocated from the smallest size class that can contain the object.

Mostly Non-copying. Since fragmentation is rare, objects are usually not moved. If a page becomes fragmented due to garbage collection, its objects are moved to another (mostly full) page containing objects of the same size.

Read Barrier. Relocation of objects is achieved by using a forwarding pointer located in the header of each object [10]. A read barrier maintains a to-space invariant (mutators always see objects in the to-space).

Arraylets. Large arrays are broken into fixed-size pieces (which we call arraylets) to bound the work of scanning or copying an array and to bound external fragmentation caused by large objects.

Fuzzy Snapshot. In order to maintain real-time bounds in the presence of a large number of threads, the requirement for an atomic snapshot of all roots is avoided by having the write barrier record both the old and the new pointers during the root scanning phase, instead of just the old pointer as is done by a conventional snapshot-at-the-beginning collector.

We use the term *collection* to refer to a complete mark-sweep-defragment cycle and the term *collector quantum* to refer to a scheduling quantum in which the collector runs. A collection consists of many collector quanta.

The system uses a *lazy read barrier*. The laziness comes from the fact that references in the stack are not updated atomically when an object is moved. To ensure termination, object references written back into the heap are forwarded to current versions as they are written. As the marking phase traverses the heap, references are also forwarded to new versions. Old versions of moved objects can not be removed until after the next collection has been completed as there may still be references to them somewhere.

The original Metronome system used an *eager* read barrier which is slightly faster but requires a fixup pass over stack frames at the end of each collector quantum during the defragmentation phase. Especially on a system with many threads, this may lead to unacceptably long collector quanta.

Metronome achieves guaranteed real-time behavior provided the application is correctly characterized by the user. In particular, the user must be able to specify the maximum amount of simultaneously live data m as well as the peak allocation rate over the time interval of a garbage collection $a(\Delta G)$. The collector is parameterized by its tracing rate R.

Given these characteristics of the mutator and the collector, the user then has the ability to tune the performance of the system using three inter-related parameters: total memory consumption s, minimum guaranteed CPU utilization u, and the resolution at which the utilization is calculated Δt.

3   Real-Time Generational Collection

The potential for reducing memory consumption and/or improving throughput by employing a generational collection technique [12,13] is well understood. The generational hypothesis states that most objects have very short lifetimes. A generational collector takes advantage of this by first allocating objects into a nursery, and then employing collection techniques optimized for low survival rates to promote survivors into the next generation. In this paper we are concerned with a model of generational collection with two generations; a nursery and a mature space.

A key property for real-time generational collection is that the work required to perform a nursery collection be $O(nursery)$, not $O(heap)$. One consequence of this is that the collector must be able to discover all pointers into the nursery from the mature area without scanning the entire mature area. This is typically accomplished by using a *write barrier*, which adds overhead to each pointer write, but keeps track of all pointers from mature objects to nursery objects in a remembered set. In combination with other roots in the system, this remembered set can be used to collect the nursery without having to consider the mature space.

Previous systems have performed generational collection synchronously [4,5], but doing so links the responsiveness of the system to the worst case nursery collection time. In many applications, there are at least some time periods where the generational hypothesis does not hold. This either forces nursery sizes to be very small (low numbers of kilobytes) or worst case pause times to be quite large (tens of milliseconds).

To make generational real-time collection more widely applicable, we must (a) make nursery collection incremental, and (b) allow nursery collections to occur at any point during a mature collection cycle. Achieving both of these design goals decouples worst case pause time from nursery size, enabling the nursery to be sized to obtain the low survival rates critical for effective generational collection.

The rest of this section outlines the key challenges in incremental nursery collection and how our system addresses them. This is not a complete description of our generational algorithm; but it does cover all of the key extensions necessary to build an incremental generational collector on top of the base Metronome system. The next subsection describes how the tri-partite nursery enables the mutator to continue allocating while a nursery collection is in progress. The second subsection describes the techniques used to collect the nursery, including the write barriers that are used to preserve the nursery root set. The final subsection discusses interactions that arise when a nursery collection occurs concurrently with a mature space collection.

3.1 Tri-partite Nursery

The fundamental goal of our algorithm is to allow the mutators to continue executing – *and therefore allocating* – while we are collecting the nursery. In order to satisfy this requirement, while retaining a reasonable model of the system, we begin allocating new objects into a separate nursery area while we perform the collection of the previous nursery. We call this new nursery the *alloc* nursery, and the nursery being collected the *collect* nursery.

Unlike the previous synchronous generational Metronome [4], the alloc nursery does not have a fixed size. Instead, it continues to grow via mutator allocation actions until it is both desirable and possible to begin the next nursery collection cycle. It is desirable to initiate a nursery collection once a certain amount of allocation – the *nursery trigger* – has occurred. However, if the previous nursery collection is still in progress when the nursery trigger is hit, the new nursery collection must be deferred until the prior nursery collection completes. During this time interval, the mutator can continue to allocate into the alloc nursery. The nursery trigger is a system parameter and can be varied to trade-off survival rate with memory consumption (see Section 4). The elasticity of the nursery size allows the system to smoothly absorb short-term spikes in the allocation rate, without resorting to *flood-gating*: direct allocation into the mature area.

Since the nursery collection is incremental, the mutator is free to create new pointers within the system. As demonstrated in detail in the following sections, this leads to the requirement to retain each nursery until the nursery after it has been collected. We call a nursery at this point in the lifecycle the *promote* nursery. A promote nursery contains no active object *data*, but simply forwarding pointers, or indirections to objects that have been promoted to the mature space.

All nursery pages are allocated out of the single global pool of pages shared with the mature space. This facilitates both the logical pre-tenuring of arraylets [4] and the development of a simple model of the system. Allocation into nursery pages is performed using a simple bump pointer. As the surviving objects are promoted into the mature space, they will be relocated to an appropriate size-segregated page.

3.2   Incremental Generational Collection

As with other generational approaches, we use a write barrier that checks on the fast path if a pointer is being created from a mature object to the nursery. Figure 1 shows the fast path of the barrier, including a call to the slow path when the collector is tracing. This part of the barrier supports incremental tracing, and, from the perspective of the mutator, comes at no additional cost over the base system as the same technique is used for both nursery and full heap traces.

```
write_barrier (source: OBJECT, slot: ADDRESS, target: OBJECT) {
    target = forward(target) // Ensure forwarded

    if (isMature(source))
        if (isNursery(target))
            call slow_path

    if (collector_tracing)
        call slow_path
}
```

Fig. 1. Write barrier pseudo-code

Throughout the detailed description of the nursery collection we use the following notation:

M: The mature region.

N$_k$: The kth nursery region.

REM$_k$: This is the remset that is processed when collecting N_k. It is filled during the period of time that N_k is the active *alloc* nursery.

ROOT$_k$: The set of roots that was captured at the start of collecting N_k. While we have an extension that allows the roots to be captured incrementally, for simplicity we describe the algorithm as if there was an atomic root snapshot.

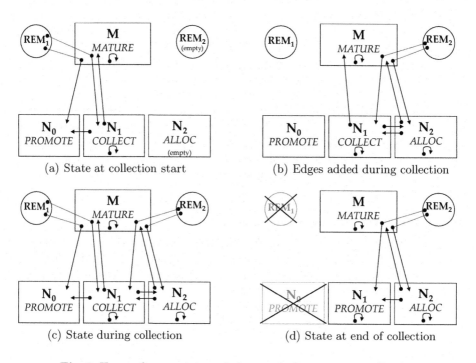

(a) State at collection start   (b) Edges added during collection

(c) State during collection   (d) State at end of collection

Fig. 2. Heap reference state and changes during a nursery collection

Consider the state of the system at the start of a collection, N_1 as shown in Figure 2a. For the initial nursery collection the *promote* nursery will be empty. We also have a remset REM_1 which will capture all references created from $M \rightarrow N_1$, and as demonstrated later, also any pointers into N_0 that were created during the collection of N_0.

As we begin to collect N_1 we perform the following steps atomically:

1. Take the remembered set REM_1 containing all references from $M \rightarrow N_1$ (and possibly $M \rightarrow N_0$),
2. Take the root set $ROOT_1$ (from stacks and other VM structures),

3. Switch all mutators to begin allocating into N_2
4. Switch all mutators to begin contributing remset entries into REM_2.
5. Turn on the tracing barrier to ensure the nursery is traced consistently.

Mutators are then allowed to continue running while N_1 is collected incrementally. It is clear that the union of REM_1 and $ROOT_1$ provide us with a complete *snapshot* of N_1. Therefore, *all* live objects in N_1 are transitively reachable from this set. Through the protection provided by the tracing barrier, this allows us to safely and completely collect the nursery. Note that all references created from N_2 into N_1 must have been obtained from somewhere captured by the snapshot. This means that it is not necessary to trace through N_2 during the collection of N_1. Figure 2b shows the references that can be *created* in mutator intervals that occur during a nursery collection. All pointers created to the mature area, or contained within an individual area will never be required to perform a nursery collection. They are shown on the figures for completeness.

The interesting references that can be created during collection are thus:

$\mathbf{M} \rightarrow \mathbf{N_1}$: We include these in REM_2. We already have a complete snapshot for N_1 in $(REM_1, ROOT_1)$. As we need to retain N_1 to deal with the unbarriered pointers from $N_2 \rightarrow N_1$ we may simply leave these values here to be updated at the next collection.

$\mathbf{M} \rightarrow \mathbf{N_2}$: We include these in REM_2: these are essentially the *normal* generational remembered set entries.

$\mathbf{N_1} \rightarrow \mathbf{N_2}$: These references are not write barriered. As the objects are promoted into the mature space, we will add appropriate entries to REM_2. The entries created on promotion correspond to the case above of $M \rightarrow N_2$.

$\mathbf{N_2} \rightarrow \mathbf{N_1}$: For objects that remain live, these references can only be discovered at the next collection (N_2). This is what requires us to retain a *promote* nursery. These references are not required to find live objects in N_1 as we have a complete snapshot for N_1 in $(REM_1, ROOT_1)$.

Figure 2c shows all references that may exist within the heap during collection. Once collection has been completed, the remset REM_1 will have been completely drained, and all objects (transitively) reachable from the mature space will have been promoted. In addition, as all references that may exist to N_0 would have existed solely in REM_1, there are now no references into N_0 and the space can be reclaimed. N_1 then becomes the *promote* nursery. This state is shown in Figure 2d. From this point the only information remaining in the promote nursery is the forwarding pointer information for promoted objects. The space is essentially closed, as all live objects have been identified and promoted.

Figure 3 shows the pointers that can be created during mutator intervals *outside* of a collection. These are simply pointers between M and N_2 (the alloc nursery), with all pointers from $M \rightarrow N_2$ captured in REM_2.

Note that after incrementing each of the indices, the state is as shown in Figure 2a when the next collection commences.

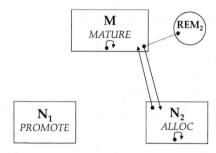

Fig. 3. Edges added outside of a nursery collection

3.3   Mature/Nursery Interaction

While the individual techniques for collecting both nursery and mature space have been shown to be correct in isolation, additional complexity is involved in combining them. In order to provide the necessary real-time guarantees, the ability for a nursery collection to occur must not be interfered with by the mature collection process. To achieve this, the mature collection leaves the system in a state where a nursery collection is possible at the end of each and every mature increment. There is no inverse requirement as the nursery collections will leave sufficient time to perform mature collection, unless the application and/or collector behavior has been incorrectly parameterized. The additional burden placed on the mature and nursery collectors must also be carefully controlled to ensure that no mature related work is performed by the nursery collector, and that the amount of additional work being performed is acceptable.

Objects are allocated with a two-field color. The color is obtained from the allocating thread and changes as the thread is scanned at the beginning of each nursery and mature collection. One field indicates the nursery epoch, while the other indicates the mature epoch. The importance of these will be understood as the following problems are discussed.

Nursery collecting out from under mature space. It is possible for objects that are live in a mature collection to be garbage from the perspective of a subsequent nursery collection. For this reason, during a mature collection, a nursery collection must keep alive the portion of the nursery that is part of the executing mature collection's snapshot. Any previously written references from the mature space to the nursery will already be captured in a remembered set. References that are subsequently lost to the nursery will be captured by the nursery's Yuasa barrier. The references to the nursery that were lost before the nursery collection began are those of interest, and these are the nursery references on the mature collection's Yuasa barrier.

The nursery treats these values as additional roots during its collection. The mature space is required to maintain nursery references separately. This avoids the nursery collector performing any mature space bounded work.

Promoting objects in the appropriate state. It is important that the nursery promotes objects into the mature space in a consistent manner. If, for example, the nursery promotes objects into the mature space as unmarked after tracing is complete, the mature space may sweep up live objects. Similarly, if the nursery promotes objects as live during tracing, references from these objects into the mature space may be missed and cause dangling pointers within the mature space.

This is the motivation for all objects being allocated with a mature epoch bit set. All objects that were allocated before the collection began will not have this bit set, and all objects allocated after the collection began will. When the nursery visits an object, it can use this bit to determine the appropriate mark state to promote with. If the object is in the previous epoch, it will either be marked by the mature collector or, interestingly, can be left as harmless garbage. If the object is in the current epoch, it is promoted as marked – which is equivalent to the allocate-black property of many snapshot collectors.

Sweeping out from under the nursery. The nursery collector maintains a remembered set of references into the nursery from the mature space. If the mature objects containing those references die, then the nursery collector would be processing garbage data looking for roots for its collection. To avoid this, the mature collector is required to sweep the remembered set, removing any references from dead objects. As these objects are garbage, any references from them into the nursery need not be traced. Additionally, when the mature space is defragmented, the nursery remset entries must be forwarded to maintain freshness.

4   Analytical Model

Intuitively, a generational collector is more efficient than a full-heap collector because processing an area in which there are many dead objects allows reclamation of more space for a given amount of GC work. However, when the survival rate η is high or even comparable to the survival rate of a full-heap collection, the generational variant will fare worse because of the cost of determining what is live as well as the actual copying. In this section, we model the behavior of the generational collector and compare it to that of the original Metronome collector and the syncopated Metronome collector.

4.1   Definitions

We begin by characterizing the garbage collector itself by the following parameters:

- R_T is the tracing rate in the heap (bytes/second);
- R_S is the sweeping rate in the heap (bytes/second);
- R_N is the collection rate in the nursery (bytes/second);

As mentioned earlier, generational collectors may be a net loss because inherently, $R_T > R_N$ (because tracing is faster than tracing together with copying). The application is characterized by the following parameters:

- a is the allocation rate (bytes/second) in mutator time (that is, allocation rate ignoring the times when garbage collection is active);
- m is the maximum live memory of the mutator (bytes);
- $\eta(N)$ is the survival rate in the nursery. Specifically, it is the portion of the objects (by bytes) that is live (taking into account the generational barrier) of the last N allocated bytes. This function is monotonically decreasing in N.

We characterize the real-time behavior of the system with the following parameters:

- Δt is the task period (seconds);
- u is the minimum mutator utilization [7] in each Δt;

4.2   Steady-State Assumption and Time Conversion

The allocation rate a and the survival ratio η in fact can vary considerably as the application runs. For the time being we will consider the case when they are smooth. However, since the nursery size varies dynamically as a central aspect of this algorithm, we model it dynamically. As in previous Metronome collectors, modeling relies on being able to convert from mutator time to GC time. For a given interval Δt, the collector may consume up to $(1 - u) \cdot \Delta t$ seconds for collection. We define the *garbage collection factor* γ as the ratio of mutator execution to useful collector work.

$$\gamma = \frac{u \cdot \Delta t}{(1 - u) \cdot \Delta t} = \frac{u}{1 - u} \tag{1}$$

Multiplying by γ converts collector time into mutator time; dividing does the reverse. Since the relationship between u in the range $[0, 1)$ and γ in the range $[0, \infty)$ is one-to-one, we also have

$$u = \frac{\gamma}{1 + \gamma} \tag{2}$$

From the above parameters, we can then derive the overall space consumption of the system. Fundamentally, for all real-time collectors, the space requirements depend on the amount of extra memory that is allocated during the time when incremental collection is being performed and the mutator is continuing to run. Thus:

- s is the space requirement (bytes) of the application in our collector, and
- e is the extra space allocated by the mutator over the course of a full-heap collection.

We will review bounds for s and e for previous collectors and then show how they relate to our collector.

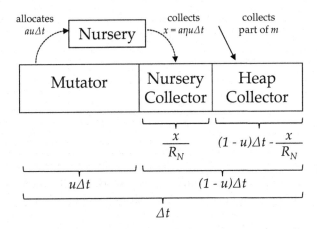

Fig. 4. Time dilation due to generational collection causes additional allocation during a major heap collection, but attenuates all allocation by the survival rate η

4.3 Bounds for Non-generational Metronome Collectors

In the absence of generational collection, the extra space e_M for Metronome (as described in [1]) is

$$e_M = a\gamma \cdot \left(\frac{m}{R_T} + \frac{s}{R_S} \right) \qquad (3)$$

which is the allocation rate multiplied by the time required to perform a collection, converted into mutator time by the γ factor.

Freeing an object in Metronome-style collectors may take as many as three collections: (1) to collect the object; (2) because the object may have become garbage immediately after a collection began, and will therefore not be discovered until the following collection cycle — floating garbage; and (3) because we may need to relocate the object in order to make use of its space. The first two aspects are common to incremental collectors; the third is specific to Metronome's approach to defragmentation.

$$s_M = (m + 3e_M) \cdot (1 + \rho) \qquad (4)$$

In other words, the maximum space required is the base memory plus three times the extra memory allocated during collection multiplied by the amount of fragmentation.

4.4 Bounds for Our Generational Collector

When performing generational collection, the time spent collecting the nursery reduces the rate of progress of the full heap collection. This in turn means that the mutator performs more allocation during collection. However, with generational collection the allocation into the mature area is also attenuated by the survival rate $\eta(N)$. This effect is shown in Figure 4, expressed by the following equations, in which we define the generational *dilation factor* δ and the corresponding extra space e_G under generational collection:

$$\delta = 1 - \frac{a\eta(N)}{R_N} \cdot \gamma \tag{5}$$

$$e_G = \frac{a\eta(N)\gamma}{\delta} \cdot \left(\frac{m}{R_T} + \frac{s}{R_S}\right) \tag{6}$$

Since our generational collector is fully incremental, we can maintain real-time behavior without limiting the size of the nursery, and therefore use a nursery size which is best suited to the survival rate of the application. However, this flexibility also leads to additional complexities in determining what that size should be.

Since $\eta(N)$ is monotonically decreasing and low η values are crucial to the success of generational collection, let us consider what happens as the nursery size varies. When the nursery size is very small, the collector will spend all its time performing nursery collections because the low survival rate leads to very unproductive nursery collections. In fact, because of the way in which the nursery grows, generational collection will not complete until the nursery grows in size until exactly all of the collection time is spent solely on minor collections at which point

$$\frac{N \cdot \eta(N)}{R_N} = \gamma \frac{N}{a} \tag{7}$$

In other words, N grows until it reaches a minimum tenable size N_{min}:

$$\eta(N_{min}) = \frac{\gamma \cdot R_N}{a} \tag{8}$$

Note that this requires that $R_N > a\eta(N)\gamma$.

When the nursery size is set above this threshold, major collections are given an opportunity to complete and there is a bound on the memory consumption. If the nursery is set arbitrarily large, overall memory consumption increases as the nursery dominates the mature space in size. Between these two extremes is a nursery size which minimizes the overall heap consumption. In order to compute this point and to compare the generational system against the non-generational version, we need to to compute the space bounds of the system.

Of course, the generational version has the additional space cost of the tripartite nursery. As a result, the space requirement of our collector paired with a given application is

$$s_G = (m + 3e_G) \cdot (1 + \rho) + 3N \tag{9}$$

The $(1 + \rho)$ factor is notably absent in the $3N$ term because of the lack of fragmentation in the nurseries. As we pointed out before, the nursery will grow in size until it passes the threshold of equation 8. If the nursery is larger than this crossover point, the heuristic will not grow the nursery in size anymore.

However, continuing to grow the nursery in size will actually diminish overall heap consumption. This can be seen because just above the crossover point, the term δ is infinitesimally positive so that s_G is arbitrarily large. Similarly, when N approaches infinity, s_G is arbitrarily large. Thus, if we hold utilization constant (because it is a target), there must exist, by continuity, a globally minimal overall heap size for some nursery size. Inverting the function to express utilization in terms of s_G gives the achievable utilization for a particular overall heap size.

Note that we are making a steady-state assumption about $\eta(N)$. Since we are collecting the nursery itself incrementally and therefore handle a wide range of nursery sizes, this is reasonable for a large class of real programs. However, there is also a class of programs that have a setup phase which precedes steady-state (or "mission") phase. For such programs the steady-state assumption, when applied to the entire program, may produce overly large nurseries. We will study an example of such a program in Section 5.4. This effect is also present in non-generational real-time collectors, but is exacerbated in generational collectors. For both types of systems, it is desirable to allow the application to explicitly delineate the setup and mission phases, and to either allow real-time bounds to be violated during the setup phase in favor of reduced memory consumption, or to perform a (potentially synchronous) memory compaction between the two phases.

4.5   Comparison with Syncopation

Generational collection in a Metronome-style collector was previously described using a technique called *Syncopation* [4]. Syncopation uses *synchronous* collection of the nursery combined with *flood-gating* — direct allocation into the mature space — when allocation and survival rates are too high for synchronous collection to be performed without violating real-time bounds.

However, with syncopation the nursery size N was not really variable, since the synchronous nursery collection places severe bounds on real-time behavior. With such small nurseries, real-world programs almost always contain spikes in the survival rate such that for all practical N, $\eta(N) \rightarrow 1$. Therefore it was generally necessary to use the largest possible nursery size such that

$$\frac{N}{R_N} = (1 - u)\Delta t \tag{10}$$

$$N = (1 - u)\Delta t R_N \tag{11}$$

The time dilation and extra space calculations then become simpler, such that

$$\delta' = 1 - \frac{N}{R_N} \cdot \gamma \tag{12}$$

$$e_S = \frac{a\gamma}{\delta'} \cdot \left(\frac{m}{R_T} + \frac{s}{R_S}\right) \tag{13}$$

and the space bound for synchronous nursery collection is

$$s_S = (m + 3e_S) \cdot (1 + \rho) + (1 - u)\Delta t R_N \tag{14}$$

Although there is no factor of 3 multiplier on the nursery as for our generational collector (equation 9), the higher survival rates incurred by the much smaller nurseries mean that the space consumption in the mature space increases significantly.

5   Experimental Evaluation

We have implemented our generational algorithm as a modification[1] to the IBM WebSphere Real Time Java virtual machine [2], which uses the non-generational Metronome-based algorithm described in Section 2. Both collectors support the complete Java semantics, including finalization and weak/soft/phantom references.

The syncopated Metronome, discussed in Section 4, is not experimentally compared. The nursery sizes required to achieve low survival rates on non-embedded applications – in the order of 1MB for SPECjvm98 – would incur pauses of at least an order of magnitude beyond the worst-case latencies for the other systems.

All experiments were run on an IBM Intellistation A Pro workstation with dual AMD Opteron 250 processors running at 2.4 GHz with a 1 MB L2 data cache. Total system memory was 4 GB RAM.

The operating system was IBM's real-time version of Linux[2] based on Red Hat Enterprise Linux 4. This includes a number of modifications to reduce latency, in particular the PREEMPT_RT patch with modifications for multi-core/multi-processor systems.

We begin our evaluation with a performance comparison of the generational and non-generational systems across a range of benchmarks. We then demonstrate the effectiveness of the dynamic nursery size at coping with short bursts of allocation. Selecting a highly generational benchmark, jess, we show the importance of large nursery sizes made possible through incremental nursery collection. We then highlight the difficulties in fairly comparing real-time collectors by observing differences between startup and steady-state behavior.

As we are interested in comparing the collector performance of two alternatives, we use a modified *second run* methodology. This methodology involves invoking a benchmark twice within a single JVM invocation, the first *warmup* run performs compilation and optimization, while results are gathered from a second *measurement* run. This methodology better isolates the performance differences due to the collector.

The JIT implementation in our system is not real-time, so it is necessary to disable it during the measurement run. Between the warmup and measurement

---

[1] In addition to adding generational capabilities, we also disabled support for the Real-Time Specification for Java (RTSJ) standard [3] and enabled defragmentation in both the base and generational configurations of the JVM. Therefore, the performance results for our base system are not directly comparable to the product.

[2] `ftp://linuxpatch.ncsa.uiuc.edu/rt-linux/rhel4u2/R1/rtlinux-src-2006-08-30-r541.tar.bz2`

runs we disable the JIT by calling `java.lang.Compiler.disable`, and pause to allow the compilation queue to drain. IBM's real-time JVM also includes an ahead-of-time compiler which could be used to factor out JIT interference, but the generated code is slower than that produced by the JIT and therefore – since the mutator is running slower – does not stress the garbage collector as much.

5.1   Generational vs. Non-generational Comparison

We performed a comparison of the generational and non-generational Metronome using the SPECjvm98 and DaCapo [11] benchmark suites. A summary of the results is shown in Table 1. For the baseline (non-generational) system we show the total run time, and the portions of time spent in mutator and collector (GC). We also show peak memory use, average memory use, and the achieved MMU (based on a target of 70%). For the generational collector, we show values relative to the baseline to facilitate comparison. Figures reported are relative times, the fraction of garbage collection time spent in nursery collection, the relative memory consumption figures, and the achieved MMU.

Table 1. Comparison of non-generational with generational Metronome collector

Bench.	Trigger (MB)	Time (s) Total	Mut.	GC	Mem. (MB) Peak	Avg.	MMU	Relative Time Total	Mut.	GC	Nur. Frac.	Rel. Mem Peak	Avg.	MMU
compress	24, 2	8.99	8.162	0.126	28.77	14.45	70%	0.99	0.98	1.87	84%	1.00	1.01	69%
jess	8, 2	8.162	6.526	1.636	12.16	8.20	69%	0.84	0.94	0.43	77%	0.69	0.80	69%
rayttrace	16, 2	4.501	3.433	1.067	29.28	19.98	69%	0.76	0.90	0.28	81%	0.99	0.55	70%
db	24, 2	13.18	12.38	0.798	32.62	20.17	67%	1.00	1.00	0.89	57%	1.09	1.04	68%
javac	24, 2	6.365	4.99	1.375	49.27	32.78	67%	1.14	1.09	1.35	92%	1.70	2.03	68%
mpegaudio	8, 2	10.24	10.24	0	2.47	2.41	100%	1.01	1.01	1.00	NA	0.78	0.77	100%
mtrt	24, 2	3.126	2.388	0.738	82.97	46.87	69%	0.88	0.97	0.61	75%	0.93	0.55	67%
jack	8, 2	4.222	3.633	0.588	10.48	6.90	69%	0.92	0.97	0.64	81%	0.82	0.90	70%
antlr	20, 4	5.426	5.063	0.362	23.64	14.26	69%	0.94	0.91	1.33	59%	1.03	1.04	68%
bloat	24, 4	30.83	26.99	3.831	45.62	20.24	69%	0.88	0.94	0.47	92%	0.56	0.83	69%
chart	36, 4	159.8	147.5	12.24	51.14	25.55	67%	0.99	1.06	0.24	80%	0.80	1.10	67%
eclipse	64, 8	90.14	77.47	12.67	80.86	66.66	56%	0.95	0.98	0.78	65%	1.23	0.75	67%
fop	24, 4	3.210	2.857	0.353	27.22	22.09	70%	1.00	1.00	0.94	82%	0.89	0.83	69%
hsqldb	144, 16	4.753	4.303	0.450	158.48	116.29	70%	1.47	1.24	3.71	100%	1.11	0.89	63%
jython	20, 4	22.44	18.53	3.911	46.72	24.89	67%	0.93	0.99	0.69	69%	0.76	0.68	63%
luindex	20, 4	17.71	16.59	1.118	21.38	14.86	68%	1.06	1.03	1.41	79%	1.02	1.04	69%
lusearch	36, 8	17.29	13.18	4.114	48.75	34.79	68%	0.97	1.00	0.88	35%	1.11	0.98	66%
pmd	48, 4	30.34	24.98	5.364	71.30	47.00	68%	0.98	0.88	1.42	89%	2.48	1.68	66%
xalan	128, 12	12.49	11.43	1.051	136.86	87.49	64%	1.16	1.11	1.80	71%	1.00	1.04	68%
geomean								0.983	0.997	0.883		0.995	0.93	

For each benchmark, the first column reports the full heap and nursery triggers used for that benchmark. The full heap triggers are based on each program's steady-state allocation rate and maximum live memory size; the nursery trigger was selected by evaluating a range of possibilities (512KB through 16MB) and picking the trigger that enabled the best time/space performance. Note that these are *triggers* and not *heap sizes*. Because of the nature of incremental collection, for a given set of parameters the system may require differing amounts of memory to run without violating its real-time requirements. When comparing stop-the-world collectors, a simpler methodology may be used in which the heap size is fixed and the resulting throughput is measured. With a real-time collector there is an additional degree of freedom, so the comparison is more complex, with an inter-relationship between total run time, total memory usage, and MMU.

The reported memory size includes both the size of the heap and the size of the nursery. This is both to make a fair comparison and it also reflects the nature of our system, in which nursery pages and heap pages are intermingled in physical memory. Note that the full heap collection trigger is with respect to this total usage – that is, it includes the memory being consumed by the nursery.

As predicted by the analytic model presented in Section 4, generational collection is better for many, but not all benchmarks. Overall, it reduces both time and space, with most of the speedup coming from reduction in time spent in the collector. However, time varies from a 24% speedup on `raytrace` to a 47% slowdown on `hsqldb` and space varies from a 44% reduction on `bloat` to a 148% increase on `hsqldb`. Real-time performance (MMU) is essentially the same, with the largest variation being 7% on `hsqldb`. Many benchmarks have short periods where they which they exhibit non-generational behavior, leading to peak memory usage higher than the non-generational system, while average usage across the whole execution is lower. An example is `eclipse`, where the generational system has a peak usage 25% higher, but average memory use is just 75% of the base system over the entire run. Overall, for programs that are at least somewhat generational in their memory allocation and usage patterns, the generational collector offered significant performance benefits. Significant degradations correlated with non-generational memory usage patterns.

5.2   Dynamic Nursery Size

The use of a single pool of pages for both the nursery and the heap, and the ability of the nursery to temporarily consume more than its trigger size, allows our collector to gracefully handle temporary spikes in the allocation rate. Table 2 shows the minimum, mean, and maximum nursery sizes for each benchmark (`mpegaudio` performs so little allocation that it never fills a 2MB nursery, so there is no data for it). Many of the benchmarks do in fact have a maximum nursery size three or more times as large as the nursery trigger, and in the case of `mtrt` the nursery is 15 times as large as the trigger size. As the nursery trigger gets larger, this effect is less dramatic but can still be seen to some degree on most of the benchmarks. These variations show that the dynamically sized nursery is highly effective at absorbing short-term allocation bursts, while maintaining overall space bounds and real-time behavior.

5.3   Parameterization Studies

In Section 4, we discussed analytically the effect of varying the nursery size on total memory consumption. Figure 5 shows the overall performance of the `jess`

Table 2. Dynamic Variation in Nursery Sizes Absorbs Uneven Allocation Rates

Benchmark	Trigger	Mean	Maximum	Std. Dev.
_201_compress	2.0	5.3	6.0	1.37
_202_jess	2.0	2.0	2.4	0.02
_205_raytrace	2.0	2.2	9.6	0.85
_209_db	2.0	2.2	6.2	0.67
_213_javac	2.0	2.9	7.1	1.31
_222_mpegaudio	—	—	—	—
_227_mtrt	2.0	2.8	31.7	3.96
_228_jack	2.0	2.0	2.1	0.01
antlr	4.0	4.05	4.31	0.05
bloat	4.0	4.05	4.31	0.02
chart	4.0	4.05	4.39	0.04
eclipse	8.0	8.04	8.97	0.07
fop	4.0	4.05	4.17	0.04
hsqldb	16.0	25.30	39.97	8.45
jython	4.0	4.11	5.48	0.20
luindex	4.0	4.03	4.06	0.004
lusearch	8	8.07	8.36	0.07
pmd	4.0	5.28	17.39	2.61
xalan	12.0	12.04	12.05	0.005

benchmark as we vary the nursery size from 256KB to 3072KB. We choose jess as it is highly generational and therefore allows us to clearly see the effect of altering the nursery trigger. Non-generational programs are likely to perform poorly on all feasible nursery sizes. Both the time and space measurements are point-wise normalized against the non-generational system. The most dramatic effect is that at low nursery sizes, the memory usage spikes upwards (beyond the range of the graph) as predicted by divergence condition in equation 7. Somewhere around a 512KB nursery size, the memory consumption of the generational and non-generational system are similar. Around 1.5MB, further increases in the nursery size do not improve the efficiency of the nursery collections so that the mature space does not decrease fast enough to compensate for the triple increase in space that the $3N$ term charges so that memory consumption begins to increase. Note that total time spent in nursery collections also monotonically decreases as we increase the nursery size as the total amount of data that is promoted decreases as $\eta(N)$ decreases. Mutator time is fairly consistent across nursery sizes and the shape of the total execution time mutedly follows the shape of the GC Time.

Figure 6 shows the dynamic behavior of memory consumption and mutator utilization of the jess benchmark when the nursery size is set to 3 different regimes. Generally, as we increase the nursery size, the overall efficiency of collection improves and total time spent in garbage collection decreases. For the very low nursery size of 256KB in sub-figure (a), all the time is spent in minor collections and the nursery is barely big enough for even a minor collection to complete. Consequently overall memory consumption is unbounded as the mature space keeps growing. The thick band shows that the utilization is always oscillating between 72% to 85% indicating that the GC has no breathing room at all. When the nursery trigger size is doubled as in sub-figure (b), the nursery

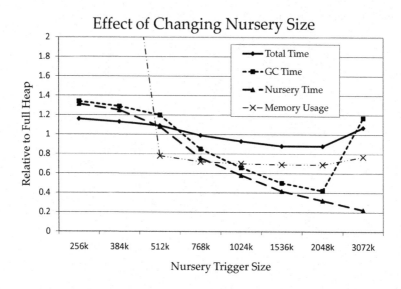

Fig. 5. Effect of changing nursery size for _202_jess with an 8m mature trigger

collections complete before the subsequent nursery is filled, allowing major collection work to occur and leading to a bounded mature heap size of around 9MB.
Utilization is not as constant as the GC does not have to work as hard so that
mutator utilization is occasionally around 90% and each major GC generally
take half a second. When nursery size is further increased as in sub-figure (c),
minor collections complete early enough that a large fraction of overall collection
time can be spent in major collection that each major collection takes only a
tenth of a second. Often, there are no active collections(either major or minor) so
that overall utilization reaches 100% and averages around 85%. Because overall
efficiency is improved, the heap consumption is 8.25MB and is actually lower
even though the nursery is larger.

5.4   Startup vs. Steady State Behavior

Figure 7 shows the memory consumption of pseudojbb under both systems.
This benchmark begins by setting up several large data structures and then
runs many transactions each of which slightly modify the pre-existing large data
structures. In the first phase, both the allocation rate and the survival rate is
high. As a result, the generational system's nursery is unable to absorb the allocation completely and must grow. During this period, as objects are promoted,
there are often two copies of portions of the long-lived data structures. In this
phase, the nurseries cause the memory consumption to be 45% higher than that
of the non-generational system. However, once we reach the "mission" phase of

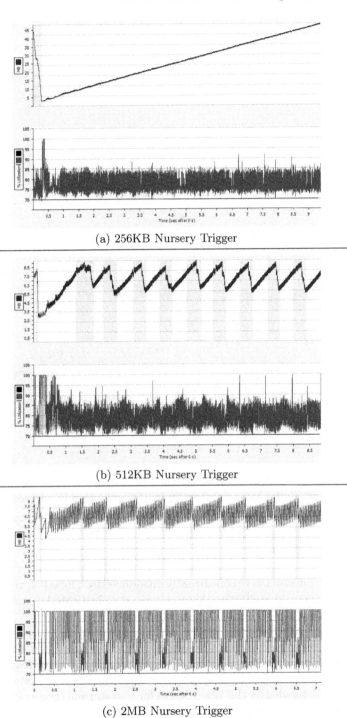

(a) 256KB Nursery Trigger

(b) 512KB Nursery Trigger

(c) 2MB Nursery Trigger

Fig. 6. Performance of _202_jess with varying nursery trigger and 8m mature trigger

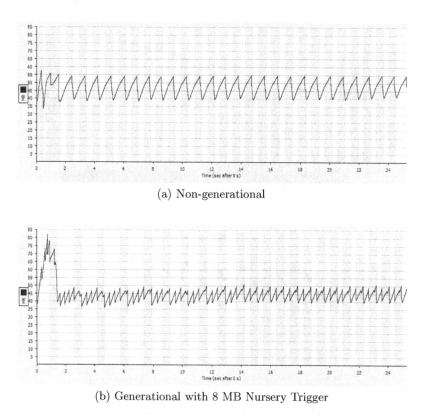

(a) Non-generational

(b) Generational with 8 MB Nursery Trigger

Fig. 7. Memory usage over time of pseudojbb under non-generational and generational collection

the application (about 1.8 seconds into the run), the greater efficiency of the generational system dominates, resulting in a 10% reduction in space consumption and less time spent in garbage collection.

6   Related Work

Generational collectors were concurrently introduced by Ungar [12] and Moon [13] and have proven to be so effective that many more sophisticated partial-heap techniques have been unable to match its performance.

A number of other systems have combined generational and concurrent collection. Doligez et al. [5] developed a collector for ML which exploited the large proportion of immutable objects by allocating them in independently collected nurseries. Nursery collection was synchronous and thread-local. Domani et al. [14] subsequently expanded on this basic design for a concurrent, non-compacting collector in which nursery collection was also concurrent. However, both collectors do not perform generational collection during tenured space collection, which is a fundamental requirement in our system for maintaining real-time behavior.

Yuasa [8] introduced a snapshot-style incremental collector. Unlike incremental update collectors, Yuasa's collector operated on a virtual snapshot of the object graph at the time collection started. Yuasa's algorithm results in more floating garbage and requires a more expensive write barrier, but is better suited to real-time collection since operations by the mutator can not "undo" the work done by the collector.

Baker [6] was the first to attack the problem of real-time garbage collection. As we discussed in Section 2, his technique fundamentally suffers from using work-based, event-triggered scheduling, and from evaluating real-time properties from the point of view of the collector rather than the application. The result is fundamentally soft real-time (best effort) rather than hard real-time (guaranteed) response.

There have been many incremental and soft real-time collectors since then, exploring various aspects of the design space, such as the use of virtual memory support [15] and coarse-grained replication with a synchronous nursery [16]. However, there is no guarantee on the maximum pause time.

While most previous work on real-time collection has focused on work-based scheduling, there are some notable exceptions. In particular, Henriksson [17] implemented a Brooks-style collector [10] in which application processes are divided into two priority levels: for high-priority tasks (assumed to be periodic with bounded compute time and allocation requirements), memory is pre-allocated and the system is tailored to allow mutator operations to proceed quickly.

Cheng and Blelloch [7] described a time-triggered real-time multiprocessor replicating collector with excellent utilization, for which they introduced the minimum mutator utilization (MMU) metric, a generic application-oriented measure of the behavior of a concurrent collector. However, MMU was measured rather than guaranteed, and space overheads were large. A generational variant was presented but the replication-based techniques and need for an atomic flip meant pointer arrays doubled in size as each logical slot required two physical slots.

The Metronome collector of Bacon et al. [1] was the first guaranteed hard real-time collector. This collector provided guaranteed MMU based on the the characterization of the application in terms of maximum live memory and allocation rate. Space overhead was usually comparable to that required by synchronous ("stop-the-world") collectors, due to incremental defragmentation and quantitative bounding of all sources of memory loss [18].

Bacon et al. [4] introduced a real-time generational collector that used a synchronous ("stop-the-world") nursery collector [4]. Though this works well for embedded benchmarks with nurseries in the tens of kilobytes, larger nurseries quickly push maximum pause times into the tens of milliseconds. This effect is exacerbated by the need to "over-sample" (collecting the nursery multiple times within a single MMU quantum) in order to avoid pathological behavior during allocation rate spikes. This forces the use of smaller nurseries, which increases survival rate and lowers the effectiveness of generational collection.

7 Conclusion

We have presented a new algorithm for performing generational collection incrementally in real-time, based on a tri-partite nursery which overlaps allocation, collection, and defragmentation. Generational collection can be interleaved with incremental real-time collection of the mature space at any point. The resulting algorithm allows the use of large nurseries that lead to low survival rates, and yet is capable of achieving sub-millisecond latencies and high worst-case utilization.

We have implemented this new algorithm in a product-based real-time Java virtual machine, and evaluated analytically and experimentally the situations under which our generational collector is superior to a non-generational real-time collector. Programs with inherently non-generational behavior and programs whose setup phase includes unusually high survival and allocation rates, will require more space to achieve the corresponding real-time bounds. However, the results show that for most programs, generational collection achieves comparable real-time bounds while leading to an improvement in space consumption, throughput, or both.

References

1. Bacon, D.F., Cheng, P., Rajan, V.T.: A real-time garbage collector with low overhead and consistent utilization. In: Proceedings of the 30th Annual ACM SIGPLAN-SIGACT Symposium on Principles of Programming Languages, New Orleans, Louisiana, pp. 285–298. ACM Press, New York (2003)
2. IBM Corporation: WebSphere Real Time Java virtual machine (August 2006) http://www.ibm.com/software/webservers/realtime
3. Bollella, G., et al,: The Real-Time Specification for Java. In: The Java Series, Addison-Wesley, UK (2000)
4. Bacon, D.F., Cheng, P., Grove, D., Vechev, M.T.: Syncopation: generational real-time garbage collection in the Metronome. In: Proceedings of the ACM Conference on Languages, Compilers, and Tools for Embedded Systems, pp. 183–192. Chicago, Illinois (June 2005)
5. Doligez, D., Leroy, X.: A concurrent generational garbage collector for a multi-threaded implementation of ML. In: Conf. Record of the Twentieth ACM Symposium on Principles of Programming Languages, pp. 113–123. ACM Press, New York (1993)
6. Baker, H.G.: List processing in real-time on a serial computer. Communications of the ACM 21(4), 280–294 (1978)
7. Cheng, P., Blelloch, G.: A parallel, real-time garbage collector. In: Proc. of the SIGPLAN Conference on Programming Language Design and Implementation, Snowbird, Utah, pp. 125–136 (June 2001)
8. Yuasa, T.: Real-time garbage collection on general-purpose machines. Journal of Systems and Software 11(3), 181–198 (1990)
9. Jones, R., Lins, R.: Garbage Collection. John Wiley and Sons, Chichester (1996)
10. Brooks, R.A.: Trading data space for reduced time and code space in real-time garbage collection on stock hardware. In: Steele, G.L. (ed.) Conference Record of the 1984 ACM Symposium on Lisp and Functional Programming, Austin, Texas, pp. 256–262. ACM Press, New York (1984)

11. Blackburn, S.M., Garner, R., Hoffmann, C., Khang, A.M., McKinley, K.S., Bentzur, R., Diwan, A., Feinberg, D., Frampton, D., Guyer, S.Z., Hirzel, M., Hosking, A., Jump, M., Lee, H., Eliot, J., Moss, B., Phansalkar, A., Stefanović, D., VanDrunen, T., von Dincklage, D., Wiedermann, B.: The dacapo benchmarks: Java benchmarking development and analysis. In: OOPSLA '06: Proceedings of the 21st annual ACM SIGPLAN conference on Object-oriented programming systems, languages, and applications, pp. 169–190. ACM Press, New York (2006)
12. Ungar, D.M.: Generation scavenging: A non-disruptive high performance storage reclamation algorithm. In: Henderson, P. (ed.) Proceedings of the ACM SIGSOFT/SIGPLAN Software Engineering Symposium on Practical Software Development Environments, Pittsburgh, Pennsylvania, pp. 157–167. ACM Press, New York (1984)
13. Moon, D.A.: Garbage collection in a large LISP system. In: Conference Record of the 1984 ACM Symposium on LISP and Functional Programming, Austin, Texas, pp. 235–246. ACM Press, New York (1984)
14. Domani, T., Kolodner, E.K., Petrank, E.: A generational on-the-fly garbage collector for Java. In: Proc. of the SIGPLAN Conference on Programming Language Design and Implementation, pp. 274–284 (June 2000)
15. Appel, A.W., Ellis, J.R., Li, K.: Real-time concurrent collection on stock multiprocessors. In: Proceedings of the SIGPLAN'88 Conference on Programming Language Design and Implementation, Atlanta, Georgia, pp. 11–20 (June 1988)
16. Nettles, S., O'Toole, J.: Real-time garbage collection. In: Proc. of the SIGPLAN Conference on Programming Language Design and Implementation, pp. 217–226 (June 1993)
17. Henriksson, R.: Scheduling Garbage Collection in Embedded Systems. PhD thesis, Lund Institute of Technology (July 1998)
18. Bacon, D.F., Cheng, P., Rajan, V.T.: Controlling fragmentation and space consumption in the Metronome, a real-time garbage collector for Java. In: Proceedings of the Conference on Languages, Compilers, and Tools for Embedded Systems, San Diego, California, pp. 81–92 (June 2003)

AS-GC: An Efficient Generational Garbage Collector for Java Application Servers

Feng Xian, Witawas Srisa-an, ChengHuan Jia, and Hong Jiang

Computer Science and Engineering
University of Nebraska-Lincoln
Lincoln, NE 68588-0115
{fxian,witty,cjia,jiang}@cse.unl.edu

Abstract. A generational collection strategy utilizing a single nursery cannot efficiently manage objects in application servers due to variance in their lifespans. In this paper, we introduce an optimization technique designed for application servers that exploits an observation that *remotable* objects are commonly used as gateways for client requests. Objects instantiated as part of these requests (*remote objects*) often live longer than objects *not created* to serve these remote requests (*local objects*). Thus, our scheme creates remote and local objects in two separate nurseries; each is properly sized to match the lifetime characteristic of the residing objects. We extended the generational collector in HotSpot to support the proposed optimization and found that given the same heap size, the proposed scheme can improve the maximum throughput of an application server by 14% over the default collector. It also allows the application server to handle 10% higher workload prior to memory exhaustion.

1 Introduction

Garbage collection (GC) is one of many features that make Java so attractive for the development of complex software systems, especially but not limited to, application servers. GC improves programmer productivity by reducing errors caused by explicit memory management. Moreover, it promotes good software engineering practice that can lead to cleaner code since memory management functions are no longer interleaved with the program logic [1, 2]. As of now, one of the most adopted GC strategies is *generational garbage collection* [3, 4].

Generational GC is based on the hypothesis that "most objects die young", and thus, concentrates its collection effort in the *nursery*, a memory area used for object creation [4]. Currently, generational collectors are configured to have only one nursery because such a configuration has proven to work well in desktop environments. However, recent studies have found the configuration to be inefficient in large server applications [5, 6] because they frequently create objects that cannot be classified as either short-lived or long-lived. Such a variance in lifespans can result in two major performance issues in any single-nursery generational collectors.

1. *A large volume of promoted objects.* If the nursery size is too small, objects with longer lifespans are promoted and then die soon after promotion. In this situation,

E. Ernst (Ed.): ECOOP 2007, LNAI 4609, pp. 126–150, 2007.
© Springer-Verlag Berlin Heidelberg 2007

the time spent in promoting objects and higher frequency of full heap collection invocations can result in longer collection pauses and more time spent in GC.

2. *Delayed collection of dead objects.* If the nursery size is large enough to allow longer living objects more time to die, short-lived objects are not collected in a timely fashion. This scenario can result in larger heap requirement, poor heap utilization, and higher paging efforts [7, 8].

1.1 This Work

We introduce the notion of *remote* and *local* objects as a framework for identifying objects with similar lifespans in application servers. The proposed framework exploits the *key objects* notion [9], which leverages temporal locality to cluster objects with similar lifespans. In Java application servers, *remotable* objects are commonly used as gateways for client requests. Once a request arrives, many more objects are created, forming a cluster, to perform the requested service. Once the request is satisfied, most of these objects die. Studies have shown that objects connected to remotable objects tend to have longer lifespans than other short-lived objects in an application [5, 6]. Thus, our technique considers these *remotable* objects as the *key* objects and any objects connected to these remotable objects as *remote objects*. We then refer to the remaining objects as *local objects*.

We then present a new generational collector based on the notion of *remote* and *local* objects. Our garbage collector is optimized based on the hypothesis that remote and local objects have different lifespan characteristics. Therefore, managing them in two separate nurseries (i.e. local nursery and remote nursery) will result in better garbage collection efficiency, as each nursery can be optimally sized based on the allocation volume and lifespan characteristic of the residing objects. Garbage collection in each nursery can be done independently of the other nursery, and the surviving objects from both nurseries are promoted to a shared mature generation. A low-overhead run-time component is used to dynamically identify and segregate remote and local objects. We have extended the generational collector in the HotSpot virtual machine (we refer to the HotSpot's collector as the *default* collector) to support the proposed optimization technique (we refer to the optimized version as the *collector for application server* or *AS-GC*). We then compared the performance of AS-GC with that of the highly tuned default collector. The results of our experiments indicate that our proposed scheme yields the following three benefits.

1. *Timely object reclamation.* The results show that the minor collectors of the local and remote nurseries are called more frequently, and each time, the percentage of surviving objects is lower than that of the default collector. Higher frequency of minor collection invocations means that our approach attempts to recycle objects quickly. Higher efficiency means that fewer objects are promoted, leading to shorter pauses, fewer major collection invocations, and less time spent in garbage collection.

2. *Higher throughput.* Given the same heap space, our collector yields 14% higher maximum throughput than that of the default collector. This improvement is achieved with negligible runtime overhead.

3. *Higher workload.* With the default collector, the throughput performance degrades significantly due to memory exhaustion when the workload reaches a certain level. Because our scheme is more memory efficient, it can operate with less heap space. Therefore, it can handle 10% higher workload before the same exhaustion is encountered.

Even though our proposed solution is domain-specific, it should have great potentials for a wider adoption by language designers and practitioners as the application server market is one of the biggest adoptors of Java [10]. It is worth noting that our approach is significantly different from the existing techniques to improve the efficiency of garbage collection (e.g. pretenuring, older-first, and Beltway [1, 11, 12, 13]). However, our approach can also be integrated with these techniques to achieve even higher GC efficiencies.

The remainder of this paper is organized as follows. Section 2 describes the preliminary studies and discusses the results that motivate this work. Section 3 provides an overview of the proposed technique and implementation details. Section 4 details the experimental environment. Section 5 describes each experiment and reports the results. Section 6 further discusses the results of our work. Section 7 provides an applicability study of this work. Section 8 highlights some of the related work, and the last section concludes this paper.

2 Why Design a Garbage Collector for Application Servers?

"It has been proven that for any possible allocation algorithm, there will always be the possibility that some application program will allocate and deallocate blocks in some fashion that defeats the allocator's strategy."

Paul R. Wilson *et al.* [14]

The same argument can be made about garbage collection. Most garbage collectors, shipped as part of any commercial Java Virtual Machines (JVMs), are based on the generational approach utilizing a single nursery. While such a collection strategy has worked well for Java over the past decade, studies have shown that objects in Java application servers may not always be short-lived [5, 6], leading to an inefficiency of any single-nursery generational collector.

Longer living objects in these server applications can degrade the efficiency of these collectors. When this happens, the throughput performance of these server applications can seriously suffer. Such inefficiency can also result in poor memory utilization [7], leading to a large number of page faults under heavy workload, ungraceful degradation of throughputs and failures [6].

In the remainder of this section, we highlight some of the differences in run-time characteristics between *desktop applications* and *application servers*. We then report the result of our experiments to investigate the lifespan characteristics in these applications and the differences in the performance of generational collection in these two types of applications.

Table 1. Comparing the basic characteristics of SPECjvm98, SPECjbb2000, and SPEC-jAppServer2004

Characteristic	SPECjvm98	SPECjbb2000 (8 warehouses)	SPECjAppServer2004 (Trans. rate = 40)
# of simultaneous threads	5 (in MTRT)	11	331
# of allocated objects	8 million (in Jess)	33 million	80 million
Amount of allocated space	231 (in db) MB	900 MB	5.1 GB
Total execution time	seconds	minutes	hours

2.1 Basic Characteristics of Application Servers

Application servers often face significant variations in service demands, the higher demands often coincide with "the times when the service has the most value" [15]. Thus, these servers are expected to maintain responsiveness, robustness, and availability regardless of the changing demands. Past studies have shown that under the heaviest workload, the resource usage can be so intense that, often times, these servers would suddenly fail with little or no warning [6, 16, 17, 18].

To better understand the differences in resource usage between desktop applications and application servers, we conducted an experiment to compare their basic runtime characteristics (see Table 1). We used SPECjvm98, SPECjbb2000, and SPEC-jAppServer2004 in our study. SPECjvm98 [19] is a commonly used benchmark suite in the research community. All applications in the suite are designed to run well in general purpose workstations. SPECjbb2000 [20] is a server benchmark designed to emulate the application server tier. It does not make any connections to external services (e.g. database connections). On the other hand, SPECjAppServer2004 [21] is a benchmark for real-world application servers designed to run on high-performance computer systems (more information about this benchmark is available in Section 4).

From Table 1, the differences in memory requirement and degree of concurrency can translate to much higher resource usage in server applications. However, they do not yield any insights into the differences in lifespan of objects between these two types of applications. Therefore, we conducted further experiments to compare their lifespan characteristics.

2.2 An Experiment to Evaluate Lifespans of Objects in Server Applications

We measured lifespan by the amount of memory allocated between birth and death (in bytes)[1]. We measured the execution progress by the accumulated amount of allocated memory (also in bytes) [11]. Figure 1 depicts our findings.

The vast majority of objects in *Jess*, a benchmark program in the SPECjvm98 suite, are short-lived; that is, most objects have lifespans of less than 10% of the maximum lifespan (as illustrated in 1a). Note that we also conducted similar studies using other

---

[1] We only accounted for objects allocated in the garbage-collected heap and ignored any objects created in the permanent space.

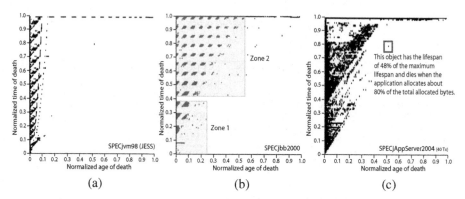

Fig. 1. Each dot in these graphs represents an object. The x-axis represents the normalized age of death, and the y-axis represents the normalized time of death. Thus, the position of each dot provides us with the age of that particular object and the time that it dies. For example, the squared object in the SPECjAppServer2004 graph (c) has a lifespan of 48% of the maximum lifespan and dies when the application allocates about 80% of the total allocated bytes.

applications in the SPECjvm98 benchmark suite and found their results to be very similar to Jess. For brevity, we do not include the results of those studies. The results of our study nicely conform to the "weak generational hypothesis" (most objects die young), which is the cornerstone of generational garbage collection [3, 4].

On the other hand, large numbers of objects in the SPECjbb2000 with 8 warehouses (Figure 1b) and SPECjAppServer2004 with 40 Tx (Figure 1c) have lifespans of up to 30% to 50% of the maximum lifespans. It is worth noting that there are more objects with longer lifespans as these programs approach termination (as indicated by the triangular patterns). This is to be expected as the amount of work in each benchmark becomes heavier as the program continues to run. For example, SPECjbb2000 starts with a single warehouse and creates one more warehouse each time it finishes making the queries. In our experiment, this process continues until 8 warehouses are created. It is worth noting that the clusters of dead objects (appeared in Figure 1b as groups of dark spots) correspond to the number of warehouses created and worked on by the application.

Our past research effort on .NET server applications also indicates a similar lifespan behavior to the Java server benchmarks [5]. We hypothesize that such behavior is a result of a high degree of concurrency in these server applications (see more discussion about this issue in Section 6). If concurrency is indeed the main factor for such a lifespan behavior, it is also possible for multithreaded desktop applications to exhibit a similar behavior. Since most of the available desktop benchmarks are not heavily multithreaded, we have yet to conduct further experiments to validate our hypothesis. Such experiments will be left for future work.

Next, we conducted an experiment to investigate the efficacy of the generational collector in the SPECjbb2000 benchmark. Our investigation focused on two execution areas: the first 40% of execution (*zone 1* of Figure 1b) where most objects are still short-lived and the last 60% of execution (*zone 2* of Figure 1b) where most objects are long-lived. We observed the following results.

1. *Generational collector performs efficiently in zone 1.* Figure 1b clearly shows that objects in this zone can be easily segregated into short-lived and long-lived. While executing in this zone, the generational scheme performs very efficiently.

2. *Generational collector is not efficient in zone 2.* Figure 1b shows that the lifespans cannot be easily classified into the short-lived and long-lived taxonomy. Therefore, the generational collector begins to lose its efficiency upon entering this zone. We also noticed that the heap size is increased dramatically even though the number of objects created in this zone is only twice as much as that of zone 1.

The lifespan behavior as depicted in zone 2 poses two important challenges to generational collectors. First, *if the nursery size is set too small, minor collection may promote a significant number of objects.* A large volume of promoted objects can cause the pause times to be long. Moreover, these promoted objects can result in more frequent collection of the older generation. This observation is reported by Xian et al. [6].

Second, the nursery may need to be set to a much larger size to allow objects with diverse lifespans sufficient time to die. Our study shows that the performance differences due to larger nursery sizes without increasing the overall heap size, are not noticeable. To yield a better performance, the entire heap space must be enlarged to provide a sufficient GC headroom. With a larger nursery, *the truly short-lived objects are not collected in a timely fashion and continue to occupy the heap space*, resulting in a much larger heap requirement, as noted in zone 2 and reported by Hertz and Berger [7].

In the next section, we provide the detailed information about the proposed generational collector designed to address these two challenges.

3   A Generational Collector for Application Servers (AS-GC)

In this section, we discuss a notion called *key objects* that is used to optimize the proposed generational strategy. We also discuss three major runtime components, dynamic objects segregation mechanism, nurseries management, and inter-type reference tracking mechanism that we implemented in HotSpot.

3.1   Defining Key Objects

Our work leverages the previous research on *Key Objects* to dynamically identify clusters of similar-lifespan objects [9]. Hayes defines *key objects* as "clusters of objects that are allocated at roughly the same time, and live for roughly the same length of time" [9]. In other words, the idea is to segregate objects into groups based on temporal locality and lifespan similarity. Our technique considers *remotable* objects as the key objects. Any objects connected to these remotable objects become part of their clusters and are assumed to have similar lifespan [9, 22, 23]. As stated earlier, these objects are referred to as remote objects, and any objects that are not part of these clusters are referred to as local objects. These two types of objects, once identified, will be managed in two separate nurseries.

3.2 Dynamic Objects Segregation

Our next step is to efficiently segregate local and remote objects. While the segregation process can be done statically [24], we chose a dynamic scheme because the distinction between remote and local objects can be easily done at run-time. Our scheme detects when remote methods are invoked. While these remote methods are still in scope, any newly allocated objects are considered remote.

In HotSpot [25], methods, classes and threads are implemented by *methodOop, KlassOop* and *Thread* objects, respectively. To segregate remote and local objects, we added a new flag bit, *is_remote* to *methodOop* to indicate that the corresponding method is remote. If a method belongs to any interfaces that extend *java.rmi.Remote* (e.g., some enterprise Beans, EJBHome or EJBObject interface), we set this flag. Otherwise, the flag remains unset.

For each thread, we also added a simple attribute *CallTreeDepth* to record the depth of the current call tree on the thread. At every method entry and exit, the *CallTreeDepth* is incremented or decremented accordingly. Particularly, when a thread first makes a remote method call, the method's information and the depth of the call tree are recorded. When a remote method call exits, the corresponding recorded information is also deleted. If a thread still maintains information about a remote method call, it means that the remote method call is still in scope, so all objects created during this time are categorized as remote objects.

There are two major sources of overhead in the type segregation process: bookkeeping of remote method calls and remote/local-type checking. In our implementation, three comparison operations are performed at every method entry and exit. In type-checking, only two comparison operations are needed to determine if an object is remote. Through experiments, we found the overhead of the type segregation process to be roughly 1% of the total execution time.

3.3 Local and Remote Nurseries

Organization: Once the type of an object is identified, the next step is to create the local and remote nurseries to host local and remote objects, respectively. Since we are extending the heap organization of HotSpot to support our proposed scheme, we first outline the heap layout adopted by HotSpot (as shown in Figure 2a).

The HotSpot VM partitions the heap into three major generations: nursery, mature, and permanent, which is not shown in Figure 2. The nursery is further partitioned into three areas: *eden* and two survivor spaces, *from* and *to*, which account for 20% of the nursery (i.e. the ratio of the eden to the survivor spaces is 4:1). Object allocations initially take place in the *eden* space. If the *eden* space is full, and there is available space in the *from* space, the *from* space is used to service subsequent allocation requests.

Figure 2b illustrates our heap organization. Our technique simply extends the existing heap organization to create two nurseries instead of just one. Within each nursery, the heap layout is similar to that of HotSpot (an eden space and two survivor spaces). The local and remote nurseries can be individually and optimally sized to match the lifespan characteristics of the local and remote objects, respectively.

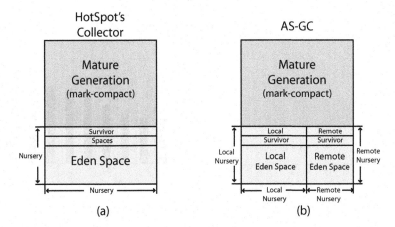

Both schemes use copying collection to promote surviving objects
from the nurseries to the mature generation.

Fig. 2. Comparing the heap organizations of HotSpot and the proposed AS-GC

Garbage collection in HotSpot. We refer to the collection scheme in HotSpot as *GenMS*. In this technique, *minor collection* is invoked when both the *eden* and *from* spaces are full. The collection process consists mainly of copying any surviving objects into the *to* space and then reversing the names of the two survivor spaces (i.e. *from* space becomes *to* space, and vice versa). Thus, the *to* space is always empty prior to a minor collection invocation [25].

The *to* space provides an aging area for longer living objects to die within the nursery, assuming that the volume of surviving objects is not larger than the size of the *to* space. If this assumption does not hold, some surviving objects are then copied directly to the mature generation. When the space in the mature generation is exhausted, *full* or *mature* collection based on mark-compact algorithm is used to collect the entire heap. It is worth noting that the aging area is only effective when the number of copied objects from the eden and the *from* spaces is small. If the number of surviving objects becomes too large (such as in application servers), most of these objects are promoted directly to the mature generation, leading to more frequent mature collection invocations.

Sizing of each nursery: The process to identify the optimal nursery sizes consists of two steps. First, we conducted a set of experiments to identify the optimal ratio between the nursery and the mature space in GenMS. We found that the nursery to mature ratio (*nursery/mature ratio*) of 1:2 (i.e. 33% nursery and 67% mature) yields the optimal throughput performance for our benchmark. This ratio is then used to further configure the local and remote nurseries; that is, the sum of the local and remote nurseries is equal to the nursery size of GenMS. As a reminder, our research objective is to show that our technique is more efficient than GenMS, given the same heap space, and thus, the same nursery size is used.

The second step involves conducting another set of experiments to identify the *local/remote ratio* (size of local nursery / size of remote nursery). We initially anticipated

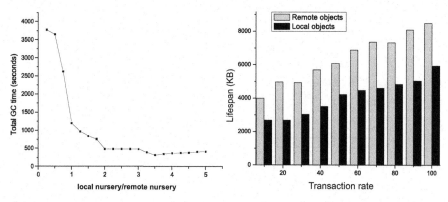

Fig. 3. Identifying optimal local/remote ratio

Fig. 4. Lifespans of remote and local objects in GenMS

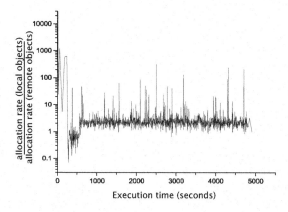

Fig. 5. Allocation rate is defined as the volume of allocated bytes over a period of time. In this experiment, we considered the allocation rates of remote and local objects separately. We then calculated the ratio of local allocation rates to remote allocation rates throughout the execution.

the remote nursery to be larger than the local nursery due to the results of previous studies indicating that the remote objects are longer living. To our surprise, the result of our experiment (depicted in Figure 3) indicates that the local nursery should be at least 3 times larger than the remote nursery.

To better understand why our result is counter-intuitive, we conducted an experiment to validate the previous claims that remote objects are longer living [5, 6]. Our result clearly shows that the claim is valid; remote objects indeed live significantly longer than local objects (see Figure 4). We then investigated the allocation behavior and discovered a valuable insight. The median allocation rate (volume of allocated objects over time) of local objects is three times higher than that of remote objects (see Figure 5). Periodically, the allocation rates of the local objects can be several hundred times higher than those of remote objects. We also noticed that during the initial phase of execution, there are no allocations of remote objects at all. This is expected as all services must be initialized locally prior to taking remote requests.

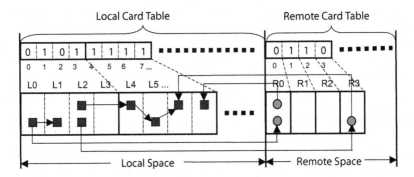

Fig. 6. Each round object represents a remote object, and each square object represents a local object. The nurseries are divided into 128-byte blocks; each block is represented by one byte card allocated in a separated card table area. Initially, each byte is set to the value of 1. When an inter-nursery reference is made (write-barrier is used to detect such a reference), the card representing the memory block that contains the inter-nursery reference becomes dirtied and is assigned the value of 0. In the example shown here, there are four inter-nursery references originated from memory blocks L0, L2, R0 and R3; thus, those cards have the value of 0.

This finding suggests that a possible dominating factor in determining the local/remote ratio is the allocation rate. It is also very likely that the allocation rate can influence the lifespans of objects in GenMS (will be discussed in Section 6).

3.4 Tracking Inter-nursery References

It is possible for objects to make inter-nursery references (i.e. a reference originated from the remote nursery to an object in the local nursery, and vice versa). Thus, we need a mechanism to track these inter-nursery references. Through a preliminary experiment, we discovered that it is common for the number of references from the remote nursery to the local nursery to be as many as 20 times higher than those from the local nursery to the remote nursery. This is likely because many of the services in these servers are done by worker threads created during the initialization. This observation led us to design a card table mechanism that uses two different scanning granularities for the local and remote nurseries to reduce scanning time. Figure 6 illustrates the organization of our card tables.

When a minor collection is invoked in the local nursery, the *remote card table* is scanned to locate any inter-nursery references coming from the remote nursery in a *fine-grained way* (byte by byte). This is because the volume of the inter-nursery references coming form the remote space tends to be very high. For each encountered dirty card, the memory block is further scanned to locate inter-nursery references. Note that the mechanism to record inter-generational references (references from the mature space to the nurseries) [4, 2] is already provided by HotSpot. Thus, we do not need to implement such a mechanism.

On the contrary, when a minor collection is invoked in the remote nursery, the *local card table* is scanned in a *coarse-grained way* (word by word[2]). This is because there

---

[2] In our experimental system, one word is corresponding to four bytes.

are fewer inter-nursery references originated from the local space. For every dirty word, the collector then identifies each dirty card within the word before proceeding to scan the corresponding memory block to locate any potential inter-nursery references. So for the local card table, each card is marked in the fine-grained way but scanned in the coarse-grained way, and thereby, reducing the cost of scanning.

4   Experimental Environment

In this section, we describe our experimental environment consisting of an application server and a benchmark program. We also provide the detailed information about the computing platforms and the operating environments in which the experiments were conducted.

4.1   Application Server and Workload Driver

There are two major software components in our experiment, the Application Servers and the workload drivers. We investigated several server benchmarks and selected JBoss [26] as our application server. JBoss is by far the most popular open-source Java Application Server (with 25% of market share and over fifteen million downloads to date). It fully supports J2EE 1.4 with advanced optimizations including object cache to reduce the overhead of object creation. Note that MySQL[3] is used as the database server in our experimental environment.

In addition to identifying the application server, we need to identify workload drivers that create realistic client/server environments. We chose an application server benchmark, jAppServer2004 from SPEC [21], which is a standardized benchmark for testing the performance of Java Application Servers. It emulates an automobile manufacturing company and its associated dealerships. The level of workload can be configured by *transaction rate* (Tx). This workload stresses the ability of the Web and EJB containers to handle the complexities of memory management, connection pooling, passivation/activation, caching, etc. The throughput of the benchmark is measured in JOPS (job operations per second).

4.2   Experimental Platforms

To deploy SPECjAppServer2004, we used three machines to construct the three-tier architecture. The client machine is an Apple PowerMac with 2x2GHz PowerPC G5 processors with 2 GB of memory and runs Mac OS-X. The application server is a single-processor 1.6 GHz Athlon with 1GB of memory. The database server is a Sun Blade with dual 2GHz AMD Opteron processors with 2GB of memory. The database machine and the application server run Fedora Core 2 Linux.

In all experiments, we used the HotSpot VM shipped as part of the Sun J2SE 1.4.2 [25] to run the JBoss application server. Unless specified differently in the next section, the heap space was limited to 2 GB (twice the amount of physical memory). The

---

[3] Visit www.mysql.com for more information.

nursery/mature ratio was set to the optimal value of 1:2, and the local/remote ratio was selected to be 3:1. We conducted all experiments in a standalone mode with all non-essential daemons and services shut down.

5   Results and Analysis

In this section, we report the experimental results focusing on the following performance metrics: garbage collection time, garbage collection efficiency and frequency, maximum throughput, memory requirement, and workload capacity.

5.1   Garbage Collection Behaviors

We first measured the GC frequency. As shown in Table 2, our collector invokes the minor collection more frequently than the GenMS approach. This is not necessarily a bad thing. Higher frequency of minor collection invocations can translate to reduced heap requirement if each of these invocations is effective in collecting dead objects. As reported in the table, the average survival rate[4] of the proposed scheme is consistently lower than that of GenMS when the same transaction rate is applied. Because the local and remote nurseries are also smaller than the nursery in GenMS, the volume of the promoted objects in our scheme is also lower.

Table 2. Comparing survival rates

Normalized workload (%)	GenMS		AS-GC			
	Minor collections	Survival rate	Minor collections		Survival rate	
			Local	Remote	Local	Remote
10	695	3.7%	976	26	3.6%	3.7%
20	1019	5.8%	1230	81	4.8%	4.9%
30	1981	6%	2204	401	5.1%	5.2%
40	2913	6.8%	3201	1098	5.6%	5.1%
50	3707	7.1%	3520	1233	6.8%	6.1%
60	4506	8.2%	4501	1622	6.9%	7.0%
70	5102	8.9%	5020	1903	7.0%	7.1%
80	6278	9.7%	6409	2411	8.2%	7.9%
90	7150	10.9%	7533	2702	9.0%	9.0%
100	8008	12.9%	8904	3202	10.1%	10.2%

More efficient minor collection translates to fewer full collection invocations (see Figure 7). At the maximum workload (Tx = 100), the reduction can be as much as 20%. Fewer full collection invocations also result in less time spent in GC; the reduction in GC time ranges from 25% to 32% when the workload is above 30 Tx (see Figure 8).

In terms of GC pauses, we report our results based on the concept of *Bounded Minimum Mutator Utilization* (BMU) [27]. Figure 9 shows BMU of GenMS and AS-GC at the initial decline of throughput (50 Tx). The x-intercept indicates the maximum pause

---

[4] The survival rate is the percentage of objects that survives each minor collection.

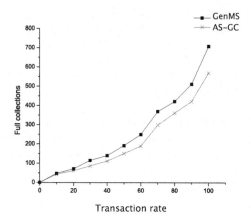

Fig. 7. Comparing major collection frequency

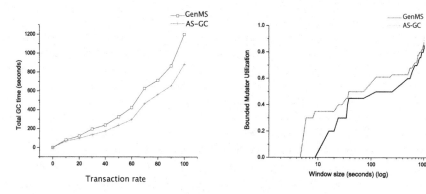

Fig. 8. Comparing overall collection times   **Fig. 9.** Comparing BMUs

time, and the asymptotic y-value indicates the fraction of the total time used for the mutator execution (average utilization). Note that we considered the additional time to track the inter-nursery references as a component of the GC time.

Full collection invocations dominate the GC pause times. On average, the pause times are usually more than 1 second. As shown in the graph, GenMS has the largest x-intercept value of around 8.83 seconds, and its utilization is about 10% lower than that of AS-GC (occurs around 200 seconds). The x-intercept of AS-GC is significantly smaller, because of less copying overhead. The overall utilization (asymptotic y-value) of AS-GC is about 5% higher than that of GenMS.

5.2   Heap Utilization

We define heap utilization as the amount of heap space needed to yield a certain through-put performance. Thus, if two systems yield the same throughput but one requires a smaller heap space, that system has better heap utilization. To evaluate this performance metric, we measured the heap space required by the two collectors to yield the same

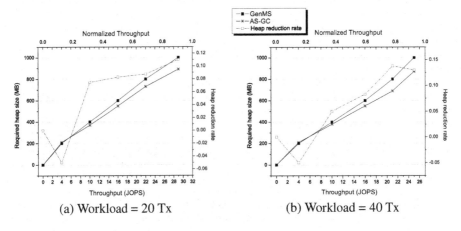

(a) Workload = 20 Tx   (b) Workload = 40 Tx

Fig. 10. Comparing heap usage between two workloads

throughput given the same workload. We chose two workload levels, 20 Tx and 40 Tx. At 20 Tx, both collectors achieve their corresponding maximum throughputs. At 40 Tx, the heap becomes tight but the application still maintains acceptable throughput performance (see Section 5.3).

For the experimental methodology, we measured the throughputs of GenMS under different heap sizes ranging from 200MB to 1GB. (We chose 1GB to minimize the effect of paging.) We then varied the heap size of AS-GC until we achieved the same throughputs as delivered by GenMS. The ratio between mature and nursery spaces is maintained at two to one.

Figure 10a reports our findings when the workload is set to 20 Tx. The solid lines in the graph illustrate the required heap sizes (left-side y-axis) of the two GC techniques to achieve the throughput specified in the lower x-axis. The dotted line is used to show the heap reduction percentage of AS-GC (right-side y-axis) over GenMS, based on the normalized throughput (top x-axis).

As shown in Figure 10a, once the heap size is large enough to handle the specified workload level (over 200 MB), AS-GC requires smaller heap space to achieve the same throughput as GenMS. When 20 Tx is used, we see the heap size reduction of 11%. When the workload is 40 Tx (see Figure 10b), AS-GC uses 13.4% smaller heap to deliver the same throughput. Since paging is not a major factor in this experiment, the main reason for better heap utilization is our collector's ability to collect dead objects more quickly and more efficiently.

5.3 Throughput

We conducted a set of experiments to measure the throughput of each collector. Each measurement was done using the same workload and the same heap size. This time, we allowed the size to be as large as 2GB so that we can evaluate the effect of AS-GC on paging. Figure 11 illustrates the throughput behavior of SPECjAppServer2004 utilizing GenMS and AS-GC. Figure 12 reports the percentage of improvement in throughput performance when AS-GC is used.

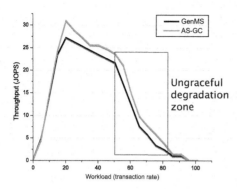

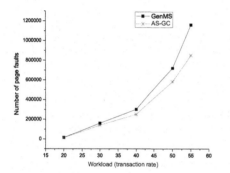

Fig. 11. Comparing throughputs

Fig. 12. Illustration of throughput performance improvement

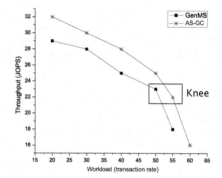

Fig. 13. Comparing paging behavior under heavy workloads

Fig. 14. Comparing throughput degradation locations

Notice that we can achieve about 14% throughput improvement when the workload is 20 Tx. Once the workload is around 50 to 55 Tx, the amount of heap space needed to execute the program exceeds the available physical memory (1GB). At this point, the system rapidly loses its ability to respond to user's requests. As the heap become tighter and tighter, the throughput improvement can range from 30% (55 Tx) to 78% (70 Tx). However, the system, when facing such high demands, is suffering from excessive paging (see Figure 13). While the percentage of improvement is large, the actual throughput delivered by the system is very small. It is worth noting that the main reason for a 30% improvement in the throughput performance when the transaction rate ranges from 55 to 65 is due to a significant reduction in the paging effort.

5.4 Ability to Handle Heavier Workload

To evaluate our collector's ability to handle varying workload, we set the initial workload to 20 Tx and the heap size to 1GB to minimize the effect of paging. We executed

SPECjAppServer2004 using this initial configuration. We then gradually increased the workload until we could precisely identify a period of execution where the throughput performance degraded sharply (Figure 11).

From Figure 14, the throughput of AS-GC degrades drastically at 55 Tx while the throughput of GenMS degrades at 50 Tx. This difference translates to 10% higher workload capacity before failure. By utilizing the heap space more efficiently, AS-GC should be able to respond to an unanticipated workload-increase better than GenMS.

6 Discussion

In this section, we provide a discussion about a runtime phenomenon called *lifespan interference* that occurs when multiple threads share the same nursery. We also discuss the feasibility of applying region-based memory management as an alternative to our approach to improve the performance of application servers.

6.1 Lifespan Interference

When a heap is shared by mulitple threads, thread scheduling performed by the underlying operating system can significantly affect lifespans of objects belonging to a thread. We refer to such an effect on lifespans due to scheduling as *lifespan interference*, which is illustrated in Figure 15.

In Figure 15a, *Thread 1* ($T1$) allocates *object a*, *object b*, and *object c* before making an I/O access. At this point, the operating system would suspend the execution of $T1$. Since there are no other threads allocating objects from the same heap as $T1$ in this scenario, the lifespan of every object in $T1$ can be easily calculated based on the object allocation pattern of $T1$. Thread scheduling by the operating system has no effect on lifespan in a single-threaded environment. Thus, the lifespan of *object a* is 3 because *objects b, c,* and d are created during the lifetime of object a.

In Figure 15b, $T1$, $T2$, and $T3$ share the same heap. Again, $T1$ is suspended by the operating system during the I/O access. Let's further assume that the scheduler picks

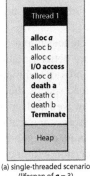

(a) single-threaded scenario
(lifespan of *a* = 3)

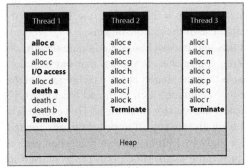

(b) multi-threaded scenario
(lifespan of *a* = any value from 3 to 17)

Fig. 15. What is the lifespan of object a?

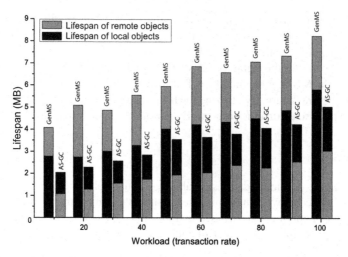

Fig. 16. Comparing the lifespans of remote and local objects when GenMS and AS-GC are used

$T2$ to run next. At this point, the lifespan of object a must include objects created by $T2$. Notice that in the example, the execution of $T1$ does not depend on any objects created by $T2$, but these objects can greatly affect the lifespans of objects created by $T1$. Depending on how long $T1$ is suspended, the lifespan of object a can be any values ranging from 3 to 17 (when both $T2$ and $T3$ complete their execution before $T1$ is resumed).

Lifespan interference is one reason why GenMS is not very efficient in large multi-threaded server applications. Objects that should be short-lived (according to the per-thread-allocation pattern) can appear to be much longer living due to scheduling. By segregating remote and local objects into two separate nurseries, the lifespans of remote and local objects are determined by the number of object allocations in remote and local nurseries, respectively. Figure 16 depicts the lifespans of objects in SPEC-jAppServer2004 when the GenMS and AS-GC approaches are used. In all workload levels, remote objects are longer living than local objects when GenMS is used. However when AS-GC is used, the lifespans of remote objects are reduced by as much as 75% (transaction rate = 20). In fact, the lifespans of the local objects are now much longer than those of the remote objects.

To put this into perspective, we compare the effect of interferences in our approach with existing approaches. It is clear that our technique provides better isolation from interferences than the shared nursery technique. On the other hand, our technique is not as isolated as techniques such as thread local heaps [28] or thread specific heaps [29], which create a subheap for each thread. However, it is unclear how well such approaches would perform given a large number of threads created in these server applications. For example, a study by [30] has shown that when each thread gets its own sub-heap, the memory utilization tends to be poor due to unused memory portion within each sub-heap. In addition, a study by [28] also reports that the run-time overhead to perform dynamic monitoring of threads may offset the improvement in garbage collection performance obtained through the thread local heap approach.

6.2 Region-Based Memory Management

Another approach to improving the performance of application servers from the memory management perspective is to utilize *region-based* memory management [31,32,33, 34] instead of or in conjunction with garbage collection. In region-based memory management, each object is created in a program specific region [31]. When a region is no longer needed, the entire area is reclaimed. One notable example of using region-based memory management in Java is scope-memory adopted in the *Real-Time Specification for Java* [35]. In this approach, a region is created for each real-time thread. The lifetime of objects created in this region is strictly bounded to the lifetime of the thread owning the region; as the thread terminates, the region is also destroyed.

As stated earlier, the lifetime of a remote object in an application server tends to be bounded by the time taken to complete a request or a task. Thus, it may be possible to bound the lifetime of a region to a task. However, our investigation of application servers also reveals many runtime factors that can make the deployment of region-based memory management in application servers challenging. First, not all objects created during a request are task-bounded. Techniques such as object caching [26] and HTTP sessions allow objects to outlive the task that creates them. Second, the time taken to complete a task can vary from a few seconds to over twenty minutes. Third, within each task there are tens to hundreds of threads that cooperate to complete a task. Fourth, within each task there can be hundreds of garbage collection attempts that yield efficient result, meaning that there is plenty of memory space to be recycled prior to the task termination. We have partially attempted a few solutions, discussed below, that can potentially address these factors.

Identifying task-bounded objects. Compile-time analysis may be employed to segregate task-bounded objects from non-task-bounded objects [31,32,33,34]. However, this implies the accessibility of source programs, which may not be made readily available by commercial software vendors. Moreover, standardized interfaces need to be established to allow VMs created by multiple vendors (e.g. Sun, BEA, IBM, etc.) to exploit the information generated by the compiler. Currently, we are extending our experimental framework to support this solution.

Reducing heap requirement. In region-based memory management, unreachable objects are not reclaimed until the end of the task. The policy of not reclaiming these objects can severely degrade performance and affect robustness of application servers especially when the memory demand is high, but the unused memory is not timely recycled [6]. One solution to conserve the heap usage is to combine region-based memory management with garbage collection [36,32,33]. It is unclear if this technique will yield higher performance improvement than the proposed AS-GC approach. We are currently experimenting with this proposed technique.

Identifying short-running tasks. Committing a memory region to a task for a long period of time may not be feasible as dead objects are not recycled promptly. However, short-running tasks may benefit from region-based memory management. The selection of the short-running tasks entails identifying threads that participate in each of these short-running tasks. Once these threads are identified, each will be directed to allocate objects in a specific region. While the idea appears to be straight-forward, a practice of thread pooling may drive up the cost of dynamically identifying these threads. With thread pooling, the analysis may have to be performed constantly as one thread can participate in both short-running and long-running tasks.

7 Applicability Study

In this section, we discuss four important issues that can greatly impact the applicability the proposed approach: generalization, alternative nursery configurations, required tuning efforts, and possible integrations with existing optimization techniques.

Generalization. To demonstrate that our solution can be generalized beyond the benchmark that was used, we conducted a preliminary study to compare the performance of AS-GC and GenMS using a different application server benchmark, SPEC-jAppServer2002. It is an outdated version of SPEC standardized application server benchmark. It conforms to the older J2EE standard (version 1.2) and also utilizes a different connection mechanism [37]. Our result indicates that we can achieve similar performance gains with AS-GC (14.8% higher maximum throughput). For future work, we will experiment with other commercial application servers as well as workload drivers to further validate the generalizability of our solution.

Nursery Configurations. In our experiments, we configured AS-GC to have the same nursery/mature ratio as GenMS throughout. However, it is possible for the performance of AS-GC to be different if other nursery/mature and local/remote ratios are used. As a preliminary study, we investigated the performance of AS-GC under two other nursery/mature heap configurations (1:3 and 1:1). We found that an additional 2% improvement in the throughput performance can be achieved with a larger nursery (1:1). This finding tells us that better results may be obtainable. As future work, we will conduct more investigation on the effect of heap configuration on the performance of the proposed AS-GC.

Tuning Efforts. Currently, heap tuning is recommended by application server vendors as a way to achieve maximum performance [5]. In our experiments, we used a standard parameter—used by practitioners for the tuning purpose—to set the nursery/mature ratio. To facilitate tuning of the local/remote ratio, we created a new command-line-configurable parameter to allow users to fully utilize our collector. While the tuning process can be tedious, it is a common procedure, and our proposed scheme only requires a small effort in addition to the current tuning practice.

Optimization. Fundamentally, our collector is a variation of copying-based generational collection. Thus, any existing techniques (e.g. pretenuring, older-first, Beltway) can be easily integrated into our scheme to further improve the performance. For example, we can have multiple belt 0s to manage clusters of objects with different lifespans. Each of these belts can be properly sized to allow just enough time for objects in the

---

[5] See http://java.sun.com/docs/performance/appserver/AppServerPerfFaq.html for tuning suggestions from Sun and http://www-03.ibm.com/servers/eserver/iseries/perfmgmt/pdf/tuninggc.pdf for tuning suggestions from IBM.

older increments to die. Pretenuring can also be applied to each sub-nursery to further improve minor collection efficiency. In addition, studies have shown that concurrent and incremental extensions can greatly improve the performance of GenMS. We foresee that if such extensions are applied to our technique, a significant performance improvement can also be expected.

8   Related Work

The main inspiration for our work is based on the concept of *Key objects* [9]. Hayes proposes the key object opportunism approach to manage longer-lived objects in a "keyed-area" [9]. This approach is based on the observation that large clusters of objects are usually allocated at the same time and also tend to die together. The main idea is to select representatives (or key objects) from the cluster and examine the reachability of these key objects more frequently than the rest of the cluster. This approach only applies when key objects exist, and they can be easily detected.

In this work, our key objects are the *remotable* objects, and any objects connected to these remotable objects (i.e. remote objects) are assumed to have similar lifespans. We can make such an assumption because the results from previous work have shown that objects connected together tend to die together [23]. To detect and segregate these remote objects, there are several options. One possible way is to use techniques such as object *colocation optimization* [24] to provide the necessary compile-time analysis to detect remote objects and the runtime component to segregate these remote objects from the local objects. We believe that the colocation technique would have worked well if these remote objects were difficult to be heuristically detected. However, this is not the case as remote objects can be easily detected by monitoring calls to remotable objects. Thus, we choose a dynamic detection technique because it can accomplish our goal at low cost. In terms of object segregation, our technique virtually accomplishes the same goal as their special allocator called *coalloc*.

In addition to the colocation technique, there are at least two additional techniques to improve the efficiency of generational GC. The first technique is *pretenuring*. The basic idea is to identify long-lived objects and create them directly in the mature generation. The goal of this technique is to reduce the promotion cost, thus reducing the GC time and improving the overall performance. Blackburn et al. [11] use a profile-based approach to select objects for pretenuring. They report a reduction in GC time of up to 32% and an improvement in the execution time by 7%. They also report a slight increase in the heap usage with pretenuring. Harris [12] uses dynamic sampling based on overflow and size to predict long-lived objects. Subsequent work to further optimize pretenuring include dynamic object sampling [38] and class based lifespan prediction [39].

The second technique is to avoid performing garbage collection on newly created objects because they may not have sufficient time to die; instead, the collection effort is mostly spent on older objects [40]. Stefanović *et.al.* [13] implements the *older-first* garbage collector that prioritizes collection of older objects to give young objects more time to die. This technique evolves to become a major part of the *Beltway* framework, introduced by Blackburn *et al.* [1]. In this framework, the heap is divided into several belts, and each belt groups one or more increments (a unit of collection) in a FIFO fashion [1]. All objects are allocated into the belt 0 (can be viewed as similar to the nursery). Beltway framework uses the older-first approach to collect the oldest increment of a belt first. All survivors are promoted to the last increment of the next higher belt. The results of their experiment show an average of 5% to 10% improvement in execution time and 35% improvement under tight heaps.

Compared to our technique, it is unclear how pretenuring and the Beltway framework would handle the lifespan characteristic of objects in application servers. If the decision is to pretenure any longer living objects, then the major collection frequency would be high. On the other hand, if the heap size is enlarged to allow more time for objects to die in the nursery, very short-lived objects are not reclaimed promptly. Similarly, each belt in the Beltway framework can be viewed as a generation. While the use of increments can avoid collection of the newly created objects, the framework still must make the decision on how to deal with the longer living objects. If belt 0 is small, these objects would be promoted to the subsequent belt, resulting in more frequent collection of the older belts. If belt 0 is large, the short-lived objects are still not collected promptly.

On the other hand, our approach invokes minor collection very frequently to quickly reclaim objects; each of our minor invocations also yields good GC efficiency. However, a major short-coming of our technique is that it does not work if objects can be easily segregated into short-lived/long-lived taxonomy. While the argument can be made for a very fine-grained segregation policy (e.g. consider segregating objects with slight differences in lifespans), the dynamic segregation overhead may offset the small benefit that can be gained. However, if clusters of objects with different lifespans can be identified, both pretenuring and the Beltway framework can be applied to further optimize our technique.

The idea of allocating objects exhibiting similar run-time behaviors into their own area is not new. Standard ML of New Jersey has been using up to 14 generations in addition to a *shared* nursery space to achieve good GC performance [41]. Each older generation consists of four arenas; each arena is used to manage a different class of objects (i.e. code objects, arrays, strings, and pairs) with different lifespans and object organizations (containing pointers vs not containing pointers). Our technique differs from this technique in several ways. First, we create two arenas in the nursery. In effect, we attempt to segregate objects at birth to improve minor collection performance. Their scheme segregates objects in the older generation to improve the full collection performance. Second, object segregation in our approach must be determined at allocation time based on the state of allocating threads (serving remote or local requests). Their technique segregates objects at GC time based on object types.

When Steensgaard introduces the thread local heaps approach [29], he also suggests that heap utilization can be improved by grouping threads that share data structures into their own sub-heap [42]. By creating a separate nursery for remote objects, our technique, in effect group threads that access remote objects into their own sub-nursery. This is somewhat similar to the suggestion by Steensgaard except that we do not create a sub-heap that includes both the nursery and the mature space. One reason for such a difference is because our optimization technique is introduced to allow the generational strategy to efficiently manage objects with diverse lifespans while Steensgaard's technique is designed to improve the allocation and garbage collection parallelism in multithreaded environments.

Recent studies have shown that once the heap size is larger than the physical memory, paging overheads can dominate the execution time and may even result in thrashing [11, 43, 8, 44]. Recent efforts have concentrated on dynamic sizing of the heap to maximize the performance of the existing GC techniques while minimizing paging [43, 8, 44, 45]. While these solutions have shown to work well, they all accept the fact that generational GC is memory inefficient, and thereby, assume that there is enough physical memory for the needed headroom. In large server applications, this assumption does not always hold. Workload variation can reduce the amount of available headroom as well as causing the heap size to be larger than the available physical memory. Nevertheless, these techniques can easily support our collector to further improve the GC performance.

9   Conclusion

In this paper, we introduce a new generational collector called AS-GC that takes advantage of an intrinsic behavior of many application servers in which *remotable* objects are commonly used as gateways for client requests. Objects instantiated as part of these requests (*remote objects*) tend to live longer than the remaining objects (*local objects*). This insight is used to create these two types of objects in two optimally sized nurseries. In doing so, the minor collection can be invoked more frequently and efficiently without increasing the heap requirement.

We have implemented the proposed AS-GC and evaluated its performance in an application server setting. We discovered that our proposed scheme can reduce the allocation interferences due to multithreading; a major reason that causes the inefficacy of single-nursery generational collectors. The experimental results show that our collector reduces the frequency of full collection invocations, paging effort, average pause time, and overall garbage collection time. As a result, our collector can yield a 14% increase in the maximum throughput and handle a 10% higher workload.

Acknowledgments

This work was sponsored in part by the National Science Foundation through award CNS-0411043 and by the Army Research Office through DURIP award W911NF-04-1-0104. We thank Mulyadi Oey and Sebastian Elbaum for their contributions in formulating the remote/local objects notion. We are grateful to Matthew Dwyer and Myra Cohen for their valuable feedback on this work. We also thank the anonymous reviewers for providing insightful comments for the final version of this paper.

References

1. Blackburn, S.M., Jones, R.E., McKinley, K.S., Moss, J.E.B.: Beltway: Getting Around Garbage Collection Gridlock. In: Proceedings of the Programming Languages Design and Implementation, Berlin, Germany, pp. 153–164 (2002)

2. Jones, R., Lins, R.: Garbage Collection: Algorithms for Automatic Dynamic Memory Management. John Wiley and Sons, Chichester (1998)
3. Lieberman, H., Hewitt, C.: A Real-Time Garbage Collector Based on the Lifetimes of Objects. Communications of the ACM 26(6), 419–429 (1983)
4. Ungar, D.: Generational Scavenging: A Non-Disruptive High Performance Storage Reclamation Algorithm. In: ACM SIGSOFT/SIGPLAN Software Engineering Symposium on Practical Software Development Environments, pp. 157–167. ACM Press, New York (1984)
5. Srisa-an, W., Oey, M., Elbaum, S.: Garbage Collection in the Presence of Remote Objects: An Empirical Study. In: Proceedings of the International Symposium on Distributed Objects and Applications, Agia Napa, Cyprus, pp. 1065–1082 (2005)
6. Xian, F., Srisa-an, W., Jiang, H.: Investigating the Throughput Degradation Behavior of Java Application Servers: A View from Inside the Virtual Machine. In: Proceedings of the 4th International Conference on Principles and Practices of Programming in Java, Mannheim, pp. 40–49 (2006)
7. Hertz, M., Berger, E.: Quantifying the Performance of Garbage Collection vs. Explicit Memory Management. In: OOPSLA '05: 20th annual ACM SIGPLAN Conference on Object-Oriented Programming Systems, Languages, and Applications, San Diego, CA, USA, pp. 313–326 (2005)
8. Yang, T., Berger, E.D., Kaplan, S.F., Moss, J.E.B.: CRAMM: Virtual Memory Support for Garbage-Collected Applications. In: OSDI'06: Proceedings of the USENIX Conference on Operating System Design and Implementation, Seattle, WA (2006)
9. Hayes, B.: Using Key Object Opportunism to Collect Old Objects. In: OOPSLA '91: Conference proceedings on Object-oriented programming systems, languages, and applications, Phoenix, AR, pp. 33–46 (1991)
10. IDC: Web services to reach $21 billion by 2007. On-line Article (2003), http://thewhir.com/marketwatch/idc020503.cfm
11. Blackburn, S.M., Singhai, S., Hertz, M., McKinely, K.S., Moss, J.E.B.: Pretenuring for Java. In: Proceedings of the OOPSLA '01 conference on Object Oriented Programming Systems Languages and Applications, Tampa Bay, FL, pp. 342–352 (2001)
12. Harris, T.L.: Dynamic Adaptive Pretenuring. In: Proceedings of International Symposium on Memory Management, Minneapolis, Minnesota, United States, pp. 127–136 (2000)
13. Stefanović, D., McKinley, K.S., Moss, J.E.B.: Age-Based Garbage Collection. In: OOPSLA '99: Proceedings of the 14th ACM SIGPLAN conference on Object-oriented Programming, Systems, Languages, and Applications, Colorado, United States pp. 370–381(1999)
14. Wilson, P.R., Johnstone, M.S., Neely, M., Boles, D.: Dynamic Storage Allocation: A Survey and Critical Review. In: IWMM '95: Proceedings of the International Workshop on Memory Management, London, UK, pp. 1–116. Springer, Heidelberg (1995)
15. Welsh, M., Culler, D.E., Brewer, E.A.: SEDA: An Architecture for Well-Conditioned, Scalable Internet Services. In: Symposium on Operating Systems Principles, pp. 230–243 (2001)
16. Hibino, H., Kourai, K., Shiba, S.: Difference of Degradation Schemes among Operating Systems: Experimental Analysis for Web Application Servers. In: Workshop on Dependable Software, Tools and Methods, Yokohama, Japan (2005)
17. Netcraft: Video iPod Launch Slows Apple Store (2005), http://news.netcraft.com/archives/2005/10/12/video_ipod_launch_slows_apple_store.html
18. Chosun Ilbo: Cyber Crime Behind College Application Server Crash. On-line article (2006), http://english.chosun.com/w21data/html/news/200602/200602100025.html
19. Standard Performance Evaluation Corporation: Spec jvm98 benchmarks (Last Retrieved: June 2005), http://www.spec.org/osg/jvm98
20. Standard Performance Evaluation Corporation: SPECjbb2000, WhitePaper (2000), http://www.spec.org/osg/jbb2000/docs/whitepaper.html

21. Standard Performance Evaluation Corporation: SPECjAppServer2004 User's Guide. On-Line User's Guide (2004), http://www.spec.org/osg/jAppServer2004/docs/UserGuide.html
22. Hirzel, M., Henkel, J., Diwan, A., Hind, M.: Understanding the Connectivity of Heap Objects. In: ISMM '02: Proceedings of the 3rd International Symposium on Memory Management, Berlin, Germany, pp. 36–49 (2002)
23. Hirzel, M., Diwan, A., Hertz, M.: Connectivity-Based Garbage Collection. In: ACM Conference on Object-Oriented Programming Systems, Languages, and Applications, pp. 359–373. ACM Press, New York (2003)
24. Guyer, S.Z., McKinley, K.S.: Finding your Cronies: Static Analysis for Dynamic Object Colocation. In: OOPSLA '04: Proceedings of the 19th annual ACM SIGPLAN Conference on Object-Oriented Programming, Systems, Languages, and Applications, Vancouver, BC, Canada, pp. 237–250. ACM Press, New York (2004)
25. Sun: Performance Documentation for the Java HotSpot VM. On-Line Documentation (Last Retrieved: June 2005), http://java.sun.com/docs/hotspot/
26. JBoss:Jboss Application Server. Product Literature (2005), http://www.jboss.org/products/jbossas
27. Sachindran, N., Moss, J.E.B.: Mark-copy: Fast Copying GC with Less Space Overhead. SIGPLAN Notices 38(11), 326–343 (2003)
28. Domani, T., Goldshtein, G., Kolodner, E.K., Lewis, E., Petrank, E., Sheinwald, D.: Thread-Local Heaps for Java. SIGPLAN Not. 38(suppl. 2), 76–87 (2003)
29. Steensgaard, B.: Thread-Specific Heaps for Multi-Threaded Programs. In: ISMM '00: Proceedings of the 2nd International Symposium on Memory Management, Minneapolis, Minnesota, United States, pp. 18–24 (2000)
30. Larson, P., Krishnan, M.: Memory Allocation for Long-Running Server Applications. In: ISMM '98: Proceedings of the 1st International Symposium on Memory Management, Vancouver, British Columbia, Canada, pp. 176–185 (1998)
31. Gay, D., Aiken, A.: Memory Management with Explicit Regions. In: PLDI '98: Proceedings of the ACM SIGPLAN 1998 Conference on Programming Language Design and Implementation, Montreal, Quebec, Canada, pp. 313–323. ACM Press, New York (1998)
32. Grossman, D., Morrisett, G., Jim, T., Hicks, M., Wang, Y., Cheney, J.: Region-Based Memory Management in Cyclone. In: PLDI '02: Proceedings of the ACM SIGPLAN 2002 Conference on Programming Language Design and Implementation, Berlin, Germany, pp. 282–293. ACM Press, New York (2002)
33. Stoutamire, D.P.: Portable, Modular Expression of Locality. PhD thesis, University of California-Berkeley, Chair-Jerome A. Feldman (1997)
34. Tofte, M., Talpin, J.P.: Region-Based Memory Management. Information and Computation 132(2), 109–176 (1997)
35. Bollella, G., Gosling, J.: The Real-Time Specification for Java. Computer 33(6), 47–54 (2000)
36. Elsman, M.: Garbage Collection Safety for Region-Based Memory Management. In: TLDI '03: Proceedings of the 2003 ACM SIGPLAN International Workshop on Types in Languages Design and Implementation, New Orleans, Louisiana, USA, pp. 123–134. ACM Press, New York (2003)
37. Standard Performance Evaluation Corporation: SPECjAppServer2002 User's Guide. On-Line User's Guide (2002), http://www.spec.org/osg/jAppServer2002/docs/UserGuide.html
38. Jump, M., Blackburn, S.M., McKinley, K.S.: Dynamic Object Sampling for Pretenuring. In: ISMM '04: Proceedings of the 4th International Symposium on Memory Management, Vancouver, BC, Canada, pp. 152–162 (2004)

39. Huang, W., Srisa-an, W., Chang, J.: Dynamic Pretenuring for Java. In: International Symposium on Performance Analysis of Systems and Software ISPASS, March 10-13, 2004, Austin, TX, pp. 133–140 (2004)
40. Clinger, W.D., Hansen, L.T.: Generational Garbage Collection and the Radioactive Decay Model. In: PLDI '97: Proceedings of the ACM SIGPLAN 1997 Conference on Programming Language Design and Implementation, Las Vegas, Nevada, United States, pp. 97–108. ACM Press, New York (1997)
41. Reppy, J.H.: A High-Performance Garbage Collector for Standard ML. Technical memorandum, AT&T Bell Laboratories, Murray Hill, NJ (1993)
42. Cohen, M., Kooi, S.B., Srisa-an, W.: Clustering the Heap in Multi-Threaded Applications for Improved Garbage Collection. In: GECCO '06: Proceedings of the 8th Annual Conference on Genetic and Evolutionary Computation, Seattle, Washington, USA, pp. 1901–1908 (2006)
43. Hertz, M., Feng, Y., Berger, E.D.: Garbage Collection Without Paging. In: PLDI '05: Proceedings of the 2005 ACM SIGPLAN Conference on Programming Language Design and Implementation, Chicago, IL, USA, pp. 143–153. ACM Press, New York (2005)
44. Yang, T., Hertz, M., Berger, E.D., Kaplan, S.F., Moss, J.E.B.: Automatic Heap Sizing: Taking Real Memory into Account. In: Proceedings of the International Symposium on Memory Management, Vancouver, BC, Canada, pp. 61–72 (2004)
45. Zhang, C., Kelsey, K., Shen, X., Ding, C., Hertz, M., Ogihara, M.: Program-Level Adaptive Memory Management. In: International Symposium on Memory Management, Ottawa, Canada, pp. 174–183 (2006)

Exception Handling: A Field Study in Java and .NET

Bruno Cabral and Paulo Marques

CISUC, Department of Informatics Engineering,
University of Coimbra Portugal
{bcabral,pmarques}@dei.uc.pt

Abstract. Most modern programming languages rely on exceptions for dealing with abnormal situations. Although exception handling was a significant improvement over other mechanisms like checking return codes, it is far from perfect. In fact, it can be argued that this mechanism is seriously limited, if not, flawed. This paper aims to contribute to the discussion by providing quantitative measures on how programmers are currently using exception handling. We examined 32 different applications, both for Java and .NET. The major conclusion for this work is that exceptions are not being correctly used as an error recovery mechanism. Exception handlers are not specialized enough for allowing recovery and, typically, programmers just do one of the following actions: logging, user notification and application termination. To our knowledge, this is the most comprehensive study done on exception handling to date, providing a quantitative measure useful for guiding the development of new error handling mechanisms.

Keywords: Exception Handling Mechanisms, Programming Languages.

1 Introduction

In order to develop robust software, a programming language must provide the programmer with primitives that make it easy and natural to deal with abnormal situations and recover from them. Robust software must be able to perceive and deal with the temporary disconnection of network links, disks that are full, authentication procedures that fail and so on.

Most modern programming languages like C#, Java or Python rely on exceptions for dealing with such abnormal events. Although exception handling was a significant improvement over other mechanisms like checking return codes, it is far from perfect. In fact, it can be argued that the mechanism is seriously limited if not even flawed as a programming construct. Problems include:

- Programmers throw generic exceptions which make it almost impossible to properly handle errors and recover for abnormal situations without shutting down the application.
- Programmers catch generic exceptions, not proving proper error handling, making the programs continue to execute with a corrupt state (especially relevant in Java). On the other hand, in some platforms, programmers do not

E. Ernst (Ed.): ECOOP 2007, LNAI 4609, pp. 151–175, 2007.

catch enough exceptions making applications crash even on minor error situations (especially relevant in C#/.NET).

- Programmers that try to provide proper exception handling see their productivity seriously impaired. A task as simple as providing exception handling for reading a file from disk may imply catching an dealing with tens of exceptions (e.g. `FileNotFoundException`, `DiskFullException`, `SecurityException`, `IOException`, etc.). As productivity decreases, cost escalates, programmer's motivation diminishes and, as a consequence, software quality suffers.
- Providing proper exception handling can be quite a challenging and error prone task. Depending on the condition, it may be necessary to enclose *try-catch* blocks within loops in order to retry operations; in some cases it may be necessary to abort the program or perform different recovery procedures. Bizarre situations, like having to deal with being thrown an exception while trying to close a file on a *catch* of a *finally* block, are not uncommon. Dealing with such issues correctly is quite difficult, error prone, not to say, time consuming.

To make things interesting, the debate about error handling mechanisms in programming languages has been recently fuelled with the launch of Microsoft's .NET platform.

Currently, the Java Platform and the .NET platform constitute the bulk of the modern development environments for commercial software applications. Curiously, Microsoft opted to have a different exception handling approach than in Java. In .NET the programmer is not forced to declare which exceptions can occur or even deal with them. Whenever an exception occurs, if unhandled, it propagates across the stack until it terminates the application. On the other hand, in Java, in most cases, the programmer is forced to declare which exceptions can occur in its code and explicitly deal with exceptions that can occur when a method is called. The rational for this is that if the programmer is forced to immediately deal with errors that can occur, or re-throw the exception, the software will be more robust. I.e. the programmer must be constantly thinking about what to do if an error occurs and acknowledge the possibility of errors.

On the .NET's camp, the arguments for not having checked exceptions that are normally used are [1]:

- Checked exceptions interfere with the programmers' productivity since they cannot concentrate in business logic and are constantly forced to think about errors.
- Since the programmer is mostly concentrated in writing business logic and not dealing with errors, it tends to shut-up exceptions, which actually makes things worse. (Corrupt state is much more difficult to debug and correct than a clean exception that terminates an application.)
- Errors should be "exonerated" by exhaustive testing. I.e. a sufficiently accurate test suite should be able to expose dormant exceptions, and corresponding abnormal situations. For the problems that remain latent, it is better that they appear as a clean exception that terminates the application than having them being swallowed in a generic *catch* statement which leads to corrupt state.

Obviously, both camps cannot be 100% right. But, overall, the important message is that in order to develop high-quality robust software, in a productive way, new advances in error handling are needed. The existing mechanisms are not adequate nor suffice.

This paper aims to contribute to the discussion by providing quantitative measures on how programmers are currently using exception handling. We examined 32 different applications, both for Java and .NET, covering 4 different software categories (*libraries*; *stand-alone applications*; *servers*; and *applications running on servers*). Overall, this corresponds to 3,410,294 lines of source code of which 137,720 are dedicated to exception handling. For this work, we have examined and processed 18,589 *try* blocks and corresponding handlers. To our knowledge, this is the most comprehensive study done to date on exception handling.

The data presented on this paper is important to guide the development of new mechanisms and approaches to exception handling. Other results will help e.g. justify the feasibility of using existent methodologies, like applying Aspect Oriented Programming (AOP) to implement exception handlers as advices.

The rest of this paper is organized as follows: Section 2 discusses related work; Section 3 describes the application set used in this study; Section 4 explains the methodology used in the analysis; Section 5 presents the results of the tests and observations about their significance; finally, Section 6 concludes the paper.

2 Related Work

Since the pioneering work of John B. Goodenough in the definition of a notation for exception handling [2] and Flaviu Cristian in defining its usage [3], the programming language constructs for handling and recovering from exceptions have not changed much. Nevertheless, programming languages designers have always suggested different approaches for implementing these mechanisms.

Several studies have been conducted over the years for validating the options taken in each different implementation. For instance, Alessandro Garcia, *et al.* did a comparative study on exception handling (EH) mechanisms available developing dependable software [4]. Alessandro's work consisted in a survey of exception handling approaches in twelve object-oriented languages. Each programming language was analyzed in respect to ten technical aspects associated with EH constructs: exception representation; external exceptions in signatures; separation between internal and external exceptions; attachment of handlers to program constructs (e.g. to statements, objects, methods, etc.); dynamism of handler binding; propagation of exceptions ; continuation of the flow control (resumption or termination); clean-up actions; reliability checks; and concurrent exception handling. After the evaluation of all the programming languages in terms of exception mechanisms, the major conclusion of the study was that "none of the existing exception mechanisms has so far followed appropriate design criteria" and programming language designers are not paying enough attention to properly supporting error handling in programming languages.

Saurabh Sinha and Mary Jean Harrold performed an extensive analysis of programs with exception handling constructs and discussed their effects on analysis techniques such as control flow, data flow, and control dependence [5]. In the analysis, the authors also presented techniques to create intraprocedural and interprocedural representations of Java programs that contain EH constructs and an algorithm for computing control dependences in their presence. Using that work, the authors performed several studies and showed that 8.1% of the methods analyzed used some kind of exception mechanism and that these constructs had an important influence in control-dependence analysis.

R. Miller and A. Tripathi identified several problems in exception handling mechanisms for Object-Oriented software development [6]. In their work, it is shown that the requirements of exception handling often conflict with some of the goals of object-oriented designs, such as supporting design evolution, functional specialization, and abstraction for implementation transparency. Being specific: object-oriented programming does not support a complete exception specification (extra information may be needed for the exception context not supported by an object interface); state transitions are not always atomic in exception handling; exception information needs to be specific, but functions can be overloaded to have a different meaning in different situations; the exception handling control flow path is different from the normal execution path and is up to the programmer to differentiate both of them. Thus, the modification of object-oriented frameworks for adaptation to exception handling can have the following effects in terms of: *Abstraction*, change of abstraction levels and the usage of partial states; *Encapsulation*, the exception context may leak information that reveals or allows the access to the exception signaler private data; *Modularity*, design evolution may be inhibited by exception conformance; *Inheritance* anomalies may occur when a language does not support exception handling augmentation in a modular way.

Martin P. Robillard and Gail C. Murphy in their article on how to design "robust Java programs with exceptions", classified exceptions as a global design problem and discussed the complexity of exception structures [7]. In their work, the authors pointed that the lack of information about how to design and implement with exceptions lead to complex and spaghetti-like exception handling code. The main factors that contribute to the difficulty of designing exception structures are the global flow of exceptions and the emergence of unanticipated exceptions. To help control these factors, the authors refined an existent software compartmenting technique for exception design and report about its usage in the rewriting of three Java programs and the consequent improvements they observed.

More recently, due to a new AOP approach to EH, two interesting studies were published emphasizing the separation of concerns in error handling code writing [8][9]. Martin Lippert and Cristina Lopes rewrote a Java application using AspectJ. Their objective was to provide a clear separation between the development of business code and exception handling code. This was achieved by applying error handling code as an *advice* (in AOP terminology) [10]. With this approach they also obtained a large reduction in the amount of exception handling code present in the application. Some of the results presented show that without aspects, the amount of code for exceptions is almost 11% of all the code; with aspects it represents only 2.9%. Lippert's paper also accounts the total number of *catch* blocks in the code and the most common exception classes used as parameters for these *catch* statements. One of the measures they present to support their AOP approach is the reduction of the number of different handlers effectively written for each one of the most commonly used exception classes. For the top 5 classes were implemented between 90.0% and 96.5% less handlers. F. Filho and C. Rubira conducted a similar study but they were not so enthusiastic in their results. The authors presented four metrics to evaluate the AOP approach to exception handling: separation of concerns; coupling between components and depth of inheritance tree; cohesion in the access to fields by pairs of method and advice; and dimension (size and number) of code. The work reports that the improvements of using AOP do not represent a substantial gain in any of the presented metrics showing that reusing handlers is much more difficult than is usually advertised. Handler reuse depends of the type of exceptions being handled, on what the handler does, the amount of contextual information needed; and what the method raising the exception returns and what the throws clause actually specifies.

The objective of this study is different from its predecessors. It does not target the quality of the mechanisms available in programming languages but the usage that programmers make of them. The emphasis is on understanding how programmers write exception handling code, how much of the code of an application is dedicated to error recovery and identifying possible flaws in their usage.

3   Workbench

The target platforms of this study were the .NET and Java environments, as well as the C# and Java programming languages.

Selecting a set of applications for the study was quite important. The code present in the applications had to be representative of common programming practices on the target platforms. Also, care had to be taken so that these would be "real world" applications developed for production use (i.e. not simply prototypes or beta versions). This was so in order not to bias the results towards immature applications where much less care with error handling exists. Finally, in order to be possible to perform different types of analyses, both the source code and the binaries of the applications had to be available.

Globally, we analyzed 32 applications divided into two sub-sets of 16 .NET programs and 16 Java programs. Each one of these sub-sets was organized in four categories accordingly to their nature:

- **Libraries:** software libraries providing a specific application-domain API.
- **Applications running on servers (Server-Apps):** Servlets, JSPs, ASPs and related classes.
- **Servers:** server programs.
- **Stand-alone applications:** desktop programs.

The complete list of applications is shown in Table 1.

Table 1. Applications listed by group

.NET	Libraries	SmartIRC4NET	IRC library
		Report.NET	PDF generation library
		Mono (corlib)	Open-source CLR implementation
		NLog	Logging library
	Server-Apps	UserStory.Net	Tool User Story tracking in Extreme Programming projects
		PhotoRoom	ASP.NET web site for managing on-line photo albums
		SharpWebMail	ASP.NET webmail application that is written in C#
		SushiWiki	WikiWikiWeb like Web application
	Servers	NeatUpload	Allows ASP.NET developers to stream files to disk and monitor progress
		Perspective	Wiki engine
		Nhost	Server for .Net objects
		DCSharpHub	Direct connect file sharing hub
	Stand-alone	Nunit	Unit-testing framework for all .NET languages
		SharpDevelop	IDE for C# and VB.NET projects
		AscGen	Application to convert images into high quality ASCII text
		SQLBuddy	SQL scripting tool for use with Microsoft SQL Server and MSDE
Java	Libraries	Thought River Commons	General purpose library
		Javolution	Real-time programming library
		JoSQL	SQL for Java Objects querying
		Kasai	Authentication and authorization framework
	Server-Apps	Exoplatform	Corporate portal and Enterprise Content Management
		GoogleTag Library	Google JSP Tag Library
		Xplanner	Project planning and tracking tool for Extreme Programming
		Mobile platform	Banks and mobile operators software for SMS and MMS services in cellular networks (not open-source)

Table 1. (*continued*)

Java	Servers	Jboss	J2EE application server
		Apache Tomcat	Servlet container
		JCGrid	Tools for grid-computing
		Berkeley DB	High performance, transactional storage engine
	Stand-alone	Compiere	ERP software application with integrated CRM solutions
		J-Ftp	Graphical Java network and file transfer client
		Columba	Email Client
		Eclipse	Extensible development platform and IDE

4 Methodology

The test applications were analyzed at source code level (C# and Java sources) and at binary level (metadata and bytecode/IL code) using different processes.

To perform the source code analysis two parsers were generated using antlr [11], for C#, and javacc [12] for Java. These parsers were then modified to extract all the exception handling code into one text file per application. These files were then manually examined to build reports about the content of exception handlers.

The source code of all application was examined with one exception. Due to the huge size of Mono, only its "corlib" module was processed.

The parsers were also used to identify and collect information about *try* blocks inside loops (i.e. detect *try* statements inside *while* and *do..while* loops). This is so because normally this type of operations corresponds to retrying a block of code that has raised an exception in order to recover from an abnormal situation.

The main objective of this article is to understand how programmers use the exception handling mechanisms available in programming languages. Nevertheless, the analysis of the applications source code is not enough by itself when trying to distinguish between the exceptions that the programmer wants to handle and the exceptions that might occur at runtime. This is so because the generated IL code/ bytecode can produce more (and different) exceptions than the ones that are declared in the applications source code by means of throw and throws statements.

To perform the analysis of the .NET assemblies and of the Java class files two different applications were developed: one for .NET and another for Java. The first one used the RAIL assembly instrumentation library [13] to access assembly metadata and IL code and extract all the information about possible method exceptions, exception handlers and exception protection blocks. The second application targeted the Java platform and used the Javassist bytecode engineering library [14] to read class files and extract exception handler information.

All data was stored on a relational database for easy statistical treatment.

Table 3. List of Assemblies and Java Packages analyzed

.NET	Java
Meebey.SmartIrc4net.dll	ThoughRiverCommons (all)
Reports.dll	Javolution (all)
mscorlib.dll	JoSQL (all)
NLog.dll	org.manentia.kasai
rq.dll (UserStory)	Exoplatform (all)
PhotoRoom.dll	GoogleTagLibrary (all)
SharpWebMail.dll	XPlanner (all)
SushiWiki.dll	Mobile platform (all)
Brettle.Web.NeatUpload.dll	JBoss (all)
Perspective.dll	org.apache
nhost.exe	JCGrid (all)
DCSharpHub.exe	Berkeley DB (all)
nunit.core.dll	org.compiere
SharpDevelop.exe	net.sf.jftp
Ascgen dotNET.exe	org.columba
SqlBuddy.exe	org.eclipse

For each application only one file (.NET) or package (and sub-packages) of classes (Java) was analyzed. Table 2 shows the names of the files and packages that were used in this study. The criterion followed to select these targets was the size of the files and their relevance in the implementation of the application core.

5 Results

In the following subsections we will present the results of this study, drawing some observations about their significance.

Nevertheless, we should caution that although the number of applications that were used was relatively large (32), it is not possible to generalize the observations to the whole .NET/Java universe. For that, it would be necessary to have a very significant number of applications, possible consisting in hundreds programs. Even so, due to the care taken in selecting the target applications, we believe that the results allow a relevant glimpse into current common programming practices in exception handling.

5.1 Error Handling Code in Applications

One important metric for understanding current error handling practices is the percentage of source code that is used in that task. For gathering this metric, we compared the number of lines of code inside all *catch* and *finally* handlers to the total number of lines of the program. The results are shown in Figure 1.

It is quite visible that in Java there is more code dedicated to error handling than in .NET. This difference can be explained by the fact that in Java it is compulsory to handle or declare all exceptions a method may throw, thus increasing the total amount of code used for error handling. Curiously, there is an exception to this pattern. In the Server Application group, the difference is almost non-existent. To explain this result we examined the applications' source code. For this class of applications, both in Java and .NET, programmers wrote quite similar code. Meaning that they expect the same kind of errors (e.g. database connections loss, communication problems, missing data, etc.) and they use the same kind of treatment (the most common handler action in this type of applications is logging the error).

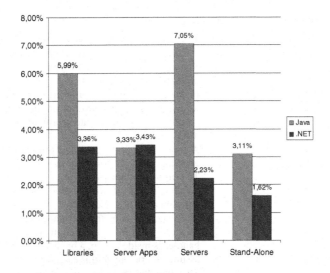

Fig. 1. Amount of error handling code

One surprising result is that the total amount of code dedicated to exception handling is much less than what would be expected. This is even more surprising in Java where using exceptions is almost mandatory even in small programs. Our results show that the maximum amount of code used for error handling was 7% in the *Servers* group. Overall, the result is 5% for Java, with a 2% standard deviation, and 3% for .NET, with a standard deviation of 1%. It should be noted the applications used in this study are quite mature, being widely used. We reason that the effort dedicated to writing error protection mechanisms is not as high as expected, even for highly critical applications like servers. The forceful of declaring and catching checked exceptions in Java effectively increases (almost doubles) the amount of error handling code written, even though it is still represents a small fraction of all the code of an application. The critical issue is that normally error handling code is being used more to alert the user, to abort the applications or to force them to continue their execution, than to actually recover from existing errors.

5.2 Code in Exception Handlers

Apart from measuring the amount of the code that deals with errors, to find out how programmers use exception handling mechanisms, it is important to know what kind of actions are performed when an error occurs.

To be able to report on this subject we had to inspect sets of ten thousand lines of application source code. As a matter of fact, we covered all the handlers (*catch* and *finally*) in all the applications except for JBoss and Eclipse. For these two, due to their dimension, only 10% of the 96,405 lines of code existing inside of exception handlers were examined. Even so, they are representative of the rest.

Table 4. Description of the Handler's actions categories

Category	Description
Empty	The handler is empty, is has no code and does nothing more than cleaning the stack
Log	Some kind of error logging or user notification is carried out
Alternative/ Static Configuration	In the event of an error or in the execution of a finally block some kind of pre-determined (alternative) object state configuration is used
Throw	A new object is created and thrown or the existing exception is re-thrown
Continue	The protected block is inside a loop and the handler forces it to abandon the current iteration and start a new one
Return	The handler forces the method in execution to return or the application to exit. If the handler is inside a loop, a break action is also assumed to belong to this category
Rollback	The handler performs a rollback of the modifications performed inside the protected block or resets the state of all/some objects (e.g. recreating a database connection)
Close	The code ensures that an open connection or data stream is closed. Another action that belongs to this category is the release of a lock over some resource
Assert	The handler performs some kind of assert operation. This category is separated because it happens quite a lot. Note that in many cases, when the assertion is not successful, this results in a new exception being thrown possibly terminating the application
Delegates (only for .NET)	A new delegate is added
Others	Any kind of action that does not correspond to the previous ones

To simplify the classification of these error handling actions we propose a small set of categories that enable the grouping of related actions. These categories are summarized in the previous table.

Note that an exception handler may contain actions that belong to more than one category. In fact, this is the common case. For instance, a handler can log an error, close a connection and exit the application. These actions are represented by three distinct categories: Log, Close and Return. Thus, in the results, this handler would be classified in all these three categories.

Since *catch* and *finally* handlers have different purposes, we opted for doing separate counts for each type of handler. Finally, the distribution of handler actions for each application was calculated as a weighted average accordingly to the number of actions found in each application. This is so that small applications do not bias the results towards their specific error handling strategy.

The results obtained for each application group are shown in next four graphs.

The graph of Figure 2 shows the average of results by application group for .NET *catch* handlers. In the four application groups 60% to 75% of the total distribution of handler actions is composed of three categories: Empty, Log and Alternative Configuration.

Empty handlers are the most common type of handler in *Servers* and the second largest in *Libraries* and *Stand-alone applications*. This result was completely unexpected in .NET programs since there are no checked exceptions in the CLR and, therefore, programmers are not obliged to handle any type of exception. Checked exceptions can sometimes lead lazy programmers to "silence exceptions" with empty handlers only to be able to compile their applications. From the analysis of the source code we concluded that its usage in .NET is not related with compilation but with avoiding premature program termination on non-fatal exceptions. A typical example is the presence of several linear protected blocks containing different ways of performing an operation. This technique assures that if one block fails to achieve its goal, the execution can continue to the next block without any error being generated.

Logging errors is also one of the most common actions in the handlers of all the applications. In fact, is the most common action in *Server-Apps* and *Stand-alone* groups? Considering web applications and desktop applications, this typically corresponds to the generation of an error log, the notification of the user about the occurrence of a problem and the abortion of the task. This idea is re-enforced by the value of the Return action category in these two application groups which is the identical and the highest of all four groups.

The number of Alternative configuration actions reports on the usage of alternative computation or object's state reconstruction when the code inside a protected block fails in achieving its objective. These actions are by far the most individualized and specialized of all. In some cases they are used to completely replace the code inside the protected block.

In the *Libraries* applications group, Assert operations are the second most common error handling action. Asserts ensure that if an error occurs, the cause of the error is well known and reported to the user/programmer.

In *Servers* there is also a high distribution value for the Others category. These actions are mainly related with thread stopping and freeing resources.

Another category of actions with some weight in the global distribution is the Throw action. This is mainly due to the layered and component based development of software. Layers and components usually have a well defined interface between them. It is a fairly popular technique to encapsulate all types of exceptions into only one type when passing an exception object between layers or software components. This is typically done with a new `throw`.

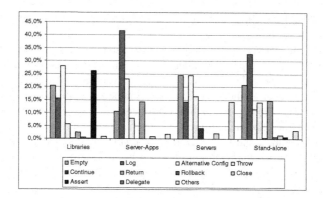

Fig. 2. Catch handler actions count for .NET programs

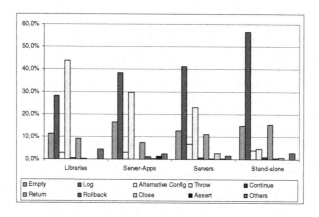

Fig. 3. Catch handlers' actions count for Java programs

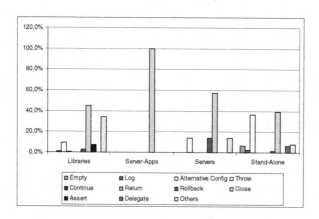

Fig. 4. Finally handlers' actions for .NET programs

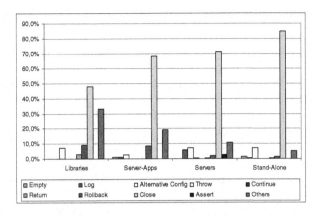

Fig. 5. Finally handlers' actions for Java programs

Empty, Log, Alternative Configuration, Throw and Return are the actions most frequently found in the *catch* handlers of .NET applications. By opposition, Continue, Rollback, Close, Assert, Delegate and Others actions are rarely used in .NET.

Figure 3 shows the results for *catch* handlers in Java programs. Only in the *Stand-alone* and *Server-Apps* groups we found some similarity with .NET. Despite this fact, it is possible to see the same type of clustering found in .NET. The cluster of categories that concentrate the highest distribution of values is composed by Empty, Log, Alternative Configuration, Throw and Continue actions.

The distribution values on the Empty category surprised us once again. This value is lower than the ones found in .NET. This suggests that the checked exception mechanism has little or no weight on the decision of the programmer to leave an exception handler empty: another reason must exist to justify the existence of empty handlers besides silencing exceptions. In .NET this happen quite frequently for building alternative execution blocks. We risk saying that in Java exception mechanisms are no longer being used only to handle "exceptional situations" but also as control/execution flow construct of the language. (Note that even the Java API sometimes forces this. For instance, the detection of an end-of-file can only be done by being thrown an exception.)

The Log actions category takes the first place for *Server-apps*, *Server* and *Stand-alone* application groups and the second place in *Libraries* group. In this last group, Log is only surpassed by Throw, another popular action in the *Server-Apps* and *Server* groups. In Java, the Log and Throw actions are highly correlated. We observed that in the majority of cases, when an object is thrown the reason why it happens is also logged.

Return is also a common action in all the application groups. Between 7% and 15% of all handlers terminate the method being executed, returning or not a value.

Figure 4 illustrates the results for *finally* handlers in .NET. The distribution of the several actions is different from the one found in *catch* handlers. Nevertheless, is visible that the most common handler action category in .NET, for all application groups, is Close. I.e. *finally* handlers, in our test suite, are mainly used to close connections and release resources.

Alternative configuration is the second mostly used handler action in all application groups with the exception of *Libraries*. A typical block of code usually found in *finally* handlers is composed by some type of conditional test that enables (or not) the execution of some predetermined configuration. In some cases, these alternative configuration is done while resetting some state. In those cases, they were classified as Rollback and not Alternative.

Another common category present in *finally* handlers of .NET applications is Others. These actions include file deletion, event firing, stream flushing, and thread termination, among other less frequent actions. In Server applications it is also common to reset object's state or rollback previously done actions.

Finally, on *Stand-alone* applications there are some empty *finally* blocks that we can not justify since they perform no easily understandable function.

In Java applications (Figure 5) the scenario is very similar to the one found in .NET. Close is the most significant category in all application groups. There are also some actions classified as Others, which are similar to the ones of .NET. In Java they have more weight in the distribution, indicating a higher programming heterogeneity in exception handling.

Rollback and Alternative configuration actions are also used as handler actions in Java *finally* handlers.

It is possible to observe that there is some common ground between application groups in Java and .NET in what concerns exception handling. For the most part, Empty and Log the most common actions in all *catch* handlers and Close is the most used action in *finally* handlers.

5.3 Exception Handler Argument Classes

After identifying the list of actions performed by handlers, we concentrated on finding out if there is some relation between *catch* handlers for the same type of exception classes. For this, we developed two programs: one to process .NET's IL code and another to process Java bytecode. These IL code/bytecode analyzers were used to discover what exceptions classes were most frequently used as *catch* statement arguments. We opted by performing this analysis at this level and not at source code level because it is simpler to obtain this information from assemblies or class files metadata than from C# or Java code.

Figure 6 shows the most common classes used as argument of catch instructions in .NET applications. The results are grouped by application type and the values represent the weighted average of the distribution among applications of the same group. Thus, programs with the largest number of handlers have more weight in the final result.

It is possible to observe that programmers prefer to use the most generic exception classes like System.Exception and System.Object for catching exceptions. Note that .NET, not C#, allows any type of object to be used as an exception argument. When the argument clause of a *catch* statement is left empty, the compiler assumes that any object can be thrown as an exception. This explains the large presence of System.Object as argument.

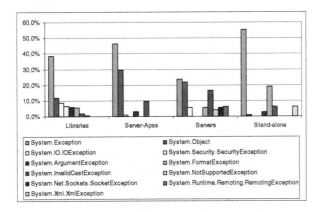

Fig. 6. .NET catch's arguments classes

The use of generic classes in *catch* statements can be related to the two of the most common actions in handlers: Logging and Return. This means that for the largest set of possible exceptions that can be thrown, programmers do not have particular exception handling requirements: they just register the exception or alert the user of its occurrence. Nevertheless, there are a lot of handlers that use more specific exception classes. These different handlers do not have any weight by themselves in the distribution but all the code that actually tries to perform some error recovery operations is concentrated around these specialized handlers.

I/O related exception handlers are fairly used in *Libraries* and *Servers*. Also invalid arguments types, number and format errors are treated as exceptions by all the applications as shown by the presence of System.ArgumentException handlers and System.FormatException handlers.

There are not many differences between Java and .NET in terms of *catch* arguments. Figure 7 shows the results for Java. It is possible to conclude that the most generic exception classes are the preferred ones: Exception, IOException, and ClassNotFoundException. We tried to found out why ClassNotFoundException is so commonly used by analyzing the source code. For the most part, most of the handlers associated to the use of this class are empty, just log the error or throw a new kind of exception. Others try to load a parent class of the class not found or another completely different class. In general, these handlers are associated with "plug-in" mechanisms or modular software components using dynamic class loading.

Finally, we did an analysis of all the applications source code to find out what was the distribution of handler actions by *catch* handler argument class for the most commonly used classes. The results can be found in Figure 8.

The results are quite different from one type of exception class to another. Even so, it is still possible to say that the dominant handler actions are the ones belonging to the categories: Empty, Log, Alternative Configuration, Throw and Return.

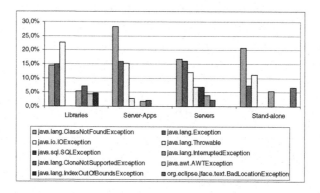

Fig. 7. Java catch's arguments classes

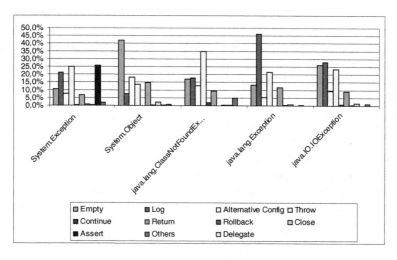

Fig. 8. Handler action distribution for the most used catch handler classes

It is interesting to notice that in .NET catch instructions with no arguments are directly associated with the largest number of Empty handlers.

In Java, in particular for ClassNotFoundException, alternative configuration actions are common. This behavior is understandable if we consider that, if a class is not found then a new one should be suggested as alternative. (This is quite common in database applications, while loading JDBC drivers.)

5.4   Handled Exceptions

On the last section, we reported the exceptions that are used in *catch* statements. Nevertheless, a *catch* statement can catch the specific exception that was listed or more specific ones (i.e. derived classes). We will now discuss exception handling code from the point of view of possible handled exceptions. As described in section 4 we used IL code/bytecode analyzers to collect all the exceptions that the applications could throw because this information is not completely available at source code level. I.e. the set of exceptions that an application can throw at runtime is not completely defined by the applications source code `throw` and `throws` statements. Therefore, a profound analysis of the compiled applications was required for gathering this information.

5.4.1 Exception Universe

In Java, thanks to the checked exception mechanism, we are able to discover and locate all the exceptions that an application can throw by analyzing its bytecode and metadata. To know what exceptions may be thrown by a method it is necessary to know:

- All the exceptions that the bytecode instructions of a method may raise accordingly to the Java specs [15]
- All the exception classes declared in the `throws` statement of the methods being called
- All the exceptions that are produced inside a protected block and are caught by one of its handlers
- All the exception classes in the method own `throws` statement

In .NET this is a more difficult task because there are no checked exceptions. To discover what exceptions a method may raise is necessary to know:

- All the exceptions that can be raised by each one of the IL instructions accordingly to the ECMA specs of the CLR [16]
- All the exceptions that the method being called may raise
- All the exception classes present in explicit `throw` statements
- All the exceptions that are produced inside a protected block and are not caught by one of its handlers

When we started to work on which exceptions could occur in .NET and Java, the results of the analysis were quite biased. This happened because:

- Almost all instructions can raise one or more exceptions, accordingly to CLR ECMA specs and Java specs, making the total number of exceptions reported grow very fast and the occurrence of other types of exceptions not directly associated with instructions almost irrelevant;
- In most cases, the exceptions that each low-level instruction could actually throw would not indeed occur since some code in the same method would prevent it (e.g. an explicit program termination if a database driver was not found, thus making all `ClassNotFoundException` exceptions for that class irrelevant). Since it is not possible to detect this code automatically, although the results could be correct, the analysis would not reflect the reality of the running application or the programming patterns of the developer.

To obtain meaningfully results we decided to perform a second analysis not using all the data from the static analysis of bytecode and IL code instructions. In particular, we filtered a group of exceptions that are not normally related to the program logic, and that the programmer should not normally handle, considering the rest. The list of exceptions that were filtered (i.e. not considered) is shown in Table 4.

Table 5. Java and .NET exception classes for bytecode and IL code instructions

JAVA	.NET
java.lang.NullPointerException	System.OverflowException
java.lang.IllegalMonitorStateException	System.Security.SecurityException
java.lang.ArrayIndexOutOfBoundsException	System.ArithmeticException
java.lang.ArrayStoreException	System.NullReferenceException
java.lang.NegativeArraySizeException	System.DivideByZeroException
java.lang.ClassCastException	System.Security.VerificationException
java.lang.ArithmeticException	System.StackOverflowException
	System.OutOfMemoryException
	System.TypeLoadException
	System.MissingMethodException
	System.InvalidCastException
	System.IndexOutOfRangeException
	System.ArrayTypeMismatchException
	System.MissingFieldException
	System.InvalidOperationException

5.4.2 Results for Handled Exceptions

Being aware of the complete list of exceptions that an application can raise and of the complete list of handlers and protected blocks, it is possible to find out which are the most commonly handled exception types. The results for .NET applications are shown in Figure 9; the values represent the average of results by application group where every application had a different weigh in the overall result according to the total number of results that they provided. It is possible to observe that the results are very different from application group to application group. For instance, in the *Libraries* group, the most commonly handled exceptions are ArgumentNullException and ArgumentException, resulting from bad parameter use in method invocations. In the remaining three groups the number one exception type is Exception, this can be a symptom of the existence of a larger and more differentiated set of exceptions that can occur. If many different exceptions can occur it is viable to assume that the most generalized type (i.e. Exception, IOException, etc.) becomes the most common one.

Seeing exception types like HttpException, MailException, SmtpException and SocketException in this top ten list and observing a distribution with such variations from application group to application group, we are confident to say that the type of exceptions that an application can raise and, in consequence, handle is strictly related with the application nature.

There is a mismatch between the type of classes used as arguments to catch instructions and the classes of the exceptions that are handled, i.e. throw statements use the exception classes that best fit the situation (exception) but the handlers that will eventually "catch" these exceptions use general exception classes like .Net's and Java's Exception as their arguments.

In Java, as in .NET, there is a large spectrum of exception types being handled. The results for Java are illustrated in Figure 10. The huge distinction helps to differentiate IOException as the most "caught" exception type in all application

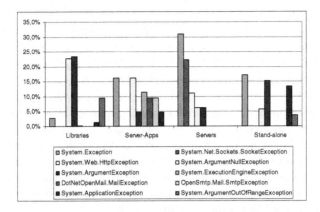

Fig. 9. Most commonly handled exception types in .NET

groups. It is also possible to observe that the exception types are tightly related to the applications. For instance in *Stand-alone* applications, three of the exception classes are from Eclipse. Due to its size Eclipse carries a large weight in its application group results and, as we are able to observe, its "private" exceptions are present in this top ten.

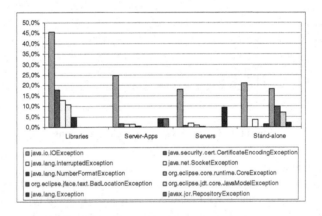

Fig. 10. Most commonly handled exceptions in Java

5.4.3 Call Stack Levels Analysis

The analysis of the applications bytecode and IL code allows us to discover the number of levels in the call stack that an exception travels before it is caught by some handler. Note that an exception is caught if the *catch* argument class is the same of the exception or a super-class of it.

One result that we can directly associate with the checked exceptions mechanism is the difference in the number of levels that an exception covers before it is caught by some handler in Java and .NET.

In Figure 11 it is possible to observe that in Java almost 80% of the exceptions are caught one level up from where they are generated, 15% two levels up, 5% three levels up and all the remaining are caught as high as five levels. On the other hand, in .NET, exceptions can cover up to seventeen levels and the distribution of the exceptions per levels covered is much sparser than in Java. The .NET programmer is not forced to catch exceptions and, as a result, exceptions can be caught much later in the call stack and most of times by exception handlers with general *catch* arguments.

In .NET, 5% of the exceptions are caught before they cover any level in the call stack. This result is unexpected and could only be explained by a detailed analysis of the IL code in the assemblies and of the source code of the programs. At first we thought that this could be the result of some code tangling at compile time but the analysis showed that the exceptions were originated in throw instructions inside the protected blocks of methods. Programmers raised these exceptions to pass the execution flow from the current point in the method to code inside a handler – i.e. they use exceptions as a flow control construct.

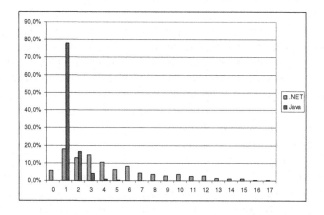

Fig. 11. Call stack levels for caught exceptions

5.4.4 Handler Size

Another interesting measure that we withdraw from the analysis of assemblies IL code and metadata was related with handler's code size or, more precisely, the count of opcodes inside a handler. This analysis could only be conducted in .NET because the metadata in the assemblies clearly identifies the *begin* and *end* instructions for each handler while in Java only the information about the beginning of a handler is available. To discover where a handler finishes we would have to do a static flow control analysis and find the join point in the code after the first instruction in the handler, which is outside of the scope of this paper.

The graph in Figure 12 shows that the largest set of handlers in *Server-Apps*, *Servers* and *Stand-alone* applications groups have 8 IL Code instructions. In the *Libraries* group more than 40% of the handlers have 3 instructions. The second largest set of handlers in all groups has 5 instructions. Obviously, there are bigger handlers but their number is so low that we excluded them from the graph to improve its reading.

These results made us curious about what was happening in these handlers and what were the instructions in question. We analyzed all the IL code in all the handlers and found some interesting facts:

- In the 526 handlers with size 8, 500 (95%) invoked a `Dispose()` method in some object; from this 500 there were two major sets of handlers with the exact same opcodes, one with 329 elements and the other with 166; the remaining 5 handlers were different between them; these handlers were all *Finally* handlers.
- In the set of handlers with 5 instructions there were 194 elements; 74 disposed of some object; 24 created and throwed a new exception; 36 stored some value.
- 484 of the 498 handlers of size 3 were *Finally* handlers; 426 handlers had exactly the same opcodes and were responsible for closing a database connection; other 34 handlers also had the same code and invoked a `Finalize` method in some object.
- The largest set of handlers with size 2 was empty handlers in the source code and its actions consisted in cleaning the stack and returning; others rethrowed the exception, and the rest called some `Assert` method.

These lead us to the conclusion that many of the handlers with few instructions are very similar between them and that the majority are *Finally* handlers that do some kind of method dispose or connection closing.

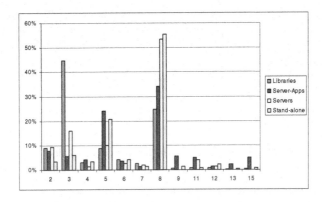

Fig. 12. Handlers size in number of IL code instructions for .NET

5.4.5 Types of Handlers

Knowing that the majority of the handlers with few instructions were *finally* blocks we tried to discover which was the relation between the total number of protected blocks, the total number of *catch* handlers and the total number of *finally* handlers.

The data in Table 5 shows that for the 1565 protected blocks found in the .NET applications there are 1630 handlers; 1144 protected bocks (73%) have *finally* handlers; but only 29% have *catch* handlers. On Java there are 18389 handlers distributed by 17024 protected blocks; 8109 protected blocks (48%) have *finally* handlers; 9402 (55%) have *catch* handlers.

Table 6. Number of protected blocks, catch handlers and finally handlers

	Protected Blocks	Handlers	Protected Blocks with Finally Handlers	Protected Blocks with Catch Handlers
.NET	1565	1630	1144	450
Java	17024	18389	8109	9402

In our test set of applications, .NET programmers use much more *finally* handlers, relatively to the total number of handlers, than Java programmers.

In the graph of Figure 13 it is possible to see that Java applications have higher maximum values of *catch* handlers per protected block, the average number of catch blocks per *try* block is almost identical in all the application groups for the two platforms and has the approximate value of one. The standard deviation values are also very low meaning that the largest number of protected blocks has only one *catch* handler.

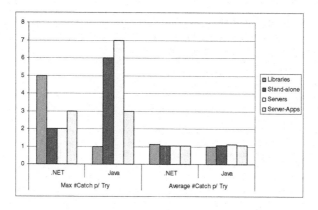

Fig. 13. Number of catch handlers per protected block.

5.4.6 Checked vs. Unchecked Exceptions

As mentioned before, the checked exceptions mechanism influences the way Java programmers use the exception detection and handling language constructs. But programmers can, alternatively, use unchecked exceptions in Java. For instance, there are some libraries specialized in using only unchecked exceptions (e.g. Java NIO).

In the programs that were analyzed, we compared the number of catch instructions that have an unchecked exception class as argument with the total number of catch instructions. The results are displayed in Table 6. It is possible to observe that except for the *Stand-Alone* application group, where the usage reaches 36.7%, for the remaining groups, values are very low, never exceeding 9%. Nevertheless, unchecked exceptions are indeed being used and, besides their extensive usage by some dedicated libraries, they are largely used to report on underlying system errors.

Table 7. Usage of Unchecked exceptions in Java catch handlers

	Unchecked
Libraries	8,90%
Servers	8,50%
Stand-Alone	36,70%
Server-Apps	6,50%

5.4.7 Retry Functionality

Neither Java or .NET have nothing like a "retry" block functionality that would enable the programmer to execute a *try* block in a cycle until it succeeds or reaches a certain condition. Other languages like Smalltalk [17] or Eiffel [18] have this kind of construct.

In Java and .NET, if a programmer wants to mimic this functionality he has to insert a protected block inside a cycle, for instance, insert a *try* block inside a *while* or *do-while* cycle.

Using source code parsers for accounting the number of protected blocks found inside cycles or loops we were able to obtain the total number of these occurrences. In Java we found 1082 cases and in .NET 16.

This analysis can be considered as some sort of blind analysis because we do not know if the programmer really intended to do a "retry". Nevertheless, 6% of all *catch* handlers were inside loops and if the programmer really intended to do a "retry", which seams to be the most reasonably reason, that would be a fairly interesting result to justify the addition of this functionality to both languages.

5.5 Making Exception Handling Work

The results discussed in the previous sections show that programmers, most of the time, do not use exception handling mechanisms correctly or, at least, they do not use them for error recovery. These practices lead to a decrease in software quality and dependability. It is clear that in order to develop high-quality robust software, in a highly productive way, new advances are needed. Some authors have already started looking for new approaches. In our line of work we are currently approaching the problem by trying to create automatic exception handling for the cases where "benign exception handling actions" can be defined (e.g. compressing a file on a disk full exception). In general, we are trying to free the programmer from the task of writing all the exception handling code by hand, forcing the runtime itself to automatically deal with the problems whenever possible. A complete description of the technique is out of scope of this paper, but the interested reader can refer to [19] for a discussion of the approach.

6 Conclusion

This article aimed to show how programmers use the exception handling mechanisms available in two modern programming languages, like C# and Java. And, although we have detailed the results individually for both platforms and found some differences, in the essential results are quite similar. To our knowledge, this is the most extensive study done on exception handling by programmers in both platforms.

We discovered that the amount of code used in error handling is much less than what would be expected, even in Java where programmers are forced to declare or handle checked exceptions.

More important is the acknowledgment that most of the exception classes used as *catch* arguments are quite general and do not represent specific treatment of errors, as one would expect. We have also seen that these handlers most of the times are empty or are exclusively dedicated to log, re-throw of exceptions or return, exit the method, or program. On the other hand, the exception objects "caught" by these handlers are from very specific types and closely tied to application logic. This demonstrates that, although programmers are very concerned in throwing the exception objects that best fit a particular exceptional situation, they are not so keen in implementing handling code with the same degree of specialization.

These results lead us to the conclusion that, in general, exceptions are not being correctly used as an error handling tool. This also means that if the programming community at large does not use them correctly, probably it is a symptom of a serious design flaw in the mechanism: exception constructs, as they are, are not fully appropriate for handling application errors. Work is needed on error handling mechanisms for programming languages. Exception handlers are not specific enough to deal with the detail of the occurring errors; the most preferable behavior is logging the problem or alerting the user about the error occurrence and abort the on-going action. Empty handlers, used to "silence" exceptions, will frequently hide serious problems or encourage bad utilization of programming language error handling constructs.

Some of the problems detected, like the duplication of code between handlers, and the mingling of business code with exceptions handling code, among other problems are still to be tackled and represent an important research target.

We now know, at least for this set of applications, what type of exceptions programmer prefer to handle and what type of exceptions are commonly caught. In the future we would like to extend our analysis to running software, actually accounting what type of exceptions do really occur and how this relates to the code programmers are forced to write for error handling.

Acknowledgments. This investigation was partially supported by the Portuguese Research Agency – FCT, through a scholarship (DB/18353/98), and by CISUC (R&D Unit 326/97).

References

1. Gunnerson, E.: C# and exception specifications. Microsoft, 2000. Available online at:http://discuss.develop.com/archives/wa.exe?A2=ind0011A&L=DOTNET&P=R32820
2. Goodenough, J.B.: Exception handling: issues and a proposed notation. Communications of the ACM, 18(12) (December 1975)
3. Cristian, F.: Exception Handling and Software Fault Tolerance. In: Proceedings of FTCS-25(reprinted from FTCS-IO 1980, 97–103) 3, IEEE (1996)

4. Garcia, A., Rubira, C., Romanovsky, A., Xu., J.: A Comparative Study of Exception Handling Mechanisms for Building Dependable Object-Oriented Software. Journal of Systems and Software 2, 197–222 (2001)
5. Sinha, S., Harrold, M.: Analysis and Testing of Programs with Exception-Handling Constructs. IEEE Transactions on Software Engineering, 26, 9 (September 2000)
6. Miller, R., Tripathi, A.: Issues with exception handling in object-oriented systems. In: Aksit, M., Matsuoka, S. (eds.) ECOOP 1997. LNCS, vol. 1241, pp. 85–103. Springer, Heidelberg (1997)
7. Robillard, M.P., Murphy, G.C.: Designing robust JAVA programs with exceptions. In: Proceedings of the 8th ACM SIGSOFT International Symposium on Foundations of Software Engineering. 25, 6 (November 2000). ACM Press (2000)
8. Lippert, M., Lopes, C.: A Study on Exception Detection and Handling Using Aspect-Oriented Programming. In: Proceedings of the 22nd International Conference on Software Engineering, Ireland 2000, ACM Press, New York, NY, USA (2000)
9. Filho, F., Rubira, C., Garcia, A.: A Quantitative Study on the Aspectization of Exception Handling. In: Black, A.P. (ed.) ECOOP 2005. LNCS, vol. 3586, Springer, Heidelberg (2005)
10. Elrad, T., Filman, R.E., Bader, A.: Aspect-Oriented Programming. Communications of the ACM, 44 (10), 29-32. (2001)
11. Parr, T.: ANTLR – Another Tool for Language Recognition. University of San Francisco (2006), Available online at:http://www.antlr.org/
12. Javacc -Java Compiler Compiler. Available online at: https://javacc.dev.java.net/
13. Cabral, B., Marques, P., Silva, L.: RAIL: Code Instrumentation for.NET. In: Preneel, B., Tavares, S. (eds.) SAC 2005. LNCS, vol. 3897, Springer, Heidelberg (2006)
14. Chiba, S.: Load-Time Structural Reflection in Java. In: Bertino, E. (ed.) ECOOP 2000. LNCS, vol. 1850, Springer, Heidelberg (2000)
15. Gosling, J., Joy, B., Steele, G., Bracha, G.: The JAVA Language Specification. Sun Microsystems, Inc, Mountain View, California, U.S.A (2000)
16. ECMA International. Standard ECMA-335 Common Language Infrastructure(CLI). ECMA Standard (2003), Available online at: http://www.ecma-international.org/publications/standards/ecma-335.htm
17. Goldberg, A., Robson, D.: Smalltalk-80: the language and its implementation. Addison-Wesley Longman Publishing Co., Inc, Boston, MA (1983)
18. Meyer, B.: Eiffel: the Language. Prentice-Hall, Inc. Upper Saddle River, NJ, USA, (1992).
19. Cabral, B., Marques, P.: Making Exception Handling Work. In: Proceedings of the Workshop on Hot Topics in System Dependability (HotDep'06), USENIX, Seattle, USA (November 2006)

On the Impact of Aspectual Decompositions on Design Stability: An Empirical Study

Phil Greenwood[1], Thiago Bartolomei[2], Eduardo Figueiredo[1], Marcos Dosea[3],
Alessandro Garcia[1], Nelio Cacho[1], Cláudio Sant'Anna[1,4], Sergio Soares[5],
Paulo Borba[3], Uirá Kulesza[4], and Awais Rashid[1]

[1] Lancaster University, United Kingdom
{p.greenwood,e.figueiredo,n.cacho,a.garcia}@lancaster.ac.uk
awais@comp.lancs.ac.uk
[2] Kiel University of Applied Sciences, Germany
thiago.bartolomei@gmail.com
[3] Federal University of Pernambuco, Brazil
{mbd2,phmb}@cin.ufpe.br
[4] Pontifical Catholic University of Rio, Brazil
{claudio,uira}@les.inf.puc-rio.br
[5] Pernambuco State University, Brazil
sergio@dsc.upe.br

Abstract. Although one of the main promises of aspect-oriented (AO) programming techniques is to promote better software changeability than object-oriented (OO) techniques, there is no empirical evidence on their efficacy to prolong design stability in realistic development scenarios. For instance, no investigation has been performed on the effectiveness of AO decompositions to sustain overall system modularity and minimize manifestation of ripple-effects in the presence of heterogeneous changes. This paper reports a quantitative case study that evolves a real-life application to assess various facets of design stability of OO and AO implementations. Our evaluation focused upon a number of system changes that are typically performed during software maintenance tasks. They ranged from successive re-factorings to more broadly-scoped software increments relative to both crosscutting and non-crosscutting concerns. The study included an analysis of the application in terms of modularity, change propagation, concern interaction, identification of ripple-effects and adherence to well-known design principles.

1 Introduction

Design stability [1-4] encompasses the sustenance of system modularity properties and the absence of ripple-effects in the presence of change. Development of stable designs has increasingly been a deep challenge to software engineers due to the high volatility of systemic concerns and their dependencies [5]. Contemporary developers often need to embrace a plethora of unexpected changes on driving design concerns, ranging from simple perfective modifications and re-factorings to more architecturally-relevant system increments. In fact, incremental development has been established as the de-facto practice in realistic software development in order to

E. Ernst (Ed.): ECOOP 2007, LNAI 4609, pp. 176–200, 2007.
© Springer-Verlag Berlin Heidelberg 2007

progressively cope with such evolving system concerns [1, 3, 5]. Some recent industrial case studies have demonstrated that around 50% of object-oriented (OO) code is altered between two releases, and 68% of change requests are accepted and implemented [1, 3].

It has been empirically observed that design stability is directly dependent on the underlying decomposition mechanisms [4-6]. For instance, certain studies have detected that the versatility of multiple inheritance is one of the main causes of ripple-effects in OO systems [6]. Interestingly, we are in an age where emerging aspect-oriented (AO) programming techniques [7] are targeted at improving software maintainability. The proponents of aspect-oriented programming argue that superior modularity and changeability of crosscutting concerns are obtained through the use of new composition mechanisms, such as pointcut-advice and inter-type declarations. It is often claimed that such AO mechanisms support enhanced incremental development [5, 6, 8], and avoid early design degradation [9].

However, there is no empirical evidence AO decompositions promote superior design stability in realistic evolutionary software development [1], especially when experiencing changes of a diverse nature. Most of the existing case-studies in the literature have reported on the positive and negative impacts of aspect-oriented programming in the upfront modularization of conventional crosscutting concerns such as: persistence [9-11], distribution [11], exception handling [12, 13], and design patterns [14-16]. More fundamentally, these evaluations do not compare the stability of AO and OO decompositions while applying heterogeneous types of changes to both crosscutting and non-crosscutting concerns. As a result, there is no empirical knowledge on how aspect-oriented programming contributes to the reduction of ripple-effects and design principle violations in incremental development scenarios.

This paper presents a case-study that quantitatively assesses the stability of OO and AO design versions of a real-life Web-based information system, called Health Watcher (HW). The OO version was implemented in Java, while the AO versions were implemented in AspectJ [17] and CaesarJ [8]. Our evaluation focused upon ten releases of the HW system, which underwent a number of typical maintenance tasks, including: re-factorings, functionality increments, extensions of abstract modules, and more complex system evolutions. Some of the crosscutting concerns were "aspectized" from the first release, while others were modularized as new HW versions were released. Very often, additive and subtractive modifications required the alteration of how two or more concerns were inter-related. The design stability of OO and AO versions was evaluated according to conventional suites of modularity and change impact metrics. Such measures allowed us to analyze the extent to which the OO and AO implementations were vulnerable to ripple-effects, and exhibited symptoms of violations of fundamental design properties, such as the narrow interfaces and the Open-Closed principle [18].

The main outcomes of our analysis *in favour* of AO designs were:

(1) the concerns aspectized upfront tended to show superior modularity stability in the AO designs; changes tended to be confined to the target module and only minor fragility scenarios were observed in the aspect interfaces;

(2) AO solutions required less intrusive modification (e.g. changes to existing operations and lines of code) even when the change focused on a non-crosscutting concern;

(3) aspectual decompositions have demonstrated superior satisfaction of the Open-Closed principle [18] in most of the maintenance scenarios;

(4) both OO and AO implementations have exhibited a significant stability of high-level design structures; however, architectural ripple effects (i.e. changes to architectural elements) were observed when persistence-related exceptions needed to be introduced in the OO design;

Alternatively, the main findings *against* aspectual decompositions were:

(1) significant incidence of violation of pivotal design principles – such as narrow interfaces and low coupling – were detected in evolutionary scenarios involving classical design patterns, such as the Command and State design patterns [19];

(2) although invasive modification was more frequent in the OO solution, the AO modifications tended to propagate to seemingly unrelated modules;

(3) in general the aspectization of exception handling has shown no improvement; in addition, certain design degeneration was observed due to the creation of artificial method signatures in order to expose contextual information to the aspectized exception handlers.

The remainder of the paper is structured as follows: Section 2 describes the experimental settings and justifies the decisions made to ensure the study is valid. Section 3 describes the Health Watcher system used as the base for this study and also describes the changes applied. The results gathered from applying modularity metrics are discussed in Section 4. Section 5 discusses how the changes propagate within each paradigm. The evolution of the concern interactions are discussed in Section 6. Other related discussions of the results are conducted in Section 7. Finally, Sections 8 and 9 conclude this paper by discussing related work and summarizing this paper's findings.

2 Experimental Settings

This section describes the configuration of our study including the choice of the target application (Section 2.1), and the evaluation methodology (Section 2.2).

2.1 Target System Selection

The first major decision that had to be made in our investigation was the selection of the target application. The chosen system is a typical Web-based information system, called Health Watcher (HW) [11]. The main purpose of the HW system is to allow citizens to register complaints regarding health issues. This system was selected because it met a number of relevant criteria for our intended evaluation. First, it is a real and non-trivial system with existing Java and AspectJ implementations (each around 4000 lines of code). The HW system is particularly rich in the kinds of non-crosscutting and crosscutting concerns present in its design. HW also involves a number of recurring concerns and technologies common in day-to-day software development, such as GUI, persistence, concurrency, RMI, Servlets and JDBC. Second, each HW design and implementation choice for both OO and AO solutions has been extensively discussed and evolved in a controlled manner. Both the OO and

AO designs (Sections 3.1 and 3.2) of the HW system were developed with modularity and changeability principles as main driving design criteria. Third, qualitative and quantitative studies of the HW system have been recently conducted [9, 11] allowing us to correlate our results with these previous studies. Finally, the first HW release of the Java implementation was deployed in March 2001, since then a number of incremental and perfective changes have been addressed in posterior HW releases; it has allowed us to observe typical types of changes in such an application domain.

2.2 Study Phases and Change Scenarios

The study was divided into three major phases: *(1)* the development and alignment of HW versions, *(2)* the implementation of change scenarios, and *(3)* the assessment of the three versions (developed in phase 1) and the successive releases (delivered in phase 2). In the first phase, we prepared the base versions of the OO and AO implementations of the HW system. The OO solution was already available and implemented in Java. Two AO implementations were assessed: one based on a pre-existing AspectJ version (implemented after the original OO implementation) [11, 17], and a newly created CaesarJ [8] version for this study. Both the Java and AspectJ implementation have been successfully used in other studies [9, 11], and so provided a solid foundation for this study. An independent post-graduate student was responsible for implementing the CaesarJ version by re-factoring the Java implementation. We would like to highlight that this study has not targeted the comparison of the two AO programming languages (i.e. AspectJ and CaesarJ). On the contrary, the objective of using more than one particular language was to allow us to yield broader conclusions that are agnostic to specific AO language features.

All three base HW versions were verified according to a number of *alignment rules* in order to assure that coding styles and implemented functionality were exactly the same. Moreover, the implementations followed the same design decisions in that best practices were applied in all implementations to ensure a high degree of modularity and reusability. This alignment and validation exercise was performed by an independent post-doc researcher. A number of test-cases were exhaustively used for all the releases of the Java, AspectJ and CaesarJ versions to ease the alignment process. These alignment procedures assure that the comparison between versions is equitable and fair. Inevitably, some minor re-factorings in the three versions had to be performed when misalignments were observed at the composition-level, interface-level, module-level or even LOC-level. When these misalignments were discovered the implementers for that particular version (in the case of the Java and AspectJ versions this was the original HW developers) were notified and instructed to correct the implementation accordingly.

The second phase involved the implementation of nine changes (Section 3.3) in all three HW versions (available from [20]). Each change involved: *(i)* the design and implementation of new modules to be included or existing modules to be removed from the system, *(ii)* the use of language mechanisms to compose such new modules with existing ones, and *(iii)* if necessary, changes to the modules already present in the previous HW release. Also, for each change, we needed to again ensure that the Java, AspectJ and CaesarJ implementations were aligned and so the alignment process described above was applied to each subsequent version of HW developed.

The goal of the third phase was to compare the design stability of AO and OO designs. In order to support a multi-dimensional data analysis, the assessment phase was further decomposed in four main stages. The first two stages (Section 4) are aimed at examining the overall maintenance effects in fundamental modularity properties through the HW releases. The third stage (Section 5) evaluates the three implementations from the perspective of change propagation. The last stage (Section 6) focuses on assessing design stability in terms of how the implementation of concern "boundaries" and their dependencies have evolved through the HW releases. Section 7 also discusses architecture-level design stability. Traditional metrics suites were used in all the assessment stages, and will be discussed in the respective sections. Although design stability is discussed in terms of these metrics, the metric measurements are a direct reflection of design changes, i.e. any variations in the metric values are evidence of changes that occurred in the code structure.

3   Health Watcher System

Both the OO and AO architectural designs of the HW system are mainly determined by the conjunctive application of both client-server and layered architectural styles [21]. The original architecture aimed at modularizing user interface, distribution, business rules, and data management concerns. Most of them are layers in both the OO and AO architectures; the only exception is the distribution concern that has been aspectized and is no longer a layer in the AO architectural design. All the corresponding OO and AO design structures that realize such driving design concerns have been successfully reused in several applications [3, 10, 11]. Fig. 1 and Fig. 2 present representative slices of both OO and AO architecture designs.

3.1   The Object-Oriented Design

In the HW system, complaints are registered, updated and queried through a Web client implemented using Java Servlets [22], represented by the components in the view layer. Accesses to the HW services are made through the *IFacade* interface, which is implemented by the *HealthWatcherFacade*. This facade works as a portal to access the business collections, such as *ComplaintRecord* and *EmployeeRecord*. Records access the data layer using interfaces, like *IComplaintRep*, which decouple the business logic from the specific type of data management in use. For example, Fig. 1 shows a *ComplaintRep* class that implements a repository for a database.

This structure prevents some code tangling, because it clearly separates some main concerns in layers. However, tangling is not completely avoided [11]. For example, the *HealthWatcherFacade* implements several concerns, including transaction management (persistence) and distribution. One possibility is the use of adapters [19] to take care of transaction functionality, but at a high price, since developers must maintain both the facade and the adapter.

The design of the OO HW system also fails to completely prevent code scattering. For example, business components implement the distribution concern; this comes from the need to implement the *Serializable* interface to allow them to be sent across a network. Furthermore, almost all components must deal with the exception handling concern. However, despite not completely separating concerns, the layered architecture gives some support to adaptability. For instance, in the system configuration used in our experiment, instead of RMI, one could use EJBs.

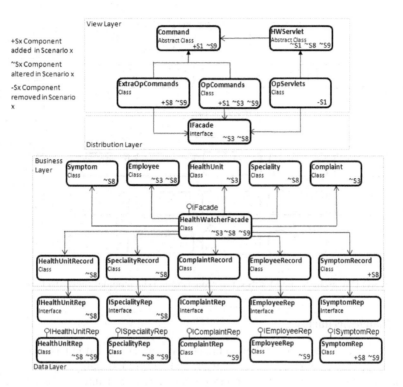

Fig. 1. OO HW architecture. A sub-set of scenarios and the modules they affect are marked.

3.2 The Aspect-Oriented Design

Fig. 2 displays a diagram that is essentially the same for both AO implementations (AspectJ and CaesarJ). The AO versions modularize some concerns that were tangled and scattered in the OO decomposition counterpart. Basically, in the first AO release of the HW system, crosscutting elements relative to distribution, persistence, and concurrency control concerns were modularized as aspects.

For instance, the concurrency control concern was removed from the layers and encapsulated in two aspects, namely *HWManagedSync* and *HWTimestamp*; each of these deals with a specific facet of concurrency control. Timestamp is a technique used to avoid object inconsistency. This problem can occur when two copies of an object are retrieved by different requests before one of them can update its version. The technique uses a timestamp field to avoid object updating if there is a newer version of it stored in the persistence mechanism.

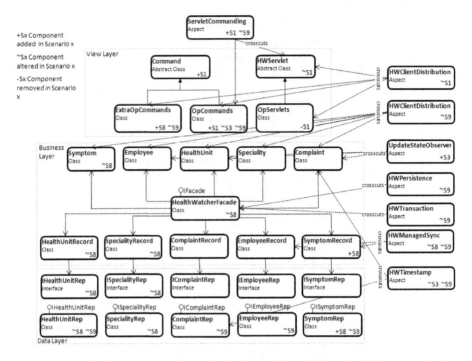

Fig. 2. AO HW architecture. A sub-set of scenarios and the modules they affect are marked.

3.3 Change Scenarios

The selected changes to be applied to the HW system are varied in terms of the types of modifications performed. Some of them add new functionality, some improve or replace functionality, and others improve the system structure for better reuse or modularity. The purpose was to expose the OO and AO implementations to distinct maintenance and evolution tasks that are recurring in incremental software development. These changes originated from a variety of sources: the experiences of the original developers of HW including changes they would like to implement (that are actually necessary) and changes from previous empirical studies [9, 12]. The remaining changes were created by the students and researchers involved in this study, where certain extensions and improvements that could be applied were identified. This ensured a variety of sources of changes was used and so would not artificially bias one paradigm. Before the changes were applied, the original developers of HW were consulted to confirm whether these changes were valid.

This wide range of modifications provide an indication as to whether one paradigm supports better design stability for certain types of change. The changes were implemented using the best possible practices in the given paradigm to ensure a fair comparison. Each of the scenarios is summarized in Table 1, a sub-set of the scenarios and the modules that they affect in the OO and AO paradigm are marked on Fig. 1 and Fig. 2 according to whether a component is added, removed or modified during a particular scenario.

Table 1. Summary of the scenarios used in the study

Scenario	Change	Impact
1	Factor out multiple Servlets to improve extensibility.	View Layer
2	Ensure the complaint state cannot be updated once closed to protect complaints from multiple updates.	View/Business Layers
3	Encapsulate update operations to improve maintainability using common software engineering practices.	Business/View Layers
4	Improve the encapsulation of the distribution concern for better reuse and customization.	View/Distribution/ Business Layers
5	Generalize the persistence mechanism to improve reuse and extensibility.	Business/Data Layers
6	Remove dependencies on Servlet response and request objects to ease the process of adding new GUIs.	View Layer
7	Generalize distribution mechanism to improve reuse and extensibility.	Business/View/ Distribution Layers
8	New functionality added to support querying of more data types.	Business/Data/View Layers
9	Modularize exception handling and include more effective error recovery behaviour into handlers.	Business/Data/View Layers

4 Modularity Analysis

We have described earlier how the assessment procedures were organized in four stages (Section 2.2). This section presents the results for the first two stages, where we primarily analyze the initial modularity of each OO and AO solutions (Section 4.1). Then we analyze their stability throughout the implemented changes (Section 4.2). Both the first and second assessment phases are supported by a metrics suite that quantified four fundamental modularity attributes, namely separation of concerns (SoC), coupling, cohesion, and conciseness [23]. Such metrics were chosen because they have already been used in several experimental studies and proven to be effective quality indicators (e.g. [9, 12, 14, 15, 24]).

The metrics for coupling, cohesion, and size were defined based on classic OO metrics [25]; the original metrics definitions were extended to be applied in a paradigm-independent way, supporting the generation of comparable results. Also, this suite introduces three new metrics for quantifying SoC. They measure the degree to which a single concern in the system maps to: (i) the design *components* (i.e. classes and aspects) – based on the CDC metric (Concern Diffusion over Components), (ii) *operations* (i.e. methods and advice) – based on the CDO metric (Concern Diffusion over Operations), and (iii) *lines of code* – based on the CDLOC metric (Concern Diffusion over Lines of Code). The majority of these metrics can be collected automatically by applying the appropriate tool [26, 27].

The separation of concern metrics had to be calculated manually. This involved a post-graduate student (not involved in the implementation phase of the study) 'shadowing' the code to identify which segment of code contributed to which concern. In circumstances when it was not clear which concern the segment contributed to, discussions between all people involved in the implementation took place to reach a common agreement. For all the employed metrics, a lower value implies a better result. Detailed discussions about the metrics are out of the scope of this work and appear elsewhere [14, 23].

4.1 Quantifying Initial Modularity

This stage evaluates the modularity of the base versions in order to have an overall understanding of the modularity attributes of the first release of each OO and AO implementation. Hence, it can support our further analysis on how the maintenance changes affected the degree of modularity initially obtained in the Java, AspectJ and CaesarJ implementations. Instead of analysing each individual metric result, we provide a general view of the meanings behind the results. Fig. 3 presents the modularity results for SoC, coupling, cohesion, and size in the base version. The *concurrency* concern is representative of all the analysed crosscutting concerns which included: concurrency, persistence, distribution and exception handling. Furthermore, other architectural and design elements were analysed using the SoC metrics that are discussed later, these elements included: view (GUI) layer, business layer and various design pattern. The metrics raw data can be found at [20].

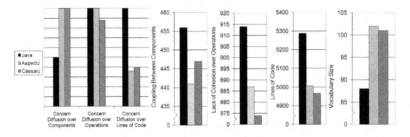

Fig. 3. Relative SoC metric values for concurrency (CDC, CDO and CDLOC), and absolute values for coupling, cohesion, lines of code and vocabulary size for the base version of Health Watcher

A careful analysis of the measures (Fig. 3) determines that the AO implementations offer superior modularity in these initial versions. Even though the base AO implementations have more modules (measured by the Vocabulary Size metric which counts the number of components) and a higher Concern Diffusion over Components (CDC), this does not automatically mean that separation of concerns is worse. It is due to the fact that additional aspectual modules have been created for the purpose of isolating certain crosscutting concerns (Section 3.2). When other values are analysed together, such as Concern Diffusion over Lines of Code (CDLOC) and over Operations (CDO), Coupling between Components (CBC), Lack of Cohesion over Operations (LCOO), it becomes clear that AO implementations create more cohesive and self-contained modules that are less coupled to each other. They create dedicated components for each concern, but they also require fewer Lines of Code (LOC), since they reduce the duplicated code. The subsequent sections will analyse how these modularity properties alter due to the application of change scenarios (Section 3.3).

4.2 Quantifying Modularity Stability

After producing an overview of the modularity attributes in the base versions we proceeded with the analysis regarding the stability of these attributes. In the following we present the most significant results for each modularity attribute.

The variations in the modularity metrics are traced back to the implementations in order to determine the causes of instability. Generally, any variation to their values is considered undesirable. Often the variations are unavoidable, particularly when a certain module is the focus of an implementation change. Thus, we categorise the variation in the values as either being unavoidable or negative. Unavoidable variations occur when a component that is directly related to the affected concern is altered. For example, if a scenario targets the GUI concern, then variations in the metric values for the view related modules are generally expected and unavoidable. However, if unrelated modules are affected, then these should be considered as being negative variation. As a result, the approach with the most stable design is the one which minimises the number of negative variations.

Concern Measures. The analyzed crosscutting concerns included concurrency, distribution, persistence, and exception handling. These were selected because they were the main modularization target either at the initial HW design decomposition (Sections 3.1 and 3.2) or subject to change when applying the scenarios described in Section 3.3. For the same reasons, other non-crosscutting concerns were also analyzed including the view and business layers of the HW architecture. Finally, the modularity of concerns relative to some key design patterns adopted during the system HW evolutions – such as the Command and State design patterns [19] – were analyzed.

From the analysis of SoC metric results, three distinct groups of concerns naturally emerged, with respect to which type of modularization paradigm presents superior stability. The following set of figures illustrates the relative variations between versions in the Java, AspectJ and Caesar implementations. When no bar for a particular implementation is present, this means no variation in that particular measure was observed for the corresponding scenario. We do not distinguish in the graphics the difference between an increase in a metric value and a drop in a metric value.

Concerns with Superior AO Design Stability. Most of the concerns that present a widely-scoped crosscutting nature have presented superior design stability when implemented using AO techniques. This includes concurrency, persistence and distribution, with the sole exclusion of exception handling (discussed later). All of these concerns were modularized into aspects from the first AspectJ and CaesarJ implementations. Fig. 4 presents the metrics results for the concurrency concern, the representative of how concerns in this group have behaved. In general, the concern diffusion over components (CDC) metric is less affected on AO implementations as the initial modules seem to cope well with newly introduced scenarios and the changes are localized in these modules.

The concern diffusion over operations (CDO) metric also presents a very superior result for the AO implementations. This difference largely comes from the quantification properties in AO, where the use of declare statements and regular expressions in pointcuts eliminates the need for some operations. For example, in the specific case of concurrency, the timestamp behaviour affects CDO in the OO implementation (particularly in Scenario 2), but has less influence on the values for AO version, where it is implemented with advice and intertype declarations (or bindings in CaesarJ). The results for concern diffusion over lines of code (CDLOC) provide evidence that AO implementations present better stability.

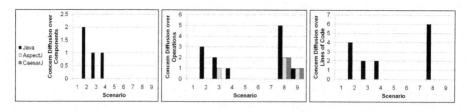

Fig. 4. Changes in the SoC metrics for the concurrency concern

Concerns with Superior OO Design Stability. Concerns that are widely scoped but that do not have a crosscutting nature, such as view and business; have presented slightly superior design stability in the OO implementation. Fig. 5 presents the metrics results for the view concern. In general, this type of concern is already well modularised by OO decompositions and this modularisation is stable throughout the changes. AO implementations do not visibly modify this OO modularisation, but the transfer of some functionality affects the stability of these concerns. Using the view results as an example, we observe that the concerns are spread over the same number of more components (CDC) in AO. That is because the AO implementations not only suffer from the same unavoidable changes as OO, but also may present some negative changes, such as new pointcuts having to be introduced to aspects related to the view layer. In contrast, the OO implementation will have the necessary functionality inserted directly to the view layer and so will not impact the CDC metric. The number of operations per concern (CDO) also shows the same general trend. The concern diffusion over lines of code (CDLOC) results provide additional evidence of the superiority of OO decompositions for these concerns, because the AO implementations are more instable with respect to how certain concerns interact with each other (Section 6).

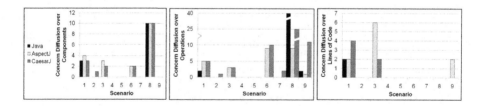

Fig. 5. Changes in the SoC metrics for the view layer

Concerns with no Stability Superiority Observed. Some concerns have not presented explicit superiority in either of the paradigms. These include the exception handling (EH) concern and also the more localized concerns, such as the Command and State patterns [19]. As can be observed in Fig. 6, both paradigms experience similar high degrees of variation in all the metrics for the EH concern. This similarity occurs for two main reasons. First, the EH concern was not explicitly modularised in the AO implementations until the last scenario (Section 3.3). Before that, the exception handlers were just aspectized when they related to other concerns that were also aspectized. For example, when concurrency was aspectized, its handlers were also removed from the base code and encapsulated in a new module. Second, AO implementations were not able to promote modularization gains in terms of this concern even in Scenario 9. The general problem with using AO to encapsulate EH is that it usually involves negative changes through the creation of artificial operations in order to expose context information for the aspectized exceptional behaviour [12].

When analysing the results for the more localized concerns we were confronted with very distinct and irregular patterns. It was not possible to generalize about their stability, because specific characteristics of the concerns and their applications play a major role on the results. For example, the State pattern was very stable and similar for all metrics in both paradigms. However, the Command pattern was stable through several scenarios but was largely affected by the last two scenarios, in a similar proportion on AO and OO. We conclude that, due to the narrow scope of these concerns, their stability largely depends on the localization of the change.

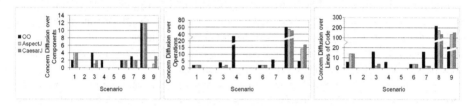

Fig. 6. Changes in the SoC metrics for the exception handling concern

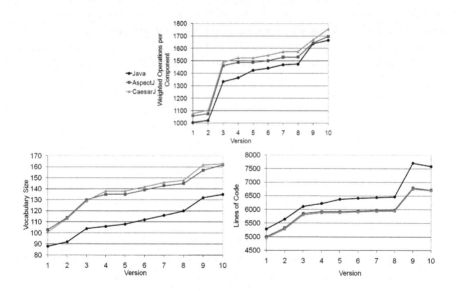

Fig. 7. Size metric variation through the 10 versions

Size Measures. Both OO and AO implementations present very similar stability with respect to size measures. Fig. 7 shows the absolute results for Weighted Operations per Component (WOC – i.e. complexity of operations based on number of parameters) and

Vocabulary Size (VS – i.e. number of components) through the versions. The VS curves show that AO implementations tend to be worse, and this difference gets larger, rendering AO less stable regarding the number of components needed to modularize the concerns. The Lines of Code (LOC) curves, present an inverted result, where AO implementations scale better, due to being able to avoid repeated code.

The WOC curves show that AO implementations are usually more complex, as they introduce pointcuts and advice that are counted as operations. In general the curves are very similar. However, AO performs better for functional changes (i.e. Scenario 9), due to better quantification, but poorly in the exception handling scenario as new advice and artificial methods must be created for each handler. As a general conclusion for the size attribute, AO is more stable with respect to LOC and for functional changes, while OO is better in VS and in exception handling.

Coupling and Cohesion Measures. Due to the strong synergy between coupling and cohesion, we will discuss these two attributes together. The Depth of Inheritance Tree (DIT) metrics are largely the same and do not bring any interesting insights. In this section we will refer to Coupling Between Components (CBC) and Lack of Cohesion over Operations (LCOO) metrics as coupling and cohesion.

Fig. 8 displays the graphs for the average cohesion and coupling per component. Observing the curves, AO implementations have generally much more stable values for both coupling and cohesion. It can be seen that most of the scenarios actually improve their values, while OO implementations are affected in different ways. The only major changes for AO occur in version three and the last two scenarios. In the former, the cohesion values are worsen due to hook methods having to be inserted in the base code for the newly added aspects to be executed correctly. In general, AO implementations were much better and more stable with respect to coupling and cohesion attributes due to the generic capabilities of AO techniques.

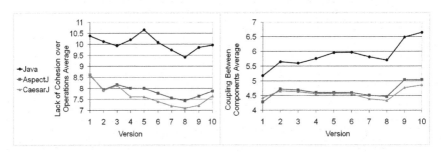

Fig. 8. Average results for cohesion (left) and coupling (right) per component throughout the versions

5   Change Impact Analysis

This section describes the third assessment stage where we quantitatively analyze to what extent each maintenance scenario entails undesirable change propagations in the AO and OO HW implementations.

5.1 Impact of the Change Nature

This phase relies on a suite of typical change impact measures [3, 4] presented in Table 2, such as number of components (aspects/classes) added or changed, number of added or modified LOC, and so forth. The purpose of using these metrics is to quantitatively assess the propagation effects, when applying the various changes, in terms of different levels of abstraction: components, operations, lines of code and relationships. The lower the change impact measures the more stable and resilient the design is to a certain change.

Table 2. Change propagation metrics for Java (J), AspectJ (A) and CaesarJ (C)

		Sc. 1	Sc. 2	Sc. 3	Sc. 4	Sc. 5	Sc. 6	Sc. 7	Sc. 8	Sc. 9
Added Components	J	24	12	2	3	4	4	4	12	5
	A	29	16	3	0	4	4	2	12	6
	C	25	16	3	0	4	4	2	12	6
Changed Components	J	2	6	14	25	1	24	2	23	46
	A	2	5	4	0	1	26	2	19	52
	C	2	4	5	0	1	25	2	18	21
Added Operations	J	4	4	10	0	0	0	0	62	5
	A	2	7	1	0	0	0	0	40	16
	C	2	7	1	0	0	0	0	32	17
Changed Operations	J	3	61	15	19	2	25	1	21	94
	A	0	57	3	0	1	25	0	10	94
	C	0	57	6	0	1	25	0	14	99
Added Pointcuts	A	5	12	8	0	2	0	2	0	16
	C	5	12	11	0	1	0	0	4	9
Changed	A	1	0	0	0	0	1	2	3	1
	C	1	0	0	0	0	1	0	4	1
Added LOC	J	72	59	123	294	6	1	0	653	109
	A	4	34	4	0	1	2	0	290	60
	C	8	35	6	0	1	2	0	300	70
Changed LOC	J	4	53	12	40	1	107	1	13	177
	A	2	50	0	0	5	110	4	9	141
	C	2	52	5	0	5	110	4	5	187

Adherence to the Open-Closed Principle. AO solutions generally require more new components to implement a change. In comparison the OO implementation require existing components to be modified more extensively to implement the same change. This behaviour is confirmed in the change propagation metrics (see Table 2) whereby much more extensive changes (in terms of added operations and LOC) occur in the OO version. Up to 30% fewer operations and up to 60% fewer LOC are added in the AO implementations throughout the scenarios. This indicates that the AO solutions conform more closely to the Open-Closed principle [18] which states that "software should be open for extension, but closed for modification".

The scenario which demonstrates this difference best is Scenario 3. The purpose of this scenario is to isolate the update method calls, which is implemented in the form of the Observer pattern [19]. This involves modifying a sub-set of the command classes in the view layer by removing the update calls. However, the OO implementation requires further modification, for example a variety of classes within the business layer require modification (marked on Fig. 1) so that the update method is called when the state of business objects alters. The AO implementation is able to quantify and capture these state changes via pointcuts and so the Observer pattern is able to be applied by introducing new components rather than modifying existing ones (the added modules are marked on Fig. 2).

In order to analyse the results more closely and to identify specific reasons for these changes the results will be split into three categories: the first examines groups of scenarios where the AO versions are superior, the second focuses on scenarios where the AO and OO implementations are comparable and the final category looks at scenarios where the OO version is superior. It is interesting to note that these categories can be mapped to particular types of change.

Propagation of Functional Changes is Superior in AO Designs. When considering the scenarios (1, 3, 8 and 9) where the AO solutions are superior, they require fewer changes to components (in terms of modified LOC, added LOC, etc). It is also clear that these changes are absorbed in other ways. For example, we can see that pointcuts must either be modified or added in these scenarios. Equally, the OO implementation requires new fields/parameters to be added directly to the base classes in order to implement the changes in these scenarios. These additions can be directly absorbed within new aspects. What is not clear from analysing these metrics in isolation is which type of change propagation is more desirable and which paradigm provides the better mechanism for absorbing these changes. When considering the earlier modularity metrics we can conclude that the AO implementation has less impact on these attributes and so AO provides better mechanisms for absorbing these changes. Note that the changes performed in Scenario 4 reflect an attempt to improve the modularity of the distribution concern, as this concern was already well modularised in the AO versions no changes were necessary.

AO and OO are Comparable when Implementing Perfective Changes. In the cases where (Scenarios 5, 6, and 7) the AO and OO implementations have similar change propagation metrics, the modifications are related to improving the design structure of HW in terms of extensibility and reusability. These improvements to the design generally target OO concepts, this can be inferred from the metrics due to the low number of pointcuts added or modified in these scenarios. For example, two of the scenarios (6 and 7) involve splitting a class implementation in two parts. As this structure is repeated in both the AO and OO implementation it is natural that they are both affected in similar ways. This is also reflected in the earlier modularity metrics.

OO Implementation of the State Pattern was Superior. Finally, the OO implementation is clearly superior in Scenario 2, which basically involves the instantiation and inclusion of the State pattern [19]. Although the added state update behaviour is crosscutting, it does require 'hook methods' to be inserted in the base components for advice to be executed at the correct events. This results not only in the same structural changes as the OO implementation (introduction of methods, fields and inheritance relationships) but also in new aspects to be added. In comparison, the OO solution can encapsulate the same behaviour using OO mechanisms and, as a consequence, reduces the need for changes across modules. There are other scenarios (such as Scenario 1) where the suitability of using AO is questionable but due to the fact that multiple concerns are involved (view and distribution), the AO solutions are able to capture these relationships more cleanly and, so, offer improvements over OO.

5.2 Overall Stability Measurements

From these change propagation metrics various attributes can be extracted that can be used to comment on the implementations' stability. One of the most significant results from these stability metrics is the number of unique components modified through the nine scenarios applied. For each paradigm 72 different modules are modified throughout all the scenarios. It may appear at first glance that because this measure is the same the stability is also the same. However, the actual number of potential modules that could be modified has to be taken into account. In the case of the OO design, this is 1113 potential classes (the cumulative figure of all classes in all versions). The AO versions have over 250 more classes/aspects that could be modified. As a result, the fact that the number of modified modules is the same for the AO versions despite this, illustrates that the AO implementations are more stable.

Similarly, when analysing the changes to the LOC that are made to these 72 modules the AO solutions again show more stability. For example, in version 10 of the OO implementation of HW there are in total 5453 LOC of which 32% of these have either been modified or added during the course of the study. This is compared to around 4000 LOC in version 10 of the AO implementations of which only 18-19% have been added or modified.

6   Concern Interaction Analysis

We have presented results concerning the first three assessment phases. This section discusses the last evaluation stage: the scalability of OO and AO solutions from the viewpoint of stability in concern interactions.

The analysis of the data gathered based on the modularity and change impact metrics (Sections 4 and 5) makes it evident that most of the concerns involved in HW are scattered and tangled with each other over the system classes. For example, the class *HealthWatcherFacade* implements a business layer facade (Fig. 1), but also incorporates code for distribution- and persistence-specific functionalities. The implementation of certain system concerns and the way they interact through the system modular decomposition change as the system evolves. As a consequence, this section discusses how the concern interactions changed over time in the three HW implementations. The goal is to observe how changes relative to a specific concern "traversed the boundaries" of other concern implementations and/or generated new undesirable inter-concern dependencies.

6.1   Concern-Interaction Categories

We have performed an analysis of AO and OO design stability when there are interactions involving two or more concerns. In order to support such an analysis, we have observed different categories of interactions involving the analyzed concerns. In the context of the HW system, there are different ways in which the concerns interact with each other: invocation-based interaction, interlacing, and overlapping. Our classification of concern interactions is based on how the concern realizations share elements in the implementation artefacts, which have been defined and exploited in previous studies [12, 15].

Invocation-based Interactions. This is the simplest form of composition. The invocation-based interaction occurs when a component realizing the first concern is connected to a component realizing another concern based on one or more method calls. An example of this form of interaction is when the business facade class calls persistence methods to invoke transaction management in the OO HW version.

Interlacing. In this case, implementations of two concerns, C1 and C2, have one or more components in common [12, 15]. However, C1 and C2 are implemented by different sets of methods, attributes and statements in the shared classes. In other words, the involved concerns have common participant components, but there is no common element implementing both. We can identify interlacing either in the component level or in the method level. Both component- and method-level interlacing produce concern tangling but at different levels of abstraction. Alternatively, in the method-level interlacing the implementations of concerns C1 and C2 have one or more methods in common. However, different pieces of code in these methods are dedicated to implement both concerns. An example of this interaction category is the concurrency control implemented in some methods of data management classes of the OO HW version. In these methods there is exception handling code that is not related to the concurrency control concern.

Overlapping. The implementations of concerns C1 and C2 share one or more statements, attributes, methods, and components. This dependency style is different from interlacing because here the shared elements contribute to both concerns rather than being disjoint. Depending on the kind of elements participating in the interaction, it can be classified as component overlapping, operation overlapping, or attribute overlapping. The update methods are examples of operation overlapping. They are used to guarantee that in a distributed environment the modified data in one (client) machine is reflected to another (server) machine and that persistence data modified in memory is also reflected to the persistence mechanism.

6.2 Concern Interactions in the Base Versions

We explore the categories of concern interactions (previous subsection) in the base version in order to provide a general idea of how each pair of concerns depends on each other. This first analysis allows us to track the stability of these dependences through the software scenarios. We have analyzed all the 15 possible pair-wise concerns of the three HW implementations (Java, AspectJ and CaesarJ) and we have found many similarities between them. The results regarding the types of interactions are essentially the same for AspectJ and CaesarJ; therefore, we discuss them as AO issues. Our first observation is that, in general, concern boundaries are wider in the OO implementation, i.e. the concerns interact in more components in OO than in AO. Although the AO compositions usually present fewer components in the concern boundaries, these components usually present more intricate interactions. Fig. 9 presents two illustrative instances of concern interactions, concurrency with distribution and concurrency with persistence. The left side of the pie chart (Fig. 9) shows that 5 components present interlacing between the concurrency and distribution concerns in the OO version, while only 3 components present interlacing of these concerns in the AO version. In this interaction, it is not clear that components in the concern boundaries of the AO design have stronger interaction. On the other hand, in the concurrency with persistence interaction (Fig. 9, right side) the same number of operations (17) realizes the interaction between these two concerns. However, AO composition has more methods with overlapping of concerns (6 against 2). Furthermore, the AO version has fewer components with interlacing which also means a stronger dependency of concurrency with persistence in these components.

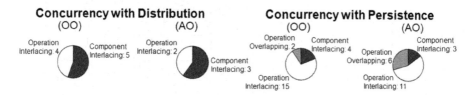

Fig. 9. Pie charts of interactions between concurrency and distribution concerns (left) and concurrency and persistence concerns (right) in the base versions

6.3 Scalability of Aspectual Decompositions

In this section we focus on the stability of each pair of concerns through the implementations. We verify for each concern the number of components it shares with other concerns. This kind of analysis supports assessment of concern modularization and stability because it shows whether the inter-concern coupling drops with the software evolution or not. Table 3 shows the obtained results for each pair-wise concern in terms of the number of components in the boundaries. Due to space limitations, this table presents only the results for the base version and Scenarios 3, 6 and 9 for all the 15 compositions. We have selected these versions because (i) they group together each 3 sequences of evolution and (ii) they represent scenarios with more extensive changes, including architectural ones.

The results in Table 3 show that, in general, concern interactions are more stable in the AO implementations through all scenarios. Only one composition, concurrency with view (see Table 3, line 9), presents stability in favour of OO. Alternatively, 5 compositions in AspectJ (and 4 in CaesarJ) present stable results: business with concurrency (line 1), concurrency with distribution (line 6), concurrency with EH (line 7), concurrency with persistence (line 8), and persistence with view (line 15). This last one is not totally stable in CaesarJ, but a minor variation occurs between the Scenarios 3 and 6. Besides, all the other AO compositions involving at least one crosscutting concern show an almost stable behaviour, such as business with persistence, distribution with view and business with distribution. This stability of AO solutions is a result of the better separation of crosscutting concerns. For instance, concurrency is far more stable in all of its compositions in AO solutions than in OO ones, which is explained by its better modularization (Section 4.2).

Similarly to concurrency, the concern interaction analysis summarized in Table 3 also shows that the distribution concern is far better separated in the AO versions. All compositions of distribution (lines 2, 6, 10, 11, and 12 of Table 3) have fewer shared components in AspectJ and CaesarJ. Although the introduction of the Adapter pattern

Table 3. Number of shared components of the pair-wise concerns through the HW implementations in Java (J), AspectJ (A) and CaesarJ (C)

Concerns Interaction		Base			Scenario 3			Scenario 6			Scenario 9		
		J	A	C	J	A	C	J	A	CJ	J	A	C
1	Bus + Conc	3	5	5	4	5	5	5	5	5	6	5	5
2	Bus + Dist	29	10	18	32	8	19	22	8	19	29	11	23
3	Bus + EH	26	30	29	28	30	29	29	30	29	38	41	40
4	Bus + Per	23	12	12	24	10	10	24	10	10	34	12	12
5	Bus + View	18	19	19	17	21	20	17	21	20	25	29	28
6	Conc + Dist	5	3	3	7	3	3	8	3	3	8	3	3
7	Conc + EH	7	11	11	9	11	11	10	11	11	11	11	11
8	Conc + Per	4	3	3	6	3	3	6	3	3	6	3	3
9	Conc + View	0	2	2	0	3	2	0	3	2	0	2	1
10	Dist + EH	40	32	32	44	29	29	33	29	29	37	31	32
11	Dist + Per	28	16	16	32	13	13	21	14	14	27	15	15
12	Dist + View	16	5	5	16	2	2	4	2	2	6	2	2
13	EH + Per	40	32	31	42	30	29	41	30	29	48	34	32
14	EH + View	20	24	24	23	28	28	23	28	28	32	38	39
15	Per + View	17	5	5	15	5	5	15	5	4	22	5	4

(Scenario 5) improves the separation of the distribution concern in the Java version and it also drops interaction of this concern, this improvement is not enough to make it superior to the AO implementations. In spite of the superiority of AO compositions of crosscutting concerns, OO is no worse in the interaction of non-crosscutting concerns. In fact, in most of compositions involving either business or view, OO is comparable to AO implementations or even better. For instance, the OO composition of concurrency with view has no shared classes in the base version and this situation remains stable in the following scenarios. This result is not surprising, as OO decomposition is suitable to modularize non-crosscutting concerns.

As mentioned earlier and also presented in Table 3, CaesarJ has very similar results to AspectJ. However, there are some exceptions which present significant difference, such as the business with distribution composition. In this composition the CaesarJ solution is worse than AspectJ, but better than Java. The difference between AspectJ and CaesarJ is due to their distinct composition mechanisms. The AspectJ solution uses declare parents construct to introduce the *Serializable* interface into classes, but CaesarJ does not provide such a construct. Therefore, this piece of code which is part of the distribution concern remains scattered in the CaesarJ implementation which contributes to the high interaction between business and distribution.

7 Discussions

7.1 Observing Ripple Effects

A further analysis performed was centred on identifying ripple-effects caused by changes that propagate between unrelated components. For example, if a change targets the Servlets then it would be hoped that these changes would be localised to the view layer. Any change which targets a particular concern and is propagated to other concerns is considered a negative change. Typically scenarios which target a crosscutting concern (i.e. Scenarios 5 and 7 which target persistence and distribution) the AO paradigm is able to localise these changes to specific components. In comparison the change has to span multiple layers/concerns in the OO version.

In scenarios which typically target the layers of the HW system the OO implementation performs better or comparable to the AO implementations. This is interesting as the AO implementation has the same core behaviour (in terms of layers) so the changes should propagate in a similar manner. As in the OO version, the AO core layers require modification but changes also propagate to other (seemingly) unrelated concerns. For example, Scenarios 1 and 6 specifically target the view layer; the OO implementation is able to contain these changes entirely within this layer. However, the AO versions require other additional concerns to be modified such as distribution and pattern implementations but not at the expense of modularity. Although the OO implementation also has these dependencies, the increased tangling prevents the modifications from spreading to multiple components but do affect more operations and LOC. A similar ripple-effect occurred between the persistence and concurrency concerns within Scenario 3, whereby the AO implementations required modification of the timestamp behaviour but the OO implementation did not due to the differences in the levels of concern locality (Section 4.2).

However, within the same scenario (Scenario 3) and Scenario 5 the OO implementation demonstrates a significant weakness that occurs in the majority of the scenarios. This is the high fragility [2, 28] of the *HealthWatcherFacade* class (see Fig. 1) which is caused by the extremely high tangling of concerns within this class. Although this may not seem a bad property due to the fact that it appears to reduce the ripple-effects it does increase the complexity and reduces the modularity.

Generally, we can conclude that ripple-effects occur in both the AO and OO versions. The improved SoC within the AO versions causes the changes to propagate to more unrelated components, making the changes less obvious as unexpected components are affected. In turn the OO version requires more extensive changes within each affected component making these changes more obvious. These differences lead to a notion of 'deep' and 'wide' ripple-effects. The AO ripple-effects tend to go 'deeper' in that the changes propagate to unrelated components. In comparison the OO ripple-effects tend to go 'wider' in that the ripple-effects tend to more extensively affect the modified components.

This notion is illustrated in Scenario 8, which focuses on modifying the business, view and data layers. The changes in the OO version tend to be located in each of these layers (marked on Fig. 1), however, the AO version requires additional behaviour to be added in seemingly unrelated components (marked on Fig. 2). The concurrency concern within OO implementation requires a concurrency manager to be inserted directly into the new classes added (hence being "wider"). In comparison the AO versions needs extra logic to determine which class is currently being accessed and then delegate to the appropriate concurrency manager and is "deeper" by affecting an unobvious component.

It would appear that wider ripple-effects were less problematic due to the changes having to be made being more obvious. However, when taking into account the earlier modularity metrics it is clear that if these ripple-effects could be identified or limited then the AO paradigm would be superior. Pointcut fragility [29] is the significant factor that contributes to these AO ripple-effects. For example, in Scenarios 6 and 8 the re-factorings and component additions that take place invalidate pointcuts that are used to apply the Observer pattern. This results in unintuitive changes having to be made. This trade-off that must be accounted for; future AO techniques should take this pointcut fragility into account and allow more expressive and semantic-based pointcuts to be specified.

7.2 Architecture Stability Analysis

Our policy to analyse design stability at the architecture level followed the same principle and relied on similar measures as in the implementation level. The analysis at the architecture level was supported by a modularity suite of metrics based on measures for SoC, component coupling and cohesion, and interface complexity. However, now the metrics are defined in terms of architecture-level abstractions, such as components, interfaces and operations [30]. First, we compared the modularity of the OO and AO HW architectures in the base version. For SoC, we assessed the scattering of the concerns over the design elements and the architecture description. The considered concerns during the analysis were: distribution, persistence, concurrency, exception handling, view, and business.

The most significant difference between the two solutions was related to the persistence concern. The persistence concern was present in many more architectural elements in the OO solution than in the AO solution. For instance, in the OO architecture more components (5 vs. 2), more interfaces (22 vs. 9) and more operations (154 vs. 45) have the persistence concern. The reason for this phenomenon is that, in the OO architecture, the persistence-specific exceptional events are propagated from components in the data layer to components in the view layer. Therefore, these persistence exception events are handled by almost all interfaces between the data, business, distribution, view layers. In the AO architecture, these exceptions are caught and treated via the persistence aspect earlier in the interfaces of the data layer and do not propagate through the other interfaces and respective layers.

After applying the metrics to the base version, we applied the metrics for both OO and AO architectures in the other versions of the HW system. The goal was to analyse the impact of the evolution changes in the architecture modularity. The scenario which changes impact most in the architecture was Scenario 8. This occurred because this scenario demanded the addition of a number of operations in the interfaces between each connected pair of layers. Note that Scenario 8 impacts the boundaries of every layer in Fig. 1 and Fig. 2. For instance, it affected *IFacade*, *HealthWatcherFacade* and *IHealthUnitRep* interfaces in the distribution, business and data layers respectively. In fact, the measures showed that the persistence concern is more stable in the AO architecture. As the persistence concern is not well modularized in the OO architecture (as stated earlier), every operation added in Scenario 8 had to address the persistence concern. Each new operation had to consider the persistence-specific exceptional events. The concern metrics highlighted that the number of operations containing the persistence concern in the OO architecture increased 38 (from 154 in the base version to 192) in the version produced after applying Scenario 8. In comparison, the increase that occurred in the AO architecture was just one operation. This result confirmed the previous results for the implementation level that Scenario 8 favours the AO implementation of the persistence concern due to the quantification mechanisms.

8 Related Work and Study Constraints

8.1 Related Work

The current body of empirical knowledge on AO techniques cannot explain the influence of compelling aspect interactions on long-term design stability. Lopes and Bajracharya [31] presented an analysis of modularity in AO design using the theory of modular design developed by Baldwin and Clark [32]. They have studied the design evolution of a Web Service application where they observed the effects of applying aspect modularisations using Design Structure Matrix and Net Option Value. It was an interesting first experiment that observed that there was added value in introducing aspects into an already modularized design. It contributes to an earlier work by Sullivan [33] by: (i) providing a realistic and modern example, and (ii) the analysis of effects of AOP on the value of the overall design. However, this study involved only the application of only two kinds of aspects: logging and authentication.

There is little related work focusing either on the quantitative assessment of AO solutions in general, or on the empirical investigation about the design stability of AO decompositions. Substantial empirical evidence is missing even for crosscutting concerns that software engineers face every day, such as persistence, distribution, and exception handling. There are several case studies in the literature involving the "aspectization" of such pervasive crosscutting concerns [10-12]. However, these studies mainly focus on the investigation on how the use of AO abstractions supports the separation of those concerns. They do not analyze other effects and stringent quality indicators in the resulting AO systems. Furthermore, they do not quantify the benefits and drawbacks of AO techniques in the presence of widely-scoped changes. A number of empirical analyses need to be carried out, since certain typical criticisms that AOP has suffered [34] and the initial studies have exhibited some controversies even when aspectizing classical crosscutting concerns, such as transaction management [10, 11], exception handling [12, 13], and design patterns [14-16].

We have previously performed a far-reaching maintenance study [24], but our target was aspects specific to multi-agent systems. In addition, the aspects used in this system have a localized scope and tend to affect a few modules; they do not have a major influence on the architectural design of the system. In addition, the introduced changes were restricted to simple changes in few classes or aspects. Also, we did not evaluate aspect interaction issues. In another study, we evaluated how AspectJ scales to modularize pattern compositions [15]. However, the stability of the aspectized pattern combinations was not assessed. Our previous study documented in [19] evaluated the scalability of the AspectJ implementation by performing some initial changes to the HW system. These changes correspond to a subset of the changes made in Scenario 8. However, this previous study did not examine concern interaction, design stability or the affect on design principles. Nevertheless, the study presented in this paper has confirmed and expanded in scope our previous findings.

8.2 Study Constraints

Although it can be argued that using a single system for such a study is a limiting factor we feel that the HW system is representative of modern systems and the scenarios applied are extensive and so reduces the necessity of additional systems. Naturally it is desirable to involve more systems and more approaches.

As stated previously one of the aims of this study was to perform a general comparison of the OO and AO paradigms. This was achieved by re-implementing HW using CaesarJ, however, a similar OO re-implementation was not performed for Java. As such the study could be viewed as a Java vs. AO comparison but we feel this would be unfair. Java is a good representative of OO techniques and re-implementing it would be a wasted exercise. Equally, it would be difficult to reproduce a similar implementation due to the techniques used in the OO implementation i.e. Servlets, etc. Fundamentally for this type of study we require good representatives of AO techniques for the base language. Unfortunately this range does not exist for other OO languages and so limits the benefits of studying other OO languages.

The concerns analysed tended to focus on ones that were more significantly affected by the changes applied in either the AO or OO versions. Due to the nature of the study and the fact that separation of concerns is central to this study the crosscutting concerns were naturally the ones which varied the most. We have also presented results of other non-crosscutting concerns (e.g. view and business layers) to provide a balanced comparison of the AO and OO paradigms.

The applicability and usefulness of some of the specific metrics used in this study has often been questioned such as the cohesion measure. We accept the criticism of such metrics. However, it is important to consider the results gathered from all metrics rather than just one metric in particular. The multi-dimensional analysis allows us to grasp which measurement outliers are significant and which are not. In fact, when drawing conclusions from the results we have considered all the gathered data and never relied upon one single piece of data from this set.

9 Concluding Remarks

The transfer of aspect-oriented technologies to mainstream software development is largely dependent on our ability to empirically understand their positive and negative effects through design changes. Software designs are often the target of unanticipated changes and, as a result, incremental development has been established as the defacto-practice in realistic software development [1, 5, 6]. This study has followed these practices to evolve a real-life application in order to assess various facets of design stability of object-oriented and aspect-oriented implementations. This included the analysis of the implementations modularity, change propagation, concern interaction analysis and identification of architectural ripple-effects.

From this analysis we have discovered a number of interesting outcomes. Firstly, the AO implementations tend to have a more stable design particularly when a change targets a crosscutting concern. Furthermore, changes tended to be much less intrusive and more simplistic to apply in the AO implementations. This indicates that aspectual decompositions are superior especially when considering the Open-Closed principle

[18] (Section 5). Significantly, both OO and AO implementations exhibited high stability in high-level design structures but with a certain architectural ripple-effect occurring within the OO design when persistence-related exceptions had to be introduced. In certain circumstances aspectual decompositions did perform worse. These tended to occur when evolutionary scenarios targeted classical design patterns such as Command and State [19], applying these design patterns violated pivotal design principles, such as narrow interfaces and low coupling. Even though as stated above the AO implementations tended to require less invasive changes, sometimes the modifications propagated to components that were not the direct target of the change scenario. The overall conclusion regarding the design stability and concern interaction analysis (Section 6) is that aspect decomposition narrows the boundaries of concern dependencies, however, with more tight and intricate interactions.

References

1. Larman, C., Basil, V.: Iterative and Incremental Development. A Brief History. IEEE Computer 36(6), 47–56 (2003)
2. Martin, R.: Engineering Notebook: Stability (1997)
3. Mohagheghi, P., Conradi, R.: Using Empirical Studies to Assess Software Development Approaches and Measurement Programs. In: Proc. Workshop on Empirical Software Engineering (WSESE'03), Rome (2003)
4. Yau, S.S., Collofello, J.S.: Design Stability Measures for Software Maintenance. IEEE Transactions on Software Engineering 11(9), 849–856 (1985)
5. Rajlich, V.: Changing the Paradigm of Software Engineering. Communications of the ACM 49(8), 67–70 (2006)
6. Casais, E.: Managing Class Evolution in Object-Oriented Systems. In: Nierstrasz, O., Tsichritzis, D. (eds.) Object-Oriented Software Composition, Prentice Hall, Englewood Cliffs (1995)
7. Kiczales, G., Lamping, J., Mendhekar, A., Maeda, C., Lopes, C.V., Longtier, J.-M., Irwin, J.: Aspect-Oriented Programming. In: Proceedings European Conference on Object-Oriented Programming, Jyväskylä, Finland, Springer, Heidelberg (1997)
8. Mezini, M., Ostermann, K.: Conquering Aspects with Caesar. In: 2nd International Conference on Aspect-Oriented Software Development (AOSD), Boston, USA (2003)
9. Kulesza, U., Sant'Anna, C., Garcia, A., Coelho, R., Staa, A., Lucena, C.: Quantifying the Effects of AOP: A Maitenance Study. In: Proc. of 9th Intl. Conference on Software Maintenance (ICSM'06), Philadelphia, USA (2006)
10. Rashid, A., Chitchyan, R.: Persistence as an Aspect. In: 2nd International Conference on Aspect-Oriented Software Development (AOSD), ACM, Boston, Massachusetts (2003)
11. Soares, S., Borba, P., Laureano, E.: Distribution and Persistence as Aspects. Software: Practice and Experience (2006)
12. Filho, F., Cacho, N., Figueiredo, E., Maranhao, R., Garcia, A., Rubira, C.: Exceptions and Aspects: The Devil is in the Details. In: International Conference on Foundations of Software Engineering (2006)
13. Lippert, M., Lopes, C.: A Study on Exception Detection and Handling Using Aspect-Oriented Programming. In: 22nd International Conference on Software Engineering (1999)
14. Garcia, A., Sant'Anna, S., Figueiredo, E., Kuleska, U., Lucena, C., Von Staa, A.: Modularizing Design Patterns with Aspects: A Quantative Study. In: 4th International Conference on Aspect-Oriented Software Development (AOSD), Chicago, USA (2005)

15. Cacho, N., Sant'Anna, C., Figueiredo, E., Garcia, A., Batista, T., Lucena, C.: Composing Design Patterns: A Scalability Study of AOP. In: AOSD, Bonn, Germany (2006)
16. Hannemann, J., Kiczales, G.: Design Pattern Implementation in Java and AspectJ. In: Proceedings of the 17th ACM SIGPLAN conference on Object-oriented programming, systems, languages, and applications (OOPSLA), ACM, Seattle, Washington (2002)
17. Kiczales, G., Hilsdale, E., Hugunin, J., Kersten, M., Palm, J., Griswold, W.: Getting Started with AspectJ. Communications of the ACM 44(10), 59–65 (2001)
18. Meyer, B.: Object-Oriented Software Construction, 1st edn. Prentice-Hall, Englewood Cliffs (1988)
19. Gamma, E., Helm, R., Johnson, R., Vlissides, J.: Design Pattern, Elements of Reusable Object-Oriented Software. Addison-Wesley Professional Computing Series, London, UK (1995)
20. Greenwood, P., et al.: Aspect Interaction and Design Stability: An Empirical Study (2007), Available from: http://www.comp.lancs.ac.uk/computing/users/greenwop/ecoop07
21. Buschmann, F., et al.: Pattern-Oriented Software Architecture: A System of Patterns. Wiley and Sons, Chichester (1996)
22. Hunter, J., Crawford, W.: Java Servlet Programming. O'Reilly and Associates Inc. 1998
23. Sant'Anna, C., Garcia, A., Chavez, C., Lucena, C., von Staa, A.: On the Reuse and Maintenance of Aspect-Oriented Software: An Assessment Framework. In: Brazilian Symposium on Software Engineering, Manaus, Brazil (2003)
24. Garcia, A., et al.: Separation of Concerns in Multi-Agent Systems: An Empirical Study. Software Engineering for Multi-Agent Systems, 2(2940) (2004)
25. Chidamber, S., Kemerer, C.: A Metrics Suite for Object-Oriented Design. IEE Transactions on Software Engineering 20(6), 476–493 (1994)
26. Bartolomei, T.T.: MuLaTo (2006), Available from: http://sourceforge.net/projects/mulato
27. Figueiredo, E., Garcia, A., Luena, C.: AJATO: An AspectJ Assessment Tool. In: European Conference on Object-Oriented Programming (ECOOP Demo), France (2006)
28. Colwell, B.: Design Fragility. Computer 37(1), 13–16 (2004)
29. Kellens, A., Mens, K., Brichau, J., Gybels, K.: Managing the Evolution of Aspect-Oriented Software with Model-based Pointcuts. In: Thomas, D. (ed.) ECOOP 2006. LNCS, vol. 4067, Springer, Heidelberg (2006)
30. Sant'Anna, C., et al.: On the Quantitative Assessment of Modular Multi-Agent System Architectures. In: NetObjectDays (MASSA) (2006)
31. Lopes, C., Bajracharya, S.: An Analysis of Modularity in Aspect-Oriented Design. In: Proc. Aspect-Oriented Software Development (AOSD), Chicago, USA (2005)
32. Baldwin, C., Clark, K.: Design Rules:The Power of Modularity. Vol 1. MIT Press, Cambridge (2000)
33. Sullivan, K., Griswold, W., Cai, Y., Hallen, B.: The Structure and Value of Modularity in Software Design. In: 8th European Software Engineering Conference, ACM Press, New York (2001)
34. Steimann, F.: The Paradoxical Success of Aspect-Oriented Programming. In: International Conference on Object-Oriented Programming, Systems, Languages and Applications (OOPSLA) (2006)

An Accidental Simula User

Luca Cardelli

Microsoft Research
luca@microsoft.com

Abstract. It was a simple choice, really, on an IBM 370 in the 70's, between APL, Fortran, Lisp 1.5, PL/1, COBOL, and Simula'67. Nothing could come close to Simula's combination of strong typing, garbage collection, and proper string processing. Separate compilation (prefix classes) and coroutines were nice bonuses. And then there were these ... "objects" but, well, nothing is perfect. Hot topics in those days were the freshly invented denotational semantics (which Simula didn't have), formal type systems (which objects didn't have), and abstract data types (which seemed to have confusingly little to do with classes). Still, Simula was the obvious choice to get something done comfortably because, after all, it was an improved Algol. It even had the functional programming feature of call-by-name by default. So, it became my first favorite language, for every reason other than it being object-oriented.

The story I am going to tell is the very, very slow realization that Simula was the embodiment of a radically different philosophy of programming, and the gradual and difficult efforts to reconcile that philosophy with the formal methods that were being developed for procedural and functional programming. Along the way, domain theory helped rather unexpectedly, at least for a while. Type theory had to be recast for the task at hand. Landin's lambda-reductionism had to be partially abandoned. Always, there seemed to be a deep fundamental mismatch between objects and procedures, well described by Reynolds, that made any unification impossibly complicated. But in the end, both object-oriented and procedural programming have benefited from the clash of cultures. And the story is far from over yet, as witnessed by the still blooming area of program verification for both procedural and object-oriented languages.

E. Ernst (Ed.): ECOOP 2007, LNAI 4609, p. 201, 2007.

Validity Invariants and Effects

Yi Lu, John Potter, and Jingling Xue

Programming Languages and Compilers Group
School of Computer Science and Engineering
University of New South Wales, Sydney
{ylu,potter,jingling}@cse.unsw.edu.au

Abstract. Object invariants describe the consistency of object states, and are crucial for reasoning about the correctness of object-oriented programs. However, reasoning about object invariants in the presence of object abstraction and encapsulation, arbitrary object aliasing and re-entrant method calls, is difficult.

We present a framework for reasoning about object invariants based on a behavioural contract that specifies two sets: the *validity invariant*—objects that must be valid before and after the behaviour; and the *validity effect*—objects that may be invalidated during the behaviour. The overlap of these two sets is critical because it captures precisely those objects that need to be re-validated at the end of the behaviour. When there is no overlap, no further validity checking is required.

We also present a type system based on this framework using ownership types to confine dependencies for object invariants. In order to track the validity invariant, the type system restricts updates to permissible contexts, even in the presence of re-entrant calls. Object referencing and read access are unrestricted, unlike earlier ownership type systems.

1 Introduction

The flexibility and extensibility offered in object-oriented programming is both a boon and a curse. Classes provide an encapsulated definition of object data and behaviour; subclassing allows the extension of existing definitions with reuse of code that depends on a parent class; heap-based allocation allows objects to persist beyond the scope of their creator; object references provide a disciplined use of pointers. However this programming flexibility comes at a cost. Reasoning about the behaviour of objects is difficult. More specifically, the presence of complex object dependencies, object aliasing, and arbitrary method call-backs (re-entrant calls) makes it difficult to reason about object-oriented code. The particular problem we focus on in this paper is how we can guarantee the validity of objects within such a programming context.

Formal verification techniques for structured programming encapsulate the program state within local variables and arguments of procedures. This makes it feasible to provide a complete axiomatic semantics based on a pre/post-condition style of reasoning about code. A critical assumption in such reasoning systems, is that the program state that is being reasoned about is encapsulated within code

E. Ernst (Ed.): ECOOP 2007, LNAI 4609, pp. 202–226, 2007.

blocks—a stack-based memory model is assumed. Such reasoning techniques cannot directly cope with reasoning about programs with pointers—the essential problem is that heap-based data may be accessed and modified indirectly via pointers. Currently the most promising approach for formally dealing with pointers appears to be Separation Logic [6,29,15,7] which supports reasoning about the distinctness of regions of the heap.

Design by contract is a technique for reasoning about objects introduced by Meyer [21] and provided with programming language support in Eiffel [20]. Design by contract relies on the specification of object behaviours via the combination of object invariants describing valid object states, and pre/post-conditions for object behaviours. Although design by contract does provide a good conceptual basis for assisting designers, its formal basis is weakened by the presence of inter-object dependencies, aliasing and call-backs.

We extend an example used by Leino and Müller [17] to illustrate the effect of call-backs on object invariants. If P calls back on m then a divide-by-zero error may occur. The problem is that P is called when the current invariant is broken, and cannot be relied on in subsequent re-entrant calls. On the other hand, if Q in n is re-entrant there is no harm, assuming it maintains invariants.

```
class C {
    int a, b;        invariant: 0 <= a < b;
    C() { a = 0;        b = 3; }
    void m() { int k = 100/(b-a);
               a = a+3;    P(...);    b = (k+4)*b; }
    void n() { int k = 100/(b-a);    Q(...); } }
```

In order to reason about this type of code, we need to be able to track the effect and dependency of possible call-backs on the current object invariant. This is our goal.

The difficulty of modular verification of object-oriented programs has been recognized for a long time [16]. Recently researchers have made some in-roads, with the use of fixed ownership-based schemes in Universe Types [24,22,13,26], and dynamic ownership used to track object validity in the Boogie methodology, as manifested in Spec# [3,17,27,4]. Our own work draws strongly on the ideas of object validity of this work. Further comparisons will follow in Section 5.

In this paper we present a general framework for tracking validity within object systems which is independent of any particular language framework. The motivation for adopting a language-free approach is to emphasize the underlying principles. The key idea of our model is to capture the effect of code blocks (such as method bodies) on the validity of the objects in the system. The approach we take requires code blocks to specify a pair of object sets $\langle \mathcal{I}, \mathcal{E} \rangle$. $\mathcal{I}$ is the *validity invariant* for the code, which specifies those objects that must be valid before and after the code executes. $\mathcal{E}$ is the *validity effect* which specifies those objects that may be invalidated during execution of the code. During execution, nested code blocks or method calls $\langle \mathcal{I}', \mathcal{E}' \rangle$ must satisfy some consistency criteria with respect to their calling context. When the sets $\mathcal{I}$ and $\mathcal{E}$ are disjoint, there is nothing to check, other than consistency criteria for the code—system validity is automatically guaranteed to hold. If $\mathcal{J}$ and $\mathcal{E}$ are not disjoint, validity of the objects within their overlap must be established by other means (presumably relying on a more detailed program logic). It is this ability to hone in on a restricted critical set of objects whose validity must be established after code execution which provides the novelty in our model. When object validity is specified *via object invariants, our model imposes certain structural constraints* that relate the form of $\mathcal{J}$ and $\mathcal{E}$ to the dependencies inherent in the object invariants.

A general model is only useful if it can be realized in some concrete form. To that end, we offer a small language, Oval, that realizes the model using an ownership-based type system. In Oval, an object's invariant can only depend on its own fields, and on other objects that it contains, as determined by the ownership structure. For simplicity, we restrict the overlap between $\mathcal{J}$ and $\mathcal{E}$ to be, at most, a single object which is always the current active object. Consequently, *only local (per-object) reasoning is necessary to establish system-wide validity.*

Within Oval, we do not impose restrictions on object reference or read access; our system does not rely on alias protection. Instead, interpreting the consistency criteria of nested code blocks (method calls) from our general model, we restrict what write access is allowed in different contexts. It is this mechanism that allows us to keep track of which objects are valid at any particular time; for example, if a call-back requires an object to be valid, we can prohibit it if that object may be invalid but allow it if we know it must be valid.

Interestingly, it is straightforward to create immutable objects in Oval. Objects high up in the ownership hierarchy are more accessible for update (and more likely to be invalid). For us, immutable objects are those created at the very bottom of the ownership hierarchy, where nothing has write access. Note that immutability is determined by the object's creation type (instantiating the object's owner to be bot) rather than the object's class (where the owner is a formal parameter, rather than a concrete context). Our system also provides a more general model than approaches based on read-only annotations. In Oval, the context of the reference holder determines its update capability.

Our system is also able to express encapsulation-aware read-only references. They typically use hidden contexts (equivalent to existentially abstract contexts) to forbid access to methods that have some write capability on the objects encapsulated by the context where the reference is held.

In summary, specific contributions of this paper include:

- a validity specification for blocks of code—defining a set of objects $\mathcal{J}$ that must be valid before and after, and a set of objects $\mathcal{E}$ that may be invalidated during code execution;
- identification of where explicit validity checks are required within code blocks, and where validity can be assumed to hold;
- a model of structure based on the object dependency implied by object invariants;
- a small language, Oval, with an ownership-based type system—where an object's invariant can only depend on an its own fields and its owned objects, and system validity can be achieved with per-object checks;

– immutable objects and a generalization of read-only annotations arise as a special case of the type system.

This paper is organized as follows. Section 2 details our general approach for describing system validity and the behavioural abstraction $\langle \mathfrak{I}, \mathcal{E} \rangle$ introduced above. In particular we outline the consistency conditions for nested code with the underlying rationale. Our initial model is descriptive, rather than focused on specific language mechanisms for programming objects. Section 3 introduces the Oval language with examples. Here, our intention is to illustrate language mechanisms and type rules to support our general model of Section 2 rather than to design a realistic programming language. Unlike most previous ownership schemes [12,11,9,8,10], we do not use the object ownership structure to restrict object references and aliasing, but rather, we use it to specify the sets of objects that must be valid, or may be invalid, during method calls. This use of ownership builds on earlier work extending the use and flexibility of ownership type systems [19,18]. With Oval we have opted for simplicity rather than a fully expressive model. Oval requires that object invariants are only invalidated one object at a time; possible extensions avoiding this limitation are discussed in this section. In Section 4 we provide a static and dynamic semantics for our language and formalize properties that demonstrate how this language implements the general model. Section 5 addresses other related work, including Boogie/Spec# and Universes, Ownership Types and read-only systems. Section 6 briefly concludes the paper.

2 A Model for Object Validity

2.1 The Validity Contract $\langle \mathfrak{I}, \mathcal{E} \rangle$

The key idea for our model is very simple: whenever an object is active, it may be invalid. If an object is not active (and still alive) then it must be valid. But what determines when an object is valid? For now, it suffices to consider an object to be valid when it satisfies its specified invariant—this is the standard notion of object validity. Later on, in Subsection 2.3, we will refine this notion somewhat, in order to handle object invariants that depend on more than one object. So, for the moment, to maintain consistency with the refined notion, we will simply assume that there is some notion of object validity, and at any time, there is a set of all valid objects, that we call the *validity set* VALID.

For any particular structured block of code, we specify a behavioural abstraction: the *validity contract* $\langle \mathfrak{I}, \mathcal{E} \rangle$. The *validity invariant* $\mathfrak{I}$ specifies a set of objects that must be valid both before and after the code executes. Clearly this imposes an obligation on the caller (see Subsection 2.2) and the code itself (see below). The *validity effect* $\mathcal{E}$ specifies those objects that may be invalidated during execution of the code.

A given validity contract $\langle \mathfrak{I}, \mathcal{E} \rangle$ for a block of code provides constraints on VALID at different execution timepoints as shown in Table 1. In the following we denote the validity set at the start of code execution by VALID_0, so that at any timepoint, $\text{VALID}_0 - \text{VALID}$ represents invalidated objects—those that were initially valid, but are currently invalid. Interpreting constraints, we first have, immediately before the code executes, that all objects in $\mathcal{I}$ must be valid. During execution, only those objects in $\mathcal{E}$ may become invalid, and so the remainder, $\mathcal{I} - \mathcal{E}$ must still be valid. At the end of execution, we have a proof obligation for the code: the validity of the *critical set* of objects $\mathcal{I} \cap \mathcal{E}$ must be checked. Then, immediately after execution, we have ensured that all objects in $\mathcal{I}$ are still valid, and that only objects in $\mathcal{E} - \mathcal{I}$ may have been invalidated. These constraints will be the basis for the rules for subcontracting, coming up next.

We have chosen our model to be flow insensitive for simplicity. It is indeed possible to provide a stronger validity contract in which we provide separate pre- and post-conditions for validity. For consistency, the post-condition would need to be stronger than the disjunction of the pre-condition and the validity effect. We leave the pursuit of this more general form of validity contract for another time.

Table 1. Validity Contract: Constraints on the Validity Set

Before:	$\mathcal{I} \subseteq \text{VALID}$
During:	$\mathcal{I} - \mathcal{E} \subseteq \text{VALID}$
	$\text{VALID}_0 - \text{VALID} \subseteq \mathcal{E}$
At End:	$\mathcal{I} \cap \mathcal{E} \subseteq \text{VALID}$ *to be checked*
After:	$\mathcal{I} \subseteq \text{VALID}$
	$\text{VALID}_0 - \text{VALID} \subseteq \mathcal{E} - \mathcal{I}$

2.2   Validity Subcontract for Nested Behaviours

With structured code, we can nest behaviours in various ways, such as by making method calls, or entering nested blocks. From a caller's perspective, we can also think of a method override as being a nested version of the overridden method. Method calls must respect the validity contract of their calling context; nested code blocks may have their own contract, but must respect the contract of their containing block; and the contract for a method override must be consistent with the contract for the method being overridden. All of these nested behaviours must conform to the contract for the surrounding behaviour in the same way.

In Design by Contract [21] there is a notion of subcontracting for subclasses, and in particular, for overridden methods. The subcontract rules (preconditions may only be weakened, postconditions may only be strengthened) provide a guarantee that the overriding behaviour conforms to the contract of the overridden method, which allows clients to reason about method calls without worrying about whether the method has been overridden in a subclass. In formal specification this notion corresponds to that of operation refinement. We adopt a similar approach for validity subcontracts, but we take into account the constraints on validity imposed by a contract, as formulated above.

Within the context of a particular validity contract $\langle \mathcal{I}, \mathcal{E} \rangle$, suppose we execute code that is known to meet another validity contract $\langle \mathcal{I}', \mathcal{E}' \rangle$. According to the constraints of Table 1, on entry to $\langle \mathcal{I}', \mathcal{E}' \rangle$ we require $\mathcal{I}' \subseteq$ VALID, but we know that during the execution of $\langle \mathcal{I}, \mathcal{E} \rangle$ that $\mathcal{I} - \mathcal{E} \subseteq$ VALID. We therefore require that $\mathcal{I}' \subseteq \mathcal{I} - \mathcal{E}$. From the perspective of $\langle \mathcal{I}, \mathcal{E} \rangle$, we do not care what becomes invalid during execution of $\langle \mathcal{I}', \mathcal{E}' \rangle$, provided that it exits satisfying the constraints imposed by $\langle \mathcal{I}, \mathcal{E} \rangle$. When $\langle \mathcal{I}', \mathcal{E}' \rangle$ exits, we know that the only objects to have been invalidated by its execution, VALID$_0'$ − VALID, lie within $\mathcal{E}' - \mathcal{I}'$. However we know that before $\langle \mathcal{I}', \mathcal{E}' \rangle$ executes, that VALID$_0$ − VALID$_0'$ is within $\mathcal{E}$. It follows that VALID$_0$ − VALID will be within $\mathcal{E}$ as required, provided $\mathcal{E}' - \mathcal{I}' \subseteq \mathcal{E}$. This reasoning leads us to the following definition for a *validity subcontract*. Note that the definition makes no mention of the validity set VALID. The subcontract definition simply relates two different validity contracts, irrespective of what the validity set may be.

Definition 1 (Validity Subcontract). $\langle \mathcal{I}', \mathcal{E}' \rangle$ *is a* validity subcontract *of* $\langle \mathcal{I}, \mathcal{E} \rangle$ *if:*

$$\mathcal{I}' \subseteq \mathcal{I} - \mathcal{E}$$
$$\mathcal{E}' - \mathcal{I}' \subseteq \mathcal{E}$$

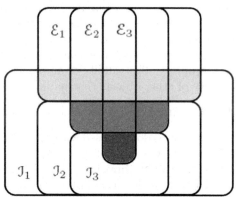

Fig. 1. Validity Subcontracts: The Relationship between Nested Contracts. Validity of objects in $\mathcal{E}_i \cap \mathcal{I}_i$ (shaded) must be separately established.

Figure 1 captures the nesting properties of the validity invariants and effects, for subcontracts. Here $\langle \mathcal{I}_3, \mathcal{E}_3 \rangle$ is a subcontract of $\langle \mathcal{I}_2, \mathcal{E}_2 \rangle$, which is, in turn, a subcontract of $\langle \mathcal{I}_1, \mathcal{E}_1 \rangle$. Intuitively, we think of this in terms of nested method calls. The validity invariant is weakened, the deeper the call structure. On successive calls it is safe to reduce the size of the validity effect. However, most interesting is where the effect may be increased. This critical set is the overlap of the validity invariant and effect for the new call. It is precisely this critical set of objects whose validity must be re-established at the end of the call.

Before introducing our language Oval, we will discuss the relationship between the validity set and object invariants for our general model.

2.3   Object Invariants and Dependency Structure

In abstract terms an object's invariant captures the commonality between the pre- and post-conditions for all of the object's methods. By specifying an object invariant, we effectively constrain the allowable behaviours of the object, thereby defining the safe or consistent states of the object. An object's invariant ultimately resolves to constraints on fields, not only of the current object, but also, possibly, of other objects. It is therefore possible for an object's invariant to be satisfied, even though it depends on another object whose invariant does not hold. To avoid this worrisome situation, we refine the idea of object validity.

Definition 2 (Object Dependency). *An object (transitively) depends on another if it's invariant depends directly, or indirectly, on the fields of the other object. We write $\succcurlyeq$ for this preorder between objects.*

Definition 3 (Object Validity). *An object is* valid *if it's invariant is satisfied and if all of the objects that it depends on are also valid. The* validity set VALID *is the largest set of objects that are valid.*

Because the definition of *valid object* is recursive, we have specified the validity set to be the largest possible set of objects satisfying the constraint.

It is possible to have objects whose invariant holds, but that are not valid by our definition. For us, the important point is that from a system-wide perspective, validity is a closed property. The validity of an object only depends on its own state, and the validity of other objects that its invariant depends on.

Property 1 (Validity Closure). *If* $o \in$ VALID *and* $o \succcurlyeq o'$ *then* $o' \in$ VALID.

This asserts that the validity set is down-closed with respect to the object dependency induced by the invariants. Consequently in specifying validity contracts, it makes sense to insist that the validity invariant $\mathcal{I}$ (valid objects) is down-closed, and that the validity effect $\mathcal{E}$ (possibly invalid objects) is up-closed with respect to object dependency. Figure 1 was drawn to illustrate the closure properties of $\mathcal{I}$ and $\mathcal{E}$, assuming that object dependency is downwards in the diagram.

We now begin to see some hope of how to achieve a syntactic representation of validity contracts in programming languages. Assuming we can explicitly list the objects at the top of $\mathcal{I}$ and the bottom of $\mathcal{E}$, and assuming we can capture the object dependency, then we should be able to reason about validity contracts syntactically. In Section 3 we do so by using ownership types to constrain the object dependency, and specifying the extrema of $\mathcal{I}$ and $\mathcal{E}$ as single objects, that is, as ownership contexts I and E respectively.

3   Oval: A Language with Ownership-Based Validity

Oval is a simple object-oriented programming language that incorporates owner-ship types to support validity contracts. Oval realises our general model by using object ownership to provide the structure for specifying validity invariants and effects. Oval presumes that object dependency (for invariants) is constrained by object ownership.

3.1   Ownership Types and Effect Encapsulation

Object encapsulation techniques hide an object's internal representation and force any access from outside to be made via the object's interface. Ownership types [28,12,11,9] improve on previous work on full encapsulation techniques [14,2] by allowing outgoing references while still preventing representation expo-sure; objects cannot be referenced from outside of the encapsulation.

In ownership type systems, each object has one fixed owning object, given at the time of creation. The ownership relation partitions objects into an *ownership tree*, whose root is a conceptual object called top in this paper. Objects are con-fined so that they can only reference or access objects owned by their (transitive and reflexive) owners.

Ownership type systems are essentially access control systems where accessi-bility is determined by the position of the target object in the ownership tree. Such systems achieve a form of information hiding. However, the problem of maintaining object validity is fundamentally a problem of effects: only updates can break object invariants. In other words, read access can always be consid-ered safe. Our earlier work on *effect encapsulation* [19] has provided a technique for encapsulating side-effects on an object without restricting referenceability or read access. Our work in this paper provides a significant extension to effect encapsulation; we allow each method to specify the validity invariant, that is, what object invariants can be expected to hold. By tracking permissible updates via the validity effect, the type system checks if each expected validity invariant can be met.

3.2   Overview of Oval

In Oval, we use ownership types to structure objects, specify validity contracts and confine dependencies for object invariants.

Oval programs specify a validity invariant and effect for each method as a *validity contract*, $\langle I, E \rangle$. I and E are ownership contexts in our type system. The corresponding validity invariant $\mathcal{I}$ is the context I and all contexts owned (transitively) by I; the corresponding effect $\mathcal{E}$ is the context E and all owning contexts of E; in the ownership order, I is the top of the down-set $\mathcal{I}$, and E is the bottom of the up-set $\mathcal{E}$ (which is a branch of the ownership tree). The only overlap allowed for $\mathcal{I}$ and $\mathcal{E}$ is the local context this. This yields just two interesting cases. When the validity invariant and effect are disjoint, the critical set is empty, and I must be strictly within E in the ownership order. Otherwise, when they overlap, they must satisfy $I = E =$ this; the critical set just contains the current object. As we shall see, the type system also checks that the subcontract rule is satisfied by any method calls. Consequently when the critical set is empty, there is no further reasoning about object validity required in the current method body. When the critical set is a single object, only the validity of the current object needs to be re-established at the end of the method body. By incorporating the idea of validity contracts in the type system, Oval provides a frame for localized reasoning about object validity.

The constraint that I and E can only overlap at the current object, allows us to keep both the syntax and type system simple in Oval. Allowing a bigger overlap is feasible: it is a trade-off between greater expressiveness and increased complexity. The added complexity arises from syntactic issues (describing sets of contexts rather than singletons), the type system (the static dependency ordering is trickier), and reasoning for re-establishment of invariants with multiple objects simultaneously. These sorts of extensions have been made for Spec# where objects may have peers, and whole peer sets can be simultaneously invalidated.

An object's invariant may only depend on its member fields and fields of (transitively) owned objects. For expressiveness, we allow fields that are not part of the object's representation to be declared nonrep. nonrep fields cannot be mentioned in the class invariant. Fields which are not explicitly declared nonrep are part of the object's representation and may participate in its object invariant. Some other languages have a similar design, for instance, Javari [5] uses the keyword mutable to annotate those nonrep fields. Because there is no object ownership structure in Javari, object invariants can never depend on mutable fields. In our language, we do allow the owning object's invariant to depend on any fields of owned objects (including nonrep fields). An object's invariant can only depend on its rep fields and objects that it (transitively) owns. So updates on rep fields may affect the target's invariant, and so (in Oval) should only be allowed by the target's own methods. Updates on nonrep fields can only affect an owner's invariant, and that owner must already have an active method that is responsible for re-establishing the owner's invariant.

A constructor must always establish its object's invariant. For simplicity, we consider constructors to have no effect on validity—they simply initialize the object in a valid state.

In addition to the usual top context, we introduce another context bot. The bot context is the bottom of the ownership hierarchy; it is inside/owned by all other contexts. We syntactically restrict its use in Oval to the validity invariant part of a contract. When a method's validity invariant is bot, it neither requires nor ensures any object validity; it provides a vacuous constraint for the validity set.

3.3   Oval by Example

The validity contract allows us to solve the re-entrancy problem discussed in the Introduction section.

```
class C {
    int a, b;
    invariant:   0 <= a < b;
    C() { a = 0; b = 3; }
    void m() <this, this> { int k =   100/(b-a);
                            a = a+3; P(...); b = (k+4)*b; }
    void n() <this, top>  { int k = 100/(b-a);
                            Q(...); } }
```

In the above example, the validity contract for method m is <this,this>, which means the method requires the current object (this) to be valid and the method is allowed to break this's invariant via either direct assignment or indirect method calls. What is interesting here is that our type system guarantees P cannot callback on m. In order for P to callback on m, P must meet the required validity invariant—this must be valid. However, object this is invalid in P because the validity effect of m has invalidated this.

On the other hand, the contract for method n is <this,top>. It does expect the current object (this) to be valid, but it does not invalidate any object except the conceptual context top. This time, Q may callback on n, because this is valid in Q and so it will be able to satisfy the required validity invariant of n on re-entry.

A method can require a validity invariant other than its target object (this), as in the following code using class C from above.

```
class D { nonrep int f; ... }
```

```
class G [p, q] where p < q {
    void ie(C<p> x, D<q> y) <p, q> { y.f = 100/(x.b-x.a); } }
```

Every class has a formal parameter which refers to the owner of the current object. By default, when the owner parameter is not used by the class definition, it may be omitted, as for class D. Moreover, since field f is declared as nonrep, updates on field f will not break the invariant of class D, because the local invariant cannot depend on its nonrep fields. But updates on f may break the invariant of its owning object, whose invariant is allowed to depend on any field of owned objects. In fact, in our type system, fields not declared to be nonrep can only be updated by the object itself.

As part of its validity contract, method ie states that p is the validity invariant; since the parameter x is owned by p, x must be valid, that is, its invariant must hold—so we know there will be no divide-by-zero error. Note that, to reason in this way, the programmer needs to know class C's invariant—C's invariant needs to be *visible*. We will discuss this in Section 5.

The method contract of ie specifies its validity effect as q; this permits q to be invalidated. Since the object in y is owned by q; assignment on y may invalidate q and any objects owning q; this is allowed by the method's validity effect.

To illustrate a more realistic use of our type system, we adopt an example from a tutorial on Spec# [30].

```
class Person {
    int freeday;
    Meeting<this> next;
    invariant: if next!=null then next.day!=freeday;
    int travel(int d) <this, this> {
        freeday = d;
        if (next!=null) next.reschedule((d+1)%7); } }

class Meeting {
    int day;
    invariant: 0 <= day < 7;
    Meeting(int d) { day = d; }
    void reschedule(int d) <this, this> { day = d; } }
```

The invariant of Person depends on the day field of the Meeting object next.
Consequently, if the day field of the Meeting object is changed, the invariant of
the Person may be broken. Ownership types capture this kind of dependency
by enforcing the Meeting object to be owned by Person—the owner argument
of next is this which refers to the current Person object.

Both the validity invariant and effect of the method reschedule in class
Meeting are the current object this. The method is allowed to update its day
field, and it will require and ensure its local invariant holds before and after the
method call.

Back to the travel method in class Person whose validity contract is also
<this, this>. The method is allowed to call next.reschedule because it can
meet reschedule's validity invariant requirement, and next.reschedule can
meet travel's requirement for validity effect. Method next.reschedule requires
next to be valid before calling it; within the method travel the local invariant
of the Person object may be violated, but all objects owned by the Person
object, including the object in next, are valid. On the other hand, method
travel's validity effect insists that only objects (transitively and reflexively)
owning this may be invalidated within its body, more precisely for this case, it
insists that the object in next must be valid after the call to next.reschedule.
The validity invariant on method next.reschedule ensures that the object in
next is validated after the call.

Linked lists are a popular example for illustrating language features dealing with restricted use of references. Ownership type systems are known to be
inadequate for expressing cross-encapsulation references such as needed by iterators, because of their restrictive reference containment. We show how iterators
are expressed in our language, explaining how our type system is able to relax
the usual ownership restriction on reference containment while still keeping the
iterators safe.

```
class List[o, d] {
  Node<this, d> head;
  void insert(Data<d> data) <this, this> { head.insert(data); }
  Iterator<o, this, d> getIterator() <bot, top> {
    return new Iterator<o, this, d>(head); } }
```

```
class Node[l, d] {
  nonrep Data<d> data;          nonrep Node<l, d> next;
  Node(Node<l, d> next, Data<d> data) {
    this.next = next;             this.data = data; }
  void insert(Data<d> data) <bot, l> {
    next = new Node<l, d>(next, data); } }

class Iterator[o, l, d] {
  nonrep Node<l, d> current;
  Iterator(Node<l, d> node) { current = node; }
  void next() <bot, o> { current = current.next; }
  int element() <bot, top> { return current.data; }
  void insert(Data<d> data) <bot, l> { current.insert(data); } }

// client code
List<o, d> list = ...;   Data<d> data = ...;    list.insert(data);
Iterator<o, *, d> iterator = list.getIterator();
while iterator.element() {
  int data = iterator.element();    iterator.next(); }
list.insert(data)     // OK
iterator.insert(data);  // error, effect is unknown in current context
Node<*, d> node = list.head; // OK, * can abstract any context
node.next = ...         // error, owner of node.next is hidden
```

The List class provides methods for adding new elements to the list and
for returning iterators for the list. The implementation of the List class is almost the same as for ownership types except the methods have been annotated
with a validity contract. Method insert will update the current object and can
be called by clients, so its validity invariant and effect are the current object.
Method getIterator's validity contract is <bot,top>; it makes no assumptions
about validity (by the bot invariant), and does not invalidate any object (by the
top effect).

In the Node class, the field next is declared to be nonrep so that it is part of
its owner's representation (the owner being the list, in this example). We can
allow the field next to be part of the node's representation if the programmer
wants that—this is an explicit design choice: if the field is part of the object's
representation, then the iterator will not be able to insert objects into the list,
because it will not be able to specify the required effect on the node as part of
its validity contract.

The field current in class Iterator may refer to the node objects owned by
list (note that the class parameter l is bound to the list object). The method
insert may add new elements into the list. The method next allows the iterator
to step to the next link in the list object. Method element will return the
data at the current position of traversal. None of these methods constrain the
validity, because the iterator has no internal representation: its fields are owned
by the list, and any invariant will be associated with the list rather than the
iterator.

3.4   Abstract Contexts and Mutability from Top to Bot

In the list example above, the client can give the correct types for list and data objects, but it cannot give the precise type for iterators. This is because the second formal parameter of the iterators is bound to the internal context of the list, which cannot be named from the client outside. To solve this problem, we use the context abstraction techniques introduced in our earlier papers [19,18] to abstract the name of list's internal context, so that the client can declare the correct type to hold a reference to the iterators. This is how our type system frees programs from the restrictive reference containment enforced by ownership type system. We allow arbitrary reference structure, yet, we ensure safety of these references. In this example, the client cannot use the iterators to insert elements into the list, because this will mutate and break the list's invariant. In order for the client to insert new elements, it must use the list's interface which allows the list's local invariant to be re-established by itself. The last two lines of the client code illustrate that the nodes of the list can be referenced by the external client code, but they cannot directly update the nodes because they cannot specify a concrete context for the owner of the nodes' fields (the list in this case).

However, our iterators are *not* read-only references. Iterators are able to return `Data` objects which can be mutated by the client. This is very different to previous read-only systems which use read-only references to allow iterators to cross the boundary of object encapsulation. More precisely, read-only references can only call pure (side-effect free) methods and return references in read-only mode. For instance, the `Data` objects returned by their read-only iterators cannot be mutated.

Moreover, our iterators are able to mutate the list's representation in its `insert` method depending on the caller's context. In this example, the client sits outside of the list context so it cannot use iterators to mutate the list. But objects inside the list may call `insert` on iterators to modify the list. In this sense, all references in our language are context-aware, they can be used to read anything, but write capability depends on the contexts where the references are held.

Oval provides the ability to create immutable objects explicitly. Immutable objects cannot be mutated after initialization. In Oval, immutable objects are those objects whose owner is the special context bot. By declaring an object to have bot as owner, the system allows any other object's invariant to depend on this object. Consequently, mutation of an object owned by bot could break the invariants of those objects. This is disallowed by prohibiting bot from being used as a validity effect. No well-formed method is capable of mutating objects owned by bot—effectively they become immutable.

There are some notable special cases for validity contracts. The validity contract for the main method is <top, top>. Validity invariant top means all objects in the heap are valid. At the beginning of the main method (before execution of the program), there is no object in the heap. At the end of the main method (after execution of the program), all objects created by the program must be valid.

Another special contract is <bot,top>. Methods with a <bot,top> contract do not require any objects to be valid, and do not break any validity that objects may have. By the subcontracting rule, any calls within such methods must obey the same contract. The <bot,top> contract can be used to default the validity contract of methods in legacy code such as Java programs; any callbacks from legacy code must be restricted to <bot,top> methods.

4   The Oval Type System

We present a type system for a core part of the Oval language to demonstrate that the general object validity model of Section 2 is realizable within a type system. The Oval type system is based on our earlier effective ownership type system [19]. There, methods are declared with an effective owner, E, which serves two purposes: it determines the write capability of the method body, and it restricts access to call contexts where E is known. In Oval, we replace the effective owner, E, with a validity contract $\langle I, E \rangle$. The Oval type system adopts our earlier scheme [19,18], based on abstraction of ownership contexts, which provides for liberal read access to owned objects in an ownership type systems.

The most important rules of the Oval type system are field assignment and method call. Method call is constrained by the subcontracting rules of Section 2.2. We do not formalize the expression of object invariants and their dependence on fields; informally, we simply require that object invariants only depend on the object's owned fields (those declared without nonrep) and on fields of other objects that it (transitively) owns. However we do formalize object validity by presenting a dynamic semantics which tracks a set Σ of valid objects, assuming that the object invariant is re-established for critical method calls (where $I = E = $ this).

4.1   Syntax and Static Semantics

The abstract syntax is given in Table 2. X ranges over formal context parameters; and x ranges over variable names including this used to reference the target object for the current call. Note that this is also used as a context. The overbar is used for a sequence of constructs; for example, $\bar{e}$ is used for a possibly empty sequence $e_1..e_n$, $\bar{T}\ \bar{x}$ stands for a possibly empty sequence of pairs $T_1\ x_1..T_n\ x_n$.

The first context argument of a type determines the actual owner of objects of the type. The abstract context * is used to hide context arguments when they are not nameable. We do not distinguish syntactically between concrete and abstract contexts in forming types. However such distinctions are important in our type rules. For example, the object creation type in a new expression must be concrete.

Programs consist of a collection of classes with an expression to be evaluated. Classes are parameterized with context parameters having some assumed ordering expressed by the where clause. The first formal context parameter of a class determines the owner of this object within the class. Like the original type systems, the owner of an object is determined by its creation type, and is fixed for

Table 2. Abstract Syntax for the Oval Source Language

T	$::= C\langle \overline{K} \rangle$	types
K, I, E	$::= X \mid \text{this} \mid \text{top} \mid \text{bot} \mid *$	contexts
P	$::= \overline{L} \ e$	programs
L	$::= \text{class } C[\overline{X}] \lhd T \text{ where } \overline{X} \prec \overline{X} \ \{\overline{F}; \ \overline{M}\}$	classes
F	$::= [\text{nonrep}]_{\text{opt}} \ T \ f$	fields
M	$::= T \ m(\overline{T} \ \overline{x}) \ \langle I, E \rangle \ \{e\}$	methods
e	$::=$	terms
	x	variable
	$\mid \text{new } T(\overline{e})$	new
	$\mid e.f$	select
	$\mid e.m(\overline{e})$	call
	$\mid e.f = e$	assignment

Table 3. Extended Syntax for Oval's Type Rules

K, I, E	$::= ... \mid ? \mid K_{\text{rep}}$	contexts
Γ	$::= \bullet \mid \Gamma, X \prec X \mid \Gamma, x : T$	environments
S	$::= \langle K, I, E \rangle$	stack frames

the lifetime of the object. Unlike the original ownership type systems we do not insist that the owner is within the other formal parameters of the class, because we do not use ownership to constrain object references. In the class production, inheritance $\lhd T$ is optional because our type system does not need a top type. Each field may optionally be declared to be nonrep, implying that the object's own invariant should *not* depend on it. Each method defines a pair of contexts $\langle I, E \rangle$ which specify the validity contract. We interpret the validity invariant as the down-set of I in the ownership ordering of contexts, and the validity effect is the up-set of E. The actual validity contract for a method call is determined by the context binding for the type of the target object (see the lookup [LKP-DEF] in Table 8). Our term syntax is kept as simple as possible; our interest is focused on field assignment and method call—the operations which can make changes, direct or indirect, to objects.

Table 3 extends the abstract syntax for use in the type system. This syntax is not expressible in programs. The context ? denotes an existential context, that is, an unknown context. It replaces the general context $*$ when a type is opened up in a dot expression for a field access or method call (see the [LKP-DEF] rule in Table 8). Different occurrences of the existential context cannot be compared, because they represent arbitrarily different, but unknown contexts. Similarly K_{rep} denotes an existential context whose owner is K. This allows us to expand the fields of a non-local object without needing to name it as a context (see the lookups [LKP-FLD-EXP], [LKP-INT'] rules in Table 8). Our earlier paper [18] has more detail on the topic of context abstractions and existential contexts.

Type environments Γ record the assumed ordering between context parameters, and the types of variables. Stack frames S keep track of the current active object and the validity contract for the active call. In the dynamic semantics K

Table 4. Type, Subtype, and Binding Rules

$$\mathsf{defin}(\mathsf{C}\langle\overline{\mathsf{K}}\rangle, \_) = \mathsf{class}\ \mathsf{C}\ ...\ \mathsf{where}\ \overline{\mathsf{K}'} \prec \overline{\mathsf{K}''}\ ...$$

[TYP-OBJ] $\dfrac{* \notin \overline{\mathsf{K}} \qquad \Gamma \vdash \overline{\mathsf{K}'} \prec \overline{\mathsf{K}''}}{\Gamma \vdash_o \mathsf{C}\langle\overline{\mathsf{K}}\rangle}$

[TYPE] $\dfrac{\Gamma \vdash_o \mathsf{T}' \qquad \vdash \mathsf{T}' < \mathsf{T}}{\Gamma \vdash \mathsf{T}}$

[SUB-EXT] $\dfrac{\mathsf{class}\ \mathsf{C}[\overline{\mathsf{X}}] \lhd \mathsf{T}'\ ... \qquad \mathsf{T} = [\overline{\mathsf{K}}/\overline{\mathsf{X}}]\mathsf{T}'}{\vdash \mathsf{C}\langle\overline{\mathsf{K}}\rangle < \mathsf{T}}$

[SUB-RFL] $\dfrac{}{\vdash \mathsf{T} < \mathsf{T}}$

[SUB-TRA] $\dfrac{\vdash \mathsf{T} < \mathsf{T}'' \qquad \vdash \mathsf{T}'' < \mathsf{T}'}{\vdash \mathsf{T} < \mathsf{T}'}$

[BIN-ABS] $\dfrac{\vdash \overline{\mathsf{K}} \subseteq \overline{\mathsf{K}'}}{\vdash \mathsf{C}\langle\overline{\mathsf{K}}\rangle <: \mathsf{C}\langle\overline{\mathsf{K}'}\rangle}$

[BIN-SUB] $\dfrac{\vdash \mathsf{T} < \mathsf{T}'' \qquad \vdash \mathsf{T}'' <: \mathsf{T}'}{\vdash \mathsf{T} <: \mathsf{T}'}$

corresponds to the current object location; in the static semantics, K is bound to this in method bodies. $\langle \mathsf{I}, \mathsf{E} \rangle$ denotes the validity contract of the current method.

The type rules proper follow in the next four tables. In addition, Table 8 defines some auxiliary definitions to be used by the type system. We put substitutions and lookups in the auxiliary definitions to keep the type rules simple.

Table 4 provides rules for type well-formedness and subtyping rules for expressible types. We introduce a separate judgement for bindability to handle types with existential contexts (which only occur in the type system after field or method lookup). For expressible types, there is no difference between subtyping and bindability. However bindability is not reflexive, because existential types can only occur on the right-hand side of the binding relation.

Concrete object types are formed by substituting concrete contexts into class definitions as in [TYP-OBJ]. This rule explicitly excludes context abstraction. By [TYPE] well-formed expressible types are those that have a valid concrete subtype. The rules for subtyping are based on substitution in class inheritance [SUB-EXT], and by reflexive and transitive closure [SUB-RFL], [SUB-TRA]. The binding rules are governed by a combination of context abstraction [BIN-ABS] and subtyping [BIN-SUB].

Table 5 defines the context ordering for concrete contexts. It also defines the rules for context abstraction. [ABS-RFL] ensures that the existential contexts ? and $\mathsf{K}_{\mathsf{rep}}$ abstract nothing. Combined with the earlier bindability rule [BIN-ABS] this ensures that types with existential contexts cannot be associated with the target of a binding. Finally [SUBCONTRACT] describes rules for enforcing validity subcontracting, which correspond to the earlier subcontracting definition of Section 2.2. The fourth case is equivalent to $\Gamma \vdash \mathsf{E} \preceq \mathsf{E}' \vee \mathsf{E} = \mathsf{owner}_\Gamma(\mathsf{E}')$. This highlights the fact that calls that affect the validity invariant can only be made from the owner context.

Table 5. Context Ordering, Abstraction and Subcontracting Rules

$$[\text{ORD-ENV}] \quad \frac{K \prec K' \in \Gamma}{\Gamma \vdash K \prec K'}$$

$$[\text{ORD-OWN}] \quad \frac{K \neq \text{bot}}{\Gamma \vdash K \prec \text{owner}_\Gamma(K)}$$

$$[\text{ORD-BOT}] \quad \frac{K \neq \text{bot}}{\Gamma \vdash \text{bot} \prec K}$$

$$[\text{ORD-REP}] \quad \frac{}{\Gamma \vdash K_{\text{rep}} \prec K}$$

$$[\text{ORD-TRA}] \quad \frac{\Gamma \vdash K \prec K' \quad \Gamma \vdash K' \prec E}{\Gamma \vdash K \prec E}$$

$$[\text{ORD-REF}] \quad \frac{\Gamma \vdash K \prec K' \quad \text{or} \quad K = K'}{\Gamma \vdash K \preceq K'}$$

$$[\text{ABS-ANY}] \quad \frac{}{\vdash K \subseteq *}$$

$$[\text{ABS-RFL}] \quad \frac{K \neq ? \quad K \neq \text{-rep}}{\vdash K \subseteq K}$$

$$[\text{SUBCONTRACT}] \quad \frac{\begin{array}{c}\Gamma \vdash I \prec E \implies \Gamma \vdash I' \preceq I \\ \Gamma \vdash I' \prec E' \implies \Gamma \vdash E \preceq E' \\ I = E \implies \Gamma \vdash I' \prec I \\ I' = E' \implies \Gamma \vdash E \preceq \text{owner}_\Gamma(E')\end{array}}{\Gamma; \langle K, I, E \rangle \vdash \langle I', E' \rangle}$$

The rules for well-formed program definitions and declarations are in Table 6. The main expression has an empty environment, and uses the top context to express the validity contract. A valid class must have valid fields and methods, assuming the given context ordering. The [METHOD] checks the validity contract is in one of the two correct forms, where the critical set is just this or is empty, and checks the method body within the appropriate stack frame. If the method is overriding a superclass method, its validity contract must be a subcontract of its parent.

Table 7 defines expression types. [EXP-NEW] requires that the object creation type is a valid object type, and that the constructor arguments are bindable. Field assignment [EXP-ASS] requires that the assigned expression type be bindable to the field type. If the field type involves a hidden context, this is not possible. For default field accessibility, the target expression e must be this, and it must be allowed to break its validity. For nonrep fields, the validity of the owner of the target expression must be able to be modified. Method call [EXP-CAL] is governed by the validity subcontracting rule; note that this check applies in the context of the call, so the same call may be allowed in some calling contexts and not in others. This contributes to the context sensitivity of the type system.

4.2   Dynamic Semantics and Properties

To formulate reduction rules, in Table 9 we extend the syntax of terms and contexts with typed object locations; they provide the runtime context bindings

Table 6. Program, Class, Method and Field Rules

[PROGRAM]
$$\frac{\vdash \overline{L} \qquad \bullet;\langle top, top, top\rangle \vdash e : T}{\vdash \overline{L}\ e}$$

[CLASS]
$$\frac{\Gamma = \overline{X'} \prec \overline{X''}, this : C\langle \overline{X}\rangle, super : T \qquad \Gamma \vdash T \qquad \Gamma \vdash \overline{M} \qquad \Gamma \vdash \overline{F}}{owner_\Gamma(this) = owner_\Gamma(super) \qquad range(\overline{F}) \cap dom(fields(T, this)) = \bullet} \\ \vdash class\ C[\overline{X}] \lhd T\ where\ \overline{X'} \prec \overline{X''}\ \{\overline{F};\ \overline{M}\}$$

[METHOD]
$$\frac{\begin{array}{c} S = \langle this, I, E\rangle \qquad \Gamma, \overline{x} : \overline{T}; S \vdash e : T'' \qquad \Gamma \vdash T, \overline{T} \qquad \vdash T'' <: T \\ I = E = this\ or\ \Gamma \vdash I \prec E \\ method(\Gamma(super), this, m) = T'\ m(\overline{T'}\ \_)\ \langle I', E'\rangle ... \implies \\ \vdash T <: T' \qquad \vdash \overline{T'} <: \overline{T} \qquad \Gamma; S \vdash \langle I', E'\rangle \end{array}}{\Gamma \vdash T\ m(\overline{T}\ \overline{x})\ \langle I, E\rangle\ \{e\}}$$

[FIELD]
$$\frac{\Gamma \vdash T}{\Gamma \vdash [nonrep]_{opt}\ T\ f}$$

Table 7. Typing Rules for Expressions

[EXP-VAR]
$$\frac{\Gamma(x) = T}{\Gamma; S \vdash x : T}$$

[EXP-NEW]
$$\frac{\Gamma \vdash_o T \qquad fields(T, ?) = \_\overline{T} \qquad \Gamma; S \vdash \overline{e} : \overline{T'} \qquad \vdash \overline{T'} <: \overline{T}}{\Gamma; S \vdash new\ T(\overline{e}) : T}$$

[EXP-SEL]
$$\frac{fields_S^\Gamma(e)(f) = T}{\Gamma; S \vdash e.f : T}$$

[EXP-ASS]
$$\frac{\begin{array}{c} \Gamma; S \vdash e.f : T \qquad \Gamma; S \vdash e' : T' \qquad \vdash T' <: T \\ f \notin nrfields_S^\Gamma(e) \implies \Gamma; S \vdash \langle bot, e\rangle \wedge S = \langle e, ..\rangle \\ f \in nrfields_S^\Gamma(e) \implies \Gamma; S \vdash \langle bot, owner_\Gamma(e)\rangle \end{array}}{\Gamma; S \vdash e.f = e' : T'}$$

[EXP-CAL]
$$\frac{\begin{array}{c} method_S^\Gamma(e, m) = T\ m\langle I, E\rangle(\overline{T}\ \_) \\ \Gamma; S \vdash \overline{e} : \overline{T'} \qquad \vdash \overline{T'} <: \overline{T} \qquad \Gamma; S \vdash \langle I, E\rangle \end{array}}{\Gamma; S \vdash e.m(\overline{e}) : T}$$

which serve to structure the heap. Objects are modeled as mappings from fields to locations (for convenience, the object type is encoded in the object's location rather than in the object itself). The heap maps locations to objects.

Amongst the extra definitions in Table 10, note that the well-formedness of the validity set requires that it contains all objects within the validity invariant I, and I itself when it is distinct from the validity effect E.

Table 11 presents a big-step reduction semantics. It is of particular interest to trace how the validity set is affected by the reductions, depending on the validity contract for method call, and how default and nonrep field assignment differ by either invalidating the target of the call or its owner.

Finally, we present some of the key properties of the type system. The main result *validity preservation* is stated together with the conventional *type preservation* property in Theorem 1. The first line of the *if-then* block is the validity

Table 8. Auxiliary Definitions for Typing Rules

$$[\text{LKP-DEF}] \quad \frac{L = \text{class } C[\overline{X}] \ \dots \qquad \overline{K'} = [?/*]\overline{K}}{\text{defin}(C\langle\overline{K}\rangle, K) = [\overline{K'}/\overline{X}, K/\textbf{this}]L}$$

$$[\text{LKP-FLD}] \quad \frac{\text{defin}(T, K) = \text{class } \dots \lhd T' \ \{[\text{nonrep}]_{\text{opt}} \ \overline{T} \ \overline{f}; \ \dots \}}{\text{fields}(T, K) = \overline{f} \ \overline{T}, \text{fields}(T', K)}$$

$$[\text{LKP-FLD-EXP}] \quad \frac{\Gamma; S \vdash e : T}{\text{fields}_S^\Gamma(e) = \text{fields}(T, \text{internal}_S^T(e))}$$

$$[\text{LKP-MUT}] \quad \frac{\text{class } C \ \dots \lhd T \ \{\dots \ \text{nonrep } \overline{T} \ \overline{f} \ \dots; \ \dots \}}{\text{nrfields}(C\langle..\rangle) = \overline{f}, \text{nrfields}(T)}$$

$$[\text{LKP-MUT-EXP}] \quad \frac{\Gamma; S \vdash e : T}{\text{nrfields}_S^\Gamma(e) = \text{nrfields}(T)}$$

$$[\text{LKP-MTH}] \quad \frac{\text{defin}(T, K) = \text{class } \dots \ T' \ m(\overline{T} \ \overline{x})\{e\} \ \dots}{\text{method}(T, K, m) = T' \ m(\overline{T} \ \overline{x})\{e\}}$$

$$[\text{LKP-MTH}'] \quad \frac{\text{defin}(T, K) = \text{class } \dots \lhd T' \ \{ \ \dots \ ; \overline{M}\} \qquad m \notin \overline{M}}{\text{method}(T, K, m) = \text{method}(T', K, m)}$$

$$[\text{LKP-MTH-EXP}] \quad \frac{\Gamma; S \vdash e : T}{\text{method}_S^\Gamma(e, m) = \text{method}(T, \text{internal}_S^T(e), m)}$$

$$[\text{LKP-OWN}] \quad \frac{\Gamma; \bullet \vdash e : T}{\text{owner}_\Gamma(e) = \text{owner}(T)}$$

$$[\text{LKP-OWN}'] \quad \frac{}{\text{owner}(C\langle K, ..\rangle) = K}$$

$$[\text{LKP-INT}] \quad \frac{S = \langle K, I, E\rangle}{\text{internal}_S^T(K) = K}$$

$$[\text{LKP-INT}'] \quad \frac{S = \langle K, I, E\rangle \qquad e \neq K \qquad K' = \text{owner}(T)}{\text{internal}_S^T(e) = K'_{\text{rep}}}$$

invariant property; and the second line of the *if-then* is the type preservation property. Corollary 1 states that all objects created by the program must be valid at the end of the execution.

Theorem 1 (Validity Preservation and Type Preservation). *Given* $\vdash P$, $\vdash H$ *and* $H \vdash S$,

$$if \begin{cases} H; S \vdash \Sigma \\ \bullet; S \vdash e : T \end{cases} and \ H; \Sigma; e \Downarrow_S H'; \Sigma'; l, \ then \begin{cases} H'; S \vdash \Sigma' \\ \bullet; S \vdash l : T', \vdash T' <: T \ and \vdash H' \end{cases}.$$

Proof. The proof proceeds by induction on the form of $H; \Sigma; e \Downarrow_S H; \Sigma; l$. Due to the limited space, we only sketch the proof for validity preservation. Let $S = \langle K, I, E\rangle$. Case [RED-SEL] is trivial. Case [RED-NEW]: we show that the newly created object is valid by the [OBJECT] rule, then by the [VALIDITY SET] rule we have the result. Case [RED-ASS]: we need to show assignments cannot invalidate objects in Σ, by the [EXP-ASS] and the [SUBCONTRACT] rules we have that the object invalidated by the assignment is equal or outside of E. Since $H \vdash S$, and by the [STACKFRAME] rule we have I is inside or equal to the invalidated object, depending on whether or not I and E are the same. Then by the [OBJECT] and

Table 9. Extended Syntax for Dynamic Semantics

l, l_T		typed locations
e	$::= ... \mid l$	terms
K, I, E	$::= ... \mid l$	contexts
o	$::= \overline{f} \mapsto \overline{l}$	objects
H	$::= \overline{l} \mapsto \overline{o}$	heaps
Σ	$::= \text{bot}, \overline{l}$	valid objects

Table 10. Auxiliary Definitions for Dynamic Features

[EXP-LOC]
$$\frac{}{\Gamma; S \vdash l_T : T}$$

[HEAP]
$$\frac{\forall l \in \text{dom}(H) \cdot \bullet; \bullet \vdash l : T \qquad H(l) = \overline{f} \mapsto \overline{l}}{\text{fields}(T, l) = \overline{f}\,\overline{T} \qquad \bullet; \bullet \vdash \overline{l} : \overline{T'} \qquad \vdash \overline{T'} <: \overline{T}}{\vdash H}$$

[STACKFRAME]
$$\frac{\{K, I, E\} \subseteq \text{dom}(H) \cup \{\text{top}\} \qquad \bullet \vdash I \prec E \text{ or } K = I = E}{H \vdash \langle K, I, E \rangle}$$

[OBJECT]
$$\frac{\bullet \vdash l' \preceq l \implies l' \in \Sigma}{\Sigma \vdash l}$$

[VALIDITY SET]
$$\frac{\Sigma \subseteq \text{dom}(H) \cup \{\text{top}\} \qquad \bullet \vdash I \prec E \implies \Sigma \vdash I \qquad I = E \implies \Sigma, I \vdash I}{H; \langle K, I, E \rangle \vdash \Sigma}$$

Table 11. Reduction Rules

[EXECUTION]
$$\frac{\bullet; \text{bot}; e \Downarrow_{\langle \text{top,top,top} \rangle} H; \Sigma; l}{\overline{L}\ e \Downarrow H; \Sigma; l}$$

[RED-CAL]
$$\frac{\begin{array}{c} H; \Sigma; e \Downarrow_S H'; \Sigma'; l \qquad H'; \Sigma'; \overline{e} \Downarrow_S H''; \Sigma''; \overline{l} \\ \text{method}(l, m) = ...\langle I, E \rangle (\_\ \overline{x})\{e'\} \qquad H''; \Sigma''; [\overline{l}/\overline{x}]e' \Downarrow_{\langle l, I, E \rangle} H'''; \Sigma'''; l' \\ l = I = E \implies \Sigma'''' = \Sigma''', l \qquad \Gamma \vdash I \prec E \implies \Sigma'''' = \Sigma''' \end{array}}{H; \Sigma; e.m(\overline{e}) \Downarrow_S H'''; \Sigma''''; l'}$$

[RED-NEW]
$$\frac{H; \Sigma; \overline{e} \Downarrow_S H'; \Sigma'; \overline{l} \qquad l_T \notin \text{dom}(H') \qquad \text{fields}(T, l_T) = \overline{f}\ \_}{H; \Sigma; \text{new } T(\overline{e}) \Downarrow_S H', l_T \mapsto \{\overline{f} \mapsto \overline{l}\}; \Sigma', l_T; l_T}$$

[RED-ASS]
$$\frac{\begin{array}{c} H; \Sigma; e \Downarrow_S H'; \Sigma'; l \qquad H'; \Sigma'; e' \Downarrow_S H''; \Sigma''; l' \\ f \notin \text{nrfields}(l) \implies \Sigma''' = \Sigma'' - l \\ f \in \text{nrfields}(l) \implies \Sigma''' = \Sigma'' - \text{owner}(l) \end{array}}{H; \Sigma; e.f = e' \Downarrow_S [l \mapsto H''(l)[f \mapsto l']]H''; \Sigma'''; l'}$$

[RED-SEL]
$$\frac{H; \Sigma; e \Downarrow_S H'; \Sigma'; l}{H; \Sigma; e.f \Downarrow_S H'; \Sigma'; H'(l)(f)}$$

[VALIDITY SET] rules, we have the result. Case [RED-CAL]: as for the [RED-ASS] case, except the target object of the call may be invalidated during the call and is re-validated after the call.

Corollary 1 (System Validity). *Given* $\vdash$ P, *if* P $\Downarrow$ H; Σ; l *then* $\Sigma = \mathrm{dom}(H)$.

Proof. After applying Theorem 1 to the [EXECUTION] rule, we have the result by the [VALIDITY SET] rule.

5   Discussion and Related Work

5.1   Boogie and Universes

Our model for object validity is general, and not tied to any particular language. The Oval language provides just one possible realization of our general model for validity contracts. It has been inspired, not only by our own attempt to use ownership types to reason about object invariants and effects [19], but by various work on the Boogie methodology [17] and Universes [24]. We now compare the Universes and Boogie approaches with our general model.

Universes uses a relatively simple ownership type system to arrange objects into layers. Object invariants may depend on objects in the same and inner layers. Read-only annotations are used to allow object dependencies between layers, without providing a general update capability. The layering of objects corresponds to our object preorder $\succcurlyeq$. The validity invariant should be interpreted as the set of layers below the currently active layer, and the validity effect corresponds to the current layer. In Universes, there is no attempt to track the (possibly) invalid call context E, and so its up-closure is not required.

The Boogie methodology, as manifested in Spec#, is based on a program logic, accompanied by a model for protecting the validity of object state, which dynamically tracks the ownership of objects. The basic model describes objects as either consistent or valid or neither. Consistent or valid objects must satisfy their own invariant, and may only own consistent objects. Within the scope of an object pack/upack block, a valid object may be updated and its invariant may be broken within that scope. For us, the validity invariant corresponds to the set of valid or consistent objects, and the validity effect corresponds to those objects that have currently been unpacked. Interestingly, this model allows dynamic transfer of ownership. For us, this implies that the preorder $\succcurlyeq$ is dynamic, so when reasoning about I and E, we need to allow for different closures as the ownership structure changes. This may require some extra consistency constraints, but we believe that our model for validity contracts as summarized in Table 1 is still applicable. This is worthy of further investigation. In general, program logics like Boogie increase the specification overhead significantly. We believe the use of an Oval-like type system can provide framing assumptions for more detailed specifications, thereby allowing those specifications to be more concise.

Ownership is useful for expressing partially ordered *one-to-many* dependency relation, that is, one object may depend on multiple other objects. This kind of dependency is particularly useful for enforcing locality in object-oriented programs to allow localized reasoning on object invariants. However, ownership is not enough for expressing cyclic, many-to-one or many-to-many dependency relations. For instance, in a double-linked list, a node object has two fields—a previous field to reference its predecessor node in the list and a next field to reference its successor. The invariant of such a node typically requires the next field in its predecessor and the previous field in its successor to reference back the node itself. As a result, the invariants of two adjacent nodes are mutual. Ownership cannot capture such an invariant precisely, instead it requires such an invariant to be maintained by the list (i.e., the owner of the nodes). This is a sound solution, but in practice, it may complicate specification and reasoning [17]. In order to verify the invariant of the list, one has to consider all node objects owned by the list, but in fact modification of one node can affect only its predecessor and successor nodes.

Universes and Boogies allow local invariants to depend on the states of objects which are not owned by the current object; those objects are typically required to be within the same owner or sufficiently unpacked. For example, a node object's invariant may mention fields in its predecessor and successor nodes. This kind of invariant is called a *visibility-based invariant* [22,17], because it requires an invariant to be visible in every method that might violate the invariant, typically restricted to be within a module or friend classes. Visibility-based invariants essentially allow programmers to trade the locality offered by ownership for flexibility in the object invariant. They need to check states which are not local, and consequently generate more complicated proof obligations. Our general model introduced in Section 2 is independent of the form of the invariant, whether ownership or visibility-based. The Oval language has only used an ownership-based invariant in demonstrating the general model. This results in several advantages including less specification overhead (only type annotations are needed) and significantly simplified proof obligations for verification. In the future, we may consider extending Oval to handle visibility-based invariants as well.

5.2 Ownership Type Systems

Ownership Types [28,12,11,9] allow programmers to enforce a tree-based encapsulation by declaring owners of objects as part of their types. Traditional object-oriented programs offer no object structure, and can be considered as special case of ownership types where all objects are owned by a single universal context top.

Effective ownership [19] allows programmers to add contexts to methods as effect owners. It is an encapsulation-aware effect system which frees ownership types from reference constraint, i.e. it allows arbitrary reference structure, but still retains a strict encapsulation on object representation. The *effect encapsulation* property guarantees that any update to an object's internal state must occur (directly or indirectly) via a call on a method of its owner. Ownership types can be generalized as a special case of effective ownership where all effect owners are the current context this.

The type system we present in this paper generalizes effective ownership by adding invariant constraints to methods. The effect owner used in effective ownership is indeed the validity effect we have used in our new type system. Effective ownership is a special case of this type system where all validity invariants are the special context bot. The actual formalization of effective ownership is slightly different, but we are able encode them in our type system. Consequently, the *effect encapsulation* property is also true in our type system.

The original ownership types hide knowledge of the identity of an object outside itself so that it cannot be named from outside. This kind of naming restriction may limit the expressiveness of ownership types. In particular, ownership types are known to be unable to express some common design patterns such as iterators or callbacks, which typically need to cross the boundary of encapsulation.

There have been a number of proposals made to improve the expressiveness of ownership types. *JOE* [10] allows internal contexts to be named through read-only local variables so that internal representation can be accessed from outside. *Ownership Domains* [1] use a similar method where read-only fields (final fields in Java) are used to name internal domains (partitions of contexts) instead of read-only variables. The *inner class* solution [9,8] allows inner classes to name the outer object directly. These proposals tend to break the strict encapsulation of ownership types, and do not support localized reasoning on object invariants.

5.3   Read-Only Systems

Read-only systems [23,25,5] use read-only references to cross the boundary of encapsulation, called *observational representation exposure* in [5]. Read-only references are considered harmless because they are restricted—they can only call pure methods (methods with no side effect) and return other read-only references. For example, they are able to express iterators by using a read-only reference to access the internal implementation of the list object.

However, these iterators can only return data elements in read-only mode, that is, the elements stored in the list cannot be updated in this way (unless using dynamic casting with its associated runtime overheads [25]). This is due to the fact that traditional read-only references are plain read-only—they are unaware of any encapsulation structure.

Our proposal here allows references to cross encapsulation boundaries but ensures these references cannot update the internal states directly, that is, any update still has to be initiated by the owner object. The novelty is that all references in our system are encapsulation-aware. A reference can never be used to mutate states encapsulated by the context where the reference is held, yet they can always be used to mutate states of or outside of the current context. For example, iterator objects in our program can be used by a client to mutate data elements stored by a list object, while still protecting the list's representation from external modification. Moreover, the iterator objects may or may not be used to update the list's internal implementation depending on the contexts where the iterators are used—the `insert` method may be called from within the list context but never from outside of the list.

6   Conclusion

In this paper, we have presented a general framework for tracking object invariants. The novelty of this model is a behavioural abstraction that specifies two sets, the *validity invariant* and the *validity effect*. The overlap of these two sets captures precisely those objects that need to be re-validated at the end of the behaviour. To support our general model, we have also presented an object-oriented programming language that uses ownership types to confine dependencies for object invariants, and restricts permissible updates to track where object invariants hold even in the presence of re-entrant calls.

Acknowledgments

We thank the anonymous reviewers for their comments, one in particular being very detailed. This work has been supported by the Australian Research Council, Grant DP0665581.

References

1. Aldrich, J., Chambers, C.: Ownership domains: Separating aliasing policy from mechanism. In: Odersky, M. (ed.) ECOOP 2004. LNCS, vol. 3086, Springer, Heidelberg (2004)
2. Almeida, P.S.: Balloon types: Controlling sharing of state in data types. In: Aksit, M., Matsuoka, S. (eds.) ECOOP 1997. LNCS, vol. 1241, pp. 32–59. Springer, Heidelberg (1997)
3. Barnett, M., DeLine, R., Fahndrich, M., Leino, K., Schulte, W.: Verification of object-oriented programs with invariants. Journal of Object Technology 3(6), 27–56 (2004)
4. Barnett, M., Naumann, D.: Friends need a bit more: Maintaining invariants over shared state. In: Mathematics of Program Construction, pp. 54–84 (2004)
5. Birka, A., Ernst, M.D.: A practical type system and language for reference immutability. In: OOPSLA '04: Proceedings of the 19th annual ACM SIGPLAN Conference on Object-Oriented Programming, Systems, Languages, and Applications, pp. 35–49. ACM Press, New York (2004)
6. Bornat, R.: Proving pointer programs in Hoare logic. In: Mathematics of Program Construction, pp. 102–126 (2000)
7. Bornat, R., Calcagno, C., O'Hearn, P., Parkinson, M.: Permission accounting in separation logic. In: Proceedings of the 32nd ACM SIGPLAN-SIGACT sysposium on Principles of programming languages, pp. 259–270 (2005)
8. Boyapati, C., Liskov, B., Shrira, L.: Ownership types for object encapsulation. In: Proceedings of the 30th ACM SIGPLAN-SIGACT Symposium on Principles of Programming Languages, pp. 213–223. ACM Press, New York (2003)
9. Clarke, D.: Object Ownership and Containment. PhD thesis, School of Computer Science and Engineering, The University of New South Wales, Sydney, Australia (2001)
10. Clarke, D.G., Drossopoulou, S.: Ownership, encapsulation and disjointness of type and effect. In: 17th Annual Conference on Object-Oriented Programming, Systems, Languages, and Applications (OOPSLA) (November 2002)
11. Clarke, D.G., Noble, J., Potter, J.M.: Simple ownership types for object containment. In: Knudsen, J.L. (ed.) ECOOP 2001. LNCS, vol. 2072, Springer, Heidelberg (2001)

12. Clarke, D.G., Potter, J.M., Noble, J.: Ownership types for flexible alias protection. In: Proceedings of the 13th ACM SIGPLAN Conference on Object-Oriented Programming, Systems, Languages, and Applications, pp. 48–64. ACM Press, New York (1998)
13. Dietl, W., Muller, P.: Universes: Lightweight ownership for JML. Journal of Object Technology (JOT) (2005)
14. Hogg, J.: Islands: aliasing protection in object-oriented languages. In: OOPSLA '91: Proceedings of Conference on Object-Oriented Programming Systems, Languages, and Applications, pp. 271–285. ACM Press, New York (1991)
15. Ishtiaq, S., O'Hearn, P.W.: Bi as an assertion language for mutable data structures. In: Proceedings of the 28th Annual ACM SIGPLAN - SIGACT Symposium on Principles of Programming Languages, ACM Press, New York (2001)
16. Leavens, G.: Modular specification and verification of object-oriented programs. Software, IEEE 8(4), 72–80 (1991)
17. Leino, K.R.M., Müller, P.: Object invariants in dynamic contexts. In: Odersky, M. (ed.) ECOOP 2004. LNCS, vol. 3086, pp. 491–516. Springer, Heidelberg (2004)
18. Lu, Y., Potter, J.: On ownership and accessibility. In: Proceedings of the 20th European Conference on Object-Oriented Programming, pp. 99–123. Springer, Heidelberg (2006)
19. Lu, Y., Potter, J.: Protecting representation with effect encapsulation. In: Proceedings of the 33th ACM SIGPLAN-SIGACT Symposium on Principles of Programming Languages, ACM Press, New York (2006)
20. Meyer, B.: Eiffel: the language. Prentice-Hall, Inc, Upper Saddle River, NJ, USA (1992)
21. Meyer, B.: Object-oriented software construction, 2nd edn. Prentice-Hall, Upper Saddle River, NJ, USA (1997)
22. Müller, P.: Modular Specification and Verification of Object-Oriented Programs. LNCS, vol. 2262. Springer, Heidelberg (2002)
23. Müller, P., Poetzsch-Heffter, A.: Universes: A type system for controlling representation exposure. In: Programming Languages and Fundamentals of Programming (1999)
24. Müller, P., Poetzsch-Heffter, A.: Universes: A Type System for Alias and Dependency Control. Fernuniv. Fachbereich Informatik (2001)
25. Müller, P., Poetzsch-Heffter, A.: Universes: A type system for alias and dependency control. Technical Report 279, Fernuniversität Hagen (2001)
26. Muller, P., Poetzsch-Heffter, A., Leavens, G.: Modular invariants for layered object structures. Science of Computer Programming (2006)
27. Naumann, D., Barnett, M.: Towards imperative modules: reasoning about invariants and sharing of mutable state. In: Logic in Computer Science, 2004. Proceedings of the 19th Annual IEEE Symposium on, pp. 313–323 (2004)
28. Noble, J., Vitek, J., Potter, J.: Flexible alias protection. In: Jul, E. (ed.) ECOOP 1998. LNCS, vol. 1445, Springer, Heidelberg (1998)
29. Reynolds, J.: Separation logic: a logic for shared mutable data structures. In: 2002. Proceedings. 17th Annual IEEE Symposium on Logic in Computer Science, pp. 55–74 (2002)
30. Schulte, W.: Towards a Verifying Compiler: The Spec# Approach. Microsoft Research (2006), http://research.microsoft.com/specsharp/

Non-null References by Default in Java: Alleviating the Nullity Annotation Burden

Patrice Chalin and Perry R. James

Dependable Software Research Group,
Dept. of Computer Science and Software Engineering,
Concordia University Montréal, Québec, Canada
chalin@encs.concordia.ca, perry@dsrg.org

Abstract. With Java 5 annotations, we note a marked increase in tools that statically detect potential null dereferences. To be effective such tools require that developers annotate declarations with nullity modifiers and have annotated API libraries. Unfortunately, in our experience specifying moderately large code bases, the use of non-null annotations is more labor intensive than it should be. Motivated by this experience, we conducted an empirical study of 5 open source projects totaling 700 KLOC which confirms that on average, 3/4 of declarations are meant to be non-null, by design. Guided by these results, we propose adopting a non-null-by-default semantics. This new default has advantages of better matching general practice, lightening developer annotation burden and being safer. We adapted the Eclipse JDT Core to support the new semantics, including the ability to read the extensive API library specifications written in the Java Modeling Language (JML). Issues of backwards compatibility are addressed.

1 Introduction

Null pointer exceptions (NPEs) are among the most common faults raised by components written in object-oriented languages. As a present-day illustration of this, we note that of the bug fixes applied to the Eclipse Java Development Tools (JDT) Core[1] between releases 3.2 and 3.3, five percent were directly attributed to NPEs. Developers increasingly have at their disposal tools that can detect possible null dereferences by means of static analysis (SA) of component source. A survey of such tools shows that the introduction in Java 5 of Annotations [30, §9.7] seems to have contributed to an increase in support for non-null static checking in Java.

It is well know that SA tools supporting *inter*-procedural analysis tend to yield a high proportion of false positives unless code and support libraries are supplemented with appropriate nullity annotations [20, 35]. This currently translates into more work for developers; adding annotations to new or existing code can be a formidable task: e.g. the Eclipse JDT Core contains approximately 11,000 declarations that are candidates for non-null annotation. It has been our experience in annotating

---

[1] The JDT Core includes the Eclipse Java compiler (incremental and batch), code assist, code search, etc.

E. Ernst (Ed.): ECOOP 2007, LNAI 4609, pp. 227–247, 2007.

moderately large code bases (including the JDT Core), that we spend most of our time constraining declarations to be non-null rather than leaving them unannotated.

Can something be done to alleviate the burden of developers? Imposing such an extra burden on developers generally translates into reduced adoption—contrast the total number of downloads, over comparable periods, of two fully automated and popular SA tools: Esc/Java2 (52,000) which requires developers to write specifications and/or annotations vs. FindBugs which doesn't (270,000)[2]. Motivated by our experiences and inspired by the success of FindBugs (built on the philosophy that simple techniques are effective too), a simple solution seemed apparent: switch the nullity interpretation of declarations to non-null by default. But since this would be contrary to the current Java default, such a switch would only be justified if significantly more than 50% of declarations are non-null in practice, and appropriate measures are taken to address backwards compatibility and migration of existing projects to the new default. We deal with both of these points in this article.

The main contribution of this paper is a carefully executed empirical study (Sections 2 and 3) confirming the following hypothesis:

In Java programs, at least 2/3 of declarations (other than local variables) that are of reference types **are meant to be non-null, based on *design intent*.**

We exclude local variables because their non-nullity can be inferred by intra-procedural analysis [2, 35]. For this study we sampled 5 open source projects totaling 722 KLOC of Java source. To our knowledge, this is the first formal empirical study of this kind—though anecdotal evidence has been mentioned elsewhere, e.g. [24, 25].

A review of languages supporting non-null annotations or types (Section 4) shows a recent trend in the adoption of non-null as a default. We believe that this, coupled with the study results, suggest that the time is ripe for non-null-by-default in Java. A second contribution of this paper is a proposal, supported by the study results, that declarations of reference types be non-null by default in Java. This new default has the advantage of better matching general practice, lightening the annotation burden of developers and being *safer* (Section 5). Our proposal also carefully addresses issues of backwards compatibility and code migration. We describe an implementation of the new default in a customized version of the Eclipse 3.3 JDT Core which supports non-null types [8, 24]. It achieves this by adopting the syntax for nullity modifiers of the Java Modeling Language (JML)—e.g. `/*@non_null*/` and `/*@nullable*/` [3]. Among other things, this choice of syntax makes it possible to support all versions of Java (not just Java 5) and non-null casts. In addition, it relieves developers from having to annotate API libraries since the tool processes the extensive collection of API specifications developed by the JML community.

Expert groups have recently been formed to look into the standardization of "Annotations for Software Defect Detection" (JSR 305) [45] and "Annotations on

---

[2] To be fair, we note that FindBugs originally only supported intra-procedural analysis. It now supports inter-procedural analysis and hence, like ESC/Java2, will require developers to provide nullity annotations when this feature is enabled.

[3] For a brief period, experimental support for such annotations (i.e. inside comments) was a part of the 3.2 build.

Java Types" (JSR 308) [17]. JSR 305 will "work to develop standard annotations (such as @NonNull) that can be applied to Java programs to assist tools that detect software defects." Making the right choice of nullity default will have an important impact on the annotation burden of developers and, we believe, can even help improve the accuracy of SA tools, particularly nullity annotation assistants (cf. Section 5.3). The next two sections cover the main contribution of the paper: the study method and study results, respectively.

2 Study

2.1 Hypothesis

The purpose of the study was to test the following hypothesis:

> In Java programs at least 2/3 of declarations (other than local variables) that are of reference types are meant to be non-null, based on design intent.

A key point of this hypothesis is that it is phrased in terms of design *intent*; i.e. whether or not the application designer intended a particular declaration to be nullable or non-null. Design intent is not something that can be reverse-engineered from the inspection of code. Tools exist which attempt to guess correct nullity annotations, but these remain guesses. As an illustration of this, consider the following interface:

```
public interface A {
  void m(Object o);
}
```

Should the parameter o be declared non-null? In the case of an interface, there is no code to inspect. While a tool might be able to analyze *current* implementations of the interface, if these happen to be accessible, that does not preclude future implementations from having different behaviors. Furthermore, let us assume that the only implementation of A has the following definition:

```
public class C implements A {
  private Object copy;
  void m(Object o) {
    copy = o.clone();
  }
}
```

Does this mean that o was meant to be non-null, or have we stumbled upon a bug in C.m()? Without knowledge of intent of the designers of A, we cannot tell. To quote Bill Pugh, FindBugs project lead, *"Static analysis tools, such as FindBugs, don't actually know what your code is supposed to do. Instead, they typically just find inconsistencies in your code"* [46].

Design intent is found most often in the heads of designers and *sometimes* recorded as documentation, inlined code comments or machine checkable annotations and specifications. Hence, it was important for us to seek study subjects supported with design documentation, that were already annotated or for which we had access to designers who could answer our questions as we added annotations to the code.

2.2 Case Study Subjects

It was our earlier work on an ESC/Java2 case study, in the specification and verification of a small web-based enterprise application framework named SoenEA [47], that provided the final impetus to initiate the study reported in this paper; i.e., the burden of having to annotate (what appeared to be) *almost all* reference type declarations of an existing code base with non-null modifiers, seemed to drive home the idea that non-null should be the default. Hence, we chose to include SoenEA as one of our case study subjects. As our next three subjects we chose the JML checker, ESC/Java2 and the tallying subsystem of Koa, a recently developed Dutch internet voting application[4]. We chose these projects because:

- We believe that they are representative of typical designs in Java applications and that they are of a non-trivial size—numbers will be given shortly.
- The sources included some inlined design documentation and were at least partly annotated with nullity modifiers; hence we would not be starting entirely from scratch.
- We were familiar with the source code (and/or had peers that were) and hence expected that it would be easier to extend or add accurate nullity annotations. Too much effort would have been required to study and understand unfamiliar and sizeable projects in sufficient detail to be able to write correct specifications[5].
- Finally, the project sources are freely available to be reviewed by others who may want to validate our specification efforts.

All of the study subjects named so far are related to work done by the JML community and could be considered "academic" projects. Since restricting our attention to such samples might bias the study results we chose the Java Development Tools (JDT) package of Eclipse 3.3 as our final study subject. This brings in a "real" industrial grade application. Furthermore, prior to this study we were in no way involved in the development of the JDT hence there could be no bias in terms of us imposing a particular Java design style on the code base.

2.3 Procedure

2.3.1 Selection of Sample Files
With the study projects identified, our objective was to add nullity annotations to all of the source files, or, if there were too many, a randomly chosen sample of files. In the latter case, we fixed our sample size at 35 since sample sizes of 30 or more are generally considered "sufficiently large" [29]. Our random sampling for a given project was created by first listing the N project files in alphabetical order, generating 35 random numbers in the range $1..N$, and then choosing the corresponding files.

Table 1 provides the number of files, lines-of-code (LOC) and source-lines-of-code (SLOC) [43] for our study subjects as well as the projects that they are subcomponents of. Aside from SoenEA, the study subjects are actually an integral (and dependant) part of a larger project. For example, the JML checker is only one of the tools provided as part of the ISU tool suite—other tools include JmlUnit and the JML run-time assertion

---

[4] Koa was used, e.g., in the 2004 European parliamentary elections.

[5] Particularly since projects tend to lack detailed design documentation.

checker compiler. The Eclipse JDT Core is one of 5 components of the Eclipse JDT, which itself is one of several subprojects of Eclipse. Overall, the source for all four projects consists of 1475 KLOC (939 KSLOC) from almost 6000 Java source files. Our study subjects account for 722 KLOC from a total population of 1644 files.

Table 1. General statistics of study subjects and their encompassing projects

Encompassing Project →	JML ISU Tools	ESC Tools	SoenEA	Koa	Eclipse JDT	Total (partial)
# of files	831	455	52	459	4124	5921
LOC (K)	243	124	3	87	1018	1475
SLOC (K)	140	75	2	62	660	939

Study subject →	JML Checker	ESC/ Java2	SoenEA	Koa Tally Subsystem	Eclipse JDT Core	Total
# of files	217	216	52	29	1130	1644
LOC (K)	86	63	3	10	560	722
SLOC (K)	58	41	2	4	365	470

```
/**
 * Performs code correction for the given IProblem,
 * reporting results to the given correction requestor.
 *
 * Correction results are answered through a requestor.
 *
 * @param problem  the problem which describe the problem to correct.
 * @param targetUnit denote the compilation unit …. Cannot be null.
 * @param requestor the given correction requestor
 * @exception IllegalArgumentException if targetUnit or
 *               requestor is null.
 *    …
 * @since 2.0
 */
public void computeCorrections(IProblem problem, ... targetUnit, ... requestor) throws ... {
    if (requestor == null) {
        throw new IllegalArgumentException(Messages.correction_nullUnit);
    }
    this.computeCorrections(
        targetUnit, problem.getID(),
        problem.getSourceStart(),
        problem.getSourceEnd(),
        problem.getArguments(),
        requestor);
}
```

Fig. 1. Excerpt from the JDT Core API class org.eclipse.jdt.core.CorrectionEngine

2.3.2 Annotating the Sample Files

We then added non-null annotations to declarations where appropriate. As an illustration of the type of situations that we faced, consider the code for the computeCorrections() method of the public API class org.eclipse.jdt.core. CorrectionEngine as shown in Figure 1. (By convention, types inside packages named internal are not to be used by client plug-ins, while all other types are assumed to be part of the JDT Core's public API, hence `CorrectionEngine` is part of the API.) In principle, clients would only read the method's Javadoc which would allow a developer to learn that `targetUnit` and `requestor` must not be null. Nothing is said about `problem` and yet this argument is dereferenced in the method body without a test for null. Hence we have detected an inconsistency between the Javadoc and the code. Further analysis actually reveals another inconsistency: an `IllegalArgumentException` is *not* thrown when `targetUnit` is null. None-the-less, the intended nullity attributes for the three formal parameters is clearly `non_null`.

A simple example of a field declaration that we would constrain to be non-null is:

```
static final String MSG1 = "abc";
```

Of course, cases in which the initialization expression is a method call require more care. Similarly we would conservatively annotate constructor and method parameters as well as method return types based on the apparent design intent. As an example of a situation where there was no supporting documentation, consider the following method:

```
String m(int paths[]) {
    String result = "";
    for(int i = 0; i < paths.length; i++) {
        result += paths[i] + ";";
    }
    return result;
}
```

In the absence of any explicit specification or documentation for such a method we would assume that the designer intended `paths` to be non-null (since there is no test for nullity and yet, e.g., the `length` field of `paths` is used). We can also deduce that the method will always return a non-null String.

2.3.3 Proper Handling of Overriding Methods

Special care needs to be taken when annotating overriding or overridden methods. We treat non-null annotations as if defining non-null types [8, 24]. In this respect, we follow Java 5 conventions and support method

- return type covariance—as is illustrated in Figure 2;
- parameter type invariance.

Hence, constraining a method return or parameter type to be non-null for an overriding method in one of our study sample files generally required adding annotations to the overridden method declaration(s) as well. This was particularly evident in the case of the JML checker code since the class hierarchy is up to 6 levels of inheritance for some files that we worked on (e.g. `JmlCompilationUnit`).

2.4 Verification and Validation of Annotations

We used two complementary techniques to ensure the accuracy of the nullity annotations that we added. Firstly, we compiled the study subjects—using the Eclipse JML JDT to be described in Section 5.1—with runtime assertion checking (RAC)

```
public abstract class Greeting
{
  protected /*@non_null*/ String nm;

  public void set(/*@non_null*/ String nm) {
    this.nm = aNm;
  }

  public /*@non_null*/ String welcome() {
    return greeting() + " " + nm;
  }

  public abstract /*@nullable*/ String greeting();

}
```

(a) Greeting **class**

```
public class EnglishGreeting extends Greeting
{
  public void set(/*@nullable*/ String nm) // error: contravariance prohibited in Java 5
  {
    ...
  }

  public /*@non_null*/ String greeting() {   // ok: covariance supported in Java 5
  {
    return "Hello";
  }
}
```

(b) EnglishGreeting **class**

Fig. 2. Illustration of nullity type variance rules for overriding methods

enabled and then ran them against each project's standard test suite. Nullity RAC ensures that a non-null declaration is never initialized or assigned null, be it for a local variable, field, parameter or method (return) declarations. In some cases the test suites are quite large—e.g. in the order of 15,000 for the Eclipse JDT, 50,000 for JML, and 600 for ESC/Java2. While the number of tests for ESC/Java2 is lower, some of the individual tests are "big": e.g. the type checker is run on itself. In addition, we ran the RAC-enabled version of ESC/Java2 on all files in the study samples. Though testing can provide some level of assurance, coverage is inevitably partial and depends highly on the scope of the test suites.

Hence, we also made use of the ESC/Java2 static analysis tool. In contrast to runtime checking, static analysis tools can verify the correctness of annotations for "all cases" (within the limits of the completeness of the tool); but this greater completeness comes at a price: in many cases, general method *specifications* (beyond mere nullity annotations) needed to be written in order to eliminate false warnings.

Using these techniques we were able to identify about two dozen (0.9%) incorrectly annotated declarations—excluding errors we corrected in files outside of the sample set. With these errors fixed, tests passing and ESC/Java2 not reporting any nullity warnings, we are very confident in the accuracy of the final annotations.

2.5 Metrics

Java reference types can be used in the declaration of local variables, fields, methods (return types) and parameters. In our study we considered all of these types of declaration except for local variables since they are outside of the scope of the study hypothesis. Unless specified otherwise, we shall use the term *declaration* in the remainder of this article to be a declaration other than that of a local variable.

We have two principal metrics in this study, both of which are measured on a per file basis:

- d is a measure of the number of declarations that are of a reference type and
- m is a measure of the number of declarations specified to be non-null (hence $m \leq d$).

The main statistic of interest, x, will be a measure of the proportion of reference type declarations that are non-null, i.e. m / d.

2.6 Statistics Tool

In order to gather statistics concerning non-null declarations we created a simple Eclipse JDT abstract syntax tree (AST) visitor which walks the Java AST of the study subjects and gathers the required statistics for relevant declarations. At an earlier point in the study, we made use of an enhanced version of the JML checker which both counted and inferred nullity annotations using static analysis driven by elementary heuristics. We decided instead to annotate all declarations explicitly and use a simple visitor to gather statistics. This helped us eliminate one threat to internal validity that arose due to completeness and soundness issues of the JML-checker based statistics-gathering tool.

2.7 Threats to Validity

2.7.1 Internal Validity
We see two threats to internal validity. Firstly, in adding non-null constraints to the sample files we may have been excessive. As was discussed earlier, we chose to be conservative in our annotation exercise. Furthermore, as was mentioned in Section 2.4, we ran the given project test suites with runtime checking enabled and we subjected the files to static analysis using ESC/Java2. Since ESC/Java2 is neither sound nor complete, this does not offer a guarantee of correctness, but it does increase our confidence in the accuracy of the annotations.

Finally, we note that the code samples (both before the exercise and after) are available for peer review: the JML checker is accessible from SourceForge (jmlspecs.sourceforge.net); ESC/Java2 and Koa are available from Joseph Kiniry's GForge site (sort.ucd.ie), Eclipse from Eclipse.org, and SoenEA (as well as the Eclipse JML JDT) are available from the authors.

2.7.2 External Validity
Can we draw general conclusions from our study results? The main question is: can our sample of source files be taken as representative of typical Java applications? There are two aspects that can be considered here: the design style used in the samples, and the application domains.

Modern object-oriented programming best-practices promote e.g., a disciplined (i.e. moderate) use of null with the Null Object pattern recommended as an alternative [27]. Of course, not all Java code is written following recommended best practices; hence our sample applications should include such "non-OO-style" code. This is the case for some of the ESC/Java2 core classes which were designed quite early in the project history and were apparently influenced by the design of its predecessor (written in Modula-3 [12]). For example, some of the classes declare their fields as public (a practice that is discouraged [3, Item 12]) rather than using getters and setters, making it very difficult to ascertain, in the absence of supporting documentation, whether a field was intended to be non-null. Also, the class hierarchy is very flat, with some classes resembling a module in the traditional sense (i.e. a collection of static methods) more than a class.

With a five-sample set, it is impossible to claim that we have coverage in application domains, but we note that the SoenEA and Koa samples represent one of the most popular uses of Java—web-based enterprise applications [28].

3 Study Results

A summary of the statistics of our study samples is given in Table 2. As is usually done, the number of files in each sample is denoted by n, and the population size by N. Note that for SoenEA, 11 of the files did not contain any declarations of reference types, hence the population size is $41 = 52 - 11$; the reason that we exclude such files from our sample is because it is not possible to compute the proportion of non-null references for files without any declarations of reference types. We see that the total number of declarations that are of a reference type (d) across all samples is 2839. The total number of such declarations constrained to be non-null (m) is 2319. The proportion of non-null references across all files is 82%.

We also computed the mean, $\bar{x}$, of the proportion of non-null declarations on a per file basis ($x_i = d_i / m_i$). The mean ranges from 79% for the Eclipse JDT Core, to 89%

Table 2. Distribution of the number of declarations of reference types

	JML Checker	ESC/ Java2	SoenEA	Koa TS	Eclipse JDT Core	Sum or Average
n	35	35	41	29	35	175
N	217	216	41	29	1130	1633
$\sum d_i$	420	989	231	566	633	2839
$\sum m_i$	362	872	196	424	465	2319
$\sum m_i / \sum d_i$	86%	88%	85%	75%	73%	82%
mean ($\bar{x}$)	89%	85%	84%	80%	79%	83%
std.dev.(s)	0.14	0.22	0.28	0.26	0.24	-
E ($\alpha=5\%$)	4.4%	6.8%	-	-	7.7%	-
$\mu_{min} = \bar{x} - E$	85%	78%	84%	80%	71%	80%

for the JML checker. Also given are the standard deviation (s) and a measure of the maximum error (E) of our sample mean as an estimate for the population mean with a confidence level of $1 - \alpha = 95\%$. The overall average and weighted average (based on N) for μ_{min} are 80% and 74%, respectively. Hence we can conclude with 95% certainty that the population means are above $\mu_{min} = 74\%$ in all cases. As was explained earlier, we were conservative in our annotation exercise, hence is it quite possible that the actual overall population mean is greater than this.

All declarations were non-null (i.e. $x = 100\%$) for 46% of the files included in our sampling: 10% of JML, 9% of ESC/Java2, 13% of SoenEA, 7% of Koa and 7% of Eclipse JDT files. The distribution of the remaining 54% of files sampled is shown in Figure 3; each bar represents the proportion of sampled files having a value of x in the given range—following standard notation, $[a,b)$ represents the interval of values v in the range $a \leq v < b$. We see that the JML checker has no files with an x in the range [0-10%). On the other hand, the JDT has the largest proportion of files in the range [80-90%).

The mean of x by kind of declaration (fields, methods and parameters) for each of the study samples is given in Figure 4. The mean is highest for parameters in all cases except for the Eclipse JDT, and it is second highest for methods in all cases except for Koa. The Eclipse JDT has the highest proportion of non-null fields; we believe that this is because Eclipse developers make extensive use of named string constants declared as static final fields.

Hence the study results clearly support the hypothesis that in Java code, over 2/3 of declarations that are of reference types are meant to be non-null—in fact, it is closer to 3/4. It is for this reason that we recently adapted the Eclipse JDT Core to support nullity modifiers and to adopt non-null as the default. We describe our enhancements to the Eclipse JDT Core in Section 5.1. In the next section we explore related work.

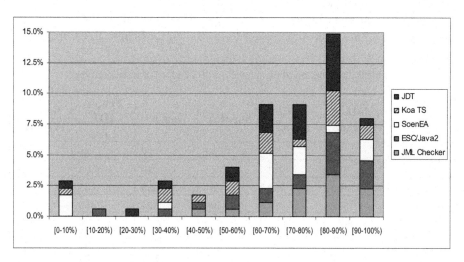

Fig. 3. Distribution of the percentage of sampled files having a value for x (the proportion of non-null declarations) in the range [0-100%). The remaining 46% of files had x = 100%.

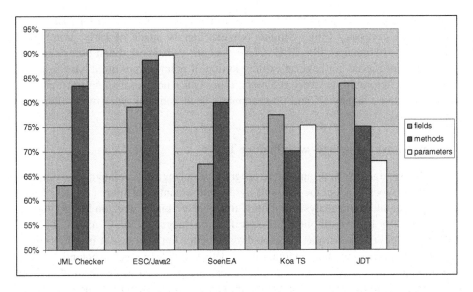

Fig. 4. Mean of x, the proportion of non-null declarations, by kind

4 Related Work: Languages and Nullity

In this section we present a summary of the languages, language extensions and tools that offer support for non-null types or annotations. This will allow us to better assess current language design trends in the treatment of nullity, and hence better establish the context for the proposal presented in Section 5.

4.1 Languages Without Pointer Types

Early promotional material for Java touted it to be an improvement over C and C++, in particular because "Java has no pointers" [26, Chapter 2], hence ridding it of "one of the most bug-prone aspects of C and C++ programming" [26, p.6]. Of course, reference types are implemented by means of pointers, though Java *disciplines* their use—e.g. the pointer arithmetic of C and C++ is prohibited in Java.

Other languages have pushed this discipline even further by eliminating null. Obvious examples are functional languages, including ML which also supports imperative features such as references and assignment. Another noteworthy example from the ML family is the Objective Caml object-oriented language. Though ML and Objective Caml support references, every reference is guaranteed to point to an instance of its base type, because the only way that a reference can be created is by taking the reference of a *value* of the base type [44]. Hence, references are (vacuously) non-null by default in these languages. Of course, a generic "pointer type" can be defined in ML or Objective Caml as a user-defined tagged union type

```
type 'a pointer = Null | Pointer of 'a ref;
```

Programmers need not go out of their way to define and use such a type since it is very seldom necessary [36]. Similar remarks can be made of early prototypical object-oriented languages like CLU. CLU (vacuously) supported non-null references by default since it did not have an explicit notion of pointers, nor did it have a special "null" value belonging to every reference type. Our study results confirm that Java developers, like Objective Caml programmers, need non-null types more often than nullable types.

4.2 Imperative Languages with Pointer Types

To our knowledge, the first imperative programming language, or language extension, with pointer types to adopt the non-null-by-default semantics is Splint [19, 21]. Splint is a "lightweight" static analysis tool for C that evolved out of work on LCLINT (a type checker of the behavioral interface specification language for C named Larch/C [18, 32]). Splint is sometimes promoted as "a better lint" because it is able to make use of programmer supplied annotations to detect a wider range of potential errors, and this more accurately, than lint. Annotations are provided in the form of stylized comments. In Splint, declarations having pointer types are assumed to be non-null by default, unless adorned with /*@null*/. Splint does nullity checking at "interface boundaries" [21, §2]: annotations can be applied to function parameters and return values, global variables, and structure fields but not to local variables [22, p.44].

While there are no other extensions to C supporting the non-null-by-default semantics, extensions for non-null annotations or types have been proposed. For example, Cyclone [38], described as a "safe dialect of C", supports the concept of never-NULL pointers, written as "$T@$" in contrast to the usual syntax "$T*$" for nullable pointers to T [31]. As another example, we note that the GNU gcc supports a form of non-null annotation for function parameters only; e.g. an annotation of the form

```
__attribute__((nonnull (1, 3)))
```

after a function signature would indicate that the first and third arguments of the function are expected to be non-null [48, §5.24].

4.3 Object-Oriented Languages (Non-Java)

4.3.1 Eiffel
The recent ECMA Standard of the Eiffel programming language introduces the notions of *attached* and *detachable* types [13]. These correspond to non-null (or non-void types, as they would be called in Eiffel) and nullable types, respectively. By default, types are attached—which, to our knowledge, makes Eiffel the first non research-prototype object-oriented language to adopt this default. Eiffel supports covariance in method return types and invariance of parameter types except with respect to parameter nullity, for which it supports contravariance [13, §8.10.26, §8.14.5]—see Table 3.

Prior to the release of the ECMA standard, types were detachable by default. Hence a migration effort for the existing Eiffel code base has been necessary. Special consideration has been given to minimizing the migration effort in the form of compiler and tool support.

Table 3. Summary of support for non-null

Language / Tool	Type (T) / Annotation (A)	Default: non-null (NN) or nullable (nu)	Member declaration modifier (prefix) for		Non-null Annotation (A) and Checking at run-time (R), or statically at compile-time (S). Abbr.: all (✓ = ARS); none (✗)					Overriding method type variance w.r.t. ...		Anno. API of std libraries?	Class modifier?	Compiler option to invert default
			non-null	nullable	method	param	field	local var	array elt	result nullity	param-eter nullity			
Splint	A	NN	/*@notnull*/	/*@null*/	AS	AS	AS	S	✗	N/A	N/A	✗	N/A	✗
Cyclone	T	nu	@, e.g. T@	(std., e.g. T*)	✓	✓	(✓)	✓	✗	N/A	N/A	✗	N/A	✗
Eiffel	T	NN	!	?	✓	✓	✓	✓	✓	covariance	contravar.	✓	✗	✓
Spec#	T	nu	! (suffix)	? (suffix)	✓	✓	✓	✓	AS	invariance	invariance	(✓)	✗	✗
Nice	T	NN	!	?	AS	AS	AS	AS	✓	covariance	contravar.	✗	✗	✗
Java support														
JML	A	NN	/*@non_null*/	/*@nullable*/	✓	✓	✓	AS	AS	covariance	**invariance**	✓	✓	✓
IntelliJ IDEA (≥ 5.1)	A	nu	@NotNull	@Nullable	AS	AS	AS	AS	✗	covariance	contravar.	✗	✗	✗
Nully (IDEA plug-in)	A	nu	@NonNull	@Nullable	✓	(✓)	✗	(✓)	✗	no restriction	no restriction	✗	✗	✗
FindBugs (≥ 0.8.8)	A	nu	@NonNull	@Check-ForNull	AS	AS	✗	S	✗	no restriction	no restriction	✗	✗	✗
JastAdd + NonNull Extension	A	nu	[NotNull]	[MayBeNull]	AS	AS	AS	AS	✗	invariance	invariance	✗	✗	✗
Eclipse JML JDT (3.3)	T	NN	/*@non_null*/	/*@nullable*/	✓	✓	✓	✓	✓	covariance	**invariance**	✓	✓	✓

4.3.2 Spec#

Spec# is an extension of the C# programming language that adds support for contracts, checked exceptions and non-null types. The Spec# compiler statically enforces non-null types and generates run-time assertion checking code for contracts [2]. The Boogie program verifier can be used to perform extended static checking of Spec# code [11]. While Spec# code cannot generally be processed by C# compilers, compatibility can be maintained by placing Spec# annotations inside stylized comments (/*^ ... ^*/) as is done with other annotation languages like Splint and JML (which use /*@ ... */).

Introduction of non-null types (vs. annotations) requires care, particularly with respect to field initialization in constructors and helper methods [23]. Open issues also remain with respect to arrays and non-null static fields, for which the Spec# compiler resorts to run-time checking to ensure type safety [1, §1.0]. For reasons of backwards compatibility, a reference type name T refers to possibly null references of type T. The notation $T!$ (or /*^ ! ^*/, with a special shorthand of /*!*/) is used to represent non-null references of type T.

As of the February 2006 release of the Spec# compiler, it is possible to use a compiler option to enable a non-null-by-default semantics. When this is done, T? can be used to denote possibly null references to T. Note, however, that Spec# has no class level modifiers which would allow the default nullity to be set for a single class. We note in passing that of all the languages discussed in this section, Spec# is the only one with annotation suffixes (i.e. that appear *after* the type name rather than before). Nullity return type and parameter type variance for overriding methods in Spec# conforms to the type invariance rules of C#—i.e., types must be the same.

4.3.3 Nice

Nice is a programming language whose syntax is superficially similar to that of Java. It can be thought of as an enriched variant of Java supporting parametric types, multimethods, and contracts, among other features [4, 5]. Nullable types are called *option types* in Nice terminology. It is claimed that Nice programs are free of null pointer exceptions. By default, a reference type name T denotes non-null instances of T. To express the possibility that a declaration of type T might be null, one prefixes the type name with a question mark, $?T$ [6].

4.4   Java Support for Non-null

4.4.1   FindBugs

The FindBugs tool does static analysis of Java class files and reports *common* programming errors; hence, by design, the tool forgoes soundness and completeness for utility; an approach that is not uncommon for static analyzers [34]. In order to increase the accuracy of error reporting related to nullity and to better be able to assign blame, support for nullity annotations for return types and parameters was recently added—annotations can be applied to local variables, but they are effectively ignored. The annotations are: @NonNull, used to indicate that the declared entity cannot be null, and @CheckForNull, indicating that a null value should be expected and hence, any attempted dereference should be preceded with a check [35].

Although FindBugs has been applied to production code (e.g. Eclipse 3.0 source), nullity annotations have not yet been used on such samples. Our study results suggest that when this happens, specifiers are likely to find themselves decorating most reference type declarations with @NonNull.

4.4.2   Nully and the IntelliJ IDEA

Nully is an IntelliJ IDEA plug-in that can be used to detect potential null dereferences at edit-time, compile-time and run-time. It can be applied to method return types and parameters as well as local variables but not fields. Nully documentation claims that it supports run-time checking of non-null constraints on local variables but this could not be confirmed. Non-null checking of parameters is only provided in the form of run-time checks [39].

There has yet to be an official release of Nully and it is not clear whether the tool is still being developed, particularly since the latest release of the IntelliJ IDEA marks the introduction of its own (proprietary) annotations @NotNull and @Nullable [37]. IDEA supports edit-time and compile-time checks, but not run-time checks of non-null. IDEA supports nullity return type covariance and parameter type contravariance. We note that this is incompatible with Java which requires invariance for parameter types.

4.4.3 JastAdd

JastAdd is an open source "aspect-oriented compiler construction system" whose architecture promises to support compiler feature development in a more modular fashion than is usually possible [14, 33]. As a demonstration of this flexibility, support for non-null types has been defined as an "add-on" to the JastAdd based Java 1.4 compiler [15]. The implemented type system is essentially that of Fähndrich and Leino [24]. In fact, they make use of the same annotations, which makes the extension incompatible with standard Java (of course, it should be rather easy to rename the annotations to be conformant to Java 5 annotation syntax). Like Spec#, nullity modifiers of overriding methods must match exactly, both for return and parameter types. To provide support for its non-null type system, JustAdd was extended with the ability to infer type nullity and rawness for APIs and other legacy code. After analyzing 100 KLOC from the Java 1.4 API, 24% of reference return types were inferred to be non-null and 70% of dereferences were found to be safe [15].

4.4.4 Java Modeling Language

The Java Modeling Language (JML) originated from Iowa State University (ISU) under the leadership of Gary Leavens. JML is currently the subject of study and use by a dozen international research teams [40]. It is a behavioral interface specification language that, in particular, brings support for Design by Contract (DBC) to Java [41]. Using JML, developers can write complete interface specifications for Java types. JML annotated Java code can be compiled with standard Java compilers because annotations are contained in stylized comments whose first character is @. JML enjoys a broad range of tool support including [7, 40]:

- Jmldoc that generates documentation in a manner that is similar to Javadoc, but incorporating JML specifications.
- jmlc, the ISU JML run-time assertion checker compiler.
- ESC/Java2, an extended static checker that provides a compiler-like interface to fully automated checking of JML specifications. Like similar tools, ESC/Java2 compromises soundness and completeness for efficacy and utility.
- LOOP tool that can be used in conjunction with PVS to perform complete verification of JML annotated Java applications.
- JmlUnit, a tool for generating JUnit test suites using JML specifications as test oracles.
- JMLKEY tool that offers support for model-driven design, principally from UML class diagrams, with JML as a design (constraint) specification language. The tool supports the complete JavaCard language.

JML has nullity modifiers (non_null and nullable) and it recently adopted a non-null-by-default semantics for reference type declarations [9].

4.5 Summary

A summary of the languages, extensions and tools covered in this section, is given in Table 3. Two key observations are that for all languages and tools *not* using Java 5 annotations there seems to be a trend in adopting

- non-null type system over non-null annotations, with
- non-null as the default.

Even well established languages like Eiffel are making the bold move of switching to the new default [42]. The apparent trend in the evolution of languages supporting pointers would seem to indicate that the time is ripe to consider a switch in Java from nullable-by-default to non-null-by-default. A concrete proposal for this is given in the next section.

5 Non-null by Default in Java

The study results suggest that an adoption of non-null-by-default in Java would have the advantage of

- Better matching general practice: the majority of declarations will be *correctly* constrained to be non-null, and hence,
- Lightening the annotation burden of developers; i.e. there are fewer declarations to explicitly annotate as nullable.

In addition, and possibly more importantly, the new default would be *safer*:

- Processing of null generally requires extra programming logic and code to be handled correctly. With the new default, an annotation now explicitly *alerts* developers that null values need to be considered.
- If a developer delays or forgets to annotate a declaration as nullable, this will at worst limit functionality rather than introducing unwanted behavior (e.g., null pointer exceptions)—also, limited functionality is generally easier to detect than potential null pointer exceptions.

5.1 An Implementation of Non-null by Default: Eclipse JML JDT

Guided by our experiences in the implementation of non-null types and non-null by default in JML tools [8], we have recently completed a similar implementation as an extension to the Eclipse JDT Core—which we will call the Eclipse JML JDT Core (or JML JDT for short). Since 3.2, the Eclipse JDT Core has supported intra-procedural flow analysis for potential null problems. The JML JDT builds upon and extends this base.

One of the first and most obvious questions which we faced was: which annotation syntax should the tool support? Until the JSR 305 [45] efforts are finalized, adhering to JML-like annotations seemed advantageous since it would allow the JML JDT to

- support nullity annotations for all versions of Java, not just Java 5 (many projects, including Eclipse, are still at Java 1.4).

- support casts to non-null (these are necessary to counter false positives). Java 5 annotations cannot be used for this purpose, though JSR 308 [17] is likely to address this limitation as of Java 7.
- naturally recognize and process the extensive collection of JML API specifications which have been developed over the years by the JML community.

Using JML syntax also means that the source files will be more easily amenable to processing by the complementary suite of JML tools (cf. Section 4.4.4). Once the standard Java 5 annotations are defined, it will be rather easy to adapt the tool to process these annotations as well.

A summary of the JML JDT Core capabilities is given at the bottom of Table 3 on page 239. In particular we note that it supports edit-time, compile-time and runtime checking of nullity annotations—see Figure 5.

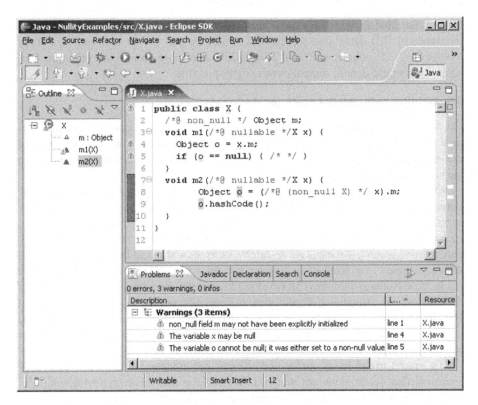

Fig. 5. Screenshot of the Eclipse JML JDT

5.2 Backwards Compatibility, and Migration to the New Default

The JML JDT supports tool-wide and project specific settings for the choice of nullity default. A finer grain of control is provided in the form of type (i.e., class or interface) scoped declaration modifiers named nullable_by_default, and `non_null_by_default`. Applying the first of these modifiers to a type enables developers to recover the nullable-by-default semantics; i.e., all reference type declarations in the class or interface that are not explicitly declared non-null are interpreted as nullable. Note that the scope of the `*_by_default` modifiers is strictly the type to which it is applied; hence, it is not inherited by subtypes.

In addition to these class- and interface-scoped modifiers, a script is available that enables developers to add the `nullable_by_default` modifier to all classes and interfaces in a given project. This allows the global project default to be non-null while, gradually, and as needed, files can be reviewed and updated one-by-one to conform to the new default by

- adding `nullable` modifiers,
- optionally removing explicit `non_null` modifiers (if there are any), and finally,
- removing the `nullable_by_default` modifier.

(This is the process which we have been following in our gradual migration of the thousands of JML-annotated source files which are part of our tool and case study repositories.) Of course, such a porting effort also drives home the importance of adopting the right default semantics as early as possible.

5.3 Helping Automated Annotation Assistants Too

The best time to add nullity annotations is when code is being created since at that time the original author is available to record his or her design intents. Adoption of non-null by default means that developers will have fewer declarations to annotate in the new code that they write.

What can be done about existing unannotated code? There exist a few fully automatic static analysis tools, called annotation assistants, which can help in adding nullity annotations (among other specification constructs) to source files. Does the existence of such tools eliminate the need to change nullity defaults? We believe not. For the most part, these annotation assistants are research prototypes and would be unable to cope with large code bases. In a recent study, Engelen lists three non-null annotation assistants [16]: the JastAdd Nullness Inferrer [15], Houdini [25] and the more recent CANAPA [10]. Of these tools, only Houdini has published performance results. Houdini makes use of ESC/Java2 to test its annotation guesses, and it is capable of processing less than 500 lines per hour (though admittedly it infers more than non-null annotations). On the other hand, the accuracy of its non-null annotations is reported at 79% [25].

Our study results have shown that we can get comparable accuracy simply by assuming that declarations are non-null. We believe that the switch to non-null by default can actually be an aid to annotation assistants. Tools can assume that declarations are non-null (and hence get a majority of annotations correct) and only opt for nullable if there is clear evidence that the declaration can be assigned null.

6 Conclusion

In this paper, we report on a novel study of five open projects (totaling over 722 KLOC) taken from various application domains. The study results have shown that on average, one can expect approximately 75% of reference type declarations to be non-null by design in Java. We believe that this report is timely, as we are witnessing the increasing emergence of static analysis (SA) tools using non-null annotations to detect potential null pointer exceptions. Before too much code is written under the current nullable-by-default semantics, it would be preferable that Java be adapted, or at least a *standard* non-null annotation-based extension be defined, in which declarations are interpreted as non-null by default. This would be the first step in the direction of an apparent trend in the modern design of languages (with pointer types), which is to support non-null types and non-null by default.

One might question whether a language as widely deployed as Java can switch nullity defaults. If the successful transition of Eiffel is any indication, it would seem that the switch can be achieved if suitable facilities are provided to ease the transition. We believe that our Eclipse JML JDT offers such facilities in the form of support for project-specific as well as fine-grained control over nullity defaults (via type-scope annotations). Until standard Java 5 nullity annotations are adopted via JSR 305, we have designed the JML JDT to recognize JML style nullity modifiers, hence allowing the tool to reuse the comprehensive set of JML API specifications (among other advantages). Adding nullity annotations is time consuming. By adopting JML-style nullity modifiers we also offer developers potentially increased payback, in that all other JML tools will be able to process the annotations as well—including the SA tool ESC/Java2 and JmlUnit, which generates JUnit test suites using JML specifications and annotations as test oracles.

As a natural continuation of our work, we have begun enhancements to the Eclipse JML JDT to allow runtime and compile-time (SA) support for Design by Contract via a core of JML's syntax.

Acknowledgments

We are grateful to Joseph Kiniry for providing access to, and assistance on, the Koa source, and for discussions about Eiffel. We thank Frederic Rioux for his contribution to the initial study efforts. Research support was provided by NSERC of Canada (261573-03) and the Quebec FQRNT (100221).

References

[1] Barnett, M., DeLine, R., Jacobs, B., Faehndrich, M., Leino, K.R.M., Schulte, W., Venter, H.: The Spec# Programming System: Challenges and Directions. In: International Conference on Verified Software: Theories, Tools, Experiments, Zürich, Switzerland (2005)

[2] Barnett, M., Leino, K.R.M., Schulte, W.: The Spec# Programming System: An Overview. In: Barthe, G., Burdy, L., Huisman, M., Lanet, J.-L., Muntean, T. (eds.) CASSIS 2004. LNCS, vol. 3362, Springer, Heidelberg (2004)

[3] Bloch, J.: Effective Java Programming Language Guide. Addison-Wesley, Reading (2001)

[4] Bonniot, D.: Using kinds to type partially-polymorphic methods. Electronic Notes in Theoretical Computer Science 75, 1–20 (2003)

[5] Bonniot, D.: The Nice programming language (2005), http://nice.sourceforge.net/

[6] Bonniot, D.: Type safety in Nice: Why programs written in Nice have less bugs (2005)

[7] Burdy, L., Cheon, Y., Cok, D.R., Ernst, M.D., Kiniry, J.R., Leavens, G.T., Leino, K.R.M., Poll, E.: An Overview of JML Tools and Applications. International Journal on Software Tools for Technology Transfer (STTT) 7(3), 212–232 (2005)

[8] Chalin, P.: Towards Support for Non-null Types and Non-null-by-default in Java. In: Proceedings of the 8th Workshop on Formal Techniques for Java-like Programs (FTfJP'06), Nantes, France (July 2006)

[9] Chalin, P., Rioux, F.: Non-null References by Default in the Java Modeling Language. In: Proceedings of the Workshop on the Specification and Verification of Component-Based Systems (SAVCBS), Lisbon, Portugal, September 2005, ACM Press, New York (2005)

[10] Cielecki, M., Fulara, J., Jakubczyk, K., Jancewicz, L.: Propagation of JML non-null annotations in Java programs. In: Proceedings of the International Conference on Principles and Practices of Programming. In Java (PPPJ'06), Mannheim, Germany (2006)

[11] DeLine, R., Leino, K.R.M., Boogie, P.L.: A Typed Procedural Language for Checking Object-Oriented Programs, Microsoft Research, Technical Report (2005)

[12] Detlefs, D.L., Leino, K.R.M., Nelson, G., Saxe, J.B.: Extended Static Checking, Compaq Systems Research Center, Research Report 159 (December 1998)

[13] ECMA International, Eiffel Analysis, Design and Programming Language, ECMA-367 (June 2005)

[14] Ekman, T.: Extensible Compiler Construction. Ph.D. thesis. CS Dept. Lund University (2006)

[15] Ekman, T., Hedin, G.: Pluggable non-null types for Java, Dept. of CS, Lund University, Technical Report (unpublished, 2006)

[16] Engelen, A.F.M.: Nullness Analysis of Java Source Code. Master's thesis. Nijmegen Institute for Computing and Information Sciences, Radboud University Nijmegen, Netherlands (2006)

[17] Ernst, M., Coward, D.: Annotations on Java Types, JCP.org, JSR 308 (2006)

[18] Evans, D.: Using Specifications to Check Source Code, MIT, MIT/LCS/TR 628 (June 1994)

[19] Evans, D.: Static Detection of Dynamic Memory Errors. In: Proceedings of the ACM SIGPLAN Conference on Programming Language Design and Implementation, Philadelphia, Pennsylvania, United States, ACM Press, New York (1996)

[20] Evans, D.: Annotation-Assisted Lightweight Static Checking. In: First International Workshop on Automated Program Analysis, Testing and Verification (February 2000)

[21] Evans, D.: Splint User Manual, Secure Programming Group, University of Virginia (June 5, 2003)

[22] Evans, D., Larochelle, D.: Improving security using extensible lightweight static analysis. IEEE Software 19(1), 42–51 (2002)

[23] Fähndrich, M., Leino, K.R.M.: Non-Null Types in an Object-Oriented Language. In: Proceedings of the Workshop on Formal Techniques for Java-like Languages, Malaga, Spain (2002)

[24] Fähndrich, M., Leino, K.R.M.: Declaring and Checking Non-null Types in an Object-Oriented Language. In: Proceedings of the 18th annual ACM SIGPLAN Conference on Object-Oriented Programming, Systems, Languages, and Applications. OOPSLA'03, pp. 302–312. ACM Press, New York (2003)

[25] Flanagan, C., Leino, K.R.M.: Houdini, an Annotation Assistant for ESC/Java. In: Oliveira, J.N., Zave, P. (eds.) FME 2001. LNCS, vol. 2021, pp. 500–517. Springer, Heidelberg (2001)

[26] Flanagan, D.: Java in a Nutshell: A Desktop Quick Reference. O'Reilly (1996)

[27] Fowler, M.: Refactoring: Improving the Design of Existing Code. Addison-Wesley, Reading (1999)
[28] Fowler, M.: Patterns of Enterprise Application Architecture. Addison-Wesley, Reading (2003)
[29] Freund, J.E., Walphole, R.E.: Mathematical Statistics. Prentice-Hall, Englewood Cliffs (1980)
[30] Gosling, J., Joy, B., Steele, G., Bracha, G.: The Java Language Specification, 3rd edn. Addison-Wesley, Reading (2005)
[31] Grossman, D., Hicks, M., Jim, T., Morrisett, G.: Cyclone: a Type-safe Dialect of C. C/C++ Users Journal 23(1) (2005)
[32] Guttag, J.V., Horning, J.J.: Larch: Languages and Tools for Formal Specification. Springer, Heidelberg (1993)
[33] Hedin, G., Magnusson, E.: JastAdd–an aspect-oriented compiler construction system. Science of Computer Programming 47(1), 37–58 (2003)
[34] Hovemeyer, D., Pugh, W.: Finding Bugs is Easy. ACM SIGPLAN Notices 39(12), 92–106 (2004)
[35] Hovemeyer, D., Spacco, J., Pugh, W.: Evaluating and Tuning a Static Analysis to Find Null Pointer Bugs. SIGSOFT Software Engineering Notes 31(1), 13–19 (2006)
[36] INRIA, "Pointers in Caml", in Caml Documentation, Specific Guides (2006), http://caml.inria.fr/resources/doc/
[37] JetBrains, "Nullable How-To", in IntelliJ IDEA 5.x Developer Documentation: JetBrains (2006)
[38] Jim, T., Morrisett, G., Grossman, D., Hicks, M., Cheney, J., Wang, Y.: Cyclone: A safe dialect of C. In: Proceedings of the USENIX Annual Technical Conference, Monterey, CA, June 2002, pp. 275–288 (2002)
[39] Lea, K.: Nully (2005), https://nully.dev.java.net/
[40] Leavens, G.T.: The Java Modeling Language (JML) (2006), http://www.jmlspecs.org
[41] Leavens, G.T., Cheon, Y.: Design by Contract with JML, Draft paper (2005)
[42] Meyer, B.: Attached Types and Their Application to Three Open Problems of Object-Oriented Programming. In: Black, A.P. (ed.) ECOOP 2005. LNCS, vol. 3586, pp. 1–32. Springer, Heidelberg (2005)
[43] Park, R.: Software Size Measurement: A Framework for Counting Source Statements, CMU, Software Engineering Institute, Pittsburgh CMU/SEI-92-TR-20 (1992)
[44] Paulson, L.C.: ML for the Working Programmer. Cambridge University Press, Cambridge (1991)
[45] Pugh, W.: Annotations for Software Defect Detection, JCP.org, JSR 305 (2006)
[46] Pugh, W.: How do you fix an obvious bug (2006), http://findbugs.blogspot.com/
[47] Rioux, F., Chalin, P.: Improving the Quality of Web-based Enterprise Applications with Extended Static Checking: A Case Study. Electronic Notes in Theoretical Computer Science 157(2), 119–132 (2006)
[48] Stallman, R.: Using the GNU Compiler Collection (GCC): GCC Version 4.1.0, Free Software Foundation (2005)

Efficiently Generating Structurally Complex Inputs with Thousands of Objects

Bassem Elkarablieh, Yehia Zayour, and Sarfraz Khurshid

The University of Texas at Austin
{elkarabl,zayour,khurshid}@ece.utexas.edu

Abstract. We present Shekoosh, a novel framework for constraint-based generation of structurally complex inputs of large sizes. Given a Java predicate that represents the desired structural integrity constraints, Shekoosh systematically explores the input space of the predicate and generates inputs that satisfy the given constraints. While the problem of generating an input that satisfies all the given constraints is hard, generating a structure at random, which may not satisfy the constraints but has a desired number of objects is straightforward. Indeed, a structure generated at random is highly unlikely to satisfy any of the desired constraints. However, it can be *repaired* to transform it so that it satisfies all the desired constraints.

Experiments show that Shekoosh can efficiently generate structures that are up to 100 times larger than those possible with previous algorithms, including those that are based on a dedicated search and also those that use off-the-shelf enumerating SAT solvers.

Keywords: Constraint-based Generation, Software Testing, Data Structure Repair, Integer Constraint Solving.

1 Introduction

Software systems are steadily growing in complexity and size. At the same time, reliability is becoming a more and more vital concern. Software failures already cost the US economy tens of billions of dollars annually [1]. To meet the ever-increasing demand for reliability, a great deal of progress is required in improving the current state-of-the-art to deliver higher quality software at a lower cost.

Software testing, the most commonly used technique for validating the quality of software, is a labor intensive process, and typically accounts for about half the total cost of software development and maintenance [2]. Automating testing would not only reduce the cost of producing software but also increase the reliability of modern software.

While testing is a conceptually simple process—just create a test suite, i.e., a set of test inputs, run them against the program, and check if each output is correct—the current approaches to testing remain expensive and ineffective. The key issue with the current practice of testing is the need to manually generate test suites.

For programs that take as inputs structurally complex data, which pervade modern software, test generation is particularly hard. Desired inputs must satisfy complex structural integrity constraints that characterize valid structures. Examples of structures

E. Ernst (Ed.): ECOOP 2007, LNAI 4609, pp. 248–272, 2007.

include text-book data structures, such as red-black trees that characterize balanced binary search trees [3], which are widely used as library classes, as well as various other structures, such as fault-trees that characterize failures of mission-critical systems [4] and intentional names that characterize properties of services in a dynamic networked environment [5], which are implemented in stand-alone applications.

There are two fundamental approaches for generating structurally complex tests: one, representation-level generation by explicitly allocating objects and setting values of their fields such that the underlying constraints are satisfied; two, abstract-level generation by a sequence of method invocations using the API. The two approaches are complementary and have their advantages and disadvantages. For example, while concrete-level generation requires the user to a priori provide constraints, abstract-level generation requires the user to first correctly implement the methods used in a sequence.

Recent years have seen a significant progress in automating both these approaches. Constraint-based techniques are able to provide efficient test enumeration at the representation level using off-the-shelf SAT solvers [6] as well as using novel search algorithms [7, 8, 9]. Efficient state matching algorithms are able to provide test enumeration at the abstract level by pruning redundant method sequences [11, 12, 10].

Much of the prior work, however, has focused on systematic generation of small structures. The motivation—inspired by traditional model checking—for that is to enable bounded exhaustive testing, where a program is tested on all (in-equivalent) inputs within a small input size. While bounded exhaustive testing does increase a developer's confidence in their software, it is not prudent to altogether ignore testing the program on larger inputs. The existing test generation techniques do not provide an efficient way to generate large structures. Note that the ability to generate large structures even enables a systematic approach to test the performance of the software.

This paper presents a novel algorithm for constraint-based generation of large inputs that represent structurally complex data. We view structures as object graphs whose nodes represent objects and edges represent fields. A key observation behind our algorithm is that while generating an object-graph that satisfies desired structural constraints is hard, generation of a connected graph at random with a desired number of nodes is straightforward. Of course, a graph generated at random is highly unlikely to satisfy any of the desired constraints and would therefore represent an invalid structure. However, we can systematically *repair* such a graph such that it satisfies all the constraints.

Our algorithm deploys an efficient repair routine that we have developed in our previous work on error recovery [13]. Given a structure that violates desired integrity constraints, the repair routine performs *repair actions*, which mutate the structure to transform it into a valid structure. The repair routine performs a systematic state-space exploration of a neighborhood of the given structure and uses *symbolic execution* [14] as well as heuristics to perform efficient and effective repair.

We have evaluated our test generation algorithm on a variety of data structure subjects, including those from the Java Collection Framework. Experimental results using our prototype implementation, Shekoosh, show that our algorithm can generate structures that are 100 times larger than those possible with previous constraint-based generation techniques, such as Korat [7] that implements a dedicated search, or TestEra [6] that uses the Alloy Analyzer [15] and off-the-shelf SAT solvers, such as mChaff [16].

We make the following contributions:

- **Repair for generation.** We introduce the idea of using data structure repair to generate structurally complex tests.
- **Algorithm to generate large inputs.** We present an efficient algorithm for constraint-based generation of large inputs that represent structurally complex data.
- **Implementation.** We present the Shekoosh tool that implements our test generation algorithm.
- **Evaluation.** We evaluate our implementation using a variety of subjects and present experimental results that show two orders of magnitude improvement over the previous state-of-the-art.

2   Example

This section describes an example that illustrates our test generation algorithm. Consider the following class declaration that declares a binary search tree, i.e., an acyclic graph that satisfies the search constraints on the values of its nodes:

```
class BinarySearchTree {
    Node root;
    int size;

    static class Node {
        int elem;
        Node left;
        Node right;
    }
}
```

Each `BinarySearchTree` object has a `root` node and stores the number of nodes in the field `size`. Each `Node` object has an integer value, called `elem`, and has a `left` and a `right` child. The structural constraints of a binary search tree can be written as a predicate that returns true if and only if its input satisfies all the constraints. Following the literature, we term such predicates `repOk` methods and for object-oriented programs, we term structural invariants class invariants [17].

The class invariant of `BinarySearchTree` can be formulated as follows.

```
boolean repOk() {
    if (!isAcyclic()) return false;
    if (!sizeOk()) return false;
    if (!searchConstraintsOk()) return false;
    return true;
}
```

When invoked on a `BinarySearchTree` object o, the predicate `repOk` traverses the object graph rooted at o and checks all the constraints that define a binary search tree. If any constraint is violated the predicate returns false; otherwise, it returns `true`. The helper methods are implemented as standard work-list-based algorithms that keep track of visited nodes [18] (Appendix A gives an implementation of the helper methods).

To generate tests, our prototype Shekoosh takes as inputs the class declarations, the `repOk` predicate and a desired structure size. For this example, for size 100, Shekoosh takes 32 milliseconds (on average) to generate a valid binary search tree; for size 10000 (respectively 100000), Shekoosh generates a structure in less than one (respectively three) seconds (on average). In comparison, TestEra [6], which uses the Alloy Analyzer fails to generate a binary search tree with twenty nodes, due to the analyzer's inability to translate the structural invariant from Alloy to a propositional formula given twenty minutes. Korat [7], which implements a specialized search fails to generate a binary search tree with thirty nodes in twenty minutes. Section 5 presents a detailed comparison for a variety of subject structures.

3   Background: Forward Symbolic Execution

Forward symbolic execution is a technique for executing a program on symbolic values [14]. There are two fundamental aspects of symbolic execution: (1) defining semantics of operations that are originally defined for concrete values and (2) maintaining a path condition for the current program path being executed. A path condition specifies necessary constraints on input variables that must be satisfied to execute the corresponding path. As an example, consider the following program that returns the absolute value of its input:

```
int abs(int i) {
    L1. int result;
    L2. if (i < 0)
    L3. result = -1 * i;
    L4. else result = i;
    L5. return result;
}
```

To symbolically execute this program, we consider its behavior on a primitive integer input, say I. We make no assumptions about the value of I (except what can be deduced from the type declaration). So, when we encounter a conditional statement, we consider both possible outcomes of the condition. To perform operations on symbols, we treat them simply as variables, e.g., the statement on L3 updates the value of result to be $-1 * I$. Of course, a tool for symbolic execution needs to modify the type of result to note updates involving symbols and to provide support for manipulating expressions, such as $-1 * I$. Symbolic execution of the above program explores the following two paths:

```
path 1:
[I < 0] L1 -> L2 -> L3 -> L5
path 2:
[I >= 0] L1 -> L2 -> L4 -> L5
```

Note that for each path that is explored, there is a corresponding path condition (shown in square brackets). While execution on a concrete input would have followed exactly one of these two paths, symbolic execution explores both.

4   Algorithm

This section describes our test generation algorithm. Our prototype implementation, Shekoosh, has three main modules: *Egor*, a random graph generator, *Juzi++*, an optimized repair framework based on our previous work on error recovery [13], and *Dicos*, a solver for difference constraints [3].

We describe the algorithm for generating a structure that has a unique root; structures that have more than one root are handled similarly [7]. Figure 1 shows the generation framework, which takes three inputs: (1) `clazz` that represents the class of the structure's root, (2) predicate `repOk` that represents the structural integrity constraints, and (3) `size`, a set of pairs, which defines the number of objects for each class in the structure. To illustrate, consider the declaration of the class `BinarySearchTree` from Section 2. To generate tree objects with 100 nodes, we set `size` = {<BinarySearch Tree, 1>, <Node, 100>}.

Shekoosh performs the following steps:

- Allocate appropriate objects using the field declarations in `clazz` and generate a random graph using these objects; indeed, this graph may not satisfy any of the desired constraints yet;
- Repair the reference fields of the random graph such that all constraints on these fields are satisfied; Juzi++ returns the constraints on the primitive variables;
- Solve the data constraints; Dicos returns a complete solution;
- Assign each data field its value; the resulting graph represents a concrete object-graph that satisfies all the desired invariants.

The rest of this section describes the details of the algorithm and its main modules.

4.1   Egor: Random Graph Generator

Egor takes an object representing the class declaration of the structure's root class, and the desired size as inputs, and generates a random graph that is allocated on the heap.

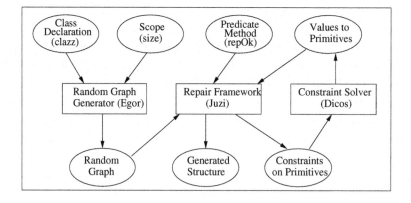

Fig. 1. Shekoosh framework for test input generation

```
Object generateRandomGraph(Class clazz, Set<Pair<Class, int>> size) {

    Random rand = new Random();
    LinkedList liveObjectWorkList = new LinkedList();
    Set deadObjectSet = new HashSet();
    LiveFieldCount liveFieldCount = new LiveFieldCount(clazz);
    CurrentSize currentSize= new CurrentSize(clazz);

    Object root = clazz.newInstance();
    liveObjectWorkList.add(root);
    liveFieldCount.update(root);

    while ( !liveObjectWorkList.isEmpty() ) {
        Object o = liveObjectWorkList.removeFirst();

        for ( Field f : fields(o) ) {
            liveFieldCount.decrement(f);
            if ( currentSize.get(f) == desiredSize(f,size) ) {
                int i = rand.nextInt(2);
                if(i == 0) f.setValue(null);
                if(i == 1) f.setValue(getRandomObject(deadObjectSet));
            }
            else {
                if ( liveFieldCount.get(f) == 0 ) {
                    Object o' = newInstance(f);
                    f.setValue(o');
                    liveObjectWorkList.add(o');
                    liveFieldCount.update(o')
                    currentSize.update(f);
                }
                else {
                    int i = rand.nextInt(3);
                    if(i == 0) f.setValue(null);
                    if(i == 1) f.setValue(getRandomObject(deadObjectSet));
                    if(i == 2) {
                        Object o' = newInstance(f);
                        f.setValue(o');
                        liveObjectWorkList.add(o');
                        liveFieldCount.update(o');
                        currentSize.update(f);
                    }
                }
            }
        }
        deadObjectSet.add(o);
    }
}
```

Fig. 2. The Egor algorithm for generating random graphs

The vertices of the graph are new objects of the given classes. The edges of the graph represent the reference fields. Figure 2 shows the pseudo-code for the Egor random graph generation algorithm.

Intuitively, the algorithm starts with an empty graph. It then allocates new objects as required to generate a graph of the desired size. For each object, the algorithm randomly assigns values to the object's reference fields, ensuring at each step that the graph can further be extended if necessary. The algorithm terminates when the graph has the desired number of objects and all the reference fields of the allocated objects have been initialized.

To explain the algorithm, we first explain the notation we use in Figure 2:

- **clazz** is an object representing the container class of the structure (for example the `BinarySearchTree` class).
- **size** is a set of pairs representing the desired size of every class in the structure. Egor provides a helper method `desiredSize` that takes a field `f` and `size`, and returns the desired size of the class that is the declared type of `f`.
- **liveObjectWorkList** is a list of objects whose reference fields are yet to be assigned a value.
- **deadObjectSet** is a set of objects whose reference fields have already been assigned a value. Egor provides a helper method `getRandomObject` that randomly returns an object from the `deadObjectSet`
- **LiveFieldCount** is a class that represents for each class the number of object fields, i.e., *live count*, that have not yet been assigned values in the structure. The live count of every class is initially set to zero. `LiveFieldCount` provides three helper methods: `get`, `update`, and `decrement`. The method `get` takes a field object and returns the live count of the field's declared class; `update` takes an object, and for each of its fields, increments the live count of the field's declared class; `decrement` takes a field object, and decrements the live count value of the field's declared class.
- **CurrentSize** is a class that represents the number of objects for each class in the structure. For each class, the current size is initially zero. The class `CurrentSize` provides two helper methods: `get` and `update`. The method `get` takes a field and returns the current size of the field's declared class; `update` takes a field and increments the size for the field's declared class.

The Egor generation algorithm first initializes its variables. Next, it creates an instance of the root class (`clazz`), adds it to the `liveObjectWorkList`, and updates the `liveFieldCount`. Next, Egor iterates until the `liveObjectWorkList` is empty. In each iteration, Egor removes the first object from the `liveObjectWorkList` and assigns values to each of the object's reference fields as follows. When assigning a field f of type t, Egor first checks the `currentSize`, and the `desiredSize` for t. If `currentSize` is equal to the `desiredSize`, Egor randomly assigns f to `null`, or to an object from the `deadObjectSet` since new objects of class t can no longer be added to the graph. If the current size is less than the desired size, Egor checks t's `liveFieldCount`. If it is zero, i.e., the graph can only be extended further by assigning a new object to f, Egor allocates a new object o' of type t, assigns o' to f, and updates the `liveFieldCount` and `currentSize` for t. If the live field count is greater than zero, Egor randomly assigns f to `null`, an object from the `deadObjectSet`, or a new object of a compatible type. After assigning all the fields of an object, Egor adds the object to the `deadObjectSet`. Figure 3 illustrates the generation of a `BinarySearchTree` with two nodes.

The generated graph satisfies two key properties: reachability, i.e., all the objects allocated are reachable from the root object, and randomness, i.e., the assignment to each field is made at random (using the Java API). Note that primitive data is left uninitialized. Determining the values for the primitive fields is performed using Dicos after the random structure is repaired by Juzi++. Figure 4 shows an example of a six node `BinarySearchTree` graph generated using Egor.

[Iteration 0]
BinarySearchTree
root?

LiveObjectList
root

DeadObjectList

	LiveFieldCount	CurrentSize	DesiredSize
BinarySearchTree	0	1	1
Node	1	0	2

[Iteration 1]
BinarySearchTree
root
N0 i0
left? right?

LiveObjectList
N0

DeadObjectList
root

	LiveFieldCount	CurrentSize	DesiredSize
BinarySearchTree	0	1	1
Node	2	1	2

[Iteration 2]
BinarySearchTree
root
N0 i0
right
N1 i1
left? right?

LiveObjectList
N1

DeadObjectList
root N0

	LiveFieldCount	CurrentSize	DesiredSize
BinarySearchTree	0	1	1
Node	2	2	2

[Resulting object–graph]
BinarySearchTree
root
N0 i0
right
N1 i1
left right

LiveObjectList

DeadObjectList
root N0 N1

	LiveFieldCount	CurrentSize	DesiredSize
BinarySearchTree	0	1	1
Node	0	2	2

Fig. 3. Egor illustration: generating a random `BinarySearchTree` object with two nodes. The algorithm takes three iterations of the while-loop. The algorithm state at the beginning of each iteration as well as the resulting object-graph are shown. The reference fields are labeled appropriately; a ' ? ' indicates the field has not yet been assigned a value by the algorithm; fields that have the value `null` are omitted for clarity. Each node is labeled with its identity (N0 or N1) and a symbolic integer value (i0 or i1).

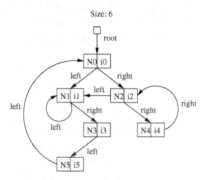

Fig. 4. Random graph with six nodes generated by Egor

4.2 Juzi++: Repair Framework

Juzi++ takes as inputs the random graph generated by Egor and `repOk`, and performs *repair actions* on the graph. Each repair action assigns a new value to an object field. Juzi++ transforms the graph so that it satisfies the desired constraints on the reference fields, and returns a set of constraints on the primitive fields of the structure. Juzi++ builds on our previous work on data structure repair and introduces new heuristics that enable repair to scale to large structures that may have a large number of corruptions. Juzi++ introduces two key heuristics: prioritizing values to use in repair as well as prioritizing fields to repair. We first describe our basic repair algorithm Juzi [13], and then explain the heuristics that Juzi++ implements.

Juzi. This section describes the basic Juzi [13] repair algorithm. Given a structure s that is to be repaired and a predicate `repOk` that represents the structural constraints, the algorithm:

- invokes `s.repOk()`.
- monitors execution of `repOk` to note the order in which fields of objects in s are accessed[1].
- if `repOk` returns false
  - backtracks and mutates s by toggling the value of the last field that was accessed by `repOk` (while maintaining the values of all other fields), and re-executes `repOk`
- else
  - outputs s (which now has been repaired)

The first invocation of `repOk` (which is on the given corrupt structure) simply follows the Java semantics. When `repOk` returns false, the repair algorithm mutates the given structure, by changing the value of the last accessed field, which is non-deterministically assigned:

- `null`, if the field value was not originally null;
- an object (of a compatible type) that was encountered during the last execution of `repOk` on the corrupt structure, if the field was not originally pointing to this object;
- a new object (of a compatible type), unless the object that the field originally pointed to was different from all objects in the structure encountered during the last execution of `repOk`;

When all the choices for a field assignment have been explored, Juzi resets the value of the last field accessed to its initial value and systematically backtracks to modify the value of the second-last field accessed and so on.

Generation of large structures requires highly efficient repair. Notice that Juzi uses backtracking to perform repair. Thus, Juzi repeatedly invokes `repOk` until the predicate returns *true*. The performance of repair depends on the number of times `repOk` is executed. When repairing a graph generated at random, the number of invocations can be prohibitively expensive. For such a graph, the number of faults are likely to be proportional to its size. Therefore, the number of times `repOk` is executed, which equals the total number of *repair actions* performed, is very high and the basic Juzi approach does not scale, say to repairing large structures, say consisting of 10000 nodes, that have a large number of faults.

Juzi++. We introduce two heuristics for prioritizing repairs to enable an efficient repair framework, which we use in Shekoosh. The heuristics are aimed to optimize repair. However they do not compromise completeness (Section 6).

---

[1] Execution of repOk is monitored by replacing field accesses with invocations of "get" methods and adding new boolean fields that are set on the first access of the corresponding field. Details are available elsewhere [13, 19].

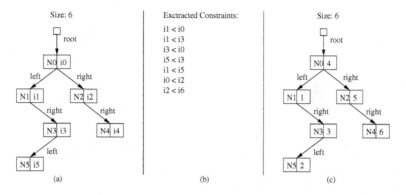

Fig. 5. (a) `BinarySearchTree` object repaired by Juzi++; primitive fields have symbolic values. (b) Difference constraints on primitive fields computed by Juzi++. (c) Solution to the constraints generated by Dicos used to assign values to the primitive fields.

The first heuristics is based on building and solving constraints on references. Juzi++ identifies equality constraint patterns of the form:

```
if ( field != value ) return false ;
```

The solution of such constraints is embedded in the negation of the condition. *Juzi++* detects and directly solves such constraints without using nondeterministic assignment. This optimization enables highly efficient solving of a variety of *local* constraints. To illustrate, the parent-child relation of a binary tree takes the following form:

```
Node left = current.left ;
if ( left.parent != current ) return false ;
```

Juzi++ keeps track of the last equality comparison between a reference field and a value, and selects the value as the first candidate to try. Thus, for the above example, Juzi++ needs to try only one value for repairing the `parent` field of a node.

The second heuristics is based on a lightweight dynamic analysis [20] of the structure. Unlike Juzi, which for each field uses the same order of nondeterministic choices, we use a dynamic ordering. The analysis identifies a set of *core* fields—fields that are used primarily to traverse the structure. When repairing core fields, our algorithm gives higher priority to selecting a new node or `null`, over selecting an already visited node. This optimization guarantees that the reachability of the structure is preserved by repair, and reduces the number of attempts required to find the repaired structure.

These two heuristics dramatically improve the performance of repair (Section 5). The search uses the most *likely* values first, which enables generation of large structures. Note that prioritization of constraints does not compromise the completeness of the algorithm: if a solution to the constraints represented by `repOk` exists for the desired size, our algorithm will generate it. Moreover, the optimizations allow Juzi++ to fix more than one corrupt field using a single execution of `repOk`—an optimization that is essential to scale repair based on imperative constraints.

To illustrate repair, recall the structure shown in Figure 4. Figure 5(a) shows the corresponding repaired structure.

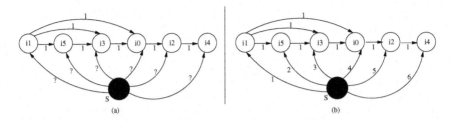

Fig. 6. (a) Data constraint graph based on the constraints from Figure 5 (b); the edges labeled with weight 1 arise from the difference constraints; s is the new reference node and edges labeled with ' ? ' indicate the new edges. (b) Solution for the difference constrains; each ' ? ' has been replaced with the value of the longest distance from s.

Juzi++ repairs the structural constraints and returns a set of data constraints, which constrain the primitive fields of the resulting structure. Juzi++ extracts the data constraints using symbolic execution. To illustrate, Figure 5(b) shows the data constraints extracted from the BinarySearchTree in Figure 5(a). The constraints returned by Juzi++ are solved by Dicos (Section 4.3), which determines an appropriate value for each primitive field.

4.3   Dicos: Data Constraint Solver

This section describes a technique for generating data values that satisfy the data constraints of the subject structure. A simple approach for generating data values is to assign the values randomly. While generating random values for the primitive fields is straightforward, such an approach is unlikely to give a valid solution in the presence of any constraints on data.

We have developed Dicos, a difference constraint solver for constraints on primitive integers. Our current implementation handles difference constraints that take the form $x < y$ and $x \leq y$ as well as equality constraints. Following a textbook algorithm [3], Dicos builds a constraint graph where the vertices are the primitive fields, and the edges are the difference constraints. Once the graph is built, the problem simplifies to finding the topological order of the nodes in the graph. The primitive values are the longest distances from a new reference node. For a directed acyclic graph with n nodes and e edges, we can compute the primitive values in $O(n + e)$ using a topological sort.

To illustrate, consider the constraints shown in Figure 5(b). Figure 6(a) shows the corresponding constraint graph. The solution of this constraint graph is shown in Figure 6(b). The values for the nodes are the longest distances from the reference node added during the graph construction.

We use the solution returned by Dicos to assign values to the data fields of the structure (Figure 5(c)).

5   Experiments

In this section we evaluate the performance of Shekoosh in generating large data structures. We first describe our experimental methodology. We present different subject structures with various complex structural and data integrity constraints. We use Shekoosh to generate the subject structures, and we compare our results with related techniques in automatic test input generation. Finally, we discuss the scalability of Shekoosh in terms of the size and the complexity of the generated structures.

5.1 Methodology

We evaluate Shekoosh by applying it to generate ten subject structures. For each subject, we evaluate the time it takes to generate one valid structure for sizes: 10, 100, 1000, 10000, and 100000. We repeat the generation using 50 different randomization seeds and report the average generation time.

Our subjects are divided into three categories: (1) subjects with simple constraints on the structure only, (2) subjects with simple constraints on both the structure as well as the primitive data (3) and subjects with highly complex structural and data constraints. Subjects in category (1) can be generated without using our constraint solver Dicos, i.e., without the need for symbolic execution for primitives, while subjects in category (2) and (3) require its use.

For solving purely structural constraints, two of the previous tools that have been shown to provide efficient solving are TestEra [6], which uses the Alloy Analyzer [21] and off-the-shelf SAT technology, and Korat [7], which implements an imperative constraint solver. For the benchmarks in category (1), we present a comparison of Shekoosh with these two tools. For the benchmarks in categories (2) and (3), TestEra and Korat are unable to compete with Shekoosh because they require explicit enumeration of primitive values and checking of their constraints—the two tools do not use any dedicated solver of constraints on primitives. We have conducted experiments to generate the structures in categories (2) and (3) using Korat and TestEra. We gave Korat and TestEra 20 minutes to generate one structure. Korat and TestEra failed to generate structures with 25 nodes within the given time. The comparison with TestEra and Korat shows that Shekoosh can generate structures of sizes that are 100 times larger.

5.2 Experimental Results

We next describe the data structure subjects and the generation results. All experiments used a 1.7 GHZ Pentium M processor with 512 MB RAM.

Category (1). Subjects in this category only have simple constraints on the structure, and no constraints on primitive data. The structural constraints are limited to reachability, acyclicity, and transposition. We use these structures to evaluate the performance of Shekoosh in comparison with TestEra and Korat. The subjects in this category are as follows:

- **Singly-linked acyclic list.** A list object has a `header` node; each list node has a `next` field. Structural integrity is acyclicity along `next`.
- **Doubly-linked circular list.** A list object has a `header` node; each list node has a `next` and a `previous` field. Structural integrity is circularity along `next` and the transpose relation between `next` and `previous`. This subject is based on the library class `java.util.LinkedList`.

Table 1. Results on solving constraints on the structure. Shekoosh is able to generate structures that are 100 times larger than those feasible with TestEra and Korat. A time of ' – ' indicates failure to generate in 20 minutes. All tabulated times are in milliseconds.

	Shekoosh			Korat	TestEra
Singly Linked List	Generation Time(msec)	Repair Time(msec)	Total Time(msec)	Total Time(msec)	Total Time(msec)
10 Nodes	1	2	3	37	3000
100 Nodes	4	4	8	334	-
1000 Nodes	8	14	22	-	-
10000 Nodes	30	33	63	-	-
100000 Nodes	199	483	682	-	-
Doubly Linked List	Generation Time(msec)	Repair Time(msec)	Total Time(msec)	Total Time(msec)	Total Time(msec)
10 Nodes	1	16	17	82	8000
100 Nodes	3	44	43	3204	-
1000 Nodes	14	271	285	-	-
10000 Nodes	50	3718	3768	-	-
100000 Nodes	396	43174	43570	-	-
Binary Tree	Generation Time(msec)	Repair Time(msec)	Total Time(msec)	Total Time(msec)	Total Time(msec)
10 Nodes	1	14	15	21	5000
100 Nodes	2	125	127	512	-
1000 Nodes	14	372	386	-	-
10000 Nodes	85	3672	3777	-	-
100000 Nodes	397	45267	45664	-	-

– **Binary tree.** A binary tree object has a `root` node; each node has a `left` and a `right` child node. Structural integrity is acyclicity along `left` and `right`.

Solving Constraints on Structure. We used Shekoosh to generate the subject structures of this category with sizes ranging from 10 to 100000 nodes. Table 1 shows the results for the subjects in category (1). For test generation, Shekoosh's performance scales essentially linearly. Singly-linked list has the simplest of the constraints and its generation is therefore the fastest. Even though doubly-linked list and binary tree have two fields each, the constraints for doubly-linked list are more complex since they involve two properties (circularity and transpose relation between `next` and `previous`) as opposed to one (acyclicity).

Notice that the generation time is essentially proportional to the number of fields in the structure. The repair time dominates the generation time as expected. The actual time to repair depends on the complexity of the underlying structural constraints.

We gave TestEra and Korat 20 minutes to generate one structure. Overall, Korat performs better than TestEra. However, Korat is unable to generate any subject structure with more than 800 nodes within the given time. Thus, Shekoosh is able to generate structures that are up to 100 times larger than those feasible with Korat and TestEra.

Table 2. Results on solving constraints on the structure as well as on data. All times are in milliseconds.

	Shekoosh			
Sorted Linked List	Structure Generation Time(msec)	Structure Repair Time(msec)	Data Generation Time(msec)	Total Time(msec)
100 Nodes	16	21	5	42
1000 Nodes	22	51	27	100
10000 Nodes	46	210	26	282
100000 Nodes	338	1423	178	1939
Binary Search Tree	Structure Generation Time(msec)	Structure Repair Time(msec)	Data Generation Time(msec)	Total Time(msec)
100 Nodes	10	142	8	160
1000 Nodes	27	422	14	463
10000 Nodes	65	4008	30	4103
100000 Nodes	446	48401	201	49048
Heap Array	Structure Generation Time(msec)	Structure Repair Time(msec)	Data Generation Time(msec)	Total Time(msec)
100 Nodes	10	11	8	29
1000 Nodes	14	37	15	66
10000 Nodes	15	124	29	168
100000 Nodes	55	1084	184	1323

Category (2). Subjects in this category are similar in complexity to those of category (1) yet they have constraints on the order of primitive data. We use these structures to evaluate our constraint solver and measure its efficiency in completing the solution. The subjects in this category are as follows:

– **Sorted linked list.** A sorted linked list is an acyclic linked list whose nodes have integer elements. Integrity constraints include acyclicity as well as ordering of elements: all elements appear in sorted order.
– **Binary search tree.** A binary search tree is a binary tree whose nodes have integer keys. Integrity constraints include acyclicity as well as ordering on keys: for each node, its key is larger than any of the keys in the left sub-tree and smaller than any of the keys in the right-sub tree.
– **Heap arrays.** Heap arrays provide an array-based implementation of the binary heap data structure that is also commonly known as a priority queue. A heap has a capacity that is the length of the underlying array and a size that is the number of elements currently in the heap. For a heap element at index i, its left child is at index $2 * i + 1$ and the right child is at index $2 * i + 2$. Integrity constraints require that size <= capacity and the heap satisfies the max-heap property: an element is larger than both its children.

Solving Constraints on Structure as well as Data. Structures in this category have constraints on the order of the data. For a sorted list, the elements are ordered in a strictly increasing/decreasing order along the next field. For a binary search tree the element in the root of a tree is larger than all the elements in the left sub-tree, and less than all the elements in the right sub-tree. For a heap array, an element at a node is larger than both its children. We used TestEra and Korat to generate these structures, and both failed to generate the first structure with 30 nodes within 20min. TestEra and Korat use a search algorithm to solve the reference constraints as well as data constraints where as in our approach we try to solve the two problems separately if possible (section 6) which allows us to use a dedicated solver for data constraints.

Table 2 tabulates the results for the subjects in category (2). We point out the efficiency of our constraint solver Dicos. The performance of Dicos scales essentially linearly with the size of the generated structures. For test generation, Shekoosh's performance still scales. Note that the structure repair time includes the time to build the constraints on the primitives. (Recall, Juzi++ returns these constraints as its result).

Category (3). Subjects in this category have more complex structural and data constraints than those in categories (1) and (2). These constraints include height balance, path coloring, sentinel reachability (all nodes should have a pointer to a sentinel node) and more. These structures are used to measure the scalability of our approach in generating large data structures, and to discover which phase has the most contribution in the generation time. Again we tried to use TestEra and Korat to generate these structures, and both tools couldn't generate the first structure of 25 nodes within the given 20min threshold. The subjects in this category are as follows:

- **Disjoint set.** The Disjoint set data structure is a linked-based implementation of the fast union-find data structure [3]; this implementation uses both path compression and rank estimation heuristics to improve efficiency. A Disjoint set object has a `header` and a `tail` node as well as a `size` field that represents the size of the set; each set node has a `next` and a `parent` field. Structural integrity constraints are acyclicity and reachability to the sentinel header node (the `parent` field of each node should point to the header node).
- **TreeMap.** TreeMap implements the Map interface using red-black trees. A TreeMap object has a `root` node; and stores the number of entries in the `size` field. A TreeMap node stores a data element in the field `key`, has a `left` and a `right` child, and also has a `parent` pointer. Furthermore, a node has a `color`, which is either RED (false) or BLACK (true). Structural integrity is acyclicity along `left` and `right`, the transpose relation between `left`, `right` and `parent`, and the natural order on the keys. Furthermore a TreeMap structure should satisfy the following constraints on the colors of its nodes:
  - red entries have black children;
  - the number of black entries on any path from the root to a leaf is the same.
- **AVL tree.** implements the intentional name trees that describe properties of services in the Intentional Naming System (INS) [22], an architecture for service location in dynamic networks. An AVL tree is a balanced binary search tree. The integrity constraints are the same as those of the binary search tree as well as the balance property where the height of the left and the right sub-trees does not differ by more than one.
- **Fibonacci heap.** A Fibonacci-Heap is a dynamic data structure that also implements a heap. A Fibonacci heap object has a `min` field that points to the minimum

Table 3. Results on large structures with very complex structural integrity constraints. All times are in milliseconds.

	Shekoosh			
Disjoint Set	Structure Generation Time(msec)	Structure Repair Time(msec)	Data Generation Time(msec)	Total Time(msec)
10 Nodes	16	4	5	25
100 Nodes	15	63	10	88
1000 Nodes	31	4255	37	4323
5000 Nodes	62	33455	87	33604
10000 Nodes	132	250485	178	250795
AVL Tree	Structure Generation Time(msec)	Structure Repair Time(msec)	Data Generation Time(msec)	Total Time(msec)
10 Nodes	16	16	10	42
100 Nodes	33	94	21	148
1000 Nodes	47	3322	48	3397
5000 Nodes	78	23313	121	23424
7000 Nodes	115	455813	201	456297
Fibonacci Heap	Structure Generation Time(msec)	Structure Repair Time(msec)	Data Generation Time(msec)	Total Time(msec)
10 Nodes	16	32	7	55
100 Nodes	31	64	9	124
1000 Nodes	47	2140	29	2204
4000 Nodes	62	97952	52	98066
7000 Nodes	94	248828	184	249106
Red Black Tree	Structure Generation Time(msec)	Structure Repair Time(msec)	Data Generation Time(msec)	Total Time(msec)
10 Nodes	16	16	10	42
100 Nodes	43	268	22	333
1000 Nodes	62	6546	53	6661
5000 Nodes	267	315671	149	316087

element in the heap, and a `size` field that stores the number of nodes. Each Fibonacci heap node has a `parent` pointer, a `child` pointer, and a `sibling` pointer. A node stores the key element in a `key` field. Detailed description of the structural and data integrity constraints of a fibonacci heap are found in [3].

Generating Structurally Complex Subjects. The results for generating the structures in categories (1) and (2) show that all the components of Shekoosh (Egor, Juzi++, and Dicos) scale linearly. Yet as expected Juzi++ dominated the time required for generation. We further test the scalability of Shekoosh when generating structures with very complex constraints on the structure (complex structures truly determine the efficiency of the repair algorithm and thus the generation approach).

Table 3 shows the results for generating the structures in category (3). Note that as the structure size increases, both Egor and Dicos scale linearly , yet the repair algorithm grows faster. This is due to the complex nature of the structures being generated. The domination of the repair algorithm over the overall generation time is clearly obvious in

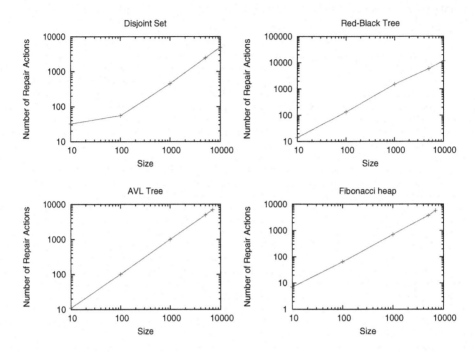

Fig. 7. Variation in the number of repair actions with the size of the structures. For all the studied subject structures, the number of repair actions grows essentially linearly with the size of the structure.

these structures. Even with the complexities, Shekoosh is still able to generate structure with thousands of nodes.

We point out that although the repair algorithm uses a search based approach (similar to Korat), it was still able to repair large structures with very complex properties (the balancing property of the AVL, the path color property of the red-black tree, the sentinel property of the disjoint sets, and the heap property of the fibonacci heap) within the threshold value that we used before terminating the generation. The next section will further investigate the scalability of Shekoosh and the performance of the repair algorithm.

5.3 Scalability of Shekoosh

The experimental results show that the scalability of Shekoosh is highly dependent on the scalability of the repair algorithm. Recall that the performance of Juzi++ is directly proportional to the number of repair actions performed while repairing the structure. We use the number of repair actions as a metric to measure the scalability of Juzi++, and thus Shekoosh. Figure 7 displays the graphs of the variation of the number of repair actions with the size of the structures. Unlike what we expected, although the performance of Juzi++ is not linear (Section 5.2), the number of repair actions grows linearly with the size of the structure. These results are justified as follows:

– First, the number of faults in the structures grows linearly with the size of the structure due to the random creation of the graph generated by Egor. The random graph acts as a partial solution that in the worst case satisfies the reachability and the size constraints of the structure.

– Second, the optimizations that were added to Juzi++ directs the search algorithm to the most likely value to repair a field, and thus the number of repair actions are closer to the number of faults as most of the fault are highly likely to be repaired with only one action.

– Third, and most important, recall that the backtracking algorithm in Juzi++ uses a stateless search space approach. Basically, with every repair action repOk is called, the original structure is re-initialized, and the state is built up to the faulty field. Using this approach the structure is reconstructed with every repair action. This causes a quadratic effect on the runtime of Juzi++ even though the number of repair actions grows linearly.

This observation about the number of repair actions shows that for the subject structures the performance of Juzi++ is more dependent on the backtracking algorithm rather than the search algorithm. An alternative approach for backtracking is to use a stateful approach similar to that used in software model checkers like the Java Path Finder (JPF) [10]. Future versions of Shekoosh will implement a stateful approach which can allow Shekoosh to generate even larger structures with complex integrity constraints.

6   Discussion

We next present some characteristics and limitations of Shekoosh and discuss some promising future directions.

Completeness of Generation. Shekoosh repairs a randomly generated structure in two steps: repair of structural constraints (using Juzi++) and repair of data constraints (using Dicos). Doing so enables efficient solving of structural constraints without the overhead of building data constraints on every execution of repOk. However, due to possible dependencies among different kinds of constraints, it is possible that a structure that satisfies its structural constraints cannot be repaired further to satisfy the data constraints without modifying the structure. In such cases, Shekoosh systematically backtracks and uses Juzi++ to generate a different structure. We point out that the algorithm is complete for difference constraints: the given structure size makes the underlying problem decidable. Even though the initial structure is generated at random, the repair by Juzi++ and Dicos is systematic. If any valid structure of the desired size exists, such a structure will be returned by Shekoosh; if no such structure exists, Shekoosh notifies the user.

Data Constraint Solving. The current implementation of Shekoosh supports solving two types of data constraints: difference constraints and equality constraints. Solving a problem that comprises additional types of constraints requires extending our solver Dicos or the use of a more sophisticated solver, such as the CVC-lite theorem prover [23].

Test Case Enumeration. We have illustrated Shekoosh for generating one structure of a desired size. Shekoosh can also be used to systematically enumerate a given number of structures. We expect a typical usage of Shekoosh to be to generate a small set of large test inputs; for inputs of large size, exhaustive generation is infeasible in principle due to the enormous number of valid structures.

Sensitivity to repOk. Repair actions performed by our algorithm depend on the formulation of repOk. Recall that Juzi++ backtracks on the last field accessed by repOk and modifies that field. Therefore, repOks that return false as soon as they determine a constraint violation without accessing remaining parts of the structure induce faster generation. Naturally written repOks have been shown to enable efficient generation [18].

Constraint-Based Generation Versus Construction Sequences. As we discussed in the introduction, an alternative to constraint-based test generation is the complementary approach of using method sequences to construct structures of a desired size. While this alternative requires an a priori implementation of the methods used in the construction sequence as well as their correct functionality, it presents a viable alternative for generating certain large structures. We have conducted experiments to compare the performance of Shekoosh with construction sequences using our subjects (Section 5). For the subjects in category (1) the performance of both approaches was similar in magnitude. Subjects in category (1) have no data elements, thus both approaches scaled linearly. The comparison for subjects in category (2) is more informative. For sorted linked list, Shekoosh outperforms construction sequences, e.g., for 100000 nodes, construction sequence takes 19800 milliseconds, which is 10 times the time Shekoosh takes. For binary search tree, the times are of a similar magnitude: for 100000 nodes, Shekoosh takes 2372 milliseconds while construction sequences take 1858 milliseconds. For heap array, construction sequences outperform Shekoosh, e.g., for 100000 nodes, construction sequences take 251 milliseconds, which is one-sixth of the time Shekoosh takes. For the structures in category (3) construction sequences outperforms shekoosh due to the complexity of the constraints being solved.

The two approaches are complementary and have their advantages and disadvantages. While construction sequences outperform Shekoosh when generating structurally complex structure, it still requires an a priori correct implementation of the methods used in the sequence. Shekoosh generically generates the structures from the given specification, but its performance is sensitive to the complexity of the structures being generated.

7   Related Work

We discuss how Shekoosh is related to other approaches in test input generation. We first survey some related work on specification-based testing. We then examine different approaches for assertion-based data structure repair. Finally we look at different methodologies for solving constraints on data.

7.1   Specification-Based Linked Structure Generation

Specification-based testing has been present in the testing literature since decades [24]. Many approaches automate test generation from specification languages such as Z specification [25], JML annotations [26], ASML specifications [27], or UML state-charts [28]. Originally these specifications did not handle complex data structures like the ones we present in this paper, yet some were extended to handle such structures.

The AsmL Test Generator (ASMLT) [27] was recently extended to handle structurally complex data using a search based approach. ASMLT transforms Asml specifications into finite state machines (FSM), and a search algorithm is performed on the FSM to generate the test inputs.

Korat [7] is a search-based test generation tool that exhaustively enumerates all non-isomorphic instances of a complex data structure up to a bound on the size. Unlike AsmlT, Korat takes the constraint written as a *Java* predicate. Korat's approach is highly favorable by programmers since there is no need to learn a new language (which is declarative in most of the cases) to write the specification. Yet the performance of Korat is highly sensitive to the way the Java predicate is written. Korat uses a search based approach that systematically explores the input space to find all the structures to satisfy the given predicate.

TestEra [29] is a test generation tool that uses the Alloy Analyzer [15] which in turn uses off-the-shelf enumerating SAT solvers [16] to generate all the structures that satisfy the integrity constraints. TestEra translates the class declarations of a structure into an Alloy model, and the Java predicate into an Alloy formula which is then fed into the Alloy Analyzer. TestEra is insensitive to the way the specifications are written since the Alloy Analyzer translates the model into a CNF formula before using a SAT solver to find the solution. The performance of TestEra is limited to the efficiency of the Alloy Analyzer when translating the Alloy model, and the performance of the SAT solver to find the solution.

Handling data constraints is a challenge for both search and SAT based approaches. Korat treats data members the same way it treats references. TestEra does not provide an efficient way to handle data elements due to the way integer types are modeled in Alloy [30].

Our generation tool, Shekoosh, differs from the above approaches as it targets generating the first structure that satisfies a given Java predicate rather than enumerating all the test cases. Although Shekoosh uses an approach similar to Korat when repairing the structures, the algorithm scales due to three factors: (1) the partial solution provided by the random graph generator (Although the graph generated by egor is random, yet it still acts as a partial solution which at least satisfies the reachability constraint of the structure), (2) the optimizations added to the repair algorithm which direct the search to the most-likely value to repair a structure, and (3) the dedicated solver (Dicos) for solving the constraints on primitives (unlike Korat).

7.2 Error Recovery

Dynamic error recovery has been part of software systems for a long time [31]. For example, state-full techniques used checkpointing [32] to recover the program state in distributed systems, and stateless techniques implemented dedicated repair routines for special faults [33]. The problem with these approaches is that they require dedicated special routines to be implemented with each system, and thus it is hard to build a robust generic repair framework using such approaches, since the developer must envision all possible bugs.

Recent work on repair proposes assertion-based techniques to repair a data structure. Assertions have long been used to describe the properties of code. Many tools and techniques make use of assertions to check the program correctness statically and dynamically [2]. The success of assertion checks in hardware verification [34] motivated the use of the same approach for software validation [35]. Most of the recent programming languages have special support for assertions, for example the `assert` keyword in `Java 1.5`. Assertions can be used to describe the structural integrity constraints of a data structure. Such a description can be written in a declarative language like first order logic, or in an imperative language as a predicate method. Although declarative languages provide a more succinct method for describing constraints, there is a large gap between the syntax and grammar of such languages and those of imperative programming languages which are commonly used by software developers and testers.

Recent techniques for repair use the structural constraints to dynamically repair data structures. Demsky and Rinard have recently proposed an constraint-based generic framework for data structure repair [36]. Given the consistency constraints in a new declarative language, their algorithm generates repair routines for each of the integrity constraints.

Juzi [13] is assertion-based framework for data structure repair [13]. However in Juzi, assertions are written in the host language (Similar to Korat). Given the structural constraints written as a `Java` predicate, Juzi systematically searches the neighborhood of the fault and mutates the structure to satisfy the integrity constraints. *Juzi* uses a dedicated search algorithm [7] to find the correct candidate that repairs an erroneous data structure. The performance of *Juzi* depends on the number of faults and the efficiency of the search algorithm in finding the correct candidate.

Shekoosh builds on the Juzi algorithm; it optimizes the search algorithm in order to scale for repairing larger structures with more faults.

7.3   Other Test Generation Techniques

Automatic test case generation is a very old idea, and there are large number of techniques on the topic. We select a couple of techniques and compare them with our approach. A straightforward method for test generation is to build structures using already existing construction sequences. Godefroid et al. proposed DART [37], an automated random testing tool that uses both static and dynamic analysis to generate test cases. Many techniques for test generation use randomized algorithms [38, 39] to generate input tests. Pargas [40] used genetic algorithms to generate a sequence of construction calls that builds up a test input. Claessen et al. [41] use specifications written in Haskell [42] to randomly generate a large number of inputs to test programs written in Haskell. All these techniques can scale to generate large structures with complex structural and data integrity constraints.

Shekoosh differs from the above techniques in that it does not require any implementation of the generated structure. Shekoosh only uses the class declaration and the predicate method describing the constraints.

8   Conclusions

We have presented Shekoosh, a novel framework for generating large data structures. Given a Java predicate that represents the desired structural and data integrity constraints, and the size of the structure to be generated, the Shekoosh test generation algorithm generates a structure that has the given size and satisfies all the constraints. Generation has three phases. The first phase generates a random graph. The second phase repairs the graph to satisfy the structural constraints using an optimized framework based on our previous work on error recovery. The third phase solves the constraints on primitive data and assigns appropriate values to the primitive fields.

Experiments on generating large data structures using subjects with complex structural and data constraints show that Shekoosh can efficiently generate structures with thousands of nodes. In comparison with two existing constraint-based generation frameworks, Shekoosh is able to generate structures that are up to 100 times larger.

We believe Shekoosh presents an exciting new approach to test generation and represents an important step towards a wider application of constraint-based approaches for automated testing and error recovery.

Acknowledgments.   We would like to thank Christine Kehyayan, Feras Karablieh, Darko Marinov, and the anonymous referees for their helpful comments on the paper. This work was funded in part by the EDGE scholar program and the NSFITR-SoD award #0438967.

References

1. National Institute of Standards and Technology. The economic impacts of inadequate infrastructure for software testing. Planning report 02-3 (May 2002)
2. Beizer, B.: Software Testing Techniques. International Thomson Computer Press (1990)
3. Cormen, T.H., Leiserson, C.E., Rivest, R.L.: Introduction to Algorithms. The MIT Press, Cambridge, MA (1990)
4. United States Nuclear Regulatory Commission. Fault Tree Handbook, NUREG-0492 (1981)
5. Adjie-Winoto, W., Schwartz, E., Balakrishnan, H., Lilley, J.: The design and implementation of an intentional naming system. In: Proc. 17th ACM Symposium on Operating Systems Principles (SOSP), Kiawah Island (December 1999)
6. Marinov, D., Khurshid, S.: TestEra: A novel framework for automated testing of Java programs. In: Proc. 16th Conference on Automated Software Engineering (ASE), San Diego, CA (November 2001)
7. Boyapati, C., Khurshid, S., Marinov, D.: Korat: Automated testing based on Java predicates. In: Proc. International Symposium on Software Testing and Analysis (ISSTA) (July 2002)
8. Khurshid, S., Pasareanu, C., Visser, W.: Generalized symbolic execution for model checking and testing. In: Garavel, H., Hatcliff, J. (eds.) ETAPS 2003 and TACAS 2003. LNCS, vol. 2619, Springer, Heidelberg (2003)
9. Sen, K., Marinov, D., Agha, G.: CUTE: a concolic unit testing engine for C. In: Proc. 13th ACM SIGSOFT International Symposium on Foundations of Software Engineering (FSE) (2005)
10. Visser, W., Pasareanu, C.S., Khurshid, S.: Test input generation with Java PathFinder. In: Proc. 2004 ACM SIGSOFT International Symposium on Software Testing and Analysis (2004)

11. Xie, T., Marinov, D., Notkin, D.: Rostra: A framework for detecting redundant object-oriented unit tests. In: Proc. 19th IEEE International Conference on Automated Software Engineering (September 2004)
12. Xie, T., Marinov, D., Schulte, W., Notkin, D.: Symstra: A framework for generating object-oriented unit tests using symbolic execution. In: Halbwachs, N., Zuck, L.D. (eds.) TACAS 2005. LNCS, vol. 3440, Springer, Heidelberg (2005)
13. Khurshid, S., García, I., Suen, Y.L.: Repairing structurally complex data. In: Proc. 12th SPIN Workshop on Software Model Checking (2005)
14. King, J.C.: Symbolic execution and program testing. Communications of the ACM 19(7) (1976)
15. Jackson, D.: Micromodels of software: Modelling and analysis with Alloy (2001), http://sdg.lcs.mit.edu/alloy/book.pdf
16. Moskewicz, M.W., Madigan, C.F., Zhao, Y., Zhang, L., Malik, S.: Chaff: Engineering an efficient SAT solver. In: Proceedings of the 39th Design Automation Conference (DAC) (June 2001)
17. Liskov, B., Guttag, J.: Program Development in Java: Abstraction, Specification, and Object-Oriented Design. Addison-Wesley, Reading (2000)
18. Marinov, D.: Automatic Testing of Software with Structurally Complex Inputs. PhD thesis, Computer Science and Artificial Intelligence Laboratory, Massachusetts Institute of Technology (2004)
19. Khurshid, S., Suen, Y.L.: Generalizing symbolic execution to library classes. In: 6th ACM SIGPLAN-SIGSOFT Workshop on Program Analysis for Software Tools and Engineering, Lisbon, Portugal (September 2005)
20. Malik, M.Z., Pervaiz, A., Khurshid, S.: Generating representation invariants of structurally complex data. In: Proc. 11th Conference on Tools and Algorithms for Construction and Analysis of Systems (TACAS), LNCS, vol. 4424, Springer, Heidelberg (March 2007)
21. Jackson, D.: Software Abstractions: Logic, Language and Analysis. The MIT Press, Cambridge, MA (2006)
22. Khurshid, S.: Exploring the design of an intentional naming scheme with an automatic constraint analyzer. Master's thesis, Laboratory for Computer Science, Massachusetts Institute of Technology (2000)
23. Barrett, C., Berezin, S.: CVC Lite: A new implementation of the cooperating validity checker. In: Alur, R., Peled, D.A. (eds.) CAV 2004. LNCS, vol. 3114, Springer, Heidelberg (2004)
24. Goodenough, J., Gerhart, S.: Toward a theory of test data selection. IEEE Transactions on Software Engineering (June 1975)
25. Horcher, H.-M.: Improving software tests using Z specifications. In: Proc. 9th International Conference of Z Users, The Z Formal Specification Notation (1995)
26. Cheon, Y., Leavens, G.T.: A simple and practical approach to unit testing: The JML and JUnit way. In: Magnusson, B. (ed.) ECOOP 2002. LNCS, vol. 2374, Springer, Heidelberg (2002)
27. Stobie, K.: Advanced modeling, model based test generation, and Abstract state machine Language (AsmL). Seattle Area Software Quality Assurance Group (January 2003), http://www.sasqag.org/pastmeetings/asml.ppt
28. Offutt, J., Abdurazik, A.: Generating tests from UML specifications. In: France, R.B., Rumpe, B. (eds.) UML '99 - The Unified Modeling Language. Beyond the Standard. LNCS, vol. 1723, Springer, Heidelberg (1999)
29. Khurshid, S., Marinov, D.: Checking Java implementation of a naming architecture using TestEra. In: Stoller, S.D., Visser, W. (eds.) Electronic Notes in Theoretical Computer Science. ENTCS, vol. 55. Elsevier Science Publishers, Amsterdam (2001)
30. Jackson, D.: Alloy: A lightweight object modeling notation. ACM Transactions on Software Engineering and Methodology (TOSEM) 11(2) (2002)

31. Smirnov, A., Chiueh, T.-c.: DIRA: Automatic detection, identification, and repair of control-hijacking attacks. In: The 12th Annual Network and Distributed System Security Symposium, February 2005, San Diego, CA (2005)
32. Kim, J.L., Park, T.: An efficient protocol for checkpointing recovery in distributed systems. IEEE Transactions on Parallel and Distributed Systems (August 1993)
33. Karablieh, F., Bazzi, R.A., Hicks, M.: Compiler-assisted heterogeneous checkpointing. In: SRDS, p. 56 (2001)
34. Wile, B., Goss, J., Roesner, W.: Comprehensive Functional Verification: The Complete Industry Cycle. Morgan Kaufmann, San Francisco (2005)
35. Synopsis. Assertion-based verification (March 2003), http://www.synopsys.com/products/simulation/assertion_based_wp.pdf
36. Demsky, B., Rinard, M.: Automatic detection and repair of errors in data structures. In: Proc. Conference on Object-Oriented Programming, Systems, Languages, and Applications (OOPSLA) (2003)
37. Godefroid, P., Klarlund, N., Sen, K.: Dart: directed automated random testing. In: PLDI '05: Proceedings of the 2005 ACM SIGPLAN conference on Programming language design and implementation (2005)
38. Cohen, D.M., Dalal, S.R., Fredman, M.L., Patton, G.C.: The AETG system: An approach to testing based on combinatorial design. IEEE Transactions on Software Engineering 23(7) (1997)
39. Jones, B.F., Sthamer, H.H., Eyres, D.E.: Automatic structural testing using genetic algorithms. Software Engineering Journal (1996)
40. Pargas, R.P., Harrold, M.J., Peck, R.: Test-data generation using genetic algorithms. Journal of Software Testing, Verification, and Reliability 9(4) (1999)
41. Claessen, K., Hughes, J.: QuickCheck: a lightweight tool for random testing of Haskell programs. ACM SIGPLAN Notices 35(9), 268–279 (2000)
42. Jones, S.P., Hughes, J.: Report on the Programming Language Haskell 98. A Non-strict Purely Functional Language (February 1999)

A   Structural Invariants for BinarySearchTree

The helper methods used in class invariant of `BinarySearchTree` can be formulated as follows.

```
// checks the acyclicity property of the tree
boolean isAcyclic () {
    Set visited = new HashSet ();
    visited.add(root);
    LinkedList workList = new LinkedList ();
    workList.add(root);

    while (!workList.isEmpty ()) {
        Node current = (Node)workList.removeFirst ();
        if (current.left != null) {
            if (!visited.add(current.left)) return false;
            workList.add(current.left);
        }
        if (current.right != null) {
            if (!visited.add(current.right)) return false;
            workList.add(current.right);
```

```
        }
    }
    return true;
}
// checks if the reachability constraint is satisfied
boolean sizeOk() {
    return size == numNodes(root);
}
// returns the number of nodes reachable from the root node
int numNodes(Node n) {
    if (n == null) return 0;
    return (1) + (numNodes(n.left))+ (numNodes(n.right));
}
// checks if the tree elements satisfy the order constraints
boolean searchConstraintsOk() {
    return isOrdered(root, MINUSINFINITY, PLUSINFINITY);
}

boolean isOrdered(Node n, Object min, Object max) {
    if ((min != null && compare(n.element, min) <=0 ) ||
    (max != null && compare(n.element, max) >=0)
        return false;
    if (n.left != null)
        if (!isOrdered(n.left, min, n.element)) return false;
    if (n.right != null)
        if (!isOrdered(n.right, n.element, max)) return false;
    return true;
}
```

Matching Objects with Patterns

Burak Emir[1], Martin Odersky[1], and John Williams[2]

[1] EPFL, 1015 Lausanne, Switzerland
`{first.last}@epfl.ch`
[2] Language Computer Corporation, Richardson TX 75080, USA
`jrw@pobox.com`

Abstract. Data in object-oriented programming is organized in a hierarchy of classes. The problem of *object-oriented pattern matching* is how to explore this hierarchy from the outside. This usually involves classifying objects by their run-time type, accessing their members, or determining some other characteristic of a group of objects. In this paper we compare six different pattern matching techniques: object-oriented decomposition, visitors, type-tests/type-casts, typecase, case classes, and extractors. The techniques are compared on nine criteria related to conciseness, maintainability and performance. The paper introduces case classes and extractors as two new pattern-matching methods and shows that their combination works well for all of the established criteria.

1 Introduction

Data in object-oriented programming is organized in a hierarchy of classes. The problem of *object-oriented pattern matching* is how to explore this hierarchy from the outside. This usually involves classifying objects by their run-time type, accessing their members, or determining some other characteristic of a group of objects. Here, we take a very general view of patterns. A pattern is simply some way of characterizing a group of objects and binding local names to objects that match some property in the classification.

A number of functional languages are built on patterns as an essential syntactic construct. Examples are SML, OCaml or Haskell. In object-oriented languages, patterns are much less common, even though some research exists [1,2,3,4]. Mainstream object-oriented languages propose to do pattern matching through encodings, such as virtual classification methods, visitors, or type-tests and type-casts.

The reason why patterns have so far played a lesser role in object-oriented languages might have to do with the object-oriented principle which states that behavior should be bundled with data and that the only form of differentiation should be through virtual method calls. This principle works well as long as (1) one can plan from the start for all patterns that will arise in an application, and (2) one only needs to decompose one object at a time.

However, these two assumptions do not always hold. The extensive literature on the expression problem [5,6,7,8] has explored many situations where access patterns are constructed a-posteriori, after the interface of the base class is fixed. Furthermore, there are access patterns where the result depends on the kinds of several objects.

E. Ernst (Ed.): ECOOP 2007, LNAI 4609, pp. 273–298, 2007.

Consider for instance symbolic manipulation of expressions. We assume a hierarchy of classes, rooted in a base class Expr and containing classes for specific forms of expressions, such as Mul for multiplication operations, Var for variables, and Num for numeric literals. Different forms of expressions have different members: Mul has two members left and right denoting its left and right operand, whereas Num has a member value denoting an integer. A class hiercharchy like this is expressed as follows (we use Scala as programming notation throughout the paper).

```
class Expr
class Num(val value : int) extends Expr
class Var(val name : String) extends Expr
class Mul(val left : Expr, val right : Expr) extends Expr
```

A particular expression would then be constructed as follows

```
new Mul(new Num(21), new Num(2))
```

Let's say we want to write a simplifier for arithmetic expressions. This program should try to apply a set of simplification rules, until no more rewrites are possible. An example simplification rule would make use of the right-neutrality of the number one. That is,

```
new Mul(x, new Num(1))   is replaced with    x .
```

The question is how simplification rules like the one above can be expressed. This is an instance of the object-oriented pattern matching problem, where objects of several variant types connected in possibly recursive data structures need to be classified and decomposed from the outside.

We will review in this paper the six techniques for this task: (1) classical object-oriented decomposition, (2) visitors, (3) type-tests/type-casts, (4) typecase, (5) case classes, and (6) extractors. Of these, the first three are well known in object-oriented languages. The fourth technique, typecase, is well known in the types community, but its extensions to type patterns in Scala is new. The fifth technique, case classes, is specific to Scala. The sixth technique, extractors, is new. It has been proposed independently by John Williams for Scala [9] and by Don Syme under the name "active patterns" for F# [10]. The basic F# design is in many ways similar to the Scala design, but Scala's treatment of parametricity is different.

Every technique will be evaluated along nine criteria. The first three criteria are concerned with conciseness of expression:

1. *Conciseness/framework*: How much "boilerplate" code needs to be written to enable classifications?
2. *Conciseness/shallow matches*: How easy is it to express a simple classification on the object's type?
3. *Conciseness/deep matches*: How easy is it to express a deep classification involving several objects?

The next three criteria assess program maintainability and evolution. In big projects, their importance often ranks highest.

4. *Representation independence*: How much of an object's representation needs to be revealed by a pattern match?
5. *Extensibility/variants*: How easy is it to add new data variants after a class hierarchy is fixed?
6. *Extensibility/patterns*: How easy is it to add new patterns after a class hierarchy is fixed? Can new patterns be expressed with the same syntax as existing ones?

Note that all presented schemes allow extensions of a system by new processors that perform pattern matching (one of the two dimensions noted in the expression problem). After all, this is what pattern matching is all about! The last three considered criteria have to do with performance and scalability:

7. *Base performance*: How efficient is a simple classification?
8. *Scalability/breadth*: How does the technique scale if there are many different cases?
9. *Scalability/depth*: How does the technique scale for larger patterns that reach several levels into the object graph? Here it is important that overlaps between several patterns in a classification can be factored out so that they need to be tested only once.

Our evaluation will show that a combination of case classes and extractors can do well in all of the nine criteria.

A difficult aspect of decomposition is its interaction with static typing, in particular type-parametricity. A subclass in a class hierarchy might have either fewer or more type parameters than its base class. This poses challenges for the precise typing of decomposing expressions which have been studied under the label of "generalized algebraic data-types", or GADT's [11,12]. The paper develops a new algorithm for recovering static type information from patterns in these situations.

Related Work. Pattern matching in the context of object-oriented programming has been applied to message exchange in distributed systems [13], semistructured data [14] and UI event handling [15].

Moreau, Ringeissen and Vittek [1] translate pattern matching code into existing languages, without requiring extensions. Liu and Myers [4] add a pattern matching construct to Java by means of a backward mode of execution.

Multi-methods [16,17,18,19] are an alternative technique which unifies pattern matching with method dispatch. Multi-methods are particularly suitable for matching on several arguments at the same time. An extension of multi-methods to predicate-dispatch [20,21] can also access embedded fields of arguments; however it cannot bind such fields to variables, so support for deep patterns is limited.

Views in functional programming languages [22,23] are conversions from one data type to another that are implicitly applied in pattern matching. They play a role similar to extractors in Scala, in that they permit to abstract from the concrete data-type of the matched objects. However, unlike extractors, views are anonymous and are tied to a particular target data type. Erwig's active patterns [24] provide views for non-linear patterns with more refined computation rules. Gostanza et al.'s active destructors [25] are closest to extractors; an active destructor corresponds almost exactly to an unapply method in an extractor. However, they do not provide data type injection, which is

```
// Class hierarchy:
trait Expr {
  def isVar: boolean = false
  def isNum: boolean= false
  def isMul: boolean = false
  def value: int        = throw new NoSuchMemberError
  def name : String   = throw new NoSuchMemberError
  def left : Expr       = throw new NoSuchMemberError
  def right: Expr       = throw new NoSuchMemberError
}
class Num(override val value: int) extends Expr {
  override def isNum = true }

class Var(override val name: String) extends Expr {
  override def isVar = true }

class Mul(override val left: Expr, override val right: Expr) extends Expr {
  override def isMul = true }

// Simplification rule:
  if (e.isMul) {
    val r = e.right
    if (r.isNum && r.value == 1) e.left else e
  } else e
```

Fig. 1. Expression simplification using object-oriented decomposition

handled by the corresponding apply method in our design. Also, being tied to traditional algebraic data types, active destructors cannot express inheritance with varying type parameters in the way it is found in GADT's.

2   Standard Techniques

In this section, we review four standard techniques for object-oriented pattern matching. These are, first, object-oriented decomposition using tests and accessors, second, visitors, third, type-tests and type-casts, and fourth, typecase. We explain each technique in terms of the arithmetic simplification example that was outlined in the introduction. Each technique is evaluated using the six criteria for conciseness and maintainability that were developed in the introduction. Performance evaluations are deferred to Section 5.

2.1   Object-Oriented Decomposition

In *classical OO decomposition*, the base class of a class hierarchy contains *test methods* which determine the dynamic class of an object and *accessor methods* which let one refer to members of specific subclasses. Some of these methods are overridden in each subclass. Figure 1 demonstrates this technique with the numeric simplification example.

The base class Expr contains test methods isVar, isNum and isMul, which correspond to the three subclasses of Expr (a **trait** is roughly a Java interface with methods optionally having default implementations). All test methods return **false** by default. Each subclass re-implements "its" test method to return **true**. The base class also contains one accessor method for every publicly visible field that is defined in some subclass. The default implementation of every access method in the base class throws a NoSuchMemberError exception. Each subclass re-implements the accessors for its own members. Scala makes these re-implementations particularly easy because it allows one to unify a class constructor and an overriding accessor method in one syntactic construct, using the syntax **override val** ... in a class parameter.

Note that in a dynamically typed language like Smalltalk, the base class needs to define only tests, not accessors, because missing accessors are already caught at runtime and are turned into NoSuchMethod messages. So the OO-decomposition pattern becomes considerably more lightweight. That might be the reason why this form of decomposition is more prevalent in dynamically typed languages than in statically typed ones. But even then the technique can be heavy. For instance, Squeak's Object class contains 35 test methods that each inquire whether the receiver is of some (often quite specific) subclass.

Besides its bulk, the object-oriented decomposition technique also suffers from its lack of extensibility. If one adds another subclass of Expr, the base class has to be augmented with new test and accessor methods. Again, dynamically typed languages such as Smalltalk alleviate this problem to some degree using meta-programming facilities where classes can be augmented and extended at run-time.

The second half of Figure 1 shows the code of the simplification rule. The rule inspects the given term stepwise, using the test functions and accessors given in class Expr.

Evaluation: In a statically typed language, the OO decomposition technique demands a high notational overhead for framework construction, because the class-hierarchy has to be augmented by a large number of tests and accessor methods. The matching itself relies on the interplay of many small functions and is therefore often somewhat ad-hoc and verbose. This holds especially for deep patterns. Object-oriented decomposition maintains complete representation independence. Its extensibility characteristics are mixed. It is easy to add new forms of matches using existing tests and accessors. If the underlying language has a concept of open classes or mixin composition, these matches can sometimes even be written using the same method call syntax as primitive matches. On the other hand, adding new subclasses requires a global rewrite of the class-hierarchy.

2.2 Visitors

Visitors [26] are a well-known design pattern to simulate pattern matching using double dispatch. Figure 2 shows the pattern in the context of arithmetic simplification. Because we want to cater for non-exhaustive matches, we use visitors with defaults [3] in the example. The Visitor trait contains for each subclass X of Expr one *case-method* named *caseX*. Every *caseX* method takes an argument of type X and yields a result of type T,

```
// Class hierarchy:
trait Visitor[T] {
    def caseMul(t: Mul): T     = otherwise(t)
    def caseNum(t: Num): T     = otherwise(t)
    def caseVar(t: Var): T     = otherwise(t)
    def otherwise(t: Expr): T  = throw new MatchError(t)
}

trait Expr {
    def matchWith[T](v: Visitor[T]): T }

class Num(val value: int) extends Expr {
    def matchWith[T](v: Visitor[T]): T = v.caseNum(this) }

class Var(val name: String) extends Expr {
    def matchWith[T](v: Visitor[T]): T = v.caseVar(this) }

class Mul(val left: Expr, val right: Expr) extends Expr {
    def matchWith[T](v: Visitor[T]): T = v.caseMul(this) }

// Simplification rule:
    e.matchWith {
        new Visitor[Expr] {
            override def caseMul(m: Mul) =
                m.right.matchWith {
                    new Visitor[Expr] {
                        override def caseNum(n: Num) =
                            if (n.value == 1) m.left else e
                        override def otherwise(e: Expr) = e
                    }
                }
            override def otherwise(e: Expr) = e
        }
    }
```

Fig. 2. Expression simplification using visitors

the generic type parameter of the Visitor class. In class Visitor every case-method has a default implementation which calls the otherwise method.

The Expr class declares a generic abstract method matchWith, which takes a visitor as argument. Instances of subclasses X implement the method by invoking the corresponding *caseX* method in the visitor object on themselves.

The second half of Figure 2 shows how visitors are used in the simplification rule. The pattern match involves one visitor object for each of the two levels of matching. (The third-level match, testing whether the right-hand operand's value is 1, uses a direct comparison). Each visitor object defines two methods: the *caseX* method corresponding to the matched class, and the otherwise method corresponding to the case where the match fails.

Evaluation: The visitor design pattern causes a relatively high notational overhead for framework construction, because a visitor class has to be defined and matchWith

```
// Class hierarchy:
trait Expr
class Num(val value : int) extends Expr
class Var(val name : String) extends Expr
class Mul(val left : Expr, val right : Expr) extends Expr
```

```
// Simplification rule:
  if (e.isInstanceOf[Mul]) {
    val m = e.asInstanceOf[Mul]
    val r = m.right
    if (r.isInstanceOf[Num]) {
      val n = r.asInstanceOf[Num]
      if (n.value == 1) m.left else e
    } else e
  } else e
```

Fig. 3. Expression simplification using type-test/type-cast

methods have to be provided in all data variants. The pattern matching itself is disciplined but very verbose, especially for deep patterns. Visitors in their standard setting do not maintain representation independence, because case methods correspond one-to-one to data alternatives. However, one could hide data representations using some ad-hoc visitor dispatch implementation in the matchWith methods. Visitors are not extensible, at least not in their standard form presented here. Neither new patterns nor new alternatives can be created without an extensive global change of the visitor framework. Extensible visitors [6] address the problem of adding new alternatives (but not the problem of adding new patterns) at the price of a more complicated framework.

2.3 Type-Test/Type-Cast

The most direct (some would say: crudest) form of decomposition uses the type-test and type-cast instructions available in Java and many other languages. Figure 3 shows arithmetic simplification using this method. In Scala, the test whether a value x is a non-null instance of some type T is expressed using the pseudo method invocation x.isInstanceOf$[T]$, with T as a type parameter. Analogously, the cast of x to T is expressed as x.asInstanceOf$[T]$. The long-winded names are chosen intentionally in order to discourage indiscriminate use of these constructs.

Evaluation: Type-tests and type-casts require zero overhead for the class hierarchy. The pattern matching itself is very verbose, for both shallow and deep patterns. In particular, every match appears as both a type-test and a subsequent type-cast. The scheme raises also the issue that type-casts are potentially unsafe because they can raise ClassCastExceptions. Type-tests and type-casts completely expose representation. They have mixed characteristics with respect to extensibility. On the one hand, one can add new variants without changing the framework (because there is nothing to be done in the framework itself). On the other hand, one cannot invent new patterns over existing variants that use the same syntax as the type-tests and type-casts.

```
// Class hierarchy:
trait Expr
class Num(val value : int) extends Expr
class Var(val name : String) extends Expr
class Mul(val left : Expr, val right : Expr) extends Expr

// Simplification rule:

e match {
  case m : Mul ⇒
    m.right match {
      case n : Num ⇒
        if (n.value == 1) m.left else e
      case _ ⇒ e
    }
  case _ ⇒ e
}
```

Fig. 4. Expression simplification using typecase

2.4 Typecase

The typecase construct accesses run-time type information in much the same way as type-tests and type-casts. It is however more concise and secure. Figure 4 shows the arithmetic simplification example using typecase. In Scala, typecase is an instance of a more general pattern matching expression of the form $expr$ **match** { $cases$ }. Each case is of the form **case** $p ⇒ b$; it consists of a pattern p and an expression or list of statements b. There are several kinds of patterns in Scala. The typecase construct uses patterns of the form $x : T$ where x is a variable and T is a type. This pattern matches all non-null values whose runtime type is (a subtype of) T. The pattern binds the variable x to the matched object. The other pattern in Figure 4 is the *wildcard pattern* _, which matches any value.

Evaluation: Pattern matching with typecase requires zero overhead for the class hierarchy. The pattern matching itself is concise for shallow patterns but becomes more verbose as patterns grow deeper, because in that case one needs to use nested *match*-expressions. Typecase completely exposes object representation. It has the same characteristics as type-test/type-cast with respect to extensibility: adding new variants poses no problems but new patterns require a different syntax.

3   Case Classes

Case classes in Scala provide convenient shorthands for constructing and analyzing data. Figure 5 presents them in the context of arithmetic simplification.

A case class is written like a normal class with a **case** modifier in front. This modifier has several effects. On the one hand, it provides a convenient notation for constructing data without having to write **new**. For instance, assuming the class hierarchy of Fig. 5, the expression Mul(Num(42), Var(x)) would be a shorthand for

// Class hierarchy:
trait Expr
case class Num(value : int) **extends** Expr
case class Var(name : String) **extends** Expr
case class Mul(left : Expr, right : Expr) **extends** Expr

// Simplification rule:
```
e match {
    case Mul(x, Num(1)) ⇒ x
    case _ ⇒ e
}
```

Fig. 5. Expression simplification using case classes

new Mul(**new** Num(42), **new** Var(x)). On the other hand, case classes allow pattern matching on their constructor. Such patterns are written exactly like constructor expressions, but are interpreted "in reverse". For instance, the pattern Mul(x, Num(1)) matches all values which are of class Mul, with a right operand of class Num which has a value field equal to 1. If the pattern matches, the variable x is bound the left operand of the given value.

Patterns
A pattern in Scala is constructed from the following elements:

- Variables such as x or right. These match any value, and bind the variable name to the value. The wildcard character _ is used as a shorthand if the value need not be named.
- Type patterns such as x : int or _ : String. These match all values of the given type, and bind the variable name to the value. Type patterns were already introduced in Section 2.4.
- Constant literals such as 1 or "abc". A literal matches only itself.
- Named constants such as None or Nil, which refer to immutable values. A named constant matches only the value it refers to.
- Constructor patterns of the form $C(p_1, \ldots, p_n)$, where C is a case class and $p_1, \ldots, p_n$ are patterns. Such a pattern matches all instances of class C which were built from values $v_1, \ldots, v_n$ matching the patterns $p_1, \ldots, p_n$.

   It is not required that the class instance is constructed directly by an invocation $C(v_1, \ldots, v_n)$. It is also possible that the value is an instance of a subclass of C, from where a super-call constructor invoked C's constructor with the given arguments. Another possibility is that the value was constructed through a secondary constructor, which in turn called the primary constructor with arguments $v_1, \ldots, v_n$. Thus, there is considerable flexibility for hiding constructor arguments from pattern matching.
- Variable binding patterns of the form $x@p$ where x is a variable and p is a pattern. Such a pattern matches the same values as p, and in addition binds the variable x to the matched value.

To distinguish variable patterns from named constants, we require that variables start with a lower-case letter whereas constants should start with an upper-case letter or special symbol. There exist ways to circumvent these restrictions: To treat a name starting with a lower-case letter as a constant, one can enclose it in back-quotes, as in **case** 'x' ⇒ ... . To treat a name starting with an upper-case letter as a variable, one can use it in a variable binding pattern, as in **case** X @ _ ⇒ ....

case (Cons(_,_), Cons(_,_)) ⇒ b1
case (Cons(_,_), Nil) ⇒ b2
case (Nil, Cons(_,_)) ⇒ b3
case (Nil, Nil) ⇒ b4

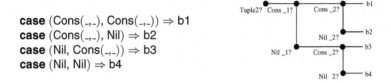

Fig. 6. Optimizing nested patterns

Optimizing Matching Expressions
A pattern match has usually several branches which each associate a pattern with a computation. For instance, a slightly more complete realistic simplification of arithmetic expressions might involve the following match:

```
t match {
    case Mul(Num(1), x) ⇒ simplify(x)
    case Mul(x, Num(1)) ⇒ simplify(x)
    case Mul(Num(0), x) ⇒ Num(0)
    case Mul(x, Num(0)) ⇒ Num(0)
    case _ ⇒ t }
```

A possible implementation for this match would be to try patterns one by one. However, this strategy would not be very efficient, because the same type tests would be performed multiple times. Evidently, one needs to test not more than once whether t matches Mul, whether the left operand is a Num, and whether the right operand is a Num. The literature on pattern matching algebraic data types discusses identification and removal of superfluous tests [27]. We adapt these results to an object-oriented setting by replacing constructor-tests with subtyping [28].

The principle is shown in Fig. 6 for a match on a pair (tuple types are explained in detail below). After preprocessing, a group of nested patterns is expressed as a decision tree. During execution of the generated code, a successful test leads to the right branch, where as a failing one proceeds downwards. If there is no down path, backtracking becomes necessary until we can move down again. If backtracking does not yield a down branch either, the whole match expression fails with a MatchError exception. Note that for this match, match failure is excluded by the _ pattern in the last case.

A vertically connected line in the decision tree marks type tests on the same value (the *selector*). This can be implemented using type-test and type-case. However, a linear sequence of type tests could be inefficient: in matches with n cases, on average $n/2$

cases might fail. For this reason, we attach integer tags to case class and translates tests on the same selector to a lookup-switch. After having switched on a tag, only a constant number of type tests (typically one) is performed on the selector. We review this decision in the performance evaluation.

Examples of Case Classes

Case classes are ubiquitous in Scala's libraries. They express lists, streams, messages, symbols, documents, and XML data, to name just a few examples. Two groups of case classes are referred to in the following section. First, there are classes representing optional values:

```
trait Option[+T]
case class Some[T](value : T) extends Option[T]
case object None extends Option[Nothing]
```

Trait Option[T] represents optional values of type T. The subclass Some[T] represents a value which is present whereas the sub-object None represents absence of a value. The '+' in the type parameter of Option indicates that optional values are covariant: if S is a subtype of T, then Option[S] is a subtype of Option[T]. The type of None is Option[Nothing], where Nothing is the bottom in Scala's type hierarchy. Because of covariance, None thus conforms to every option type.

For the purpose of pattern matching, None is treated as a named constant, just as any other singleton object. The **case** modifier of the object definition only changes some standard method implementations for None, as explained in Section 4. A typical pattern match on an optional value would be written as follows.

```
v match {
    case Some(x) ⇒ "do something with x"
    case None ⇒ "handle missing value"
}
```

Option types are recommended in Scala as a safer alternative to **null**. Unlike with **null**, it is not possible to accidentally assume that a value is present since an optional type must be matched to access its contents.

Tuples are another group of standard case classes in Scala. All tuple classes are of the form:

```
case class Tuplei[T1, ..., Ti](_1 : T1, ..., _i : Ti)
```

There's also an abbreviated syntax: $(T_1, ..., T_i)$ means the same as the tuple type Tuple$i[T_1, ..., T_i]$ and analogous abbreviations exist for expressions and patterns.

Evaluation: Pattern matching with case classes requires no notational overhead for the class hierarchy. As in functional programming languages, the matching code is concise for shallow as well as nested patterns. However, also as in functional programmin, case classes expose object representation. They have mixed characteristics with respect

284 B. Emir, M. Odersky, and J. Williams

to extensibility. Adding new variants is straightforward. However, it is not possible to define new kinds of patterns, since patterns are in a one to one correspondence with (the types of) case classes. This shortcoming is eliminated when case classes are paired with extractors.

4 Extractors

An extractor provides a way for defining a pattern without a case class. A simple example is the following object Twice which enables patterns of even numbers:

```
object Twice {
    def apply(x :Int) = x∗2
    def unapply(z :Int) = if(z%2==0) Some(z/2) else None
}
```

This object defines an apply function, which provides a new way to write integers: Twice(x) is now an alias for x ∗ 2. Scala uniformly treats objects with apply methods as functions, inserting the call to apply implicitly. Thus, Twice(x) is really a shorthand for Twice.apply(x).

The unapply method in Twice reverses the construction in a pattern match. It tests its integer argument z. If z is even, it returns Some(z/2). If it is odd, it returns None. The unapply method is implicitly applied in a pattern match, as in the following example, which prints "42 is two times 21":

```
val x = Twice(21)
x match {
    case Twice(y) ⇒ Console.println(x+" is two times "+y)
    case _ ⇒ Console.println("x is odd") }
```

In this example, apply is called an *injection*, because it takes an argument and yields an element of a given type. unapply is called an *extraction*, because it extracts parts of the given type. Injections and extractions are often grouped together in one object, because then one can use the object's name for both a constructor and a pattern, which simulates the convention for pattern matching with case classes. However, it is also possible to define an extraction in an object without a corresponding injection. The object itself is often called an *extractor*, independently of the fact whether it has an apply method or not.

It may be desirable to write injections and extractions that satisfy the equality F.unapply(F.apply(x)) == Some(x), but we do not require any such condition on user-defined methods. One is free to write extractions that have no associated injection or that can handle a wider range of data types.

Patterns referring to extractors look just like patterns referring to case classes, but they are implemented differently. Matching against an extractor pattern like Twice(x) involves a call to Twice.unapply(x), followed by a test of the resulting optional value. The code in the preceding example would thus be expanded as follows:

```
val x = Twice.apply(21)   // x = 42
Twice.unapply(x) match {
  case Some(y) ⇒ Console.println(x+" is two times "+y)
  case None ⇒ Console.println("x is odd")
}
```

Extractor patterns can also be defined with numbers of arguments different from one. A nullary pattern corresponds to an unapply method returning a boolean. A pattern with more than one element corresponds to an unapply method returning an optional tuple. The result of an extraction plays the role of a "representation-object", whose constituents (if any) can be bound or matched further with nested pattern matches.

Pattern matching in Scala is loosely typed, in the sense that the type of a pattern does not restrict the set of legal types of the corresponding selector value. The same principle applies to extractor patterns. For instance, it would be possible to match a value of Scala's root type Any with the pattern Twice(y). In that case, the call to Twice.unapply(x) is preceded by a type test whether the argument x has type int. If x is not an int, the pattern match would fail without executing the unapply method of Twice. This choice is convenient, because it avoids many type tests in unapply methods which would otherwise be necessary. It is also crucial for a good treatment of parameterized class hierarchies, as will be explained in Section 6.

Representation Independence
Unlike case-classes, extractors can be used to hide data representations. As an example consider the following trait of complex numbers, implemented by case class Cart, which represents numbers by Cartesian coordinates.

```
trait Complex
case class Cart(re: double, im: double) extends Complex
```

Complex numbers can be constructed and decomposed using the syntax Cart(r, i). The following injector/extractor object provides an alternative access with polar coordinates:

```
object Polar {
  def apply(mod: double, arg: double): Complex =
    new Cart(mod * Math.cos(arg), mod * Math.sin(arg))

  def unapply(z: Complex): Option[(double, double)] = z match {
    case Cart(re, im) ⇒
      val at = atan(im / re)
      Some(sqrt(re * re + im * im),
           if (re < 0) at + Pi else if (im < 0) at + Pi * 2 else at)
  }
}
```

With this definition, a client can now alternatively use polar coordinates such as Polar(m, e) in value construction and pattern matching.

```scala
// Class hierarchy:
trait Term
class Num(val value: int) extends Term
class Var(val name: String) extends Term
class Mul(val left: Term, val right: Term) extends Term

object Num {
  def apply(value: int) = new Num(value)
  def unapply(n: Num) = Some(n.value)
}
object Var {
  def apply(name: String) = new Var(name)
  def unapply(v: Var) = Some(v.name)
}
object Mul {
  def apply(left: Term, right: Term) = new Mul(left, right)
  def unapply(m: Mul) = Some (m.left, m.right)
}

// Simplification rule:

  e match {
    case Mul(x, Num(1)) ⇒ x
    case _ ⇒ e
  }
```

Fig. 7. Expression simplification using extractors

Arithmetic Simplification Revisited

Figure 7 shows the arithmetic simplification example using extractors. The simplification rule is exactly the same as in Figure 5. But instead of case classes, we now define normal classes with one injector/extractor object per each class. The injections are not strictly necessary for this example; their purpose is to let one write constructors in the same way as for case classes.

Even though the class hierarchy is the same for extractors and case classes, there is an important difference regarding program evolution. A library interface might expose only the objects Num, Var, and Mul, but not the corresponding classes. That way, one can replace or modify any or all of the classes representing arithmetic expressions without affecting client code.

Note that every X.unapply extraction method takes an argument of the alternative type X, not the common type Term. This is possible because an implicit type test gets added when matching on a term. However, a programmer may choose to provide a type test himself:

```scala
  def unapply(x: Term) = x match {
    case m:Mul ⇒ Some {m.left, m.right}
    case _ ⇒ None
  }
```

```
class Mul(_left: Expr, _right: Expr) extends Expr {
    // Accessors for constructor arguments
    def left = _left
    def right = _right

    // Standard methods
    override def equals(other: Any) = other match {
        case m: Mul ⇒ left.equals(m.left) && right.equals(m.right)
        case _ ⇒ false
    }
    override def hashCode = hash(this.getClass, left.hashCode, right.hashCode)
    override def toString = "Mul("+left+", "+right+")"
}
object Mul {
    def apply(left: Expr, right: Expr) = new Mul(left, right)
    def unapply(m: Mul) = Some(m.left, m.right)
}
```

Fig. 8. Expansion of case class Mul

This removes the target type from the interface, more effectively hiding the underlying representation.

Evaluation: Extractors require a relatively high notational overhead for framework construction, because extractor objects have to be defined alongside classes. The pattern matching itself is as concise as for case-classes, for both shallow and deep patterns. Extractors can maintain complete representation independence. They allow easy extensions by both new variants and new patterns, since patterns are resolved to user-defined methods.

Case Classes and Extractors
For the purposes of type-checking, a case class can be seen as syntactic sugar for a normal class together with an injector/extractor object. This is exemplified in Figure 8, where a syntactic desugaring of the following case class is shown:

case class Mul(left: Expr, right: Expr) **extends** Expr

Given a class C, the expansion adds accessor methods for all constructor parameters to C. It also provides specialized implementations of the methods equals, hashCode and toString inherited from class Object. Furthermore, the expansion defines an object with the same name as the class (Scala defines different name spaces for types and terms; so it is legal to use the same name for an object and a class). The object contains an injection method apply and an extraction method unapply. The injection method serves as a factory; it makes it possible to create objects of class C writing simply $C(\ldots)$ without a preceding **new**. The extraction method reverses the construction process. Given an argument of class C, it returns a tuple of all constructor parameters, wrapped in a Some.

However, in the current Scala implementation case classes are left unexpanded, so the above description is only conceptual. The current Scala implementation also compiles pattern matching over case classes into more efficient code than pattern matching using extractors. One reason for this is that different case classes are known not to overlap, i.e. given two patterns $C(\ldots)$ and $D(\ldots)$ where C and D are different case classes, we know that at most one of the patterns can match. The same cannot be assured for different extractors. Hence, case classes allow better factoring of multiple deep patterns.

5   Performance Evaluation

In this section, we measure relative performance of the presented approaches, using three micro-benchmarks. All benchmarks presented here were carried out on a Pentium 4 machine running Ubuntu GNU/Linux operating system using the HotSpot server VM and Sun's JDK 1.5 and the Scala distribution v2.3.1. They can be run on any runtime environment supported by the Scala compiler and are available on the first author's website. The BASE benchmark establishes how the techniques perform for a single pattern. The DEPTH benchmark shows how factoring out common cases affects performance. Finally, the BREADTH benchmarks tests how the number of alternatives affects performance. Since typecase is equivalent cast after translation, we do not list it separately in the benchmarks.

BASE Performance

We assess base performance by running the arithmetic simplification rule from the introduction. This benchmark measures execution time of $2 * 10^7$ successful matches, in milliseconds. The simplification is not applied recursively.

The results are given below. They are graphically represented in the left half of Fig. 9. We use the abbreviations oo for object-oriented decomposition, vis for visitor, cast for test-and-cast, ccls for case classes, ext for extractors returning tuples. Finally, ext+ shows extractors in a modified example where classes extend product interfaces, such that the extraction can return the same object and avoid constructing a tuple.

Discussion: No difference is observed between the object-oriented, test-and-cast and case class approaches. The visitor and the extractor approaches suffer from having to create new objects. In ext+, we diminish this penalty by making the data classes implement the Product2 interface and returning the same object instead of a tuple.

The DEPTH Benchmark

When several patterns are tested side-by-side, a lot of time can be saved by factoring out common tests in nested patterns. If this is done by hand, the resulting code becomes hard to read and hard to maintain.

This benchmark measures execution time of 10^5 applications of several arithmetic simplification rules that are applied side-by-side and recursively. The results are graphed in the right side of Fig. 9.

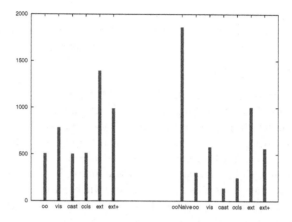

Fig. 9. Results on BASE and DEPTH benchmarks, in ms

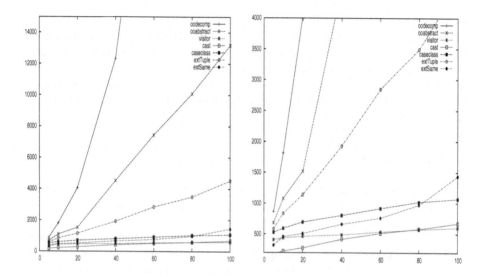

Fig. 10. Diagrams for BREADTH benchmark

Discussion: The ooNaive column shows that a readable, semantically equivalent program with redundant type tests can be 6 times slower than the hand-optimized oo version. But cast and ccls improve on both. Again, vis, ext and ext+ suffer from object
construction. After factoring out common tests and removing object construction, ext+
is twice as fast as ext and on a par with vis.

The BREADTH Benchmark

Finally, we study how performance of a pattern match is related to the number of cases
in a matching expression. For a fixed number n, the BREADTH benchmark defines n

generated subclass variants and a matching expression that covers all cases. Applying the match 25000 times on each term of a list of 500 randomly generated terms yields the result (the terms and the order are the same for all approaches). The data is shown in Fig. 10 using two scales.

Discussion: Chained if-statements used by oodecomp fail $n/2$ on average. We also see that ooabstract that dispatching to a virtual method in an abstract class is faster than to one in an interface. The visitor approach vis is predictably unaffected by the number of cases, because it uses double-dispatch. Surprisingly, cast performs on a par with vis. It seems that HotSpot recognizes sequences of type-tests as an idiom and translates it efficiently. Unaware of this VM optimization, we tried to achieve the same using integer tags caseclass on which we switch before doing the instanceOf. Extractions returning new tuples as results extTuple are affected negatively, but still outperform object-oriented decomposition. Finally, saving on object constructions in extSame achieves performance similar to caseclass.

Summary

The results show that the HotSpot VM is good at optimizing the output resulting from translation of pattern matching. While providing for much more readable code, case classes and unapply methods in long-running computations have performance that is not inferior to the performance of standard techniques. Hotspot optimizes sequences of type tests, which shows that we can reconsider our implementation strategy to take advantage of this fact.

6   Parametricity

Up to now, we have studied only hierarchies of monomorphic classes. The problem becomes more interesting once we consider classes with type parameters. An example is the typed evaluator for lambda expressions given in Figure 11.

There is an abstract base trait Term with subclasses Var for variables, Num for numbers, Lam for lambda abstractions, App for function applications, and Suc for a pre-defined successor function. The abstract base trait is now parameterized with the type of the term in question. The parameters of subclasses vary. For instance Var is itself generic with the same type parameter as Term, whereas Num is a Term of int, and Lam is a Term of b $\Rightarrow$ c where both b and c are type parameters of Lam.

The challenge is now how to write – in a statically type-safe way – an evaluation function that maps a term of type Term[a] and an environment to a value of type a. Similar questions have been explored in the context of "generalized algebraic data types" (GADT's) in functional languages such as Haskell [29] and Omega [30]. Kennedy and Russo [12] have introduced techniques to simulate GADT's in an extension of C# using visitors and equational constraints on parameters. We show here how GADT's can be simulated using typecase as the decomposition technique. This provides a new perspective on the essence of GADTs by characterizing them as a framework for exploiting

```
//Class hierarchy
trait Term[a]
class Var[a]    (val name : String)                    extends Term[a]
class Num       (val value : int)                      extends Term[int]
class Lam[b, c] (val x : Var[b], val e : Term[c])      extends Term[b ⇒ c]
class App[b, c] (val f : Term[b ⇒ c], val e : Term[b]extends Term[c]
class Suc       ()                                     extends Term[int ⇒ int]

// Environments:
abstract class Env {
  def apply[a](v : Var[a]): a

  def extend[a](v : Var[a], x : a) = new Env {
    def apply[b](w : Var[b]): b = w match {
      case _: v.type ⇒ x        // v eq w, hence a = b
      case _ ⇒ Env.this.apply(w)
}}}

object empty extends Env {
  def apply[a](x : Var[a]): a = throw new Error("not found: "+x.name) }

// Evaluation:
def eval[a](t : Term[a], env : Env): a = t match {
  case v : Var[b]   ⇒ env(v)                              // a = b
  case n : Num      ⇒ n.value                             // a = int
  case i : Suc      ⇒ { y : int ⇒ y + 1 }                 // a = int ⇒ int
  case f : Lam[b, c] ⇒ { y : b ⇒ eval(f.e, env.extend(f.x, y)) } // a = b ⇒ c
  case a : App[b, c] ⇒ eval(a.f, env)(eval(a.e, env))     // a = c
}
```

Fig. 11. Typed evaluation of simply-typed lambda calculus

type-overlaps. It goes beyond previous work by also providing a way to write update-able polymorphic functions. Such functions are used in several forms in denotational and operational semantics, for instance they can implement stores or environments.

Figure 11 shows an evaluation function eval which uses typecase for pattern matching its term argument t. The first observation from studying this function is that we need to generalize our previous concept of a typed pattern. Given a term of type Term[a] and pattern of form f : App[...], what type arguments should be provided? In fact, looking at a term's static type we can determine only the second type argument of App (which must be equal to a), but not the first one. The first type argument needs to be a fresh, completely undetermined type constant. We express this by extending the syntax in a type pattern:

A type pattern can now consist of types and *type variables*. As for normal patterns, we have the convention that type variables start with a lower-case letter whereas references to existing types should start with an upper-case letter. (The primitive types int, char, boolean, *etc* are excepted from this rule; they are treated as type references, not variables).

However, Scala currently does not keep run-time type information beyond the top-level class, i.e. it uses the same erasure module for generics as Java 1.5. Therefore, all type arguments in a pattern must be type variables. Normally, a type variable represents a fresh, unknown type, much like the type variable of an opened existential type. We enforce that the scope of such type variables does not escape a pattern matching clause. For instance, the following would be illegal:

```
def headOfAny(x: Any) = x match {
    case xs : List[a] ⇒ xs.head  // error: type variable 'a' escapes its scope as
}                                 // part of the type of 'xs.head'
```

The problem above can be cured by ascribing to the right-hand side of the case clause a weaker type, which does not mention the type variable. Example:

```
def headOfAny(x: Any): Any = x match {
    case xs : List[a] ⇒ xs.head  // OK, xs.head is inferred to have type 'Any', the
}                                 // explicitly given return type of 'headOfAny'
```

In the examples above, type variables in patterns were treated as fresh type constants. However, there are cases where the Scala type system is able to infer that a pattern-bound type variable is an alias for an existing type. An example is the first case in the eval function in Figure 11.

```
def eval[a](t: Term[a], env: Env): a = t match {
    case v : Var[b]    ⇒ env(v) ...
```

Here, the term t of type Term[a] is matched against the pattern v :Var[b]. From the class hierarchy, we know that Var extends Term with the same type argument, so we can deduce that b must be a type alias for a. It is essential to do so, because the right-hand side of the pattern has type b, whereas the expected result type of the eval function is a. Aliased type variables are also not subject to the scoping rules of fresh type variables, because they can always be replaced by their alias.

A symmetric situation is found in the next case of the eval function:

```
case n : Num ⇒ n
```

Here, the type system deduces that the type parameter a of eval is an alias of int. It must be, because class Num extends Term[int], so if a was any other type but int, the Num pattern could not have matched the value t, which is of type Term[a]. Because a is now considered to be an alias of int, the right-hand side of the case can be shown to conform to eval's result type.

Why is such a reasoning sound? Here is the crucial point: the fact that a pattern matched a value tells us something about the type variables in the types of both. Specifically, it tells us that there is a non-null value which has both the static type of the selector and the static type of the pattern. In other words, the two types must *overlap*. Of course, in a concrete program run, the pattern might not match the selector value, so any deductions we can draw from type overlaps must be restricted to the pattern-matching case in question.

We now formalize this reasoning in the following algorithm **overlap-aliases**. Given two types t_1, t_2 which are known to overlap, the algorithm yields a set $\mathcal{E}$ of equations of the form $a = t$ where a is a type variable in t_1 or t_2 and t is a type.

Algorithm: overlap-aliases

The algorithm consists of two phases. In the first phase, a set of type equalities is computed. In the second phase, these equalities are rewritten to solved form, with only type variables on the left-hand side. We consider the following subset of Scala types:

1. Type variables or parameters, a.
2. Class types of form $p.C[\bar{t}]$. Here, p is a *path*, i.e. an immutable reference to some object, C names a class which is a member of the object denoted by p, and $\bar{t}$ is a (possibly empty) list of type arguments for C.
3. Singleton types of form $p.\textbf{type}$ where p is a path. This type denotes the set of values consisting just of the object denoted by p.

Every type t has a set of basetypes denoted $\textbf{basetypes}(t)$. This is the smallest set of types which includes t itself, and which satisfies the following closure conditions:

- if t is a type variable with upper bound u, $\textbf{basetypes}(t) \subseteq \textbf{basetypes}(u)$,
- if t is a singleton type $p.\textbf{type}$, where p has type u, $\textbf{basetypes}(t) \subseteq \textbf{basetypes}(u)$,
- if t is a class type $p.C[\bar{u}]$, $\textbf{basetypes}(t)$ includes all types in the transitive supertype relation of t [31].

The class extension rules of Scala ensure that the set of basetypes of a type is always finite. Furthermore, it is guaranteed that if $p.C[\bar{t}]$ and $q.C[\bar{u}]$ are both in the basetypes of some type t', then the two prefix paths are the same and corresponding type arguments are also the same, i.e. $p = q$ and $\bar{t} = \bar{u}$.

This property underlies the first phase of the algorithm, which computes an initial set of type equalities $\mathcal{E}$:

$$
\begin{aligned}
&\textbf{for} - \textbf{all } t \text{ of form } p.C[\bar{t}] \in \textbf{basetypes}(t_1) \\
&\quad \textbf{for} - \textbf{all } u \text{ of form } q.D[\bar{u}] \in \textbf{basetypes}(t_2) \\
&\qquad \textbf{if } C = D \\
&\qquad\quad \mathcal{E} := \mathcal{E} \cup \{t = u\}
\end{aligned}
$$

The second phase repeatedly rewrites equalities in $\mathcal{E}$ with the following rules, until no more rules can be applied.

$$
\begin{aligned}
p.C[\bar{t}] = q.C[\bar{u}] \quad &\longrightarrow \quad \{p = q\} \cup \{\bar{t} = \bar{u}\} \\
p = q \quad &\longrightarrow \quad t = u \qquad\qquad \textbf{if } p : t, q : u \\
t = a \quad &\longrightarrow \quad a = t \qquad\qquad \textbf{if } t \text{ is not a type variable}
\end{aligned}
$$

Note that intermediate results of the rewriting can be path equalities as well as type equalities. A path equality $p = q$ is subsequently eliminated by rewriting it to a type equality between the types of the two paths p and q.   □

Returning to the type-safe evaluation example, consider the first clause in function eval. The type of the selector is Term[a], the type of the pattern is Var[b]. The basetypes of these two types have both an element with Term as the class; for Var[b] the basetype is Term[b], whereas for Term[a] it is Term[a] itself. Hence, the algorithm yields the equation Term[b] = Term[a] and by propagation b = a.

Now consider the second clause in function eval, where the type of the pattern is Num. A basetype of Num is Term[int], hence **overlap-aliases**(Num, Term[a]) yields the equation Term[int] = Term[a], and by propagation a = int.

As a third example, consider the final clause of eval, where the type of the pattern is App[b, c]. This type has Term[c] as a basetype, hence the invocation **overlap-aliases**(App[b, c], Term[a]) yields the equation Term[c] = Term[a], and by propagation c = a. By contrast, the variable b in the pattern rests unbound; that is, it constitutes a fresh type constant.

In each case, the overlap of the selector type and the pattern type gives us the correct constraints to be able to type-check the corresponding case clause. Hence, the type-safe evaluation function needs no type-cast other than the ones implied by the decomposing pattern matches.

Polymorphic Updateable Functions

The evaluator in question uses environments as functions which map lambda-bound variables to their types. In fact we believe it is the first type-safe evaluator to do so. Previous type-safe evaluators written in Haskell [29], Omega [30] and extended C# [12] used lambda expressions with DeBrujn numbers and represented environments as tuples rather than functions.

In Figure 11, environments are modeled by a class Env with an abstract polymorphic apply method. Since functions are represented in Scala as objects with apply methods, instances of this class are equivalent to polymorphic functions of type $\forall a.\text{Var[a]} \Rightarrow a$. Environments are built from an object empty representing an empty environment and a method extend which extends an environment by a new variable/value pair. Every environment has the form

$$\text{empty.extend}(v_1, x_1). \dots .\text{extend}(v_n, x_n)$$

for $n \geq 0$, where each v_i is a variable of type $\text{Var}[T_i]$ and each x_i is a value of type T_i.

The empty object is easy to define; its apply method throws an exception every time it is called. The implementation of the extend method is more difficult, because it has to maintain the universal polymorphism of environments. Consider an extension env.extend(v, x), where v has type Var[a] and x has type a. What should the apply method of this extension be? The type of this method is $\forall b.\text{Var[b]} \Rightarrow b$. The idea is that apply compares its argument w (of type Var[b]) to the variable v. If the two are the same, the value to return is x. Otherwise the method delegates its task by calling the apply method of the outer environment env with the same argument. The first case is represented by the following case clause:

case _: v.**type** $\Rightarrow$ x .

This clause matches a selector of type Var[b] against the singleton type v.**type**. The latter has Var[a] as a basetype, where a is the type parameter of the enclosing extend method. Hence, **overlap-aliases**(v.**type**, Var[b]) yields Var[a] = Var[b] and by propagation a = b. Therefore, the case clause's right hand side x of type a is compatible with the apply method's declared result type b. In other words, type-overlap together with singleton types lets us express the idea that if two references are the same, their types must be the same as well.

A pattern match with a singleton type p.**type** is implemented by comparing the selector value with the path p. The pattern matches if the two are equal. The comparison operation to be used for this test is reference equality (expressed in Scala as eq). If we had used user-definable equality instead (which is expressed in Scala as == and which corresponds to Java's equals), the type system would become unsound. To see this, consider a definition of equals in some class which equates members of different classes. In that case, a succeeding pattern match does no longer imply that the selector type must overlap with the pattern type.

Parametric Case-Classes and Extractors

Type overlaps also apply to the other two pattern matching constructs of Scala, case-classes and extractors. The techniques are essentially the same. A class constructor pattern $C(p_1, ..., p_m)$ for a class C with type parameters $a_1, \ldots, a_n$ is first treated as if it was a type pattern $\_: C[a_1, \ldots a_n]$. Once that pattern is typed and aliases for the type variables $a_1, \ldots, a_n$ are computed using algorithm **overlap-aliases**, the types of the component patterns $(p_1, ..., p_m)$ are computed recursively. Similarly, if the pattern $C(p_1, ..., p_n)$ refers to a extractor of form

```
object C {
  def unapply[a₁, ..., aₙ](x : T) ...
  ...
},
```

it is treated as if it was the type pattern $\_: T$. Note that T would normally contain type variables $a_1, \ldots, a_n$.

As an example, here is another version of the evaluation function of simply-typed lambda calculus, which assumes either a hierarchy of case-classes or extractors for every alternative (the formulation of eval is the same in each case).

```
def eval[a](t : Term[a], env : Env): a = t match {
  case v @ Var(name)     ⇒ env(v)
  case Num(value)        ⇒ value
  case Suc               ⇒ { y : int ⇒ y + 1 }
  case Lam(x : Var[b], e) ⇒ { y : b ⇒ eval(e, env.extend(x, y)) }
  case App(f, e)         ⇒ eval(f, env)(eval(e, env)) }
```

7 Conclusion

We described and evaluated six techniques for object-oriented pattern matching along nine criteria. The evaluations of the preceding sections are summarized in Table 1. The table classifies each technique for each criterion in three categories. We should empha-size that this is more a snapshot than a definitive judgment of the different techniques. All evaluations come from a single language on a single platform, with two closely

Table 1. Evaluation summary

	oodecomp	visitor	test/cast	typecase	caseclass	extractor
Conciseness						
framework	−	−	+	+	+	−
shallow matches	o	−	−	+	+	+
deep matches	−	−	−	o	+	+
Maintainability						
representation independence	+	o	−	−	−	+
extensibility/variants	−	−	+	+	+	+
extensibility/patterns	+	−	−	−	−	+
Performance						
base case	+	o	+	+	+	−
scalability/breath	−	+	+	+	+	−
scalability/depth	−	o	+	+	+	−

related implementations. Conciseness might vary for languages with a syntax different from Scala. Performance comparisons might be different on other platforms, in particular if there is no JIT compiler.

However, the evaluations can serve for validating Scala's constructs for pattern matching. They show that case classes and extractors together perform well in all of the criteria. That is, every criterion is satisfied by either case-classes or extractors, or both. What is more, case-classes and extractors work well together. One can conceptualize a case class as syntactic sugar for a normal class with an injector/extractor object, which is implemented in a particularly efficient way. One can also switch between case classes and extractors without affecting pattern-matching client code. The typecase construct plays also an important role as the type-theoretic foundation of pattern matching in the presence of parametricity. Extractor matching generally involves implicit pattern matches with type patterns. Typecase is thus useful as the basic machinery on which the higher-level constructs of case classes and extractors are built.

Acknowledgments. We thank Craig Chambers, William Cook, Christian Plesner Hansen, and Urs Hölzle for discussions about previous pattern matching constructs, which led to the extractor design described here. We thank Don Syme for discussing the fine points of active patterns. Andrew Kennedy and Lex Spoon provided feedback on a previous version of the paper.

References

1. Moreau, P.E., Ringeissen, C., Vittek, M.: A Pattern Matching Compiler for Multiple Target Languages. In: Hedin, G. (ed.) CC 2003 and ETAPS 2003. LNCS, vol. 2622, pp. 61–76. Springer, Heidelberg (2003)
2. Oderksy, M., Wadler, P.: Pizza into Java: Translating theory into practice. In: Proc. of Principles of Programming Languages (POPL) (1997)
3. Zenger, M., Odersky, M.: Extensible Algebraic Datatypes with Defaults. In: Proc. of Int. Conference on Functional Programming (ICFP) (2001)

4. Liu, J., Myers, A.C.: JMatch: Iterable Abstract Pattern Matching for Java. In: Dahl, V., Wadler, P. (eds.) PADL 2003. LNCS, vol. 2562, pp. 110–127. Springer, Heidelberg (2002)
5. Cook, W.: Object-oriented programming versus abstract data types. In: de Bakker, J.W., Rozenberg, G., de Roever, W.-P. (eds.) Foundations of Object-Oriented Languages. LNCS, vol. 489, Springer, Heidelberg (1991)
6. Krishnamurthi, S., Felleisen, M., Friedman, D.P.: Synthesizing Object-Oriented and Functional Design to Promote Re-use. In: Jul, E. (ed.) ECOOP 1998. LNCS, vol. 1445, Springer, Heidelberg (1998)
7. Torgersen, M.: The expression problem revisited. In: Odersky, M. (ed.) ECOOP 2004. LNCS, vol. 3086, Springer, Heidelberg (2004)
8. Zenger, M., Odersky, M.: Independently Extensible Solutions to the Expression Problem. In: Workshop on Foundations of Object-Oriented Languages (FOOL) (2005)
9. Williams, J.: (April 2006), `http://article.gmane.org/gmane.comp.lang.scala/1993`
10. Syme, D.: `http://blogs.msdn.com/dsyme/archive/2006/08/16/activepatterns.aspx`
11. Xi, H., Chen, C., Chen, G.: Guarded recursive datatype constructors. In: Proc. of Principles of Programming Languages (POPL), January 2003, New Orleans, pp. 224–235 (2003)
12. Kennedy, A., Russo, C.: Generalized Algebraic Data Types and Object-Oriented Programming. In: Proc. of Object-Oriented Programming Systems and Languages (OOPSLA) (2005)
13. Lee, K., LaMarca, A., Chambers, C.: HydroJ: Object-oriented Pattern Matching for Evolvable Distributed Systems. In: Proc. of Object-Oriented Programming Systems and Languages (OOPSLA) (2003)
14. Gapeyev, V., Pierce, B.C.: Regular Object Types. In: Cardelli, L. (ed.) ECOOP 2003. LNCS, vol. 2743, Springer, Heidelberg (2003)
15. Chin, B., Millstein, T.: Responders: Language Support for Interactive Applications. In: Thomas, D. (ed.) ECOOP 2006. LNCS, vol. 4067, Springer, Heidelberg (2006)
16. Castagna, G., Ghelli, G., Longo, G.: A Calculus for Overloaded Functions with Subtyping. In: Lisp and Functional Programming, June 1992, pp. 182–192 (1992)
17. Chambers, C.: Object-Oriented Multi-Methods in Cecil. In: Madsen, O.L. (ed.) ECOOP 1992. LNCS, vol. 615, pp. 33–56. Springer, Heidelberg (1992)
18. Millstein, T., Bleckner, C., Chambers, C.: Modular typechecking for hierarchically extensible datatypes and functions. ACM Transactions on Programming Languages and Systems (TOPLAS) 26(5), 836–889 (2004)
19. Clifton, C., Millstein, T., Leavens, G.T., Chambers, C.: MultiJava: Design Rationale, Compiler Implementation, and Applications. ACM Transactions on Programming Languages and Systems 28(3), 517–575 (2006)
20. Ernst, M., Kaplan, C., Chambers, C.: Predicate dispatching: unified theory of dispatch. In: Jul, E. (ed.) ECOOP 1998. LNCS, vol. 1445, pp. 186–211. Springer, Heidelberg (1998)
21. Millstein, T.: Practical Predicate Dispatch. In: Proc. of Object-Oriented Programming Systems and Languages (OOPSLA), pp. 245–364 (2004)
22. Wadler, P.: Views: A way for pattern matching to cohabit with data abstraction. In: Proc. of Principles of Programming Languages (POPL) (1987)
23. Okasaki, C.: Views for Standard ML. In: SIGPLAN Workshop on ML, pp. 14–23 (1998)
24. Erwig, M.: Active patterns. In: Kluge, W. (ed.) IFL 1996. LNCS, vol. 1268, pp. 21–40. Springer, Heidelberg (1997)
25. Gostanza, P.P., Pena, R., Nunez, M.M.: A new look at pattern matching in abstract data types. In: Proceedings of Int. Conference on Functional Programming (ICFP) (1996)
26. Gamma, E., Helm, R., Johnson, R., Vlissides, J.: Design Patterns. Addison-Wesley, Reading (1995)

27. Fessant, F.L., Maranget, L.: Optimizing pattern matching. In: Proc. of International Conference on Functional Programming (ICFP), pp. 26–37 (2001)
28. Emir, B.: Translating Pattern Matching in a Java-like Language. In: Proc. of Third International Kyrgyz Conference on Computers and Electronics (IKECCO) (2005)
29. Weirich, S.: A statically type-safe typechecker for haskell. Manuscript, communicated at Dagstuhl seminar, September 2004 (unpublished)
30. Pasalic, E., Linger, N.: Meta-programming with typed object-language representations. In: Proc. of Generative Programming and Component Engineering (GPCE) (October 2004)
31. Cremet, V., Garillot, F., Lenglet, S., Odersky, M.: A core calculus for scala type checking. In: Proc. of Mathematical Foundations for Computer Science (MFCS) (2006)

DirectFlow: A Domain-Specific Language for Information-Flow Systems

Chuan-kai Lin and Andrew P. Black

Department of Computer Science
Portland State University
{cklin,black}@cs.pdx.edu

Abstract. Programs that process streams of information are commonly built by assembling reusable *information-flow components*. In some systems the components must be chosen from a pre-defined set of primitives; in others the programmer can create new custom components using a general-purpose programming language.

Neither approach is ideal: restricting programmers to a set of primitive components limits the expressivity of the system, while allowing programmers to define new components in a general-purpose language makes it difficult or impossible to reason about the composite system. We advocate defining information-flow components in a domain-specific language (DSL) that enables us to infer the properties of the components and of the composed system; this provides us with a good compromise between analysability and expressivity.

This paper presents DirectFlow, which comprises a DSL, a compiler and a runtime system. The language allows programmers to define objects that implement information-flow components without specifying how messages are sent and received. The compiler generates Java classes by inferring the message sends and methods, while the run-time library constructs information-flow networks by composition of DSL-defined components with standard components.

1 Introduction

Systems that stream information continuously from source to sink are commonplace; examples include software routers for network traffic [1], data stream query systems [2], surveillance systems, real-rate video streaming [3], and highway loop detector data analysis [4]. Hart and Martinez survey more than 50 current examples of environmental sensor networks, and argue that the ability to construct systems that stream environmental data continuously from the field to the scientists' laboratories will revolutionize earth system science [5]. We refer to this wide class of systems as information flow applications.

A popular strategy for building information-flow applications is by composing reusable components. Systems based on this strategy include Aurora [2], the Click modular router [1], Krasic's media streaming system [3], StreamIt [6], Spidle [7], and our own Infopipes system [4,8]. In these systems, each component has a set of input ports (inports) and output ports (outports), which connect to information flows. Since each application has distinct data-processing

E. Ernst (Ed.): ECOOP 2007, LNAI 4609, pp. 299–322, 2007.
© Springer-Verlag Berlin Heidelberg 2007

requirements, many information-flow programming systems allow programmers to define custom components.

In component-based systems, programmers construct an information-flow application by connecting the ports of components with channels, which specify the flow of data packets. In an object-oriented program, message sends directly determine how the thread of control passes between objects. In contrast, a channel connecting two ports determines only how data packets flow: it says nothing (directly) about how the thread passes between components. Control may pass from upstream to downstream or the other way around: the choice depends on not only the nature of the connected components, but also the context in which the components appear. These dependencies make managing the control flow of an information-flow application a difficult and labor-intensive task: the relationship between a component's data-flow behaviour and its control-flow interaction with other components is understood only for linear components [9]. Moreover, the context-sensitivity of components means that a local code change may have a great influence on the global control-flow.

Manually managing the control flow distracts programmers from organizing the data flow in an application, and a practical information-flow programming system should relieve programmers of this burden with the following feature:

F0. *Automatic invocation of components.* The system should handle the invocation of components in response to runtime data flow. The programmer should not have to specify how a component invokes, or is invoked by, neighboring components.

In addition to this software-engineering feature, we will argue that a practical information-flow programming system should also support the following three *information-flow* features:

F1. *Expressive custom components.* The system should allow the creation of custom components with multiple inports and outports that can add packets to or remove packets from a flow.
F2. *Control over data-transfer latency between components.* The system should connect components with unbuffered channels to avoid introducing arbitrary latency between components.
F3. *Choice of processing mode.* Two different modes of processing are possible: data-driven processing invokes a component when a data packet arrives at one of its inports, while demand-driven processing invokes a component when a data request arrives at one of its outports. The system should allow both modes of processing to coexist in one application.

Unfortunately, no previous information flow systems support all four features F0–F3 because this rich combination of features can allow programmers to connect components in a way that has no reasonable implementation.

In this article we describe DirectFlow, which does support all four features. How do we achieve this? DirectFlow allows programmers to define custom components using a domain-specific language (DSL). The DirectFlow compiler checks the DSL modules to see if they satisfy a context condition (discussed in Sect. 3.2). If they do, the compiler generates one or more Java classes for each module. The DirectFlow runtime system allows programmers to compose these custom components with standard library components; further consistency checks are applied at composition time. The effect of the checks is to eliminate unimplementable pipelines. The composed pipeline is then instantiated in a set-up phase, and can finally be used in an ordinary Java program to perform information-flow processing tasks.

In Sect. 2 we fill-in some background about the four features listed above and explain why it is hard to support them all. The DirectFlow domain-specific language is described in Sect. 3. Section 4 describes the way that we ascertain the possible processing modes for the components defined in the DSL, and how we generate Java code. Section 5 discusses the DirectFlow Framework, which brings together library code, generated Java code, and hand-crafted Java code into deployable pipelines.

The specific technical contributions of this work are as follows:

- A CSP-inspired programming model that supports both data-driven and demand-driven data processing in a uniform manner.
- A general characterization of how the thread of control traverses through ports of information-flow components connected by unbuffered data-driven and demand-driven channels.
- A control-flow analysis algorithm that infers automatically how the thread of control enters and exits an information-flow component.
- The DirectFlow DSL based on our programming model.
- A compiler that generates several different Java implementations of a component from the DirectFlow definition, one for each possible flow of control.
- A run-time system that allows programmers to compose DirectFlow components, while ensuring that they are composed consistently.

We also show that the ideas behind DirectFlow lead to an alternative formulation of objects that does not involve methods.

2   Background

The information-flow features F1–F3 are important because of situations that naturally arise in information-flow applications. We illustrate these situations by example; here and throughout this paper we will refer to the custom components depicted in Fig. 1.

A *filter* transforms individual packets in a flow. For example, a filter can decompress an MPEG video block into an 8×8 block of pixels.

A *prioritizer* buffers packets in a flow. On request, it outputs the packet with the highest priority. The output thus depends not only on the content of the flow but also on the timing of the input and output events. Krasic uses such a component to provide high-quality video playback over an unstable network connection [3].

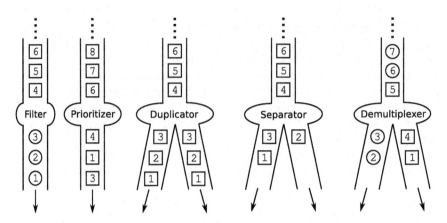

Fig. 1. Five example components

A *duplicator* sends each packet in the input flow to two output flows. A programmer might use it to copy a stream for logging.

A *separator* sends each packet in the input flow to one of two output flows. The chosen flow is the one that is ready to receive the packet first. A separator allows us to connect a "ticket dispenser" component that produces unique numbers to multiple clients.

A *demultiplexer* sends each packet in the input flow to one of two output flows depending on the packet's contents. For example, a demultiplexer can extract video and audio streams from an MPEG system stream.

2.1   Why the Information-Flow Features Are Important

If an information-flow system is to allow programmers to define custom components like these examples, it must exhibit features F1–F3. Without F1 (expressivity), there is no way to implement a demultiplexer because it has two outports with different data rates. Without F2 (latency-control), the system is no longer compositional: splitting a component into two components can introduce arbitrary latency [8, §2.1]. Moreover, buffered channels change the behaviour of the prioritizer because they alters the timing of input and output operations and thus interfere with the priority-reordering.

The result of sacrificing F3 (choice of processing mode) depends on the specifics of the system. If the system supports only data-driven processing, there is no way to build a separator without buffering or blocking. If the system supports only demand-driven processing, there is no way to use a duplicator or a demultiplexer without buffering or blocking.

Full support of F3 permits not only pure data-driven and demand-driven components but also components that are partially data-driven and partially demand-driven. For example, the prioritizer has a data-driven inport and a demand-driven outport; it stores packets whenever they arrive and outputs one whenever a request is received from downstream. If a system does support F3, components like the filter and duplicator present additional complications: they can naturally work in multiple processing modes, and the programming system ought to support this generality. While the case of multi-mode single-inport, single-outport components is well understood [8,10], there is little discussion of the general case in the literature beyond the statement that the problem is "complicated" [9].

2.2   Information-Flow Features in Existing Systems

Given the importance of features F1–F3, it seems clear that an information-flow programming system should aim to provide them. Unfortunately, all of the systems we surveyed have given up some of F1–F3 in order to support F0 (automatic invocation). The consequences of supporting F0–F3 depend on system design:

1. Systems such as Click [1], which use buffered channels and rely on a runtime scheduler to invoke components, can run into deadlocks or unbounded buffer growth.
2. In thread-transparent Infopipes [9], adding components with multiple inports or outports introduces the risk of resuming a stale coroutine.
3. Shivers' and Might's online transducers with multiple inports or outports [11] risk using stale channel continuations.

These problems show up only in specific pipeline configurations (for example, connecting a data-driven outport to a demand-driven inport); they suggest that the combination of F1–F3 allows programmers to specify pipelines that are internally inconsistent and for which there is no reasonable implementation. Existing systems get around these problems by sacrificing one of the information-flow features, or by giving up F0 and requiring the programmer to specify the control-flow interaction of components.

Instead of sacrificing one of F1–F3 to achieve F0, DirectFlow allows programmers to define internally inconsistent pipelines but uses a context condition to detect these cases at compile time. It is the restricted expressivity of the DSL that makes this possible.

2.3   Comparison with Infopipes

DirectFlow evolved from the Infopipes middleware system [8]; following the terminology developed there, we call a component a *pipe* and a composition of components a *pipeline*. (To avoid confusion, we reserve "Infopipes" exclusively for the previous Smalltalk-based system.) The Infopipes system sits on top of an object-oriented language; it represents a pipe as an object and implements inter-pipe packet transfer with message send.

Infopipes support features F1–F3, but require programmers to manually arrange the invocation of pipes by declaring their *polarity configurations*. A polarity configuration defines the control-flow interface of a pipe by assigning a positive or negative polarity to each port. A positive port transfers data by sending a message (push for outports and pull for inports), and a negative port transfers data when it receives a message. Specifying the polarity configuration of a pipe is more complicated than merely writing a declaration: for each negative port the programmer has to define a method to run in response to messages received. Thus, the polarity configuration dictates how the functionality of the pipe must be divided into methods. Moreover, there are no general rules to help programmers decide what polarity configurations a pipe can have; although multi-mode ("polymorphic") pipes can be constructed, all of the methods necessary to make them work must be written by hand, and the programmer is responsible for ensuring that the data-driven and demand-driven behaviours are the same.

DirectFlow differs from Infopipes in three main ways. First, DirectFlow programmers define their components at a higher level; rather than defining *objects* that implement both the data-flow and the control-flow behaviour of their pipes, they define only the data-flow behaviour using a DSL. The DirectFlow compiler infers the control flow and generates the objects (specifically, Java classes). Second, DirectFlow deals with composition more consistently than did Infopipes: composite pipelines can be treated in exactly the same way as custom pipes, since they can be instantiated as many times as needed. Third, while both Infopipes and DirectFlow use ports, their role is different in the two systems. Infopipe ports are objects that exist at runtime: all packets flowing into or out of a pipe have to pass though a port. In DirectFlow, ports exist at configuration time, but they are eliminated before runtime, thus also eliminating a level of indirection in the information flow.

3   The DirectFlow DSL

The DSL component of DirectFlow is an embedded language for programming information-flow components. We developed the language under the following assumptions:

A1. A pipe transfers data packets through a fixed set of inports and outports.

A2. Pipes are *reactive*. A pipe does not own a thread of control: it runs only in response to external data transfer requests.

A3. An outport of an upstream pipe is connected to a single inport of a downstream pipe by an unbuffered channel.

A4. At most one thread of control is executing in a pipeline at a given time.

A5. The thread moves from one pipe to another along with the data; this is similar to the way that message sends in an object-oriented system cause the thread of control to move from one object to another.

We introduced assumption A1 to simplify the design of DirectFlow, while assumptions A3 and A5 are inherited from the Infopipes system. Assumptions A2 and A4, which may seem rather strong, apply not to the entire information-flow application, but only to individual segments implemented in DirectFlow. Programmers can implement any segment of the system that they wish to run without scheduling overhead as a DirectFlow pipeline and then create higher-level logic to connect these segments. For example, a voice-mail server might use separate pipelines to serve separate clients, and each client might have its own pipeline that takes packets from the network, decrypts them, and presents audio to the user. Even though A2 and A4 still hold within each pipeline, the application as a whole involves multiple threads and run-time scheduling.

3.1 Language Overview and Syntax

The DirectFlow language is inspired by Hoare's Communicating Sequential Processes (CSP) [12] and therefore bears some resemblance to occam [13]. Using CSP abstracts away from the polarity configurations of the objects; programmers see a DirectFlow module as a sequentially executed thread that uses input and output statements to perform data transfers. Like occam, DirectFlow supports nondeterministic branches, so a DirectFlow module can perform concurrent blocking I/O operations in the style of the POSIX select system call.

DirectFlow is not a complete, stand-alone programming language; for example, it contains no support for arithmetic or other data manipulation operations. To be useful the DSL must be embedded into a general-purpose programming language, which we call the *host language*. This embedded design strategy has the benefit of reducing the work of language design (there is no need to reinvent all the wheels and do a bad job). It also simplifies the task of porting an existing program to DirectFlow: the data input–output interface will need to be changed, but the code that actually manipulates the data can be brought over from the host language unchanged.

In the work described here we embedded the DirectFlow DSL into Java, and matched DirectFlow's concrete syntax to that of Java. However, it is a simple matter to change the concrete syntax when integrating DirectFlow with another host language: we developed a previous prototype using Smalltalk syntax and integrated it with Squeak.

The syntax of the DirectFlow /Java language is shown in Fig. 2. A DirectFlow /Java module contains the name of the pipe, an optional Java superclass

---

module	::= pipe name (extends super)? '{' *portdecl*+ process '{' *stmt*+ '}' '}'
portdecl	::= (inport | outport) *port* (',' *port*)+ ';'
var	::= JAVA VARIABLE IDENTIFIER
expr	::= JAVA EXPRESSION
stmt	::= JAVA STATEMENT | *alternative* | *input* | *output*
alternative	::= alt *stmt* (with *stmt*)+
input	::= *var* = *port* '?' ';'
output	::= *port* '!' *expr* ';'

Fig. 2. DirectFlow /Java syntax in Backus-Naur form extended with ? (indicating 0 or 1 repetitions), and + (indicating 1 or more repetitions). We list only those grammar rules that augment Java syntax. The top level nonterminal symbol is *module*; the *alternative*, *input*, and *output* statements can appear at any place in a DirectFlow module at which an ordinary Java statement can appear.

declaration (discussed in Sect. 4.4), port declarations, and a data-processing process block. The process block defines how the pipe performs input–output and processes data packets in each iteration; there is an implicit unbounded loop around the block. Code in the block can make use of three new kinds of primitive statement: *alternative*, *input* and *output*.

alternative. The meaning of alt $stmt_1$ with $stmt_2$ with $stmt_3$ is that one of the branches $stmt_1$, $stmt_2$ or $stmt_3$ is executed. The programmer of a pipe has no direct control over which; this is determined at run time based on the outstanding input and output requests from other pipes. The meaning of an alt statement does not depend on the order of the branches.

input. The meaning of $var = port$? is that the pipe inputs a packet from the inport *port* and stores the packet in the variable *var*.

output. The meaning of $port$! $expr$ is that the pipe evaluates the expression *expr* and outputs the result through the outport *port*.

The primitive statements in our DSL correspond closely to those of CSP, but with a few modifications. For example, a DirectFlow module has no way to invoke itself, or indeed any other DirectFlow module. We have also eliminated the CSP parallel composition operator ‖ because it is not useful in our context (due to A4). In contrast with the CSP choice operator ⟦, which requires that the first statement in each branch performs a distinct input or output operation, the alt statement in the DirectFlow DSL does not restrict the first statements in the branches.

3.2   The Context Condition

To ensure that a DirectFlow module corresponds to a reactive pipe, we introduce one *context condition* restricting how the pipe performs input–output through its ports. Before we can state the context condition we need to introduce two definitions.

- An *alt specialization* of a module is the module that results from replacing each alternative statement by one of its branches. For example, the module { a; alt b; with c; } has two alt specializations: { a; b; } and { a; c; }.
- A port is an *index port* of an alt specialization if the port is accessed exactly once in the execution of the alt specialization, regardless of control flow, and if the port is *not* accessed in any *other* alt specialization of the module. It does not matter if the port is an inport or an outport.

The context condition we impose on DirectFlow is that *every alt specialization in a valid module must have at least one index port*. The motivation behind this requirement is twofold. First, we want to ensure that every alt specialization is triggered by data transfer at a certain port. The index port of the alt specialization is that port; transferring data through the index port executes the alt specialization. Second, we need to determine which branch of an alt to execute. By requiring that each alt specialization has an *exclusive* index port not accessed elsewhere, we can always make this determination when a data transfer request arrives at an index port. In essence, this rule lets us implement angelic nondeterminism, *i.e.*, we make alt choices not arbitrarily but in a way that ensures that the pipe can conduct the necessary data transfer.

```
pipe Filter {              pipe Duplicate {           pipe Separate {
    inport in;                 inport in;                 inport in;
    outport out;               outport out0, out1;        outport out0, out1;

    process {                  process {                  process {
        Object packet;             Object packet;             Object packet;
        packet = in ?;             packet = in ?;             packet = in ?;
        out ! packet;              out0 ! packet;             alt    out0 ! packet;
    }                              out1 ! packet;             with  out1 ! packet;
}                              }                          }
                           }                          }
```

Fig. 3. DirectFlow modules for the Filter, Duplicate and Separate pipes of Sect. 2

Fig. 3 shows three pipes in DirectFlow /Java. Port names in a pipe are not values in the host language and thus cannot be stored in variables; they can be used only as the subjects of the ? and ! constructs.

Since the Filter module does not contain an alt statement, its alt specialization is trivially the same as the module itself. Both in and out are index ports of this program, and thus it satisfies the context condition. Likewise, the alt specialization of the Duplicate module is the same as itself. Ports in, out0 and out1 are all index ports, and the module satisfies the context condition. The Separate module has two alt specializations: { Object packet; packet = in ?; out0 ! packet; } and { Object packet; packet = in ?; out1 ! packet; }. The first has out0 as an index port; the second has out1 as an index port. Note that the port in appears in *both* alt specializations, so it cannot be an index port of either.

```
pipe Switch {
    inport in0, in1;
    outport out0, out1;

    process {
        Object packet;
        alt    packet = in0 ?;
        with  packet = in1 ?;
        alt    out0 ! packet;
        with  out1 ! packet;
    }
}
```

Fig. 4. This Switch pipe definition is not a valid DirectFlow module because none of its alt specializations has an index port

The Switch module in Fig. 4 is an example of an invalid DirectFlow module. It has four alt specializations: { packet = in0 ?; out0 ! packet; }, { packet = in0 ?; out1 ! packet; }, { packet = in1 ?; out0 ! packet; }, and { packet = in1 ?; out1 ! packet; }. However, none of these alt specializations has an index port because each port is accessed in two different specializations.

4 Compiling DirectFlow Modules

In the previous section we described how DirectFlow uses a CSP-inspired programming model to eliminate the polarity-declaration requirement in Infopipes. Instead the DirectFlow compiler infers the polarity configurations of a pipe and generates the pipe objects. In this section we first discuss the inference process conceptually, and then present the details of our inference algorithm. Finally, we explain how the compiler generates code.

4.1 Principles of the Compilation Process

An object is characterized by its behaviour: its protocol (the messages that it can understand), and the responses that it makes to those messages. Most "object-oriented" languages, including Java, specify both of these things by defining a set of methods: the names of the methods define the protocol, and the bodies of the methods define the response to each message. So we have:

$$\text{methods in an object} \implies \begin{cases} \text{messages the object can understand} \\ \text{code to run when receiving a message} \end{cases}$$

However, this is not the only way of defining the behaviour of an object. Direct-Flow modules can also be viewed as defining objects. Their protocol is limited to a subset of the messages push and pull, while the response to these messages is given implicitly by the DirectFlow module. The task of the compiler is to determine if the object corresponding to a DirectFlow module understands push, pull, or both, and to generate Java methods that implement the data-processing functionality defined in the DirectFlow code. So we start by inverting the diagram above:

$$\text{methods in the object} \impliedby \begin{cases} \text{messages an object can understand} \\ \text{code to run when receiving a message} \end{cases}$$

How can we decide what messages a pipe object can understand? The DirectFlow code might say that a pipe performs output on a certain port, but it does not explicitly say whether the port is positive or negative. If the port is positive, it will *send* messages to transfer data to or from some other pipe, but will never *receive* messages. Only negative ports can receive messages: negative inports receive push messages and negative outports receive pull messages. Thus, if we can determine the possible polarity configurations of a DirectFlow program, we can infer its protocol. Can we also infer the body of the method to execute in

Infopipe	in	out0	out1
	−	+	+
Duplicate	+	−	+
	+	+	−
Separate	+	−	−

Fig. 5. Polarity configurations of the Duplicate and Separate pipes in Fig. 3

response to an incoming message? We can, *provided that*, for each negative port, there is a single piece of code that executes a data transfer on the port. So we constrain valid polarity configurations to ensure that each negative port must be associated with one alt specialization, and that it is accessed exactly once in the execution of one cycle of the pipe. In other words, a port can be negative only if it is an index port as defined in Sect. 3.2.

Thus the following strategy lets us derive an implementation for a DirectFlow module as a Java class:

> For each alt specialization, mark one of its index ports with negative polarity. Mark all other ports with positive polarity. The code to run when receiving a message through a negative port is the alt specialization that accesses the port.

This strategy determines how many polarity configurations a pipe has. The context condition of Sect. 3.2 ensures that a DirectFlow module has at least one polarity configuration, but some pipes have more than one. Consider the Filter pipe in Fig. 3. Because both in and out are index ports, applying this strategy to Filter produces the data-driven and demand-driven polarity configurations as documented in the filter design pattern [10]. Fig. 5 shows the results of applying this strategy to the Duplicate and the Separate pipes.

4.2 Mapping an Invalid DirectFlow Module to Objects

Let us try to implement the Switch DirectFlow module in Fig. 4 (which violates the context condition) as a pipe object. We will fail, but it is instructive to see why. We start by considering which ports should have negative polarity.

- Suppose that in0 and in1 are negative, and the other ports are positive. Since branches in the second alt construct do not access any negative ports (out0 and out1 are both positive), the object cannot use the received message to decide whether to send the outgoing packet through out0 or out1.
- Suppose ports in0, in1, and out0 are negative. This pipe cannot respond to data request on out0 in a useful way because it has no way of requesting data from upstream, but must instead block until an upstream pipe pushes data in (which may never happen).
- Suppose that ports in1 and out0 are negative. With this polarity configuration we can eliminate the blocking behaviour by making the object pull from in0 when it receives a pull message associated with out0, and push to out1

when it receives a push message associated with in1. However, such an object does not implement the Switch Infopipe faithfully because our arbitrary choice rules out the execution paths in0 — out1 and in1 — out0.
- Suppose that all ports are positive. Since pipe objects do not have their own threads, and this pipe object does not have a thread entrance, it will never acquire a thread and will just sit idly doing nothing. This behaviour is quite useless, so we disallow the all-positive configuration.

Even though these discussions are based on our intuitive understanding of reactive objects, they all relate back to the context condition. These lines of reasoning should help programmers to understand the cause of the problem when the DirectFlow compiler rejects a module that violates the context condition, or why the compiler does not allow a pipe to have a specific polarity configuration.

4.3   Inferring Polarity Configurations of DirectFlow Modules

The compilation process reflects the preceding discussion. It starts by identifying the alt specializations of the module using a mechanism called *alt lifting*. It then determines if each alt specialization has one or more index ports; if there is no index port, the context condition has been violated. The next step is to *compute the polarity configurations* by selecting one index port from each alt specialization and marking it as a negative port. The compiler can then generate a pipe object with a push method and a pull method. The push method contains alt specializations with negative inports, and the pull method contains alt specializations with negative outports. If the pipe has multiple polarity configurations, we generate a separate pipe object for each configuration. We now describe the processes of alt lifting and of computing the polarity configurations in more detail.

Code pattern	Rewrite result	
alt $\langle s_1, ..., s_m \rangle$; t	alt $\langle s_1 ; t, ..., s_m ; t \rangle$	(seq-a)
s ; alt $\langle t_1, ..., t_n \rangle$	alt $\langle s ; t_1, ..., s ; t_n \rangle$	(seq-b)
if (c) { alt $\langle s_1, ..., s_m \rangle$ } t	alt $\langle$ if (c) s_1 t, ..., if (c) s_m $t \rangle$	(if-a)
if (c) s { alt $\langle t_1, ..., t_n \rangle$ }	alt $\langle$ if (c) s t_1, ..., if (c) s $t_n \rangle$	(if-b)
alt $\langle s_1, ..., $ alt $\langle t_1, ..., t_n \rangle, ..., s_m \rangle$	alt $\langle s_1, ..., t_1, ..., t_n, ..., s_m \rangle$	(alt)

Fig. 6. The rewrite rules for alt lifting in an abstract-syntax notation. We enclose alt branches in angle brackets separated by commas. The semicolon (;) in the seq rules is the statement sequence operator.

Alt Lifting. The alt lifting procedure computes the alt specializations of a DirectFlow module through a series of rewrites. The rewrite rules, listed in Fig. 6, make use of the property that conditional and statement sequencing constructs all distribute over alt, so we can "lift" alt up without changing the meaning of the module. Since code duplicated by the rewrites goes into different alt branches, and an alt construct always executes only one branch, the duplication cannot cause multiple executions of the same statement. The procedure

```
pipe Separate {                         pipe Switch {
  inport in;                              inport in0, in1;
  outport out0, out1;                     outport out0, out1;

  process {                               process {
    alt {                                   alt {
      Object packet;                          Object packet;
      packet = in ?;                          packet = in0 ?;
      out0 ! packet;                          out0 ! packet;
    } with {                                } with {
      Object packet;                          Object packet;
      packet = in ?;                          packet = in1 ?;
      out1 ! packet;                          out0 ! packet;
    }                                       } with {
  }                                           Object packet;
}                                             packet = in0 ?;
                                              out1 ! packet;
                                            } with {
                                              Object packet;
                                              packet = in1 ?;
                                              out1 ! packet;
                                            }
                                          }
                                        }
```

Fig. 7. The Separate and Switch pipes after alt lifting. The original DirectFlow source for these two pipes are shown in Figs. 3 and 4.

repeatedly rewrites the module until all alt constructs are at the top level, at which point each alt branch would be an alt specialization. The observant reader will notice that there is no rule for loops. A module that contains an alt in a loop always violates the context condition, so the compiler never needs to lift it.

Example: Applying alt Lifting to Separate and Switch. We illustrate the alt lifting procedure by applying it to two examples. The Separate pipe in Fig. 3 contains only one alt construct and the rewrite terminates in one step. The Switch pipe in Fig. 4 contains two alt constructs; the rewrite starts by lifting either of the alt constructs and then proceeds by flattening the nested alt constructs using the alt rewrite rule. Fig. 7 shows the pipes after alt lifting; each top-level alt branch corresponds to an alt specialization of the module.

Computing Polarity Configurations. The DirectFlow compiler computes the polarity configurations of a DirectFlow module by first identifying the index ports of each alt specialization, and then computing the Cartesian product of the sets of index ports. The algorithm proceeds as follows.

Step 1. Let B be the set of alt specializations of the program; for each $b \in B$, compute the set P_b of all the ports accessed in b.

Step 2. For each $b \in B$, compute the set Q_b using the following equation:

$$Q_b = P_b - \bigcup_{i \in B - \{b\}} P_i$$

Q_b is the set of ports that are accessed in the alt specialization b and nowhere else.

Step 3. For each $b \in B$, eliminate from Q_b all ports accessed in a loop, accessed in only one branch of an if construct, or accessed multiple times in an execution path. This step is a simple control-flow analysis that enforces the "exactly once" part of the definition of index ports. The resulting sets Q_b contain the index ports of the alt specializations in B.

Step 4. We compute the negative ports in a polarity configuration by choosing one port from the set Q_b for each specialization b. We represent a polarity configuration by a tuple of its negative ports, and the set N of configurations is given by

$$N = \prod_{i \in B} Q_i$$

where $\prod$ represents Cartesian product on sets.

In our experience, the crude control-flow analysis algorithm in Step 3 works fairly well. If it later turns out that imprecision in this algorithm rules out some polarity configurations on useful DirectFlow modules, we can apply more sophisticated control-flow analysis algorithms. (These could, for example, recognize mutually exclusive if conditions to infer a larger set of polarity configurations.)

Example: Polarity configurations of Separate. We number the alt branches in Fig. 7 according to their order of appearance and use the module to demonstrate how to compute polarity configurations.

Step 1. $P_1 = \{ \text{in}, \text{out0} \}$, $P_2 = \{ \text{in}, \text{out1} \}$
Step 2. $Q_1 = P_1 - P_2 = \{ \text{out0} \}$, $Q_2 = P_2 - P_1 = \{ \text{out1} \}$
Step 3. No changes to Q_1 and Q_2
Step 4. $N = Q_1 \times Q_2 = \{ \langle \text{out0}, \text{out1} \rangle \}$

The set N has only one element, so Separate has one polarity configuration. The ports out0 and out1 are negative, and hence in is positive.

Example: Polarity Configurations of Switch. We now apply the same constraint solving process to the lifted Switch pipe in Fig. 7.

Step 1. $P_1 = \{ \text{in0}, \text{out0} \}$, $P_2 = \{ \text{in1}, \text{out0} \}$, $P_3 = \{ \text{in0}, \text{out1} \}$, $P_4 = \{ \text{in1}, \text{out1} \}$
Step 2. $Q_1 = Q_2 = Q_3 = Q_4 = \emptyset$

At this point we can conclude that the Switch DirectFlow module does not have a polarity configuration because none of its alt specializations has an index port, and the Cartesian product of any set with an empty set is empty. In this case the compiler reports an error instead of continuing with the code generation process.

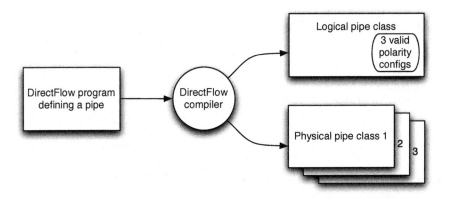

Fig. 8. Defining a DirectFlow pipe using the domain-specific language

4.4 Generating Code for Pipe Objects

When a DirectFlow module is compiled, the compiler analyses the module, determines how many polarity configurations are possible for the pipe that it defines, and (assuming that there is at least one legal configuration) outputs several Java class definitions. A Java *logical* pipe class is always created; the logical pipe is like an abstract model of the pipe's behaviour. Inside this class, amongst other things, is a method validConfigurations that returns a set of polarity configurations; in Fig. 8 we assume that there are three. For each configuration, the compiler outputs a Java class definition for a *physical* pipe class. We don't yet know which of these classes will be used, because this depends on the context into which the pipe is eventually deployed, so the most useful thing to do is to generate all of them.

Each physical pipe Java class implements the data-processing functionality of the DirectFlow module. In addition to the ability to transfer data packets to and from other pipe objects, a DirectFlow physical pipe object can:

1. invoke methods in Java objects,
2. maintain persistent state between executions, and
3. make its persistent state accessible from other Java objects.

In this subsection we describe the design of physical pipe objects and how the DirectFlow compiler generates these objects from a DirectFlow module.

At the core of a physical pipe object are its push and pull methods. The push method accepts a port number and a data packet; the pull method accepts a port number and returns a data packet. (The compiler translates port names in DirectFlow to port numbers.) Both methods contain a top-level test of the port number, and execute a different segment of code depending on the port through which data transfer occurred; see SeparatePhysicalPipePNN in Fig. 9 for an example. Each of these segments is derived from one alt specialization, and the derivation depends on whether the specialization has a negative inport

```
public class DuplicatePhysicalPipeNPP {
   public void push(int index, Object input) {
      if (index == 0) {
         Object packet;
         packet = input;                          public class SeparatePhysicalPipePNN {
         out0.push(packet);                          public Object pull(int index) {
         out1.push(packet);                             Object output;
         return;                                        if (index == 1) {
      }                                                    Object packet;
   }                                                       packet = in.pull();
}                                                          output = packet;
                                                           return output;
public class DuplicatePhysicalPipePNP {                 }
   public Object pull(int index) {                      if (index == 2) {
      Object output;                                       Object packet;
      if (index == 1) {                                    packet = in.pull();
         Object packet;                                    output = packet;
         packet = in.pull();                               return output;
         output = packet;                               }
         out1.push(packet);                          }
         return output;                            }
      }
   }
}
```

Fig. 9. Excerpt of physical pipe objects compiled from the DirectFlow modules in Fig. 3. We show only two of the three classes generated from the Duplicate pipe because the PPN case is analogous to the PNP one (left bottom).

or a negative outport. If an alt specialization has a negative *inport*, it works in data-driven mode and therefore the code belongs in the push method (because an upstream component will push data into this component). If an alt specialization has a negative *outport*, it works in demand-driven mode and the code belongs in the pull method.

This translation realizes our intuition that negative ports act as thread entrances, while positive ports act as thread exits. Since each index port (and therefore, each negative port) is accessed exactly once, we can be certain that each invocation of a data-driven alt specialization consumes one data packet, and each invocation of a demand-driven alt specialization produces one data packet. Fig. 9 shows the physical pipes generated from the Duplicate and the Separate Infopipes.

We use the generation-gap pattern [14] in the physical pipe objects to integrate the code generated from the DirectFlow DSL with ordinary Java code written by hand. The original formulation of the generation-gap pattern puts machine-generated code in a superclass of the hand-written code; this allows the machine-generated code to be customized by subclassing. Such an approach does not quite work in our case because the compiler can generate *multiple* physical pipe classes from a DirectFlow module, and because the number of generated physical pipe classes may change with the contents of the DirectFlow module. Instead we make the machine-generated classes *subclasses* of the hand-written code; this allows all of the generated classes to reuse the same hand-written code. This is the purpose of the extends *superclass* clause mentioned in Sect. 3.1: it defines the name of the hand-written class from which the generated physical pipe classes should inherit. We call this variant the *inverse generation-gap* pattern.

The inverse generation-gap pattern enables a physical pipe object to maintain persistent state in the fields of its superclass; it also allows other Java objects to access that persistent state through the public methods of the superclass. The DirectFlow compiler copies all Java statements in a DirectFlow module into the translated alt specializations in the physical pipe classes, so the programmer is able to invoke other Java methods from within the DirectFlow module.

5   The DirectFlow Framework

The DirectFlow framework is designed to help the programmer build an information flow system in several steps. Although this may at first sight appear unnecessarily complicated, the stepwise development allows for maximal reuse. Let us draw an analogy with object-oriented programming languages. If what one wants is objects, classes may seem like an unnecessary complication — why not define objects directly? However, it turns out that classes are quite useful when one needs to make many objects that are almost the same. Similarly, generic classes may seem like an unnecessary complication, but they turn out to be quite useful when one needs to make several classes that differ parametrically.

5.1   Building a Pipeline

The first step in using DirectFlow is to define any custom pipes that are necessary for the application at hand. There is a library of standard pipes, which we expect to grow over time, but let us assume that at least one custom pipe is required, for example, a pipe that diverts suspicious data packets (say, into a log) to help track down a suspected sensor malfunction.

As described in Sect. 4.4, the result of compiling these custom pipe modules is a collection of logical and physical pipe classes. The next step is to take these generated classes and to write a Java program that composes them with appropriate library classes to build the desired information pipeline. This process is illustrated in Fig. 10 for the simple case of a pipeline containing only two components. The thread configuring the pipeline first creates a CompositeFactory object, and then creates the two logical pipes, src and sink, that will be its components. src and sink are added to the factory, and the appropriate connections between the output port of src and the input port of sink are set up. Incremental checks are performed during this process; for example, we check to make sure that two outports are not connected together. At this stage it is also possible to specify that an internal port of one of the components is "forwarded" to become an external port of the whole composition. When the programmer has completed the "wiring up" of the composite factory, the factory is told to

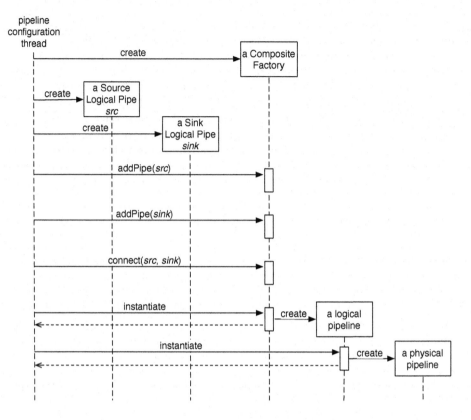

Fig. 10. A UML Sequence diagram showing how a physical pipeline is created

instantiate the composition. Some non-local checks can now be carried out, for example, to ensure that there are no disconnected ports inside the composition. If all is well, the result of instantiation is another *logical* pipeline.

The composite logical pipeline has no open ports, so it can be instantiated as a physical pipeline: a pipeline that can actually carry data. This is not a simple matter, because the appropriate mode of processing of each component in the composition depends on the mode of its neighbors. Now we see the value of building the logical pipeline first: it provides an abstract model of the composite pipeline that can be explored to gain a global understanding of the whole pipeline. This makes it possible to select the best physical pipe class to implement each logical pipe.

5.2 Composite Pipes

The DirectFlow system supports two kinds of pipes — simple pipes and composite pipes — and goes to some lengths to treat them on an equal footing. Simple pipes are created by instantiating a logical pipe object, which is an instance of the logical pipe class generated by the DirectFlow compiler. Composite pipes, which are compositions of other pipes, are constructed by instantiating a logical pipeline object, but in this case the logical pipe object is created by a composite factory.

To construct a composite pipe, the programmer starts by creating a CompositeFactory object and then invokes its methods to describe the structure of the desired composite pipe.

- addPipe(String n, LogicalPipe op) This method adds an internal pipe op with name n to the composite pipe.
- newInport(String ident) and newOutport(String ident)   These methods adds an input port or an output port to the composite pipe. A composite pipe with ports can be further composed with other pipes.
- connect(Channel c) A Channel object identifies a pair of ports, each in a specific component. The connect method connects the two ports described by c. The programmer can connect an inport of the composite pipe to an inport of an internal pipe, an outport of an internal pipe to an inport of an internal pipe, or an outport of an internal pipe to a outport of the composite pipe.

Finally, invoking the instantiate() method on the CompositeFactory creates a CompositeLogicalPipe object. The resulting CompositeLogicalPipe object is like any other logical pipe object, and the programmer can pass it to addPipe to compose it with other pipes.

To create a physical pipe object that can perform data processing operations, the programmer *terminates* a logical pipe by connecting its inports and outports to special Source and Sink logical pipes, and then instantiates the logical pipe to produce a CompositePhysicalPipe object.

Because the resulting physical pipe has no open ports, it cannot be sent push or pull messages. Instead we use the getInternal method to obtain references to the Source and Sink physical pipes, and use these objects to inject data and control into the pipeline. This design hides the communication protocol between physical pipe objects and allows it to evolve without changing the public interface of the pipeline.

6   Related Work

Historical Information-Flow Systems. Computer programs have long been structured to process streams of information from external devices. The idea of a stream as a first-class object can be traced back to Stoy and Strachey's OS6 operating system [15]. OS6 also incorporated stream functions, which could be applied to an argument stream to construct another stream (with different contents) as the result. A related I/O system using (bidirectional) streams appeared in Unix [16]. In both OS6 and Unix, the stream subsystem is regarded as peripheral to the "main program", and it incurs high overhead due to the reliance on runtime scheduling and the need to move data across process boundaries.

Coordination Languages. Our work bears some resemblance to control-based coordination languages [17] in that they model a program as a collection of entities connected by point-to-point channels. Unlike existing coordination languages, which treat processes as purely computational entities, DirectFlow also captures the communication aspects of a component by addressing it separately from the computation aspects of the component.

Communicating Sequential Processes. DirectFlow is inspired by Hoare's CSP [12]. Unlike libraries such as JCSP [18], which faithfully implement the semantics of CSP, DirectFlow eliminates certain restrictions (such as the prohibition against different alt branches starting with the same operation) while adding others (such as the context condition) to better support the development of information-flow programs.

Design Patterns. The way we build information-flow programs by exchanging messages between Infopipe objects has been documented under the name *filter pattern* [10]. The filter pattern literature describes (data-driven) sink filters and (demand-driven) source filters, but it does not discuss how to generalize these two cases to filters with multiple inputs or outputs. DirectFlow provides a more general and more elegant mechanism for building filters because it relieves the programmer from the responsibility of implementing both the data-driven and demand-driven variants of a filter.

Information-Flow Systems Without F1. Some information-flow programming systems achieve automatic component invocation by restricting the form or the behaviour of custom components. Both thread-transparent Infopipes [9] and StreamIt [6] require a component to have exactly one inport and one outport, and Spidle [7] requires all channels to have the same data rate.

Information-Flow Systems Without F2. Some information-flow programming systems connect components with buffered channels and achieve automatic invocation by runtime scheduling. Click [1] and StreamIt [6] both fall into this category. Such designs suffer from three problems. First, the reliance on runtime scheduling makes it difficult to understand the interaction between components and to ensure liveness. Second, channel buffering introduces latency and therefore breaks compositionality. Finally, buffering interferes with components such as a prioritizer whose operation depends on the interleaving of input and output.

Information-Flow Systems Without F3. Some information-flow programming systems achieve automatic component invocation by supporting only data-driven or only demand-driven processing. The Eden operating system [19] explored making streams asymmetric by eliminating active output (data-driven) operations. Reactive objects in O'Haskell [20,21] eliminate active input (demand-driven) operations. Dataflow languages like SISAL [22] and lazy streams, which typically appear in programs written in functional languages like Scheme or Haskell, support only data-driven operation. These systems cannot support the prioritizer described in Sect. 2, which uses both data-driven and demand-driven data processing.

Polarity-Polymorphic Ports. Our previous Infopipes system [8] supports a feature called *polarity polymorphism* which allows an Infopipe object to assume multiple polarity configurations. In the system, an Infopipe defines a polarity-polymorphic port by providing it with both push and pull methods and specifying its polarity using a variable that is instantiated to either $+$ or $-$. For example, a filter has polarity configuration $\alpha \rightarrow \bar{\alpha}$ that is instantiated to $+ \rightarrow -$ or $- \rightarrow +$. The runtime system determines the polarity configuration of an Infopipeline by unifying the polarity specifications of connected ports.

The Click modular router [1] uses *agnostic ports* for the same purpose. The agnostic polarity specifies that the port can work in either demand-driven or data-driven mode, and the programmer is required to specify a *flow code* for any processing element that contains agnostic ports to help the runtime system decide the polarity configurations of the element. A flow code is a sequence of *port codes* that specify the internal dataflow of an element; if the codes of two ports share the same letter, data packets arriving from one port may exit from the other. For example, a filter has flow code "x/x" indicating that packets arriving from the inport can exit from the outport. We do not completely understand how Click computes the polarity configurations of an element from its flow code, but the design of agnostic ports appears to be similar to polarity polymorphism. Both designs share the following drawbacks.

1. When defining a component, the programmer must identify the ports that can assume either polarity and provide additional information on the relationship between the polarity of ports. There is no tool support for checking whether the supplied information is consistent with the behaviour of the component, and therefore the programmer is solely responsible for the correctness of the port polarity specifications.
2. The programmer must implement both push and pull methods for each polymorphic/agnostic port and ensure that the component exhibits the same information flow behaviour regardless of whether it is used with push or pull.
3. The mechanisms used to specify port polarity relations are not general enough to capture the polarity relations of components with more than two ports. There is no way to define a polymorphic Infopipe that works in all three configurations of the duplicate pipe in Fig. 5. Likewise, even though a duplicator, a separator, and a demultiplexer all have different information-flow behaviour and polarity configurations, they cannot be distinguished in the Click system because they share the same flow code "x/xx".

In comparison, our proposed technique both requires less programmer intervention (by automatically inferring the information flow behaviour of a pipe and generating the methods corresponding to each polarity configuration) and works in more general contexts (because it can distinguish between and correctly characterize duplicators, separators, and demultiplexers).

7   Experiences

We first prototyped DirectFlow as a Smalltalk-embedded language and then adapted it for embedding in Java. We implemented a DirectFlow /Java compiler in Haskell [23] and a corresponding run-time library in Java. Excluding comments and blank lines, the compiler is about 400 lines of Haskell, and the run-time library is about 600 lines of Java. The implementation is available through http://infopipes.cs.pdx.edu/.

One of the design goal for DirectFlow is to allow programmers to define pipes that correspond to data stream operators like those in the Aurora Stream Query Algebra (SQuAl) [2]. SQuAl defines a wide variety of primitive operators, which include standard relational algebra operators like Map (projection) and Union, generalized relational algebra operators like Filter (selection-based demultiplexing), and data-stream-specific operators like Resample. Some of these operators have multiple inports, some have multiple outports; only Map has a fixed relationship between its input data rate and its output data rate.

We studied SQuAl and concluded that DirectFlow is expressive enough to support all its operators. The only difficulty is that implementing SQuAl operators with variable arity requires a daisy-chain of pipes. For example, SQuAl has an n-stream union operation; because a DirectFlow pipe has a fixed set of ports, this must be implemented using a chain of two-stream unions components. However, since this can be implemented by a $1..n$ loop at pipeline configuration time, we do not see this as a problem.

Our study further suggests that using DirectFlow can improve the expressivity of existing data-stream management systems. To simplify system design and implementation, data-stream management systems such as Niagara and Aurora support only data-driven components. While they work well with data sources that produce infrequent discrete events, they are not well-suited for data sources that produce a continuous stream of time-varying data, such as thermometers or light sensors. Such sources are most naturally demand-driven: operating them in data-driven mode requires that they produce frequent updates, which wastes resources when the user does not need those values. However, reducing the frequency of updates compromises data freshness. DirectFlow naturally supports both data-driven and demand-driven components, so it would allow a data-stream management system to request data from continuous sources on demand, achieving the best of both worlds.

8   Conclusions and Future Work

Abstraction mismatch between the programming language and the application domain makes software development unnecessarily complicated. This is because making programmers use a language that exposes aspects of the system that are irrelevant to the domain forces over-specification and thus reduces reusability. Dually, a language that hides aspects of the system that *are* relevant to the domain makes it more difficult to define and to reason about system behaviour in domain-specific terms.

We investigated the problem of abstraction mismatch in the information-flow domain and proposed the DirectFlow language to address the shortcomings of programming this domain with objects. By allowing programmers to define pipes without specifying their polarity configurations, DirectFlow eliminates the need to define and maintain multiple pipe objects that differ only in their polarity configurations.

The design of DirectFlow seeks a balance between language expressivity and implementation efficiency. The language allows a pipe to alter its input–output behaviour based on its internal state, which makes it possible to define de-multiplexers and reordering buffers, components that are commonly found in information-flow programs. At the same time, DirectFlow is sufficiently restrictive to permit the compiler to perform static analysis on DirectFlow modules and to compile them to objects. DirectFlow is expressive enough to implement the Aurora stream algebra; whether it will be equally successful on other information-flow tasks is a question that we plan to explore in our future work.

In this paper we have demonstrated that DirectFlow simplifies the development of information-flow components by hiding the control flow interaction between them. It remains to be seen if DirectFlow facilitates reasoning about information-flow programs. We hope that deeper understanding of the semantics of DirectFlow will lead to progress in quality-of-service verification and in thread allocation for information pipelines.

Acknowledgments. This work is partially supported by the National Science Foundation of the United States under grants CCR–0219686 and CNS–0523474.

References

1. Kohler, E., Morris, R., Chen, B., Jannotti, J., Kaashoek, M.F.: The Click modular router. ACM Transactions on Computer Systems 18(3), 263–297 (2000)
2. Abadi, D.J., Carney, D., Çetintemel, U., Cherniack, M., Convey, C., Lee, S., Stonebraker, M., Tatbul, N., Zdonik, S.: Aurora: a new model and architecture for data stream management. International Journal on Very Large Data Bases 12(2), 120–139 (2003)
3. Krasic, C., Walpole, J., Feng, W.: Quality-adaptive media streaming by priority drop. In: Papadopoulos, C., Almeroth, K.C. (eds.) Network and Operating System Support for Digital Audio and Video, 13th International Workshop, NOSSDAV 2003, June 2003, pp. 112–121 (2003)
4. Murphy-Hill, E., Lin, C., Black, A.P., Walpole, J.: Can Infopipes facilitate reuse in a traffic application? In: Companion to the 20th Annual ACM SIGPLAN Conference on Object-Oriented Programming, Systems, Languages, and Applications, October 2005, pp. 100–101. ACM Press, New York (2005)
5. Hart, J.K., Martinez, K.: Environmental sensor networks: A revolution in the earth system science? Earth-Science Reviews 78, 177–191 (2006)
6. Thies, W., Karczmarek, M., Amarasinghe, S.: StreamIt: a language for streaming applications. In: Horspool, R.N. (ed.) CC 2002 and ETAPS 2002. LNCS, vol. 2304, pp. 179–195. Springer, Heidelberg (2002)
7. Consel, C., Hamdi, H., Réveillère, L., Singaravelu, L., Yu, H., Pu, C.: Spidle: a DSL approach to specifying streaming applications. In: Pfenning, F., Smaragdakis, Y. (eds.) GPCE 2003. LNCS, vol. 2830, pp. 1–17. Springer, Heidelberg (2003)
8. Black, A.P., Huang, J., Koster, R., Walpole, J., Pu, C.: Infopipes: an abstraction for multimedia streaming. Multimedia Systems 8(5), 406–419 (2002)

9. Koster, R., Black, A.P., Huang, J., Walpole, J., Pu, C.: Thread transparency in information flow middleware. In: Guerraoui, R. (ed.) Middleware 2001. LNCS, vol. 2218, pp. 121–140. Springer, Heidelberg (2001)
10. Grand, M.: 6. In: Patterns in Java: a catalog of reusable design patterns illustrated in UML, vol. 1, pp. 155–163. John Wiley & Sons, Chichester (1998)
11. Shivers, O., Might, M.: Continuations and transducer composition. In: PLDI'06: Proceedings of the 2006 ACM SIGPLAN Conference on Programming Language Design and Implementation, June 2006, pp. 295–307. ACM Press, New York (2006)
12. Hoare, C.A.R.: Communicating Sequential Processes. In: Series in Computer Science, Prentice-Hall International, Upper Saddle River, NJ, USA (1985)
13. SGS-THOMSON Microelectronics Ltd.: occam 2.1 Reference Manual (1995)
14. Vlissides, J.: 3. In: Pattern Hatching: Design Patterns Applied, pp. 85–101. Addison-Wesley, Reading (1998)
15. Stoy, J.E., Strachey, C.: OS6 — an experimental operating system for a small computer. Part 2: input/output and filing system. Computer Journal 15(3), 195–203 (1972)
16. Ritchie, D.M.: A stream input-output system. AT&T Bell Laboratories Technical Journal 63(8), 1897–1910 (1984)
17. Papadopoulos, G.A., Arbab, F.: Coordination Models and Languages. In: The Engineering of Large Systems, September 1998. Advances in Computers, vol. 46, pp. 329–400. Academic Press, London (1998)
18. Welch, P.H.: Process oriented design for Java: concurrency for all. In: Arabnia, H.R. (ed.) Proceedings of the International Conference on Parallel and Distributed Processing Techniques and Applications (PDPTA 2000), June 2000, vol. 1, pp. 51–57. CSREA Press (2000)
19. Black, A.P.: An asymmetric stream communication system. In: Proceedings of the Ninth ACM Symposium on Operating System Principles, October 1983, pp. 4–10. ACM Press, New York (1983)
20. Nordlander, J., Carlsson, M.: Reactive objects in a functional language: an escape from the evil "I". In: Proceedings of the Third Haskell Workshop (June 1997)
21. Nordlander, J., Jones, M.P., Carlsson, M., Kieburtz, R.B., Black, A.P.: Reactive objects. In: Proceedings of the Fifth IEEE International Symposium on Object-Oriented Real-Time Distributed Computing, April 2002, pp. 155–158. IEEE Computer Society Press, Los Alamitos (2002)
22. Feo, J.T., Cann, D.C., Oldehoeft, R.R.: A report on the Sisal language project. Journal of Parallel and Distributed Computing (Special issue: data-flow processing) 10(4), 349–366 (1990)
23. Jones, S.P. (ed.): Haskell 98 Language and Libraries: The Revised Report. Cambridge University Press, Cambridge, UK (2003)

A Relational Model of Object Collaborations and Its Use in Reasoning About Relationships*

Stephanie Balzer[1], Thomas R. Gross[1], and Patrick Eugster[2]

[1] Department of Computer Science, ETH Zurich
[2] Department of Computer Science, Purdue University

Abstract. Understanding the *collaborations* that arise between the instances of classes in object-oriented programs is important for the analysis, optimization, or modification of the program. Relationships have been proposed as a programming language construct to enable an explicit representation of these collaborations. This paper introduces a *relational model* that allows the specification of systems composed of classes and relationships. These specifications rely in particular on *member interposition* (facilitates the specification of relationship-dependent members of classes) and on *relationship invariants* (facilitate the specification of the consistency constraints imposed on object collaborations). The notion of a *mathematical relation* is the basis for the model. Employing relations as an abstraction of relationships, the specification of a system can be formalized using discrete mathematics. The relational model allows thus not only the specification of object collaborations but also provides a foundation to reason about these collaborations in a rigorous fashion.

1 Introduction

The *collaborations* between objects are the key to understanding large object-oriented programs. Software systems do not accomplish their tasks with a single object in isolation, but only by employing a collection of objects — most likely instances of different classes — that exchange messages [1]. Unfortunately, class-based object-oriented programming languages do not provide sufficient means to explicitly specify these collaborations. Today's languages allow the description of objects through the programming language abstraction of a class, yet they lack a peer abstraction for object collaborations. Programmers must resort to the use of *references* to indicate collaborations and thereby often hide the intent and, at the same time, further complicate any analysis of a program since references are a powerful, all encompassing programming construct.

Conceptual modeling languages, such as the Unified Modeling Language (UML) [2] and the Entity-Relationship (ER) model [3], allow explicit representation of object collaborations through associations and relationships, respectively.

---

* This work was partially supported by the National Competence Center in Research on Mobile Information and Communication Systems (NCCR-MICS), a center supported by the Swiss National Science Foundation under grant number 5005-67322.

E. Ernst (Ed.): ECOOP 2007, LNAI 4609, pp. 323–346, 2007.

The benefits of explicit representation of object collaborations also at the level of the programming language have been gaining increasing acceptance [4,5,6,7,8]. Languages devised in this spirit provide, in addition to classes, the programming language abstraction of a *relationship*. As classes allow the description of a collection of individual objects, relationships allow the description of a collection of groups of interacting objects. In both cases, the description involves the declaration of attributes and methods. Relationships furthermore indicate the classes of which the interacting objects are instances to delimit the scope of the collaboration.

The benefits of explicit representation of object collaborations through relationships at the level of the programming language are diverse [4,5,6,7,8]. Relationship-based implementations allow a *declarative* description of object collaborations. Class-based object-oriented implementations employ an *imperative* style since they represent object collaborations through references. The scope of a collaboration, for example, is explicitly declared in a relationship-based implementation. In a class-based object-oriented implementation, programmers must analyze the reference structure of the program to deduce the scope of the collaboration. Relationships are furthermore intrinsically bilateral, as both collaborators are known to the relationship. A class-based object-oriented implementation must deliberately introduce this bilateralism by providing a reference at each site of the collaboration. Relationship-based languages also allow the declaration of multiplicities (consistency constraints). In class-based object-oriented implementations, such multiplicities must be hand-coded by implementing the appropriate checks to enforce the constraints. These checks are most likely distributed among the classes participating in the collaboration, and this distribution carries the risk of introducing inconsistencies when the classes are updated. Relationships furthermore support the declaration of collaboration members. In class-based object-oriented implementations, such members must be taken care of manually. It appears overall that, as nicely put by Rumbaugh [5], "class-based object-oriented implementations of object collaborations *hide the semantic information* of collaborations but *expose their implementation details*" (emphasis added).

Unfortunately, the concepts supported by current relationship-based languages are not sufficient to specify object collaborations satisfactorily. Based on the example of an information system of a university (variations of this example can be found in several related publications [4,7,8,9]), we show which requirements of the system cannot be accommodated. Figure 1 shows the complete list of requirements for the university information system. Figure 2 depicts the corresponding UML class diagram of the system, and Fig. 3 sketches its implementation in a relationship-based language. There are several requirements that call for concepts not supported by current relationship-based languages. For example, the constraints that faculty members can neither substitute themselves nor each other (R7) and that students cannot assist courses they attend (R4) cannot be expressed through multiplicities. Also the restriction of the possible values attributes may assume, such as the year of study (R2), cannot be specified declaratively. The existence of entity properties that only apply when the

R1 The entities of the system are *students*, *courses*, and *faculty members*.

R2 For every student the *name*, a unique registration *number*, and the current *year* of study must be retained. The year of study cannot exceed 10. Courses must indicate their *titles*. Faculty members must list their *names*.

R3 Enrolled students must *attend* courses. When attending a course students can get a *mark* between 1 and 6.

R4 Students can *assist* courses as teaching assistants. Students cannot assist courses they are attending themselves. For every teaching assistant the *language of instruction* must be recorded. For every assisted course a maximal *group size* can be defined, which restricts the number of students that are assisted by a single teaching assistant. In case a maximal group size is prescribed for a course, then it must be guaranteed that the number of students assisted by a single teaching assistant must not exceed the maximal group size defined for that course.

R5 Students can *work for* a faculty member as research assistants, provided that they are at least in their third year. For every research assistant the *grant amount* paid can be retained.

R6 Every course must be *taught* by at least one faculty member.

R7 Every faculty member must name at least one other faculty member as *substitute*. No faculty member can be its own substitute, and two distinct faculty members cannot substitute each other.

Fig. 1. Requirements for the information system of a university

entity fulfills a particular role, such as the language of instruction for students assisting courses (R4), is a further example of an issue that can only be dealt with in current relationship-based languages by resorting to the introduction of auxiliary classes and further levels of indirection.

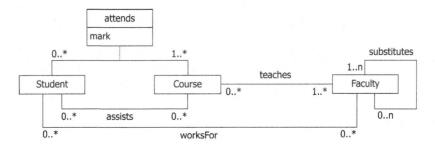

Fig. 2. UML class diagram modeling the simplified version of the information system of a university. The diagram uses an association class to allow the association `attends` to declare its own members.

In this paper, we show how to *specify object collaborations* in an *explicit* and *declarative* way. Our presentation is based on relationships but extends current relationship-based languages with concepts appropriate to accommodate the typical kinds of requirements imposed on software systems. In particular, we introduce *member interposition*, a concept allowing the specification of

```
relationship
  Attends (0-* Student learner, 1-* Course lecture) {
    int mark;
}
relationship
  Assists (0-* Student ta, 0-* Course course) {}

relationship
  WorksFor (0-* Student ra, 0-* Faculty supervisor) {}

relationship
  Teaches (1-* Faculty lecturer, 0-* Course lecture) {}

relationship
Substitutes (1-* Faculty substitute, 0-* Faculty substituted){}
```

Fig. 3. Implementation of the running example in a language supporting relationships. The code combines features present in RelJ [4] and/or the Data Structure Manager (DSM) [5]. Details not relevant to the discussion have been omitted.

relationship-dependent members of classes, and *relationship invariants*, a concept allowing the specification of the consistency constraints of relationships. Since we use *mathematical relations* as the fundamental abstractions to reason about relationships, we can express relationship invariants by means of the mathematical properties of the relations underlying the relationships. The abstraction of a relation furthermore allows a formalization of the concepts we introduce relying entirely on discrete mathematics.

The remainder of the paper is organized as follows: Sect. 2 introduces relations, the abstractions underlying the relational model. Sects. 3 and 4 detail member interposition and relationship invariants, respectively. Sect. 5 discusses further issues related to the presented concepts. Sect. 6 provides design guidelines for a programming language accommodating specifications as presented in this paper. Sect. 7 lists the related work and Sect. 8 concludes the paper.

2   Relations

In this section we introduce relations, the driving forces underlying the concepts presented in this paper. We also set up our terminology.

2.1   Abstracting Object Collaborations

The existence of an appropriate abstraction to reason about systems composed of classes and relationships is a prerequisite to their specification. We use the notion of a *mathematical relation* as an abstraction of a relationship. Figure 4 depicts the relationships Attends and Teaches. As classes describe the common properties of a collection of individual objects, we abstract them as *sets of objects*.

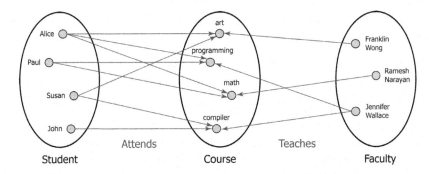

Fig. 4. Graphical representation of the `Attends` and `Teaches` relationship: classes (ellipses) are sets of objects (circles) and relationships (arrows in between ellipses) are sets of object tuples

As relationships describe the common properties of a collection of groups of collaborating objects, we abstract them as *sets of object tuples* and consequently as *relations*. Figure 4 thus contains the sets

$Student = \{\ Alice,\ Paul,\ Susan,\ John\}$
$Course\ =\ \{\ art,\ programming,\ math,\ compiler\}$
$Faculty\ =\ \{\ Franklin\ Wong,\ Ramesh\ Narayan,\ Jennifer\ Wallace\}$

and the relations

$Attends = \{\ Paul \mapsto programming,\ Paul \mapsto math,\ John \mapsto compiler,$
$\qquad\qquad Alice \mapsto art,\ Alice \mapsto programming,\ Alice \mapsto math,$
$\qquad\qquad Susan \mapsto art,\ Susan \mapsto compiler\}$
$Teaches = \{\ Jennifer\ Wallace \mapsto programming,\ Jennifer\ Wallace \mapsto compiler,$
$\qquad\qquad Ramesh\ Narayan \mapsto math,\ Franklin\ Wong \mapsto art\}$

Thanks to mathematical relations we can model a system composed of classes and relationships using discrete mathematics. The resulting *relational model* of a system then allows us to reason about a system composed of classes and relationships in a rigorous fashion. From its model, we can derive the specification of a system. The university information system yields the following initial model:

$$Attends \subseteq Student \times Course$$
$$Assists \subseteq Student \times Course$$
$$WorksFor \subseteq Student \times Faculty$$
$$Teaches \subseteq Faculty \times Course$$
$$Substitutes \subseteq Faculty \times Faculty$$

2.2 Terminology and Restrictions

Before continuing the presentation of the specification of object collaborations based on relations, we briefly set up the terminology used in this paper. We restrict the specification of object collaborations to the non-concurrent case and — because of space constraints — we do not discuss inheritance either.

Class: We consider classes as *types* and also as *sets*. Such a set contains objects that are instances of the type defined by the class declaration.

Relationship: We consider a relationship to be both a *type* and a *relation*. The relation contains the *object tuples* that are instances of the type defined by the relationship declaration.

Participants: The participants of a relationship are the *carrier sets* (i.e., classes) of the relation defining the relationship.

Roles: The participants of a relationship declaration can be named to indicate the conceptual *role* the particular class plays in the relationship.

3 Member Interposition

Some properties of objects only apply when the object is fulfilling a particular role [10]. The attributes instructionLanguage (see Fig. 1, R4) and grantAmount (R5) are examples of such properties since these properties are required only for teaching and research assistants, respectively, but not for all students. Thus, the selection of properties that are required for an object depends on the relationship(s) the object takes part in.

3.1 Problem Description and Solution

Member interposition accommodates relationship-dependent properties of objects. Member interposition allows us to define properties as part of the role a particular class fulfills in a relationship. Figure 5 gives an example. Both the attributes instructionLanguage and grantAmount are declared in the relationships on which these attributes depend and as part of the roles played by the classes to which these attributes apply (are interposed into). Attribute instructionLanguage is declared in relationship Assists for the role teaching assistant (ta), attribute grantAmount in relationship WorksFor for the role research assistant (ra).

Without member interposition, we would have to use the role object [11] and extension object [12] design patterns, respectively. We then would subclass Student to provide specializations both for teaching and research assistants and would need to introduce an additional level of indirection to represent the possible roles students can play and to allow dynamic casts between these roles. Member interposition, on the other hand, allows us to accommodate relationship-dependent properties of classes without resorting to inheritance and role classes.

Relationships can declare both interposed members and non-interposed members. Attribute mark in relationship Attends is an instance of a member that is not interposed. Whereas an interposed member describes a class that plays a particular role in a relationship, a non-interposed member describes the

```
relationship Attends
  participants (Student learner, Course lecture) {
  int mark;
}
relationship Assists
  participants (Student ta, Course course) {
    // attribute interposed into role ta
  String >ta instructionLanguage;
}
relationship WorksFor
  participants (Student ra, Faculty supervisor) {
    // attribute interposed into role ra
  int >ra grantAmount;
}
```

Fig. 5. Relationship members are declared either at the level of the relationship or, through *member interposition*, at the level of a participating role. Interposed members are declared using the ">" symbol and are depicted underlined.

collaboration that exists between the participants of a relationship. We therefore also refer to interposed members as *participant-level* members and to non-interposed members as *relationship-level* members. Intuitively (see Fig. 4), we can imagine an interposed member as being attached to each object (circle) of the class (ellipse) that is the target of interposition. A non-interposed member, on the other hand, is attached to each object tuple (arrow) of the relationship. In the current specification, the attribute instructionLanguage records per teaching assistant the language of instruction. If we interposed attribute instructionLanguage into the role course instead of the role ta, we could indicate in what language a particular course must be assisted. A third option would be to declare attribute instructionLanguage as a non-interposed member. In this case, teaching assistants would be allowed to use different languages for different courses.

Like non-interposed members, interposed members are part of the interface[1] of their defining relationships (and not part of the interface of the classes they are interposed into). This treatment has two consequences. First, the names of interposed members must be unique only within their defining relationship. An interposed member can therefore be named the same as a member of the class that is the target of interposition or the same as an interposed member of a different relationship that has the same target of interposition. In both cases, separate copies of these members are maintained. Second, operations to access interposed members must be called on the relationship and are not allowed to be called directly on the targeted class. According to Snyder [14], encapsulation in class-based object-oriented programming languages aims to minimize the module interdependences through the application of strict external interfaces. Since

---

[1] We use the term interface as introduced by Parnas [13].

member interposition leaves the interfaces of the classes being the target of interposition unchanged, the encapsulation of these classes remains unaffected.

3.2 Formalization

Using the abstraction of a relation and the means provided by discrete mathematics we can formalize the interposed and non-interposed attributes of Fig. 5 as follows:

$$Attends\_mark \in Attends \nrightarrow [1 .. 6] \qquad (3.1)$$

$$Assists\_instructionLanguage \in \mathrm{dom}(Assists) \rightarrow String \qquad (3.2)$$

$$WorksFor\_grantAmount \in \mathrm{dom}(WorksFor) \nrightarrow \mathbb{N} \qquad (3.3)$$

As illustrated by (3.1), we can model a relationship-level attribute as a relation from a relation to the set of possible values the attribute may assume (see Table 1 for an explanation of the notation used). In the example, the relationship-level attribute mark is a partial function from the relation *Attends* to the set of integer numbers ranging from 1 to 6. Note that we restrict the range of the function to [1 .. 6] as imposed by R3 in Fig. 1. Participant-level attributes (3.2) and (3.3), on the other hand, are relations from the domain or range of a relation to the set of possible values the attribute may assume. The interposed attribute instructionLanguage (3.2), for example, is a relation that has the domain of the relation *Assists* — which is a subset of the set *Student* — as its domain, and a set of strings as its range. Note that we use a total function for the relation since we need to retain the language of instruction for every student assisting a course (R4).

Table 1. Mathematical notation as defined in [15]

Symbol	Description
$\mapsto$	Pair constructing operator
$S \leftrightarrow T$	Set of binary relations from S to T
$S \leftrightarrow\!\!\!\!\rightarrow T$	Set of surjective relations from S to T
$S \leftrightarrow\!\!\!\!\leftrightarrow T$	Set of total relations from S to T
$S \nrightarrow T$	Set of partial functions from S to T
$S \rightarrow T$	Set of total functions from S to T
$S \,;\, T$	Forward composition of relations S and T
S^{-1}	Inverse of relation S
$\mathrm{dom}(S)$	Domain of relation S
$\mathrm{ran}(S)$	Range of relation S
$S[m]$	Image of the set m under the relation S
$\mathrm{card}(m)$	Number of elements of set m
$\mathrm{id}(m)$	Identity relation built on set m

Since member interposition targets at the role of a participant rather than at the class as a whole, it is possible to selectively add properties to objects that are instances of the same class, but play different roles in the same relationship (relationship Substitutes, for example). In such a case, we formalize the relation defining the relationship as a relation from one subset of the participant to another subset of the participant, with each subset containing the objects that play a particular role in the relationship.

4   Relationship Invariants

Current relationship-based languages do not provide the appropriate means to declare consistency constraints other than multiplicities. As demonstrated by the running example of this paper, the existence of more elaborate constraints, such as the restriction that students cannot assist courses they are attending (Fig. 1, R4), are an important trait of object collaborations. We introduce the concept of *relationship invariants* to express consistency constraints required for the specification of object collaborations.

Invariants proved viable for the specification of consistency constraints in a number of class-based object-oriented programming and specification languages, such as the Eiffel programming language [16,17], the Spec# programming system [18], and the behavioral interface specification language for Java, JML (Java Modeling Language), and its verification tools [19,20]. Whereas invariants of class-based object-oriented programming languages are imposed on individual objects (object invariants) or on the class as a whole (static class invariants) [21], we allow invariants to range over several classes by imposing them on one or several relationships. As we maintain a set-oriented view of classes and relationships, invariants implicitly quantify over the objects or object tuples contained in the set the invariants are imposed on. Classical invariants of class-based object-oriented programming and specification languages are different: such invariants are restricted to individual objects and classes, respectively. The restricted scope of classical invariants makes the verification of invariants particularly challenging in case an invariant involves references [22,23].

We distinguish between *intra-relationship* and *inter-relationship* invariants, and between *value-based* and *structural* invariants. The first category denotes the scope of the invariant. An intra-relationship invariant is imposed on a single relationship and thus restricts the collaboration of the participants within that relationship. An inter-relationship invariant involves several relationships and thus defines how relationships relate to each other. The second category distinguishes whether values that relationships or participating classes assume for their members are taken into account for the invariant specification. A value-based invariant defines the values or the range of values the elements in the scope of the invariant declaration are allowed to assume for the specified members. A structural invariant restricts the possible ways different elements in the scope of the invariant declaration can be paired up irrespective of the values these elements assume for their members. The two categories are orthogonal, yielding four kinds of invariants. We provide a formalization of each kind of invariant using the abstraction of a relation for a relationship.

4.1 Structural Invariants

We start the presentation of the different kinds of invariants with structural invariants as they are similar to multiplicity restrictions. In fact, multiplicity restrictions are a subset of structural intra-relationship invariants.

Structural Intra-Relationship Invariants. The requirements document of the university information system (see Fig. 1) lists several structural invariants, such as the restrictions that enrolled students must attend courses (R3) and that every faculty member must name at least one other faculty member as substitute (R7). These restrictions, expressed by *multiplicities* in current relationship-based programming languages, define the structural characteristics of a relationship and can thus be formalized by indicating the structural properties of the relations defining the relationship. For example, the $(0..*,1..*)$ multiplicity of the relationship Attends can be formalized as a total relation, and the $(1..*,0..*)$ multiplicity of the relationship Substitutes can be formalized as a surjective relation, as outlined by (4.1) and (4.5), respectively, in the following:

$$Attends \in Student \leftrightarrow Course \tag{4.1}$$
$$Assists \in Student \leftrightarrow Course \tag{4.2}$$
$$WorksFor \in Student \leftrightarrow Faculty \tag{4.3}$$
$$Teaches \in Faculty \leftrightarrow Course \tag{4.4}$$
$$Substitutes \in Faculty \leftrightarrow\!\!\!\to Faculty \tag{4.5}$$

There are additional structural invariants present in the running example, for example, that no faculty member can be his or her own substitute and that two distinct faculty members cannot substitute each other (R7). These structural constraints, not expressible through multiplicities, define the asymmetry (4.6) and irreflexiveness (4.7) of the Substitutes relationship and can be formalized as follows:

$$Substitutes \cap Substitutes^{-1} = \varnothing \tag{4.6}$$
$$Substitutes \cap \mathrm{id}(Faculty) = \varnothing \tag{4.7}$$

Based on the example of the Substitutes relationship, Fig. 6 illustrates how structural intra-relationship invariants can be specified as part of relationship declarations.

Structural Inter-Relationship Invariants. According to the requirements document of the university information system (see Fig. 1) students are not allowed to assist courses they are attending themselves (R4). This requirement also represents a structural invariant, but, in contrast to the invariants discussed in the previous section, this invariant encompasses several relationships:

```
relationship Substitutes
  participants (Faculty substitute, Faculty substituted) {

  invariant
    surjectiveRelation(Substitutes) &&
    asymmetric(Substitutes) &&
    irreflexive(Substitutes);
}
```

Fig. 6. Relationship Substitutes with a structural intra-relationship invariant: the relation defining the relationship is surjective, asymmetric, and irreflexive

the relationship Assists ("students are not allowed to *assist* courses...") and the relationship Attends ("...they are *attending* themselves"). To satisfy the requirement, the two defining relations of the relationships must be disjoint:

$$Attends \cap Assists = \varnothing \tag{4.8}$$

Figure 7 illustrates how the structural inter-relationship invariant (4.8) can be specified as part of a program composed of classes and relationships. Unlike an intra-relationship invariant, which can be directly listed as part of the relationship declaration, an inter-relationship declaration appears outside of the scope of the relationship declarations it is imposed on.

```
invariant (Attends, Assists) attendsAssistsDisjointness:
  Attends intersection Assists == emptySet;
```

Fig. 7. Structural inter-relationship invariant guaranteeing that teaching assistants cannot attend the courses they are assisting. An inter-relationship invariant can be named and indicates the relationships it is imposed on in parentheses.

4.2   Value-Based Invariants

Value-based intra- and inter-relationship invariants bear resemblance to traditional invariants of class-based object-oriented programming languages as traditional invariants are assertions on the values the fields of an object or a class may assume. Value-based invariants, however, exceed the scope of traditional invariants as they range over several classes and relationships.

Value-Based Intra-Relationship Invariants. The requirements document of the university information system (see Fig. 1) demands that students must be at least in their third year to become research assistants (R5). This requirement can be expressed through a value-based intra-relationship invariant. As demonstrated by (4.10) below we can formalize the invariant by requiring that

```
relationship WorksFor
  participants (Student ra, Faculty supervisor) {
    // attribute interposed into role ra
    int >ra grantAmount;

  invariant
    relation(WorksFor) &&
    ra.year > 2 &&
    partialFunction(grantAmount) in N;
}
```

Fig. 8. Relationship invariant consisting of a structural intra-relationships invariant **relation**(WorksFor) and two value-based intra-relationship invariants guaranteeing that research assistants are at least in their third year of study (ra.year > 2) and that the amount of funding the student receives is optional and a natural number (**partialFunction**(grantAmount) in **N**)

the range of the forward composition $WorksFor^{-1}$; $Student\_year$ is a subset of the set of integer numbers ranging from 3 to 10. The forward composition yields the set of pairs of faculty members and integer numbers, with one pair for each group of research assistants that are supervised by the same faculty member and that share the same year of study. The relation $Student\_year$ (4.9) abstracts the attribute year of class Student.

$$Student\_year \in Student \rightarrow [1 .. 10] \tag{4.9}$$

$$\mathrm{ran}(WorksFor^{-1} ; Student\_year) \subseteq [3 .. 10] \tag{4.10}$$

Interestingly, the invariant (4.10) involves a member of a participant and not a member of a relationship. As the constraint imposed on the member depends on the relationship — the year of study needs to be considered only for research assistants but not for students in general — it cannot be declared as a class invariant (see Sect. 5.2) but must be declared as a relationship invariant. In a mere class-based implementation of the running example with support for traditional invariants, the definition of the constraint would have to account for this dependence. To guard the evaluation of the invariant, a resulting object invariant would most likely introduce an implication of the form supervisor !=
null ==> **this**.year > 2.

Figure 8 illustrates how the value-based intra-relationship invariant (4.10) can be specified as part of the declaration of relationship WorksFor. The figure furthermore reveals that an invariant declaration can consist of several kinds of invariants. Besides the value-based intra-relationship invariant imposing the constraint just discussed, Fig. 8 lists the structural intra-relationship invariant **relation**(WorksFor) and a further value-based intra-relationship invariant **partialFunction**(grantAmount) in **N** defining the nature of the interposed member grantAmount. The corresponding formalization of the attribute grantAmount was introduced in Sect. 3.2.

```
invariant (Attends, Assists) enoughAssistants:
  forAll c (isDefined(Assists.select(course==c).maxGroupSize)
    ==> numberOf(Attends.lecture.select(c)) <=
      numberOf(Assists.course.select(c)) *
      Assists.select(course==c).maxGroupSize);
```

Fig. 9. Value-based inter-relationship invariant guaranteeing that there are enough teaching assistants per course. The use of role names as in `Attends.lecture` allows the retrieval of the set of objects participating in the relationship and playing the indicated role. The **select** operator allows the retrieval of the set of objects (when applied to a role) or set of object tuples (when applied to the relationship) that match the condition indicated in parentheses. For further details see Sect. 6.

Value-Based Inter-Relationship Invariants. The requirements document of the university information system (see Fig. 1, R4) prescribes that the number of students assisted by a single teaching assistant for a particular course does not exceed the maximal group size defined for that course, if defined at all. This requirement guarantees that enough teaching assistants are recruited for a particular course. We can formalize this restriction by requiring that, for every course, the number of students attending the course ($\mathrm{card}(Attends^{-1}[\{c\}])$) is less than or equal to the number of assistants assisting the course ($\mathrm{card}(Assists^{-1}[\{c\}])$) multiplied by the maximal group size for the course ($Assists\_maxGroupSize(c)$). As indicated by the implication in (4.11), the inequality is evaluated for a course only that is currently assisted and for which the attribute maxGroupSize is defined.

$$\forall c \cdot (c \in \mathrm{dom}(Assists\_maxGroupSize) \Rightarrow$$
$$\mathrm{card}(Attends^{-1}[\{c\}]) \leq \qquad (4.11)$$
$$\mathrm{card}(Assists^{-1}[\{c\}]) * Assists\_maxGroupSize(c))$$

Figure 9 shows the corresponding program specification of the value-based inter-relationship invariant (4.11). In the example, we need to introduce explicit quantification as the invariant must hold only for selected constituent objects of the tuples involved.

5 Discussion

The use of relationships together with the concepts introduced in this paper influences not only the specification of object collaborations but also the development of programs composed of classes and relationships in general. In this section, we discuss some consequences.

5.1 References

The introduction of relationships changes the purpose of references. In class-based object-oriented programs references allow the implementation of object collaborations. For example, students keep references to the list of courses they attend. With explicit relationships, on the other hand, classes no longer need to maintain references to (instances of) the classes they collaborate with as the description of this collaboration is "out-sourced" to the corresponding relationship.

Relationships, however, need a kind of reference to access the objects that participate in a relationship. It is questionable, though, whether traditional references are the appropriate means to implement the "awareness" of a relationship of its participants. To answer this question, we must consider what the characteristics of references are and which traits of these characteristics are required in the case of relationships. References can be used in two different ways: (i) to access the *artifact* that the reference refers to and (ii) to read or change the *value* (object identifier in a class-based object-oriented context) of the reference. With respect to relationships, the first use of references is clearly desired — it must be possible to access the objects that participate in a relationship. However, an object tuple should not be allowed to change its identity by replacing (or possibly erasing) any of its constituent objects. Relationships therefore need *restricted forms* of references that allow access of the constituent objects but prohibit direct manipulation of the values assigned to references. Role names, for example, can serve that purpose.

Of course, it must be possible to change the participation of objects in relationships. Because we consider classes and relationships as sets — sets of objects and sets of object tuples, respectively — changes in relationship participation break down to adding and removing object tuples to and from relationships. These operations encompass the relationship as a whole and must therefore be executed outside of the scope of the targeted relationship (see Sect. 6.1).

5.2   Class Invariants

A specification of programs composed of classes and relationships must include the declaration of class invariants besides the declaration of relationship invariants. *Class invariants* allow the specification of the consistency constraints that are imposed on the instances of individual classes. Since classes do not describe their collaborations with other classes, class invariants have an *intra-class* scope and are purely *value-based*. To restrict the possible values objects can assume for their members, we abstract object members as relations from classes (sets) to the sets of possible values their members may assume. The mathematical properties of these relations then express the class invariant.

Equations (5.1), (5.2), and (5.3) show the relations abstracting the members of class Student. Equation (5.2) uses a total injection from the set *Student* to the set of natural numbers to express that every student must have a number which is unique.

$$Student\_name \in Student \rightarrow String \qquad (5.1)$$

$$Student\_number \in Student \rightarrowtail \mathbb{N} \qquad (5.2)$$

$$Student\_year \in Student \rightarrow [1 .. 10] \qquad (5.3)$$

```
class Student {
  String name;
  int number;
  int year;

  invariant
    totalFunction(name) &&
    totalInjection(number) in N &&
    totalFunction(year) in [1..10];
}
```

Fig. 10. Specification of the class invariant of Student restricting the possible values class members can assume

Figure 10 shows the corresponding declaration of the class invariants of class Student. The invariant that specifies that student numbers must be unique highlights the benefits of treating classes and class members as sets and relations, respectively. As opposed to its counterpart in a class-based implementation, it is simple and clear-cut. In a class-based setting, on the other hand, the specification of the same constraint would demand a more extensive invariant. To express the injectivity of the relation *Student_number*, a static class invariant would need to be declared which uses explicit quantification to range over all instances of the class and to make sure that the attribute number is different for every instance.

5.3   Invariant Preservation

The use of invariants as part of the declaration of classes and relationships raises the question of their verification. Irrespective of the approach taken — run-time verification (*dynamic*) or compile-time verification (*static*) — the invariants imposed on a system composed of classes and relationships must be preserved from one state to the other along state transitions of the system.

The relational model can help to substantially decrease the number of transitions that must be inspected to verify the invariant. Thanks to the categorization of invariants we can identify for each kind of invariant the operations that cause state transitions that potentially endanger the invariant. For structural invariants, for example, the operations causing such transitions are the addition to and removal of objects from classes, and the addition to and removal of object tuples from relationships. If we consider, in addition to its category, also the mathematical properties of an invariant, we can delimit the cases in which state transitions occur that potentially endanger the invariant.

In the most general case of a relation as a structural intra-relationship invariant the following interdependence between the relationship and its participants exists:

$$R \in A \leftrightarrow B \Leftrightarrow \forall a, b \cdot (a \mapsto b \in R \Rightarrow a \in A \land b \in B) \tag{5.4}$$

From (5.4) we can delimit the following invariant-endangering operations:

- the removal of an object from a class if the object participates in a relationship with the class being a participant of that relationship
- the addition of an object tuple if the constituent objects are not part of the participants of the relation.

The number of invariant-endangering operations increases with the restrictiveness of the relation. In case of a total relation, for example, we can delimit the following invariant-endangering operations:

- the addition of an object to a class that is the domain of the total relation
- the removal of an object from a class that is the domain of the total relation
- the addition of an object tuple if the constituent objects are not part of the participants of the total relation
- the removal of an object tuple from the total relation if no other object tuple exists in that relation that contains the first constituent object of the tuple to be removed.

The handling of these invariant-endangering operations must be left to the respective programming language or system that implements the specification concepts introduced in this paper. An implementation could, for example, deal with certain invariant-endangering operations by executing a corresponding corrective action to maintain the invariant. A further implementation concern is to determine the granularity of atomic sequences of operations. Most likely, an implementation will provide the means to combine several invariant-endangering operations in one atomic unit and thus allow a further decrease of the verification load.

We expect the relational model of object collaborations to be helpful with verifying invariants statically. Thanks to its foundation in discrete mathematics, a relation model describing a concrete system composed of classes and relationships could easily be transformed to the input required by a theorem prover or model checker, which then would allow the verification of the system.

6 Language Design Issues

In this section we sketch the main features of a programming language that incorporates the specification concepts introduced in this paper.

6.1 Three Dimensions of Problem Decomposition

In their seminal paper on programming with abstract data types, Liskov et al. [24] introduce two forms of programming language abstractions: procedures (functional abstraction) and operation clusters (abstract data types). We regard the separation of functional decomposition from data decomposition to be valuable as it allows us to separate the definition of artifacts from their use. Due to our focus on the specification of object collaborations, we complement the abstractions introduced by Liskov et al. with the abstraction representing object collaborations. A programming language that incorporates the specification concepts introduced in this paper thus needs to support the following language abstractions:

- *Class (data decomposition)*: Programming language abstraction representing classes as defined in Sect. 2.2.
- *Relationship (collaboration decomposition)*: Programming language abstraction representing relationships as defined in Sect. 2.2.
- *Application (functional decomposition)*: Programming language abstraction comprising a number of procedures to manipulate the sets of objects and object tuples contained in a program.

6.2   Language Definition

A programming language that incorporates the specification concepts introduced in this paper must support the types *ValueType*, *ClassName*, *RelationshipName*, *Object⟨ClassName⟩*, and *Query⟨Set⟩*. A *ValueType* is a type with a value type semantics. Whereas both *ClassName* and *RelationshipName* are types that denote sets, *Object⟨ClassName⟩* is a parameterized type that stands for a particular instance of the class provided as an argument. A *Query⟨Set⟩* is also a parameterized type that represents sets of objects or object tuples. Possible arguments to a query type are class names, relationship names, or any expressions composed of relationship names and relational operators yielding a set as a result. Both parameterized types are instances of *HandleType*, which represents a Java final-like reference to either an object or a set of objects and object tuples, respectively.

Like Bierman and Wren [4] we use tables and maps (see Fig. 11) to formalize the declarations appearing in a program devised in the language under discussion. We have tables for classes, relationships, inter-relationship invariants, and for applications. Each table is a map from a name (class name, for example) to a definition (class definition, for example). Definitions are tuples with the elements being sets or further maps. For example, a class definition is a tuple $(\mathcal{A}, \mathcal{M}, ci)$ where $\mathcal{A}$ is a map from attribute names to attribute types, $\mathcal{M}$ is a map from method names to method definitions, and ci is the class invariant body. The signature definitions in Fig. 11 reveal an important characteristic of the programming language: both the attributes of classes and relationships are of value type only (see Sect. 5.1 for a further discussion). As relationships must have access to their participating objects, *RelMethodMap* lists the set *RoleName* in its range. Unlike classes and relationships, applications are neither types nor do they declare invariants. Applications are mere procedural modules that consist of a number of variables and procedures. As these procedures need to instantiate classes and need to add to and remove objects from classes and object tuples from relationships, respectively, applications can declare variables of type *HandleType*.

6.3   Creation, Addition, Removal, and Retrieval

An appropriate programming language must provide built-in operators to *instantiate* classes, to *add* to and *remove* objects from classes, and to add to and

$$ClassTable \in ClassName \rightarrow AttrMap \times ClMethodMap \times ClassInvBody$$

$$RelationshipTable \in RelationshipName \rightarrow RoleMap \times AttrMap \times RelMethodMap$$
$$\times RelInvBody$$

$$InterRelInvTable \in (InvName \times (RelationshipName \times \cdots \times RelationshipName))$$
$$\rightarrow InterRelInvBody$$

$$ApplicationTable \in ApplicationName \rightarrow VarMap \times ProcedureMap$$

$$RoleMap \in RoleName \rightarrow ClassName$$

$$AttrMap \in AttrName \rightarrow ValueType$$

$$ClMethodMap \in MethodName \rightarrow ArgMap \times LocalMap \times ValueType \times MethodBody$$

$$RelMethodMap \in MethodName \rightarrow ArgMap \times LocalMap \times RoleName \times ValueType$$
$$\times MethodBody$$

$$ArgMap \in ArgName \rightarrow ValueType$$

$$LocalMap \in VarName \rightarrow ValueType$$

$$VarMap \in VarName \rightarrow (ValueType \cup HandleType)$$

$$ProcedureMap \in ProcName \rightarrow ProcArgMap \times ProcLocalMap$$
$$\times (ValueType \cup HandleType) \times ProcBody$$

$$ProcArgMap \in ArgName \rightarrow (ValueType \cup HandleType)$$

$$ProcLocalMap \in VarName \rightarrow (ValueType \cup HandleType)$$

Fig. 11. Signatures of class, relationship, and application tables and associated maps

remove object tuples from relationships. As both classes and relationships are sets, the addition and removal operators are conceptually equivalent with set union and set subtraction.

Figure 12 shows a program fragment implementing the running example. The fragment consists of several class and relationship declarations and one application declaration. Class Student declares a constructor to allow creation of a single object. The constructor is called in procedure initialize in application UniversityInformationSystem and assigned to the object handle alice. The object denoted by alice is then added to class Student in line 27. For every course Alice is attending, a corresponding student-course pair is added to the relationship Attends (28-30). In the examples, the **add** operator is used to add single objects and single object tuples, respectively. The **add** operator, however, can also be used to add a set of objects and a set of object tuples to a class and relationship, respectively. The same explanations apply likewise to the **remove** operator.

An appropriate programming language must further provide built-in operators to *retrieve* sets of objects and sets of object tuples. These operators must enable the retrieval of the set of objects playing a particular role in a relationship and the retrieval of the set of objects or object tuples that satisfy a given condition.

Figure 12 illustrates the use of the **select** operator to retrieve the set of object tuples that match the condition provided as an argument. In line 21, all faculty-course pairs are retrieved with the object denoted by the handle

```
   class Student {
 2   Object<Student> Student(String name, int number, int year) {
       this.name = name;
 4     this.number = number;
       this.year = year;
 6   }...
   }...
 8 relationship Attends
     participants (Student learner, Course lecture) {...}
10 ...
   application UniversityInformationSystem {
12   // handles to objects
     Object<Student> alice, john, susan, paul;
14   Object<Faculty> jenniferWallace, rameshNarayan, franklinWong;
     Object<Course> programming, math, compiler, art;
16   ...
     void main() {
18   initialize();
       // assign all students of Franklin Wong the grade 6
20   Query<Teaches.lecture> coursesFw;
       coursesFw = Teaches.select(lecturer==franklinWong).lecture;
22   Attends.select(lecture==coursesFw).setMark(6);
     }
24   void initialize() {
       ...
26     alice = new Student("Alice", 778, 1);
       Student.add(alice);
28     Attends.add(alice, programming);
       Attends.add(alice, math);
30     Attends.add(alice, art);
     }...
32 }
```

Fig. 12. Program fragment consisting of several class and relationship declarations and one application declaration. The fragment shows the creation of an object (26), the addition of an object to a class (27), and the addition of object pairs to a relationship (28-30). Line 20 illustrates the use of queries as handles to a set that contains the result of a retrieval operation. Line 22, furthermore highlights the set-oriented character of the language: method setMark is called on the set of student-course pairs such that the students contained in the set attend a class taught by Franklin Wong.

franklinWong playing the role of the lecturer. On this result set, the role operator lecture is applied to return only the set of courses that are taught by Franklin Wong. Of interest in the example is also the declaration of a *query type* in line 20. According to the argument of the type, the query coursesFw is a handle to a set of objects that are instances of type Course. Queries are a powerful construct as they allow us to type intermediate retrieval results. In the example, the query encompasses only one relationship, however, as a query accepts any argument that is a set, any expression composed of relationship names and relational operators yielding a set as a result can be declared as an argument of a query.

As demonstrated by the instructions on line 20-22, relationships ease the handling of object collections. Willis et al. [25] introduced a prototype extension to Java that supports the concept of first-class queries to dispose of iterators otherwise needed to traverse object collections. However, such first-class queries still need to explicitly indicate the matching attributes that establish the "join" condition. With relationships, on the other hand, queries do not have to indicate the join conditions as they are implicitly established through the relationship declaration.

6.4   Atomic Procedures

Separating application declarations from class and relationship declarations allows us furthermore to separate the declaration of invariants from their verification. As the procedures of applications are the only ones to manipulate classes and relationships, they are also the only ones to endanger the invariants established on the classes and relationships. Therefore, in a programming language that incorporates the specification concepts introduced in this paper, the body of an application procedure defines the granularity of atomic sequences of operations. Invariants, consequently, must hold only on entry and exit of procedures, but not during procedure execution. In Fig. 12, for example, the structural intra-relationship invariant of relationship Attends is temporarily violated after the addition of the object denoted by alice to class Student in line 27 (relationship Attends is defined by a total relation). Only after the addition of the first student-course pair to the relationship Attends for a course Alice is attending, the invariant is re-established and preserved until the end of the procedure.

7   Related Work

In this section we discuss the related work. To be consistent with previous sections, we use our terminology for the discussion and indicate the actual terms used in the respective publication(s), if different, in parentheses.

Rumbaugh [5] first discovered the important role relationships (relations) play in object-oriented programming and thus introduces an object-oriented programming language, the Data Structure Manager (DSM), that complements classes with relationships. Classes in DSM can declare role names for their identification in a relationship, a concept we adopted for the specification of object collaborations. Rumbaugh also perceives relationships as sets of object tuples, however, he does not further exploit his observation. Our work, in contrast, goes further and links relationships to discrete mathematics, allowing the use of mathematical relations to define invariants, a concept more powerful than the multiplicities (cardinalities) supported in DSM. Furthermore, we support relationship members and member interposition, both concepts not present in Rumbaugh's work. The missing support for member interposition is also the reason why Rumbaugh introduces qualified relations. A qualified relation is a special instance of a ternary relationship that allows the addition of a distinguishing attribute to one of the two participants of the relationship. With member interposition, on the other hand, the need for a ternary relationship in such cases fades as the distinguishing attribute can be interposed into the respective participant.

Albano et al. [6] develop a strongly typed object-oriented database programming language with explicit support for relationships (associations) that is specifically tailored to fit the requirements of database applications. Like our work, the language Albano et al. devised allows the declaration of relationship attributes; however, it does not support relationship methods, nor member interposition. In contrast to Rumbaugh, the authors allow programmers not only to declare multiplicities (cardinality and surjectivity) but also to indicate how these constraints must be maintained, i.e., whether to cascade an operation that endangers the constraint or whether to prevent it from being executed. Like DSM, however, the language of Albano et al. lacks support for expressing constraints other than multiplicities.

The main contribution of the work by Bierman and Wren [4] is to provide the type system and the operational semantics of a Java-like language that supports relationships. In this way, the authors describe how a strongly typed class-based object-oriented language, like Java, can be extended to support relationships. Bierman and Wren further introduce relationship inheritance, a concept not considered in this paper. Again, our work mainly differs from the work by Bierman and Wren in its support for member interposition and relationship invariants.

Pearce and Noble [7,8] show how to use aspects [26,27] to implement relationships and multiplicities in a class-based object-oriented language. In an aspect-based implementation, relationship members can then be interposed into participants through inter-type declarations.

Noble and Grundy [28] describe ways of persisting relationships from the modeling to the implementation stage in object-oriented development by transforming analysis relationships into corresponding classes. Their approach is purely class-based and does not mention language support for relationships.

Helm et al. [29] use contracts to specify the behavioral compositions in class-based object-oriented systems. Similar to relationships, these contracts allow the programmer to explicitly state which classes collaborate with each other. The focus of the work by Helm et al., however, is the specification of collaborative behavior. A contract, for example, can declare actions that need to be executed by the participants and can impose an ordering on the execution.

Aksit et al. [30] propose Abstract Communication Types (ACTs), classes describing object interactions, as a means to encapsulate these interactions at the programming language level. ACTs rely on composition filters for their integration with the remaining system and act in response to calls issued from the underlying classes that are forwarded and possibly adapted by these filters. Relationships, on the contrary, are self-contained and independent of the events happening in the participating classes.

Herrmann [31] describes a Java-like language supporting Object Teams, the modules encapsulating multi-object collaborations. The focus of Herrmann's work is the a posteriori integration of collaborations into existing systems. The language thus allows the programmer to forward method calls from teams to base classes and offers advice-like constructs, known from aspect-oriented programming [26], to override methods of base classes.

Reenskaug [10] introduces role models to describe the structure of cooperating objects along with their static and dynamic properties. Role models are purely conceptual and focus on message-based interactions; however, they could assist in the identification of relationships during system design as relationships can be regarded as representations of particular role models.

8   Concluding Remarks

Relationships capture the collaborations between objects and provide a key to understanding large-scale object-oriented systems. This paper introduces mathematical relations as an abstraction of relationships and develops the concept of member interposition (which points out those members of classes that participate in a relationship). Once relationships are explicit in a program, it is possible to express invariants that extend beyond the inside of a class (or class instance). Invariants can be classified along two orthogonal dimensions: there are intra-relationship and inter-relationship invariants as well as value-based and structural invariants.

Understanding and reasoning about object-oriented programs remains a difficult issue, and many approaches have been suggested to help the programmer in this task. Mathematical relations as a formal model of relationships provide a solid foundation to deal with the object collaborations in such a program. Relationships that are explicit widen the view of the programmer (and ultimately the view of tools) so that it is possible to reason (and optimize) beyond class boundaries.

Acknowledgments

We thank Jean-Raymond Abrial, Peter Müller, and Laurent Voisin for their feedback.

References

1. Goldberg, A., Robson, D.: Smalltalk-80: The Language and Its Implementation. Addison-Wesley, Reading (1983)
2. Jacobson, I., Booch, G., Rumbaugh, J.E.: The Unified Software Development Process. Addison-Wesley, Reading (1999)
3. Chen, P.P.S.: The entity-relationship model - toward a unified view of data. ACM Transactions on Database Systems (TODS) 1(1), 9–36 (1976)
4. Bierman, G.M., Wren, A.: First-class relationships in an object-oriented language. In: Black, A.P. (ed.) ECOOP 2005. LNCS, vol. 3586, pp. 262–286. Springer, Heidelberg (2005)

5. Rumbaugh, J.: Relations as semantic constructs in an object-oriented language. In: 2nd ACM Conference on Object-Oriented Programming Systems, Languages and Applications (OOPSLA '87), pp. 466–481. ACM Press, New York (1987)

6. Albano, A., Ghelli, G., Orsini, R.: A relationship mechanism for a strongly typed object-oriented database programming language. In: 17th International Conference on Very Large Data Bases (VLDB'91), pp. 565–575. Morgan Kaufmann Publishers Inc. San Francisco (1991)

7. Pearce, D.J., Noble, J.: Relationship aspects. In: 5th International Conference on Aspect-Oriented Software Development (AOSD '06), pp. 75–86. ACM Press, New York (2006)

8. Pearce, D.J., Noble, J.: Relationship aspect patterns. In: 11th European Conference on Pattern Languages of Programs (EuroPLoP'06) (2006)

9. Booch, G.: The Unified Modeling Language User Guide. Addison-Wesley, Reading (1999)

10. Reenskaug, T., Wold, P., Lehne, O.A.: Working with Objects: The OOram Software Engineering Method. Manning/Prentice Hall, Englewood Cliffs (1996)

11. Bäumer, D., Riehle, D., Siberski, W., Wulf, M.: The role object pattern. In: 4th Conference on Pattern Languages of Programs (PLoP'97) (1997)

12. Gamma, E.: The extension objects pattern. In: 3rd Conference on Pattern Languages of Programs (PLoP'96) (1996)

13. Parnas, D.L.: On the criteria to be used in decomposing systems into modules. Communications of the ACM 15(12), 1053–1058 (1972)

14. Snyder, A.: Encapsulation and inheritance in object-oriented programming languages. In: 1st ACM Conference on Object-Oriented Programming Systems, Languages and Applications (OOPSLA '86), vol. 21, pp. 38–45. ACM Press, New York (1986)

15. Abrial, J.R.: The B-Book: Assigning Programs to Meanings. Cambridge University Press, Cambridge (1996)

16. Meyer, B.: Object-Oriented Software Construction, 2nd edn. Prentice-Hall, Englewood Cliffs (1997)

17. Meyer, B.: Eiffel: The Language. Prentice-Hall, Englewood Cliffs (1991)

18. Barnett, M., Leino, K.R.M., Schulte, W.: The Spec# programming system: An overview. In: Barthe, G., Burdy, L., Huisman, M., Lanet, J.-L., Muntean, T. (eds.) CASSIS 2004. LNCS, vol. 3362, pp. 49–69. Springer, Heidelberg (2004)

19. Leavens, G.T., Baker, A.L., Ruby, C.: Preliminary design of JML: A behavioral interface specification language for java. Technical Report 98-06-rev29, Iowa State University (2006)

20. Burdy, L., Cheon, Y., Cok, D.R., Ernst, M.D., Kiniry, J.R., Leavens, G.T., Leino, K.R.M., Poll, E.: An overview of jml tools and applications. International Journal on Software Tools for Technology Transfer (STTT'05) 7(3), 212–232 (2005)

21. Leino, K.R.M., Müller, P.: Modular verification of static class invariants. In: Fitzgerald, J.A., Hayes, I.J., Tarlecki, A. (eds.) FM 2005. LNCS, vol. 3582, pp. 26–42. Springer, Heidelberg (2005)

22. Jacobs, B., Kiniry, J., Warnier, M.: Java program verification challenges. In: de Boer, F.S., Bonsangue, M.M., Graf, S., de Roever, W.-P. (eds.) FMCO 2002. LNCS, vol. 2852, pp. 202–219. Springer, Heidelberg (2003)

23. Leavens, G.T., Leino, K.R.M., Müller, P.: Specification and verification challenges for sequential object-oriented programs. Formal Aspects of Computing (to appear, 2006)

24. Liskov, B., Zilles, S.: Programming with abstract data types. In: ACM SIGPLAN Symposium on Very High Level Languages, pp. 50–59. ACM Press, New York (1974)
25. Willis, D., Pearce, D.J., Noble, J.: Efficient object querying for java. In: Thomas, D. (ed.) ECOOP 2006. LNCS, vol. 4067, pp. 28–49. Springer, Heidelberg (2006)
26. Kiczales, G., Lamping, J., Mendhekar, A., Maeda, C., Lopes, C., Loingtier, J.-M., Irwin, J.: Aspect-oriented programming. In: Aksit, M., Matsuoka, S. (eds.) ECOOP 1997. LNCS, vol. 1241, pp. 220–242. Springer, Heidelberg (1997)
27. Kiczales, G., Hilsdale, E., Hugunin, J., Kersten, M., Palm, J., Griswold, W.G.: An overview of AspectJ. In: Knudsen, J.L. (ed.) ECOOP 2001. LNCS, vol. 2072, pp. 327–353. Springer, Heidelberg (2001)
28. Noble, J., Grundy, J.: Explicit relationships in object-oriented development. In: Conference on the Technology of Object-Oriented Languages and Systems (TOOLS'95), pp. 211–226. Prentice-Hall, Englewood Cliffs (1995)
29. Helm, R., Holland, I.M., Gangopadhyay, D.: Contracts: specifying behavioral compositions in object-oriented systems. In: European Conference on Object-Oriented Programming on Object-Oriented Programming Systems, Languages, and Applications (OOPSLA/ECOOP '90), pp. 169–180. ACM Press, New York (1990)
30. Aksit, M., Wakita, K., Bosch, J., Bergmans, L., Yonezawa, A.: Abstracting object interactions using composition filters. In: Guerraoui, R., Riveill, M., Nierstrasz, O. (eds.) Object-Based Distributed Programming. LNCS, vol. 791, pp. 152–184. Springer, Heidelberg (1994)
31. Herrmann, S.: Object teams: Improving modularity for crosscutting collaborations. In: Aksit, M., Mezini, M., Unland, R. (eds.) NODe 2002. LNCS, vol. 2591, pp. 248–264. Springer, Heidelberg (2003)

JavaGI: Generalized Interfaces for Java

Stefan Wehr[1], Ralf Lämmel[2], and Peter Thiemann[1]

[1] Institut für Informatik, Universität Freiburg
{wehr,thiemann}@informatik.uni-freiburg.de
[2] Microsoft Corp., Redmond
ralf.lammel@microsoft.com

Abstract. JavaGI is an experimental language that extends Java 1.5 by generalizing the interface concept to incorporate the essential features of Haskell's type classes. In particular, generalized interfaces cater for retroactive and constrained interface implementations, binary methods, static methods in interfaces, default implementations for interface methods, interfaces over families of types, and existential quantification for interface-bounded types. As a result, many anticipatory uses of design patterns such as Adapter, Factory, and Visitor become obsolete; several extension and integration problems can be solved more easily. JavaGI's interface capabilities interact with subtyping (and subclassing) in interesting ways that go beyond type classes. JavaGI can be translated to Java 1.5. Its formal type system is derived from Featherweight GJ.

1 Introduction

What are the distinguishing characteristics of Haskell compared to other programming languages? An informed answer will eventually mention type classes.

Type classes have been invented for dealing with overloading in functional programming languages in a non–ad-hoc manner [20,37]. To the surprise of their inventors, type classes provide powerful means for solving various software-design problems. For instance, sufficiently powerful type classe systems address various software extension and integration problems [23]—in fact, a range of problems for which previously a whole array of techniques and programming language extensions has been proposed.

The observation that type classes and Java-style interfaces are related is not new [32,23]. In this context, the following questions arise: (i) What part of type-class expressiveness corresponds to interfaces? (ii) What is the exact value of additional type-class expressiveness for an OO language? (iii) What is a viable OO language design with interfaces that cover most if not all type-class expressiveness? The paper answers these questions by proposing the design of JavaGI (Java with Generalized Interfaces) as a language extension of Java 1.5.

Type classes vs. interfaces. Let us recall Haskell's type classes and relate them to OO interfaces. A type class is a named abstraction for the signatures of *member functions* that share one or more type parameters. Here is a type class Connection for database connections with a member exec to execute SQL commands:

E. Ernst (Ed.): ECOOP 2007, LNAI 4609, pp. 347–372, 2007.

```
class Connection conn where
   exec :: conn -> String -> IO QueryResult
   {- further members elided -}
```

The type parameter conn abstracts over the implementing type. An *instance definition* instantiates the type parameter(s) of a type class and provides specific implementations of the member functions. Here is an instance for PostgreSQL, assuming the existence of a type PostgreSQLConnection and a function pgsqlExec of type PostgreSQLConnection -> String -> IO QueryResult:

```
instance Connection PostgreSQLConnection where
   exec = pgsqlExec
```

This kind of abstraction is familiar to OO programmers. A Java programmer would create a Connection interface and provide different classes that implement the interface, *e.g.*, a class for PostgreSQL:

```
interface Connection {
   QueryResult exec(String command);
   /* further members elided */
}
class PostgreSQLConnection implements Connection {
   public QueryResult exec(String command) { ... }
}
```

Type-class–bounded vs. interface polymorphism. The Connection example indicates that interfaces and type classes have some common ground. But there are differences such as the mechanics of using type classes and interfaces when devising signatures for functions and methods. Here is a Haskell function using the Connection type class for inserting a customer:

```
newCustomer conn customer = do let command = ...
                               exec conn command
```

The use of a member functions from a type class (such as exec) abstracts over different implementations. An implementation (*i.e.*, instance) is chosen on the grounds of the types of the used members. The selection happens at compile time, if types are sufficiently known. Otherwise, it is deferred till run time. Let us consider the (inferred or declared) Haskell signature for newCustomer:

```
newCustomer :: Connection a => a -> Customer -> IO QueryResult
```

The *type variable* a serves as a placeholder for a connection type, which is restricted by the *constraint* Connection a to be an instance of Connection. ('=>' separates all constraints from the rest of the signature.) In contrast, a Java signature treats the interface Connection as a type. Thus:

```
class UseConnection {
   static QueryResult newCustomer(Connection conn, Customer customer) {
      String command = ...;
      return conn.exec(command);
   }
}
```

To summarize, polymorphism based on Haskell's type classes uses (the names of) type classes to form bounds on type variables in function signatures, whereas polymorphism based on Java's interfaces (or .NET's interfaces for that matter) uses (the names of) interfaces as types, while type variables still serve their role as type parameters for OO generics.

This difference has several consequences that we discuss in the paper. For instance, type-class–bounded polymorphism naturally provides access to the "identity" of an implementing type, thereby enabling, among others, binary methods. (A binary method [3] is a method with more than one argument of the implementing type.) For example, Haskell's type class Eq declares a binary method, (==), for equality:

class Eq a **where** (==) :: a −> a −> Bool

The interfaces of Java 1.5 (or .NET) cannot directly express that the types of the two formal arguments of the equality function must be identical because the type implementing the corresponding interface cannot be referenced. A non-trivial extension of Java with self types [4] addresses the problem. For Java 1.5, there is an encoding that requires a rather complicated, generic interface with recursive bounds [1].

Once we commit to a style that makes the implementing type of an interface explicit, it is natural to consider multiple implementing types. Such a generalization of interfaces corresponds to multi-parameter type classes in Haskell [30]. Accordingly, an implementation of a "multi-parameter" interface is not tied to a specific receiver type but rather to a family of interacting types.

Contributions

1. We generalize Java 1.5 interfaces to unleash the full power of type classes in JavaGI, thereby enabling retroactive and constrained interface implementations, binary methods, static methods in interfaces, default implementations for interface methods, and interfaces over families of types.
2. We conservatively extend Java's interface concept. We clarify that interface-oriented programming is sufficient for various scenarios of software extension and integration. We substantiate that interface orientation is of crucial help in mastering self types, family polymorphism, and class extension.
3. We retrofit Java's interface types as bounded existential types, where the bound is the interface. In general, constraint-bounded existential types are more powerful than interface types. JavaGI's existentials are non-intrusive because they come with implicit pack and unpack operations.
4. We exploit interesting feature interactions between interface polymorphism and OO subclassing to demonstrate that JavaGI goes beyond a mere transposition of Haskell type classes to Java. Further, interfaces over multiple types require an original grouping mechanism "per receiver".

Outline. Sec. 2 motivates generalized interfaces and describes JavaGI's language constructs through a series of canonical examples. Sec. 3 describes a simple translation of JavaGI back to Java 1.5. Sec. 4 develops the type system of Core–JavaGI as an extension of Featherweight GJ [17]. Related work is discussed in Sec. 5. Finally, Sec. 6 concludes the paper and gives pointers to future work.

2   JavaGI by Examples

This section introduces JavaGI through a series of examples addressing common
OO programming problems that cannot be addressed in the same satisfactory
manner with just Java 1.5. As JavaGI is a conservative extension of Java, JavaGI
code refers to common classes and interfaces from the Java 1.5 API.

2.1   Example: Retroactive Interface Implementation

Recall the interface for database connections from the introductory section. Suppose we have to make existing code (such as newCustomer from class UseConnection)
work with a MySQL database where a library class MySQLConnection provides the
desired functionality, although under a different name:

```
class MySQLConnection { QueryResult execCommand(String command) { ... } }
```

The library author was not aware of the Connection interface, and hence did
not implement the interface for the MySQLConnection class. In Java, we cannot retroactively add such an implementation. Hence, we need to employ the
Adapter pattern: a designated adapter class wraps a MySQLConnection object
and implements Connection by delegating to MySQLConnection. This approach is
tedious and suffers from problems like object schizophrenia [31].

Inspired by Haskell, JavaGI supports *retroactive interface implementation* such
that the implementation of an interface does no longer need to be coupled with
the implementing class. Here is the *implementation definition* for the Connection
interface with the MySQLConnection class acting as the *implementing type* (enclosed in square brackets '[...]'):

```
implementation Connection [MySQLConnection] {
    QueryResult exec(String command) { return this.execCommand(command); }
}
```

In the body of the method exec, **this** has static type MySQLConnection and refers
to the receiver of the method call. Thanks to the implementation definition just
given, the newCustomer method can now use a MySQLConnection:

```
MySQLConnection conn = ...;
QueryResult result = UseConnection.newCustomer(conn, someCustomer);
```

2.2   Example: Preserved Dynamic Dispatch

Methods of a Java 1.5 interface are virtual, *i.e.*, subject to dynamic dispatch.
JavaGI preserves this capability for methods of retroactive interface implementations. This expressiveness implies extensibility in the operation dimension so
that we can solve the expression problem [36]. Compared to existing solutions
in Java 1.5 (or C# 2.0) [33], JavaGI's solution is simple and more perspicuous.

Consider a class hierarchy for binary trees with strings at the leaves:

```
abstract class BTree {}
class Leaf extends BTree { String information; }
class Node extends BTree { BTree left, right; }
```

Now suppose the classes for binary trees are in a compiled package, but we want to implement a count method on trees that returns the number of inner nodes. As we cannot add count to the classes, we introduce an interface Count with the count method and implement the interface for the tree hierarchy.

```
interface Count { int count(); }
implementation Count [BTree] { int count() { return 0; } } // works also for Leaf
implementation Count [Node] {
   int count() { return this.left.count() + this.right.count() + 1; }
}
class CountTest { int doCount(BTree t) { return t.count(); } }
```

In a recursive invocation of count in the implementation for Node, the static type of the receiver is BTree. Without dynamic dispatch, the recursive calls would count 0. Fortunately, JavaGl supports dynamic dispatch for retroactive interface implementations, so the recursive invocations return indeed the number of inner nodes of the subtrees.

The default implementation for BTree is required because retroactively added methods must not be abstract. See Sec. 3 for an explanation and further restrictions on the distribution of implementations over different compilation units.

Adding new operations and new data variants is straightforward. For a new operation, an interface and the corresponding implementations suffice.

```
// A new operation that collects the string information stored in the tree.
interface Collect { void collect(List<String> l); }
implementation Collect [BTree] { void collect(List<String> l) { return; } }
implementation Collect [Node] {
   void collect(List<String> l) { this.left.collect(l); this.right.collect(l); }
}
implementation Collect [Leaf] {void collect(List<String> l) {l.add(this.information);} }
```

A new data variant corresponds to a new subclass of BTree and interface implementations for existing operations, unless the default for the base class is acceptable.

```
// A new data variant that stores information in inner nodes.
class InformationNode extends Node {
   String information;
   void collect(List<String> l) { this.left.collect(l); l.add(this.information); this.right.collect(l); }
}
implementation Collect [InformationNode]
// The implementation of Count for Node also works for InformationNode.
```

JavaGl is amenable to another solution to the expression problem, which requires slightly more encoding effort. That is, we can transpose a Haskell-based recipe to JavaGl exploiting its regular type-class–like power [23], without taking any dependency on subtyping (and virtual methods): (i) designate an interface instead of a class as the root of all data variants; (ii) define data variants as generic classes that implement the root interface and are parameterized by the types of the immediate subcomponents; (iii) define subinterfaces of the root interface for the operations; (iv) provide implementations for all the data variants. This recipe does not require default implementations for the root of the hierarchy, and it does not put restrictions on the distribution over compilation units.

2.3   Example: Binary Methods

Java 1.5 defines a generic interface for comparing values:

```
interface Comparable<X> { int compareTo(X that); }
```

If we wanted to ensure that the (formal) argument type coincides with the type implementing the interface, then the above signature is too permissive. We would need to define compareTo as a *binary method* [3]. In Java 1.5, we can still constrain uses of the permissive signature of compareTo by a generic type with a recursive bound. For instance, consider a generic method max that computes the maximum of two objects using Comparable [2]:

```
<X extends Comparable<X>> X max(X x1, X x2) {
  if (x1.compareTo(x2) > 0) return x1;
  else return x2;
}
```

The recursive type bound X **extends** Comparable<X> expresses the intuition that the argument type of compareTo and the type implementing Comparable are the same. Any class C that is to be used with max must implement Comparable<C>.

In contrast, JavaGI supports binary methods (in interfaces) and enables the programmer to define the less permissive signature for compareTo directly:

```
interface MyComparable { int compareTo(This that); }
```

The type variable **This** (*cf.* compareTo's argument) is implicitly bound by the interface. It denotes the type implementing the interface. The type of compareTo results in a simpler and more comprehensible signature for the maximum method:

```
<X> X myMax(X x1, X x2) where X implements MyComparable {
  if (x1.compareTo(x2) > 0) return x1;
  else return x2;
}
```

The switch to a constraint-based notation **where** X **implements** MyComparable is reminiscent of .NET generics [21,39]. To type check an implementation, **This** is replaced with the implementing type. Here is an implementation for Integer:

```
implementation MyComparable [Integer]
```

This implementation need not provide code for compareTo because Integer already has a method int compareTo(Integer that). Assuming type inference for generalized interfaces, we can call myMax as follows:

```
Integer i = myMax(new Integer(1), new Integer(2));
```

Let us bring subtyping into play. For instance, consider an implementation of MyComparable for Number, which is the (abstract) superclass of Integer.

```
implementation MyComparable [Number] {
  int compareTo(Number that) { /* Convert to double values and compare */ }
}
```

Suppose that x and y are of static type Number, so the call x.compareTo(y) is valid. Which version of compareTo should be invoked when both x and y have dynamic type Integer? JavaGI takes an approach similar to multimethods [10] and selects the most specific implementation dynamically, thereby generalizing the concept of virtual method calls. Hence, the compareTo method of the implementation for Integer is invoked. In all other cases, the compareTo version for Number is chosen (assuming that there are no other implementations for subclasses of Number).

2.4   Example: Constrained Interface Implementations

If the elements of two given lists are comparable, then we expect the lists themselves to be comparable. JavaGI can express this implication with a constrained interface implementation.

```
implementation<X> MyComparable [LinkedList<X>] where X implements MyComparable {
  int compareTo(LinkedList<X> that) {
    Iterator<X> thisIt = this.iterator(); Iterator<X> thatIt = that.iterator();
    while (thisIt.hasNext() && thatIt.hasNext()) {
      X thisX = thisIt.next(); X thatX = thatIt.next();
      int i = thisX.compareTo(thatX); // type checks because X implements MyComparable
      if (i != 0) return i;
    }
    if (thisIt.hasNext() && !thatIt.hasNext()) return 1;
    if (thatIt.hasNext() && !thisIt.hasNext()) return -1;
    return 0;
  }
}
```

If now x and y have type LinkedList<Integer>, then the call myMax(x, y) is valid.

The implementation of MyComparable for LinkedList<X> is parameterized over X, the type of list elements. The constraint X implements MyComparable of the implementation makes the compareTo operation available on objects of type X and ensures that only lists with comparable elements implement MyComparable.

There is no satisfactory solution to the problem of constrained interface implementations in Java 1.5. Here are two suboptimal solutions. (i) Implement Comparable<LinkedList<X>> directly in class LinkedList<X>. But then we either could no longer assemble lists with incomparable elements (if X has bound Comparable<X>), or we would need run-time casts for the comparison of elements (if X is unbounded). (ii) Plan ahead and use a designated class, CmpList, for lists of comparable elements.

```
class CmpList<X extends Comparable<X>> implements Comparable<CmpList<X>> { ... }
```

But this is another instance of the Adapter pattern with its well-known short-comings. In addition, this technique results in a prohibitive proliferation of helper classes such as CmpList because other interfaces than Comparable may exist.

2.5   Example: Static Interface Members

Many classes need to implement parsing such that instances can be constructed from an external representation. (Likewise, in the XML domain, XML data needs to be de-serialized.) Hence, we would like to define an interface of parseable types with a parse method. However, parse cannot be defined as an instance method because it behaves like an additional class constructor. To cater for this need, JavaGI (but not Java 1.5) admits static methods in interfaces:

```
interface Parseable { static This parse(String s); }
```

Again, **This** (in the result position) refers to the implementing type. For example, consider a generic method to process an entry in a web form (*cf.* class Form) using the method String getParameter(String name) for accessing form parameters:

```
class ParseableTest {
    <X> X processEntry(Form f, String pname) where X implements Parseable {
        String s = f.getParameter(pname);
        return Parseable[X].parse(s);
    }
    Integer parseMyParam(Form f) { return processEntry<Integer>(f, "integer parameter"); }
}
```

The expression Parseable[X].parse(s) invokes the static method parse of interface Parseable with X as the implementing type, indicated by square brackets '[...]'. The parseMyParam method requires a Parseable implementation for integers:

```
implementation Parseable [Integer] {
    static Integer parse(String s) { return new Integer(s); }
}
```

In Java 1.5, we would implement this functionality with the Factory pattern. The Java solution is more complicated than the solution in JavaGI because boilerplate code for the factory class needs to be written and an additional factory object must be passed around explicitly.

2.6   Example: Multi-headed Interfaces

Traditional subtype polymorphism is insufficient to abstract over relations between conglomerations of objects and their methods. *Family polymorphism* [12] has been proposed as a corresponding generalization. It turns out that interfaces can be generalized in a related manner.

Consider the Observer pattern. There are two participating types: subject and observer. Every observer registers itself with one or more subjects. Whenever a subject changes its state, it notifies its observers by sending itself for scrutiny. The challenge in modeling this pattern in a reusable and type-safe way is the mutual dependency of subject and observer. That is, the subject has a register method which takes an observer as an argument, while the observer in turn has an update method which takes a subject as an argument.

JavaGI provides a suitable abstraction: *multi-headed interfaces*. While a classic OO interface concerns a single type, a multi-headed interface relates multiple implementing types and their methods. Such an interface can place mutual requirements on the methods of all participating types. The following multi-headed interface captures the Observer pattern:

```
interface ObserverPattern [Subject, Observer] {
  receiver Subject {
    List<Observer> getObservers();
    void register(Observer o) { getObservers().add(o); }
    void notify() { for (Observer o : getObservers()) o.update(this); }
  }
  receiver Observer { void update(Subject s); }
}
```

With multiple implementing types, we can no longer use the implicitly bound type variable **This**. Instead, we have to name the implementing types explicitly through type variables Subject and Observer. Furthermore, the interface groups methods by receiver type because there is no obvious default.

The example illustrates that generalized interfaces may contain default implementations for methods, which are inherited by all implementations that do not override them. The default implementations for register and notify rely on the list of observers returned by getObservers to store and retrieve registered observers. (Default implementations in interfaces weaken the distinction between interface and implementation. They are not essential to JavaGl's design, but they proved useful in Haskell).

Here are two classes to participate in the Observer pattern:

```
class Model { // designated subject class
  private List<Display> observers = new ArrayList<Display>();
  List<Display> getObservers() { return observers; }
}
class Display { } // designated observer class
```

An implementation of ObserverPattern only needs to define update:

```
implementation ObserverPattern [Model, Display] {
  receiver Display { void update (Model m) { System.out.println("model has changed"); } }
}
```

All other methods required by the interface are either implemented by the participating classes or inherited from the interface definition.

The genericUpdate method of the following test class uses the constraint [S,O] **implements** ObserverPattern to specify that the type parameters S and O must together implement the ObserverPattern interface.

```
class MultiheadedTest {
  <S,O> void genericUpdate(S subject, O observer) where [S,O] implements ObserverPattern {
    observer.update(subject);
  }
  void callGenericUpdate() { genericUpdate(new Model(), new Display()); }
}
```

The Observer pattern can also be implemented in Java 1.5 using generics for the subject and observer roles with complex, mutually referring bounds. In fact, the subject part must be encoded as a generic class (as opposed to a generic interface) to provide room for the default methods of subjects. A concrete subject class must then extend the generic subject class, which has to be planned ahead and is even impossible if the concrete subject class requires another superclass.

The notation for single-headed interfaces used so far is just syntactic sugar. For example, JavaGI's MyComparable interface (Sec. 2.3) is fully spelled out as:

interface MyComparable [**This**] { **receiver This** { int compareTo(**This** that); } }

2.7   Example: Bounded Existential Types

In the preceding examples, we have used interfaces such as Connection (Sec. 2.1) and List (Sec. 2.2) as if they were types. This view aligns well with Java 1.5. But multi-headed interfaces, introduced in the preceding section, do not fit this scheme. For instance, simply using ObserverPattern as a type does not make sense.

To this end, JavaGI supports *bounded existential types* in full generality. Take **exists** X **where** [Model,X] **implements** ObserverPattern . X as an example. This bounded existential type (*existential* for short) comprises objects that acts as an observer for class Model. Here is an example that calls the update method on such objects:

```
class ExistentialTest {
    void updateObserver((exists X where [Model,X] implements ObserverPattern . X) observer) {
        observer.update(new Model()); /* implicit unpacking */
    }
    void callUpdateObserver() { updateObserver(new Display()); /* implicit conversion */ }
}
```

The example also demonstrates that existential values are implicitly unpacked (*e.g.*, the update method is invoked directly on an object of existential type), and that objects are implicitly converted into an existential value (*e.g.*, an object of type Display is used directly as an argument to updateObserver).

This treatment of bounded existential types generalizes the requirement for backwards compatibility with Java interface types, which are only syntactic sugar for existentials. For instance, the type Connection is expanded into **exists** X **where** X **implements** Connection . X, whereas type List<Observer> is an abbreviation for **exists** X **where** X **implements** List<Observer> . X.

Support for multi-headed interfaces is not the only good reason to have bounded existential types. They have other advantages over Java interface types:

– They allow the general composition of interface types. For example, the type **exists** X **where** X **implements** Count **and** X **implements** Connection . X is the intersection of types that implement both the Count and Connection interfaces. Java 1.5 can denote such types only in the bound of a generic type variable as in X **extends** Count & Connection.
– They encompass Java wildcards [35]. Consider List<? **extends** Connection>, a Java 1.5 type comprising all values of type List<X> where X **extends** Connection. (This type is different from the fully heterogeneous type List<Connection>, where each list element may have a different type.) In JavaGI, this type is denoted as **exists** X **where** X **implements** Connection . List<X>. Torgersen, Ernst, and Hansen [34] investigate the relation between wildcards and existentials.

3   Translation to Java

This section sketches a translation from JavaGI to Java 1.5, which follows the scheme for translating Haskell type classes to System F [15]. We first demonstrate the general idea (Sec. 3.1), then explain the encoding of retroactively defined methods (Sec. 3.2) and of multi-headed interfaces (Sec. 3.3), show how existentials are translated (Sec. 3.4), and finally discuss interoperability with Java (Sec. 3.5).

3.1   Translating the Basics

We first explain the general idea of the translation under the simplifying assumption that the implementing types of an implementation definition provide all methods required, so that the definition itself contains only static methods.[1]

An interface $I\langle\overline{X}\rangle[\overline{Y}]$ is translated into a *dictionary interface* $I^{\mathrm{dict}}\langle\overline{X},\overline{Y}\rangle$. The interface I^{dict} supports the same method names as I, but static methods of I are mapped to non-static methods and I's non-static methods for implementing type Y_i get a new first argument this\$ of type Y_i.

As an example, consider the translation of the interfaces MyComparable and Parseable (Sec. 2.3 and 2.5).

```
interface MyComparableDict<This> { int compareTo(This this$, This that); }
interface ParseableDict<This> { This parse(String s); }
```

A constraint $[\overline{T}]$ **implements** $I\langle\overline{U}\rangle$ in a class or method signature is translated into an additional constructor or method argument, respectively, that has type $I^{\mathrm{dict}}\langle\overline{T},\overline{U}\rangle$. The additional argument allows the class or method to access a *dictionary object* (*i.e.*, an instance of the dictionary class) that provides all methods available through the constraint. In case of a class constraint, the dictionary object is stored in an instance variable.

For example, here is the translation of myMax and processEntry (Sec. 2.3 and 2.5):

```
<X> X myMax(X x1, X x2, MyComparableDict<X> dict) {
   if (dict.compareTo(x1, x2) > 0) return x1; else return x2;
}
<X> X processEntry(Form f, String pname, ParseableDict<X> dict) {
   String s = f.getParameter(pname); return dict.parse(s);
}
```

A definition **implementation**$\langle\overline{X}\rangle I\langle\overline{T}\rangle[\overline{U}]\{\dots\}$ (ignoring constrained implementations for a moment) is translated into a *dictionary class* $C^{\mathrm{dict},\overline{U}}\langle\overline{X}\rangle$ that implements $I^{\mathrm{dict}}\langle\overline{T},\overline{U}\rangle$. Methods of I^{dict} corresponding to static methods in the original interface are implemented by translating their bodies (discussed shortly). The remaining methods of I^{dict} are implemented by delegating the call to the corresponding implementing type, which is available through the argument this\$.

---

[1] The following conventions apply: I ranges over interface names; I^{dict} and $C^{\mathrm{dict},\overline{U}}$ represent fresh interface and class names, respectively; X and Y range over type variables; T and U range over types; overbar notation denotes sequencing (*e.g.*, $\overline{T}$ denotes $T_1,\dots,T_n$).

The next example shows the translation of the implementation definitions for
MyComparable and Parseable with implementing type Integer (Sec. 2.3 and 2.5).

```
class MyComparableDict_Integer implements MyComparableDict<Integer> {
    public int compareTo(Integer this$, Integer that) {
        return this$.compareTo(that); // Integer has a compareTo method
    }
}
class ParseableDict_Integer implements ParseableDict<Integer> {
    public Integer parse(String s) { return new Integer(s); }
}
```

A constrained implementation is translated similarly, with every constraint
$[T]$ **implements** $I\langle\overline{U}\rangle$ giving rise to an extra constructor argument and an instance
variable of type $I^{\text{dict}}\langle\overline{T}, \overline{U}\rangle$ for the dictionary class. These dictionary objects
serve the same purpose as the additional arguments introduced for constraints
in class or method signatures.

The translation of the implementation of MyComparable for LinkedList (Sec.2.4)
looks as follows:

```
class MyComparableDict_LinkedList<X> implements MyComparableDict<LinkedList<X>> {
    private MyComparableDict<X> dict;
    MyComparableDict_LinkedList(MyComparableDict<X> dict) { this.dict = dict; }
    public int compareTo(LinkedList<X> this$, LinkedList<X> that) {
        /* ... */ X thisX = thisIt.next(); X thatX = thatIt.next();
                int i = this.dict.compareTo(thisX, thatX); /* ... */
    }
}
```

The translation of statements and expressions considers every instantiation of a
class and every invocation of a method. If the class or method signature contains
constraints, the translation supplies appropriate dictionary arguments.

Here are translations of sample invocations of myMax and of parseMyParam
(Sec. 2.3, 2.4, and 2.5).[2]

```
void invokeMyMax(LinkedList<Integer> x, LinkedList<Integer> y) {
    Integer j = myMax(new Integer(1), new Integer(2), new MyComparableDict_Integer());
    LinkedList<Integer> z = myMax(x, y, new MyComparableDict_LinkedList<Integer>(
                                    new MyComparableDict_Integer()));
}
Integer parseMyParam(Form f) {
    return processEntry(f, "integer parameter", new ParseableDict_Integer());
}
```

3.2   Translating Retroactively Defined Methods

The preservation of dynamic dispatch is the main complication in the translation
of retroactively defined methods (*e.g.*, non-static methods of retroactive interface
implementations). For example, consider the implementations of Count for BTree
and its subclass Node from Sec. 2.2. The translation creates a dictionary interface
CountDict and two dictionary classes CountDict_BTree and CountDict_Node. Because
count is a retroactively defined method, its invocations in the implementation

---

[2] Repeated allocations of dictionary objects can be avoided by using a caching mechanism.
For simplicity, we omit this optimization in this section.

for Node must be translated such that an instance of CountDict_BTree acts as the receiver. But this means that the definition of count in CountDict_BTree must take care of dynamically dispatching to the correct target code.

MultiJava's strategy for implementing external method families [11] solves the problem. The dictionary CountDict_BTree uses the **instanceof** operator to dispatch on this$, which represents the receiver of the call in the untranslated code. If this$ is an instance of Node, the call is delegated to an instance of CountDict_Node. Otherwise, the code for BTree is used. If there are further arguments of the implementing type, then they must be included in the dispatch.

Fig. 1 contains an application of this strategy. For simplicity, the code ignores the possibility that some subclass of Node or Leaf overrides count internally. The MultiJava paper explains how this situation is handled.

To allow for modular compilation, we impose two restrictions. (i) Retroactively defined methods must not be abstract. (ii) If an implementation of interface I in compilation unit U retroactively adds a method to class C, then U must contain either C's definition or any implementation of I for a superclass of C.

The first restriction corresponds to MultiJava's restriction R2 [11, p. 542]. It ensures that there is a default case for the **instanceof** tests on this$ (**return** 0; in Fig. 1). The second restriction guarantees that all possible branches for the **instanceof** tests can be collected in a modular way. It corresponds to MultiJava's restriction R3 [11, p. 543].

3.3   Translating Multi-headed Interfaces

Fig. 2 shows the translation of the multi-headed interface ObserverPattern (Sec. 2.6). The dictionary interface ObserverPatternDict has two type parameters, one for each implementing type. Grouping by receiver type, in JavaGI achieved through the **receiver** keyword, translates to different types for the first argument this$.

The abstract class ObserverPatternDef contains those methods for which default implementations are available. A class such as ObserverPattern_ModelDisplay, which

```
// Dictionary interface corresponding to JavaGI's Count interface
interface CountDict<This> { int count(This this$); }
// Implementations of the dictionary interface
class CountDict_BTree implements CountDict<BTree> {
  public int count(BTree this$) {
    if (this$ instanceof Node) return new CountDict_Node().count( (Node) this$);
    else return 0;
  }
}
class CountDict_Node implements CountDict<Node> {
  public int count(Node this$) {
    return new CountDict_BTree().count(this$.left) +
        new CountDict_BTree().count(this$.right) + 1;
  }
}
```

Fig. 1. Translation of interface Count and its implementations (Sec. 2.2) to Java 1.5

```
// Dictionary interface corresponding to JavaGI's ObserverPattern interface
// (without default methods)
interface ObserverPatternDict<Subject,Observer> {
  // methods with receiver type Subject
  List<Observer> getObservers(Subject this$);
  void register(Subject this$, Observer o);
  void notify(Subject this$);
  // methods with receiver type Observer
  void update(Observer this$, Subject s);
}
// Abstract class holding the default methods of the ObserverPattern interface
abstract class ObserverPatternDef<Subject,Observer>
              implements ObserverPatternDict<Subject,Observer> {
  public void register(Subject this$, Observer o) { getObservers(this$).add(o); }
  public void notify(Subject this$) { for (Observer o : getObservers(this$)) update(o, this$); }
}
// Implementation of the dictionary interface
class ObserverPatternDict_ModelDisplay extends ObserverPatternDef<Model, Display> {
  public List<Display> getObservers(Model this$) { return this$.getObservers(); }
  public void update(Display this$, Model m) { System.out.println("model has changed"); }
}
// Test code
class MultiheadedTest {
  <S,O> void genericUpdate(S subject, O observer, ObserverPatternDict<S,O> dict) {
    dict.update(observer, subject);
  }
  void callGenericUpdate() {
    genericUpdate(new Model(), new Display(), new ObserverPatternDict_ModelDisplay());
  }
}
```

Fig. 2. Translation of the multi-headed interface ObserverPattern, its implementation, and its use (Sec. 2.6) to Java 1.5

implements the dictionary interface, inherits from the abstract class to avoid code duplication and to allow redefinition of default methods.

3.4   Translating Bounded Existential Types

The translation of a bounded existential type is a wrapper class that stores a witness object and the dictionaries for the constraints in instance variables. The types of these instance variables are obtained by translating the original witness type and the constraints from JavaGI to Java, replacing every existentially quantified type variable with Object.

Fig. 3 shows the class Exists1 resulting from translating the JavaGI type **exists X where X implements** Count . X. The class uses a static, generic create method to return new Exists1 instances for a witness of type X and a CountDict<X> dictionary, because a constructor cannot be generic unless the class is generic.

A method call on an existential value is translated to Java by invoking the corresponding method on one of the existential's dictionaries, passing the witness as first argument. For example, if x has type **exists X where X implements** Count

```
class Exists1 {
  // Type Object stands for the existentially quantified type variable
  Object witness; CountDict<Object> dict;
  private Exists1(Object witness, CountDict<Object> dict) {
    this.witness = witness; this.dict = dict;
  }
  // "type-safe" constructor method
  static <X> Exists1 create(X witness, CountDict<X> dict) {
    return new Exists1(witness, (CountDict) dict); // CountDict is a raw type
  }
}
```

Fig. 3. Java 1.5 class corresponding to the bounded existential type **exists** X **where** X **implements** Count . X in JavaGI

. X in JavaGI, then x has type Exists1 in Java, and the call x.count() is translated into x.dict.count(x.witness).

3.5   Interoperability with Java

The main source of incompatibility between JavaGI and Java is that Java uses interface names as types, whereas JavaGI uses them only in constraints (if we ignore JavaGI's syntactic sugar). As discussed in Sec. 2.7, a Java interface type I is interpreted as the existential **exists** X **where** X **implements** I . X. We face two problems: (i) it must be possible to pass objects of this type from JavaGI to a Java method expecting arguments of type I; (ii) JavaGI must be prepared to invoke methods of I on objects coming from the Java world, *i.e.*, objects that are not instances of the existential's wrapper class but implement I in the Java-sense.

How are these problems solved? Let $T = \mathbf{exists}\,\overline{X}\,\mathbf{where}\,\overline{Q}\,.\,Y$ where $\overline{Q}$ is a sequence of constraints and class C be the translation of T. To solve the first problem, C implements each Java interface $I\langle\overline{U}\rangle$ that appears in $\overline{Q}$ as Y **implements** $I\langle\overline{U}\rangle$. To solve the second problem, we adjust the translation for method calls on objects of existential type. If a method declared in a Java interface is called on an object of type T (assuming a suitable constraint in $\overline{Q}$), the modified translation leaves the call unchanged because the object may not be an instance of C. The translated call is also valid for C because C implements the Java interface. In all other cases, the translation treats the call as in Sec. 3.4.

Wrapping objects is problematic because operations involving object identity (*e.g.*, ==) and type tests (*e.g.*, **instanceof**) in Java code may no longer work as expected. (Translating such operations away does not work because they may be contained in some external Java library not under our control.) It is, however, somewhat unavoidable if retroactive interface implementation is to be supported and changing the JVM is not an option. (For example, the translation of expanders [38] to Java suffers from the same problem.) Eugster's uniform proxies [14] might solve the problem for type tests because they would allow the wrapper to be a subclass of the run-time class of the witness and to implement all interfaces the witness implements through a regular Java **implements** clause.

4 A Formal Type System for JavaGI

This section formalizes a type system for the language Core–JavaGI, which captures the main ingredients of JavaGI and supports all essential features presented in Sec. 2. The static semantics of Core–JavaGI is based on Featherweight GJ (FGJ [17]) and on Wild FJ [34].

4.1 Syntax

Fig. 4 shows the syntax of Core–JavaGI.[3] A program *prog* consists of a sequence of class definitions *cdef*, interface definitions *idef*, implementation definitions

$$
\begin{array}{rcl}
prog & ::= & \overline{def}\ e \\
def & ::= & cdef \mid idef \mid impl \\
cdef & ::= & \textbf{class}\ C\langle\overline{X}\rangle\ \textbf{extends}\ N\ \textbf{where}\ \overline{Q}\ \{\,\overline{T\ f}\ \ \overline{m:mdef}\,\} \\
idef & ::= & \textbf{interface}\ I\langle\overline{X}\rangle\ [\overline{X}]\ \textbf{where}\ \overline{Q}\ \{\,\overline{m:\textbf{static}\ msig}\ \ \overline{itsig}\,\} \\
impl & ::= & \textbf{implementation}\langle\overline{X}\rangle\ K\ [\overline{T}]\ \textbf{where}\ \overline{Q}\ \{\,\overline{m:\textbf{static}\ mdef}\ \ \overline{itdef}\,\} \\
itsig & ::= & \textbf{receiver}\ \{\,\overline{m:msig}\,\} \qquad\qquad S,T,U,V ::= X \mid N \mid \exists \overline{X}\ \textbf{where}\ \overline{Q}\,.\,T \\
itdef & ::= & \textbf{receiver}\ \{\,\overline{m:mdef}\,\} \qquad\qquad N \qquad\ ::= C\langle\overline{T}\rangle \mid Object \\
msig & ::= & \langle\overline{X}\rangle\,\overline{T\,x} \to T\ \textbf{where}\ \overline{Q} \qquad\quad K \qquad\ ::= I\langle\overline{T}\rangle \\
mdef & ::= & msig\ \{e\} \qquad\qquad\qquad\qquad\qquad P,Q \quad\ ::= \overline{T}\ \textbf{implements}\ K \\
e & ::= & x \mid e.f \mid e.m\langle\overline{T}\rangle(\overline{e}) \mid K[\overline{T}].m\langle\overline{T}\rangle(\overline{e}) \mid \textbf{new}\ N(\overline{e}) \mid (N)\,e
\end{array}
$$

$$
\begin{array}{lll}
X,Y,Z \in TyvarName & C,D \in ClassName & I,J \in IfaceName \\
m \in MethodName & f \in FieldName & x \in VarName
\end{array}
$$

Fig. 4. Syntax of Core–JavaGI

impl, and a "main" expression *e*. We omit constructors from class definitions, and assume that every field name is defined at most once. Methods of classes are written as *m : mdef* where *mdef* is a method signature *msig* with a method body. An interface definition contains static method signatures *m : **static** msig* and signatures *itsig* for methods supported by particular implementing types. Implementation definitions provide the corresponding implementations *m : **static** mdef* and *itdef*.

Core–JavaGI does not support default methods in interface definitions. Moreover, signatures *itsig* and definitions *itdef* refer to their implementing type by position. We assume that the name of a method defined in some interface is unique across method definitions in classes and other interfaces. Interface implementations must provide explicit definitions for all methods of all implementing types. It is straightforward but tedious to lift these restrictions.

---

[3] The notation $\overline{\xi}^n$ (or $\overline{\xi}$ for short) denotes the sequence $\xi_1, \ldots, \xi_n$ for some syntactic construct ξ, $\cdot$ denotes the empty sequence. At some points, we interpret $\overline{\xi}$ as the set $\{\xi_1, \ldots, \xi_n\}$. We assume that the identifier sets *TyvarName*, *ClassName*, *IfaceName*, *MethodName*, *FieldName*, and *VarName* are countably infinite and pairwise disjoint.

$$\boxed{\Theta; \Delta \vdash T \text{ ok} \qquad \Theta; \Delta \vdash K[\overline{T}] \text{ ok} \qquad \Theta; \Delta \vdash Q \text{ ok} \qquad \Theta; \Delta \vdash [\overline{T/X}] \text{ ok under } \overline{Q}}$$

$$\frac{X \in \Delta}{\Theta; \Delta \vdash X \text{ ok}} \qquad \Theta; \Delta \vdash Object \text{ ok} \qquad \frac{\Theta; \Delta, \overline{X}, \overline{Q} \vdash \overline{Q}, T \text{ ok}}{\Theta; \Delta \vdash \exists \overline{X} \text{ where } \overline{Q}. T \text{ ok}}$$

$$\frac{\textbf{class } C\langle \overline{X} \rangle \textbf{ extends } N \textbf{ where } \overline{Q} \{ \dots \} \in \Theta}{\Theta; \Delta \vdash [\overline{T/X}] \text{ ok under } \overline{Q}} \qquad \frac{\textbf{interface } I\langle \overline{X} \rangle [\overline{Y}] \textbf{ where } \overline{Q} \{ \dots \} \in \Theta}{\Theta; \Delta \vdash [\overline{S/X}, \overline{T/Y}] \text{ ok under } \overline{Q}}$$
$$\frac{}{\Theta; \Delta \vdash C\langle \overline{T} \rangle \text{ ok}} \qquad \frac{}{\Theta; \Delta \vdash I\langle \overline{S} \rangle [\overline{T}] \text{ ok}}$$

$$\frac{\Theta; \Delta \vdash K[\overline{T}] \text{ ok}}{\Theta; \Delta \vdash \overline{T} \textbf{ implements } K \text{ ok}} \qquad \frac{(\forall i) \; \Theta; \Delta \Vdash [\overline{T/X}] Q_i \qquad \Theta; \Delta \vdash \overline{T} \text{ ok}}{\Theta; \Delta \vdash [\overline{T/X}] \text{ ok under } \overline{Q}}$$

Fig. 5. Well-formedness

A method signature $msig$ has the form $\langle \overline{X} \rangle \, \overline{T} \, \overline{x} \to T$ **where** $\overline{Q}$ where $\overline{T}$ are the argument types and T is the result type. Types T in Core–JavaGI are either type variables X, class types N, or bounded existential types $\exists \overline{X}$ **where** $\overline{Q}. T$. The latter are considered equivalent up to renaming of bound type variables, reordering of type variables and constraints, addition and removal of unused type variables and constraints, and merging of variable-disjoint, adjacent existential quantifiers. Finally, $\exists \cdot$ **where** $\cdot . T$ is equivalent to T, so that every type can be written as an existential $\exists \overline{X}$ **where** $\overline{Q}. T$ where T is a type variable or class.

K abbreviates an instantiated interface $I\langle \overline{T} \rangle$ and P, Q range over constraints. Core–JavaGI does not support class bounds in constraints.

Core–JavaGI expressions e are very similar to FGJ expressions. The new expression form $K[\overline{T}].m(\overline{e})$ invokes static interface methods. The types $\overline{T}$ select the implementation of method m. The target type of a cast must be a class type N, so that constraints need not be checked at runtime.[4]

4.2 Typing Judgments

The typing judgments of Core–JavaGI make use of three different environments. A program environment Θ is a set of program definitions def and constraint schemes of the form $\forall \overline{X} . \overline{Q} \Rightarrow P$. The constraint schemes result from the **interface** and **implementation** definitions of the program (to be defined in Fig. 9). A type environment Δ is a sequence of type variables and constraints. Its domain, written $\text{dom}(\Delta)$, consists of only the type variables. The extension of a type environment is written $\Delta, \overline{X}, \overline{Q}$ assuming $\text{dom}(\Delta) \cap \overline{X} = \emptyset$. A variable environment Γ is a finite mapping from variables to types, written $\overline{x} : \overline{T}$. The extension of a variable environment is denoted by $\Gamma, x : T$ assuming $x \notin \text{dom}(\Gamma)$.

Fig. 5 establishes well-formedness predicates on types, instantiated interfaces with implementing types, constraints, and substitutions. The judgment $\Theta; \Delta \vdash [\overline{T/X}]$ ok under $\overline{Q}$ ensures that the (capture avoiding) substitution $[\overline{T/X}]$ replaces

---

[4] Interoperability with Java requires support for casts to certain bounded existential types whose constraints are easily checkable at runtime.

$$\boxed{\Theta; \Delta \Vdash Q \qquad \Theta; \Delta \vdash T \leq T}$$

$$\frac{Q \in \Delta}{\Theta; \Delta \Vdash Q} \qquad \frac{\forall \overline{X}.\, \overline{Q} \Rightarrow P \in \Theta \qquad (\forall i)\ \Theta; \Delta \vdash [\overline{T/X}] \text{ ok under } Q_i}{\Theta; \Delta \Vdash [\overline{T/X}]P}$$

$$\Theta; \Delta \vdash T \leq T \qquad \Theta; \Delta \vdash T \leq Object \qquad \frac{\Theta; \Delta \vdash S \leq T \qquad \Theta; \Delta \vdash T \leq U}{\Theta; \Delta \vdash S \leq U}$$

$$\frac{\text{class } C\langle \overline{X}\rangle \text{ extends } N \ldots \in \Theta}{\Theta; \Delta \vdash C\langle \overline{T}\rangle \leq [\overline{T/X}]N} \qquad \frac{\Theta; \Delta, \overline{X}, \overline{Q} \vdash T \leq U \qquad \Theta; \Delta \vdash U \text{ ok}}{\Theta; \Delta \vdash \exists \overline{X} \text{ where } \overline{Q}.\, T \leq U}$$

$$\frac{(\forall i)\ \Theta; \Delta \Vdash [\overline{U/X}]Q_i \qquad \Theta; \Delta \vdash \exists \overline{X} \text{ where } \overline{Q}.\, T \text{ ok}}{\Theta; \Delta \vdash [\overline{U/X}]T \leq \exists \overline{X} \text{ where } \overline{Q}.\, T}$$

Fig. 6. Entailment and subtyping

$\overline{X}$ with well-formed types $\overline{T}$ that respect the constraints $\overline{Q}$. Its definition uses the entailment judgment $\Theta; \Delta \Vdash Q$ discussed next. We abbreviate multiple well-formedness predicates $\Theta; \Delta \vdash \xi_1$ ok$, \ldots, \Theta; \Delta \vdash \xi_n$ ok to $\Theta; \Delta \vdash \overline{\xi}$ ok.

Fig. 6 defines the entailment and the subtyping relation. Entailment $\Theta; \Delta \Vdash Q$ establishes the validity of constraint Q. A constraint is only valid if it is either contained in the local type environment Δ, or if it is implied by a constraint scheme of the program environment Θ. There is no rule that allows us to conclude T implements I if all we know is T' implements I for some supertype T' of T. Such a conclusion would be unsound because the implementing type of I might appear in the result type of some method.[5] Similarly, a constraint such as $(\exists X \text{ where } X \text{ implements } I \,.\, X)$ implements I is only valid if there exists a corresponding implementation definition; otherwise, invocations of methods with the implementing type of I in argument position would be unsound.[6]

The subtyping judgment $\Theta; \Delta \vdash T \leq U$ is similar to FGJ, except that there is a top rule $\Theta; \Delta \vdash T \leq Object$ and two rules for bounded existential types. These two rules allow for implicit conversions between existential and non-existential values. The first allows opening an existential on the left-hand side if the quantified type variables are sufficiently fresh (guaranteed by the premise $\Theta; \Delta \vdash U$ ok). The second rule allows abstracting over types that fulfill the constraints of the existential on the right-hand side.

The relation $\text{mtype}_{\Theta; \Delta}(m, T) = msig$, defined in Fig. 7, determines the signature of method m invoked on a receiver with static type T. The first rule is similar to the corresponding rules in FJG, except that it does not ascend the inheritance tree; instead, Core–JavaGI allows for subsumption on the receiver type (see the typing rules for expressions in Fig. 8). The second rule handles the case of invoking a method defined in an interface implemented by the receiver. The

---

[5] To ensure interoperability with Java, we generate suitable implementation definitions for all Java classes that "inherit" the implementation of an interface from a superclass.

[6] Interoperability with Java requires us to generate implementation definitions for I and all its superinterfaces with implementing type $\exists X \text{ where } X \text{ implements } I \,.\, X$.

$$\boxed{\text{mtype}_{\Theta;\Delta}(m, T) = msig \qquad \text{smtype}_{\Theta;\Delta}(m, K[\overline{T}]) = msig}$$

$$\frac{\textbf{class } C\langle \overline{X}\rangle \textbf{ extends } N \textbf{ where } \overline{Q}\{\dots\ \overline{m : msig\ \{e\}}\} \in \Theta}{\text{mtype}_{\Theta;\Delta}(m_j, C\langle \overline{T}\rangle) = [\overline{T/X}]msig_j}$$

$$\frac{\begin{array}{c}\Theta;\Delta \Vdash \overline{T} \textbf{ implements } I\langle \overline{V}\rangle\\ \textbf{interface } I\langle \overline{X}\rangle\,[\overline{Y}] \textbf{ where } \overline{Q}\{\dots\ \overline{itsig}\} \in \Theta \qquad itsig_j = \textbf{receiver } \{\overline{m : msig}\}\end{array}}{\text{mtype}_{\Theta;\Delta}(m_k, T_j) = [\overline{V/X}, \overline{T/Y}]msig_k}$$

$$\frac{\Theta;\Delta \Vdash \overline{T} \textbf{ implements } I\langle \overline{S}\rangle \quad \textbf{interface } I\langle \overline{X}\rangle\,[\overline{Y}] \textbf{ where } \overline{Q}\{\overline{m : \textbf{static } msig}\ \dots\} \in \Theta}{\text{smtype}_{\Theta;\Delta}(m_j, I\langle \overline{S}\rangle[\overline{T}]) = [\overline{S/X}, \overline{T/Y}]msig_j}$$

Fig. 7. Method types

$$\boxed{\Theta;\Delta;\Gamma \vdash e : T}$$

$$\frac{\Theta;\Delta;\Gamma \vdash e : T \qquad \text{bound}(T) = \exists \overline{X} \textbf{ where } \overline{Q}\,.\,N \qquad \text{fields}_\Theta(N) = \overline{U\,f}}{\Theta;\Delta;\Gamma \vdash e.f_i : \exists \overline{X} \textbf{ where } \overline{Q}\,.\,U_i}$$

$$\frac{\begin{array}{c}\Theta;\Delta;\Gamma \vdash e_0 : T_0 \qquad \Theta;\Delta \vdash T_0 \le \exists \overline{X} \textbf{ where } \overline{Q}\,.\,T'_0\\ (\forall i)\ \Theta;\Delta;\Gamma \vdash e_i : S_i \qquad \text{mtype}_{\Theta;\Delta,\overline{X},\overline{Q}}(m, T'_0) = \langle \overline{Y}\rangle\,\overline{U\,x} \to U \textbf{ where } \overline{P}\\ \Theta;\Delta \vdash \overline{V} \textbf{ ok} \qquad (\forall i)\ \Theta;\Delta,\overline{X},\overline{Q} \Vdash [\overline{V/Y}]P_i \qquad (\forall i)\ \Theta;\Delta,\overline{X},\overline{Q} \vdash S_i \le [\overline{V/Y}]U_i\end{array}}{\Theta;\Delta;\Gamma \vdash e_0.m\langle \overline{V}\rangle(\overline{e}) : \exists \overline{X} \textbf{ where } \overline{Q}\,.\,[\overline{V/Y}]U}$$

$$\frac{\begin{array}{c}\Theta;\Delta \vdash K[\overline{T}] \textbf{ ok} \qquad \text{smtype}_{\Theta;\Delta}(m, K[\overline{T}]) = \langle \overline{X}\rangle\,\overline{U\,x} \to U \textbf{ where } \overline{Q}\\ \Theta;\Delta \vdash [\overline{V/X}] \textbf{ ok under } \overline{Q} \qquad (\forall i)\ \Theta;\Delta;\Gamma \vdash e_i : S_i \qquad (\forall i)\ \Theta;\Delta \vdash S_i \le [\overline{V/X}]U_i\end{array}}{\Theta;\Delta;\Gamma \vdash K[\overline{T}].m\langle \overline{V}\rangle(\overline{e}) : [\overline{V/X}]U}$$

Fig. 8. Expression typing. The remaining rules are similar to those for FGJ [17] and thus omitted.

judgment $\text{smtype}_{\Theta;\Delta}(m, K[\overline{T}]) = msig$, also shown in Fig. 7, defines the type of a static method invoked on instantiated interface K for implementing types $\overline{T}$.

The typing judgment for expressions $\Theta;\Delta;\Gamma \vdash e : T$ (Fig. 8) assigns type T to expression e under the environments Θ, Δ, and Γ. Its definition is very similar to the corresponding FGJ judgment, so we show only those rules that are new (rule for static method invocation) or significantly different (rules for field lookup and non-static method invocation). Following Wild FJ [34], the rules for field lookup and non-static method invocation propagate the existentially bounded type variables and the constraints of the receiver type to the conclusion to ensure proper scoping. Furthermore, the rule for non-static method invocation allows subsumption on the receiver type. This change was necessary because entailment does not take subtyping into account (see the discussion on page 364), so without subsumption on the receiver type, it would not be possible to invoke a retroactively defined method on a receiver whose static type is a subtype of the type used in the corresponding implementation definition.

$$\boxed{\Theta;\Delta;\Gamma \vdash \mathit{mdef}\ \mathsf{ok} \qquad \Theta;\Delta \vdash \mathit{msig} \leq \mathit{msig}}$$

$$\frac{\Delta' = \Delta, \overline{X}, \overline{Q} \qquad \Theta;\Delta' \vdash \overline{T}, U, \overline{Q}\ \mathsf{ok} \qquad \Theta;\Delta';\Gamma, \overline{x:T} \vdash e :_{\leq} U}{\Theta;\Delta;\Gamma \vdash \langle \overline{X} \rangle\, \overline{T}\, x \to U\ \mathbf{where}\ \overline{Q}\, \{e\}\ \mathsf{ok}}$$

$$\frac{(\forall i)\ \Theta;\Delta, \overline{X}, \overline{Q} \Vdash [\overline{X/Y}]P_i \qquad (\forall i)\ \Theta;\Delta, \overline{Y}, \overline{P} \Vdash [\overline{Y/X}]Q_i}{(\forall i)\ \Theta;\Delta, \overline{X}, \overline{Q} \vdash [\overline{X/Y}]U_i \leq T_i \qquad (\forall i)\ \Theta;\Delta, \overline{X}, \overline{Q} \vdash T \leq [\overline{X/Y}]U}{\Theta;\Delta \vdash \langle \overline{X} \rangle\, \overline{T}\, x \to T\ \mathbf{where}\ \overline{Q} \leq \langle \overline{Y} \rangle\, \overline{U}\, x \to U\ \mathbf{where}\ \overline{P}}$$

$$\boxed{\Theta;\Delta \vdash m : \mathit{mdef}\ \mathsf{ok\ in}\ N \qquad \mathsf{override\text{-}ok}_{\Theta;\Delta}(m : \mathit{msig}, N) \qquad \Theta \vdash \mathit{cdef}\ \mathsf{ok}}$$

$$\frac{\Theta;\Delta;\mathit{this}:N \vdash \mathit{msig}\,\{e\}\ \mathsf{ok} \qquad \mathsf{override\text{-}ok}_{\Theta;\Delta}(m : \mathit{msig}, N)}{\Theta;\Delta \vdash m : \mathit{msig}\,\{e\}\ \mathsf{ok\ in}\ N}$$

$$\frac{(\forall N')\ \mathsf{if}\ \Theta;\Delta \vdash N \leq N'\ \mathsf{and}\ \mathsf{mtype}_{\Theta;\Delta}(m, N') = \mathit{msig}'\ \mathsf{then}\ \Theta;\Delta \vdash \mathit{msig} \leq \mathit{msig}'}{\mathsf{override\text{-}ok}_{\Theta;\Delta}(m : \mathit{msig}, N)}$$

$$\frac{\Delta = \overline{X}, \overline{Q} \qquad \Theta;\Delta \vdash N, \overline{Q}, \overline{T}\ \mathsf{ok} \qquad (\forall i)\ \Theta;\Delta \vdash m_i : \mathit{mdef}_i\ \mathsf{ok\ in}\ C\langle \overline{X} \rangle}{\Theta \vdash \mathbf{class}\ C\langle \overline{X} \rangle\ \mathbf{extends}\ N\ \mathbf{where}\ \overline{Q}\, \{\, \overline{T\, f}\ \overline{m : \mathit{mdef}}\, \}\ \mathsf{ok}}$$

$$\boxed{\Theta;\Delta \vdash \mathit{msig}\ \mathsf{ok} \qquad \Theta;\Delta \vdash \mathit{itsig}\ \mathsf{ok} \qquad \Theta \vdash \mathit{idef}\ \mathsf{ok}}$$

$$\frac{\Delta' = \Delta, \overline{X}, \overline{Q} \qquad \Theta;\Delta' \vdash \overline{T}, U, \overline{Q}\ \mathsf{ok}}{\Theta;\Delta \vdash \langle \overline{X} \rangle\, \overline{T}\, x \to U\ \mathbf{where}\ \overline{Q}\ \mathsf{ok}} \qquad \frac{(\forall i)\ \mathit{msig}_i\ \mathsf{ok}}{\Theta;\Delta \vdash \mathbf{receiver}\, \{\overline{m : \mathit{msig}}\}\ \mathsf{ok}}$$

$$\frac{\Delta = \overline{X}, \overline{Y}, \overline{Q} \qquad \Theta;\Delta \vdash \overline{Q}, \overline{\mathit{msig}}, \overline{\mathit{itsig}}\ \mathsf{ok}}{\Theta \vdash \mathbf{interface}\ I\langle \overline{X} \rangle\, [\overline{Y}]\ \mathbf{where}\ \overline{Q}\, \{\, \overline{m : \mathbf{static}\ \mathit{msig}\ \mathit{itsig}}\, \}\ \mathsf{ok}}$$

$$\boxed{\Theta;\Delta \vdash \mathit{mdef}\ \mathsf{implements}\ \mathit{msig} \qquad \Theta;\Delta \vdash \mathit{itdef}\ \mathsf{implements}\ \mathit{itsig} \qquad \Theta \vdash \mathit{impl}\ \mathsf{ok}}$$

$$\frac{\Theta;\Delta;\Gamma \vdash \mathit{msig}\,\{e\}\ \mathsf{ok} \qquad \Theta;\Delta \vdash \mathit{msig} \leq \mathit{msig}'}{\Theta;\Delta;\Gamma \vdash \mathit{msig}\,\{e\}\ \mathsf{implements}\ \mathit{msig}'}$$

$$\frac{(\forall i)\ \Theta;\Delta;\Gamma \vdash \mathit{mdef}_i\ \mathsf{implements}\ \mathit{msig}_i}{\Theta;\Delta;\Gamma \vdash \mathbf{receiver}\, \{\overline{m : \mathit{mdef}}\}\ \mathsf{implements}\ \mathbf{receiver}\, \{\overline{m : \mathit{msig}}\}}$$

$$\frac{\begin{array}{c}\Delta = \overline{X}, \overline{Q} \qquad \Theta' = \Theta \setminus \{\forall \overline{X} . \overline{Q} \Rightarrow \overline{S}\ \mathsf{implements}\ I\langle \overline{T} \rangle\} \\ \Theta';\Delta \vdash I\langle \overline{T} \rangle[\overline{S}], \overline{Q}\ \mathsf{ok} \qquad \mathbf{interface}\ I\langle \overline{Y} \rangle\, [\overline{Z}]\ \mathbf{where}\ \overline{P}\, \{\, \overline{m : \mathbf{static}\ \mathit{msig}\ \mathit{itsig}}\, \} \in \Theta \\ (\forall i)\ \Theta;\Delta;\emptyset \vdash \mathit{mdef}_i\ \mathsf{implements}\ [\overline{T/Y}, \overline{S/Z}]\mathit{msig}_i \\ (\forall i)\ \Theta;\Delta;\mathit{this}:S_i \vdash \mathit{itdef}_i\ \mathsf{implements}\ [\overline{T/Y}, \overline{S/Z}]\mathit{itsig}_i\end{array}}{\Theta \vdash \mathbf{implementation}\langle \overline{X} \rangle\ I\langle \overline{T} \rangle\, [\overline{S}]\ \mathbf{where}\ \overline{Q}\, \{\, \overline{m : \mathbf{static}\ \mathit{mdef}\ \mathit{itdef}}\, \}\ \mathsf{ok}}$$

$$\boxed{\mathit{def} \Mapsto \Theta \qquad \vdash \mathit{prog}\ \mathsf{ok}}$$

$$\mathit{cdef} \Mapsto \emptyset$$

$$\mathbf{interface}\ I\langle \overline{X} \rangle\, [\overline{Y}]\ \mathbf{where}\ \overline{Q}^n\, \{\ldots\} \Mapsto \{\forall \overline{XY} . \overline{Y}\ \mathsf{implements}\ I\langle \overline{X} \rangle \Rightarrow Q_i \mid 1 \leq i \leq n\}$$

$$\mathbf{implementation}\langle \overline{X} \rangle\ K\, [\overline{T}]\ \mathbf{where}\ \overline{Q}\, \{\ldots\} \Mapsto \{\forall \overline{X} . \overline{Q} \Rightarrow \overline{T}\ \mathsf{implements}\ K\}$$

$$\frac{(\forall i)\ \mathit{def}_i \Mapsto \Theta_i \qquad \Theta = \overline{\mathit{def}} \cup \cup_i \Theta_i}{(\forall i)\ \Theta \vdash \mathit{def}_i\ \mathsf{ok} \qquad \mathsf{well\text{-}founded}(\Theta) \qquad \mathsf{no\text{-}overlap}(\Theta) \qquad \Theta;\cdot;\cdot \vdash e : T}{\vdash \overline{\mathit{def}}\ e\ \mathsf{ok}}$$

Fig. 9. Program typing

In the rule for field lookup, $\mathsf{fields}_\Theta(N)$ denotes the fields of N and its superclasses (as in FGJ), and $\mathsf{bound}(T)$ denotes the upper bound of T. It is defined as $\mathsf{bound}(N) = N$, $\mathsf{bound}(X) = \mathit{Object}$, and $\mathsf{bound}(\exists \overline{X}\ \mathbf{where}\ \overline{Q}\,.\,T) = \exists \overline{X}\ \mathbf{where}\ \overline{Q}\,.\,\mathsf{bound}(T)$.

Fig. 9 defines the program typing rules. They differ from FGJ because FGJ defines only a method and a class typing judgment. The first part of the figure defines well-formedness of method definitions and a subtyping relation on method signatures.[7] The next three parts check that class, interface, and implementation definitions are well-formed. The last part defines the two judgments $\mathit{def} \Mapsto \Theta$ and $\vdash \mathit{prog}$ ok. The first judgment collects the constraint schemes resulting from the definitions in the program: a class definition contributes no constraint schemes, an interface definition contributes constraint schemes for all of its superinterfaces because every implementation of the interface must respect the superinterface constraints, and an implementation definition contributes a single constraint scheme. The judgment $\vdash \mathit{prog}$ ok first collects all constraint schemes, then checks the definitions of the program, and finally types the main expression. The predicate $\mathsf{well\text{-}founded}(\Theta)$ only holds if the class and interface hierarchies of program Θ are acyclic. The predicate $\mathsf{no\text{-}overlap}(\Theta)$ ensures that program Θ does not contain overlapping implementation definitions, *i.e.*, no implementation definition in Θ is a substitution instance of some other implementation definition.

5 Related Work

PolyTOIL [7] and $\mathcal{LOOM}$ [6] are both object-oriented languages with a MyType type as needed for binary methods: an occurrence of MyType refers to the type of **this**. PolyTOIL achieves type safety by separating inheritance from subtyping, whereas $\mathcal{LOOM}$ drops subtyping completely. However, both languages support matching, which is more general than subtyping. The language LOOJ [4] integrates MyType into Java. It ensures type safety through exact types that prohibit subtype polymorphism. Compared with these languages, JavaGI does not support MyType in classes but only in interfaces. As a consequence, JavaGI allows unrestricted subtype polymorphism on classes; only invocations of binary methods on receivers with existential type are disallowed. JavaGI also supports retroactive and constrained interface implementations, as well as static interface methods; these features have no correspondence in PolyTOIL, $\mathcal{LOOM}$, or LOOJ. $\mathcal{LOOM}$ supports "hash types", which can be interpreted as match-bounded existential types in the same way as JavaGI's interface types are interpreted as interface-bounded existential types. Hash types, though, are tagged explicitly.

The multi-headed interfaces of JavaGI enable a statically safe form of family polymorphism (dating back to BETA's [24] virtual types). Other work on family polymorphism either use path-dependent types [12], virtual classes [13], or a generalized form of MyType [5] that deals with a mutually recursive system of classes. Scala's abstract types together with self type annotations [28,27] can

---

[7] Interoperability with Java requires a second relation specifying covariant return types, only.

also be used for family polymorphism. Helm and collaborators' contracts [16] specify how groups of interdependent objects should cooperate, thus allowing some form of family polymorphism.

JavaGI's generalization of Java interfaces is systematically inspired by Haskell's type-class mechanism [37,29,30]: (multi-headed) interface and implementation definitions in JavaGI play the role of (multi-parameter) type classes and instance definitions in Haskell (so far without functional dependencies). A notable difference between JavaGI and Haskell is that Haskell does not have the notion of classes and objects in the object-oriented sense, so methods are not tied to a particular class or object. Thus, methods of Haskell type classes correspond to static methods of JavaGI's interfaces; there is no Haskell correspondence to JavaGI's non-static interface methods. Another difference is the absence of subtyping in Haskell, which avoids the question how subtyping and instance definitions should interact. However, Haskell supports type inference, whereas JavaGI requires explicit type annotations. Finally, Haskell's existentials are notoriously inconvenient since they are bound to data-type constructors and lack implicit pack and unpack operations.

Siek and collaborators have developed a related notion of concepts for grouping and organizing requirements on a type [32]. In particular, they have also formalized this notion in F^G, an extension of System F, receiving inspiration from Haskell type classes. F^G also includes associated types (*i.e.*, types functionally depending on other types). In contrast, JavaGI supports self types, bounded existential types, defaults for interface methods, and it interacts with subtyping. It has been noted that a limited form of concepts can be also realized with C#'s interface support [19], while the primary application domain of concepts (*i.e.*, generic programming) requires extra support for associated types and constraint propagation. We note that constraint propagation [19] is related to our notion of constraint entailment.

There is an impressive number of approaches for some form of open classes— means to extend existing classes. The approaches differ with regard to the "extension time" and the restrictions imposed on extensions. Partial classes in C♯ 2.0 provide a primitive, code-level modularization tool. The different partial slices of a class (comprising superinterfaces, fields, methods, and other members) are merged by a preprocessing phase of the compiler. Extension methods in C♯ 3.0 [25] support full separate compilation, but the added methods cannot be virtual, and members other than methods cannot be added. Aspect-oriented language implementations such as AspectJ [22] typically support some sort of open classes based on a global program analysis, a byte-code–level weaving technique, or more dynamic approaches.

MultiJava [11] is a conservative Java extension that adds open classes and multimethods. We adopted MultiJava's implementation strategy to account for retroactive interface implementations and for implementing binary methods [3] by specializing the argument types in subclasses. The design of Relaxed Multi-Java [26] might help to lift the restrictions imposed by our compilation strategy. Expanders [38] comprise an extra language construct (next to classes and interfaces) for adding new state, methods and superinterfaces to existing classes in a modular manner. JavaGI does not support state extension. Expanders do not deal with family polymorphism, static interface methods, binary methods, and some other aspects of JavaGI.

The expander paper [38] comprises an excellent related work discussion looping in all kinds of approaches that are more or less remotely related to class extensions: mixins, traits, nested inheritance, and Scala views.

6   Conclusion and Future Work

We have described JavaGI, a language that generalizes Java's interfaces in various dimensions to enable clearer program designs, stronger static typing, and extra forms of software extension and integration. Our generalization is based on Haskell's type class mechanism. The design of JavaGI shows that the combination of type classes and bounded existential types with implicit pack and unpack operations subsumes Java-like interfaces. We have watched out for feature interactions with existing uses of interfaces, subtyping, and subclassing. In particular, JavaGI is the first satisfactory example of a language where type classes (interfaces) and subtyping coexist. In this language-design process, we realized that a convenient form of existential quantification needs to become part of the extended Java type system. All of the scenarios that JavaGI can handle have been previously identified in other work; however, using separate language extensions with unclear interaction. There is no single proposal that would match the expressiveness of JavaGI. Hence, we do not apply for an originality award but we hope to score with the uniformity and simplicity of generalized interfaces.

The formalization of JavaGI presented in this article consists of only a type system for a core language. In future work, we would like to complete the formalization. In particular, this includes the specification of an operational semantics, its soundness proof, an algorithmic formulation of subtyping, the adoption of Java's inference algorithm for type parameters, the completeness proof for representing Java generics in JavaGI's existential-based type system, and a proper formalization of the translation to Java. Furthermore, we are working on a prototype compiler for JavaGI from which we also expect real-world data on the overhead caused by the translation semantics. We also would like to lift the restrictions imposed by our compilation strategy, and we are investigating state extension for JavaGI. Another challenging aspect is the potential of multiple type parameters of generalized interfaces (both implementing types and regular type parameters). Such multiplicity has triggered advanced extensions for Haskell's type classes [18,9,8] to restrict and direct instance selection and type inference. In the context of JavaGI, the existing restriction for generics—that a certain type can implement a generic interface for only one type instantiation—may be sufficient for practical purposes.

Acknowledgments. We thank the anonymous reviewers for their detailed comments, which helped to improve the presentation significantly.

References

1. Bracha, G.: Generics in the Java programming language (July 2004),
   http://java.sun.com/j2se/1.5/pdf/generics-tutorial.pdf
2. Bracha, G., Odersky, M., Stoutamire, D., Wadler, P.: Making the future safe for the past: Adding genericity to the Java programming language. In: Proc. 13th ACM Conf. OOPSLA, Vancouver, BC, October 1998, pp. 183–200. ACM Press, New York (1998)
3. Bruce, K.B., Cardelli, L., Castagna, G., Eifrig, J., Smith, S.F., Trifonov, V., Leavens, G.T., Pierce, B.C.: On binary methods. Theory and Practice of Object Systems 1(3), 221–242 (1995)
4. Bruce, K.B., Foster, J.N.: LOOJ: Weaving LOOM into Java. In: Odersky, M. (ed.) ECOOP 2004. LNCS, vol. 3086, pp. 389–413. Springer, Heidelberg (2004)
5. Bruce, K.B., Odersky, M., Wadler, P.: A statically safe alternative to virtual types. In: Jul, E. (ed.) ECOOP 1998. LNCS, vol. 1445, pp. 523–549. Springer, Heidelberg (1998)
6. Bruce, K.B., Petersen, L., Fiech, A.: Subtyping is not a good "match" for object-oriented languages. In: Aksit, M., Matsuoka, S. (eds.) ECOOP 1997. LNCS, vol. 1241, pp. 104–127. Springer, Heidelberg (1997)
7. Bruce, K.B., Schuett, A., van Gent, R., Fiech, A.: PolyTOIL: A type-safe polymorphic object-oriented language. ACM Trans. Prog. Lang. and Systems 25(2), 225–290 (2003)
8. Chakravarty, M.M.T., Keller, G., Jones, S.P.: Associated type synonyms. In: Pierce, B.C. (ed.) Proc. Intl. Conf. Functional Programming 2005, Tallinn, Estonia, September 2005, pp. 241–253. ACM Press, New York (2005)
9. Chakravarty, M.M.T., Keller, G., Jones, S.P., Marlow, S.: Associated types with class. In: Abadi, M. (ed.) Proc. 32nd ACM Symp. POPL, Long Beach, CA, USA, January 2005, pp. 1–13. ACM Press, New York (2005)
10. Chambers, C.: Object-oriented multi-methods in Cecil. In: Madsen, O.L. (ed.) ECOOP 1992. LNCS, vol. 615, pp. 33–56. Springer, Heidelberg (1992)
11. Clifton, C., Millstein, T., Leavens, G.T., Chambers, C.: MultiJava: Design rationale, compiler implementation, and applications. ACM Trans. Prog. Lang. and Systems 28(3), 517–575 (2006)
12. Ernst, E.: Family polymorphism. In: Knudsen, J.L. (ed.) ECOOP 2001. LNCS, vol. 2072, pp. 303–326. Springer, Heidelberg (2001)
13. Ernst, E., Ostermann, K., Cook, W.R.: A virtual class calculus. In: Jones, S.P. (ed.) Proc. 33rd ACM Symp. POPL, Charleston, South Carolina, USA, January 2006, pp. 270–282. ACM Press, New York (2006)
14. Eugster, P.: Uniform proxies for Java. In: Proc. 21th ACM Conf. OOPSLA, Portland, OR, USA, pp. 139–152. ACM Press, New York (2006)
15. Hall, C.V., Hammond, K., Jones, S.L.P., Wadler, P.L.: Type classes in Haskell. ACM Trans. Prog. Lang. and Systems 18(2), 109–138 (1996)
16. Helm, R., Holland, I.M., Gangopadhyay, D.: Contracts: specifying behavioral compositions in object-oriented systems. In: Conf. OOPSLA / ECOOP, Ottawa, Canada, October 1990. SIGPLAN Notices, vol. 25(10), pp. 169–180 (1990)

17. Igarashi, A., Pierce, B.C., Wadler, P.: Featherweight Java: a minimal core calculus for Java and GJ. ACM Trans. Prog. Lang. and Systems 23(3), 396–450 (2001)
18. Jones, M.P.: Type classes with functional dependencies. In: Smolka, G. (ed.) ESOP 2000 and ETAPS 2000. LNCS, vol. 1782, pp. 230–244. Springer, Heidelberg (2000)
19. Järvi, J., Willcock, J., Lumsdaine, A.: Associated types and constraint propagation for mainstream object-oriented generics. In: Proc. 20th ACM Conf. OOPSLA, pp. 1–19. ACM Press, New York (2005)
20. Kaes, S.: Parametric overloading in polymorphic programming languages. In: Ganzinger, H. (ed.) ESOP 1988. LNCS, vol. 300, pp. 131–144. Springer, Heidelberg (1988)
21. Kennedy, A., Syme, D.: Design and implementation of generics for the .NET common language runtime. In: Proc. 2001 PLDI, Snowbird, UT, United States, June 2001, pp. 1–12. ACM Press, New York, USA (2001)
22. Kiczales, G., Hilsdale, E., Hugunin, J., Kersten, M., Palm, J., Griswold, W.G.: An Overview of AspectJ. In: Knudsen, J.L. (ed.) ECOOP 2001. LNCS, vol. 2072, pp. 327–353. Springer, Heidelberg (2001)
23. Lämmel, R., Ostermann, K.: Software extension and integration with type classes. In: GPCE '06, pp. 161–170. ACM Press, New York (2006)
24. Madsen, O.L., Møller-Pedersen, B., Nygaard, K.: Object-Oriented Programming in the BETA Programming Language. Addison-Wesley, Reading (1993)
25. Microsoft Corp. C# Version 3.0 Specification (May 2006), http://msdn2.microsoft.com/en-us/vcsharp/aa336745.aspx
26. Millstein, T., Reay, M., Chambers, C.: Relaxed MultiJava: Balancing extensibility and modular typechecking. In: Proc. 18th ACM Conf. OOPSLA, Anaheim, CA, USA, pp. 224–240. ACM Press, New York (2003)
27. Odersky, M.: The scala language specification version 2.0, Draft (November 2006), http://scala.epfl.ch/docu/files/ScalaReference.pdf
28. Odersky, M., Zenger, M.: Scalable component abstractions. In: Proc. 20th ACM Conf. OOPSLA, San Diego, CA, USA, 2005, pp. 41–58. ACM Press, New York (2005)
29. Jones, S.P.(ed.): Haskell 98 Language and Libraries, The Revised Report. Cambridge University Press, Cambridge (2003)
30. Jones, S.P., Jones, M., Meijer, E.: Type classes: An exploration of the design space. In: Launchbury, J. (ed) Proc. of the Haskell Workshop, Amsterdam, June 1997, The Netherlands (1997)
31. Sekharaiah, K.C., Ram, D.J.: Object schizophrenia problem in object role system design. In: Bellahsène, Z., Patel, D., Rolland, C. (eds.) OOIS 2002. LNCS, vol. 2425, pp. 494–506. Springer, Heidelberg (2002)
32. Siek, J., Lumsdaine, A.: Essential language support for generic programming. In: Proc. 2005 ACM Conf. PLDI, June 2005, pp. 73–84. ACM Press, New York (2005)
33. Torgersen, M.: The expression problem revisited — four new solutions using generics. In: Odersky, M. (ed.) ECOOP 2004. LNCS, vol. 3086, Springer, Heidelberg (2004)
34. Torgersen, M., Ernst, E., Hansen, C.P.: Wild FJ. In: International Workshop on Foundations of Object-Oriented Languages, informal proceedings (2005)
35. Torgersen, M., Ernst, E., Hansen, C.P., von der Ahé, P., Bracha, G, Gafter, N.: Adding wildcards to the java programming language. Journal of Object Technology 3(11), 97–116 (2004)
36. Wadler, P.: The expression problem, Posted on Java Genericity mailing list (1998)

37. Wadler, P., Blott, S.: How to make ad-hoc polymorphism less ad-hoc. In: Proc. 16th ACM Symp. POPL, Austin, Texas, January 1989, pp. 60–76. ACM Press, New York (1989)
38. Warth, A., Stanojevic, M., Millstein, T.: Statically scoped object adaptation with expanders. In: Proc. 21th ACM Conf. OOPSLA, Portland, OR, USA, 2006, pp. 37–56. ACM Press, New York (2006)
39. Yu, D., Kennedy, A., Syme, D.: Formalization of generics for the .NET common language runtime. In: Leroy, X. (ed.) Proc. 31st ACM Symp. POPL, Venice, Italy, January 2004, pp. 39–51. ACM Press, New York (2004)

Metaprogramming with Traits

John Reppy and Aaron Turon

University of Chicago
{jhr,adrassi}@cs.uchicago.edu

Abstract. In many domains, classes have highly regular internal structure. For example, so-called business objects often contain boilerplate code for mapping database fields to class members. The boilerplate code must be repeated per-field for every class, because existing mechanisms for constructing classes do not provide a way to capture and reuse such member-level structure. As a result, programmers often resort to *ad hoc* code generation. This paper presents a lightweight mechanism for specifying and reusing member-level structure in Java programs. The proposal is based on a modest extension to traits that we have termed *trait-based metaprogramming*. Although the semantics of the mechanism are straightforward, its type theory is difficult to reconcile with nominal subtyping. We achieve reconciliation by introducing a hybrid structural/nominal type system that extends Java's type system. The paper includes a formal calculus defined by translation to Featherweight Generic Java.

1 Introduction

In mainstream object-oriented languages, programming amounts to class creation. While a programmer may write classes from scratch, good style dictates that existing code be used when possible. Several mechanisms exist to aid the programmer in this endeavor: inheritance combines existing classes with extensions or modifications; mixins and traits capture such extensions, allowing them to be reused; and generic classes are instantiated with type parameters to produce specialized classes. Each of these mechanisms allows programmers to capture and reuse useful structure at the level of classes, but they provide limited support for capturing structure at the level of class members.

In many domains, classes have highly regular *internal* structure. As a simple example, consider a thread-safe class in which all methods obtain a single lock before executing. Manually writing this boilerplate code results in clutter and rigidity: the locking strategy cannot easily be changed after the fact. In Java, thread-safe methods were considered important enough to warrant the **synchronized** keyword, but adding keywords is a kind of magic that only the language designer, not the language user, can perform. In this paper, we propose a mechanism that allows programmers to capture, reuse, and modify such *member-level patterns* in a coherent way.

The **synchronized** pattern consists of behavior common to otherwise unrelated members of a class. Another common member-level pattern is when a class

E. Ernst (Ed.): ECOOP 2007, LNAI 4609, pp. 373–398, 2007.

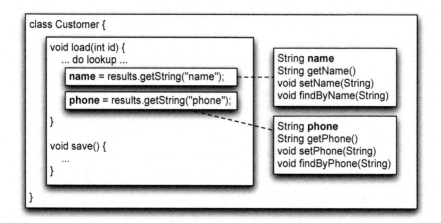

Fig. 1. A more complex member-level pattern

contains collections of similar members that are intended to match a domain model. For example, consider a `Customer` class that provides access to a customer table in a database. For each field present in the table, the `Customer` class will contain a cluster of members: for the `name` field, the `Customer` class might contain an instance variable `name` and methods `getName`, `setName`, and `findByName`. Moreover, the class will provide `load` and `save` methods that load and store the class's instance variables. This situation is shown diagrammatically in Figure 1. While additional behavior may be needed for particular fields, it is desirable to abstract the common structure and implementation; once defined, the abstraction answers the question "what does it mean for a class to provide access to a database field?" We show how this can be done with our mechanism at the end of Section 3.

Our proposal is based on a modest extension to *traits* [9] that allows programmers to write *trait functions*, which are parameterized by member names. Trait functions are applied at compile time to build classes, supporting what we term *trait-based metaprogramming*. In describing our mechanism as a form of metaprogramming, we mean that (1) it operates entirely at compile-time and (2) it allows both *generation* and *introspection* of code.[1] There are many frameworks available for metaprogramming; our proposal's strength is its singular focus on member-level patterns. We believe that the territory between classes and individual class members is a fruitful place to do metaprogramming, and by focusing our efforts there, we are able to provide a succinct mechanism with good guarantees about the generated code. A detailed discussion of related work is given in Section 5.

The language design is presented informally in Section 3. In Section 4 we model our mechanism as an extension to Featherweight Generic Java (FGJ), giving our semantics as a translation to FGJ. While the translation is very simple,

---

[1] This paper focuses on generation; we discuss introspection in a technical report [28].

its type theory is difficult to reconcile with nominal subtyping because abstraction over member labels is allowed. We achieve reconciliation by introducing a hybrid structural/nominal type system that extends Java's type system. The type system is not strongly tied to our broader proposal, and we hope that the ideas will find broad application in metaprogramming systems for nominally-subtyped languages, a possibility we discuss in Section 5.2.

2 Background

Traits were originally introduced by Schärli *et al.* in the setting of Smalltalk [9] as a mechanism for sharing common method definitions between classes. In their proposal, a trait is simply a collection of named methods. These methods cannot directly reference instance variables; instead, they must be *"pure behavior."* The methods defined in a trait are called the *provided methods*, while any methods that are referenced, but not provided, are called *required methods*. An important property of traits is that while they help structure the implementation of classes, they do not affect the inheritance hierarchy. In particular, traits are distinguished from mixins [5] because they can be composed without the use of inheritance.[2] Traits can be formed by definition (*i.e.*, listing a collection of method definitions) or by using one of several trait operations:

Symmetric sum merges two disjoint traits to create a new trait. [3]

Override forms a new trait by layering additional methods over an existing trait. This operation is an asymmetric sum. When one of the new methods has the same name as a method in the original trait, the override operation replaces the original method.

Alias creates a new trait by adding a new name for an existing method. This operation is *not* renaming, in that it does not replace references to the old name with the new one.

Exclusion forms a new trait by removing a method from an existing trait. Combining the alias and exclusion operations yields a renaming operation, although the renaming is shallow.

The other important operation on traits is *inlining*, the mechanism whereby traits are integrated with classes. This operation merges a class C, a trait, and additional fields and methods to form a new subclass of C. Often, the additional methods, called *glue methods* [9], provide access to the newly added fields. The glue methods, plus the methods inherited from C, provide the required methods of the trait. An important aspect of traits is that the methods of a trait are only loosely coupled; they can be removed and replaced by other implementations.

Traits provide a lightweight alternative to multiple inheritance, and they have been the focus of much recent interest, including formal calculi [11,20] and other

---

[2] Bracha's *Jigsaw* [4], one of the first formal presentations of mixins, supports a similar notion of composition, but most other constructs under the name "mixin" do not.

[3] Smalltalk traits allow name conflicts, but replace the conflicting methods with a special method body **conflict** that triggers a run-time error if evaluated.

language designs for traits [24,27,23,14]. While the details of these various mechanisms vary, they all share a focus on sharing common method implementations across unrelated classes. Our design shifts the focus toward sharing member-level patterns that can occur within a single class.

3   A Design for Trait-Based Metaprogramming

We present our design in the setting of Java, though there is little that is Java-specific. Like other language designs that incorporate traits, a trait in our language has a collection of members it *provides* and a collection of members it *requires*. What is new in our design is that traits may be parameterized over the names and types of these members: our traits are really *trait functions*. The basic form of a trait is as follows:

> **trait** *trait-name* (*member-name parameters*, *type parameters*, *value parameters*)
> **requires** { *requirements* }
> **provides** { *member definitions* }

Note that traits may be parameterized over values, such as constant values that vary between instances of a member-level pattern. Member-name parameters are prefixed with "$" so that member-name variables never shadow actual member names; in our experience, having a clear distinction between `obj.foo` and `obj.$foo` makes trait code easier to understand.

The **requires** and **provides** sections also differ from previous designs. In addition to giving the signatures of required class members, the requirements section is also used to place constraints on type parameters, as illustrated in the `DelegateT` example near the end of this section. Another departure in our design is that the **provides** section can contain field declarations. When such declarations are inlined in a class, the class's constructors are responsible for initializing them. Traits are inlined using the **use** construct, which is syntactically just another form of member definition. Since traits are actually functions, the **use** construct applies the trait function to its arguments and inlines the resulting member definitions. As shown below, the **provides** section of a trait can also have **use** declarations, which is how traits are composed. Conflicting method or field declarations within the body of a trait or class, whether defined directly or inlined from traits, are rejected by the type system.

3.1   Some Illustrative Examples

In the remainder of this section, we present a series of examples that illustrate our mechanism and the kinds of patterns it captures. We begin by with the notion of a "property" — a field along with getter and setter methods. In this example, the variables `$f`, `$g`, and `$s` range over field and method names, while the variable `T` ranges over types. The access modifiers **public** and **private** determine the visibility the members will have after they are inlined into a class:

```
trait PropT ($f, $g, $s, T)
  provides {
    private T $f;
    public void $s (T x) { $f = x; }
    public T $g () { return $f; }
  }
```

We can use `PropT` to define a 2D point class by *"using"* it twice with different member names:

```
class Point2 {
  use PropT (x, getX, setX, int);
  use PropT (y, getY, setY, int);
  Point2 () { x = 0; y = 0; }
}
```

Note also that the `Point2` constructor initializes the fields introduced by the traits.

Next, we revisit the **synchronized** example from Section 1:

```
trait SyncT ($op, R, A...)
  requires {
    ThisType implements {
      Mutex lock;
      R $op (A...);
    }
  }
  provides {
    override public R $op (A...) {
      lock.acquire();
      R res = outer.$op (...);
      lock.release();
      return res;
    }
  }
```

This example illustrates several features of our design. Often, as here, we use a trait to wrap behavior around methods in a way that does not depend on the parameters or return type of the method. Since Java does not treat parameter sequences as tuples, we introduce the notation "x..." as a way to name parameter sequences with heterogeneous types, where the arity may vary from instance to instance. This notation can be used in the signatures of methods; within their bodies, the actual value of the parameter sequence is denoted by "...". When the trait is inlined, a tuple of types is given for the parameter sequence, as in the following example that synchronizes a string comparison method:

```
use SyncT (compare, int, (String, String));
```

The second feature to note is the **ThisType** keyword, which denotes the class that is using the trait. Here, we use **ThisType** to state the requirement that the class provides the `lock` field and an implementation of the `$op` method to be overridden by the trait. The scope of **ThisType** acts is the entire trait, so it may appear as an argument or return type of a method, for example. In particular, this means that traits can provide binary methods.

The last feature is the use of the **override** and **outer** keywords in the declaration of the provided method. The **override** keyword states that the method is replacing an existing method in the class, which could either be inherited or locally defined. The **outer** keyword is used to invoke the version of the method that is being overridden. The **outer** keyword is similar to **super**, except that it may only be used to invoke methods that have the **override** annotation. After a method is overridden by inlining a trait, it is considered locally defined, and so it can be overridden again by inlining another trait; this technique can be used to concatenate partial method implementations from multiple traits, as we show in a later example.

The following class uses the `SyncT` trait to implement an atomic test-and-set operation:

```
class C {
  private boolean x;
  private Mutex lock;
  boolean testAndSet () { boolean t = x; x = true; return t; }
  use SyncT (testAndSet, boolean, ());
  C () { lock = new Mutex(); x = false; }
}
```

Note that without the **override** annotation in the `SyncT` trait, there would be a conflict between the definition of `testAndSet` given in the body of C and the one provided by `SyncT`.

The **requires** clause of a trait can also be used to impose constraints on any type parameters the trait might have. These constraints can be *nominal* (using **extends**) or *structural* (using **implements**), with the latter allowing us to capture patterns like delegation, as in the following example:

```
trait DelegateT ($m, $f, T, A..., R)
  requires {
    T implements { R $m (A...); }
    ThisType implements { T $f; }
  }
  provides {
    R $m (A...) { return $f.$m(...); }
  }
```

We conclude with a more substantial example: the `Customer` class from Section 1. Classes like `Customer` are quite common in database applications, where relational databases are mapped onto the class hierarchy. Usually, such classes include large amounts of boilerplate code for performing this mapping. Numerous mechanisms have been proposed to alleviate this burden, including

```
trait BObjectT(String table)
  provides {
    protected void loadData(ResultSet r) {}
    protected void findBy(String whereClause) throws DataNotFound {
      Connection con = ... open connection to database ...
      Statement stmt = con.createStatement();
      String sql = "SELECT * FROM " + table + " WHERE " + whereClause;
      ResultSet r = stmt.executeQuery(sql);
      if (r.next()) {
        loadData(r);
      } else {
        throw new DataNotFound();
      }
    }
  }

trait StringFieldT($f, $g, $s, $fBy, String fieldName, int length)
  requires {
    ThisType implements {
      void loadData(ResultSet r);
      void findBy(String whereClause) throws DataNotFound;
    }
  }
  provides {
    use PropT($f, $g, $s, String);
    override String $s(String x) throws FieldTooSmall {
      if (x.length() > length) throw new FieldTooSmall();
      outer.$s(x);
    }
    override void loadData(ResultSet r) {
      $f = r.getString(fieldName);
      outer.loadData(r);
    }
    void $fBy(String x) throws DataNotFound, FieldTooSmall {
      if (x.length() > length) throw new FieldTooSmall();
      findBy(fieldName + " = '" + x + "'");
    }
  }

class Customer {
  use BObjectT("customers");
  use StringFieldT(name, getName, setName, findByName, "name", 40);
  use StringFieldT(addr, getAddr, setAddr, findByAddr, "address", 40);
  use StringFieldT(phone, getPhone, setPhone,
                   findByPhone, "phone_num", 40);
  ... etc ...
}
```

Fig. 2. Business objects: a sketch

code generation and other forms of metaprogramming; sophisticated frameworks like *Hibernate*[4] and *Ruby on Rails*[5] are currently used to automate this mapping.

Figure 2 presents a code fragment using trait-based metaprogramming to tackle the mapping problem. Our solution uses two related traits: `BObjectT` factors out the code needed to query an SQL database, and `StringFieldT` maps a field in an object to a string field in a database. The latter is a trait function with value parameters: `fieldName` and `length`. As a whole, the example demonstrates an idiom allowing traits to define "partial methods:" a base trait(`BObjectT`) is used to seed a class with an empty implementation of a method (`loadData`). Then a trait function (`StringFieldT`) is applied multiple times, each time extending the method's behavior before invoking the **outer** implementation.

3.2   From No Parameters to Too Many?

7One apparent downside of the proposed mechanism is that, having introduced parameters, we need too many of them in order to encode interesting patterns. The `StringFieldT` trait, for example, takes a total of six parameters, and one can easily imagine adding more for a more sophisticated implementation. This problem is exacerbated by parameter sequences, where the user of a trait must tediously spell out a tuple of types. In many of these cases, however, the appropriate value for a parameter can be inferred or explicitly computed. For instance, if the `$f` parameter to `StringFieldT` is `name`, we can derive that `$g` should be `getName`, `$s` should be `setName`, and so on. Given a few primitives for label manipulation, these rules are easy to write down. Likewise, the type arguments to the `SyncT` trait can be inferred based on the actual method that the trait overrides, as long as no method overloading has occurred. Having the compiler infer these arguments makes our mechanism less cumbersome to use, and we take up the idea in a companion technical report [28]; as it turns out, this leads directly to a powerful form of *pattern matching* for trait functions.

4   A Formal Model: Meta-trait Java

Having informally described trait-based metaprogramming, we proceed to the formal model. The primary goal of this model is to study the type theory of our mechanism in the context of Java's nominal type system. Thus, we model only the core features of our proposal: we drop **super**, **outer**, and variable-arity parameters, since they do not substantially alter the type system, but do clutter its presentation. In earlier work, we presented a detailed semantics for compiling traits with hiding and renaming [25]; here, we give a simpler semantics that performs renaming only through trait functions. The relationship between the two models is discussed in Section 5.3.

---

[4] http://www.hibernate.org/
[5] http://www.rubyonrails.org/

$$C ::= \textbf{class } c\texttt{<}\overline{\alpha} \lhd \overline{N}\texttt{>} \lhd N \ \{K \ \overline{D}\} \qquad \text{class declaration}$$
$$K ::= c(\overline{T} \ \overline{f}) \ \{\textbf{super}(\overline{f}) \, ; \ \textbf{this}.\overline{f} = \overline{f}; \} \qquad \text{constructor declaration}$$

$$A ::= \textbf{trait } t(\overline{\$l}, \ \overline{\alpha}) \ \textbf{req } \{\overline{R}\} \ \textbf{prov } \{\overline{D}\} \qquad \text{trait function decl.}$$
$$R ::= \alpha \lhd N \ \textbf{implements } \{\overline{F} \ \overline{S}\} \qquad \text{trait requirement decl.}$$
$$S ::= \texttt{<}\overline{\alpha} \lhd \overline{N}\texttt{>} \ T \ m(\overline{T} \ \overline{x}) \, ; \qquad \text{method signature decl.}$$
$$E ::= t(\overline{l}, \ \overline{T}) \qquad \text{trait function application}$$
$$| \quad E \ \textbf{drop } l \qquad \text{member exclusion}$$
$$| \quad E \ \textbf{alias } m \ \textbf{as } m \qquad \text{method aliasing}$$

$$D ::= F \ | \ M \ | \ \ \textbf{use } E; \qquad \text{member declaration}$$
$$F ::= T \ f; \qquad \text{field declaration}$$
$$M ::= T \ m(\overline{T} \ \overline{x}) \ \{\textbf{return } e;\} \qquad \text{method declaration}$$

$$e ::= x \ | \ e.f \ | \ e.m(\overline{e}) \ | \ \textbf{new } N(\overline{e}) \qquad \text{expression}$$
$$v ::= \textbf{new } N(\overline{e}) \qquad \text{value}$$

$$N, P ::= c\texttt{<}\overline{T}\texttt{>} \qquad \text{nonvariable type name}$$
$$T, U ::= N \ | \ \alpha \qquad \text{type name}$$

Fig. 3. MTJ: syntax

Our calculus, MTJ, is essentially an extension of Featherweight Generic Java (FGJ); we drop FGJ's type casts and method type parameters since they do not interact with our type system in any interesting way.[6] Featherweight Java was designed to capture the minimal essence of Java, with particular focus on its type system and proof of soundness, and FGJ extends FJ with generics [17]. Our calculus adds traits and trait functions to FGJ, along with the additional type-theoretic machinery needed to support those features. Like FGJ, we omit assignment, interfaces, overloading, and **super**-sends. MTJ is not equipped with its own dynamic semantics; instead, we define a translation from MTJ programs to FGJ programs. The type system, however, is given directly, and it conservatively extends FGJ's type system.

4.1   Syntax

The syntax of MTJ is given in Figure 3; portions highlighted in grey are extensions to FGJ's syntax. For the calculus, we abbreviate **extends** to $\lhd$, **requires** to **req**, and **provides** to **prov**. The metavariables c and d range over class names and t ranges over trait names. For field names and method names (collectively called *labels*), we separate variables from concrete names, as follows:

---

[6] For the remainder of this paper, when we refer to FGJ, we mean this restricted calculus.

	Concrete	Variable	Either
Field names	f, g	$f	f
Method names	m	$m	m
Member names (labels)	l	$l	l, k

Note we assume the sets of field and method names are disjoint. Object is a class name, but cannot be defined in an MTJ program; **this** is a variable name, but cannot occur as a parameter.

To keep notation compact, we make heavy use of overbar sequence notation: $\bar{f}$ denotes the possibly empty sequence $f_1, \ldots, f_n$, for example. Pairs of sequences are interleaved: $\overline{T}\,\bar{f}$ stands for $T_1\,f_1, \ldots, T_n\,f_n$, and **this**.$\bar{f} = \bar{f}$; stands for **this**.$f_1 = f_1$; $\ldots$; **this**.$f_n = f_n$;. Sequences are delimited as necessary to match Java syntax. Sequences of parameters are also assumed to contain no duplicate names. The empty sequence is denoted by $\bullet$, and sequence concatenation by the $\cdot$ operator. Finally, sequences with named elements are sometimes used as finite maps taking names to sequence elements. Thus, $\overline{D}(\texttt{foo})$ denotes the field or method declaration in $\overline{D}$ named $\texttt{foo}$ (unambiguous because method and field names must be distinct).

A class table CT is a map from class names c to class declarations. Likewise, a trait table TT maps trait names t to trait declarations. A program is a triple (CT, TT, e). In defining the semantics of MTJ, we assume fixed, global tables CT and TT. We further assume that these tables are *well-formed*: the class table must define an acyclic inheritance hierarchy, and the trait table must define an acyclic trait use graph.

4.2   Translation to FGJ

An FGJ program is an MTJ program with an empty trait table (and thus no trait use declarations). The semantics of MTJ are given by a translation function $[\![-]\!]$ that takes MTJ class declarations to FGJ class declarations. The translation *flattens* trait use declarations into sequences of FGJ member declarations, incorporating the bodies of traits into the classes in which they are used. As a consequence, the so-called *flattening property* [22] holds by construction: class members introduced through traits cannot be distinguished from class members defined directly within a class.[7]

Much of the work of translation is performed by substitution. Since trait functions are strictly first-order, the definitions of the various substitution forms (types for types, labels for labels, *etc.*) are straightforward and hence omitted.

The details of the translation are shown in Figure 4. Class declarations are translated by flattening the class body, keeping track of the name of the class so that any occurrences of **ThisType** can be replaced by it. Fields and methods are already "flat," so the only interesting member-level translation is for trait use declarations. To flatten a trait function application, we first substitute the actual parameters for the formal parameters within the trait body, and then

---

[7] A similar property, called the *copy principle*, has been defined for mixins [2].

$$[\![\textbf{class } c\texttt{<}\overline{\alpha}\texttt{>} \triangleleft \overline{N}\texttt{>} \triangleleft N \ \{K \ \overline{D}\}]\!] = \textbf{class } c\texttt{<}\overline{\alpha}\texttt{>} \triangleleft \overline{N}\texttt{>} \triangleleft N \ \{K \ [\![\overline{D}]\!]_{c\texttt{<}\overline{\alpha}\texttt{>}}\}$$

$$[\![F]\!]_N = F$$
$$[\![M]\!]_N = M$$
$$[\![\textbf{use } E;]\!]_N = [\![E]\!]_N$$

$$[\![t(\overline{\mathsf{l}}, \ \overline{T})]\!]_N = [\![[\overline{\mathsf{l}}/\overline{\$\mathsf{l}}], \ \overline{T}/\overline{\alpha}, N/\textbf{ThisType}]\overline{D}]\!]_N$$
$$\text{where } \mathrm{TT}(t) = \textbf{trait } t(\overline{\$\mathsf{l}}, \ \overline{\alpha}) \ \textbf{req } \{\overline{R}\} \ \textbf{prov } \{\overline{D}\}$$
$$[\![E \ \textbf{drop } \mathsf{l}]\!]_N = [\![E]\!]_N \setminus \mathsf{l}$$
$$[\![E \ \textbf{alias } \mathsf{m} \textbf{ as } \mathsf{m}']\!]_N = [\![E]\!]_N \cdot [\mathsf{m}'/\mathsf{m}]([\![E]\!]_N(\mathsf{m}))$$

Fig. 4. MTJ to FGJ translation

flatten the result. To drop a member for an inlined trait, we simply remove it from the flattened collection of member delcarations. There is a subtlety in the semantics for aliasing: when recursive methods are aliased, do their recursive invocations refer to the original method or to the alias? We have chosen the latter interpretation, following Liquori and Spiwack [20]. This choice does not affect our type system, but does affect finer-grained type systems that track individual method requirements [25].

Note that translation is guaranteed to terminate, since the trait use graph is required to be acyclic.

4.3   Types in MTJ

We now turn to the static semantics for MTJ. One approach for constructing a type system for traits is to defer type checking of trait members until the trait is used in a class, then check the trait members as if they were declared within that class [20]. While this approach is pleasantly simple, requiring no changes to the existing type system for classes, it has at least one significant downside: type errors in a trait function may not be detected until that function is used, perhaps by a programmer using a library of such trait functions.

Our goal, in contrast, is to subsume FGJ's type system while *separately* type checking trait definitions, expressions, and uses. To achieve this goal, our calculus must give types to traits and trait expressions. Trait types must also be available at the expression level, because **this** and **ThisType** may appear in trait method bodies. In a structural type system, these requirements can be easily met by introducing *incomplete* object types to track trait requirements and assigning these types to traits [11,3]; the type of a trait would then be a (structural) supertype of all classes that include that trait. Determining the status of trait types in a nominal type system is more difficult. One route is to associate a type name with each trait declaration [27], as is done for class declarations. Typing trait expressions involving aliasing or exclusion, however, is awkward with this approach.

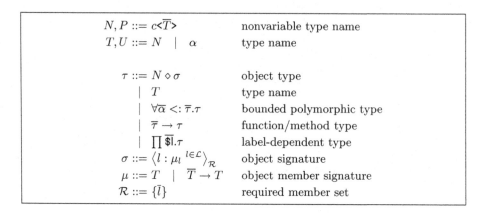

$$
\begin{array}{lll}
N, P ::= c\mathord{<}\overline{T}\mathord{>} & & \text{nonvariable type name} \\
T, U ::= N \mid \alpha & & \text{type name} \\[1em]
\tau ::= N \diamond \sigma & & \text{object type} \\
\quad \mid T & & \text{type name} \\
\quad \mid \forall \overline{\alpha} <: \overline{\tau}.\tau & & \text{bounded polymorphic type} \\
\quad \mid \overline{\tau} \rightarrow \tau & & \text{function/method type} \\
\quad \mid \prod \overline{\$l}.\tau & & \text{label-dependent type} \\
\sigma ::= \langle l : \mu_l{}^{l \in \mathcal{L}} \rangle_{\mathcal{R}} & & \text{object signature} \\
\mu ::= T \mid \overline{T} \rightarrow T & & \text{object member signature} \\
\mathcal{R} ::= \{\overline{l}\} & & \text{required member set}
\end{array}
$$

Fig. 5. MTJ: type syntax

The situation in MTJ is further complicated by the fact that trait functions are abstracted over labels and types, and may constrain their type parameters to implement interfaces that include abstract labels (Section 3). In principle these features could be supported in a purely nominal way, but we believe that the resulting type system would be too brittle and cumbersome, and would limit the programmer's ability to use existing classes as type parameters to traits.

In view of these concerns, we propose a hybrid structural/nominal type system. Purely nominal type systems must still check the structure of types to ensure soundness; the pertinent structure does not appear in the syntax of the types, but rather through auxiliary machinery (*e.g.*, *fields* and *mtype* in FGJ). Our type system exposes structural types syntactically: an object type $N \diamond \sigma$ is a pair of a type name N and an object signature σ. If an object has type $N \diamond \sigma$, then it is *nominally* a subtype of N, and *structurally* a subtype of σ. The nominal component is used for checking method arguments and return values, because in FGJ these constructions impose nominal subtyping constraints, while the structural component is used for checking field accesses and method invocations, corresponding to the structural-checking machinery in FGJ. The full syntax of MTJ types is given in Figure 5.

Of course, there is a relationship between the two components of an object type: for each nominal type N — for each class — there is a signature σ_N giving its interface. We call this signature the *canonical signature for N*. The purpose of the signature component in an object type is to impose *additional* structural constraints on the type of the object, beyond those already imposed by its canonical signature. These additional constraints can only be introduced through the **requires** and **provides** declarations in a trait function; thus, the constraints are only placed on type variables (including **ThisType**, which we treat as a type variable). The type variables in a trait are replaced by class names when trait function application is translated to FGJ. Our type system ensures that the constraints on these type variables are satisfied by the eventual class name arguments, ensuring the type-safety of the resulting FGJ code.

Notice that types τ include both object types and type names. A type name is either a nonvariable type name (which is a class name, possibly applied to type parameters) or a type variable. A nonvariable type name N stands for the object type $N \diamond \sigma_N$ that includes the canonical signature of the class. A type variable α stands for an unknown (but bounded) object type. The surface syntax of the language prevents trait and class member declarations from introducing new object types: member declarations can only refer to named types. Thus, in the type syntax, object signatures are constrained to use type names rather than arbitrary object types. This constraint allows us to give a tidy account of recursive object types, as we shall see later.

An object signature σ is annotated with a set $\mathcal{R}$ of member names. In the object type for a trait, this set contains the name of all required members. For example, consider the following trait BarT, which requires a foo method and provides a bar method:

```
trait BarT
  requires { ThisType implements { Object foo(Object x); } }
  provides { Object bar(Object x) { return foo(foo(x)); } }
```

The type of BarT is $\mathtt{Object}\diamond\langle \mathtt{foo : Object} \rightarrow \mathtt{Object, bar : Object} \rightarrow \mathtt{Object}\rangle_{\{\mathtt{foo}\}}$. The nominal component of the type is Object because BarT places no nominal constraints on **ThisType**. Note that expression-level typing does not distinguish between the provided and required members of an object type, because traits are ultimately incorporated into classes that must provide all required members.

Classes are also given object types, as with the following polymorphic class [17]:

```
class Pair<X ◁ Object, Y ◁ Object> ◁ Object {
  Pair(X fst, Y snd) { super(); this.fst=fst; this.snd=snd; }
  X fst; Y snd;
  Pair<X,Y> setfst(X newfst) { return new Pair<X,Y>(newfst, snd); }
}
```

Our type system will give the following type to Pair:

$$\forall \mathtt{X} <: \mathtt{Object} \diamond \langle\rangle_\emptyset, \mathtt{Y} <: \mathtt{Object} \diamond \langle\rangle_\emptyset \ . \ \mathtt{Pair<X,Y>} \diamond \left\langle \begin{array}{l} \mathtt{fst : X, \ snd : Y,} \\ \mathtt{setfst : X} \rightarrow \mathtt{Pair<X,Y>} \end{array} \right\rangle_\emptyset$$

Trait functions add an additional complication: the result *type* of a trait function may depend on its label parameters, but these labels are unknown *values*, not unknown types. We introduce a very limited form of *dependent types* [15] to address this issue. In our calculus, the dependent type $\prod \$l.\tau$ represents a function that takes a label parameter and yields a value of type τ, where $\$l$ may occur free in τ. For example, consider the following trait function:

```
trait GetterT ($f, $g, T)
  requires { ThisType implements { T $f; } }
  provides { T $g() { $f; } }
```

In MTJ, GetterT has the type

$$\prod \$f, \$g \ . \ \forall \mathtt{T} <: \mathtt{Object} \diamond \langle\rangle_\emptyset \ . \ \mathtt{Object} \diamond \langle \$f : \mathtt{T}, \$g : \bullet \rightarrow \mathtt{T}\rangle_{\{\$f\}}$$

Nominal subtyping: $\boxed{\Delta \vdash T \lessdot T}$

$$\frac{\mathrm{CT}(c) = \mathbf{class}\ c\langle\overline{\alpha}\ \triangleleft\ \overline{N}\rangle\ \triangleleft\ N\ \{\dots\}}{\Delta \vdash c\langle\overline{T}\rangle \lessdot [\overline{T}/\overline{\alpha}]N} \qquad \frac{\Delta(\alpha) = N \diamond \sigma}{\Delta \vdash \alpha \lessdot N}$$

$$\frac{\Delta \vdash T_1 \lessdot T_2 \qquad \Delta \vdash T_2 \lessdot T_3}{\Delta \vdash T_1 \lessdot T_3} \qquad \frac{}{\Delta \vdash T \lessdot T}$$

Structural subtyping: $\boxed{\Delta \vdash \sigma <: \sigma}$

$$\frac{\mu_m = \overline{T} \rightarrow T \qquad \mu'_m = \overline{T} \rightarrow T' \qquad \Delta \vdash T \lessdot T'}{\Delta \vdash \langle m : \mu_m,\ l : \mu_l\ {}^{l \in \mathcal{L}} \rangle_{\mathcal{R}} <: \langle m : \mu'_m,\ l : \mu_l\ {}^{l \in \mathcal{L}} \rangle_{\mathcal{R}}}$$

$$\frac{\mathcal{L}_1 \supseteq \mathcal{L}_2 \qquad \mathcal{R}_1 \subseteq (\mathcal{R}_2 \cup (\mathcal{L}_1 \setminus \mathcal{L}_2))}{\Delta \vdash \langle l : \mu_l\ {}^{l \in \mathcal{L}_1} \rangle_{\mathcal{R}_1} <: \langle l : \mu_l\ {}^{l \in \mathcal{L}_2} \rangle_{\mathcal{R}_2}} \qquad \frac{\Delta \vdash \sigma_1 <: \sigma_2 \qquad \Delta \vdash \sigma_2 <: \sigma_3}{\Delta \vdash \sigma_1 <: \sigma_3}$$

General subtyping: $\boxed{\Delta \vdash \tau <: \tau}$

$$\frac{\Delta \vdash N_1 \lessdot N_2 \qquad \Delta \vdash \sigma_1 <: \sigma_2}{\Delta \vdash N_1 \diamond \sigma_1 <: N_2 \diamond \sigma_2} \qquad \frac{}{\Delta \vdash \alpha <: \Delta(\alpha)} \qquad \frac{\Delta \vdash \tau_1 <: \tau_2 \qquad \Delta \vdash \tau_2 <: \tau_3}{\Delta \vdash \tau_1 <: \tau_3}$$

Fig. 6. MTJ: subtyping

To give the typing judgments of the system, we need a few definitions. A *context* Γ is a sequence of abstract labels $\$l$ and variable typings $x : T$; we write $\$l \in \Gamma$ and $\Gamma(x) = T$, respectively, to denote their occurrence in Γ. Each label or variable may only occur once in Γ. A *type context* Δ is a finite map from type variables α to types τ. Just as we fixed class and trait tables in the translation semantics, we fix a global class type table CTy and trait type table TTy for the static semantics. The former takes class names to types, the latter takes trait names to types. These tables play a role similar to a store typing: they give each class and trait a presumed type, allowing us to check mutually-recursive class definitions. Ultimately, we ensure that the actual type of each class and trait matches the type given in the table. Formally, we regard the tables as implicit contexts for our typing judgments.

4.4 Subtyping

MTJ has three forms of subtyping: *nominal subtyping*, written $\Delta \vdash N_1 \lessdot N_2$, *structural subtyping*, written $\Delta \vdash \sigma_1 <: \sigma_2$, and *general subtyping*, written $\Delta \vdash \tau_1 <: \tau_2$. These relations are defined in Figure 6.

The nominal subtyping relation is just FGJ's subtyping relation: it defines inheritance-based subtyping, which is the reflexive-transitive closure of the **extends** relation.

Structural subtyping applies to object signatures. We support both depth and width subtyping. For depth subtyping, we follow FGJ (and GJ) in providing only covariant subtyping on methods. We also consider a signature with fewer requirements to be a subtype of the same signature with more requirements; the reasons for this choice will become clear in Section 4.7.

General subtyping is defined so that the nominal and structural components of an object type may vary independently. In particular, it is sometimes necessary for the nominal component of a type to be promoted without affecting the structural component, as in the following example:

```
class HasFoo { Object foo; }
trait NeedsFooA requires { ThisType implements {foo : Object} }
trait NeedsFooB requires { ThisType ⊲ HasFoo } provides { use NeedsFooA; }
```

In NeedsFooB, **ThisType** is bounded by $\text{HasFoo} \diamond \langle \text{foo} : \text{Object} \rangle_{\{\text{foo}\}}$. In NeedsFooA, however, **ThisType** is bounded by $\text{Object} \diamond \langle \text{foo} : \text{Object} \rangle_{\{\text{foo}\}}$, so a promotion of the nominal component of the bound is needed. Note that foo is marked required for NeedsFooA because it is not *provided* by the trait—in particular, it cannot be removed using **drop**—but is expected to be present in any class using the trait.

4.5 Static Semantics: Expressions

We present the static semantics of MTJ starting with expressions and working our way upwards.

As usual for a type system without a subsumption rule, we include a promotion function bound_Δ for computing the least nonvariable supertype of a given type, given in Figure 7. At the expression level, all types are named, so bound_Δ is only defined on type names. The type *computed* by bound_Δ, however, is always an object type. Thus, using bound_Δ on a nonvariable type name corresponds to an iso-recursive "unfold:" the signature component of $\text{bound}_\Delta(N)$, *i.e.*, the canonical signature of N, is the one-step expansion of N. We use the function "type" to compute the canonical type; that function, in turn, uses the class table to discover the appropriate canonical signature. As in FGJ, we have a well-formedness check for type names, written $\Delta \vdash T$ OK, which ensures that the type parameters for a class respect their bounds.

The expression typing rules (Figure 7) are similar to their counterparts in FGJ, with a few notable differences. Most importantly, field access and method invocation are checked via object signatures, rather than separate machinery. These rules are the motivation for our hybrid type system, making it possible to type traits and classes in a uniform way. Our rule for method invocation is somewhat simpler than in FGJ, because we do not model generic methods. A final point to observe is that all premises involving subtyping use the *nominal* subtyping relation. Each such premise corresponds to a proposition that must hold, using FGJ's (nominal) subtyping relation, after translation of the expression.

Bound of type name:

$$\text{type}(N) \quad = [\overline{T}/\overline{\alpha}]\tau_0 \ \text{when} \ \text{CTy}(c) = \forall \overline{\alpha} <: \overline{\tau}.\tau_0$$
$$\text{bound}_\Delta(N) = \text{type}(N)$$
$$\text{bound}_\Delta(\alpha) = \Delta(\alpha)$$

Well-formed type names: $\boxed{\Delta \vdash T \ \text{OK}}$

$$\frac{\alpha \in \text{dom}(\Delta)}{\Delta \vdash \alpha \ \text{OK}}$$ $$\frac{\text{CTy}(c) = \forall \overline{\alpha} <: \overline{\tau}.\tau_0 \quad \Delta \vdash \overline{T} \ \text{OK} \quad \Delta \vdash \text{bound}_\Delta(\overline{T}) <: [\overline{T}/\overline{\alpha}]\overline{\tau}}{\Delta \vdash c{<}\overline{T}{>} \ \text{OK}}$$

Expression typing: $\boxed{\Delta; \Gamma \vdash e \ : \ T}$

$$\frac{}{\Delta; \Gamma \vdash x \ : \ \Gamma(x)}$$ $$\frac{\Delta; \Gamma \vdash e_0 \ : \ T_0 \quad \text{bound}_\Delta(T_0) = N \diamond \sigma}{\Delta; \Gamma \vdash e_0.f \ : \ \sigma(f)}$$

$$\frac{\Delta; \Gamma \vdash e_0 \ : \ T_0 \quad \text{bound}_\Delta(T_0) = N \diamond \sigma \quad \sigma(m) = \overline{T} \to T' \quad \Delta; \Gamma \vdash \overline{e} \ : \ \overline{U} \quad \Delta \vdash \overline{U} \lessdot \overline{T}}{\Delta; \Gamma \vdash e_0.m(\overline{e}) \ : \ T'}$$

$$\frac{\Delta \vdash N \ \text{OK} \quad \text{fields}(N) = \overline{T} \ \overline{f} \quad \Delta; \Gamma \vdash \overline{e} \ : \ \overline{U} \quad \Delta \vdash \overline{U} \lessdot \overline{T}}{\Delta; \Gamma \vdash \mathbf{new} \ N(\overline{e}) \ : \ N}$$

Fig. 7. MTJ: expression typing

4.6   Static Semantics: Member Declarations and Trait Expressions

Type checking for classes and traits begins at the member level: the judgment $\Delta; \ \Gamma \vdash D \ : \ \tau$, given in Figure 8, assigns each member declaration an *object* type. This type should be understood as the least upper bound for the type of objects containing the declaration. For field and method declarations, the nominal component of the type will always be Object, while the structural component will give the label and type for that member. Trait use declarations are assigned the type of their trait expression, which may include nominal requirements.

Member declaration typing checks that any abstract labels are in scope ($\Gamma \vdash l \ \text{OK}$). Notice that method bodies are checked via the expression typing judgment, and the type given to the body is (as usual) required to be a nominal subtype of the expected return type. We also check that any types appearing in the program text are well-formed.

Trait expression typing is fairly straightforward; here, our type system resembles Fisher and Reppy's [11]. Recall that, when trait function applications are translated, a class name is substituted for ThisType (Section 4.2); really, ThisType is an implicit type parameter to every trait. Thus, when checking a trait function application, we substitute the type of **this** (as given by Γ) for

Label checking: $\boxed{\Gamma \vdash l \text{ OK}}$

$$\frac{}{\Gamma \vdash \mathsf{l} \text{ OK}} \qquad \frac{\$\mathsf{l} \in \Gamma}{\Gamma \vdash \$\mathsf{l} \text{ OK}}$$

Member declaration typing: $\boxed{\Delta; \Gamma \vdash D \ : \ \tau}$

$$\frac{\Delta \vdash T \text{ OK} \qquad \Gamma \vdash f \text{ OK}}{\Delta; \Gamma \vdash T \ f; \ : \ \mathsf{Object} \diamond \langle f \ : \ T \rangle_\emptyset} \qquad \frac{\Delta; \Gamma \vdash E \ : \ \tau}{\Delta; \Gamma \vdash \mathbf{use} \ E; \ : \ \tau}$$

$$\frac{\Delta \vdash T_0, \overline{T} \text{ OK} \qquad \Gamma \vdash m \text{ OK} \qquad \Delta; \Gamma, \overline{x} : \overline{T} \vdash e \ : \ U \qquad \Delta \vdash U \lessdot T_0}{\Delta; \Gamma \vdash T_0 \ m(\overline{T} \ \overline{x}) \ \{\mathbf{return} \ e;\} \ : \ \mathsf{Object} \diamond \langle m : \overline{T} \to T_0 \rangle_\emptyset}$$

Trait expression typing: $\boxed{\Delta; \Gamma \vdash E \ : \ \tau}$

$$\frac{\mathrm{TTy}(t) = \prod \overline{\$\mathsf{l}}. \forall \overline{\alpha} <: \overline{\tau} \ . \ N \diamond \sigma \qquad \Delta \vdash \overline{T} \text{ OK} \qquad \Gamma \vdash \overline{l} \text{ OK}}{\Delta \vdash \mathrm{bound}_\Delta(\overline{T}) <: [\overline{l}/\overline{\$\mathsf{l}}, \overline{T}/\overline{\alpha}, \Gamma(\mathbf{this})/\mathbf{ThisType}]\overline{\tau}}$$
$$\frac{}{\Delta; \Gamma \vdash t(\overline{l}, \ \overline{T}) \ : \ [\overline{l}/\overline{\$\mathsf{l}}, \overline{T}/\overline{\alpha}, \Gamma(\mathbf{this})/\mathbf{ThisType}]N \diamond \sigma}$$

$$\frac{\Delta; \Gamma \vdash E \ : \ T \diamond \langle l : \mu_l{}^{l \in \mathcal{L}} \rangle_\mathcal{R} \qquad m \in \mathcal{L} \setminus \mathcal{R} \qquad m' \notin \mathcal{L} \qquad \Gamma \vdash m' \text{ OK}}{\Delta; \Gamma \vdash E \ \mathbf{alias} \ m \ \mathbf{as} \ m' \ : \ T \diamond \langle m' : \mu_m, \ l : \mu_l{}^{l \in \mathcal{L}} \rangle_\mathcal{R}}$$

$$\frac{\Delta; \Gamma \vdash E \ : \ T \diamond \langle l : \mu_l{}^{l \in \mathcal{L}} \rangle_\mathcal{R} \qquad k \in \mathcal{L} \setminus \mathcal{R}}{\Delta; \Gamma \vdash E \ \mathbf{drop} \ k \ : \ T \diamond \langle l : \mu_l{}^{l \in \mathcal{L}} \rangle_{\mathcal{R} \cup \{k\}}}$$

Fig. 8. MTJ: member-level typing

ThisType in the trait type. We also substitute the explicit type arguments, checking that they respect their bounds.

The **alias** operation requires that the method to be aliased is actually provided by the trait, and that no method with the aliased name is provided or required by the trait. Likewise, for **drop** we check that the member to be dropped is provided by the trait. Because the member might be mentioned in a method provided by the trait, we do not simply drop it from the trait signature, but rather mark it as required. A more precise type can be given if member requirements are tracked for each provided method [25], but this comes at a cost: it leaks fine-grained implementation details about the trait into its signature.

4.7 Static Semantics: Classes and Traits

When typing a class or trait declaration, we attempt to find the meet (greatest lower bound) of its member declaration types. If the meet is defined, it gives us the type for the class or trait; if it is not defined, there is a type error. For example, consider the following class:

```
class C {
  int x;
  int getX() { return x; }
}
```

The types of the member declarations are

$$\texttt{Object} \diamond \langle \texttt{x : int} \rangle_\emptyset \quad \text{and} \quad \texttt{Object} \diamond \langle \texttt{getX} : \bullet \to \texttt{int} \rangle_\emptyset$$

respectively. The greatest lower bound of these types is

$$\texttt{Object} \diamond \langle \texttt{x : int, getX} : \bullet \to \texttt{int} \rangle_\emptyset$$

Replacing `Object` in the nominal component of this type with `C`, we have the type of the class.

As another example, suppose we have a trivial trait that provides nothing, but requires a method `foo`:

```
trait ReqT
  requires { ThisType implements { Object foo(); } }
  provides {}
```

Notice that the type of `ReqT` is $\texttt{Object} \diamond \langle \texttt{foo} : \bullet \to \texttt{Object} \rangle_{\{\texttt{foo}\}}$. We can then define a class `A` that uses `ReqT`:

```
class A ◁ Object {
  A foo() { return this; }
  use ReqT;
}
```

Taking the meet of `ReqT`'s type with the type of `foo` defined in `A` yields the type $\texttt{Object} \diamond \langle \texttt{foo} : \bullet \to \texttt{A} \rangle_\emptyset$. This is why types with fewer required members are "smaller" according to the subtyping relation: when we take the meet of two types, one requiring a member and one providing it, the resulting type lists the member as provided. In the above example, the type of the required member was lowered as well. On the other hand, the class `B` is not well-typed.

```
class B ◁ Object {
  Object foo(Object x) { return x; }
  use ReqT;
}
```

The requisite meet is not defined for `B`, because its type for `foo` has no lower bound in common with `ReqT`.

The meet of two object types, written $\tau_1 \wedge_\Delta \tau_2$, is defined in Figure 9. In addition, we define *object type concatenation*, written $\tau_1 \oplus_\Delta \tau_2$, which yields the meet of its operands but also checks that they provide disjoint sets of members.

The judgment $\Delta; \Gamma \vdash R \Rightarrow \alpha <: \tau$ is used to gather trait requirements into type constraints. Recall that both nominal and structural requirements can be specified. Object type concatenation is used to compute a type encompassing

Requirements:

$$\operatorname{reqs}\left(N \diamond \left\langle l : \mu_l \,^{l \in \mathcal{L}}\right\rangle_{\mathcal{R}}\right) = N \diamond \left\langle l : \mu_l \,^{l \in \mathcal{R}}\right\rangle_{\mathcal{R}}$$

Object type meet: $\boxed{N \diamond \sigma \wedge_\Delta N \diamond \sigma = N \diamond \sigma}$

$$\frac{\Delta \vdash N_i \lessdot N_j \text{ with } i,j \in \{1,2\}}{\Delta \vdash \sigma <: \sigma_1 \quad \Delta \vdash \sigma <: \sigma_2 \quad \Delta \vdash \sigma' <: \sigma_1, \Delta \vdash \sigma' <: \sigma_2 \implies \Delta \vdash \sigma' <: \sigma}{N_1 \diamond \sigma_1 \wedge_\Delta N_2 \diamond \sigma_2 = N_i \diamond \sigma}$$

Object type concatenation: $\boxed{N \diamond \sigma \oplus_\Delta N \diamond \sigma = N \diamond \sigma}$

$$\frac{\sigma_1 = \left\langle l : \mu_l \,^{l \in \mathcal{L}_1}\right\rangle_{\mathcal{R}_1} \quad \sigma_2 = \left\langle l : \mu_l \,^{l \in \mathcal{L}_2}\right\rangle_{\mathcal{R}_2} \quad (\mathcal{L}_1 \cap \mathcal{L}_2) \subseteq (\mathcal{R}_1 \cup \mathcal{R}_2)}{N_1 \diamond \sigma_1 \oplus_\Delta N_2 \diamond \sigma_2 = N_1 \diamond \sigma_1 \wedge_\Delta N_2 \diamond \sigma_2}$$

Method signature declaration typing: $\boxed{\Delta; \Gamma \vdash S \ : \ \tau}$

$$\frac{\Delta \vdash T_0, \overline{T} \text{ OK} \quad \Gamma \vdash m \text{ OK}}{\Delta; \Gamma \vdash T_0 \ m(\overline{T} \ \overline{x}) \ ; \ : \ \mathsf{Object} \diamond \left\langle m : \overline{T} \to T_0 \right\rangle_\emptyset}$$

Requirement constraints: $\boxed{\Delta; \Gamma \vdash R \Rightarrow \alpha <: \tau}$

$$\frac{\Delta \vdash N \text{ OK} \quad \Delta; \Gamma \vdash \overline{F} \ : \ \overline{\tau_f} \quad \Delta; \Gamma \vdash \overline{S} \ : \ \overline{\tau_s}}{\mathrm{bound}_\Delta(N) \wedge_\Delta \left(\bigoplus_\Delta \overline{\tau_f} \cdot \overline{\tau_s}\right) = N \diamond \left\langle l : \mu_l \,^{l \in \mathcal{L}}\right\rangle_\emptyset}{\Delta; \Gamma \vdash \alpha \triangleleft N \text{ implements } \{\overline{F} \ \overline{S}\} \Rightarrow \alpha <: N \diamond \left\langle l : \mu_l \,^{l \in \mathcal{L}}\right\rangle_\mathcal{L}}$$

Trait function declaration typing: $\boxed{A \ : \ \tau}$

$$\frac{\Delta; \overline{\$l} \vdash \overline{R} \Rightarrow \overline{\alpha} <: \overline{\tau} \quad \Delta; \overline{\$l} \vdash R_0 \Rightarrow \mathsf{ThisType} <: \tau_0'}{\Delta = \overline{\alpha} <: \overline{\tau}, \mathsf{ThisType} <: \tau_0 \quad \Delta; \overline{\$l}, \mathbf{this} : \mathsf{ThisType} \vdash \overline{D} \ : \ \overline{\tau_{\mathsf{decl}}}}{\tau_0 = \tau_0' \oplus_\Delta \left(\bigoplus_\Delta \overline{\tau_{\mathsf{decl}}}\right) \quad \Delta \vdash \tau_0' <: \mathrm{reqs}(\tau_0)}{\mathbf{trait} \ t(\overline{\$l}, \ \overline{\alpha}) \ \mathbf{req} \ \{R_0 \ \overline{R}\} \ \mathbf{prov} \ \{\overline{D}\} \ : \ \prod \overline{\$l} . \forall \overline{\alpha} <: \overline{\tau} . \tau_0}$$

Class declaration typing: $\boxed{C \ : \ \tau}$

$$\frac{K = c(\overline{U} \ \overline{\mathsf{g}}, \ \overline{T} \ \overline{\mathsf{f}}) \ \{\mathbf{super}(\overline{\mathsf{g}}) \ ; \ \mathbf{this}.\overline{\mathsf{f}} = \overline{\mathsf{f}}; \}}{\mathrm{fields}(N) = \overline{U} \ \overline{\mathsf{g}} \quad \mathrm{fields}(c<\overline{\alpha}>) = \overline{U} \ \overline{\mathsf{g}}; \ \overline{T} \ \overline{\mathsf{f}}}{\Delta = \overline{\alpha} <: \mathrm{type}(\overline{N}) \quad \Delta \vdash \overline{N}, N \text{ OK} \quad \Delta; \mathbf{this} : c<\overline{\alpha}> \vdash \overline{D} \ : \ \overline{\tau}}{P \diamond \sigma = \bigoplus_\Delta \overline{\tau} \quad \sigma = \left\langle l : \mu_l \,^{l \in \mathcal{L}}\right\rangle_\mathcal{R} \quad N \diamond \sigma_N = \mathrm{type}(N)}{\Delta \vdash \sigma <: (\sigma_N \restriction (\mathcal{L} \setminus \mathcal{R})) \quad \mathcal{R} \subseteq \mathrm{dom}(\sigma_N) \quad \Delta \vdash c<\overline{\alpha}> \lessdot P}{\mathbf{class} \ c<\overline{\alpha} \triangleleft \overline{N}> \triangleleft N \ \{K \ \overline{D}\} \ : \ \forall \overline{\alpha} <: \mathrm{type}(\overline{N}) . \ c<\overline{\alpha}> \diamond \sigma \wedge_\Delta N \diamond \sigma_N}$$

Fig. 9. MTJ: class and trait typing

the given structural requirements, while checking that there is at most one requirement for any member name. The rule takes the meet of this type with the nominal requirement, allowing structural requirements to refine, but not conflict with, its canonical signature. Thus, for instance, a trait cannot both require **ThisType** to be a subclass of `String` and also provide a `length` method that returns a `boolean`. The type constraint given by the judgment includes the labels of all required members in its requirement set.

The typing rule for trait function declarations is given in a declarative style: it uses a type context Δ mentioning types that are in turn checked under Δ. This is necessary for two reasons. First, a **requires** clause for one type parameter may mention any of the trait function's type parameters, so requirements must be checked under the the constraints they denote. Likewise, the upper bound for **ThisType** is needed for type checking member declarations, but the types given to those declarations are used to constrain **ThisType**. The result type of the trait function, τ_0, is the concatenation of the types of the provided and required members of the trait. Using concatenation rather than meet ensures that the trait does not contain multiple definitions of a member.

Note that a trait function t may use other traits without fulfilling their requirements. In this case, we insist that t explicitly state the unfulfilled requirements in its **ThisType** constraints, which is checked by the hypothesis $\Delta \vdash \tau_0' <: \text{reqs}(\tau_0)$, where τ_0' is the bound t places on **ThisType** and τ_0 is the result type of the trait function.

Class declaration typing is similar to trait function typing: the types of the class's member declarations are used to partially determine the class's type via concatenation. There are several important differences, however. For one, the class type includes the canonical signature of its immediate superclass (σ_N in the rule). If a class overrides any members of its superclass, the overriding definitions must be subtypes of the originals. Hence, we check that the signature of the superclass, σ_N, restricted to the members defined in the class body, $\mathcal{L} \setminus \mathcal{R}$, is a supertype of the signature for the class body, σ. Another difference is that all trait requirements must be fulfilled by the class. This is checked in two ways. First, the set of required members from the class body, $\mathcal{R}$, must be a subset of the members provided by the superclass, $\text{dom}(\sigma_N)$. Second, class itself is required to be a nominal subtype of any nominal requirements introduced by the traits it uses ($\Delta \vdash c\texttt{<}\overline{\alpha}\texttt{>} \lessdot P$).

4.8   Soundness

The semantics of MTJ is given by a translation to FGJ, but the resulting FGJ class table is *also* a valid MTJ class table. Thus, our soundness result is broken into two steps, one taking place entirely within MTJ and one relating the two calculi. We briefly survey the result here, with a detailed version of the proof available in a companion technical report [28].

Definition 1. *A class C is **flat** if it contains no trait use declarations.*

Note that limiting the syntax of MTJ to flat class declarations yields the syntax of FGJ, modulo the features that we dropped (casts and generic methods).

To prove soundness, we need to ensure that the presumed class and trait types from the class type and trait type tables agree with the actual classes and traits in CT and TT.

Definition 2. *A class type table CTy **agrees** with a class table CT, written $CT \vdash CTy$, if $dom(CT) = dom(CTy)$ and for all $c \in dom(CT)$, we have $CT(c) :$ $CTy(c)$. We write $TT \vdash TTy$ for the same property relating the trait tables.*

We can now show a typical soundness result purely in terms of MTJ; here, translation acts as the "dynamic semantics" for MTJ and we prove that any well-typed program will successfully translate to a program with the same type.

Theorem 1 (Soundness of translation). *If $CT \vdash CTy$ and $TT \vdash TTy$ then, for all $c \in dom(CT)$, we have that $C = [\![CT(c)]\!]$ is defined, that C is flat, and that $C : CTy(c)$. Furthermore, if $\vdash e : T$ under CT, then $\vdash e : T$ under the translated class table.*

This theorem is straightforward to prove. First, we prove a series of standard lemmas for weakening of the context and type and label substitution. These are sufficient to prove the theorem, since translation is essentially trait function application. A minor twist comes in the lemma showing type preservation for member declaration translation. The type of the original member is not always the same as the translated member: if the original member is a trait use declaration, and the trait places requirements on **ThisType**, those requirements will not appear in the flattened trait body. Thus, the translation preserves only the *provided* elements of a member declaration type. Theorem 1 still holds, however, because the class typing rule ensures that there are no residual requirements, so the type of the class as a whole is preserved under translation.

We then show the following result, relating MTJ to FGJ.

Theorem 2 (Well-typed, flat MTJ programs are well-typed FGJ programs). *If $(CT, \bullet, e)$ is an MTJ program with only flat class declarations and $CT \vdash CTy$, $TT \vdash TTy$, and $\vdash_{MTJ} e : T$, then (CT, e) is a well-typed FGJ program and $\vdash_{FGJ} e : T$.*

This theorem is even easier to prove: we prove that our canonical type signatures give the same results as FGJ's machinery (*e.g.*, the *mtype* function), and then prove by a series of inductive arguments that our typing judgments imply the corresponding judgments in FGJ. Taking the two theorems together, we have that a type-safe MTJ program translates to a type-safe FGJ program.

5   Discussion

5.1   Related Work: Metaprogramming

Broadly speaking, metaprogramming consists of writing (meta) programs that manipulate (object) programs.Compilers are the best-known metaprograms, but the technique is also useful for generating high-level code. In particular, *generative programming* has been proposed as a paradigm for building families of related systems: code and other artifacts are generated from a high-level model or specification, automating much of the software development process [6]. Metaprogramming, of course, is a crucial element of this process. Since metaprogramming raises the level of abstraction and can arbitrarily modify the meaning of code, it is important that metaprogramming frameworks strike a good balance between expressiveness, invasiveness, readability, and safety guarantees.

Draheim *et al.* give a good summary of several metaprogramming frameworks for Java and similar languages, focusing specifically on their utility for generative programming [7]. A typical approach is to use so-called meta-objects to represent and alter code entities (classes, methods, *etc.*). The implementation of the meta-objects gives rise to a *meta-object protocol* (MOP) that can be overridden or extended with new features [18]. MOP frameworks have been used both to generate code and to modify the semantics of language mechanisms such as multiple inheritance. They are extremely flexible, but require manipulation of ASTs and provide very few guarantees about generated code.

An alternative approach is to incorporate metaprogramming constructs directly into the language. SafeGen [16], for example, extends Java with *cursors* and *generators*. Cursors pick out a collection of entities within the code of a program, while generators, guided by cursors, output code fragments. Generators are written in a quasi-quotation style, giving the system a great deal of flexibility. Perhaps the most interesting aspect of SafeGen is that generators are statically checked for safety, using a theorem prover to check short first-order sentences produced by the type checker. Programmers are insulated from the theorem-proving process: from their perspective, it is just another type system.

Aspect-oriented programming (AOP) is another form of metaprogramming, where *advice* is *weaved* into existing code [19]. Our proposal has significant similarities with AOP, but also significant differences. Trait functions enable programmers to abstract "cross-cutting concerns" in a way similar to aspects; advice often wraps methods with new behavior, just as we do with examples like SyncT. The most important difference is a matter of control: aspects control their own application to classes through *pointcuts*, but traits are explicitly included in classes.

Fähndrich *et al.* have described an elegant pattern-based approach to metaprogramming, similar to AOP, but focused on generating new class members, rather than modifying existing behavior [10]. Their system is template-based, but uses pattern matching to determine how to instantiate the templates. The patterns provide constraints that lead to strong static guarantees about the templates. In our technical report, we sketch a design inspired by this idea: the member requirements for a trait function are matched against the members defined in a class, and the trait is automatically applied for each match [28]. This brings trait-based metaprogramming much closer to AOP, but the control of trait application still remains in the hands of the class designer, who must explicitly request the pattern matching to take place. Moreover, our design has a much coarser-grained notion of pointcuts than AOP, since traits cannot be inserted at arbitrary points in the control-flow of a method.

Most similar to our proposal, the Genoupe framework [8] for C# supports code generation through parameterized classes. Classes are parameterized over types and values, and may contain code that inspects their parameters at compile-time, generating code as it does so. For example, classes can use a **@foreach** keyword to loop over the fields or methods of a type parameter. The code within the **@foreach** will be generated repeatedly for each match. Genoupe includes some static type checking of parameterized classes, but it cannot guarantee the well-formedness of the generated code. Moreover, generation results in complete classes, which cannot be combined in a single-inheritance language.

In general, the novelty of our approach is its particular focus on *member-level patterns* and its strength is in simplicity. Typed traits are composable, incomplete class implementations, and with our extension, they offer a uniform, expressive, and type-safe way to do metaprogramming without resorting to AST manipulation. In addition, the result of this metaprogramming is always just a trait, leaving ultimate control of the code to the class designer.

5.2 Related Work: Type Systems

Nominal subtyping is a refinement of structural subtyping: type names are placed in a nominal subtyping relationship, but the types these names represent must be structurally related to guarantee type safety. In purely nominal type systems, types must be always be named, and subtyping always explicitly stated; "combining" structural and nominal subtyping amounts to relaxing these requirements. Moby [13] and Unity [21] relax them entirely, allowing the use of arbitrary structural subtyping. In Moby, there are *object types* and *class types*, the latter naming a specific class. Subtyping on class types is based on the explicit inheritance hierarchy, and so is essentially nominal, while object types are compared structurally. Unity is closer to our type system in that object types include a nominal component (called a *brand*) *and* a structural component. In both type systems, as with ours, nominal types have associated "canonical" structural types describing their interface. Programmers can choose whether to constrain types structurally or nominally, or, with Unity, both.

Our proposal also allows arbitrary structural subtyping, but only at the trait function level; subtyping for expressions is strictly nominal. We believe this paradigm to be widely applicable: a metalanguage with flexible, structural subtyping can be used to generate code for an object language with a more rigid, nominal type system. Moreover, since traits are just (incomplete) collections of class members, our type system can be used for other metaprogramming frameworks that do not make traits an explicit programming construct but still assemble classes from partial implementations. Though type parameters will not be tied to trait functions in such frameworks, they can still be used at the metaprogramming level with purely structural constraints, since they will not be present in generated code.

In Ancona *et al.*'s *polymorphic bytecode* proposal, compilation units are type-checked without complete knowledge of the inheritance hierarchy: type-checking results in a set of structural and nominal constraints to be satisfied by the eventual, dynamically-linked class hierarchy [1]. The combination of nominal and structural constraints resembles our object types, and the system retains Java's purely nominal subtyping after linking is performed. Polymorphic bytecode, in order to respect Java's type system, must place nominal constraints on types any time a method is invoked: it has no analog to our trait functions, which allow purely structural constraints to be imposed and discharged.

5.3   Related Work: Traits

The introduction of traits for Smalltalk [9] prompted a flurry of work on traits for statically-typed languages. Fisher and Reppy developed the first formal model of traits in a statically-typed setting [12], subsequently extending it to support polymorphic traits and stateful objects [11]. The model type checks traits in isolation from classes. The structural component of our type system is essentially a variant of Fisher and Reppy's type system. In our previous workshop paper [25], we reformulated the Fisher-Reppy trait calculus using Riecke-Stone dictionaries [26], giving a semantics for member renaming and hiding operations on traits. The calculus renames members by modifying a dictionary, rather than substituting labels in program code. Thus, it provides a foundation for the separate compilation of trait functions in Moby, which already uses such dictionaries in its implementation. Separate compilation in Java remains future work.

Multiple designs extending Java with traits have been proposed. Smith and Drossopoulou describe a family of three such extensions, called Chai [27]. They support separate type checking of traits by introducing trait names into Java's type system; in essence, traits define interfaces, and the classes that use them are considered to have "implemented" those interfaces. As discussed in Section 4, this approach is probably too brittle to support trait functions. Another proposed design is *FeatherTrait Java* [20], which adds traits to Featherweight Java, but defers all type checking until traits have been included in a class. There are strong similarities between traits and *mixins* [5]; a good discussion of their relationship can be found in [14].

5.4   Conclusion

We have presented a language design for *metaprogramming with traits*. We believe our proposal hits a sweet spot for metaprogramming: while its semantics are very simple, it is capable of capturing a wide variety of patterns occurring at the member level of class definitions. In modeling our mechanism formally, we have developed a type system which incorporates a mixture of structural and nominal subtyping, and proved the soundness of the resulting calculus. An implementation is underway, written as a source-to-source translator for Java.

Acknowledgments. We thank the anonymous reviewers for their help in catching mistakes and improving the overall presentation.

References

1. Ancona, D., Damiani, F., Drossopoulou, S., Zucca, E.: Polymorphic bytecode: compositional compilation for Java-like languages. In: POPL'05, pp. 26–37 (2005)
2. Ancona, D., Lagorio, G., Zucca, E.: Jam–designing a Java extension with mixins. TOPLAS 25(5), 641–712 (2003)
3. Bono, V., Bugliesi, M., Liquori, L.: A Lambda Calculus of Incomplete Objects. In: MFCS, pp. 218–229 (1996)
4. Bracha, G.: The Programming Language Jigsaw: Mixins, Modularity and Multiple Inheritance. PhD thesis, University of Utah (March 1992)
5. Bracha, G., Cook, W.: Mixin-based inheritance. In: ECOOP'90, October 1990, pp. 303–311. ACM Press, New York (1990)
6. Czarnecki, K., Eisenecker, U.W.: Generative programming: methods, tools, and applications. ACM Press/Addison-Wesley Publishing Co, New York (2000)
7. Draheim, D., Lutteroth, C., Weber, G.: An Analytical Comparison of Generative Programming Technologies. Technical Report B-04-02, Institute of Computer Science, Freie Universität Berlin (January 2004)
8. Draheim, D., Lutteroth, C., Weber, G.: A Type System for Reflective Program Generators. In: Glück, R., Lowry, M. (eds.) GPCE 2005. LNCS, vol. 3676, pp. 327–341. Springer, Heidelberg (2005)
9. Ducasse, S., Nierstrasz, O., Schärli, N., Wuyts, R., Black, A.: Traits: A Mechanism for fine-grained Reuse. TOPLAS 28(2), 331–388 (2006)
10. Fähndrich, M., Carbin, M., Larus, J.R.: Reflective program generation with patterns. In: GPCE'06, pp. 275–284. ACM Press, New York, USA (2006)
11. Fisher, K., Reppy, J.: Statically typed traits. Technical Report TR-2003-13, Dept. of Computer Science, U. of Chicago, Chicago, IL (December 2003)
12. Fisher, K., Reppy, J.: A typed calculus of traits. In: FOOL11 (January 2004)
13. Fisher, K., Reppy, J.H.: Extending Moby with Inheritance-Based Subtyping. In: ECOOP'00, pp. 83–107 (2000)
14. Flatt, M., Findler, R.B., Felleisen, M.: Scheme with Classes, Mixins, and Traits. In: Kobayashi, N. (ed.) APLAS 2006. LNCS, vol. 4279, Springer, Heidelberg (2006)
15. Hofmann, M.: Syntax and Semantics of Dependent Types. In: Semantics and Logics of Computation, vol. 14, pp. 79–130. Cambridge University Press, Cambridge (1997)
16. Huang, S.S., Zook, D., Smaragdakis, Y.: Statically Safe Program Generation with SafeGen. In: Glück, R., Lowry, M. (eds.) GPCE 2005. LNCS, vol. 3676, pp. 309–326. Springer, Heidelberg (2005)
17. Igarashi, A., Pierce, B.C., Wadler, P.: Featherweight Java: a minimal core calculus for Java and GJ. TOPLAS 23(3), 396–450 (2001)
18. Kiczales, G., des Rivieres, J., Bobrow, D.G.: The art of metaobject protocol. MIT Press, Cambridge, MA, USA (1991)
19. Kiczales, G., Lamping, J., Menhdhekar, A., Maeda, C., Lopes, C., Loingtier, J.-M., Irwin, J.: Aspect-Oriented Programming. In: Aksit, M., Matsuoka, S. (eds.) ECOOP 1997. LNCS, vol. 1241, pp. 220–242. Springer, Heidelberg (1997)
20. Liquori, L., Spiwack, A.: Feathertrait: A modest extension of featherweight java. TOPLAS (to appear, 2007)
21. Malayeri, D., Aldrich, J.: Combining Structural Subtyping and External Dispatch. In: FOOL/WOOD'07 (2007)
22. Nierstrasz, O., Ducasse, S., Schärli, N.: Flattening Traits. Journal of Object Technology 5(4), 129–148 (2006)

23. Odersky, M., Altherr, P., Cremet, V., Dragos, I., Dubochet, G., Emir, B., McDirmid, S., Micheloud, S., Mihaylov, N., Schinz, M., Stenman, E., Spoon, L., Zenger, M.: An overview of the Scala programming language. 2nd edn. Technical Report LAMP-REPORT-2006-001, EPFL, Lausanne, Switzerland (May 2006)
24. Quitslund, P.J.: Java traits — improving opportunities for reuse. Technical Report CSE 04-005, OGI School of Science & Engineering (September 2004)
25. Reppy, J., Turon, A.: A foundation for trait-based metaprogramming. In: FOOL/WOOD'06 (2006)
26. Riecke, J.G., Stone, C.A.: Privacy via subsumption. INC (A preliminary version appeared in FOOL5) 172(1), 2–28 (2002)
27. Smith, C., Drossopoulou, S.: Chai: Traits for Java-Like Languages. In: Black, A.P. (ed.) ECOOP 2005. LNCS, vol. 3586, pp. 453–478. Springer, Heidelberg (2005)
28. Turon, A.: Metaprogramming with Traits. Honors thesis, forthcoming as a University of Chicago technical report (2007)

Morphing: Safely Shaping a Class in the Image of Others

Shan Shan Huang[1,2], David Zook[1], and Yannis Smaragdakis[2]

[1] Georgia Institute of Technology, College of Computing
{ssh,dzook}@cc.gatech.edu
[2] University of Oregon, Department of Computer and Information Sciences
yannis@cs.uoregon.edu

Abstract. We present MJ: a language for specifying general classes whose members are produced by iterating over members of other classes. We call this technique "class morphing" or just "morphing". Morphing extends the notion of genericity so that not only types of methods and fields, but also the *structure* of a class can vary according to type variables. This offers the ability to express common programming patterns in a highly generic way that is otherwise not supported by conventional techniques. For instance, morphing lets us write generic proxies (i.e., classes that can be parameterized with another class and export the same public methods as that class); default implementations (e.g., a generic do-nothing type, configurable for any interface); semantic extensions (e.g., specialized behavior for methods that declare a certain annotation); and more. MJ's hallmark feature is that, despite its emphasis on generality, it allows modular type checking: an MJ class can be checked independently of its uses. Thus, the possibility of supplying a type parameter that will lead to invalid code is detected early—an invaluable feature for highly general components that will be statically instantiated by other programmers.

1 Introduction

The holy grail of software construction is *separation of concerns*: aspects of program behavior should be treated independently, so that complexity can be decomposed into manageable pieces. Decomposition techniques have been the goal of programming languages for several decades, both with standard object-oriented techniques, as well as with "aspect" languages such as AspectJ [19] or JBoss AOP [6]. Nevertheless, all mechanisms offer a fundamental trade-off between generality and safety: if a mechanism is general, then it is hard to check that it is valid for all possible inputs. In this paper, we present a powerful modularity technique called *class morphing* or just *morphing*. We discuss morphing through MJ—a reference language that demonstrates what we consider the desired expressiveness and safety features of an advanced morphing language. MJ morphing can express highly general object-oriented components (i.e., generic classes) whose exact members are not known until the component is parameterized with concrete types. For a simple example, consider the following MJ class, implementing a standard "logging" extension:

E. Ernst (Ed.): ECOOP 2007, LNAI 4609, pp. 399–424, 2007.
© Springer-Verlag Berlin Heidelberg 2007

```
class MethodLogger<class X> extends X {
  <Y*>[meth]for(public int meth (Y) : X.methods)
  int meth (Y a) {
    int i = super.meth(a);
    System.out.println("Returned: " + i);
    return i;
  }
}
```

MJ allows class `MethodLogger` to be declared as a subclass of its type parameter, `X`. The body of `MethodLogger` is defined by static iteration (using the `for` statement) over all methods of `X` that match the pattern `public int meth(Y)`. `Y` and `meth` are pattern variables, matching any type and method name, respectively. Additionally, the `*` symbol following the declaration of `Y` indicates that `Y` matches any number of types (including zero). That is, the above pattern matches all `public` methods that return `int`. The pattern variables are used in the declaration of `MethodLogger`'s methods: for each method of the type parameter `X`, `MethodLogger` declares a method with the same name and type signature. (This does not have to be the case, as shown later.) Thus, the exact methods of class `MethodLogger` are not determined until it is type-instantiated. For instance, `MethodLogger<java.io.File>` has methods `compareTo` and `hashCode`: these are the only `int`-returning methods of `java.io.File` and its superclasses.

"Reflective" program pattern matching and transformation, as in the above example, are not new. Several pattern matching languages have been proposed in prior literature (e.g., [2,3,4,25]) and most of them specify transformations based on some intermediate program representation (e.g., abstract syntax trees) although the patterns resemble regular program syntax. Compared to such work, MJ is quite unique for two reasons:

- MJ makes reflective transformation functionality a natural extension of Java generics. For instance, our above example class `MethodLogger` appears to the programmer as a regular class, rather than as a separate kind of entity, such as a "transformation". Using a generic class is a matter of simple type-instantiation, which produces a regular Java class, such as `MethodLogger<java.io.File>`.
- MJ generic classes support modular type checking—a generic class is type-checked independently of its type-instantiations, and errors are detected if they can occur with *any* possible type parameter. This is an invaluable property for generic code: it prevents errors that only appear for some type parameters, which the author of the generic class may not have predicted. This problem has been the target of some prior work, such as type-safe reflection [10], compile-time reflection [11], and safe program generation [13]. Yet none of these mechanisms offer MJ's modular type checking guarantees. For instance, the Genoupe [10] approach has been shown unsafe, as the reasoning depends on properties that can change at runtime; CTR [11] only captures undefined variable and type incompatibility errors, does not offer a formal system or proof of soundness, and has limited expressiveness compared to MJ

(especially with respect to method arguments); SafeGen [13] has no soundness proof and relies on the capabilities of an automatic theorem prover—an unpredictable and unfriendly process from the programmer's perspective.

For an example of modular type checking, consider a "buggy" generic class:

```
class CallWithMax<class X> extends X {
  <Y>[meth]for(public int meth (Y) : X.methods)
  int meth(Y a1, Y a2) {
    if (a1.compareTo(a2) > 0) return super.meth(a1);
    else return super.meth(a2);
  }
}
```

The intent is that class CallWithMax<C>, for some C, imitates the interface of C for all single-argument methods that return int, yet adds an extra formal parameter to each method. The corresponding method of C is then called with the greater of the two arguments passed to CallWithMax<C>. It is easy to define, use, and deploy such a generic transformation without realizing that it is not always valid: not all types Y will support the compareTo method. MJ detects such errors when compiling the above code, independently of instantiation. In this case, the fix is to strengthen the pattern with the constraint <Y extends Comparable<Y>>:

```
<Y extends Comparable<Y>>[meth]for(public int meth (Y) : X.methods)
```

Additionally, the above code has an even more insidious error. The generated methods in CallWithMax<C> are not guaranteed to correctly override the methods in its superclass, C. For instance, if C contains two methods, int foo(int) and String foo(int,int), then the latter will be improperly overridden by the generated method int foo(int,int) in CallWithMax<C> (which has the same argument types but an incompatible return type). MJ statically catches this error. This is an instance of the complexity of MJ's modular type checking when dealing with unknown entities.

2   Language Overview and Motivation

MJ adds to Java the ability to include reflective iteration blocks inside a class or interface declaration. The purpose of a reflective iteration block is to *statically iterate* over a certain subset of a type's methods or fields, and produce a declaration or statement for each element in the iterator. By *static* iteration, we mean that no runtime reflection exists in compiled MJ programs. All declarations or statements within a reflective block are "generated" at compile-time.

2.1   Language Basics

A reflective iteration block (or reflective block) has similar syntax to the existing for iterator construct in Java. There are two main components to a reflective block: the iterator definition, and the code block for each iteration. The following is a class declaration with a very simple reflective block:

```
class C<T> {
  for ( static int foo () : T.methods ) {|
    public String foo () { return String.valueOf(T.foo()); }
  |}
}
```

We overload the keyword `for` for static iteration. The iterator definition immediately follows `for`, delimited by parentheses. This defines the set of elements for iteration, which we call the *reflective range* (or just *range*) of the iterator. The iterator definition has the basic format *pattern : reflection set*. The *reflection set* is defined by applying the `.methods` or `.fields` keywords to a type, designating all methods or fields of that type. The *pattern* is either a method or field signature pattern, used to filter out elements from the reflection set. Only elements that match the pattern belong in the reflective range. In the example above, the reflective range contains only `static` methods of type `T`, with name `foo`, no argument, and return type `int`.

The second component of a reflective block is delimited by {|...|}, and contains either method/field declarations or a block of statements. The reflective block is itself syntactically a declaration or block of statements, but we prevent reflective blocks from nesting. In case of a single declaration (as in most examples in this paper), the delimiters can be dropped. The declarations or statements are "generated", once for each element in the reflective range of the block. In the example above, a method `public String foo() { ... }` is declared for each element in the reflective range. Thus, if `T` has a method `foo` matching the pattern `static int foo()`, a method `public String foo()` exists for class `C<T>`, as well.

The reflective block in the previous example is rather boring. Its reflective range contains at most one method, and we know statically the type and name of that method. For more flexible patterns, we can introduce type and name variables for pattern matching. Pattern matching type and name variables are defined right before the `for` keyword. They are only visible within that reflective block, and can be used as regular types and names. For example:

```
class C<T> {
  T t;
  C(T t) { this.t = t; }

  <A>[m] for (int m (A) : T.methods )
  int m (A a) { return t.m(a); }
}
```

The above pattern matches methods of *any* name that take one argument of *any* type and return `int`. The matching of multiple names and types is done by introducing a type variable, `A`, and a name variable, `m`. Name variables match *any* identifier and are introduced by enclosing them in [...]. The syntax for introducing pattern matching type variables extends that for declaring type parameters for generic Java classes: new type variables are enclosed in <...>. We can give type variable `A` one or more bounds: `<A extends Foo & Bar>`, and the bounds can contain `A` itself: `<A extends Comparable<A>>`. Multiple type variables can be introduced, as well: `<A extends Foo,B extends Bar>`. In addition to the

Java generics syntax, we can annotate a type parameter with keywords `class` or `interface`. For instance `<interface A>` declares a type parameter `A` that can only match an interface type. (This extension also applies to non-pattern-matching type parameters, in which case `A` can only be instantiated with an interface.) A semantic difference between pattern matching type parameters and type parameters in Java generics is that a pattern matching type parameter is not required to be a non-primitive type. In fact, without any declared bounds or `class`/`interface` keyword, `A` can match any type that is not `void`—this includes primitive types such as `int`, `boolean`, etc. To declare a type variable that only matches non-primitive types, one can write `<A extends Object>`.

The type and name variables declared for the reflective block can be used as regular types and names inside the block. In the example above, a method is declared for each method in the reflective range, and each declaration has the same name and argument types as the method that is the current element in the iteration. The body of the method calls method `m` on a variable of type `T`—whatever the value of `m` is for that iteration, this is the method being invoked.

Often, a user does not care (or know) how many arguments a method takes. It is only important to be able to faithfully replicate argument types inside the reflective block. We provide a special syntax for matching *any* number of types: a `*` suffix on the pattern matching type variable definition. For instance, if a pattern matching type variable is declared as `<A*>`, then `String m (A)` is a method pattern that matches any method returning `String`, no matter how many arguments it takes (including zero arguments), and no matter what the argument types are. Even though `A*` is technically a vector of types, it can only be used as a single entity inside of the reflective block. MJ provides no facility for iterating over the vector of types matching `A`. This relieves us from having to deal with issues of order or length.

MJ also offers the ability to construct *new* names from a name variable, by prefixing the variable with a constant. MJ provides the construct `#` for this purpose. To prefix a name variable `f` with the static name `get`, the user writes `get#f`. Note that `get` cannot be another name variable. Creating names out of name variables can cause possible naming conflicts. In later sections, we discuss in detail how the MJ type system ensures that the resulting identifiers are unique. MJ also offers the ability to create a string out of a name variable (i.e., to use the name of the method or field that the variable currently matches as a string) via the syntax *var*.`name`. The example below demonstrates these features:

```
class C<T> {
  T t;
  C(T t) { this.t = t; }

  <R,A*>[m] for (public R m (A) : T.methods )
  R delegate#m (A a) {
    System.out.println("Calling method "+ m.name + " on "+ t.toString());
    return t.m(a);
  }
}
```

The above example shows a simple proxy class that declares methods that mimic the (non-void-returning) public methods of its type parameter. Declared method names are the original method names prefixed by the constant name delegate. Declared methods call the corresponding original methods after logging the call.

In addition to the above features, MJ also allows matching arbitrary modifiers (e.g., final, synchronized or transient), exception clauses, and Java annotations. MJ has a set of conventions to handle modifier, exception, and annotation matching so that patterns are not burdened with unnecessary detail—e.g., for most modifiers, a pattern that does not explicitly mention them matches regardless of their presence. We do not elaborate further on these aspects of the language, as they represent merely engineering conveniences and are orthogonal to the main MJ insights: the morphing language features, combined with a modular type-checking approach.

2.2 Applications

MJ opens the door for expressing a large number of useful idioms in a general, reusable way. This is the power of morphing features: we can shape a generic class or interface according to properties of the members of the type it is parameterized with. The morphing approach is similar to reflection, yet all reasoning is performed statically, there is syntax support for easily creating new fields and methods, and type safety is statically guaranteed.

Default Class. Consider a general "default implementation" class that adapts its contents to any interface used as a type parameter. The class implements all methods in the interface, with each method implementation returning a default value. This functionality is particularly useful for testing purposes—e.g., in the context of an application framework (where parts of the hierarchy will be implemented only by the end user), in uses of the Strategy pattern [12] with "neutral" strategies, etc. (Note that keyword throws in the pattern does not prevent methods with no exceptions from being matched, since E is declared to match a possibly-zero length vector of types.)

```
class DefaultImpl<interface T> implements T {
    // For each method returning a non-primitive type, make it return null
    <R extends Object,A*,E*>[m] for( R m (A) throws E : T.methods )
    public R m ( A a ) throws E { return null; }

    // For each method returning a primitive type, return a default value
    <A*,E*>[m]for( int m (A) throws E : T.methods )
    public int m (A a ) throws E { return 0; }

    ... // repeat the above for each primitive return type.

    // For each method returning void, simply do nothing.
    <A*,E*>[m] for ( void m (A) throws E : T.methods )
    public void m (A a) throws E { }
}
```

One can easily think of ways to enrich the above example with more complex default behavior, e.g., returning random values or calling constructor methods, instead of using statically determined default values. The essence of the technique, however, is in the iteration over existing methods and special handling of each case of return type. This is only possible because of MJ's morphing capabilities. In practice, random testing systems often implement very similar functionality (e.g., [8]) using unsafe run-time reflection. Errors in the reflective or code generating logic are thus not caught until they are triggered by the right combination of inputs, unlike in the MJ case.

Sort-by. A common scenario in data structure libraries is that of supporting sorting according to multiple fields of a type. Although one can use a generic sorting routine that accepts a comparison function, the comparison function needs to be custom-written for each field of a type that we are interested in. Instead, a simpler solution is to morph comparison functions based on the fields of a type. Consider the following implementation of an ArrayList, modeled after the ArrayList class in the Java Collections Framework:

```
public class ArrayList<E> extends AbstractList<E>
    implements List<E>, RandomAccess, Cloneable, java.io.Serializable {
    ...// ArrayList fields and methods.

    // For each Comparable field of E, declare a sortBy method
    <F extends Comparable<F>>[f]for(public F f : E.fields)
    public void sortBy#f () {
      Collections.sort(this,
                   new Comparator<E> () {
                     public int compare(E e1, E e2) {
                       return e1.f.compareTo(e2.f);
                     }
                   });
    }
}
```

ArrayList<E> supports a method sortBy#f for every field f of type E. The power of the above code does not have to do with comparing elements of a certain *type* (this can be done with existing Java generics facilities), but with calling the comparison code on the exact fields that need it. For instance, a crucial part that is not expressible with conventional techniques is the code e1.f.compareTo(e2.f), for any field f.

The examples above illustrate the power of MJ's morphing features. Yet more examples from the static reflection or generic aspects literature [10,11,13,19] can be viewed as instances of morphing and can be expressed in MJ. For instance, the CTR work [11] allows the user to express a "transform" that iterates over methods of a class that have a @UnitTestEntry annotation and generate code to call all such methods while logging the unit test results. The same example can be expressed in MJ, with several advantages over CTR: MJ is better integrated in the language, using generic classes instead of a "transform" concept; MJ is a more expressive language, e.g., allowing matching methods with an arbitrary number and types of arguments; MJ offers much stronger guarantees of modular type safety, as its type system detects the possibility of conflicting definitions (CTR only concentrates on preventing references to undefined entities) and we offer a proof of type soundness.

3   Type System: A Casual Discussion

Higher variability always introduces complexity in type systems. For instance, polymorphic types require more sophisticated type systems than monomorphic types, because polymorphic types can reference type "variables", whose exact values are unknown at the definition site of the polymorphic code. In MJ, in addition to type variables, there are also *name* variables—declarations and references can use names reflectively retrieved from type variables. Thus, the exact values of these names are not known when writing a generic class. Yet, the author of the generic class needs to have some confidence that his/her code will work correctly with any parameterization in its intended domain. The job of MJ's type system is to ensure that generic code does not introduce static errors, for *any* type parameter that satisfies the author's stated assumptions. Pattern matching type and name variables present two challenges: 1) how do we determine that declarations made with name variables are unique, i.e., there are no naming conflicts, and 2) how do we determine that references always refer to declared members and are well-typed, when we know neither the exact names of the members referenced, or the exact names of the members declared. In this section, we present through examples the main problems and insights related to MJ's modular type checking.

3.1   Uniqueness of Declarations

Simple Case: Consider a simple MJ class:

```
class CopyMethods<X> {
  <R,A*>[m] for( R m (A) : X.methods )
  R m (A a) { ... }
}
```

CopyMethods<X>'s methods are declared within one reflective block, which iterates over all the methods of type parameter X. For each method returning a non-void type, a method with the same signature is declared for CopyMethods<X>.

How do we guarantee that, given any X, CopyMethods<X> has unique method declarations (i.e., each method is uniquely identified by its ⟨name, argument types⟩ tuple)? Observe that X can only be instantiated with another well-formed type (the base case being Object), and all well-formed types have unique method declarations. Thus, if a type merely copies the method signatures of another well-formed type, as `CopyMethods<X>` does, it is guaranteed to have unique method signatures, as well. The same principle also applies to reflective field declarations.

It is important to make sure that reflective declarations copy *all* the uniquely identifying parts of a method or field. For example, the uniquely identifying parts of a method are its name *together with* its argument types. Thus, a reflective method declaration that only copies either name or argument types would not be well-typed. For example:

```
class CopyMethodsWrong<X> {
  <R,A*>[m] for( R m (A) : X.methods )
  R m () { }
}
```

The reflective declaration in `CopyMethodsWrong<X>` only copies the return type and the name of the methods of a well-formed type. This would cause an error if instantiated with a type with an overloaded method:

```
class Overloaded {
  int bar (int a);
  int bar (String s);
}
```

`CopyMethodsWrong<Overloaded>` would have two methods, both named `bar`, taking no arguments.

Beyond Copy and Paste: Morphing of classes and interfaces is not restricted to copying the members of other types. Matched type and name variables can be used freely in reflective declarations and statements. For example:

```
class ChangeArgType<X> {
  <R,A extends Object>[m] for ( R m (A) : X.methods )
  R m ( List<A> a ) { /* do for all elements */ ... }
}
```

In `ChangeArgType<X>`, for each method of X that takes one non-primitive type argument A and returns a non-void type R, a method with the same name and return type is declared. However, instead of taking the same argument type, this method takes a `List` instantiated with the original argument type. Even though `ChangeArgType<X>` does not copy X's method signatures exactly, we can still guarantee that all methods of `ChangeArgType<X>` have unique signatures, no matter what X is. The key is that a reflective declaration can manipulate the uniquely identifying parts of a method, (i.e., name and argument types), by using them in type (or name) compositions, as long as these parts remain in the uniquely identifying parts of the new declaration. The following is an example of an *illegal* manipulation of types:

```
class IllegalChange<X> {
  <R,A>[m] for ( R m (A) : X.methods )
  A m ( R a ) { ... }
}
```

In the above example, the uniquely identifying part of X's method is no longer the uniquely identifying part of `IllegalChange<X>`'s method: the argument type

of X's method is no longer part of the argument type of IllegalChange<X>'s
method. IllegalChange<Overloaded> (using the Overloaded class defined above)
will cause an error in the generated code.

Multiple Reflective Blocks: We have discussed how to determine uniqueness
within one reflective block. When there are multiple reflective blocks in the same
type declaration, we need to guarantee that the declarations in one block do not
conflict with the declarations in another block. One way to accomplish this is to
guarantee that the blocks have iterators that produce *disjoint declaration ranges.*

Recall that the reflective range of an iterator is the set of entities it iterates
over. Accordingly, we define the *declaration range* of an iterator to be the set
of declarations it produces. Two ranges are disjoint if they contain no common
members. Consider the following MJ class with two reflective blocks whose declaration ranges are disjoint:

```
class TwoBlocks<X> {
  <R>[m] for ( R m (String) : X.methods )
  R m (String a) { ... }

  <R>[m] for ( R m (Number) : X.methods )
  R m (Number a) { ... }
}
```

The first block's reflective range contains all methods of X that take one argument of type String. The second block's reflective range contains all methods of
X that take one argument of type Number. Thus, no methods in the first range can
possibly be in the second range, and vice versa. Just as in previous examples, the
uniqueness of entities in the reflective ranges implies the uniqueness of entities in
the declaration ranges (since these use the same ⟨name, argument types⟩ tuple).
Once we have guaranteed that declarations are unique both within and across
reflective blocks, we can guarantee that all declarations within TwoBlocks<X> are
unique, no matter what X is.

When using type variables as components of other types, disjointness is often
hard to establish. Consider the following example:

```
class ManipulationError<X> {
  <R>[m] for ( R m (List<X>) : X.methods )
  R m (List<X> a) { ... }

  <R>[m] for ( R m (X) : X.methods )
  R m (List<X> a) { ... }
}
```

In the two reflective blocks of ManipulationError<X>, different manipulations
are applied to the uniquely identifying parts—in the first block, no manipulation
is applied, while in the second block, the argument type is changed to List<X>
from X. Even though the two reflective blocks have disjoint iteration ranges, they
do *not* have disjoint declaration ranges. One instantiation that would cause a
static error is the following:

```
class Overloaded2 {
  int m1 ( List<Overloaded2> a ) { ... }
  int m1 ( Overloaded2 a ) { ... }
}
```

`ManipulationError<Overloaded2>` would contain two methods named `m1`, both taking argument `List<Overloaded2>`.

In general, we can guarantee the uniqueness of declarations across reflective blocks by proving either type signature or name uniqueness. A general way to establish the uniqueness of declarations is by using unique static prefixes on names. (For static prefixes to be uniquely identifying, they must not be prefixes of each other.) For instance, our earlier example can be rewritten correctly as:

```
class Manipulation<X> {
  <R>[m] for ( R m (List<X>) : X.methods )
  R list#m (List<X> a) { ... }

  <R>[m] for ( R m (X) : X.methods )
  R nolist#m (List<X> a) { ... }
}
```

Reflective and Regular Methods Together: Declaration conflicts can also occur when a class has both regular and reflectively declared members. For example, in the following class declaration, we cannot guarantee that the methods declared in the reflective block do not conflict with method `int foo()`.

```
class Foo<X> {
  int foo () { ... }

  <R,A*>[m]for ( R m (A) : X.methods )
  R m (A a) { ... }
}
```

Just as in the case of multiple iterators, the main issue is establishing the disjointness of declaration ranges, with the regular methods acting as a constant declaration range. Again, the easiest way to guarantee disjointness is through static prefixes such that all declarations produced by the reflective iterator have names distinct from `foo`.

Proper Method Overriding and Mixins: Proper overriding means that a subtype should not declare a method with the same name and arguments as a method in a supertype, but a non-covariant return type. Ensuring proper method overriding is again a special case of declaration range disjointness.

One case that deserves some discussion is that of a type variable used as a supertype. (In case the type is a class, it is implicitly assumed to be non-final.) This is sometimes called a *mixin* pattern [5,22]. Since the supertype could potentially be any type, we have no way of knowing its declarations. For instance, the following class is unsafe and will trigger a type error, as there is no guarantee that the superclass does not already contain an incompatible method `foo`.

```
class C<class T> extends T {
  int foo () { ... }
}
```

Static prefixes are similarly insufficient to guarantee that subtype methods do not conflict with supertype methods. As a result, any legal type extending its type parameter can contain *no* members other than reflective iterators over its supertype that declare overriding versions for (some subset of) the supertype's methods.

3.2   Validity of References

Another challenge of modular type checking for a morphing language is to ensure the validity of references. We use the term "validity" to refer to the property that a referenced entity has a definition, and its use is well-typed. The following example demonstrates the complexities in checking reference validity in MJ:

```
class Reference<X> {
  Declaration<X> dx;
  ... // code to set dx field
  <U*>[n] for( String n (U) : X.methods )
  void n (U a) { dx.n(a); }
}
class Declaration<Y> {
  <V,W*>[m] for( V m (W) : Y.methods )
  void m (W a) { ... }
}
```

We would like to check the validity of method invocation `dx.n(a)`. There are multiple unknowns in this invocation that make checking its validity difficult:

- `dx` has type `Declaration<X>`, which has reflectively declared methods. We don't know statically these methods' names, argument types, or return types.
- the name of the method being invoked, `n`, is a name variable, reflectively matched to the method names in `X`, which is a type variable. Again, we do not know what these names may be.
- the type of the argument, `a`, is another type variable, `U`.

The intuition behind the checking logic is that if for every method `n` in `X` that takes any argument types `U`, and returns `String` (i.e., for every method in the range of the reflective block in `Reference<X>`) there is a method in `Declaration<X>` with the same name, taking the same types of arguments, then this reference is valid. The key to solving this problem is determining range *subsumption*. A range R_1 subsumes another range R_2 if all the entities in R_2 are also in R_1. We have already seen reflective ranges of an iterator and a declaration. We can easily expand the concept of range to other syntactic entities, such as arbitrary names and types. The range of a pattern matching type variable consists of all the types it matches in a given reflective iterator. Non-pattern-matching types have ranges with one element (themselves). The range of a name variable consists of all the names it matches in a given reflective iterator.

To determine the validity of `dx.n(a)`, we need to determine that the range of n in `Reference<X>` is subsumed by the declaration range of methods in `Declaration<X>`, and the range of U, the actual argument type, is subsumed by the range of the formal argument type for methods in `Declaration<X>`. The range of n in `Reference<X>` consists of the names of methods in X that return a `String` type. The method names in `Declaration<X>` are the names of all methods in X, regardless of return type. Thus, the latter range subsumes the former. This guarantees that `Declaration<X>` does have a method matching each n. Similarly, the range of U consists of the argument types of methods in X that return `String`. The range of the argument types of methods in `Declaration<X>` consists of the argument types of all methods in X. The latter range subsumes the former. Therefore, we conclude that the call `dx.n(a)` is well-typed.

Subsumption of ranges in the MJ type system is checked by unification of names and type variables in the reflective predicates, followed by checking of type bounds (i.e., the known supertypes of type variables) for compatibility. The next section formalizes this type checking approach more precisely.

4   Formalization

We formalize a core subset of MJ's features. This formalization (FMJ) is based on the FGJ [16] formalism, with differences (other than the simple addition of our extra environment, Λ) highlighted in gray . Figures in which all rules are new to our formalism (Figures 4,5) are not highlighted at all, for better readability.

4.1   Syntax

The syntax of FMJ is presented in Figure 1. We adopt many of the notational conventions of FGJ: C,D denote constant class names; X,Y denote type variables; N,P,Q,R denote non-variable types; S,T,U,V,W denote types; f denotes field names; m denotes non-variable method names; x,y denote argument names. In addition, we use u or v to denote name variables, while n denotes either variable or non-variable names.

We use the shorthand $\overline{T}$ for a sequence of types $T_0, T_1, \ldots, T_n$, and $\overline{x}$ for a sequence of unique variables $x_0, x_1, \ldots, x_n$. We use : for sequence concatenation. For example, $\overline{S}:\overline{T}$ is a sequence that begins with $\overline{S}$, followed by $\overline{T}$. We use $\in$ to mean "is a member of a sequence" (in addition to set membership). Thus, $T \in \overline{T}$ means that T is in the sequence $\overline{T}$. We use _ or ... for values of no particular significance to a rule. We use $\triangleleft$ and $\uparrow$ as shorthands for the keywords **extends** and **return**, respectively. Note that all classes must declare a superclass, which can be `Object`.

```
T  ::= X | N
N  ::= C<T̄>
CL ::= class C<X̄◁N̄>◁ T {T̄ f̄; M̄}
     | class C<X̄◁N̄>◁ T {T̄ f̄; 𝔐̄ }
M  ::= T m (T̄ x̄) {↑e;}
𝔐  ::= <Ȳ◁P̄>[ū] for(M:X.methods) U n (Ū x̄) {↑e;}
𝕄  ::= V n (V̄)
e  ::= x | e.f | e.n(ē) | new C<T̄>(ē) | (T)e
```

Fig. 1. Syntax

The goal of our formalization is to show that a type system in which both declarations and references can be made by reflecting over an unknown type can be sound. To keep the formalism comprehensible and concentrate on the core question, we left out some of MJ's language features. Most notable of these features is the ability to add static prefixes to name variables. Leaving this feature out prevents us from formalizing the declaration of both static and reflective methods in the same class or through inheritance, and from formalizing reflective iteration over different type variables.[1] We also do not formalize non-variable types as reflective parameters. This is a far less interesting case than reflecting over type variables, since all types and names are statically known. The zero or more length type vectors T* are also not formalized, without loss of generality. These type vectors are a matching convenience. They are treated as single types where they are used. Thus, safety issues regarding declaration and reference using vector types are covered by regular, non-vector types. Additionally, our formalism only includes reflectively declared methods, not fields—type checking reflectively declared fields is a strict adaptation of the techniques for checking methods. Lastly, polymorphic methods are not formalized.

Just like in FGJ, a program in FMJ is an (e, CT) pair, where e is an FMJ expression, and CT is the class table. We place the same conditions on CT as FGJ does. Every class declaration class C... has an entry in CT; Object is not in CT. In addition, the subtyping relation derived from CT must be acyclic, and the sequence of ancestors of every instantiation type is finite. (The last two properties can be checked with the algorithm of [1] in the presence of mixins.)

4.2 Typing Judgments

The main typing rules of FMJ are presented in Figure 2, with auxiliary definitions presented in Figure 3, 4, 5, and 6. The core of this type system is in

---

[1] We could formalize the declaration of static and reflective methods in the same class (or through inheritance), but it would only be well-formed if the reflective methods are defined using *constant* method names (instead of name variables), and the constant names are different from all statically declared method names. This is technically uninteresting, and we leave it out of our formalism for simplicity. The same is true for formalizing reflective iteration over different type variables.

determining range subsumption and disjointness. Thus, we begin our discussion with an overview of the general typing rules, and follow with a detailed explanation of *subsumes* and *disjoint*, both defined in Figure 4.

There are three environments in our typing judgments:

- Δ: Type environment. Δ maps type variables to their upper bounds. Type variables can be introduced by class declarations (e.g., class `C<`$\overline{\text{X}}$◁$\overline{\text{N}}$`>` ... introduces type variables $\overline{\text{X}}$), or by reflective iterator definitions (e.g., `<`$\overline{\text{Y}}$◁$\overline{\text{P}}$`>[`$\overline{\text{u}}$`]` `for(...)` introduces type variables $\overline{\text{Y}}$).
- Γ: Variable environment. Γ maps variables (e.g., x) to their types.
- Λ: Reflective iteration environment. Λ is introduced with each reflective block. Λ maps a type T to a tuple of $\langle \overline{\text{Y}}, \overline{\text{u}}, \text{M} \rangle$. T is the reflective parameter whose methods form the reflective set. M is the pattern used to filter the reflective set. $\overline{\text{Y}}$ and $\overline{\text{u}}$ are the pattern matching type and name variables introduced for use in M and the body of the reflective block. Since our syntax does not allow nested reflective loops, Λ contains at most one mapping.

A fourth environment, M, is sometimes used in the auxiliary definitions. M maps pattern matching type variables (e.g., those introduced by a reflective block) to other types, which may be pattern matching type variables, or non-pattern-matching types.

We use the $\mapsto$ symbol for mappings in the environments. For example, $\Delta = \dots, \text{X} \mapsto \text{C}<\overline{\text{T}}>$ means that $\Delta(\text{X}) = \text{C}<\overline{\text{T}}>$. We require every type variable to be bounded by a non-variable type. The function $bound_\Delta(\text{T})$ returns the upper bound of type T in Δ. $bound_\Delta(\text{N}) = \text{N}$, if N is not a type variable. And $bound_\Delta(\text{X}) = bound_\Delta(\text{S})$, where $\Delta(\text{X}) = \text{S}$.

In order to keep our type rules manageable, we make two simplifying assumptions. First, to avoid burdening our rules with renamings, we assume that pattern matching type variables have globally unique names (i.e., are distinct from pattern matching type variables in a different reflective environment, as well as from non-pattern-matching type variables). Secondly, we assume that all pattern matching type and name variables introduced by a reflective block are bound (i.e., used) in the corresponding pattern. Checking this property is easy and purely syntactic.

Uniqueness of Names: One of the main challenges of this type system is guaranteeing the uniqueness of declaration names. The uniqueness guarantee is simpler in our formalism than discussed in Section 3, since, in FMJ, a class can declare either static or reflective methods, but not both. Thus, we do not have to consider the case when static and reflective names conflict. We do, however, have to make sure that reflectively declared names do not conflict with each other. Rules T-METH-R and T-CLASS-R place conditions on well-typed methods and classes to prevent such naming conflicts.

T-METH-R ensures that methods declared within one reflective block should not conflict with 1) each other, and 2) methods in the superclass (i.e., there is proper overriding). The first condition is partly guaranteed by our syntax: a reflectively declared method must have the same name as the name in the method pattern for its enclosing reflective block.[2] Since a well-formed class can only be instantiated with other well-formed classes (WF-CLASS), and all well-formed classes have uniquely declared method names, we can be sure that method names reflectively retrieved from any type parameter through the pattern are unique.

The second condition is enforced using *override* (Figure 3). *override*(n, T, $\overline{U} \rightarrow U_0$) determines whether method n, defined in some *subclass* of T with type signature $\overline{U} \rightarrow U_0$, properly overrides method n in T. If method n exists in T, it must have the exact same argument and return types as n in the subclass.[3] Additionally, the reflective range of n in the subclass must be either completely subsumed by one of T's reflective ranges, or disjoint from all the reflective ranges of T (and, transitively, T's superclasses). This condition is enforced using $\Delta \vdash validRange(\Lambda, T)$ (Figure 4).

T-CLASS-R ensures that the reflective blocks within a well-typed class do not have declarations that conflict with each other. There are two key conditions: 1) all reflective blocks have the same reflective parameter (X_k), and 2) the ranges of reflective blocks are disjoint pairwise. Since all blocks reflect over the same reflective parameter, which itself has unique method names, and no blocks overlap in their reflective ranges, the names used across all blocks are unique, as well. T-CLASS-R relies on the definition of *disjoint* to handle much of its complexity.

Valid Invocations: A second challenge in this type system is the validity of references to reflectively declared methods. T-INVK (Figure 2) specifies conditions for a well-typed method invocation. It uses $\Delta; \Lambda \vdash mtype(n, T)$ (Figure 3) to retrieve the type of method n in T, under the assumptions of Δ and Λ. We next highlight the *mtype* rules.

MT-VAR-R covers the case when we are looking for the type of method n in a type variable X, where X is the reflective parameter for the current reflective environment Λ. If the method pattern for the current reflective iterator uses n as its method name, $mtype(n, X)$ is simply the type specified by the method pattern. MT-VAR-S covers the case when method n is *not* a method covered by the method pattern of the current reflective environment. In this case, we look for the type of n in the non-variable bound of X.

Rules MT-CLASS-S and MT-SUPER-S apply when we look for n in C<$\overline{T}$>, where C<$\overline{X}$> has only statically declared methods. MT-CLASS-S states that if n is not a name variable used in the current reflective environment Λ (as determined by $\Lambda \vdash constn(n)$, Figure 4), and it is the name of a statically declared method in

---

[2] This is a slightly different requirement than what is necessary in the implementation. In the formalization, there is no method name overloading, hence the uniquely identifying part of a method consists of its name only.

[3] Again, this is a simplification inherited from the FGJ formalism. In practice, one can overload method names with different argument types. We also made an extra simplification over FGJ: FGJ allows a covariant return type for overriding methods, whereas we disallow it to simplify the pattern matching rules in Figure 5.

Expression typing:

$$\Delta; \Gamma; \Lambda \vdash \mathtt{x} \in \Gamma(\mathtt{x}) \qquad\qquad \text{(T-VAR)}$$

$$\frac{\Delta; \Gamma; \Lambda \vdash \mathtt{e}_0 \in \mathtt{T}_0 \quad fields(bound_\Delta(\mathtt{T}_0)) = \overline{\mathtt{T}}\ \overline{\mathtt{f}}}{\Delta; \Gamma; \Lambda \vdash \mathtt{e}_0 . \mathtt{f}_i \in \mathtt{T}_i} \qquad \text{(T-FIELD)}$$

$$\frac{\Delta; \Gamma; \Lambda \vdash \mathtt{e}_0 \in \mathtt{T}_0 \quad \Delta; \Lambda \vdash mtype(\mathtt{n}, \mathtt{T}_0) = \overline{\mathtt{T}} \to \mathtt{T} \quad \Delta; \Gamma; \Lambda \vdash \overline{\mathtt{e}} \in \overline{\mathtt{S}} \quad \Delta \vdash \overline{\mathtt{S}} <: \overline{\mathtt{T}}}{\Delta; \Gamma; \Lambda \vdash \mathtt{e}_0 . \mathtt{n}(\overline{\mathtt{e}}) \in \mathtt{T}} \qquad \text{(T-INVK)}$$

$$\frac{\Delta \vdash \mathtt{C} \mathtt{<} \overline{\mathtt{T}} \mathtt{>}\ ok \quad fields(\mathtt{C} \mathtt{<} \overline{\mathtt{T}} \mathtt{>}) = \overline{\mathtt{U}}\ \overline{\mathtt{f}} \quad \Delta; \Gamma; \Lambda \vdash \overline{\mathtt{e}} \in \overline{\mathtt{S}} \quad \Delta \vdash \overline{\mathtt{S}} <: \overline{\mathtt{U}}}{\Delta; \Gamma; \Lambda \vdash \mathtt{new}\ \mathtt{C} \mathtt{<} \overline{\mathtt{T}} \mathtt{>}(\overline{\mathtt{e}}) \in \mathtt{C} \mathtt{<} \overline{\mathtt{T}} \mathtt{>}} \qquad \text{(T-NEW)}$$

$$\frac{\begin{array}{c} \Delta; \Gamma; \Lambda \vdash \mathtt{e}_0 \in \mathtt{T}_0 \quad \Delta \vdash \mathtt{T}\ ok \\ \Delta \vdash bound_\Delta(\mathtt{T}_0) <: bound_\Delta(\mathtt{T}) \quad \text{or} \quad \Delta \vdash bound_\Delta(\mathtt{T}) <: bound_\Delta(\mathtt{T}_0) \end{array}}{\Delta; \Gamma; \Lambda \vdash (\mathtt{T})\mathtt{e}_0 \in \mathtt{T}} \qquad \text{(T-CAST)}$$

$$\frac{\begin{array}{c} \Delta; \Gamma; \Lambda \vdash \mathtt{e}_0 \in \mathtt{T}_0 \quad \Delta \vdash \mathtt{T}\ ok \\ \Delta \nvdash bound_\Delta(\mathtt{T}_0) <: bound_\Delta(\mathtt{T}) \quad \text{and} \quad \Delta \nvdash bound_\Delta(\mathtt{T}) <: bound_\Delta(\mathtt{T}_0) \end{array}}{\Delta; \Gamma; \Lambda \vdash (\mathtt{T})\mathtt{e}_0 \in \mathtt{T}} \qquad \text{(T-SCAST)}$$

Method typing:

$$\frac{\begin{array}{c} \Delta = \overline{\mathtt{X}} <: \overline{\mathtt{N}} \quad \Gamma = \overline{\mathtt{x}} \mapsto \overline{\mathtt{T}}, \mathtt{this} \mapsto \mathtt{C} \mathtt{<} \overline{\mathtt{X}} \mathtt{>} \quad \boxed{\Lambda = \emptyset} \\ \Delta \vdash \overline{\mathtt{T}}, \mathtt{T}_0\ ok \quad \Delta; \Gamma; \Lambda \vdash \mathtt{e}_0 \in \mathtt{S}_0 \quad \Delta \vdash \mathtt{S}_0 <: \mathtt{T}_0 \\ CT(\mathtt{C}) = \mathtt{class}\ \mathtt{C} \mathtt{<} \overline{\mathtt{X}} \mathtt{\lhd} \overline{\mathtt{N}} \mathtt{>} \mathtt{\lhd}\ \mathtt{T}\ \{\ldots\} \quad \Delta; \Lambda \vdash override(\mathtt{m}, \mathtt{T}, \overline{\mathtt{T}} \to \mathtt{T}_0)) \end{array}}{\mathtt{T}_0\ \mathtt{m}\ (\overline{\mathtt{T}}\ \overline{\mathtt{x}})\ \{\ \uparrow\!\mathtt{e}_0;\ \}\ \text{OK IN}\ \mathtt{C} \mathtt{<} \overline{\mathtt{X}} \mathtt{\lhd} \overline{\mathtt{N}} \mathtt{>}} \qquad \text{(T-METH-S)}$$

$$\frac{\begin{array}{c} \Delta = \overline{\mathtt{X}} <: \overline{\mathtt{N}}, \overline{\mathtt{Y}} <: \overline{\mathtt{P}} \quad \Gamma = \overline{\mathtt{x}} \mapsto \overline{\mathtt{V}}, \mathtt{this} \mapsto \mathtt{C} \mathtt{<} \overline{\mathtt{X}} \mathtt{>} \quad \Lambda = \mathtt{X}_i \mapsto \langle \overline{\mathtt{Y}}, \overline{\mathtt{u}}, \mathtt{U}_0\ \mathtt{n}\ (\overline{\mathtt{U}}) \rangle \\ \mathtt{X}_i \in \overline{\mathtt{X}} \quad \Delta \vdash \overline{\mathtt{P}}, \mathtt{U}_0, \overline{\mathtt{U}}, \mathtt{V}_0, \overline{\mathtt{V}}\ ok \quad \Delta; \Gamma; \Lambda \vdash \mathtt{e} \in \mathtt{S}_0 \quad \Delta \vdash \mathtt{S}_0 <: \mathtt{U}_0 \\ CT(\mathtt{C}) = \mathtt{class}\ \mathtt{C} \mathtt{<} \overline{\mathtt{X}} \mathtt{\lhd} \overline{\mathtt{N}} \mathtt{>} \mathtt{\lhd} \mathtt{T}\ \{\ \ldots\ \} \quad \Delta; \Lambda \vdash override(\mathtt{n}, \mathtt{T}, \overline{\mathtt{V}} \to \mathtt{V}_0) \end{array}}{\langle \overline{\mathtt{Y}} \mathtt{\lhd} \overline{\mathtt{P}} \mathtt{>} [\overline{\mathtt{u}}] \mathtt{for}(\mathtt{U}_0\ \mathtt{n}\ (\overline{\mathtt{U}}) : \mathtt{X}_i . \mathtt{methods})\ \mathtt{V}_0\ \mathtt{n}\ (\overline{\mathtt{V}}\ \overline{\mathtt{x}})\ \{\uparrow\!\mathtt{e};\}\ \text{OK IN}\ \mathtt{C} \mathtt{<} \overline{\mathtt{X}} \mathtt{\lhd} \overline{\mathtt{N}} \mathtt{>}} \quad \text{(T-METH-R)}$$

Class typing:

$$\frac{\Delta = \overline{\mathtt{X}} <: \overline{\mathtt{N}} \quad \Delta \vdash \overline{\mathtt{N}}, \mathtt{T}, \overline{\mathtt{T}}\ ok \quad \overline{\mathtt{M}}\ \text{OK IN}\ \mathtt{C} \mathtt{<} \overline{\mathtt{X}} \mathtt{\lhd} \overline{\mathtt{N}} \mathtt{>}}{\mathtt{class}\ \mathtt{C} \mathtt{<} \overline{\mathtt{X}} \mathtt{\lhd} \overline{\mathtt{N}} \mathtt{>} \mathtt{\lhd}\ \mathtt{T}\ \{\ \overline{\mathtt{T}}\ \overline{\mathtt{f}};\ \overline{\mathtt{M}}\}\ \text{OK}} \qquad \text{(T-CLASS-S)}$$

$$\frac{\begin{array}{c} \Delta = \overline{\mathtt{X}} <: \overline{\mathtt{N}} \quad \Delta \vdash \overline{\mathtt{N}}, \mathtt{T}, \overline{\mathtt{T}}\ ok \quad \overline{\mathfrak{M}}\ \text{OK IN}\ \mathtt{C} \mathtt{<} \overline{\mathtt{X}} \mathtt{\lhd} \overline{\mathtt{N}} \mathtt{>} \quad \mathtt{X}_k \in \overline{\mathtt{X}} \\ \text{for all}\quad \mathfrak{M}_i, \mathfrak{M}_j \in \overline{\mathfrak{M}}, \\ \mathfrak{M}_i = \langle \overline{\mathtt{Y}} \mathtt{\lhd} \overline{\mathtt{P}} \mathtt{>} [\overline{\mathtt{u}}] \mathtt{for}(\mathtt{U}_0\ \mathtt{n}_i\ (\overline{\mathtt{U}}) : \mathtt{X}_k . \mathtt{methods}) \ldots \\ \mathfrak{M}_j = \langle \overline{\mathtt{Z}} \mathtt{\lhd} \overline{\mathtt{Q}} \mathtt{>} [\overline{\mathtt{v}}] \mathtt{for}(\mathtt{V}_0\ \mathtt{n}_j\ (\overline{\mathtt{V}}) : \mathtt{X}_k . \mathtt{methods}) \ldots \\ \Lambda_i = \mathtt{X}_k \mapsto \langle \overline{\mathtt{Y}}, \overline{\mathtt{u}}, \mathtt{U}_0\ \mathtt{n}_i\ (\overline{\mathtt{U}}) \rangle \quad \Lambda_j = \mathtt{X}_k \mapsto \langle \overline{\mathtt{Z}}, \overline{\mathtt{v}}, \mathtt{V}_0\ \mathtt{n}_j\ (\overline{\mathtt{V}}) \rangle \\ \text{implies}\quad \Delta, \overline{\mathtt{Y}} <: \overline{\mathtt{P}}, \overline{\mathtt{Z}} <: \overline{\mathtt{Q}} \vdash disjoint(\langle \Lambda_i, \mathtt{n}_i, \mathtt{X}_k \rangle, \langle \Lambda_j, \mathtt{n}_j, \mathtt{X}_k \rangle) \end{array}}{\mathtt{class}\ \mathtt{C} \mathtt{<} \overline{\mathtt{X}} \mathtt{\lhd} \overline{\mathtt{N}} \mathtt{>} \mathtt{\lhd} \mathtt{T}\ \{\ \overline{\mathtt{T}}\ \overline{\mathtt{f}};\ \overline{\mathfrak{M}}\}\ \text{OK}} \qquad \text{(T-CLASS-R)}$$

Well-formed types:

$$\Delta \vdash \mathtt{Object}\ ok \qquad \text{(WF-OBJECT)} \qquad\qquad \frac{\mathtt{X} \in dom(\Delta)}{\Delta \vdash \mathtt{X}\ ok} \qquad \text{(WF-VAR)}$$

$$\frac{CT(\mathtt{C}) = \mathtt{class}\ \mathtt{C} \mathtt{<} \overline{\mathtt{X}} \mathtt{\lhd} \overline{\mathtt{N}} \mathtt{>} \mathtt{\lhd}\ \mathtt{T}\ \{\ \ldots\} \quad \Delta \vdash \overline{\mathtt{T}}\ ok \quad \Delta \vdash \overline{\mathtt{T}} <: [\overline{\mathtt{T}}/\overline{\mathtt{X}}] \overline{\mathtt{N}}}{\Delta \vdash \mathtt{C} \mathtt{<} \overline{\mathtt{T}} \mathtt{>}\ ok} \qquad \text{(WF-CLASS)}$$

Fig. 2. Typing Rules

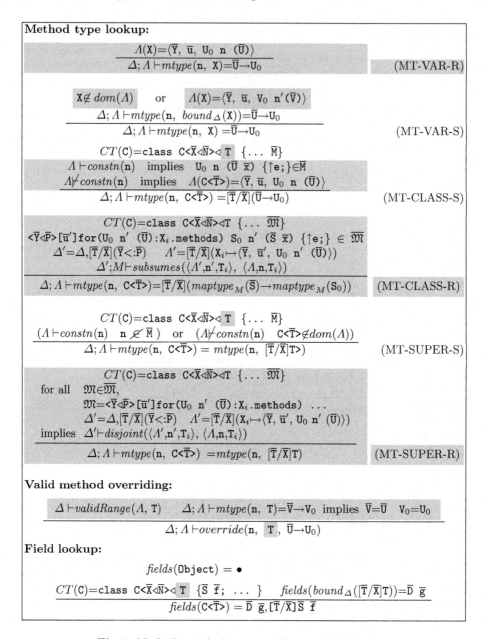

Method type lookup:

$$\frac{\Lambda(\mathtt{X})=\langle\overline{\mathtt{Y}},\ \overline{\mathtt{u}},\ \mathtt{U}_0\ \mathtt{n}\ (\overline{\mathtt{U}})\rangle}{\Delta;\Lambda\vdash mtype(\mathtt{n},\ \mathtt{X})=\overline{\mathtt{U}}\to\mathtt{U}_0}\qquad\text{(MT-VAR-R)}$$

$$\frac{\mathtt{X}\notin dom(\Lambda)\quad\text{or}\quad \Lambda(\mathtt{X})=\langle\overline{\mathtt{Y}},\ \overline{\mathtt{u}},\ \mathtt{V}_0\ \mathtt{n}'(\overline{\mathtt{V}})\rangle \qquad \Delta;\Lambda\vdash mtype(\mathtt{n},\ bound_\Delta(\mathtt{X}))=\overline{\mathtt{U}}\to\mathtt{U}_0}{\Delta;\Lambda\vdash mtype(\mathtt{n},\ \mathtt{X})=\overline{\mathtt{U}}\to\mathtt{U}_0}\qquad\text{(MT-VAR-S)}$$

$$\frac{\begin{array}{c}CT(\mathtt{C})=\texttt{class C<}\overline{\mathtt{X}}\triangleleft\overline{\mathtt{N}}\texttt{>}\triangleleft\ \mathtt{T}\ \{\ldots\ \overline{\mathtt{M}}\}\\ \Lambda\vdash constn(\mathtt{n})\quad\text{implies}\quad\mathtt{U}_0\ \mathtt{n}\ (\overline{\mathtt{U}}\ \overline{\mathtt{x}})\ \{\uparrow\mathtt{e};\}\in\overline{\mathtt{M}}\\ \Lambda\not\vdash constn(\mathtt{n})\quad\text{implies}\quad\Lambda(\mathtt{C<}\overline{\mathtt{T}}\texttt{>})=\langle\overline{\mathtt{Y}},\ \overline{\mathtt{u}},\ \mathtt{U}_0\ \mathtt{n}\ (\overline{\mathtt{U}})\rangle\end{array}}{\Delta;\Lambda\vdash mtype(\mathtt{n},\ \mathtt{C<}\overline{\mathtt{T}}\texttt{>})=[\overline{\mathtt{T}}/\overline{\mathtt{X}}](\overline{\mathtt{U}}\to\mathtt{U}_0)}\qquad\text{(MT-CLASS-S)}$$

$$\frac{\begin{array}{c}CT(\mathtt{C})=\texttt{class C<}\overline{\mathtt{X}}\triangleleft\overline{\mathtt{N}}\texttt{>}\triangleleft\mathtt{T}\ \{\ldots\ \overline{\mathfrak{M}}\}\\ \texttt{<}\overline{\mathtt{Y}}\triangleleft\overline{\mathtt{P}}\texttt{>}[\overline{\mathtt{u}}']\texttt{for(}\mathtt{U}_0\ \mathtt{n}'\ (\overline{\mathtt{U}})\texttt{:}\mathtt{X}_i\texttt{.methods)}\ \mathtt{S}_0\ \mathtt{n}'\ (\overline{\mathtt{S}}\ \overline{\mathtt{x}})\ \{\uparrow\mathtt{e};\}\in\overline{\mathfrak{M}}\\ \Delta'=\Delta,[\overline{\mathtt{T}}/\overline{\mathtt{X}}](\overline{\mathtt{Y}}\texttt{<:}\overline{\mathtt{P}})\quad\Lambda'=[\overline{\mathtt{T}}/\overline{\mathtt{X}}](\mathtt{X}_i\mapsto\langle\overline{\mathtt{Y}},\ \overline{\mathtt{u}}',\ \mathtt{U}_0\ \mathtt{n}'\ (\overline{\mathtt{U}})\rangle)\\ \Delta';M\vdash subsumes(\langle\Lambda',\mathtt{n}',\mathtt{T}_i\rangle,\ \langle\Lambda,\mathtt{n},\mathtt{T}_i\rangle)\end{array}}{\Delta;\Lambda\vdash mtype(\mathtt{n},\ \mathtt{C<}\overline{\mathtt{T}}\texttt{>})=[\overline{\mathtt{T}}/\overline{\mathtt{X}}](maptype_M(\overline{\mathtt{S}})\to maptype_M(\mathtt{S}_0))}\qquad\text{(MT-CLASS-R)}$$

$$\frac{\begin{array}{c}CT(\mathtt{C})=\texttt{class C<}\overline{\mathtt{X}}\triangleleft\overline{\mathtt{N}}\texttt{>}\triangleleft\ \mathtt{T}\ \{\ldots\ \overline{\mathtt{M}}\}\\ (\Lambda\vdash constn(\mathtt{n})\quad\mathtt{n}\not\in\overline{\mathtt{M}})\quad\text{or}\quad(\Lambda\not\vdash constn(\mathtt{n})\quad\mathtt{C<}\overline{\mathtt{T}}\texttt{>}\notin dom(\Lambda))\end{array}}{\Delta;\Lambda\vdash mtype(\mathtt{n},\ \mathtt{C<}\overline{\mathtt{T}}\texttt{>})=mtype(\mathtt{n},\ [\overline{\mathtt{T}}/\overline{\mathtt{X}}]\mathtt{T})}\qquad\text{(MT-SUPER-S)}$$

$$\frac{\begin{array}{c}CT(\mathtt{C})=\texttt{class C<}\overline{\mathtt{X}}\triangleleft\overline{\mathtt{N}}\texttt{>}\triangleleft\mathtt{T}\ \{\ldots\ \overline{\mathfrak{M}}\}\\ \text{for all}\ \mathfrak{M}\in\overline{\mathfrak{M}},\\ \mathfrak{M}=\texttt{<}\overline{\mathtt{Y}}\triangleleft\overline{\mathtt{P}}\texttt{>}[\overline{\mathtt{u}}']\texttt{for(}\mathtt{U}_0\ \mathtt{n}'\ (\overline{\mathtt{U}})\texttt{):}\mathtt{X}_i\texttt{.methods)}\ \ldots\\ \Delta'=\Delta,[\overline{\mathtt{T}}/\overline{\mathtt{X}}](\overline{\mathtt{Y}}\texttt{<:}\overline{\mathtt{P}})\quad\Lambda'=[\overline{\mathtt{T}}/\overline{\mathtt{X}}](\mathtt{X}_i\mapsto\langle\overline{\mathtt{Y}},\ \overline{\mathtt{u}}',\ \mathtt{U}_0\ \mathtt{n}'\ (\overline{\mathtt{U}})\rangle)\\ \text{implies}\quad\Delta'\vdash disjoint(\langle\Lambda',\mathtt{n}',\mathtt{T}_i\rangle,\ \langle\Lambda,\mathtt{n},\mathtt{T}_i\rangle)\end{array}}{\Delta;\Lambda\vdash mtype(\mathtt{n},\ \mathtt{C<}\overline{\mathtt{T}}\texttt{>})=mtype(\mathtt{n},\ [\overline{\mathtt{T}}/\overline{\mathtt{X}}]\mathtt{T})}\qquad\text{(MT-SUPER-R)}$$

Valid method overriding:

$$\frac{\Delta\vdash validRange(\Lambda,\ \mathtt{T})\quad\Delta;\Lambda\vdash mtype(\mathtt{n},\ \mathtt{T})=\overline{\mathtt{V}}\to\mathtt{V}_0\ \text{implies}\ \overline{\mathtt{V}}=\overline{\mathtt{U}}\quad\mathtt{V}_0=\mathtt{U}_0}{\Delta;\Lambda\vdash override(\mathtt{n},\ \mathtt{T},\ \overline{\mathtt{U}}\to\mathtt{U}_0)}$$

Field lookup:

$$fields(\texttt{Object})=\bullet$$

$$\frac{CT(\mathtt{C})=\texttt{class C<}\overline{\mathtt{X}}\triangleleft\overline{\mathtt{N}}\texttt{>}\triangleleft\ \mathtt{T}\ \{\overline{\mathtt{S}}\ \overline{\mathtt{f}};\ \ldots\ \}\quad fields(bound_\Delta([\overline{\mathtt{T}}/\overline{\mathtt{X}}]\mathtt{T}))=\overline{\mathtt{D}}\ \overline{\mathtt{g}}}{fields(\mathtt{C<}\overline{\mathtt{T}}\texttt{>})=\overline{\mathtt{D}}\ \overline{\mathtt{g}},[\overline{\mathtt{T}}/\overline{\mathtt{X}}]\overline{\mathtt{S}}\ \overline{\mathtt{f}}}$$

Fig. 3. Method type lookup, overriding and field lookup

$\mathtt{C<}\overline{\mathtt{X}}\texttt{>}$, then $mtype$ is defined to be the statically declared type of $\mathtt{n}$, with proper type substitutions of $\overline{\mathtt{T}}$ for $\overline{\mathtt{X}}$. However, if $\mathtt{n}$ *is* a name variable in Λ, and $\mathtt{C<}\overline{\mathtt{T}}\texttt{>}$ is the type that Λ iterates over, then the type of method covered by this name variable is exactly the type defined in the method pattern of Λ. MT-SUPER-S

Method range subsumption:

$$\frac{\Delta \vdash T_1 <: T_2 \qquad \overline{Y} = pmVars(\Lambda_1)}{\Delta; \Lambda_1 \vdash mtype(n_1, \ T_1) = \overline{U} \to U_0 \qquad \Delta; \Lambda_2 \vdash mtype(n_2, \ T_2) = \overline{V} \to V_0} \\ \frac{\Delta; M; \overline{Y} \vdash tunify(U_0 : \overline{U}, \ V_0 : \overline{V}) \qquad \langle \Lambda_2, n_2 \rangle \sqsubseteq_{id} \langle \Lambda_1, n_1 \rangle}{\Delta; M \vdash subsumes(\langle \Lambda_1, n_1, T_1 \rangle, \ \langle \Lambda_2, n_2, T_2 \rangle)}$$

Method range disjointness:

$$\frac{\Lambda_1 \vdash constn(n_1) \qquad \Lambda_2 \vdash constn(n_2) \qquad n_1 \neq n_2}{\Delta \vdash disjoint(\langle \Lambda_1, n_1, T_1 \rangle, \ \langle \Lambda_2, n_2, T_2 \rangle)} \qquad \text{(DS-NAME)}$$

$$\frac{\Delta; \Lambda_1 \vdash mtype(n_1, \ T_1) = \overline{U} \to U_0 \qquad \Delta; \Lambda_2 \vdash mtype(n_2, \ T_2) = \overline{V} \to V_0}{\Lambda_1 \nvdash constn(n_1) \ \text{or} \ \Lambda_2 \nvdash constn(n_2) \qquad \Delta \vdash T_1 <: T_2 \ \text{or} \ \Delta \vdash T_2 <: T_1} \\ \frac{\overline{Y} = pmVars(\Lambda_1) \qquad \overline{Z} = pmVars(\Lambda_2)}{\text{for no } M, \quad \Delta; M; \overline{Y}, \overline{Z} \vdash tunify(U_0 : \overline{U}, \ V_0 : \overline{V})} \\ \frac{}{\Delta \vdash disjoint(\langle \Lambda_1, n_1, T_1 \rangle, \ \langle \Lambda_2, n_2, T_2 \rangle)} \qquad \text{(DS-TYPE)}$$

Subtype range validity:

$$\Delta \vdash validRange(\emptyset, \ T) \quad \text{(VR-NOREFL)} \qquad \Delta \vdash validRange(X \mapsto \langle \dots \rangle, \ X) \quad \text{(VR-VAR)}$$

$$\frac{\begin{array}{c} CT(C) = \texttt{class } C < \overline{X} \triangleleft \overline{N} > \triangleleft S \ \{ \ \dots \ \overline{\mathfrak{M}} \} \\ \Delta \vdash validRange(\Lambda, \ [\overline{T}/\overline{X}]S) \qquad \Lambda = T \mapsto \langle \_, n, \_ \rangle \\ \text{for all } \mathfrak{M} \in \overline{\mathfrak{M}} \\ \mathfrak{M} = < \overline{Z} \triangleleft \overline{Q} > [\overline{u}'] \ \texttt{for} \ (S_0 \ n' \ (\overline{S}) \ : \ X_i.\texttt{methods}) \ \dots \\ \Delta' = \Delta, \overline{Z} <: [\overline{T}/\overline{X}]\overline{Q} \qquad \Lambda' = [\overline{T}/\overline{X}](X_i \mapsto \langle \overline{Z}, \ \overline{u}', \ S_0 \ n' \ (\overline{S}) \rangle) \\ \text{implies} \begin{cases} \Delta; M \vdash subsumes(\langle \Lambda', n', T_i \rangle, \ \langle \Lambda, n, T \rangle) \ \text{for some } M \ \text{ or} \\ \Delta \vdash disjoint(\langle \Lambda', n', T_i \rangle, \ \langle \Lambda, n, T \rangle) \end{cases} \end{array}}{\Delta \vdash validRange(\Lambda, \ C < \overline{T} >)} \quad \text{(VR-CLASS)}$$

Identifier subrange rules:

$$\frac{\Lambda_2 \vdash constn(n_2) \ \text{implies} \ (\ \Lambda_1 \vdash constn(n_1) \ \text{and} \ n_1 = n_2 \ )}{\langle \Lambda_1, \ n_1 \rangle \sqsubseteq_{id} \langle \Lambda_2, \ n_2 \rangle}$$

Constant name:

$$\frac{\Lambda = X \mapsto \langle \_, \overline{u}, \_ \rangle \ \text{implies} \ n \notin \overline{u}}{\Lambda \vdash constn(n)} \qquad \text{(N-CONST)}$$

Pattern matching type variables of Λ:

$$pmVars(\emptyset) = \bullet \qquad\qquad pmVars(T \mapsto \langle \overline{Y}, \dots \rangle = \overline{Y}$$

Type mapping application:

$$\frac{T \notin dom(M)}{maptype_M(T) = T} \quad \text{(TM-VAR1)} \qquad \frac{M(X) = T}{maptype_M(X) = maptype_M(T)} \quad \text{(TM-VAR2)}$$

$$\frac{maptype_M(\overline{T}) = \overline{S}}{maptype_M(C < \overline{T} >) = C < \overline{S} >} \qquad \text{(TM-CLASS)}$$

Fig. 4. Reflection related auxiliary functions

states that the type of n in $C < \overline{T} >$ is the same as its type in $C < \overline{T} >$'s superclass, T, when n is a constant name, but not the name of a statically defined method in $C < \overline{X} >$, or when n is a name variable, but $C < \overline{T} >$ is not the type Λ iterates over.

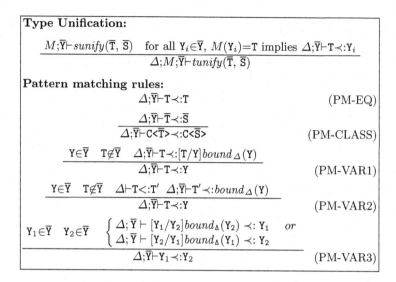

Fig. 5. Type unification and pattern matching rules

$$\text{Subtyping rules:}$$
$$\Delta \vdash T <: T \qquad \text{(S-REFL)} \qquad \Delta \vdash X <: \Delta(X) \qquad \text{(S-VAR)}$$

$$\frac{\Delta \vdash S<:T \quad \Delta \vdash T<:U}{\Delta \vdash S<:U} \quad \text{(S-TRANS)}$$

$$\frac{CT(C)=\texttt{class } C<\overline{X}\triangleleft\overline{N}>\triangleleft T \ \{\ldots\}}{\Delta \vdash C<\overline{T}> \ <: \ [\overline{T}/\overline{X}]T} \quad \text{(S-CLASS)}$$

Fig. 6. Subtyping rules

Rules MT-CLASS-R and MT-SUPER-R apply when we look for n in C<$\overline{T}$>, where C<$\overline{X}$> has reflectively declared methods. As we explained in Section 3, the key in determining whether a reflectively declared method exists is in determining that the range of n in the reference reflective environment is subsumed by the range of some name in the declaration reflective environment. If subsumption holds, the type of n is simply the type of the method whose name subsumes n, with the proper type substitutions of $[\overline{T}/\overline{X}]$, as well as the substitutions in mapping environment M. (The substitution for type T using M is defined as $maptype_M(T)$, in Figure 4. It is a straightforward application of type mappings.) MT-SUPER-R says that when the range of n in Λ is disjoint from every declared method range in C<$\overline{T}$>, n has the same type as it does in C<$\overline{T}$>'s superclass.

Subsumption: $\Delta;M \vdash subsumes(\langle \Lambda_1, n_1, T_1 \rangle, \langle \Lambda_2, n_2, T_2 \rangle)$, defined in Figure 4, determines whether, under the assumptions of Δ and M, the range of methods represented by n_1 in type T_1 subsumes the range of methods represented by n_2 in type T_2, under their respective reflective iteration environments.

There are three conditions for subsumption. First, T_1 must be a subtype of T_2. It only makes sense to compare ranges of methods if they are methods coming from the same class. Additionally, in defining reflective iterators, we interpret methods of a class (e.g., X.methods) to be the methods declared in the class and all of its superclasses, transitively. Thus, a subclass has more methods than its superclass, potentially yielding a larger range.

Secondly, the name n_1 must be less strict than the name n_2. Since all name variables can match any name, the only restriction on n_2 is when n_1 is a constant. In this case, n_2 must be equal to n_1 (see $\sqsubseteq_{id}$ in Figure 4).

Lastly, M must be a *one-way* unification mapping that maps the type signature of the larger range ($\overline{U} \rightarrow U_0$) onto that of the smaller range ($\overline{V} \rightarrow V_0$). This is a one-way unification because we want to ensure that one range is larger than the other and not just that their intersection is non-empty. *subsumes* uses $\Delta;M;\overline{Y} \vdash tunify(U_0:\overline{U}, V_0:\overline{V})$ to determine whether M is a proper unification mapping. We discuss *tunify* in detail shortly. But the main point to note is that its rules are quite general, and determine whether M is a *two-way* unification between its arguments, using the given pattern matching type variables. We use *tunify* to check one-way unification by using only $\overline{Y}$ (the pattern matching type variables in the larger range) as the variables with respect to unification, ignoring the pattern matching type variables of Λ_2, which are considered constants.

Disjointness: *disjoint* (Figure 4) takes the same arguments as *subsumes*. The goal of *disjoint* is to determine the non-overlap of the *names* of the two method ranges. DS-NAME describes the easy case, when both ranges use constant names in their method patterns, but the names are not equal to each other. DS-TYPE describes disjointness conditions when at least one of the names is not a constant. First, it stipulates that there can be no unification mapping between the types of the two method ranges. Here again, we use *tunify*. However, note that we pass the pattern matching type variables from both reflective ranges ($\overline{Y}$ and $\overline{Z}$) to *tunify*— we are looking for a two-way unification, in contrast to the one-way unification that *subsumes* looks for. Lack of unification between the two type signatures means that there is no method whose type signature is in both ranges. However, this is not enough to determine the disjunction of the names covered by these ranges—if the methods range over classes from completely different inheritance hierarchies, they could have disjoint method types, but still the same names. Thus, DS-TYPE requires that either T_1 be a subtype of T_2, or vice versa. If methods from the same inheritance hierarchy have different types, then they definitely have distinct names.

Unification: $\Delta;M;\overline{Y} \vdash tunify(\overline{T}, \overline{S})$, defined in Figure 5, determines whether $\overline{T}$ and $\overline{S}$ can be unified by unification mapping M, using $\overline{Y}$ as the pattern matching type variables. Δ is the type environment under which $\overline{Y}$, $\overline{T}$, and $\overline{S}$ are properly defined. *tunify* first checks that M is a proper *syntactic* unifying mapping. Syntactic unification is a common two-way unification such that, after the mapping is applied to $\overline{T}$ and $\overline{S}$, the resulting type sequences $\overline{T}'$ and $\overline{S}'$ are syntactically equivalent. The precise definition of *sunify* is elided for space reasons. Interested readers can obtain the specifics from the technical report [14].

What syntactic unification does not check, however, is whether a mapping from pattern matching type variable Y to type T conforms to the bound of Y in Δ. Thus, *tunify* uses the pattern matching relation, $\prec:$, to check that T can indeed be matched by Y.

The pattern matching relation, $\Delta;\overline{Y}\vdash T\prec:S$ (Figure 5), holds if there exists a type that can be matched by both T and S. $\overline{Y}$ are the pattern matching type variables, and Δ is the type environment under which all types are well-formed. The interesting case is in determining whether a non-pattern-matching type T can be matched by a pattern matching type Y. The intuition is that T can be matched by Y if it is within the bound of Y. This means that, with proper type substitutions, either T can be matched by the bound of Y (PM-VAR1), or T's superclass can be matched by the bound of Y (PM-VAR2). We use PM-VAR3 to determine whether there is a type that can be matched by two pattern matching type variables, Y_1 and Y_2. The intuition is that if there exists a type that can be matched by both $bound_\Delta(Y_1)$ and Y_2 (or $bound_\Delta(Y_2)$ and Y_1), then there is a type that can be matched by both Y_1 and Y_2.

4.3 Soundness

We prove soundness using the familiar subject reduction and progress theorems.

Theorem 1 [Subject Reduction]: If $\Delta;\Gamma;\Lambda\vdash e\in T$ and $e \rightarrow e'$, then $\Delta;\Gamma;\Lambda\vdash e'\in S$ and $\Delta\vdash S<:T$ for some S.

Theorem 2 [Progress]: Let e be a well-typed expression. 1. If e has **new** C<$\overline{T}$>($\overline{e}$).f as a subexpression, then $fields(C<\overline{T}>) = \overline{U}\ \overline{f}$, and f = f_i. 2. If e has **new** C<$\overline{T}$>($\overline{e}$).m($\overline{d}$) as a subexpression, then $mbody(m,\ C<\overline{T}>) = (\overline{x}, e_0)$ and $|\overline{x}| = |\overline{d}|$.

In addition, we must prove a lemma regarding the uniqueness of names—can there be multiple methods declared with the same name? A closer inspection of the MT-CLASS-R rule shows that there appears to be some non-determinism: the second condition of the rule specifies that one of the reflective blocks in $\overline{\mathfrak{M}}$ makes the conditions that follow true. We prove in the following lemma that there can *only* be one such $\mathfrak{M}$ in class C:

Lemma 1 [Name Uniqueness]: If C<$\overline{T}$> ok, $CT(C)$=**class** C<$\overline{X}\lhd\overline{N}$>$\lhd$T { ... $\overline{\mathfrak{M}}$}, then there can be at most one $\mathfrak{M}_i\in\overline{\mathfrak{M}}$ such that $\Delta;\Lambda\vdash mtype(n,\ C<\overline{T}>)=\overline{U}\rightarrow U_0$.

Full text of the proofs, reduction rules, and related functions are defined in the technical report version of this paper[14].

5 Discussion

Design Discussion. MJ can be viewed as part of a general effort to bring meta-programming constructs to mainstream programming languages, with smooth integration of features and modular type checking guarantees. In this sense, it is interesting to discuss MJ's design and implementation decisions in comparison with our other concurrent project: cJ [15]. cJ is an extension of Java with a static-if construct, allowing the configuration of generic classes based on properties of their type parameters. For instance, cJ can express a `List<X>` class that implements `Serializable` only when its type parameter `X` implements `Serializable`.

cJ adds to Java a reflective "if", whereas MJ adds a reflective "for", as well as the ability to create declarations with non-constant names. Thus, it should not be a surprise that MJ is a more ambitious language with significantly more complexity. This is reflected clearly in our design decisions. cJ is designed with backward compatibility in mind, enabling an erasure-based translation. cJ language constructs can be "erased" producing regular Java code in a one-to-one correspondence between cJ generic classes and Java generic classes. Additionally, cJ interacts smoothly with advanced features in the Java type system, such as variance [24,17] and polymorphic methods. In contrast, MJ takes a more radical approach, favoring feature-richness and integration of ideas over backward compatibility and implementation integration. This difference is most evident in MJ's implementation, which employs an expansion-based translation. MJ generic classes produce one regular non-generic Java class per instantiation. This implementation approach is harder to support in conjunction with some of Java's features (e.g., dynamic loading) but yields more power—e.g., to express mixins as generic subclasses. Furthermore, we have not concerned ourselves with supporting features such as variance and polymorphic methods. Considering the interaction of these features with MJ is part of future work. Overall, we do not view MJ as a language extension that can be easily integrated in standard Java. (After all, integrating with standard Java seems a near-hopeless proposition even for more modest research proposals, as the Java language has matured and the rate of change has decreased dramatically.) Instead, we view MJ as a more radical idea, intended to demonstrate the principles of morphing and to influence future language designers. Our goal with MJ is to show the first morphing language with a sound modular type checking system, and a smooth integration of concepts in an object-oriented framework.

Contrast with Meta-Programming and AOP Tools. Generally, few language mechanisms allow expressing what MJ does: writing one piece of code and having it be applied to multiple methods with different signatures. In the past, this has been the hallmark property of Meta-Object Protocols [9,18] and later Aspect-Oriented Programming [20]. Neither mechanism offers modular safety guarantees, however. The same capabilities can be achieved with traditional reflection and program generation but with lower-level means of syntax-matching and, again, no safety guarantees.

An interesting special case of program generation is *staging languages* such as MetaML [23] and MetaOCaml [7]. These languages offer modular type safety: the generated code is guaranteed correct for any input, if the generator type-checks.

Nevertheless, MetaML and MetaOCaml do not allow generating identifiers (e.g., names of variables) or types that are not constant. Generally, staging languages target program specialization rather than full program generation: the program must remain valid even when staging annotations are removed. It is interesting that even recent meta-programming tools, such as Template Haskell [21] are explicitly not modularly type safe—its authors acknowledge that they sacrifice the MetaML guarantees for expressiveness.

6 Future Work and Conclusions

There are several interesting directions of further work on MJ. A major one is the introduction of anti-patterns in addition to patterns. Several modular type checking scenarios require not just matching all entities that satisfy a pattern, but also ensuring that no entity exists that matches a certain other pattern. Anti-patterns increase the expressiveness of a morphing language significantly. For instance, they expand the possibilities for generating methods and fields with guarantees that they will not conflict with existing members of a type. Our introduction of anti-patterns will be based on the same type checking insights as patterns, namely on checking of range disjointness and subsumption.

Overall, we consider MJ and the idea of morphing to be a significant step forward in the expressiveness of modern programming languages. Morphing can be viewed as an aspect-oriented technique, allowing the extension and adaptation of existing code components, and enabling a single enhancement to affect multiple code sites (e.g., all methods of a class, regardless of name). Yet morphing is also deeply different from aspect-oriented programming, and can perhaps be seen as a bridge between AOP and generic programming. Morphing does not introduce functionality to unsuspecting code. Instead, it ensures that any extension is under the full control of the programmer. The result of morphing is a new class or interface, which the programmer is free to integrate in the application at will. Morphing strives for smooth integration in the programming language, all the way down to modular type checking. Thus, reasoning about morphed classes is possible, unlike reasoning about and type checking of generic aspects, which can typically only be done after their application to a specific code base. We thus view morphing as an exciting new direction in programming language research and MJ as an excellent ambassador of the approach.

Acknowledgments

This work was supported by the National Science Foundation under Grant No. CCR-0238289. We thank the Eugene Running Company, Leon Trotsky, and Eugene area pubs for inspiration. Opinions presented in this paper do not necessarily reflect those of the NSF. Or of Leon Trotsky.

References

1. Allen, E., Bannet, J., Cartwright, R.: A first-class approach to genericity. In: Proc. of the 18th annual ACM SIGPLAN conference on Object-oriented Programming, Systems, Languages, and Applications, Anaheim, CA, USA, pp. 96–114. ACM Press, New York (2003)
2. Bachrach, J., Playford, K.: The Java syntactic extender (JSE). In: Proc. of the 16th ACM SIGPLAN conference on Object Oriented Programming, Systems, Languages, and Applications, Tampa Bay, FL, USA, pp. 31–42. ACM Press, New York (2001)
3. Baker, J., Hsieh, W.C.: Maya: multiple-dispatch syntax extension in Java. In: Proc. of the ACM SIGPLAN Conference on Programming Language Design and Implementation, Berlin, Germany, pp. 270–281. ACM Press, New York (2002)
4. Batory, D., Lofaso, B., Smaragdakis, Y.: JTS: tools for implementing domain-specific languages. In: Proc. of the Fifth Intl. Conf. on Software Reuse, Victoria, BC, Canada, pp. 143–153. IEEE Computer Society Press, Los Alamitos (1998)
5. Bracha, G., Cook, W.: Mixin-based inheritance. In: OOPSLA/ECOOP '90: Proc. of the European conference on object-oriented programming on Object Oriented Programming Systems, Languages, and Applications, Ottawa, Canada, pp. 303–311. ACM Press, New York (1990)
6. Burke, B., et al.: JBoss AOP Web site (Accessed April 2007), http://www.jboss.org/products/aop
7. Calcagno, C., Taha, W., Huang, L., Leroy, X.: Implementing multi-stage languages using ASTs, gensym, and reflection. In: Pfenning, F., Smaragdakis, Y. (eds.) GPCE 2003. LNCS, vol. 2830, pp. 57–76. Springer, Heidelberg (2003)
8. Csallner, C., Smaragdakis, Y.: JCrasher: An automatic robustness tester for Java. Software—Practice and Experience 34(11), 1025–1050 (2004)
9. Danforth, S., Forman, I.R.: Reflections on metaclass programming in SOM. In: Proc. of the 9th ACM SIGPLAN conference on Object Oriented Programming, Systems, Languages, and Applications, pp. 440–452. ACM Press, New York (1994)
10. Draheim, D., Lutteroth, C., Weber, G.: A type system for reflective program generators. In: Glück, R., Lowry, M. (eds.) GPCE 2005. LNCS, vol. 3676, pp. 327–341. Springer, Heidelberg (2005)
11. Fähndrich, M., Carbin, M., Larus, J.R.: Reflective program generation with patterns. In: Proc. of the 5th Intl. conference on Generative Programming and Component Engineering, Portland, OR, USA, pp. 275–284. ACM Press, New York (2006)
12. Gamma, E., Helm, R., Johnson, R.: Design Patterns. Elements of Reusable Object-Oriented Software. Addison-Wesley, Reading (1995)
13. Huang, S.S., Zook, D., Smaragdakis, Y.: Statically safe program generation with SafeGen. In: Glück, R., Lowry, M. (eds.) GPCE 2005. LNCS, vol. 3676, pp. 309–326. Springer, Heidelberg (2005)
14. Huang, S.S., Zook, D., Smaragdakis, Y.: Morphing: Safely shaping a class in the image of others. Technical report (2006), http://www.cc.gatech.edu/~ssh/mjfull.pdf
15. Huang, S.S., Zook, D., Smaragdakis, Y.: cJ: Enhancing Java with safe type conditions. In: Proc. of the 6th Intl. Conf. on Aspect-Oriented Software Development, Vancouver, Canada, ACM Press, New York (2007)
16. Igarashi, A., Pierce, B., Wadler, P.: Featherweight Java: A minimal core calculus for Java and GJ. In: Meissner, L. (ed.) Proc. of the 14th ACM SIGPLAN conference on Object-oriented Programming, Systems, Languages, and Applications, vol. 34(10), pp. 132–146 (1999)

17. Igarashi, A., Viroli, M.: Variant parametric types: A flexible subtyping scheme for generics. ACM Trans. Program. Lang. Syst. 28(5), 795–847 (2006)
18. Kiczales, G., des Rivieres, J., Bobrow, D.G.: The Art of the Metaobject Protocol. MIT Press, Cambridge (1991)
19. Kiczales, G., Hilsdale, E., Hugunin, J., Kersten, M., Palm, J., Griswold, W.G.: An overview of AspectJ. In: Knudsen, J.L. (ed.) ECOOP 2001. LNCS, vol. 2072, pp. 327–353. Springer, Heidelberg (2001)
20. Kiczales, G., Lamping, J., Menhdhekar, A., Maeda, C., Lopes, C., Loingtier, J.-M., Irwin, J.: Aspect-oriented programming. In: Aksit, M., Matsuoka, S. (eds.) ECOOP 1997. LNCS, vol. 1241, pp. 220–242. Springer, Heidelberg (1997)
21. Sheard, T., Jones, S.P.: Template meta-programming for Haskell. In: Proc. of the ACM SIGPLAN workshop on Haskell, Pittsburgh, Pennsylvania, pp. 1–16. ACM Press, New York (2002)
22. Smaragdakis, Y., Batory, D.: Implementing layered designs with mixin layers. In: Jul, E. (ed.) ECOOP 1998. LNCS, vol. 1445, pp. 550–570. Springer, Heidelberg (1998)
23. Taha, W., Sheard, T.: Multi-stage programming with explicit annotations. In: Proc. of the 1997 ACM SIGPLAN symposium on Partial Evaluation and semantics-based Program Manipulation, Amsterdam, The Netherlands, pp. 203–217. ACM Press, New York (1997)
24. Torgersen, M., Hansen, C.P., Ernst, E., von der Ahe, P., Bracha, G., Gafter, N.: Adding wildcards to the java programming language. In: Proc. of the 2004 ACM Symposium on Applied Computing, Nicosia, Cyprus, pp. 1289–1296. ACM Press, New York (2004)
25. Visser, E.: Program transformation with Stratego/XT: Rules, strategies, tools, and systems in Stratego/XT 0.9. In: Lengauer, C., Batory, D., Consel, C., Odersky, M. (eds.) Domain-Specific Program Generation. LNCS, vol. 3016, pp. 216–238. Springer, Heidelberg (2004)

A Higher Abstraction Level Using First-Class Inheritance Relations

Marko van Dooren and Eric Steegmans

Department of Computer Science, K.U.Leuven
Marko.vanDooren@cs.kuleuven.be
Eric.Steegmans@cs.kuleuven.be

Abstract. Although classes are a fundamental concept in object-oriented programming, a class itself cannot be built using general purpose classes as building blocks in a practical manner. High-level concepts like associations, bounded values, graph structures, and infrastructure for event mechanisms which form the foundation of a class cannot be reused conveniently as components for classes. As a result, they are implemented over and over again.

We raise the abstraction level of the language with a code inheritance relation for reusing general purpose classes as components for other classes. Features like mass renaming, first-class relations, high-level dependencies, component parameters, and indirect inheritance ensure that maximal reuse can be achieved with minimal effort.

A case study shows a reduction of the code between 21% and 36%, while the closest competitor only reduces the size between 3% and 12%.

1 Introduction

Although increasing the reusability of software is one of the main goals of object-oriented software development, an important group of software elements still cannot be reused in a practical manner. These elements are implemented over and over again, resulting in massive code duplication and all its related problems.

A class often consists of application specific functionality written on top of general purpose characteristics like associations, values lying within bounds, lockable values, graph structures, and infrastructure for event listeners. Most of them are well-known high-level concepts which are easy to use during the design phase. But during the implementation phase, these concepts are transformed into low-level code because current reuse mechanisms cannot cope with such reuse in a convenient manner.

Most reuse mechanisms [4,6,7,9,42,32,35,39] differ little from a regular inheritance relation with subtyping and code inheritance. But the requirements for building a class from components differ in important areas from those for creating a subtype. Reusing a class as a building block for another class requires activities such as removing unwanted methods, wiring method dependencies, and especially renaming methods. But for creating subtypes, the first activity is forbidden, the second one is not required, and the third one is required only infrequently. In addition, methods of different building blocks are usually separated even if they have the same definition, while they are usually merged in case of a multiple/repeated subtyping relation.

E. Ernst (Ed.): ECOOP 2007, LNAI 4609, pp. 425–449, 2007.

Reuse mechanisms that focus on composition [26,36] create only shallow compositions; the composition is just the sum of the parts. But a class is more than the sum of its components; it adds application specific code and gives the components an application specific meaning; it creates an abstract data type.

In this paper, we present an inheritance mechanism with two relations. The subtyping relation is used for traditional subtyping inheritance. The component relation allows general purpose characteristics to be encapsulated in classes and be reused conveniently as configurable building blocks for other classes. We analyze the requirements necessary to realize this kind of reuse, and then introduce the required new features. We introduce renaming parameters for mass renaming, and make the inheritance relation first-class for accessing hidden functionality, treating components as separate objects, and resolving method dependencies using high-level component connections. We evaluate the mechanism in a case study, where it is compared to existing approaches. We also created a formal type system and proved the type soundness of the mechanism, but due to space constraints, the formalization is not presented in this paper.

In Section 2, we analyze the requirements for the reuse mechanism, and discuss existing mechanisms. In Section 3, we present the *component relation*, which is used for code inheritance. In Section 4, we present the impact on the subtyping relation. We evaluate the inheritance mechanism in Section 5 with an example and a case study. We discuss related work and future work in Sections 6 and 7, and conclude in Section 8.

2   Requirements Analysis

In this section, we analyze which features are required in order to conveniently reuse general purpose classes as a building block for other class. We use a simple banking application to illustrate the requirements.

In this paper, we illustrate the features of the inheritance mechanism mostly with components for modeling associations, which use a simple protocol to keep the association consistent. The proposed inheritance mechanism, however, can reuse general abstract data types – which can use arbitrarily complex protocols – as components.

Figure 1 illustrates the application. It contains classes for persons, bank accounts, and bank cards. The rectangles inside a class represent its characteristics. For example, an account has a balance, which is a number that lies between the credit limit and an upper bound. In addition, it has a unidirectional association with its account number, and a bidirectional association with its owner. The associations for the parents and children of a person form a graph offering different traversal strategies. Dependencies between characteristics are represented by dashed arrows. For example, the owner and accounts components need each other's methods to keep the association consistent.

Figure 2 shows a Java implementation of class BankAccount. More advanced functionality like sending events, and constraints on the associations is not shown.

The problem with the implementation is that it consists entirely of functionality that has already been implemented millions of times before. Associations and constrained values are common characteristics, and although the exact names of the methods and the used types may differ, the behavior is always the same.

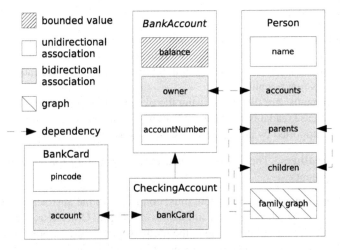

Fig. 1. High-level design of an application

```
class BankAccount {                          private long balance;
  public BankAccount(int number) {           private long upperLimit;
    this.creditLimit = -1000;                private long creditLimit;
    this.upperLimit = 1000000;
    this.accountNumber = number;             public long getBalance() {
  }                                            return balance;
  private Person owner;                      }
  public Person getOwner() {                 public void deposit(long amt) {
    return owner;                              if((amt > 0) &&
  }                                              (balance<=Long.MAX_VALUE-amt)
  public void setOwner(Person owner) {           &&(balance + amt <= upperLimit))
    if(this.owner != owner) {                        balance += amt;
      registerOwner(owner);                  }
      if(owner != null)                      public void withdraw(long amt) {
        owner.registerAccount(this);           if((amt > 0) &&
    }                                            (balance>=Long.MIN_VALUE+amt)
  }                                              &&(balance - amt >= creditLimit))
  protected void registerOwner(Person owner) {      balance -= amt;
    if (this.owner != null)                  }
      this.owner.unregisterAccount();        public long getUpperLimit() {
    this.owner = owner;                        return upperLimit;
  }                                          }
  protected void unregisterOwner() {         public long getCreditLimit() {
    owner = null;                              return creditLimit;
  }                                          }
  private final int accountNumber;         }
  public int getAccountNumber() {
    return accountNumber;
  }
}
```

Fig. 2. The Java version of `BankAccount`

2.1   Requirements

The goal is to construct a reuse mechanism that allows high-level concepts to be encapsulated and reused to build a class. The reusable entity is called a *component*. The mechanism must minimize the effort required to reuse a component, and maximize the reusability of its functionality.

The requirements[1] are illustrated using the example from Figures 1 and 2. They are grouped to increase readability, but some features can be placed in multiple groups. We omit features supported by all mechanisms, such as parameterized types.

Mandatory Features. The following features are mandatory for building a class by reusing components.

1. **ADT Components:** A component must contribute to the abstract data type of the reusing class, which rules out a simple *has-a* relation. Otherwise, the composition is too difficult to use. For example, the methods of `Person` would be spread over several objects at different depths depending on the nesting of the components, and have names that are almost meaningless in the context of the application.
2. **Multiple Reuse:** A class must be able to reuse code from more than one component. For example, class `BankAccount` has three general characteristics.
3. **Repeated Reuse:** Because a class can reuse multiple components of the same kind, it must be able to reuse a component more than once. For example, class `Person` has three bidirectional associations.
4. **Renaming:** Renaming is required to solve name conflicts caused by repeated reuse, give the reused methods a meaningful name in the context of the reusing class, and merge features. Name conflicts will occur because components can be reused more than once by a single class, as for example in class `Person`.

Expressivity Features. These features reduce the amount of work needed to reuse a component. The impact of a feature is shown using big $\mathcal{O}$ notation as *activity* : $\mathcal{O}_{without} \rightarrow \mathcal{O}_{with}$. It shows the amount of work required for an activity without and with that feature when reusing a component. Note that the activities are not independent of each other. $\mathcal{M}$ is the number of methods in the component, $\mathcal{F}$ the number of fields. $\mathcal{M}_s$ and $\mathcal{F}_s$ are the number of methods and fields exported in the interface of the reusing class, $\mathcal{M}_{ns}$ and $\mathcal{F}_{ns}$ the number of non-exported methods and fields. The required work of some features is explained further on in this paper, and is denoted with '...' for now. Note that $\mathcal{F}_s + \mathcal{F}_{ns} = \mathcal{F}, \mathcal{M}_s + \mathcal{M}_{ns} = \mathcal{M}$, and usually $\mathcal{F}_s \leqslant \mathcal{F} \ll \mathcal{M}_s < \mathcal{M}$.

5. **State Reuse:** *Declaring fields:* $\mathcal{O}(\mathcal{F}) \rightarrow \mathcal{O}(1)$ Reusing the state of a component prevents a lot of duplication. For example, the state of an association is almost always a simple reference. It makes no sense to force a developer to separately provide that state every time he uses an association component.
6. **Interface Reuse:** *Constructing interface:* $\mathcal{O}(\mathcal{M}_s + \mathcal{F}_s) \rightarrow \mathcal{O}(1)$ Reusing the component interface prevents duplication of its signatures. Aside from the exact method names and types, which can be configured using renaming and type parameters, the signatures in the reusing class are the same as those in the component interface.

---

[1] Many of the requirements are presented in related work under slightly different names.

7. **Selective Interface Reuse:** *Resolving conflicts:* $\mathcal{O}(\mathcal{M} + \mathcal{F}) \rightarrow \mathcal{O}(\mathcal{M}_s + \mathcal{F}_s)$
A developer will usually expose only a part of the component interface based on the intended use of the reusing class. Exposing its entire interface makes the reusing class harder to understand if the component has a lot of functionality. In addition, it can cause a large amount of name conflicts that must be solved even if the involved methods and fields are not relevant in the context of the reusing class.

8. **Powerful Selection:** *Selecting exported methods/fields:* $\mathcal{O}(\mathcal{M}_s + \mathcal{F}_s) \rightarrow \mathcal{O}(\ldots)$
Being able to select which methods and fields are exported in the interface of the reusing class is not enough. If hiding or selecting is done individually for each method, it requires too much work.

9. **Default Separation:** *Separating components:* $\mathcal{O}(\mathcal{M}_{ns} + \mathcal{F}_{ns}) \rightarrow \mathcal{O}(1)$ By default, components – and thus their methods and instance variables – must be separated, since that is how they are typically used. For example, the methods and fields of the association components of `Person` must be kept separate. Separating all methods manually is error-prone and requires separation of non-selected methods.

10. **Mass Renaming:** *Renaming:* $\mathcal{O}(\mathcal{M}_s + \mathcal{F}_s) \rightarrow \mathcal{O}(\ldots)$ Many components have patterns in the names of their methods. For example, the methods for associations are typically named `getX`, `setX`, `isValidX`, and so on. If such a pattern can be exploited, all of its occurrences can be replaced with a single declaration.

11. **High-level Dependencies:** *Resolving method dependencies:* $\mathcal{O}(\mathcal{D}_\mathcal{M}) \rightarrow \mathcal{O}(\ldots)$
Some components depend on methods of other components. For example, a component for bidirectional associations needs the method of the other end of the association to maintain consistency, but it does not know their final names. Resolving these dependencies individually is tedious and error-prone. In addition, if additional dependencies are added between two components, all classes that reuse them must add additional wiring code. By directly connecting entire components to each other, all dependencies between them are resolved at once, and additional dependencies require no additional wiring code. In the formula, $\mathcal{D}_\mathcal{M}$ is the number of method dependencies of the reused component.

Completeness Features. The following features increase the amount of functionality of a component that can be reused.

12. **Reuse of Hidden Functionality:** Methods that are not exposed in the interface of the reusing class – to prevent conflicts and interface bloat – may still be valuable to clients. They should still be reusable, unless the developer explicitly forbids clients to access them. Examples are advanced iteration methods for associations.

13. **Reuse of Component Type:** If an object cannot somehow be used as if it were of the type of one of its components, certain methods cannot be reused. For example, class `BoundedValue` has a method to transfer the remaining value to another `BoundedValue`. If that method cannot be used to transfer the remaining money from one bank account to another, it must be duplicated even though `BankAccount` offers all required methods and fields. But if the bounded value component of `BankAccount` can be used as a real `BoundedValue`, the transfer method can be reused.

Methodological Features. The following features prevent errors and confusion.

14. **Reuse Without Subtyping:** Mandatory subtyping causes confusion in case of repeated reuse, and it does not make sense for most components. For example, class BankAccount is no bi/uni-directional association, or a bounded value. Similarly, class Person is not three times a bidirectional association.
15. **No Surprises:** The mechanism must never automatically resolve a name conflict unless one of the candidates overrides all others. Otherwise, methods are overridden based only on the form of their signature, causing unexpected behavior at run-time [37]. A good reuse mechanism exposes such errors, instead of hiding them.

Applicability Features. The last set of features concerns the applicability of the reuse mechanism. They allow the reuse of a component even if it was not anticipated.

16. **No Separate Concept:** If a developer needs to reuse a class as a component, he must be allowed to do so, even if such reuse was not anticipated. In addition, it must be possible to instantiate non-abstract components. For example, there is no reason to complicate the creation of an object that represents a bounded value. If components and classes are the same, they are not limited to a single kind of reuse.
17. **Override State:** If the state of a component is not appropriate for the reusing class, e.g. because it can be computed, it must be possible to override the state. Otherwise, that class cannot reuse the component.
18. **Merge State:** The state of components can overlap in the context of the reusing class. But if the overlapping parts cannot be merged, the components cannot be reused. For example, if a class has two values lying within the same limits, and there is no specific component offering such behavior, it must be possible to use two BoundedValue components and merge their upper and lower limits.

2.2   Existing Reuse Mechanisms

Figure 3 shows the features that are supported by different reuse mechanisms. For languages with a separate code inheritance relation, we used that relation in the table. For the other languages, the standard inheritance relation is used. The mechanisms are discussed in more detail in the related work in Section 6.

For delegation, the major problem is that the interface of a component cannot be reused. Every method must be redefined in the reusing class to invoke the corresponding method on the delegatee. The case study shows that this is a big disadvantage. Whether or not state can be overridden or merged depends on the programming language.

The inheritance techniques – with or without subtyping – have poor support for the required features, and very poor support for the expressivity and completeness features. Only two mechanisms support the minimal requirements, and certain important expressivity and completeness features are not supported by any of them. In the columns of features that save of lot of work, there is a big gaping hole.

Our inheritance mechanism supports all the features, and makes the implementation of the *entire* application as big as the traditional implementation of BankAccount.

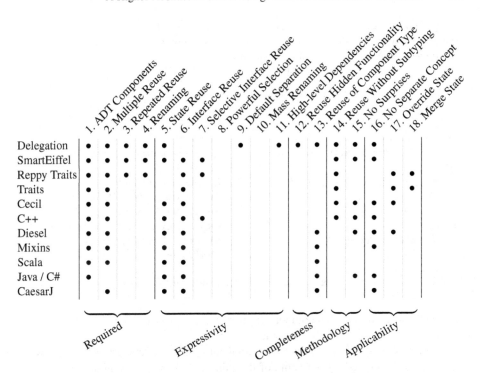

Fig. 3. Feature matrix for different code reuse mechanisms

3   The Component Relation

The component relation is a code inheritance relation for easily reusing existing components in a new class. To simplify the customization of general components for use in a class, the relation offers a number of new features which are explained further on in this section. We introduce renaming parameters for mass renaming the methods of the component. We then turn the component relation into a first-class relation. The relation can be given a name, which can be used to access non-selected functionality, use components as separate objects, and resolve dependencies on a high level. These features allow programmers to work easily with components on a high level of abstraction instead of implementing them with low-level code.

Using the component relation, the banking application of Figure 1 can be implemented by using a component relation for each component. This is illustrated in Figure 4 for the class of bank accounts. The component relations state that the class of bank accounts has a component named `owner` that behaves like a bidirectional association with multiplicity 1, a component named `balance` that behaves like a bounded value, and a component named `accountNumber` that behaves like a unidirectional association. The assignments are used for renaming, and in this case rename many methods at once by assigning values to renaming parameters. The `owner` component is connected to the component at the other end of the bidirectional association by

component BidiAssociation-1-Side<Account,Person> owner (accounts) [X=Owner]
component BoundedValue<long> balance [X=Balance,LOW=LowerLimit,HI=UpperLimit];
component UniAssociation-1<int> accountNumber
      [X=AccountNumber, **export private** {setAccountNumber}]

Fig. 4. The component relations of BankAccount

ComponentClause:
  AccessMod? **component** *Type Config?*
Config:
  Name? CompParams? ConfigBlock?
Name:
  AccessMod? Identifier
CompParams:
  "("Identifier (, Identifier) ")"*

ConfigBlock:
  "[" ConfigClause (, ConfigClause) "]"*
ConfigClause:
  Identifier = Identifier?
  override *"{" IdentifierList "}"*
  undefine *"{" IdentifierList "}"*
  export *AccessMod "{" IdentifierList "}"*
  direct *"{" IdentifierList "}"*
  indirect *"{" IdentifierList "}"*

Fig. 5. Grammar for component relations

passing the name of the other component (accounts) to the relation. Finally, the setter method for the account number is made private.

Figure 5 shows the syntax of the component relation. It consists of the keyword component followed by the name of the inherited class, including any generic parameters. There can optionally be a name, component parameters, and a configuration block. The access modifier of the relation determines if the type of the component is visible to the client, which provides valuable information about its behavior. The access modifier of the name determines if he can use the name of a visible component relation to access it as a separate object or resolve dependencies. The configuration block is similar to that of Eiffel. The assignment is used for renaming which is further explained in Section 3.2, override if a feature[2] is overridden, undefine to undefine a feature in case features are merged, and export for changing the visibility of a feature. The inheritance name, component parameters, and direct and indirect clauses are further discussed in Section 3.3.

3.1 General Semantics

If class A has a component relation with class B, A inherits the features of B, but not its type. For example, the class of bank accounts inherits all features of a bounded value, but a bank account is no bounded value. Despite the absence of subtyping, however, both methods and instance variables[3] must conform to all features they override, because the methods of the inherited class expect them to behave according to their original signatures and contracts.

If a feature is inherited via different inheritance paths, a choice must be made to decide if the feature is inherited once, or multiple times. The default policy for features

---

[2] The features of a class are its instance variables and methods.

[3] Instance variables are properties that can be overridden and merged.

inherited via a component relation is duplication because, generally, the components do not overlap. This means that if a feature is inherited via a component relation and again via another inheritance relation, there is a conflict, even if the definitions are the same. This conflict must be resolved explicitly, e.g. via merging or renaming. To avoid an explosion of the number of renaming clauses, we introduce *renaming parameters* in Section 3.2 and *indirect inheritance* in Section 3.3.

As in SmartEiffel, binding of features in inherited methods is done within the inheritance relation through which they are inherited. This is required to allow separation of the components. For example, `CheckingAccount` inherits the getter method of `BidiAssociation-1-Side` twice: once for the association with the owner, and once for the association with the bank card. Both getters must of course use the instance variable of their own component.

3.2 Renaming Parameters

Without intervention, using duplication as the default for the component relation would force a developer to explicitly rename almost every method of the component. The case study in Section 5 shows that renaming is a significant problem. We introduce a *lightweight macro system* to minimize the effort of renaming features.

The names in the features of a component often exhibit patterns. For example, the names of the methods of the N side of an association are `getX`, `addX`, `removeX`, `replaceX`, `containsX`, and so on. To avoid these patterns from getting lost in the implementation, we introduce *renaming parameters*. A renaming parameter can be written in the names of non-private features, and allows an inheriting class to rename all features that use the parameter with a single renaming declaration.

A renaming parameter is a parameter of a class and is written between square brackets. It can be given a default value; otherwise its name serves as the default value. The parameter can be used in feature names by writing its name between % characters. An inheriting class can assign a value to the parameter in the configuration block of the inheritance relation. The value of the parameter can be any string that is valid for all feature names containing the parameter – which are all visible to the inheriting class.

Figure 6 illustrates the use of renaming parameters. Parameter X is used as the name of the other end of the association and is initialized to the empty string. Parameter XS represents the plural of X and by default equals the value of X appended with an 's'. For the `children` component of `Person` both parameters are assigned because the default value of XS is not appropriate.

We can now determine the amount of work required for renaming. $\mathcal{P}_s$ is the number of renaming parameters in the selected features. $\mathcal{M}_{s,np}$ and $\mathcal{F}_{s,np}$ are the number of selected methods and fields without renaming parameters. The impact of renaming parameters is $\mathcal{O}(\mathcal{M}_s + \mathcal{F}_s) \rightarrow \mathcal{O}(\mathcal{P}_s + \mathcal{M}_{s,np} + \mathcal{F}_{s,np})$.

More details about renaming parameters can be found in the technical report [46].

3.3 First-Class Component Relations

In this section, we introduce first-class component relations to solve a number of problems. We use them to connect components without resolving every individual depen-

```
class BidiAssociation-N-Side <FROM,TO> ...  [X=,XS=%X%s] {
    Set<TO> get %XS% {...}
    void add %X% (TO x) {...}
    void remove %X% (TO x) {...}
    void replace %X% (TO x, TO y) {...}
    ...
}

class Person
    component BidiAssociation-N-Side<Person, BankAccount> ...  [X=Account]
    component BidiAssociation-N-Side<Person, Person> ...  [X=Parent]
    component BidiAssociation-N-Side<Person, Person> ...  [X=Child,XS=Children]
    {...}
```

Fig. 6. Using renaming parameters

```
class BankAccount
    component BidiAssociation-1-Side<BankAccount, Person> owner ...
    ...
class Person
    component BidiAssociation-N-Side<Person, BankAccount> accounts ...
    ...
```

Fig. 7. First-class component relations

dency, to access functionality that is not exposed in the interface of the reusing class, and to use components as if they were separate objects.

A component relation can have a name, which typically represents the role of the component in the reusing class. Figure 7 illustrates this for classes BankAccount and Person. The association components of BankAccount and Person are named owner and accounts.

Direct and Indirect Inheritance. As presented in Section 2, selective reuse of the interface of a component is required for two reasons.

First, it prevents interface bloat in the reusing class. Take for example the association components. In order to maximize code reuse, it is best to put many features in the association classes. Examples include applying some action to all referenced elements, a universal and an existential quantifier, accumulation, and validation. But for an inheriting class, this means that either its interface gets bloated, or its developer must do a lot of work to hide the functionality, preventing reuse.

Second, because not all method and field names use renaming parameters, there are still many name conflicts. For example, features like equals and hashCode in the top-level class cause conflicts in every component relation. But if these features are not interesting in the inheriting class, which is usually the case, the developer should not have to resolve their conflicts.

To solve both problems, we make a distinction between *directly* and *indirectly* inherited features. A directly inherited feature is present in the interface of the inheriting class, while an indirectly inherited feature is not, and thus cannot cause a conflict.

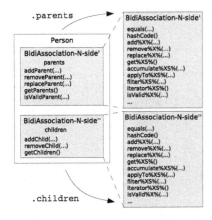

Person sandra = ... ;
Person bruno = ... ;
Person kato = ... ;

// two identical method calls
sandra .children.add (kato);
sandra .addChild (kato);

bruno.addChild(kato);
kato.parents.applyTo(. . .);

Fig. 8. Indirect Inheritance   **Fig. 9.** Using indirectly inherited features

An indirectly inherited feature, however, *can still be accessed* if the component relation has been given a name. The feature can then be invoked as `myObject.inheritanceName.feature` using its original name. It is *as if* the component is an object referenced by a field in the reusing class. This way, the client resolves the conflict by using the name of the component relation. It is, of course, the responsibility of the programmer to give the reusing class a meaningful interface. Using inheritance names to access features must not be the standard way of using a class.

Figures 8 and 9 illustrate this for class `Person`. For the `children` component, only the `add`, `remove`, and `get` methods are inherited directly. The `parents` component additionally inherits the `replace` and `isValid` methods. The other methods must be invoked indirectly via the name of the inheritance relation. Note that the invocations of `children.add` and `addChild` in Figure 9 are identical even if the method has been overridden in `Person`.

The inheriting class must specify which features are inherited directly. This is done in the configuration block either by including them with a `direct` declaration, or by renaming or overriding them. All other features are inherited indirectly.

To facilitate selecting directly inherited features, the features of a class can be put in groups as in Eiffel, Smalltalk, and C#. This way, inheriting classes can directly inherit an entire group of methods with little effort. For example, the basic functionality of a class can be put in one group while more advanced functionality can be put in others. To select which features or groups are inherited directly, the programmer can use `direct` and `indirect` declarations in the configuration block of the component relation. A feature is inherited directly if it is listed in a `direct` declaration, and indirectly if it is listed in an `indirect` declaration. If a feature is not listed in such a clause, it is inherited directly if they are part of a group that is listed in a `direct` declaration, and indirectly if its are part of a group that is listed in an `indirect` declaration. Every component relation implicitly has a `direct` declaration for the group named `default`. This is illustrated in Figure 10. The mechanism can be made more flexible, but that is not in the scope of this paper.

```
class BidiAssociation-N-Side<FROM,TO> ... [X,XS=%X%s]
    boolean equals(Object other) {...}
    int hashCode() {...}
    group default {
        Set<TO> get%XS% {...}
        void add%X%(TO x) {...}
        void remove%X%(TO x) {...}
        void replace%X%(TO x, TO y) {...}
    }
    group iteration {
        filter%XS%(...) {...}
        applyTo%XS%(Command<TO>) {...}
        ...
    }
}

class Person
    component BidiAssociation-N-Side<Person,Person> children (parents)
            [X=Child,XS=Children, indirect{replaceChild}]
    component BidiAssociation-N-Side<Person,Person> parents (children)
            [X=Parent, direct{isValidParent}]
    ...
```

Fig. 10. Selecting directly inherited features

The impact of indirect inheritance is $\mathcal{O}(\mathcal{M}_s + \mathcal{F}_s) \rightarrow \mathcal{O}(\mathcal{G}_s + \mathcal{M}_{s,ng} + \mathcal{M}_{ns,g} + \mathcal{F}_{s,ng} + \mathcal{F}_{ns,g})$ with $\mathcal{G}_s$ the number of selected groups, $\mathcal{M}_{s,ng}$ and $\mathcal{F}_{s,ng}$ the selected methods and fields not in such a group, and $\mathcal{M}_{ns,g}$ and $\mathcal{F}_{ns,g}$ the unwanted methods and fields in the selected groups.

Component References. Using indirect inheritance, the features of a component can be accessed *as if* the component were an object referenced by an immutable[4] instance variable. To allow even more reuse, we allow the name of a component relation to be *actually* used as a reference to the subobject representing that component, similar to casts in C++ [39]. Because we already require conformance between the actual component and the inherited class, type-safety is not endangered.

Component references make it possible to reuse methods of which a formal parameters has a type that is used as a component. For example, the class representing bounded values has methods to compare it with another bounded value, to transfer the remaining value to another bound value. Another example is the `equals` method for an association, which takes a similar association as its argument, to verify if two association reference the same elements. Without component references, these features cannot be reused if the class is used as a component for another class because there is no subtyping relation between the reusing class and the component.

Figure 11 shows how such methods can be reused using component references. The methods cannot take a `Person` or `BankAccount` as an argument, but by using the names of the component relations, the components can be passed to the method.

---

[4] Only the reference itself is immutable, the referenced object can still be modified.

```
boolean eq = sandra.children.equals( bruno.children );
yourAccount.balance.transferRemainingValueTo( myAccount.balance );
```

Fig. 11. Using component references

Being able to use component references has an influence on how `this` is treated in the context of a component relation. When a class A is reused through a component relation by class B, its `this` reference acts as if it were substituted by `this.inheritanceName`. Otherwise, `this` would have type A in the context of type B, which is not type-safe since B is not a subtype of A.

Consequently, a component cannot use the `this` reference to obtain a reference to the object of the reusing class because that is a reference to the subobject for that component. For example, the components for bidirectional associations need an object of type FROM – a generic parameter – to pass it to the other end of the association. Various techniques can be used to obtain that reference, e.g. storing it explicitly in a field, self types as used in Eiffel, or a variant of the self types in Scala. More details on techniques to obtain a reference to the object of the reusing class can be found in the technical report [46].

Dependency Resolution. Some components depend on methods of other components. Examples are the methods to set up and break down bidirectional associations, as shown in Figure 12. The `setOwner` method of `BankAccount` must know which `register` method to invoke on the `Person` to keep the association consistent. Similar dependencies exist for the other methods. Because `Person` has multiple associations, these dependencies cannot be resolved automatically. The developer of `BankAccount` must connect these methods to the appropriate methods in `Person`. With existing inheritance mechanisms, this must be done with wiring code for each individual method dependency.

To resolve these dependencies more elegantly, we use the names of the component relations. Figure 13 illustrates the approach. The `owner` component of `BankAccount` and the `accounts` component of `Person` are connected by resolving a single high-level dependency on each side.

To specify high-level dependencies, a class can declare formal *component parameters* . They are declared after the generic parameters of a class between parentheses, and have the form $T \rightarrow C$ cparam. In this declaration, $T \rightarrow C$ is a constraint on the

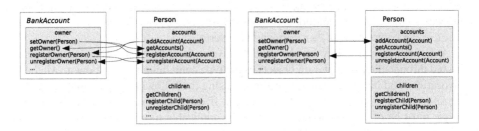

Fig. 12. Low-level dependencies   **Fig. 13.** High-level dependencies

class BidiAssociation-1-Side<FROM,TO> (TO → BidiAssociation<TO,FROM> otherEnd)
    subtype BidiAssociation<FROM,TO> (otherEnd){

  private TO other;
  public void setX(TO other) {
    . . .
    other@otherEnd.register *(expression for the object on this side of the association)*;
    . . .
  }
  protected void register(TO other) {. . . }
  . . .
}

Fig. 14. Component parameters

  class BankAccount
    component BidiAssociation-1-Side<BankAccount,Person> owner   (accounts) . . .
    . . .

  class Person
    component BidiAssociation-N-Side<Person,BankAccount> accounts (owner) . . .
    . . .

Fig. 15. Implementing high-level dependency resolution

component relation passed through the parameter. T is the type *containing* the relation, and C is the target type *of* the relation. Finally, cparam is the name of the parameter.

Figure 14 illustrates the declaration of a component parameters. The formal parameter expects the name of a relation that *a)* is a relation of the class at the other side of the association (TO), and *b)* is a BidiAssociation representing an association in the opposite direction (from TO to FROM). Figure 15 illustrates how two association components are connected to each other. If we substitute the generic parameters, we see that component relation owner requires the name of a component relation with type BidiAssociation<Person, BankAccount> that is contained in Person. Since the accounts component of Person satisfies these constraints, we can connect the owner component to the accounts component. Similarly, the owner component satisfies the constraints of the accounts component. Consequently, the owner component of BankAccount can be connected to the accounts component of Person, and vice versa.

A component parameter can be used to invoke features of the actual component passed through the parameter on objects of the type containing the component. Method invocations and field accesses are performed using the following expressions: expr@ cparam.m(args) and expr@cparam.f. If cparam has T → C as constraint, expr must be of type T, and m or f must be applicable to type C. In the context of a component relation where actual component parameter aparam is used, cparam is replaced with aparam. As a result, method aparam.m(args) or field access aparam.f are invoked on the result of expr. Note that any renaming or overriding of these features in the run-time type of expr is taken into account. We use a symbol different from the dot to emphasize the difference with a regular invocation. In addition, this avoids confusion about the meaning of expr.cparam if a feature with name cparam is added to T.

The setX method in Figure 14 shows how the component parameter is used to invoke methods. The invocation of register is applied to the otherEnd component of other. The method that will be invoked, is the register method of the actual component relation passed through the parameter, which may be overridden or renamed in the actual class TO. In the example of Figure 15, the setOwner method inherited by BankAccount will invoke the registerAccount method inherited by Person.

This approach has a number of advantages. First, it saves a lot of work by replacing the individual dependencies with a smaller number of high-level dependencies. The impact is $\mathcal{O}(\mathcal{D}_\mathcal{M}) \rightarrow \mathcal{O}(\mathcal{D}_\mathcal{C})$ with $\mathcal{D}_\mathcal{C}$ the number of component dependencies and $\mathcal{D}_\mathcal{C} \leqslant \mathcal{D}_\mathcal{M}$. Second, it ensures that the required methods are provided by a single component and not by methods of different components, which is crucial in this example. Third, if additional dependencies are added between two types of components, the reusing classes need no modifications. For example, we can add an isSibling method to BidiAssociation to check if some object is its sibling. This method would invoke the contains method on the other end of the association, introducing another dependency. Inheriting classes, however, do not need to be modified.

Visibility. By default, component relations are public because they are typically used for the characteristics of a class. A public client can see their name, type, and configuration. If a programmer knows the behavior of class C, he also knows the behavior of a component of type C. But if the relation is not visible, he must study the contracts of the inherited features again in order to understand their behavior. If the component relation is used for traditional code inheritance, for example to implement a Stack using an Array, it should be hidden from the client.

4 The Subtyping Relation

In this section, we briefly explain the most important differences with the subtyping relation of SmartEiffel. The details can be found in the technical report [46].

Figure 16 shows the syntax of the subtyping relation. It consists of the keyword subtype followed by the name of the super type, including any generic parameters. There can optionally be a name for the relation, and a configuration block. The component parameters are used to transfer compent parameters to the superclass, similar to generic parameters. To ensure consistency, component parameters passed to the same class via different subtyping relations must be identical. This is similar to the rule for generic parameters in Java and SmartEiffel.

Because the subtyping relation is no longer used for pure code reuse, it can be simplified. Duplication is forbidden since it is inappropriate for subtyping, avoiding confusion for diamond inheritance. In addition, the rule-of-dominance (as in C++ [39]) is used to avoid needless undefine clauses to select a version of a method when there is a single most specific version.

SubtypeClause:
    subtype *Type Identifier? CompParams? ConfigBlock?*

Fig. 16. Grammar for the subtyping relation

4.1 Overriding and Merging Components

For the same reasons why overriding and merging of state is required to ensure that a component can always be reused, as discussed in Section 2, it must also be possible to override and merge component relations. Similar to overriding and merging methods, either an overriding component must be defined, or an existing one must be selected.

In both cases, the overriding or selected component must satisfy two rules. First, standard subtyping conformance is required. The overriding component must not only be a subtype of the target class of the component relation, but also of all overridden components. Second, conformance of the component interface is required. This means that every feature that is inherited directly in an overridden component relation must be inherited directly in the overriding component relation. In addition, corresponding features must be given the same name.

4.2 Reducing Hierarchy Dependencies

In [35], it is argued that `super` calls in languages with multiple inheritance increase the dependency of code on the class hierarchy. In such languages, multiple methods with the same name can be inherited by a class, so in order to disambiguate super calls to such methods, they must be qualified with the name of the direct super class containing the method that must be invoked. Examples of languages using this approach are C++, Cecil, Eiffel, and SmartEiffel. This problem does not occur with inheritance mechanisms that linearize the class hierarchy, or in the prototype-based language Self [8], where super calls can be directed to a named parent slot.

These dependencies can be removed by also giving a name to a subtyping relation. It is possible to qualify a super call using the name of that inheritance relation instead of the name of the super class. Consequently, the call remains valid if the actual super class for that relation is changed, as long as an appropriate method is available in the new super class. The name of a subtyping relation is private since only the inheriting class can invoke super calls.

Technically, reuse variables in Timor also reduce this dependency, but in their paper [19], the authors do not present this insight.

5 Evaluation

In this section, we evaluate the complexity and the effectiveness of the proposed inheritance mechanism.

5.1 Complexity

Even though our inheritance mechanism introduces a number of new features, it is still easy to use, and it reduces overall complexity. Programmers already deal with high-level characteristics, dependencies, and name patterns, but they must encode them using complicated low-level code instead of writing simple high-level code. The features introduced in this paper allow programmers to easily reuse, configure, and connect components to build a class. With the creation of a graphical editor, this can even be done by simply drawing a diagram similar to Figure 1. Components can be dropped on classes, configured by filling in the type and name patterns, and connected to each other.

As an additional advantage, the subtyping inheritance relation can be simplified as it is no longer used just for code reuse. More specifically, forbidding duplication prevents confusion in case of diamond inheritance, and the rule-of-dominance resolves unnecessary conflicts that must otherwise be resolved by the programmer.

5.2   The Banking Application

Figure 17 shows the *entire* implementation of Figure 1. The names of the association classes are abbreviated for reasons of space. The implementation is done almost completely by configuring existing components. Only the constructors are actually implemented. This is an important result, because it means that this implementation can be done by drawing a class diagram, and filling in the parameters. Although the example does not contain any application specific behavior, it illustrates what can be achieved with our approach. A realistic case study is presented further on.

In addition, the high-level concepts of the diagram cannot get lost because they are directly present in the code. In current CASE tools, such concepts can get lost because they are translated into low-level code, leading to synchronization problems.

5.3   Case Study

We compared our inheritance mechanism with manual delegation, and the inheritance mechanisms of Java, SmartEiffel, and Reppy traits, which support repeated inheritance [32], by comparing their impact on the size of an application. We used *Jnome* [43], our metamodel for Java, and *Chameleon* [43], our framework for metamodels of programming languages. Together they contain 9763 lines of Java code. We must note that the reduction in code size is *not* the same as the reduction in complexity. Renaming clauses and manual delegation are much simpler than the reused methods.

We modified the Java programs using our inheritance mechanism[5], and then *calculated* the size for the other techniques based on the overhead of renaming, dependency resolution, encapsulation of state, and manual delegation for each technique. Note that *only the inheritance relations and wiring code* differ for the participating mechanisms. All other code is identical, so all effects are due to differences in the reuse mechanisms.

To study the impact of the size and the nature of extensions of the components, we repeated the experiment for two kinds of extensions. In the first extension, all associations send events when they are modified. This extension is application independent because managing the listeners and invoking `notify` is always the same. In the second

---

[5] We must note that the resulting code does not currently compile because our compiler is not yet complete.

```
class BankAccount
  component BoundedValue<long> balance
              [Value=Balance, Lower=Credit, increaseBalance=deposit,
              decreaseBalance=withdraw,
              export private {setUpperLimit,setLowerLimit,setBalance}]
  component Bidi-1-Side<BankAccount,Person> owner (accounts) [X=Owner]
  component Uni-1<int> accountNumber
              [X=AccountNumber, export private {setAccountNumber}]
{
  public BankAccount(int accountID) {
    balance.super(0,-1000,1000000);
    accountNumber.super(accountID);
  }
}


class CheckingAccount
  subtype BankAccount
  component Bidi-1-Side<CheckingAccount, BankCard> bankCard (account) [X=BankCard]
{
  public BankAccount(int number) {
    super(number);
  }
}


class Person
  component Bidi-N-Side<Person,BankAccount> accounts (owner) [X=Accounts]
  component Bidi-N-Side<Person,Person> parents (children) [X=Parents]
  component Bidi-N-Side<Person,Person> children (parents) [X=Children]
  component Uni-1<String> [X=Name]
  component Graph<Person> family (parents,children)
{
  public Person(String name, Person mother, Person father) {
    setName(name);
    addParent(mother);
    addParent(father);
  }
}


class BankCard
  component Bidi-1-Side<BankCard,CheckingAccount> account (bankCard) [X=Account]
  component Uni-1<int> [X=PinCode]
{}
```

Fig. 17. Implementation of the banking application of Figure 1

extension, which builds on the first one, the associations also check the validity of the elements. For this extension, the validity condition is application specific and must be overridden, while other supporting code can be reused.

T: Reppy Traits   **J**: Java   **E**: SmartEiffel   **D**: Delegation   **C**: Components

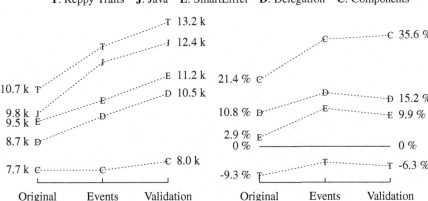

Fig. 18. Lines of Code   **Fig. 19.** Reduction Compared to Java

Figure 18 shows the code size for the different techniques and code bases. Figure 19 shows the reduction in size compared to Java. Almost all of the reduction is obtained in the domain model, which takes up 70% of the software. The other 30% consists of input and output algorithms.

Both figures clearly show that our inheritance mechanism results in a much bigger reduction than the other mechanisms. The difference is caused by the additional overhead mentioned above. Manual delegation and code inheritance in SmartEiffel reduce the size much less than our mechanism, but are still a big improvement over the Java version. Using Reppy traits, however, the code size even increases. The additional getter and setter methods – traits cannot contain state – cause so much additional overhead that the application becomes even bigger than the original Java application.

An important result is the impact of adding functionality that is not overridden in the application. Adding support for sending events requires *no modification* of the version using our inheritance mechanism. The renaming parameters, component parameters, and indirect inheritance avoid the need for additional code if all methods and variables added to the `default` group contain existing renaming parameters. With the other techniques, code must be added to the applications for renaming clauses, manual delegations, dependency methods, or state encapsulation. The more functionality is offered by the component, the more modifications are required by other techniques. This is a very important practical result. It shows that the developer of a component can usually add functionality without breaking client code if it is not added to the `default` group or if it uses renaming parameters. In addition, he can now provide lots of functionality without putting a huge burden on his clients.

Another important result shows up if validation is added to the associations, and specific validation rules are implemented in the applications. The version using our inheritance mechanism is the only one in which less code must be added than in the Java version, as shown by the gradients in the right part of Figure 19. This means that it is still beneficial to reuse small components, or small parts of bigger components, using our inheritance mechanism. Using the other techniques, the additional overhead makes reuse unattractive in these scenarios.

6   Related Work

In [28], Odersky and Zenger identify three scalable component abstractions for removing hard references from components to increase their reusability: *abstract type members*, *selftype annotations*, and *modular mixin composition*. Abstract type members and selftypes specify the required services of a component, and mixins perform the composition. But while these abstractions are scalable with respect to the size of the components, they are not scalable in the way components are used. The problem is that both selftypes, and mixins as used in Scala, prohibit any composition involving multiple components of the same kind, or components containing features with the same name. Despite the claim that these abstractions can lift an arbitrary assembly of static program parts to a component system, they already fail for our simple example application, which is little more than an assembly of four kinds of static program parts. The authors argue that nesting of classes is essential because otherwise, the amount of wiring would become substantial. This contradicts our findings. In this paper, we built an application using components without using nested classes. So while nested classes provide certain benefits, they are not a requirement for component composition.

In [44], we introduced anchored exception declarations to remove hard references from the exceptional specification of a component. They allow the exceptional specification of a method to be declared relative to other methods. This increases both the adaptability and reusability of code using checked exceptions. In the context of this paper, they allow a component to specify its exceptional behavior in terms of the exceptional behavior of its dependencies. As a result, the compiler can determine more precisely which exceptions can be thrown for a particular composition.

In [3], Bierman and Wren present a language construct for first-class full-blown relationships. A similar construct is advocated by Rumbaugh in [33]. With our inheritance mechanism, it can be replaced by a library of classes. In this paper, we used relationships without attributes, but classes for full-blown relationships can be built on top of them. An example implementation is given in the technical report [46]. Another language construct that can be replaced by a class are C# events [13].

In [31], Pearce and Noble provide support for relationships using AspectJ [20]. The authors offer a library of relationship aspects, similar to our association components, which are inserted into the application using a point-cut for each relationship in the model. Support for static relationships – relationships that are part of the participating classes – is limited because name conflict for the introduced methods and fields cannot be resolved. As such, AspectJ cannot be used to create and reuse abstract data type components. An advantage of the approach is that components can be added externally to existing classes, but using a form of higher order hierarchies as in [29,30,14,27,28], this can also be achieved with an object-oriented approach.

In the 1997 version of Eiffel [25], the inheritance relation is used both for subtyping and code inheritance. It is possible to duplicate features when inheriting more than once from the same class, which is confusing for subtyping. The resulting diamond problem for repeated inheritance is often considered to make the language more difficult [4,34]. In addition, a subclass can use covariant argument types for a method, or even remove features, which makes a whole program analysis required to ensure type safety.

In SmartEiffel 2.2 [9] and the new Eiffel specification [42], the inheritance mechanism has been extended with non-conforming inheritance. In SmartEiffel 2.2, duplication of features and narrowing their visibility is no longer permitted. Using covariant argument types, however, remains possible. SmartEiffel ensures type-safety by type-checking the code of an inserted class in the context of the inheriting class, but this violates the modularity principle. Because sharing is the default policy for the *insert* relation, accidental merging of components is possible.

Timor [19] and Sather [40] separate types and classes, and the relations between them. Types can inherit from multiple other types. Classes can *include* other classes for code inheritance, and they can implement types. Timor further uses named subtyping relations [19] to support repeated inheritance. We think it is very confusing for an object to be 1.9 times a `CassettePlayer`, as in their example. They also use the inheritance names to disambiguate conflicting names, but for reusing components this approach is not practical. A severe problem with their mechanism is that name conflicts are automatically resolved by removing direct access to the involved methods. As a result, adding a subtyping relation, or even adding a method to an inherited type can break existing clients without even a warning because conflicts can be introduced. Timor also has support for *reuse variables*. Features of the classes referenced by such variables are inherited if they are needed for the types implemented by the class. If they are not inherited, however, they are not available to clients since they are not part of the types via which the class can be used. The mechanism can be seen as delegation-by-value. Reuse variables also reduce the dependency of the implementation of a class on its hierarchy, but the authors do not present this insight.

Traits [35] not only use a separate relation for code inheritance, but also a separate concept – a *trait* – for a set of methods that can be reused via code inheritance. Unlike traits, we do not have a separate concept to represent a component, it is just a class. If the component relation could only be used with special building blocks, unanticipated reuse would be impossible. On top of that, programmers must deal with an extra concept which is just a degenerate abstract class. Another motivation for our choice is the possibility to instantiate components. We see no reason to forbid a programmer to create an object that represents a bounded value. In addition, classification of characteristics is necessary. To reuse almost any kind of association, it is necessary to create a hierarchy of association classes. The relation between classes capturing choices like mutability and arity, and the class `Association` is a subtyping relation, not just a code inheritance relation. Methods inherited via traits automatically override methods inherited from classes although there is no relation between them. This form of structural subtyping can lead to bugs that are hard to find. In addition, dependencies of traits must be resolved individually, and repeated trait-inheritance is not possible. As such, traits allow far less code reuse than our inheritance mechanism.

In [32], Reppy and Turon present trait-based metaprogramming. They add renaming and hiding to traits to allow using a trait more than once in a class. Similar to SmartEiffel, name conflicts and dependencies must be resolved one at a time. But because traits cannot contain state, the overhead is larger than in SmartEiffel.

Languages like CLOS [12], most mixin-based [4] languages like Scala [28], and many others use linearized multiple inheritance. The linearization of the class hierarchy, however, complicates its use [37,8,35]. It is not possible to determine the meaning of a single inheritance relation of a class without looking at the others because some of its methods may be overridden by methods of other classes that happen to have the same name. This makes it easy for methods to be overridden by accident [37]. Repeated inheritance, which is required for composition of classes is impossible in these languages. The abstract super class of a mixin, however, allows for reusable refinements, which cannot easily be created using our approach.

Cecil [6] supports multiple inheritance. Repeated inheritance, however, is forbidden, and name conflicts result in compilation errors. The language uses properties for instance variables, making it possible to override them. Subtyping and code inheritance relations can be used both separately or combined.

In Self [8], inheritance relations are given a priority. For relations with identical priorities, name conflicts result in an error. For relations with different priorities, conflicts are resolved automatically by inheriting the feature of the relation with the highest priority. The *Sender Path Tiebreaker Rule* resolves additional conflicts by giving priority to methods within the same inheritance path in case of ambiguities. Renaming is not supported. Directed resends do not increase the dependency between the implementation and the inheritance hierarchy because they are sent to named slots, which is very similar to using named inheritance relations.

C++ [39] has limited support for repeated inheritance. A class cannot inherit from the same base class more than once, making it unsuitable for building classes from components. In addition, it has no support for renaming, forcing clients to resolve name conflicts. The language supports separation of subtyping and code inheritance through public and private inheritance.

Some design patterns can benefit from the component relation, but most cannot. Patterns that require the introduction of certain methods benefit from using a component for each of the participants. Examples are *composite, singleton, observer*, and *memento*. Frequently used *template method* patterns, such as patterns for caching and locking, can also be captured in a component. The *visitor* and *iterator* patterns benefit from the use of association or relationship components which provide navigation methods. The *state* and *adapter* patterns cannot currently benefit from our approach because the component would have to be interchangeable at run-time as in Darwin and Lava [21].

A split object [2] consists of a collection of *pieces*. Pieces represent particular viewpoints or roles of the split object, and are organized in a delegation hierarchy. Unlike the split object, however, pieces have no identity. Invoking methods is done by selecting a viewpoint to send the message to. The main difference with our approach is that component relations are used to build an abstract data type, whereas pieces are used to model different viewpoints on an object. This difference in purpose results in additional technical differences. The hierarchies of both approaches have an opposite order with respect to overriding. For pieces, the leaves are the most specific parts, whereas for component relations, the root – the composition – is the most specific part. In addition, features in pieces cannot be merged, whereas features inherited through different component relations can be merged. Finally, pieces are added dynamically, whereas component relations are declared statically.

7   Future Work

An important task is to finish our compiler and create a library of reusable components. These include, but are not limited to, a hierarchy of association classes allowing choices like multiplicity, value or reference semantics, mutability, constraints. With these associations, graphs can be built to reuse any iteration over an object structure.

The error handling strategy of a class is fixed at this moment. For example, class `BoundedValue` must choose how to deal with invalid input: use preconditions, throw exceptions, or provide a default behavior. That means that to provide all choices to an application developer, we need three versions of the same characteristic. It would be more interesting to have a single version that provides a number of strategies for dealing with errors, and allowing the application developer to choose one.

8   Conclusion

We have shown that current object-oriented programming languages do not offer the abstraction level required to use general purpose classes as building blocks for other classes in a practical manner. This prevents a developer from reusing high-level concepts like associations, bounded values, and graphs.

We showed which features are required to encapsulate and reuse such concepts, categorized them, and showed how current reuse mechanisms support them. We then integrated those features in a new inheritance mechanism.

Our inheritance mechanism is the first to make this kind of reuse practical. By using renaming parameters and making component relations first-class citizens, we eliminate the problems encountered with existing mechanisms. They allow a programmer to easily exploit name patterns, connect components, provide both a simple class interface and lots of functionality, and use components as if they were separate objects. Together, these improvements raise the abstraction level of the programming language, since it is no longer required to create a new language construct or write lots of low-level code to reuse a high-level characteristic. Of course, the component relation can also be used for traditional code inheritance as used in traits, SmartEiffel, and Cecil.

The case study confirms that our inheritance mechanism yields much better results (21% to 36% reduction) than other inheritance mechanisms (3% to 12% reduction), and delegation (11% to 17% reduction). It also shows that our inheritance mechanism is more robust with respect to extensions of components. In addition, it is still beneficial to reuse small components, or small parts of big components with our inheritance mechanism, contrary to the other techniques.

Acknowledgments

We especially thank Adriaan Moors, Jan Smans, and Tom Schrijvers for their advice. We thank the anonymous reviewers for their insightful comments. We thank Dominique Colnet, Guillem Marpons, and Frederic Merizen of the SmartEiffel team for their valuable feedback. We also want to thank Bart Jacobs, Jeroen Boydens, Sven De Labey, Kurt Schelfthout, and Koen Vanderkimpen, who provided many insightful comments.

References

1. America, P.: Inheritance and subtyping in a parallel object-oriented language. In: Proceedings of ECOOP '87, pp. 234–242. Springer, Heidelberg (1987)
2. Bardou, D., Dony, C.: Split objects: a disciplined use of delegation within objects. In: Proceedings of OOPSLA '96, pp. 122–137. ACM Press, New York (1996)
3. Bierman, G.M., Wren, A.: First-class relationships in an object-oriented language. In: Black, A.P. (ed.) ECOOP 2005. LNCS, vol. 3586, pp. 262–286. Springer, Heidelberg (2005)
4. Bracha, G., Cook, W.: Mixin-based inheritance. In: Proceedings of OOPSLA/ECOOP '90, pp. 303–311 (1990)
5. Bracha, G., Lindstrom, G.: Modularity meets inheritance. In: Proceedings of the IEEE International Conference on Computer Languages, pp. 282–290. IEEE Computer Society Press, Los Alamitos (1992)
6. Chambers, C.: The Cecil language specification and rationale: Version 3.2 (2004)
7. Chambers, C.: The Diesel language specification and rationale: Version 0.2 (2006)
8. Chambers, C., Ungar, D., Chang, B.-W., Hölzle, U.: Parents are shared parts of objects: inheritance and encapsulation in SELF. Lisp Symb. Comput. 4(3), 207–222 (1991)
9. Colnet, D., Marpons, G., Merizen, F.: Reconciling subtyping and code reuse in object-oriented languages: Using inherit and insert in SmartEiffel, the GNU Eiffel compiler. In: Morisio, M. (ed.) ICSR 2006. LNCS, vol. 4039, Springer, Heidelberg (2006)
10. Colnet, D., Ribet, P., Adrian, C., Merizen, F., Marpons, G.: SmartEiffel 2.2 (2005), http://smarteiffel.loria.fr
11. Cook, W.R., Hill, W., Canning, P.S.: Inheritance is not subtyping. In: Proceedings of POPL '90, pp. 125–135 (1990)
12. DeMichiel, L.G., Gabriel, R.P.: The common lisp object system: An overview. In: Bézivin, J., Hullot, J.-M., Lieberman, H., Cointe, P. (eds.) ECOOP 1987. LNCS, vol. 276, pp. 151–170. Springer, Heidelberg (1987)
13. ECMA Technical Committee 39 (TC39) Task Group 2 (TG2). C# Language Specification. ECMA, 2 edn. (December 2002)
14. Ernst, E.: Higher-order hierarchies. In: Cardelli, L. (ed.) ECOOP 2003. LNCS, vol. 2743, pp. 303–329. Springer, Heidelberg (2003)
15. Gamma, E., Helm, R., Johnson, R., Vlissides, J.: Design patterns: elements of reusable object-oriented software. Addison-Wesley Longman Publishing Co., Inc. (1995)
16. Goldberg, D.S., Findler, R.B., Flatt, M.: Super and inner: together at last! In: Proceedings of OOPSLA '04, pp. 116–129 (2004)
17. Gosling, J., et al.: The Java Language Specification, 2nd edn. Addison-Wesley Longman Publishing Co., Inc. (2000)
18. Igarashi, A., Pierce, B.C., Wadler, P.: Featherweight Java: a minimal core calculus for Java and GJ. ACM Trans. Program. Lang. Syst. 23(3), 396–450 (2001)
19. Keedy, J.L., Heinlein, C., Menger, G.: Inheriting multiple and repeated parts in Timor. Journal of Object Technology 3(10), 99–120 (2004)
20. Kiczales, G., Hilsdale, E., Hugunin, J., Kersten, M., Palm, J., Griswold, W.G.: An overview of AspectJ. In: Knudsen, J.L. (ed.) ECOOP 2001. LNCS, vol. 2072, pp. 327–353. Springer, Heidelberg (2001)
21. Kniesel, G.: Type-safe delegation for run-time component adaptation. In: Guerraoui, R. (ed.) ECOOP 1999. LNCS, vol. 1628, pp. 351–366. Springer, Heidelberg (1999)
22. Knudsen, J.L.: Name collision in multiple classification hierarchies. In: Gjessing, S., Nygaard, K. (eds.) ECOOP 1988. LNCS, vol. 322, pp. 93–109. Springer, Heidelberg (1988)
23. Leino, K.R.M.: Data groups: specifying the modification of extended state. In: Proceedings of OOPSLA '98, pp. 144–153 (1998)

24. Liskov, B., Wing, J.M.: A new definition of the subtype relation. In: Nierstrasz, O. (ed.) ECOOP 1993. LNCS, vol. 707, pp. 118–141. Springer, Heidelberg (1993)
25. Meyer, B.: Object-oriented software construction, 2nd edn. Prentice-Hall, Inc., Englewood Cliffs (1997)
26. Mezini, M., Ostermann, K.: Integrating independent components with on-demand remodularization. In: Proceedings of OOPSLA '02, pp. 52–67 (2002)
27. Nystrom, N., Chong, S., Myers, A.C.: Scalable extensibility via nested inheritance. In: Proceedings of OOPSLA '04, pp. 99–115 (2004)
28. Odersky, M., Zenger, M.: Scalable component abstractions. In: Proceedings of OOPSLA '05, pp. 41–57 (2005)
29. Ossher, H., Harrison, W.: Combination of inheritance hierarchies. In: Proceedings of OOPSLA '92, pp. 25–40 (1992)
30. Ostermann, K.: Dynamically composable collaborations with delegation layers. In: Magnusson, B. (ed.) ECOOP 2002. LNCS, vol. 2374, pp. 89–110. Springer, Heidelberg (2002)
31. Pearce, D.J., Noble, J.: Relationship aspects. In: Proceedings of AOSD '06, pp. 75–86. ACM Press, New York (2006)
32. Reppy, J., Turon, A.: A foundation for trait-based metaprogramming. In: International Workshops on Foundations of Object-Oriented Languages (2006)
33. Rumbaugh, J.: Relations as semantic constructs in an object-oriented language. In: Proceedings of OOPSLA '87, pp. 466–481 (1987)
34. Sakkinen, M.: Disciplined inheritance. In: ECOOP, pp. 39–56 (1989)
35. Schärli, N., Ducasse, S., Nierstrasz, O., Black, A.: Traits: Composable units of behavior. In: Cardelli, L. (ed.) ECOOP 2003. LNCS, vol. 2743, pp. 248–274. Springer, Heidelberg (2003)
36. Seco, J.C., Caires, L.: A basic model of typed components. In: Bertino, E. (ed.) ECOOP 2000. LNCS, vol. 1850, pp. 108–128. Springer, Heidelberg (2000)
37. Snyder, A.: Encapsulation and inheritance in object-oriented programming languages. In: Proceedings of OOPSLA '86, pp. 38–45 (1986)
38. Stata, R., Guttag, J.V.: Modular reasoning in the presence of subclassing. In: Proceedings of OOPSLA '95, pp. 200–214 (1995)
39. Stroustrup, B.: The C++ programming language, 2nd edn. Addison-Wesley Longman Publishing Co., Inc., Boston, MA, USA (1991)
40. Szypersky, C., Omohundro, S., Murer, S.: Engineering a programming language: The type and class system of Sather. Technical Report TR-93-064, Berkeley, CA (1993)
41. Taivalsaari, A.: On the notion of inheritance. ACM Comput. Surv. 28(3), 438–479 (1996)
42. Technical Group 4 of Technical Committee 39. ECMA-367 Standard: Eiffel Analysis, Design and Programming Language. ECMA International (2005)
43. van Dooren, M., Smeets, N.: Jnome (2006), http://www.cs.kuleuven.be/~marko/jnome/
44. van Dooren, M., Steegmans, E.: Combining the robustness of checked exceptions with the flexibility of unchecked exceptions using anchored exception declarations. In: Proceedings of OOPSLA '05, pp. 455–471 (2005)
45. van Dooren, M., Steegmans, E.: Language constructs for improving reusability in object-oriented software. In: Companion to proceedings of OOPSLA '05, pp. 118–119 (2005)
46. van Dooren, M., Steegmans, E.: Abstract data type components. Technical Report CW 439, K.U.Leuven (March 2006), http://www.cs.kuleuven.be/publicaties/rapporten/cw/CW439.pdf

Assuring Object-Oriented Architecture

Jonathan Aldrich

Carnegie Mellon University, Pittsburgh, PA 15213, USA
jonathan.aldrich@cs.cmu.edu

"Architecture is the fundamental organization of a system, embodied in its components, their relationships to each other and the environment, and the principles governing its design and evolution" - ANSI/IEEE Std 1471-2000.

Getting the architecture of a software system right is increasingly recognized as crucial to that system's success. Effective software architects must not only make appropriate architectural decisions, but also assure that the final system correctly embodies those decisions. This task is especially difficult for object-oriented systems, for two reasons. First, much of software architecture's design terminology derives from hardware circuit diagrams, which might be a reasonable match for C programs but are a far cry from today's highly dynamic object architectures. Second, the same facilities that make object-oriented software robust and flexible—dynamism, aliasing, inheritance, and reentrancy—greatly complicate the assurance of architectural properties.

This talk explores architectural abstractions for object-oriented programs, and approaches for recognizing and assuring those abstractions in object-oriented code. Studying a number of real-world systems and frameworks provides insight into what kinds of structural and behavioral properties are important in object-oriented architectures. I will discuss how common approaches to assuring software architecture, while successful in other settings, are often incompatible with essential object-oriented architectural practices. Overcoming these incompatibilities requires new abstractions both for expressing and assuring software architectures. Several recently developed abstractions show promise in capturing architectural design intent, but a number of challenges to realizing the full potential of object-oriented architecture remain.

E. Ernst (Ed.): ECOOP 2007, LNAI 4609, p. 450, 2007.

MAO: Ownership and Effects for More Effective Reasoning About Aspects

Curtis Clifton[1], Gary T. Leavens[2], and James Noble[3,4]

[1] Rose-Hulman Institute of Technology, Terre Haute, Indiana, USA
[2] Iowa State University, Ames, Iowa, USA
[3] Imperial College, London, UK
[4] Permanent: Victoria University of Wellington, New Zealand

Abstract. Aspect-oriented advice increases the number of places one must consider during reasoning, since advice may affect all method calls and field accesses. MAO, a new variant of AspectJ, demonstrates how to simplify reasoning by allowing programmers, if they choose, to declare limits on the control and heap effects of advice. Heap effects, such as assignment to object fields, are specified using *concern domains*—declared partitions of the heap. By declaring the concern domains affected by methods and advice, programmers can separate objects owned by the base program and by various aspects. When desired, programmers can also use such concern domain annotations to check that advice cannot interfere with the base program or with other aspects. Besides allowing programmers to declare how concerns interact in a program, concern domains also support a simple kind of semantic pointcut. These features make reasoning about control and heap effects easier.

1 Introduction

Serve the People![1]

Aspect-oriented software development [13] (and its conjugates such as subjectivity, generative programming, Model-Driven Architecture and so on) are changing the way programs are structured. Rather than a program being a hierarchy, with each module or class defined in one place, a program becomes a heterarchy, where multiple crosscutting aspects contribute to the definition of multiple components. Aspect-oriented designs can help increase cohesion by reducing code scattering and tangling. This can positively affect a system's maintainability; each crosscutting concern can be dealt with in a single module, making it much easier to change the policies that govern that concern.

In this paper we describe Modular Aspects with Ownership, MAO, a variant of AspectJ 5 that helps programmers state and enforce restrictions on control and heap effects. Control effects are caused by advice that perturbs the program's control flow. Heap effects are modifications to object fields. Giving programmers the ability to state and enforce restrictions on these effects allows more effective reasoning in MAO than

---

[1] Mao Tse-tung's quotes are from http://art-bin.com/art/omaotoc.html. Use of these quotations in no way indicates our approval of Mao or his actions.

E. Ernst (Ed.): ECOOP 2007, LNAI 4609, pp. 451–475, 2007.

is generally possible in aspect-oriented languages such as ApsectJ. By "reasoning" we mean both informal checks, including desk-checking of code, and formal proofs.

MAO makes the following contributions:

1. **Surround Advice.** We introduce **surround** and **curbing** advice annotations that allow programmers to declare that their advice makes no (or limited) changes to the advised control flow. Surround advice can be used in spectator aspects to ensure they do not perturb the control flow of the base program [7, 9].
2. **Concern Domains.** We use a shallow ownership type and effect system [2, 5] to identify explicitly the concerns that own each object or aspect in the program. Programmers and tools can inspect the domain declarations and so statically determine how an aspect will interact with objects, or if two aspects may potentially interfere.
3. **Writes Pointcut Designator.** We introduce a new semantic pointcut designator, **writes**, which uses the ownership and effect system to provide a robust declaration for advice that matches all join points that may modify a particular concern domain.
4. **Spectator Aspects.** We state precise conditions on **spectator** aspects [7, 9]. Spectator aspects write only their own concern domains and use only surround advice, ensuring that they cannot affect the observable behavior of any other aspect or class in the program.

MAO's design is supported by MiniMAO$_3$, a formal model of MAO. The full details of MiniMAO$_3$ are described within Clifton's dissertation [7], including details we omit, such as a proof of type soundness and an ownership invariant for concern domains.

The paper proceeds as follows: The next section briefly presents the problem. Then, we informally introduce our solution with three sections describing the design of MAO. We give a high-level overview of our formal results and discuss a practical evaluation of our work. Finally, we conclude with a comparison to related work.

2   A Tale of Two Aspects

New things always have to experience difficulties and setbacks as they grow.

The key problem this paper addresses is reasoning about whether one module (class, method, aspect, advice) may potentially affect the behavior of another module. This is especially interesting for aspect-oriented programs, since interference among aspects and between aspects and other code can be quite subtle. Consider the venerable asteroids game [3]. The positions and vectors of a spaceship and some asteroids are managed by an N-body simulation — the spaceship can be influenced by player input. A Model class runs the simulation and stores spaceships, asteroids, missiles and so on.

Adding a user interface to this game is done with the OutputWindow aspect in Fig. 1. This aspect's advice runs after the simulation updates, when it reads data from the model, and then updates its output window. Reasoning about this aspect requires some assumptions that are not explicit in its code.

First, suppose we want to find control effects of the OutputWindow aspect. A *control effect* is a perturbation of the program's flow of control, such as throwing an exception, or stopping the call of a method. Since this aspect uses **after** advice, it does not seem to have any control effects. But that reasoning is not sufficient — we also have to

```
aspect OutputWindow {
  private SpacewarWindow w = new SpacewarWindow();

  after(Model m): target(m) && (call(void Model.set*())
                          || call(void Model.moveShip())
                          || call(void Model.updateAsteroids())) {
    w.reset();
    Spaceship s = m.getSpaceship();
    w.drawSpaceship(s.getX(), s.getY(), s.getHeading());
    for (Asteroid a : m.getAsteroids()) {
      w.drawAsteroid(a.x, a.y, a.size); }
    w.update();
}}
```

Fig. 1. The OutputWindow aspect

determine that the advice will not throw an exception that may affect the continuation of the program after the advice returns. This requires determining what exceptions can be thrown by the methods called in the advice, which are not explicit if the code calls methods that can throw unchecked exceptions.

Second, suppose we want to find the heap effects of the OutputWindow aspect. A *heap effect* is an assignment to some object fields.[2] The advice has no direct assignments to object fields, but we must also determine the potential side effects of the methods it calls. Methods like reset presumably have heap effects, and methods like getSpaceship presumably do not, though in practice we would need to verify that. Once we determine what method calls may have side effects the question becomes, what objects are affected? It matters if the object affected is owned by the advice, such as the window w, or not. In this case only w seems to be affected, but determining the heap effects of methods is not obvious from the code.

Finally, to determine when the advice will execute, we must understand its pointcut. The pointcut specifies when the display is to be updated. It does this by matching methods that may change the state of the model. This is quite a large design-level dependency on the program — we assume that the execution of any setter methods, plus a couple of specific methods on the Model class (such as moveShip or updateAsteroids) capture all effects on the model that need to be reflected. The problems with explicit naming and syntactic patterns are well known [21, 30]. The core issue here is that the pointcut specification is at the wrong level of abstraction. This advice should not match *"all calls where the first three characters of the method name are 'set', or where the method is named* moveShip *or* updateAsteroids", instead what we need to express is: *"all calls to methods that may change the* Model." Such a *heap effect dependency* cannot be expressed directly in AspectJ. While it could be expressed with XPIs [15, 31], the XPI mechanism for expressing this is again an AspectJ pointcut, and does not provide a way of checking that the methods in the pointcut accurately express the dependency.

We can compare the benign OutputWindow aspect with the Cheat aspect in Fig. 2 on the following page. This aspect aims to override the collision detection function in the

---

[2] Heap effects implicitly include I/O, since object fields are used to represent I/O devices.

program, so that when the player's Spaceship hits something the collision is ignored and the ship's shields are activated, rather than the ship being destroyed and the player losing! Compared with the OutputWindow aspect there are three main differences. First, the aspect certainly has control effects: the around advice may return "false" rather than calling proceed. Second, by looking at the code of raiseShields we could determine that the advice also has heap effects on objects in the base program. On the other hand, the pointcut in this aspect — which matches calls to the collision method — is not expressing a heap effect dependency: it simply picks out a single method's execution.

```
aspect Cheat {
  boolean around(Model m, Thing one, Thing two) :
    call(boolean Model.collision(Thing,Thing)) && target(m) && args(one,two) {
  if ((one == m.getSpaceship()) || (two == m.getSpaceship())) {
      m.getSpaceship().raiseShields();
      return false;
  } else { return proceed(m, one, two); }
}}
```

Fig. 2. The Cheat aspect

These two aspects illustrate the three problems we address in this paper:

1. How can programmers find the control effects of advice?
2. How can programmers find the heap effects of advice?
3. How can programmers select join points according to their effects on the heap?

MAO provides solutions to each of these problems: control-limited advice mitigates control effects, concern domains describe heap effects, and effect pointcut designators select join points according to their effects on the heap. Compared with other work, MAO is designed as an extension to AspectJ, rather than as a more idealized AO language [11], and relies on types and annotations that can be checked locally, rather than global control and dataflow analyses [19, 29].

3   Control-Limited Advice

We cannot do without freedom, nor can we do without discipline.

The first problem we address is how to make finding the control effects of advice easier. All kinds of advice in AspectJ can cause control effects directly by throwing exceptions. (However, we do not consider errors, which inherit from Error, to be exceptions. Since errors indicate failures of the virtual machine, they are outside the scope of our analysis.) Around advice can also perturb control flow by not calling **proceed**, or by calling it several times. It is also convenient to consider changing the result returned by a computation (in around advice) to be a control effect. In AspectJ one can also change the target (receiver) object in a method call with around advice, which causes a control effect. The Cheat aspect in section 2 has two kinds of control effects, since it does not call **proceed** in some cases, and in those cases it supplies a new return value.

MAO allows programmers to declare that a piece of advice (or a whole aspect) has no control effects, or that those effects are limited to exceptional cases. We call such advice *control-limited advice*. MAO has two annotations for declaring that a piece of advice is control-limited: @surround and @curbing.

Advice marked with @surround has no control effects. When invoked in a particular state, @surround advice will proceed to the same join point, with the same arguments, and return the same value or throw the same exception, as it would in absence of the advice. (Note that this allows extra join points to be introduced, both within the advice and within the advised code.) For example, the advice in the OutputWindow (Fig. 1 on page 453) could have been declared using @surround, but not the Cheat aspect (of Fig. 2).

Advice whose only control effects are potentially to throw one or more exceptions that would not have been thrown otherwise can be marked with the @curbing annotation. Curbing advice can stop control flowing through a join point, but cannot augment it or change it in any other way. Curbing advice can be used, for example, to check authorizations or preconditions. The @surround and @curbing annotations can also be applied to entire aspects: thus requiring all their advice to be curbing or surrounding.

MAO uses simple desugarings and conservative criteria to modularly check that advice declared as control-limited actually is control-limited. These checks work differently for different kinds of advice.

For **before** and **after** advice annotated with @surround, MAO translates the advice body in such a way that all exceptions that might potentially be thrown out of their bodies are caught and discarded. The user does not have to write code to catch these exceptions, though she certainly may. But MAO automatically places the body inside a statement of the form "**try** /*body*/ **catch** (Exception e) { ; }", which discards all exceptions that might otherwise perturb the control flow.

Since **around** advice is inherently more powerful, it requires stronger checks. MAO checks that the advice has a body that is the sequential composition of a before part, a top-level call to **proceed**, and an after part that returns the result of the call to proceed (if any). No call to **proceed** may occur in either the before or the after part. MAO statically checks that surround advice always proceeds exactly once to the advised join point, unless the before part fails to terminate (e.g., loops forever). MAO automatically translates the before and after parts, as above, to automatically discard exceptions that occur in the code before and after the mandatory **proceed** call. Because the call to proceed is at the top-level, exceptions from the call to proceed cannot be caught; they must be propagated up the call stack as they would be in the absence of the advice. Fig. 3 on the following page gives an example satisfying the restrictions.

MAO checks that any arguments passed to the join point are always the original arguments and that the original arguments are declared to be **final** and @readonly (see Sec. 4.4), so surround advice cannot mutate the arguments and cannot pass along new arguments. The result returned from executing a piece of surround advice must be (if the return type is not **void**) saved in a final, @readonly variable named **reply**, and must be returned at the end of the after part. The after part expression has read-only access to **reply**. From these restrictions it follows that the before and after parts of surround advice are evaluated solely for their heap effects. Another way to think of such around

```
@surround Object around() : call( Object *(..) ) {
    // before part
    int event_no = Logger.nextEventNumber();
    this.log.append("before" + event_no);

    // mandatory proceed to advised code
    @readonly final Object reply = proceed();

    // after part
    this.log.append("after" + event_no + "reply:" + reply);
    return reply;
}
```

Fig. 3. Example of @surround for **around** advice

advice is as paired before and after advice, where the before part can declare variables that the after part can access.

Checks on @curbing advice also differ depending on the advice type. Before or after advice declared to be @curbing is unchanged from AspectJ, since control effects that cause exceptions are permitted. Around advice that is declared to be @curbing must satisfy all of MAO's checks for @surround advice, but does not have exceptions that arise in the before and after parts automatically caught and discarded. In particular it must have the form illustrated in Fig. 3, so that it proceeds exactly once (unless the before part throws an exception).

Control-limited advice makes reasoning about aspect-oriented programs easier in three ways. First, by declaring a piece of advice as @surround or @curbing, programmers can express guaranteed limits on the control effects of their advice. MAO can ensure an advice's implementation matches the annotations on its declaration with an efficient, local analysis. The straightforward tests required — and the error messages MAO will produce if advice does not meet the conditions — should be easily comprehensible by programmers. Because the syntactic conditions can be checked locally, requiring only the code of the advice, changes to other parts of the program will not affect whether a particular piece of advice is surrounding or curbing.[3]

Second, because @surround and @curbing annotations are part of the interface of advice, programmers can immediately tell, by examining that interface, whether the advice does perturb the existing control flow. Thus when reasoning about control effects, one can simply ignore @surround advice. Furthermore one only has to look at @curbing advice in reasoning about exceptions; when reasoning about other kinds of control flow perturbation, one can also ignore @curbing advice.

Third, on a larger scale the search for control effects can be limited to non-spectator and non-surround aspects, since only such aspects may contain non-@surround advice. All of these represent some modest gains in effectiveness of reasoning.

---

[3] Of course, other advice that is not control-limited can cause control effects that occur at join points within control-limited advice. However, those control effects can be blamed on the advice that is not control-limited; that is, if all advice in a program is control-limited advice, then no control effects will affect the base program code.

4   Concern Domains

Qualitatively different contradictions
can only be resolved by qualitatively different methods.

To identify the heap effects of advice and ease reasoning about interference among and between aspect and base program code, MAO uses an ownership type-and-effect system we call *concern domains*. As with other ownership and confined type systems [2, 4, 12, 24, 27] concern domains require programmers to identify objects with a particular owner — in this case, a particular concern domain. For this reason, concern domains partition the program's heap, and so help answer the question of what object fields may be read and written by a piece of advice.

4.1   Declaring Concern Domains

Concern domains themselves are declared by classes or aspects. Unlike many ownership systems (but more like confined types [32]), concern domains are static: a particular system configuration will have a fixed set of concern domains. Following Generic Confinement and Generic Ownership, we reify domains using inert marker classes [27, 28].

Programmers explicitly declare concern domains by declaring an empty, **final** class that implements the interface Domain. Explicitly declared domains may be either publicly available, or may be private to a class or aspect [2]. To keep them static, however, they cannot be inner classes, although they can be static, nested classes.

Each concrete aspect implicitly defines a concern domain; that is the name of a concrete aspect can be used as a concern domain. This is appropriate because each such aspect is often associated with a concern in a well-designed program. Note that all instances of a particular non-singleton aspect, such as instances created per-cflow, all share a common concern domain. This sharing does not cause problems for MAO's effect analysis, though it does make it coarser.

MAO's concern domain World owns all objects not owned by other domains.

4.2   Using Concern Domains

Every object creation expression names the new object's owner, which may be a public concern domain, or a private one visible in the class (or aspect) instantiating the object. The ownership domain of every expression is statically tracked by the ownership type system, and objects owned by private domains are inaccessible outside the scope of those private domains (i.e. the class or package declaring the private domain).

The types of objects in the program can be annotated to describe the concern domains to which they belong. Classes and abstract aspects can be made ownership-parametric — in class and abstract aspect declarations a list of concern domain variables are given following the class or aspect name. The first concern domain variable listed, typically called Owner, represents the owner domain for instances of the class or aspect, that is, the domains to which they belong. Other concern domain variables allow referencing objects in other domains.

For example, the following code shows how the Model class could be defined with a domain parameter named Owner. The Spaceship and Vectors of Asteroids within Model are all stored in the same domain (Owner) as the Model object containing them.

```
class Model<Owner extends Domain> {  /* ... */
  private Spaceship<Owner> s = new Spaceship<Owner>();
  private Vector<Owner,Asteroids<Owner>> v =
    new Vector<Owner,Asteroids<Owner>>();
}
```

Then we declare a new concern domain MODEL and in it allocate a new Model instance.

```
final class MODEL implements Domain {}
static Model<MODEL> myModel = new Model<MODEL>();
```

Thanks to the field declarations in the Model class, a new Spaceship and Vector are also instantiated in the MODEL domain.

Instances of classes declared without domain annotations are owned by World.

4.3   Concern Domains and Aspects

As with classes, MAO aspects require ownership parameters to give them access to concern domains. Because MAO extends AspectJ 5, generic (and hence abstract) aspects cannot be instantiated directly, rather a concrete aspect extends the generic aspect while instantiating the generic aspect's type parameters. Thus, a concrete aspect cannot have ownership parameters (or any other type parameters), rather, the concrete aspect binds parameters of a generic aspect from which it inherits. Finally, so that aspects can have their own private data, each concrete aspect has its own domain, and the name of the concrete aspect is the name of that domain.

We rewrite the OutputWindow example (compare Fig. 1) in Fig. 4 on the next page, using the ownership type parameter Owner for the aspect's own concern domain, and parameter Other for the type of the exposed context m.[4] Note how the ownership types describe the concern domains to which each variable or argument must belong. For example the private field w belongs to the same concern domain as the aspect (its Owner) while the model m is in the Other domain. To use this aspect, we instantiate it by making a concrete aspect, binding the domain variables:

```
aspect ConcreteOutputWindow extends OutputWindow<ConcreteOutputWindow,MODEL>{}
```

the Owner variable is bound to the aspect's domain, and the Other variable to the MODEL domain. The Other domain could alternatively have been bound to any (public) domain in the program, including the default World domain, or a public domain belonging to another aspect (to support mutually-crosscutting aspects).

4.4   Effect Declarations

Concern domains and domain parameters separate expressions owned by different domains via their types: within the annotated OutputWindow aspect, we know which expressions belong to the aspect (concern domain Owner) and which to the base program (Other). To track aspect interference, we also need to determine when a method or advice execution may have a potential heap effect on the fields in a particular domain. For

---

[4] AspectJ 1.5.3 does not allow Other to be used as a type parameter in advice formals and PCDs. We leave compilation techniques that overcome this limitation as future work.

```
@readonlyDomains({"Other"})  @depends({ @varies({"Owner", "Other"}) })
abstract aspect OutputWindow<Owner extends Domain,
                             Other extends Domain> {
  private SpacewarWindow<Owner> w = new SpacewarWindow<Owner>();

  @curbing @writes({"Owner"})
  after(@readonly Model<Other> m):
          target(m) && call(void Model<Other>.*()) && writes(Other) {
    w.reset();
    Spaceship<Other> s = m.getSpaceship();
    w.drawSpaceship(s.getX(), s.getY(), s.getHeading());
    for (Asteroid<Other> a : m.getAsteroids()) {
      w.drawAsteroid(a.x, a.y, a.size); }
    w.update();
}}
```

Fig. 4. The OutputWindow aspect with annotations

this we augment the ownership type system with effects [5]. The basic effect annotations are @writes, which is attached to method and advice declarations, and @readonly, which is a type modifier.

The @writes annotation declares the concern domains that a particular method or piece of advice can potentially mutate. Due to limitations of Java 5 annotations, this annotation contains an array literal, with a comma-separated list of strings naming concern domains or parameters. For example, the advice in the above example is allowed to write into the Owner domain (which will be the ConcreteOutputWindow domain in that concrete subaspect). Since Other is not named by this @writes annotation, however, the advice is not allowed to write that domain—or MODEL in the concrete subaspect. (Due to the inherent differences in how one reasons about methods, which are explicitly called, and advice, which is triggered implicitly, we do not consider the effects of **proceed** as belonging to the effects of the advice. These effects do play a role in domain dependencies discussed below).

The @readonly annotation applies to types. Read-only fields and parameters cannot be written into, although they can be read from. For example, the model m in the above example is read-only, and hence the advice cannot mutate any field of an object reachable through that reference — so @readonly is transitive.

As a shorthand, a method (or piece of advice) can be annotated with @pure, meaning that all of its parameters (or variables in an advice's exposed context) are read-only. It is an error for a @pure method (or advice) to have a @writes annotation.

The programmer declares an ownership parameter of a class or aspect to be read-only using the @readonlyDomains annotation; this annotation is then effective wherever that parameter is used.[5] Such a read-only concern domain cannot be mentioned in a @writes annotation, making the whole concern domain read-only within the scope of that ownership parameter's declaration. If a method or advice has no @writes annotation, then by default it can write to any non-read-only concern domain in scope.

---

[5] Planned Java enhancements (JSR 308) will allow @readonly annotations on type parameters.

In Fig. 4, for example, the advice is annotated @writes("Owner") because it writes to the output window, which is allocated within the aspect's own concern domain. The important point is that the Other domain — representing the base program holding the model — is a read-only domain, to which the aspect cannot write. In this way, the effect annotations let programmers make their intentions clear and checkable. (The fact that the Other domain is read-only means that the @readonly annotation on m's type is actually redundant in this example).

Programmers using MAO can state their intention in another way also. In Fig. 4, the @depends annotation on the aspect says that the Owner domain is allowed to vary whenever Other may. This *dependency declaration* allows the after advice in the example to mutate the Owner domain while advising methods that mutate the Other domain. This dependency is used both to check the @writes annotation on the advice and to reason about potential effects without considering the internal details of the advice.

The effect annotations illustrate a key benefit of MAO's ownership types: by inspecting only the aspects and their annotations, we can be sure that OutputWindow does not change any object owned by the base program. MAO's type system enforces a non-interference property so that a static, signature-level search can identify all the code that might mutate a particular concern domain. By "static" we mean that the search can be confined to areas of the program where the concern domain in question is visible, either because it is directly visible or because it was passed as a domain parameter. By "signature-level", we mean that only method and advice headers, and not their bodies, must be considered. In fact, if a programmer is just concerned about the effects of aspects on a method call, she can consider just the headers of aspects apart from their advice. Thus MAO statically identifies code tangling, based on a separation of concerns defined by the programmer.

Finally, we can combine concern domains with the control-limited advice from Sec. 3 to define *spectator aspects* [10]. A @spectator aspect contains advice that is (implicitly) @surround, all ownership parameters other than Owner are (implicitly) @readonly, and the concrete concern domain used to instantiate a spectator aspect cannot be shared. Thus, a spectator aspect concisely specifies advice that has no control effects, and whose heap effects are confined within the aspect's own concern domain. In Sec. 6, we formally show that spectator aspects do not cause heap interference. Since lack of control effects is direct from the definition of @surround advice, spectators do not affect the execution of the base program in any way.

4.5 Annotating Base Code

We consider that annotating *aspects* with ownership types and effects is a necessary price to pay for the tighter granularity of reasoning.

An important advantage of AOP, however, is that aspects can be attached to base code that is oblivious to the aspects, that is the base code should *not* need to be changed to have aspects applied to it. Thus it will often be infeasible to annotate preexisting base code. MAO's World domain, and the default that instances of unannotated classes are owned by this domain, offers a broad brush solution to this problem. Because all objects created in the base program are owned by World, the base program still type checks. Despite the coarseness of the World domain, MAO still has more than enough information to separate base program objects from objects belonging to aspects, as the OutputWindow example above illustrates.

5   Effect Pointcut Designators

If you want knowledge, you must take part in the practice of changing reality.

To select join points according to their effects on the heap, MAO introduces a new kind of pointcut designator (PCD), **writes**. It allows programmers to use concern domain declarations to refine their aspect's pointcut definitions. We call this PCD an *effects* PCD, as it matches join points with heap effects on a given concern domain. Unlike AspectJ **set** and **get** PCDs, which describe heap effects and accesses syntactically (in terms of concrete field names or patterns), effects PCDs describe effects semantically (in terms of concern domains). Another difference is that they can work at the level of methods and advice, instead of just at the lower level of individual operations on fields.

A MAO PCD of the form **writes**(D) expresses heap effect dependencies by matching all join points that may write to concern domain D. MAO statically calculates the heap effect of field sets based on the owner domain of the field type. MAO also statically calculates the heap effect of a method or advice, either from an explicit @writes or @pure annotation, or from its default (see Sec. 4.4). Note that these PCDs do not describe method or advice call or execution join points that actually *do* write to a specific concern domain, but to those that may possibly write to that concern domain.

For example, MAO's **writes** PCD lets programmers express the heap effect dependency implicit in Fig. 1 on page 453. Instead of saying that the call should be to methods whose name matches a method pattern (set*) or one of the two named methods (moveShip or updateAsteriods), we can rewrite this PCD as in Fig. 4 on page 459, using the Other concern domain:

```
target(m) && call(void Model<Other>.*()) && writes(Other)
```

Given that the set*, moveShip, and updateAsteriods methods and so on are annotated with effects annotations, and that the OutputWindow aspect is instantiated with an appropriate domain binding (see Sec. 4.3), then this pointcut will match exactly the same methods as the previous explicit pointcut from Fig. 1. More importantly, if there are other methods that are declared as writing the Other concern domain, this pointcut will match those methods too. As the program evolves, if more methods are added that write that domain, this pointcut will stay valid. Because the effect PCDs are tied to the appropriate concern domain (MODEL which is bound to Other), these kind of pointcut designators are more closely tied to the program's semantics and can be automatically checked. Automatic checking ensures they are maintained when the program changes, unlike other, programmer-constructed pointcut abstractions, such as explicit advice points from open modules [1] or design rules [15].

The main disadvantage of effects pointcuts is that currently they can only apply to classes (and aspects) that have been annotated with concern domains and effect clauses. Defaulting base programs to a single World domain — while very effective for separating aspects from unmodified based programs — is almost completely ineffective here: we can assign all base program objects to a single domain only because that assignment

is so indiscriminate. We expect that using a confined-types-style analysis [16] to assign
e.g., individual Java packages into their own domain, should make enough distinctions
to be useful in many cases.

6   Formal Model: MiniMAO$_3$

When we look at a thing, we must examine its essence . . .

MiniMAO$_3$ provides a formal model of MAO's design, building on Clifton's and
Leaven's earlier formal model (MiniMAO$_1$) that described around advice [8]. Space
constraints keep us from fully detailing MiniMAO$_3$ here, but we aim to illuminate the
important issues. Clifton's dissertation [7] provides full details of MiniMAO$_3$.

6.1   The MiniMAO$_3$ Language

The object-oriented core of MiniMAO$_3$ is based on Featherweight Java (FJ) [18]. As
such, a MiniMAO$_3$ program includes of a list of class declarations followed by an expression, which represents the main method in a Java program. Like FJ, class declarations in MiniMAO$_3$ contain a list of field declarations and a list of method declarations.

MiniMAO$_3$ departs from FJ in several ways to support our study of heap effects
in aspect-oriented programs. As described in our earlier work on MiniMAO$_1$ [8], we
use an imperative formal language with features from Classic Java [14]. Among other
things, this choice admits **null** values for fields, so we omit constructors from the language. MiniMAO$_3$ includes concern domain annotations on types and class declarations. It also includes declaration forms that model MAO's aspects, spectator aspects,
around and surround advice, domain dependencies, and ground concern domains.

Figure 5 gives the surface syntax of MiniMAO$_3$. A program consists of a series of
declarations—of classes, regular aspects, and spectator aspects. These type declarations
are followed by a list of public concern domain declarations, like **domain** MODEL. The
public concern domains form the set of ground domains for the program and correspond to MAO's inert classes that implement the Domain interface. After the public
concern domain declarations, a program gives a list of aspect instantiation statements,
like **use** OutputWindow⟨**self**, MODEL⟩, that model MAO's generic aspect instantiation.
In our formalism, all classes and aspects are polymorphic with respect to concern domains. Class and aspect declarations give a list of concern domain variables, denoted by
the metavariable G in Figure 5. These variables are instantiated with ground domains
when the program is evaluated. The usual **new** expression instantiates a class; the new
use statement instantiates an aspect.

As mentioned, class and aspect declarations include a list of concern domain variables, ⟨G^*⟩, following the class or aspect name. The first concern domain variable listed
represents the home domain for instances of the class or aspect. The remaining variables are used to endow instances with permission to access objects in other domains,
like concern domain parameters in MAO. For spectator aspects, we always write **self**
as the first concern domain variable. This is a special variable that represents the private
concern domain of the spectator. Each spectator instance has its own unique concern
domain as in MAO. Only the spectator instance, and any objects it creates in **self**, may

$$P ::= decl^* \ \{domain^* \ asp^* \ e\}$$
$$decl ::= \texttt{class} \ c\langle G^*\rangle \ \texttt{extends} \ c\langle G^*\rangle \ \{field^* \ meth^*\}$$
$$\qquad | \ \texttt{aspect} \ a\langle G^*\rangle \ \{dep^* \ field^* \ adv^*\}$$
$$\qquad | \ \texttt{spectator} \ a\langle\texttt{self}, G^*\rangle \ \{field^* \ surr^*\}$$
$$field ::= t \ f;$$
$$meth ::= t \ m(form^*) \ eff \ \{e\}$$
$$dep ::= \gamma \ \texttt{varies with} \ \gamma;$$
$$adv ::= t \ \texttt{around}(form^*) \ eff \ : \ pcd \ \{e\}$$
$$surr ::= \texttt{surround} \ (form^*) \ : \ pcd \ \{e; \ \texttt{proceed}; \ e\}$$
$$eff ::= \texttt{writes} \ \langle\gamma^*\rangle$$
$$pcd ::= \texttt{call}(pat) \ | \ \texttt{execution}(pat) \ | \ \texttt{writes}(\gamma^*) \ | \ \texttt{args}(form^*)$$
$$\qquad | \ \texttt{this}(form) \ | \ \texttt{target}(form) \ | \ pcd \ \texttt{\&\&} \ pcd \ | \ \texttt{!} \ pcd \ | \ pcd \ \texttt{||} \ pcd$$
$$pat ::= t \ idPat(..)$$
$$form ::= t \ var, \text{where} \ var \notin \{\texttt{this}, \texttt{reply}\}$$
$$e ::= \texttt{new} \ c\langle\gamma^*\rangle() \ | \ var \ | \ \texttt{null} \ | \ e.m(e^*) \ | \ e.f \ | \ e.f = e$$
$$\qquad | \ \texttt{cast} \ t \ e \ | \ e; \ e \ | \ e.\texttt{proceed}(e^*)$$
$$t, s, u ::= \delta^* \ T\langle\gamma^*\rangle$$
$$\delta ::= \varepsilon \ | \ \texttt{readonly}, \text{where} \ \varepsilon \ \text{represents the empty string}$$
$$T ::= c \ | \ a$$
$$\gamma ::= g \ | \ G \ | \ \texttt{self}$$
$$domains ::= \texttt{domain} \ g;, \text{where} \ g \notin \mathcal{G}_{\texttt{self}}$$
$$asp ::= \texttt{use} \ a\langle g^*\rangle; \ | \ \texttt{use} \ a\langle\texttt{self}, g^*\rangle;, \text{where} \ g \notin \mathcal{G}_{\texttt{self}}$$

$G \in \mathcal{G}_{var}$, the set of concern domain variable names

$\mathcal{G}_{\texttt{self}} = \{\texttt{self}_{loc} \cdot loc \in \mathcal{L}\}$, the set of private concern domain names

$g \in \mathcal{G} \cup \mathcal{G}_{\texttt{self}}$, where $\mathcal{G}$ is the set of public concern domain names

$c, d, a, f, m \in \mathcal{I}$, the set of identifiers

$var \in \{\texttt{this}, \texttt{reply}\} \cup \mathcal{V}$, where $\mathcal{V}$ is the set of variable names

$idPat \in \mathcal{IP}$, the set of identifier patterns

Fig. 5. Surface Syntax of MiniMAO$_3$

write to this private domain. Furthermore, the spectator and its progeny may *only* write to this domain. These restrictions are enforced by MiniMAO$_3$'s static type system.

Like MAO, regular aspects in MiniMAO$_3$ include dependency declarations. These declarations allow an aspect to declare that one concern domain may be modified when code is executed that might modify some other domain. This allows an aspect to modify its own accessible concern domains, like a concrete output window, when advising code that modifies another concern domain, like the model in our game example. We would indicate this like ConcreteOutputWindow **varies with** MODEL. Dependency declarations allow—thanks to the aspect instantiation instructions—a static analysis of what

$$e ::= \ldots \mid v \mid (l\,(e^*)) \mid \langle e \rangle_{\delta,\hat{\gamma}} \mid e \frown e$$
$$\quad \mid \; \texttt{joinpt}\; j(e^*) \mid \texttt{chain}\; \bar{B}, j(e^*) \mid \texttt{under}\; e$$
$$v ::= loc_{\delta*} \mid null_{\delta*} \qquad\qquad\qquad \hat{\gamma} \in \mathcal{P}(\mathcal{G} \cup \mathcal{G}_{var} \cup \mathcal{G}_{\texttt{self}})$$
$$l ::= \texttt{fun}\; m\langle var^* \rangle . e : \tau \centerdot \hat{\gamma} \qquad\qquad \hat{g} \in \mathcal{P}(\mathcal{G} \cup \mathcal{G}_{\texttt{self}})$$
$$\tau ::= t \times \ldots \times t \to t$$
$$t, s, u ::= \ldots \mid \top$$

Fig. 6. Syntax Extensions for the Operational Semantics of MiniMAO$_3$

domains might be modified by any operation. Spectator aspects do not include dependency declarations, because we assume a spectator's private concern domain can always vary. But since objects not owned by the spectator cannot observe the private concern domain, this mutability does not matter for reasoning.

The **writes** clause specifies all the concern domains that a method or advice declaration may modify. The type system ensures that only these domains, and those transitively reachable through dependency declarations, can be modified when the method or advice executes. These features ensure that the modifiable domains for any operation can be determined from a global "signature-level" analysis of the code, the bodies of methods and advice need not be considered. The bodies are checked through local rules.

Spectator aspects may only include surround advice. Surround advice differs from around advice by syntactically enforcing the restrictions described above for MAO's @surround advice. Note that in MiniMAO$_3$, the proceed that separates the before and after parts of surround advice is not an expression. It merely serves as a mnemonic for the semantics of surround advice, which is to evaluate the before part, proceed to the advised join point with the original arguments, evaluate the after part for its side-effects, then return the value from the advised join point. The after part may use the reserved variable reference **reply** to refer to the result of the advised code. Because of this semantics no return type is declared for surround advice. Furthermore, surround advice does not include a **writes** clause; every piece of surround advice implicitly writes **self** and no other concern domains.

Types in MiniMAO$_3$ have the form $\delta^* \, T\langle \gamma_1, \ldots, \gamma_q \rangle$, where δ is either **readonly** or the empty string, T is a valid class or aspect name, and γ ranges over concern domain variables and ground domains. Since **readonly** is idempotent, using δ^* for multiple such annotations lets us write **readonly** t to confer read-only status on any type t.

Other than including our new **writes** pointcut descriptor, the join point model for MiniMAO$_3$ is standard. Similarly, its expressions need no additional explanation.

6.2   Operational Semantics

Like most small-step operational semantics, that of MiniMAO$_3$ relies on some additional syntax to represent intermediate states of computation. Figure 6 presents these syntax extensions. We give the intuition behind these expressions here.

Two new expressions, $loc_{\delta*}$ and $null_{\delta*}$, represent values. The meta-variable v ranges over values. The store in MiniMAO$_3$, denoted by S, maps locations, $loc \in \mathcal{L}$, to objects. Values carry a subscript δ^* that denotes whether the reference is read-only.

The other new expressions represent intermediate computation states. To model method execution independently from method calls [8], we use a *function application expression*, $(l(e^*))$, that represents a method and its operands. The meta-variable l ranges over method representations. A context-sensitive translation converts method declarations to more convenient method representations. For example, the declaration

boolean collision(Thing one, Thing two) **writes** $\langle$cache$\rangle$ { **false** }

inside a class Model is represented by

fun collision $\langle$one,two$\rangle$.**false** :
    Model $\times$ Thing $\times$ Thing $\rightarrow$ **boolean** . {cache}.

Tagged expressions, written $\langle e \rangle_{\delta,\hat{\gamma}}$, propagate effect constraints through the semantics (necessary for the soundness proof). In a tagged expression, the set $\hat{\gamma}$ says which concern domains may be mutated during the evaluation of e, and the subscript δ gives the read-only status of any value that results from any (non-divergent) evaluation.

Leap expressions, written $e_1 \curvearrowright e_2$, represent intermediate evaluation of surround advice, with e_1 representing the advised code and e_2 the after part of the advice. The semantics first evaluates e_1, then e_2 for its side effects, replacing any occurrences of **reply** in e_2 with the value of e_1. The result of the whole expression is the value arrived at from evaluating e_1—the value of e_1 "leaps" over the value of e_2.

As in MiniMAO$_1$ [8], **joinpt**, **chain**, and **under** expressions are used to represent the intermediate stages of advice matching, execution, and proceeding to advised code. A **joinpt** expression reifies a join point for advice binding. The meta-variable j ranges over join points and records a join point kind and optional data including things like the current **this** object, the method executing, and the writable concern domains in the current context. The operational semantics also maintains a *join point stack*, a list of join points that records dynamic context information needed for advice matching. The join point stack is a formal analogue of the call stack information that can be matched by AspectJ advice. A **chain** expression records the bodies of all advice matched at a join point. The meta-variable B ranges over advice body representations. We elide the details here, but it suffices to think of the advice body representations as like the method representations in that they record all necessary context-sensitive information about advice needed during evaluation. Finally, the operational semantics uses **under** expressions to pop join points from the join-point stack when evaluation of the code under the join point is complete.

The evaluation relation for MiniMAO$_3$ has the form: $\langle e, J, S \rangle \hookrightarrow \langle e', J', S' \rangle$. It takes an expression, a join point stack, and a store and produces a new expression or an exception, plus a new stack and a new store. The exceptional results, NullPointer-Exception and ClassCastException, handle dereferencing null pointers and bad casts.

6.3   Static Semantics of MiniMAO$_3$

The static semantics of MiniMAO$_3$ checks the restrictions of the concern domains type system, read-only annotations, and effects clauses.

Like Featherweight Java [18], a global class table, denoted CT, records all the class declarations in a MiniMAO$_3$ program. MiniMAO$_3$ extends the class table to record aspect declarations as well. Additionally, an evaluation dependency table, DT, records the information embedded in the "varies with" dependency declarations, reified according to the aspect instantiation instructions. A dependency table is a reflexive, transitive relation on concern domain names and variables. It has the type $(\mathcal{G} \cup \mathcal{G}_{var} \cup \mathcal{G}_{\texttt{self}}) \rightarrow (\mathcal{G} \cup \mathcal{G}_{var} \cup \mathcal{G}_{\texttt{self}})$. Intuitively, for any pair of concern domain names $(g, g') \in DT$, code that is allowed to mutate g may also trigger mutation of g'.

We use the notation $t \preccurlyeq s$ to denote that the type t is a subtype of the type s. The subtyping relationship starts with the reflexive and transitive closure induced by the extends declarations of classes, with every type a subtype of $\top$. To this we add a few additional tweaks. A couple of these handle read-only objects: $t \preccurlyeq$ readonly t, allowing writable objects to be passed where read-only ones are expected, but not the converse; and $t \preccurlyeq s$ implies that readonly $t \preccurlyeq$ readonly s, allowing a read-only object of a subtype to be passed where a read-only object of a supertype is expected, which is necessary for subsumption. The other tweak handles concern domains: following Aldrich and Chambers [2], a subtype must have at least as many concern domains as its supertype and the concern domains must be positionally invariant. For example, $\texttt{IterImpl}\langle\texttt{H,E,D}\rangle \preccurlyeq \texttt{Iterator}\langle\texttt{H,E}\rangle$.

The typing judgment for expressions in MiniMAO₃ has the form $\Gamma \cdot \hat{\gamma} \vdash_{DT} e : t$. This says that, given the type environment Γ, the set of writable concern domain domains $\hat{\gamma}$, and the concern dependency table DT, we can derive that the expression e has type t.

For example, the typing rule for set expressions is:

T-SET

$$\frac{\gamma_1 \in \hat{\gamma} \qquad \textit{fieldsOf}\,(T\langle\gamma_1,\ldots,\gamma_n\rangle)\,(f) = t \qquad \Gamma \cdot \hat{\gamma} \vdash_{DT} e_2 : s \qquad s \preccurlyeq t}{\Gamma \cdot \hat{\gamma} \vdash_{DT} e_1.f = e_2 : s}$$

with $\Gamma \cdot \hat{\gamma} \vdash_{DT} e_1 : T\langle\gamma_1,\ldots,\gamma_n\rangle$

This is mostly standard except for the hypothesis $\gamma_1 \in \hat{\gamma}$ that ensures that the domain containing the object to be mutated is in the set of writable concern domains.

As another example, the typing rule for method calls is:

T-CALL

$$\frac{\begin{array}{c} \Gamma \cdot \hat{\gamma} \vdash_{DT} e_0 : \delta\, T_0\langle\gamma_1,\ldots,\gamma_p\rangle \qquad \forall i \in \{1..n\} \cdot \Gamma \cdot \hat{\gamma} \vdash_{DT} e_i : u_i \\ \textit{methodType}(\delta\, T_0\langle\gamma_1,\ldots,\gamma_p\rangle, m) = t_1 \times \ldots \times t_n \rightarrow t \\ \textit{writable}(\delta\, T_0\langle\gamma_1,\ldots,\gamma_p\rangle, m) = \hat{\gamma}' \\ \textit{depClose}_{DT}\,(\hat{\gamma}') \subseteq \hat{\gamma} \qquad (\delta = \texttt{readonly}) \implies (\hat{\gamma}' = \emptyset) \qquad \forall i \in \{1..n\} \cdot u_i \preccurlyeq t_i \end{array}}{\Gamma \cdot \hat{\gamma} \vdash_{DT} e_0.m(e_1,\ldots,e_n) : t}$$

Again, much of this is standard. Interestingly, if the read-only status δ of the receiver expression is in fact **readonly**, the second to last hypothesis ensures that no domains are writable in the body of the called method. The hypothesis $\textit{depClose}_{DT}\,(\hat{\gamma}') \subseteq \hat{\gamma}$ ensures that the potentially writable domains in the body of the method form a subset of those writable in the context of the method call. The dependency closure function, $\textit{depClose}_{DT}$, operates on a dependency table and a set of concern domains. It places a bound on the concern domains that might be modified by a given method call in the presence of a given set of advice.

$$depClose_{DT}\,(\hat{\gamma}) = \{\gamma' \cdot \exists \gamma \in \hat{\gamma} \cdot (\gamma, \gamma') \in DT\}$$
$$\cup \{\texttt{self}_{loc} \cdot (\exists loc \in \mathcal{L} \cdot (\texttt{self}_{loc}, \texttt{self}_{loc}) \in DT)\}.$$

6.4 Meta-theory of MiniMAO₃

This section highlights the key theorems in the meta-theory of MiniMAO₃. These include static type safety and two theorems related to effects and the (un-)observability of mutations made by spectators.

Type safety is proved using the standard subject reduction and progress theorems.

In the meta-theory, the type environment maps variables and store locations to types. Additionally, the type environment records the ground concern domains, so that for a ground concern domain g, $\Gamma(g) = $ domain. A type environment Γ is *concern complete* for a program P if every ground concern domain in P is in the domain of Γ.

A type environment Γ is *consistent with a store* S, written $\Gamma \approx S$, if all objects in the store conform to their types, both as declared and as given by Γ, and if the sets of locations in the domains of both Γ and S are the same. A *valid store* for a program P contains objects (with the appropriate concrete concern domains) representing every aspect instantiated in P. Additionally, for a store to be valid there must exist some type environment consistent with it. Similarly, a join point stack J is *consistent with a store* S, written $J \approx S$, if all locations named in J appear in S's domain.

The Subject Reduction theorem says that, given a configuration that meets appropriate initial conditions including having a well-typed expression, single-step evaluation results in a new configuration that satisfies the same conditions and that has an expression that is a subtype of the original expression.

Theorem 1 (Subject Reduction). *Given a well-typed program P with public concern domains $\hat{g}$ and private concern domains $\hat{g}'$, for an expression e, a valid store S, a stack J consistent with S, a concern-complete type environment Γ consistent with S, a set of concern domains $\hat{\gamma}$ with $\hat{g}' \subseteq \hat{\gamma} \subseteq (\hat{g} \cup \hat{g}')$, and the evaluation dependency table, DT, of P, if $\Gamma \cdot \hat{\gamma} \vdash_{DT} e : t$ and $\langle e, J, S \rangle \hookrightarrow \langle e', J', S' \rangle$, then $J' \approx S'$, S' is valid, and there exist concern-complete $\Gamma' \approx S'$ and $t' \preccurlyeq t$, such that $\Gamma' \cdot \hat{\gamma} \vdash_{DT} e' : t'$.*

The Progress theorem says that, given a configuration that meets these same conditions, the expression is either a value or can be evaluated in a single step to a configuration giving a new expression or an exception.

Theorem 2 (Progress). *Given a well-typed program, P, with public concern domains $\hat{g}$ and private concern domains $\hat{g}'$, for an expression e, a valid store S, a stack J consistent with S, a concern-complete type environment Γ consistent with S, a set of concern domains $\hat{\gamma}$ such that $\hat{g}' \subseteq \hat{\gamma} \subseteq (\hat{g} \cup \hat{g}')$, and the evaluation dependency table DT, such that the triple $\langle e, J, S \rangle$ is reached in the evaluation of P, if $\Gamma \cdot \hat{\gamma} \vdash_{DT} e : t$ then either:*

- *$e = loc_\delta$ for some δ and $loc \in dom(S)$,*
- *$e = \texttt{null}_\delta$ for some δ, or*
- *one of the following hold:*

- $\langle e, J, S \rangle \hookrightarrow \langle e', J', S' \rangle$,
- $\langle e, J, S \rangle \hookrightarrow \langle \texttt{NullPointerException}, J', S' \rangle$, or
- $\langle e, J, S \rangle \hookrightarrow \langle \texttt{ClassCastException}, J', S' \rangle$.

The Type Safety theorem says that a well-typed program either diverges or evaluates to a value or exception.

Theorem 3 (Type Safety). *Given a program P, with main expression e, concern domains $\hat{g}$, $\vdash P$ OK, and a valid store S_0, then either the evaluation of e diverges or else $\langle e, \bullet, S_0 \rangle \overset{*}{\hookrightarrow} \langle x, J, S \rangle$ and one of the following hold for x:*

- $x = loc_\delta$ *for some δ and $loc \in dom(S)$,*
- $x = null_\delta$ *for some δ,*
- $x = \texttt{NullPointerException}$, *or*
- $x = \texttt{ClassCastException}$

Besides static type safety, MiniMAO$_3$ provably enforces the constraints given by effects clauses and concern domain dependency declarations. The central theorem here is called Tag Frame Soundness. It states that for any concern domain g that is not directly or transitively declared to be mutable for a given expression e, the portion of the store corresponding to g will be unchanged when e is evaluated to a value.

The formal statement of this theorem demands just a bit more terminology. Like Classic Java, we use evaluation context rules, denoted by $\mathbb{E}$ to implicitly define the congruence rules and give a non-constructive definition of evaluation order [14]. The rules are completely standard and are omitted here. To refer to the portion of the store S corresponding to a particular ground concern domain g, we write $S|g$, which is the set of all mappings in the store where the owner domain of the mapped object is g.

Theorem 4 (Tag Frame Soundness). *Let P be a well-typed program with concern domains $\hat{g}$ and evaluation dependency table DT. If the configuration $\langle \mathbb{E}[\langle e \rangle_{\delta,\hat{\gamma}}], J, S \rangle$ appears in an evaluation of P, then either the evaluation diverges or $\langle \mathbb{E}[\langle e \rangle_{\delta,\hat{\gamma}}], J, S \rangle \overset{*}{\hookrightarrow} \langle \mathbb{E}[v], J', S' \rangle$, where $\forall g \in (\hat{g} \setminus depClose_{DT}(\hat{\gamma})) \cdot S|g = S'|g$.*

The last theorem we discuss here applies to programs that meet a particular restriction, discussed below. In such programs, no mutation is possible by dereferencing a read-only location. This is different than Tag Frame Soundness in that it says a read-only reference may not be used for mutation *even if* it points to a writable domain.

The formal statement of this theorem uses several auxiliary functions. Intuitively, $domains_S(loc)$ gives the set of ground concern domains for the object pointed to by loc in the store S; $locations(e)$ gives every location appearing syntactically in e; $\mathbb{G}_S(loc)$ is the "object graph" of a location, whose nodes are locations and whose edges are field references; $rep_S(loc)$ gives the nodes in $\mathbb{G}_S(loc)$; and $writeReach(S)$ is the reflexive, transitive closure of all the write-enabled field references in the store. That is, $(loc, loc') \in writeReach(S)$ implies that a program with a reference to loc can obtain a write-enabled reference to loc' by a series of field references.

Given all that, the theorem assumes an intermediate state with expression e in the evaluation of a program and some location loc that only names public, not private, concern domains. Then—supposing that any references from e to loc are read-only (assumption 1), that e does not have any aliases into the object graph of loc (assumption 2), and certain restrictions on the program hold (assumption 3)—we can conclude that the evaluation of e to a value will not mutate the object graph of loc.

Theorem 5 (Read-only Soundness). *Suppose the configuration* $\langle \mathbb{E}[e], J, S \rangle$ *appears in the evaluation of a well-typed program* P. *Let* loc *be a location in* $dom(S)$ *such that* $domains_S(loc) \subset \mathcal{G}$, *i.e.,* $S(loc)$ *only names public concern domains. Let* $\mathbb{G}_S(loc) = (L, E)$, *and let the following assumptions hold:*

1. $\forall \delta \cdot (loc_\delta \in locations(e)) \implies (\delta = \texttt{readonly})$.
2. $\forall loc'_\delta \in locations(e) \cdot$
   $$(\delta = \varepsilon) \implies (\forall loc'' \in rep_S(loc) \cdot (loc', loc'') \notin writeReach(S)).$$
3. $\forall loc' \in dom(S) \cdot S(loc') = [t \cdot F] \implies isClass(t) \vee isSpectator(t)$.

If $\langle \mathbb{E}[e], J, S \rangle \xrightarrow{*} \langle \mathbb{E}[v], J', S' \rangle$, *then* $\mathbb{G}_S(loc) = \mathbb{G}_{S'}(loc)$.

So what is this restricted class of programs? Just those that do not contain regular aspects! These non-spectator aspects can "leak" pointers into the computation without being explicitly referenced. Thus, the restrictions on aliasing in assumption 2, which are sufficient without regular aspects, are not sufficient in their presence.

By Read-only Soundness, spectators can be used in a program without breaking the read-only references mechanism. The first two assumptions of the theorem are local properties of an expression. The other assumption just restricts the sorts of programs that are considered. So the statement of the theorem can be viewed as a formalization of local reasoning about the expression. Said another way, we need whole-program knowledge at the level of effects clauses, aspect instantiation, and dependency declarations to reason about the effects of regular aspects. But with just spectator aspects, we can reason about the effects of a method call solely based on its effects clause—aspect instantiation and dependency declarations are not necessary.

The Tag Frame Soundness theorem allows unseen, private concern domains to be modified during method or advice execution, since the dependency closure of the evaluation dependency table includes all private concern domains. However, because of the (elided) Respect for Privacy theorem—which states that only a spectator and objects directly or transitively created by the spectator may appear in or reference the spectator's private concern domain—one can still reason about the effects of a method or piece of advice. To reason about the execution of a method or piece of advice one must know its signature including its effects clause, the concern domains of the target object, and the configuration of non-spectator aspects in the program, as represented by the aspect instantiation instructions and dependency declarations. By Respect for Privacy, if the concern domains of the target object do not include any private concern domains, then no changes made by unseen spectators will be visible in the code being considered. The side effects of spectators are effectively sequestered. Thus, spectators can be used non-invasively.

7   Evaluation

Many things ... may become encumbrances if we cling to them blindly and uncritically.

The theoretical analysis above demonstrates the soundness of MAO's effect specifications. However, this says nothing about MAO's *usefulness* — that is, the extent to which MAO's annotations benefit programmers. In this section, we present a small case study that attempts to give a preliminary answer to this question.

Our case study is based on packages in version 1.5.3 of the *AspectJ Programmer's Guide* [3]. We omitted `introduction` and `ltw`, since these very small packages are just for demonstrating AspectJ tools. For the other 7 packages, we specified each aspect using MAO annotations, and then examined the result to determine how much these specifications aided reasoning. The case study's files are available at `http://www.cs.iastate.edu/~leavens/modular-aop/ajpg-153-examples/`.

7.1   Case Study Data

This subsection presents the raw data from our case study in a pair of tables. The subsequent subsection analyzes the data.

Basic statistics about the packages we studied are presented in Table 1. We counted: (1) the number of `.java` files, but in the `tracing` package we only counted files for version 3; (2) the number of lines in these files, with the first 12 lines for each file (a copyright notice) omitted; (3) the number of aspects and (4) abstract aspects; (5) the number of lines (determined by inspection) in the original AspectJ code that would need to be searched to determine control and heap effects of the aspect's advice — this equals the number of lines in advice and method bodies in all aspects[6]; (6) the number of lines (by inspection) in the MAO code that would need to be searched for control effects — this is 0 for @surround advice, and 1 for @curbing advice, and otherwise includes all lines in advice and method bodies called, if those are part of the aspect; and (7) the number of lines (by inspection) in the MAO code that would need to be searched for heap effects — this is 1 for advice or methods with @writes or @pure annotations, otherwise it includes all lines in other advice and method bodies.

Table 2 presents some statistics on the use of various features in MAO. We counted: (1) the number of times the @surround annotation was used — not counting implicit uses in spectator aspects (2) the number of times @curbing was used, (3) the number of times @writes was used as a method or advice annotation — we only used this within aspects and did not count implicit uses in spectator aspects, (4) the number of times @spectator was used, (5) the number of lines that would have to be searched in AspectJ, within the relevant classes, to determine all the methods that would correspond to the **writes** PCDs that the MAO code used. The MAO code used **writes** once in each of the two relevant packages.

7.2   Lessons Learned from the Case Study

Table 2 contains lessons about MAO annotation usage. We found many instances of @surround advice, especially if one counts the implicit uses of @surround in aspects

---

[6] This assumes, pessimistically, that all code in an aspect can have control and heap effects.

Table 1. Basic statistics about the packages studied

Package	Original Files	Original Lines	Aspects	Abstract aspects	AspectJ lines to search for effects	MAO search for control effects	MAO search for heap effects
tjp	2	62	1		17	0	1
tracing (v3)	6	352	2	1	18	0	0
bean	3	203	1		9	2	2
observer	8	164	2	1	9	0	1
telecom	13	593	3		20	0	4
spacewar	19	2049	8		177	19	23
coordination	8	673	1	1	118	0	0

Table 2. Usage statistics on the packages studied

Package	MAO count use of @surround	MAO count use of @curbing	MAO count use of @writes	MAO count use of @spectator	AspectJ lines to search for equivalent of @writes PCDs
tjp	1		1		
tracing (v3)	0			2	
bean	0		3	1	
observer	1		2		18
telecom	4		4	1	
spacewar	5	2	27		27
coordination				1	

that are annotated with @spectator or @surround. By contrast, @curbing was only used twice. There were also many uses of @writes, especially in spacewar's Debug aspect. Moreover, each of the uses of @spectator on an aspect suppresses several uses of the @writes annotation. While we found several spectators, we found three aspects, like spacewar's Debug aspect, do not qualify, principally because they perform I/O and have heap effects on the GUI. For these three aspects it was convenient to use @surround at the aspect-level, which is a shorthand for listing @surround on each piece of advice.

Lessons about reasoning can be drawn from Table 1. First, the use of MAO's features significantly cuts down the number of lines that need to be inspected to determine control and heap effects. This is important, as we noticed that for examples as large as the telecom package or larger it becomes quite difficult to determine the control and heap effects of advice by hand. Thus we believe that a person trying to understand a program, even of such a modest size as telecom, would benefit from the use of annotations on advice. The real problem here is not the efficiency of the analysis: it is that without MAO's modular aspect interfaces, any analysis to determine control and heap effects must depend upon fine implementation details of advice body code. Relatively sophisticated static techniques [11, 29] can certainly compute these dependencies, and IDEs present it to programmers [6, 22] but these dependencies will be *fragile*: whenever the configuration of the system, the implementation of the base program, and (especially) the internals of an aspect changes, then this analysis must be repeated and the results may change in nonlocal, unpredictable ways. The advantage of MAO's effect specifications are, ultimately, that they provide *aspects* with specifications that act both as a unit of analysis and as a boundary to changes. By writing such specifications in MAO annotations, a programmer can make their intentions clear: a tracing aspect can be declared be a spectator upon the program, with no control nor heap effects. If subsequent evolution of the aspect invalidates this intention, the change can be detected statically.

We also found that using the default ownership domain of World for everything outside an aspect worked well. This gives some hope that the annotation burden may mostly fall on aspects, and not on the base program, which is usually much larger. It also gives some hope that annotations are not necessary for Java libraries.

In summary, the case study gives some preliminary indications that the features of MAO help in reasoning about control and heap effects in aspect-oriented code. The case study does not contain enough places where the **writes** pointcut designator is used to make even much of a preliminary estimate as to its utility.

8   Related Work

All reactionaries are paper tigers. In appearance, the reactionaries are terrifying, but in reality they are not so powerful.

Mulet, Malenfant, and Cointe [25] identified a similar problem: composing metaobjects. They offer language mechanisms that make composition possible, but offer no language mechanisms to help programmers control interference.

Dantas and Walker's Harmless Advice [11] is probably the closest formal system to MAO. Harmless advice is similar to our notion of spectators but allows advice to have "curbing" control effects and to write to what we would call a system I/O domain. So, while technically spectators are more restrictive than harmless aspects, both restrict aspects to make reasoning about heap effects easier. Harmless Advice is formalized using an information flow analysis that establishes that the computation in advice cannot affect the base program's computation. As the name implies, all the advice in this system is harmless, and the user-level calculus offers only one protection domain for the base program. MAO does not restrict advice to be harmless, as it can document different kinds of advice. MAO also has a more precise set of annotations, separately documenting control and heap effects, and allowing more fine-grained specification of heap effects. Thus MAO allows specification of control and heap effects that are outside the range allowed by Harmless Advice, but are useful in AspectJ programs (for example, in the spacewar example). MAO's explicit domain declarations and aspect domain parameters allow concern domains to cross-cut the program's modularity structure, whereas the protection domain structure of Harmless Advice is tied to the program's structure.

Kiczales and Mezini [22] take a different approach to the problem of reasoning about aspect-oriented software, by introducing "aspect-aware interfaces." These interfaces are computed from a whole program's configuration and provide a bi-directional mapping from methods to associated advice, and from advice to advised methods. This certainly is helpful in reasoning about control effects of advice that may apply at a given join point or program point. As such it could be used in conjunction with MAO's annotations to determine whether the advice being applied has potential control effects. Aspect-aware interfaces give no help in reasoning about potential heap effects of advice or in reasoning, apart from helping one find what advice might have to be considered. By contrast MAO's annotations can provide more help with such questions.

Another route towards helping people reason about aspect-oriented software is provided by research that establishes interfaces for aspect-oriented program modules. Generally, these systems attach interfaces to base code elements that either permit or prohibit advice from being applied, or describe what advice has been applied. So, Pointcut Interfaces [17], Open Modules [1, 26], Aspectual Collaborations [23], and XPIs [15, 31] all require code to declare or specify the join points to which aspects may be attached. In contrast our focus is on specifying *aspects* and their effects. That is, MAO allows programmers to specify aspects to make reasoning about their effects easier, instead of restricting what they can do. Thus, in MAO, rather than describing potential pointcuts in the base code, programmers describe the important properties of their designs, such as what concerns exist, what advice writes what concerns, etc. These annotations are contained within existing interfaces in their code. MAO allows the use of some of these annotations in writing semantic PCDs, with its **writes** PCD. Furthermore, MAO's statically checked annotations help make reasoning about control and heap effects easier.

MAO is also related to a range of work on categorizing and classifying aspects [19, 20, 29]. Generally, this work identifies a number of (relatively) fine-grained aspect categories, either via manual or automatic analysis. MAO, however, does not address categorization per se: rather, our aim is to provide practical language constructs programmers can use to express properties of their aspects.

In terms of language mechanisms, MAO and especially its concern domains are closely related to other ownership and confined type systems [2, 4, 5, 12, 16, 24, 27, 28, 32]. MAO's novelty here is in demonstrating how ownership types can be used to capture the concerns in an aspect-oriented system: the techniques providing concern domains (a statically fixed set of ownership domains; objects tied to domains by type parameterization and defaults; domains for effect disjointness) are now well known. MAO shows how even a such a simple ownership type and effect system can aid reasoning about the subtle heap effects that may occur in aspect-oriented systems.

9   Conclusion

Conclusions invariably come after investigation, and not before.

In this paper, we have presented Modular Aspects with Ownership, MAO. MAO makes four contributions to the design of Aspect-Oriented languages, to make it easier for programmers to determine how aspects will affect the base code of the program, and how they interfere with each other.

First, surround advice uses simple syntactic restrictions so that programmers can ensure that an aspect will not perturb the control flow of the program to which it is bound. Second, concern domains provide an ownership type and effect system to make clear whether aspects modify data structures in the base program, and if so, what parts of the data they modify. Third, the **writes** PCD leverages concern domains to provide succinct, precise designations for pointcuts that modify data. Finally, MAO is underpinned with a formal model and demonstrates that spectator aspects (defining only surround advice, and writing only their own concern domain) cannot materially affect the execution of other classes or aspects in the program.

Using MAO, programmers can specify the full range of their aspects' interactions with the base program and their interference with one another, making aspect oriented programs more precisely documented and easier to reason about.

Acknowledgments

The work of Clifton and Leavens was supported in part by NSF grant CCF-0428078. The work of Leavens was also supported in part by NSF grant CCF-0429567. The work of Noble was supported in part by a gift from Microsoft Research, by an IBM Eclipse Innovation Grant, by the EPSRC grant Practical Ownership Types for Objects and Aspect Programs, EP/D061644/1, and by the Royal Society of New Zealand Marsden Fund. Thanks to many anonymous reviewers for comments on prior drafts of this work.

References

[1] Aldrich, J.: Open modules: Modular reasoning about advice. In: Black, A.P. (ed.) ECOOP 2005. LNCS, vol. 3586, Springer, Heidelberg (2005)

[2] Aldrich, J., Chambers, C.: Ownership domains: Separating aliasing policy from mechanism. In: Odersky, M. (ed.) ECOOP 2004. LNCS, vol. 3086, Springer, Heidelberg (2004)

[3] AspectJ Team: The AspectJ programming guide, Version 1.5.3. (2006), Available from http://eclipse.org/aspecti

[4] Boyapati, C., Liskov, B., Shrira, L.: Ownership types for object encapsulation. In: POPL, pp. 213–223 (2003)

[5] Clarke, D., Drossopoulou, S.: Ownership, Encapsulation, and the Disjointness of Type and Effect. In: OOPSLA (2002)

[6] Clement, A., Colyer, A., Kersten, M.: Aspect-oriented programming with AJDT. In: Cardelli, L. (ed.) ECOOP 2003. LNCS, vol. 2743, Springer, Heidelberg (2003)

[7] Clifton, C.: A design discipline and language features for modular reasoning in aspect-oriented programs. PhD thesis, Iowa State (2005)

[8] Clifton, C., Leavens, G.T.: MiniMAO$_1$: Investigating the semantics of proceed. Sci. Comput. Programming 63(3), 321–374 (2006)

[9] Clifton, C., Leavens, G.T.: Observers and assistants: A proposal for modular aspect-oriented reasoning. In: FOAL (2002)

[10] Clifton, C., Leavens, G.T.: Spectators and assistants: Enabling modular aspect-oriented reasoning. Technical Report TR #02-10, Dept. of Computer Science, Iowa State University (October 2002)

[11] Dantas, D.S., Walker, D.: Harmless advice. In: POPL (2006)

[12] Dietl, W., Müller, P.: Universes: Lightweight ownership for JML. Journal of Object Technology 4(8), 5–32 (2005)

[13] Filman, R.E., Elrad, T., Clarke, S., Akşit, M. (eds.): Aspect-Oriented Software Development. Addison-Wesley, Reading (2005)

[14] Flatt, M., Krishnamurthi, S., Felleisen, M.: A programmer's reduction semantics for classes and mixins. In: Formal Syntax and Semantics of Java, ch. 7, pp. 241–269. Springer, Heidelberg (1999)

[15] Griswold, W.G., Sullivan, K., Song, Y., Shonle, M., Tewari, N., Cai, Y., Rajan, H.: Modular software design with crosscutting interfaces. IEEE Software, 51–60 (January/February 2006)

[16] Grothoff, C., Palsberg, J., Vitek, J.: Encapsulating Objects with Confined Types. In: OOPSLA, pp. 241–255 (2001)

[17] Gudmundson, S., Kiczales, G.: Addressing practical software development issues in AspectJ with a pointcut interface. In: Knudsen, J.L. (ed.) ECOOP 2001. LNCS, vol. 2072, Springer, Heidelberg (2001)

[18] Igarashi, A., Pierce, B., Wadler, P.: Featherweight Java. A minimal core calculus for Java and GJ. ACM Trans. Prog. Lang. Syst. 23(3), 396–459 (2001)

[19] Katz, S.: Aspect categories and classes of temporal properties. In: Rashid, A., Aksit, M. (eds.) Transactions on Aspect-Oriented Software Development I. LNCS, vol. 3880, Springer, Heidelberg (2006)

[20] Katz, S., Gil, Y.: Aspects and superimpositions. In: Guerraoui, R. (ed.) ECOOP 1999. LNCS, vol. 1628, Springer, Heidelberg (1999)

[21] Kiczales, G.: The fun has just begun. AOSD'03 Keynote Address (2003), available from http://www.cs.ubc.ca/~gregor

[22] Kiczales, G., Mezini, M.: Aspect-oriented programming and modular reasoning. In: ICSE, pp. 49–58. ACM Press, New York (2005)

[23] Lieberherr, K., Lorenz, D.H., Ovlinger, J.: Aspectual collaborations: Combining modules and aspects. The Computer Journal 6(5), 542–565 (2003)

[24] Lu, Y., Potter, J.: Protecting representation with effect encapsulation. In: POPL, pp. 359–371 (2006)

[25] Mulet, P., Malenfant, J., Cointe, P.: Towards a methodology for explicit composition of metaobjects. In: OOPSLA, pp. 316–330. ACM, New York (1995)

[26] Ongkingco, N., Avgustinov, P., Tibble, J., Hendren, L., de Moor, O., Sittampalam, G.: Adding open modules to AspectJ. In: AOSD (2006)

[27] Potanin, A., Noble, J., Clarke, D., Biddle, R.: Generic ownership for generic Java. In: OOPSLA, pp. 311–324 (2006)

[28] Potanin, A., Noble, J., Clarke, D., Biddle, R.: Featherweight Generic Confinement. Journal of Functional Programming 16(6), 793–811 (2006)

[29] Rinard, M., Salcianu, A., Bugrara, S.: A classification system and analysis for aspect-oriented programs. In: Roy, B., Meier, W. (eds.) FSE 2004. LNCS, vol. 3017, Springer, Heidelberg (2004)

[30] Steimann, F.: The paradoxical success of aspect-oriented programming. In: OOPSLA, pp. 481–497 (2006)

[31] Sullivan, K., Griswold, W., Song, Y., Cai, Y., Shonle, M., Tewari, N., Rajan, H.: Information hiding interfaces for aspect-oriented design. In: FSE, pp. 166–175 (May 2005)

[32] Vitek, J., Bokowski, B.: Confined types in Java. S—P&E 31(6), 507–532 (2001)

Joinpoint Inference from Behavioral Specification to Implementation

Thomas Cottenier[1,2], Aswin van den Berg[1], and Tzilla Elrad[2]

[1] Motorola Software Group, Motorola
1303 E. Algonquin Rd, 60196 Schaumburg, IL, USA
[2] Concurrent Programming Research Group, Illinois Institute of Technology,
3100 S. Federal Street, 60696 Chicago, IL, USA
{thomas.cottenier,aswin.vandenberg}@motorola.com,
{cotttho,elrad}@iit.edu

Abstract. Aspect-Oriented Programming languages allow pointcut descriptors to quantify over the implementation points of a system. Such pointcuts are problematic with respect to independent development because they introduce strong mutual coupling between base modules and aspects. This paper introduces a new joinpoint selection mechanism based on state machine specifications. Module interfaces include behavioral specifications defined as protocol state machines. These specifications are not defined with respect to potential aspects, but are used to model and simulate the architecture of a system and act as behavioral contracts between the modules of the system. We show how a smart joinpoint selection mechanism is able to infer points that might be located deep inside the implementation of a module, given pointcuts that are expressed entirely in terms of behavioral specification elements. We present a tool, the Motorola *WEAVR*, which implements this technique in a Model-Driven Engineering environment.

Keywords: Aspect-Oriented Software Development, Model-Driven Software Engineering, Modules and Interfaces.

1 Introduction

Since the inception of Aspect-Oriented Software Development (AOSD) in 1997, it has been known that Aspect-Oriented Programming (AOP) languages introduce strong coupling between base modules and aspects. AOP languages allow pointcut descriptors to refer directly to the implementations of modules to capture joinpoints, points where aspects inject behavior through advices. This practice is problematic with respect to modularity and independent development. Modules that are advised by aspects become hard to evolve independently. Small refactorings are susceptible to modify the way an aspect interacts with a module, breaking the semantics of the aspect. Consequently, the deployment of AOP practices has been mostly restricted to small cohesive teams of expert programmers.

E. Ernst (Ed.): ECOOP 2007, LNAI 4609, pp. 476–500, 2007.

There are three main research directions in addressing this problem. The first direction of research advocates restricting the expressiveness of aspects by forfeiting the obliviousness of modules. Approaches such as Open Modules [1] or Crosscutting Interfaces [2] propose to move aspect pointcut descriptors from the aspect definition to the interfaces of modules. Aspects are only allowed to advice joinpoints that are explicitly published in modules interfaces. These approaches prepare modules for specific, anticipated aspects by making a commitment about particular points in the module implementation, or by organizing the structure of the module in a way that these points are easily captured by specific aspects [3].

A second approach favors investigating alternative ways to modular reasoning in the presence of aspects. In [4], the authors argue that a global analysis of the system configuration is required before the interfaces of the system modules can be determined. The approach supports modular reasoning after aspect deployment but is not applicable to design-time interfaces, and hence, it does not support independent development well.

Coupling between base system and aspects is closely related to the fragility of the pointcut descriptors used in AOP languages. A third direction of research focuses on methods that allow pointcut descriptors to be defined at a higher level of abstraction, in terms of the program semantics [5].

The approach presented in this paper is in line with the last direction of research. We propose a technique to *infer* joinpoints located deep inside the implementation of modules from pointcut descriptors that are defined in terms of behavioral descriptions of the system modules.

Traditional interfaces are generally not sufficient to enable independent development of the sub-components of large complex systems. System modules interact according to specific protocols, which need to be publicized in their interfaces. These protocols are generally captured as state machine contracts, called Protocol State Machines. They describe the observable behavior of a module and the effects of method invocations on its state in an intuitive and precise way.

We show through some non-trivial examples that it is possible to derive implementation level joinpoints from pointcut descriptors that capture properties of the behavioral description of a module. The approach therefore maintains much of the expressiveness of aspects without compromising the modularity of base modules.

Behavioral specifications do not need to be defined with respect to potential aspects. They appear naturally in the early stages of the software development lifecycle. This approach works particularly well in the context of Model-Driven Software Engineering (MDSE), especially in domains where the use of state machines is well established, such as in the telecom industry.

Yet, the approach could be generalized to programming languages using interface specifications such as typestates [6], predicates or interfaces expressed in domain-specific languages.

The paper is organized as follows. First, we introduce some of the model-driven engineering practices in industry to develop large telecom infrastructure software. We distinguish between protocol state machines, used for modeling and system validation, and implementation-level state machines, used for system verification and code generation. We present an aspect-oriented modeling tool for the UML 2.0, the Motorola *WEAVR*. The tool performs weaving of aspects at the modeling level, before code generation, and is currently being deployed in production at Motorola, in the network infrastructure business unit.

Section 3 illustrates the approach through examples that take on some of the concerns presented in the AO Challenge paper [7]. The AO Challenge consists of a series of fine-grained concerns that are required to implement fault tolerance through transactional mechanisms. These concerns depend on each other and interact in subtle ways which makes their aspect-oriented implementation problematic. The solution presented is fully implemented in terms of the behavioral specification of the system but addresses the problem in a way that would be difficult, if not impossible to match using an AOP language such as AspectJ.

Section 4 details the joinpoint selection mechanism that enables the *WEAVR* to infer implementation points of the system in terms of its specification and some of the issues associated with the selection mechanism are discussed.

Section 5 discusses related work and finally, Section 6 concludes this paper.

2   Aspect-Oriented and Model-Driven Software Engineering

2.1   Model-Driven Software Engineering

A model of a system is an abstract specification of its structure and behavior. A model defines the observable behavior of the system components and specifies how they interact, without detailing how the different tasks of the system are performed. System modeling aims at defining and validating the architecture of the system. Validation of the system architecture is performed by executing the system models in a simulation environment. Once the architecture has been validated, the component models define a contract that must be honored by the component implementations.

In this paper, Model-Driven Software Engineering (MDSE) is discussed in the context of fully automated code generation from precise behavioral models, a.k.a *translation* of models into executable artifacts [8]. The style of UML modeling used is highly influenced by the ITU Specification and Description Language (SDL) [9]. Abstract models of the system are iteratively refined and transformed until they can be executed on the target platforms.

The telecom industry has a long tradition of MDSE. It pioneered the field starting in the 70's, with the SDL. The SDL was initially conceived as a specification language to unambiguously describe the behavior of reactive, discrete systems in terms of communicating extended finite state machines. Since then, it was extended with mechanisms supporting object-orientation and has adopted a formal semantics described in terms of abstract state machines.

The use of the SDL has rapidly expanded from the area of system specification and documentation to the realm of system design and implementation. The unambiguous semantics of the SDL has enabled the industry to develop powerful code generators that take models as input and deliver highly optimized platform specific code, mostly in C and C++. Optimizing code generation has had an important effect on the system development process. The structure of the generated code is very different from the structure of the system models and prohibits the manual refinement of the system at the level of the code.

The UML 2.0 has adopted many of the language features of the SDL, including the composite-structure architecture diagrams, support for transition-oriented state machines, and parts of the SDL action language semantics. This makes it possible to interpret UML 2.0 models as SDL-like specifications using a lightweight profile, and automatically generate executables. This is exactly what is performed by tools such as Telelogic TAU [10] and the Motorola Mousetrap code generator [11].

The next section presents the different phases of development lifecycle used in this context, and discusses the use of AOSD.

2.2 System Modeling and Simulation

The requirements of the system are captured using use cases expressed as Message Sequence Charts (MSC) or UML sequence diagrams. These use cases are translated into test case definitions expressed in a notation such as the TTCN (Testing and Test Control Notation) [12]. The test case definitions drive the design and implementation process at different levels of granularity.

It is absolutely essential to be able to validate the system design and architecture as early as possible in the lifecycle. For large systems, validation is essentially performed through modeling, simulation and testing. There is therefore an important emphasis on the executability of early system models. Executability in conformance with the test cases is an important property that needs to be maintained through all phases of the development process.

The architecture of the system is defined using composite-structure diagrams, protocol state machines along with class diagrams.

2.2.1 Composite-Structure Diagrams

During the architectural phase, composite-structure diagrams are used to identify and model the different subcomponents of the system. These subcomponents generally become the basic units of independent development of the system. Composite-structure diagrams define a hierarchical run-time decomposition of the system. They define the internal run-time structure of an active class (a process definition), in terms of other active classes instances, referred to as parts. A Connector specifies a medium that enables communication between parts of an active class or between the environment of an active class and one of its parts.

Figure 1 illustrates the composite structure diagram of a simple resource access server. An instance of a server is composed of two subcomponents, one dispatcher and a pool of request handlers. The dispatcher is responsible for forwarding external requests to a request handler picked from the pool. Request handlers maintain sessions through a context id, (CID_t) and access resources delivered by resource managers, identified by a resource id (RID_t).

This architecture is typical for high-availability distributed system, as well as general-purpose web servers. For this example, we assume that we can reuse the implementation of a dispatcher to drive the simulation and we focus on the models of a request handler and a resource manager.

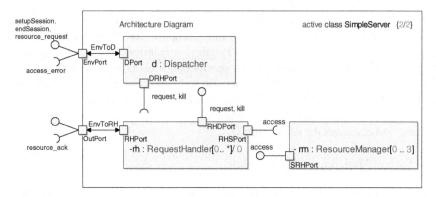

Fig. 1. Composite-structure architecture diagram for a simple resource access server

2.2.2 Protocol State Machines

The observable behavior of each part is specified using protocol state machines. These state machines are not fully executable. They specify what the state transitions of the system are, their triggers and what output they produce. They do not define how this output is produced or what actions are executed along state transitions. Yet, such models can be simulated.

In its initial phases, the simulation is initially performed by stepping through of the execution of the model, while manually taking decisions about the completion of the execution whenever the system is not fed with enough information. During this phase the initial architecture is refined as to satisfy the requirement use-cases. Once the architecture converges, different execution paths are encoded into tests to drive the simulation automatically and perform analysis.

Figure 2 shows the interfaces for a request handler and a resource manager, along with their protocol state machine specifications. The state machine of Figure 2.a defines a transition that is triggered by a request and produces a resource access. The state machine of Figure 2.b defines two distinct transitions triggered by an access, one transition to a 'success' state and another to a 'failure' state. It does not specify how the decision is made whether a resource access occurred successfully or not. The path followed during execution needs to be provided either by the user or by the test case that drives the simulation. Figure 3 shows a trace that has been generated by the simulator during validation, in the case of a successful resource access.

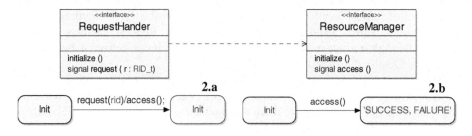

Fig. 2. Protocol state machines for request handlers and resource managers

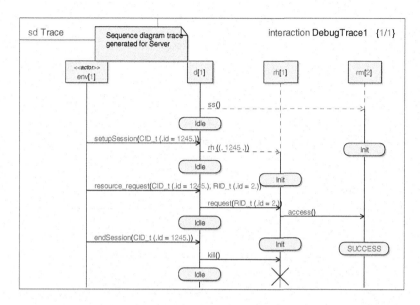

Fig. 3. Trace generated by the model simulator for the validation of the system model

2.2.3 State Machine Refinement, Inheritance and Realization Mappings

State machines can inherit from other state machines. A specialized state machine may add features or change features of the original state machine. Features that may be added include states, transitions, variables and other entities that can be declared in a state machine. State machine inheritance is a natural way to refine protocol state machines down to the implementation.

In addition, we propose a particular type of realization relationship between protocol state machines. A state machine can be the realization of a more abstract state machine according to a *realization mapping*. Figure 4 shows two protocol state machines for two different types of resource managers, *LinkManagerIf* in Figure 4.a and *ChannelManagerIf* in Figure 4.b. Both protocol state machines can be mapped to the *ResourceManager* state machine specification by mapping the transitions of *LinkManagerIf* and *ChannelManagerIf* to the transitions of *ResourceManager*. This mapping is a function from transitions of one state machine to transitions of another.

State machine realization relationships offer a powerful abstraction mechanism. A protocol state machine can be a particular perspective of another one. This perspective focuses on the properties that are relevant to the concern captured by the specification. Transitions that are not relevant can be omitted from the mapping. State machine specifications can realize multiple other specifications, each of those focusing on a different property.

Realization of state machines also favors reuse. Third party components can be integrated in system by mapping their protocol state machine to an abstract protocol state machine. For example, the interaction of the request handler with the LinkManager and ChannelManager resource managers can be expressed in terms of the resource manager specification given the realization mappings illustrated in Figure 4.

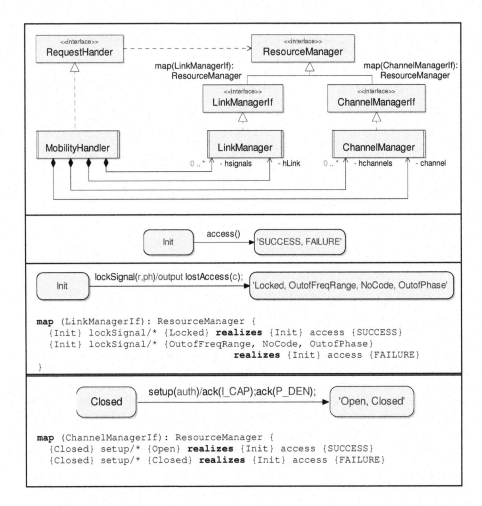

Fig. 4. Realization relationship between the protocol state machines of link and channel managers and the protocol state machine of a resource manager

2.3 System Implementation and Verification

The implementation state machines that define the behavior of the LinkManager and ChannelManager resource managers inherit from the specification state machines of the LinkManagerIf and ChannelManagerIf interfaces. This inheritance relationship enforces that the transitions defined in the specifications are maintained at the level of the implementation. This enforcement is critical to the verification of the system, ensuring that the implementation of the system conforms to its specification.

The implementation of LinkManager and ChannelManager are defined using *transition-oriented* state machines, as illustrated in Figure 5. Transition-oriented state machines provide a better view of the control flow and the communication aspects of state transitions. They are used for defining the detailed internal behavior of a reactive component. Transition-oriented state machines use explicit symbols for different actions that can be performed during the transition. They make the control flow explicit using decision actions, represented as diamonds.

The behavior of the request handler is defined in Figure 5.a. It starts up by instantiating some resources (i.0). Upon receiving a request, it accesses a resource that is indexed by a resource id (i.1), instantiates it if necessary (i.1.i), and accesses some of its own resources (i.2, i.3).

The behavior of LinkManager and ChannelManager is partially defined in Figure 5.b and 5.c. We only illustrate the behavior that is relevant to this discussion.

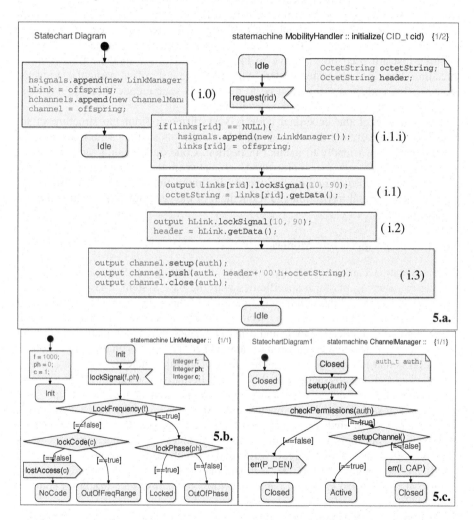

Fig. 5. Partial implementations of RequestHandler, LinkManager and ChannelManager as transition-oriented state machines

Access to the resources triggers internal state transitions, whose outcome is controlled by a decision tree. These decisions are internal to the component behavior and are not exposed in its behavioral interface. Yet, decision actions capture important semantics because they determine the outcome of a transition and directly affect the future behavior of the component.

2.4   Model Translation and Code Generation

Once the system has been validated and thoroughly tested in the simulator, the models are translated into platform-specific executables and tested in the field. The code generators used can be highly optimized for different target platforms. They handle the specificities and the configurations of the platforms and integrate additional concerns that are not explicitly handled in the models. In particular, the specific libraries that are used do not have to be referred to in the models. Examples are threading libraries, operating system API's or the use of a particular transport protocol. The code generation also performs various source code level optimizations that involve code motion and dead code elimination.

The structure of the generated code is very different from the structure of the models. Code generators do not map modeling concepts such as state machines into structures that are friendly to manual inspection. Code optimization further destroys the structural and syntactic correspondence between the system models and the generated code and may modify the overall decomposition of the system to improve performance. Manual inspection and refinement of the generated code is therefore not a viable practice.

2.5   Weaving Aspects into Models

Code generation can automatically integrate crosscutting concerns such as tracing, logging or recurring platform specificities with the base system. These concerns are activated and deployed through the configuration of the code generator. Yet, there are concerns, such as fault tolerance, security or timing constraints that are highly dependent on the application logic and cannot be handled in a systematic way through code generation. The implementation of these concerns depends on the application.

Concerns that interact with the control flow of multiple state machines are hard to modularize using the abstractions of the UML. Alternative use cases or fault tolerance concerns tend to introduce new states and new decision actions in multiple state machines, across different development teams. State machine inheritance mechanisms do not support these kinds of refinements. Each development team therefore needs to re-implement this logic within multiple state machines. In practice, different teams implement the same concern slightly differently, which leads to inconsistencies and a significant replication of effort. We estimate that model size could be reduced by an average 40% if the replication of behavior within and across state machines could be avoided [28].

There is therefore a strong motivation to provide a means to modularize application level concerns that interact with the control flow of state machines at multiple locations. For the reasons mentioned in the previous section, the use of an AOP language at the level of the generated code is not an option. Generated code lacks the necessary structure to apply aspects. Crosscutting concerns need to be fully coordinated with the base system at the level of the models. The Motorola WEAVR is a model transformation engine that enables aspects to be defined at the modeling level and to be completely woven with the base models before code generation.

3   Motorola WEAVR: Weaving Aspects into Models

The Motorola *WEAVR* provides language constructs to capture aspects in UML 2.0 and perform weaving of state machines before code generation. In a large industrial setting, the most important benefits from aspect orientation are obtained when aspects can be deployed across components of a system that are developed by independent development teams. These components communicate through well defined interfaces, with which state machines are associated.

The state machines that define the implementation of those components evolve quickly from one iteration to another. In this context, it is critical that aspects be defined exclusively in terms of the specification elements of the system.

This section illustrates by example how joinpoints that might be located deep inside the implementation of a module can be inferred from state machine specifications. This capability is essential to apply the full expressiveness of aspects in a context where information hiding is strictly enforced. We also illustrate the language constructs used in WEAVR and some of its more advanced features. The joinpoint selection mechanism itself is discussed in detail in Section 4.

The examples presented are simplified interpretations of some the AO Challenge [7] concerns applied in a distributed setting. The concerns handled relate to exception handling and recovery, applied to the example presented in Section 2. The aspects presented are Exception Handling, Recoverability, Atomicity and Distributed Transaction. Each of those aspects depends on the functionality introduced by the previous one.

3.1 WEAVR Pointcuts Descriptors

WEAVR support two distinct types of pointcut descriptors: action pointcuts and transition pointcuts. The pointcut descriptors strictly refer to actions and transition declared in the protocol state machines of the system.

The notation used for both types of pointcuts is identical: a pointcut is always represented as a transition from a set of source states to a set of target states, triggered by an input expression. The transition can contain one action expression. Wildcards can be used to quantify over both the source and target states of the transition. The trigger and action expressions are used to match the signatures of transition triggers and the signatures of actions executed in the context of a transition. Figure 6 illustrates a pointcut descriptor that matches two types of joinpoints. When interpreted as an action pointcut, it matches all actions executed in the context of any transition. When interpreted as a transition pointcut, it matches all transitions that execute any action in their context. The context relationship between action and transition joinpoints could also be extended to a cflow relationship when needed.

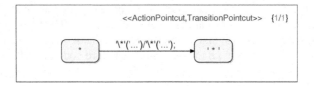

Fig. 6. A WEAVR pointcut descriptor

3.2 Exception Handling Aspect

The protocol state machine of Figure 2.b indicates that a resource access can either succeed or fail. This specification corresponds to a particular mapping, or interpretation of what is considered a failure in the context of the application. The specification does not constrain what the response of the resource is in case of failure.

The exception handling aspect enforces this response across all the components of the system. In case of exception handling, it is important to abort the execution as early as possible, from the point at which the exception is inevitable. This example illustrates how the joinpoint selection mechanism introduces advices within the implementation body of the module, at locations that are inferred from protocol state machines.

Figure 7 defines a WEAVR aspect. It states that whenever the system is about to reach a state considered as a failure in the specification of Figure 2.b, an acknowledgement containing an error code should be sent back to sender of the access request, without proceeding with the execution of the transition.

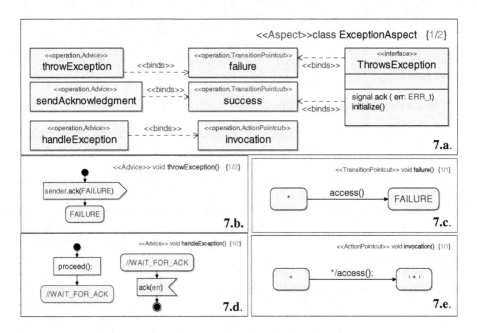

Fig. 7. The Exception Aspect binding diagram, the *failure* pointcut and the *throwException* advice, the *invocation()* pointcut and the *handleException()* advice

The aspect introduces a new interface, *ThrowsException*, which is bound to the object instance that contains joinpoints for the *success* and *failure* pointcuts. This interface declares the acknowledgement signal and the corresponding error codes. The aspect also includes pointcuts and advices. Advices are bound to pointcuts through a dependency that is annotated with the *binds* stereotype. Advices are instantiated for each joinpoint that matches a pointcut descriptor. The binding dependency specifies how arguments and parameters are passed from joinpoints to instances of the advice.

The *failure* pointcut of Figure 7.c matches a selection of execution paths in the state machines. These selections are shown in Figure 8. The shaded thin rectangles delimit portions of the execution paths that match the pointcut of Figure 7.c. The marks that occur first in the execution path correspond to *before* joinpoints whereas the second marks correspond to the *after* joinpoints.

The joinpoint selection mechanism places the *before* mark at the first location in the execution paths for which the only reachable next states match the target state of the pointcut descriptors, from a state that matches its initial state, when triggered by a signal that matches the trigger of the pointcut definition. The matching mechanism is resolved with respect to the realization mappings.

Figure 7.b illustrates an advice that is connected to the execution statements that precede the selection, aborts the current execution (it does not call the *proceed* keyword) and forces the state machine in a state that is already defined in the state machine implementation where it is instantiated, the failure state (*Failure* is declared in the pointcut it is bound to). The paths selections are deleted by the advice and replaced by a direct transition to the failure state. In particular, the *lockCode()* decision action is not executed anymore in Figure 8.a.

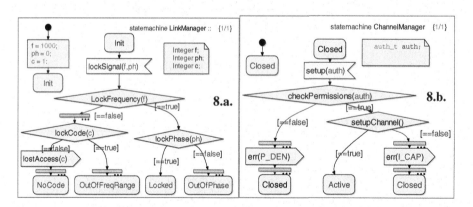

Fig. 8. The shaded thin rectangles delimit selections of executions paths in the state machine that match the pointcut of Figure 7.c

Property. Transition pointcuts can capture joinpoints that might be located deep inside the implementation of state machines. These pointcuts are entirely defined in terms of protocol state machines. The joinpoint selection mechanism performs static control flow analysis to determine the earliest points in the implementation that match the pointcut definition, according to the mappings that are defined in the system.

Figure 7.d illustrates the use of action pointcuts. The *invocation* pointcut selects send signal actions, remote procedure calls (calls to active classes) or simple method invocations (calls to passive classes) that match the *access* methods of the *ResourceManager* interface. The *handleException* advice waits for the response provided by the resource manager and recovers the returned value in the *err* variable.

Property. Caller side pointcuts can abstract from the particular invocation mechanism. This is achieved through the use of implicit states followed by a trigger (as shown by the commented out state name). In the case where the pointcut matches a send signal action, the joinpoint is replaced by a remote procedure call.

3.3 Recovery Aspect

The *Recovery* aspect is dependent on the *ThrowsException* Aspect. It illustrates the ability to introduce new transitions in state machines.

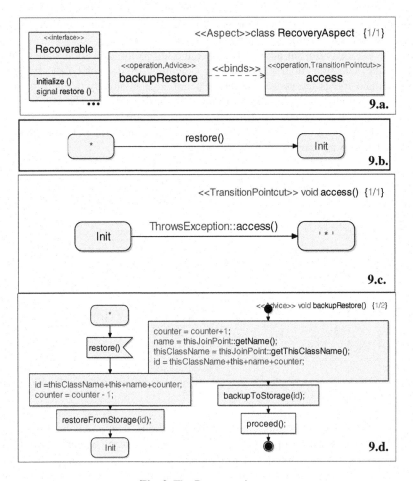

Fig. 9. The Recovery Aspect

The Recovery aspect backs up the state of resource instances before an *access* invocation is processed. The *backupRestore* advice of Figure 9.d. is applied before any transition proceeds, from the *Init* state to any other state, as indicated by the wildcard used in the name of the target state of pointcut 9.c. The advice also adds the ability to respond to a restore trigger to recover the state of the system, by calling the *.restoreFromStorage* method. It introduces new transitions from any state back to the *Init* state. The restore transition is publicized in the protocol state machine of Figure 9.b., defined in the interface of aspect.

Property. The effects of the advice on the behavior of the base models are specified as protocol state machines. This makes it possible to reason about aspect/base composition in terms of specification elements: the interface of the system, the interfaces of aspects and their pointcuts.

3.4 Atomicity Aspect

The Atomicity Aspect ensures that all the transitions that access resources proceed in an atomic way. When a resource access fails, the aspect ensures that the resources previously accessed along that transition are restored to the state in which they where before the transition was triggered.

This aspect depends on the deployment of the Exception Handling Aspect and the Recovery Aspect. A resource must notify the caller that an exception occurred and needs to provide the recovery capability. The Atomicity Aspect illustrates how aspects can introduce new states and new labels into state machines. Labels are represented as ellipses. They correspond to *goto* labels and are used to organize transitions into transition sections. State and label introduction is a powerful mechanism that allows aspects to build up complex static control flow structures.

Figure 10 depicts the Atomicity Aspect. The pointcut of Figure 10.b intercepts the access to recoverable resource managers. The advice of Figure 10.c builds up a static control flow structure that handles the failure of a resource access. A resource access failure is handled by recovering all the resources previously accessed along the current state transition execution. The advice of Figure 10.d builds up the *rollback* transition. Figure 11 *illustrates* the result of weaving the Exception Handling, Recovery and Atomicity Aspects in the request handler model. In practice, woven models are not supposed to be manually inspected. The weaving really occurs on the model, and is not applied to its presentation entities.

A state or label introduction occurs when an advice refers to a state or a label that is not declared in the pointcut descriptor it is bound to. When introducing states and labels into state machines, the scope of the introduction needs to be specified. States and labels can be introduced per State Machine, per Transition or per Joinpoint.

A state that is introduced per state machine, thisStateMachine<state_name>, is shared among all advice instances in the scope of a same state machine. A state that is introduces per transition, thisTransition<state_name> is shared by all advice instances bound to joinpoints of the same transition. A state that is introduced per Joinpoint, thisJoinPoint<state_name>, is unique to the advice instance bound to a specific joinpoint.

The joinpoints of a transition are partially ordered. In the case of per Joinpoint states, it is possible to refer to states that have been introduced by the advice bound to the previous joinpoint. This is accomplished using the previousJoinPoint<state_name, default_state> notation, which resolves to a default state in the case the previous joinpoint is not defined (the joinpoint is the first joinpoint occurring in a transition).

When referring to states or labels introduced by previous joinpoints the WEAVR can construct control structure statically, as shown in Figure 11 or dynamically. In the general case, this can only be achieved dynamically as discussed in Section 4.6.

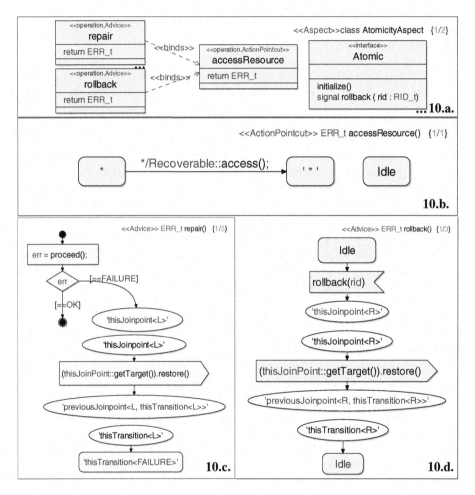

Fig. 10. The Atomicity Aspect

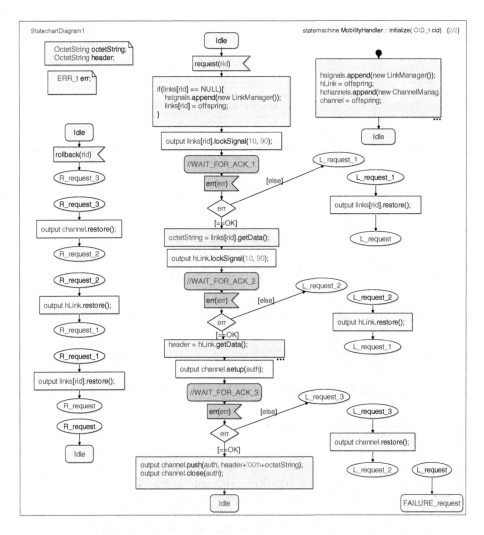

Fig. 11. Representation of the result of weaving the Exception Handling, Recovery and Atomicity Aspects in the request handler

Property. The control flow structures provided by state machines (states, decision actions and labels) make it possible to declare flow dependencies that span multiple advice instantiations. This allows aspects to introduce complex execution paths in the system. In the case of Atomicity, the aspect is able to introduce the repair and rollback functionality directly, while AOP implementations would need to define runtime structures explicitly in the advice implementation and perform application monitoring.

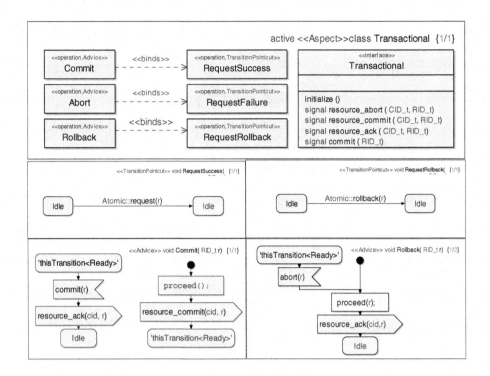

Fig. 12. Implementation of the Two-Phase Commit Aspect

3.5 Distributed Transaction Aspect

The deployment of the Atomicity Aspect provides the necessary structure that allows a distributed transactional protocol such as Two-Phase Commit to be deployed transparently on the resource handlers. The aspect for Two-Phase Commit is presented in Figure 12. The aspect only needs to introduce a per Transition Ready state, which delimits the first phase of the protocol and declare the signals that drive the phases of the protocol and send acknowledgements to the transaction coordinator.

3.6 Discussion

The Two-Phase Commit problem presented in the previous section is a simplified representation of a real problem encountered in production models. One of the systems under development is composed of a large number of distributed subcomponents. For an interaction to occur successfully, all those components need to operate in a synchronized fashion. If one resource or communication channel in the system cannot be accessed safely, the interaction needs to be aborted or delayed. As a result, each component needs to implement a variant of 2PC, for each component it communicates with, which amounts to a number of 2PC request handlers that is quadratic to the number of components. Each development team needs therefore to re-implement 2PC in the context of the specific resources that are managed. In practice, different teams would implement the same concern slightly different, which leads to inconsistencies and important replication of effort.

Transparent deployment of fault tolerance behavior is not considered as a practice that is desirable through aspect-oriented programming techniques [7]. We believe that aspect-oriented techniques can achieve a better separation of concerns at the level of state machines compared with code level techniques, especially in the domains of fault tolerance and concurrency. State machine specifications provide more information about the behavior of the modules, which allows aspects to get a better semantic grip on the module. The awareness of the base model with respect to the fault tolerance is implicitly captured by its state machine specification. This specification should not be declared with respect to potential aspects, but should appear naturally in the early design phases. Aspects can also introduce new state machine specifications and realization mappings in the system. Aspects can therefore explicitly declare the perspective of the system that is relevant to the behavior injected by the aspect. Section 4 details some of the mechanisms of joinpoint inference used in the Motorola WEAVR.

4   Inference of Joinpoints from Specification to Implementation

4.1   Joinpoint Model and Selection

The weaver needs to perform a mapping between specifications that describe *what* state transitions are to be triggered and the logic that implements *how* these transitions are executed. A transition from a state S to a state T, triggered by an event i, $(S \xrightarrow{i} T)$ corresponds to a tree of possible runtime *traces,* whose roots are *triggers* from state S and whose leaves are *next state actions* to state T. The nodes of this tree are points in the execution where the control flow affects the reachability of states. These are either decision actions or jumps statements to labels. This tree of possible traces maps to *execution paths* in the state machine implementation. The unit of weaving is a *selection* of those execution paths. A selection corresponds to a subtree of possible traces, whose leaves are next state actions.

The correspondence between the tree of traces and the graph of execution paths in the state machine can be obtained by performing a depth-first search on the state machines, starting from triggers that match the pointcut designator.

Definition. The pointcut designator $pct(S \xrightarrow{i} *)$ refers to transitions from state S to any state, triggered by an event i. It matches a tree of traces whose root is a trigger i from state S. The corresponding execution paths are obtained by performing a DFS, starting from a root trigger i from state S. The leaves of the DFS tree are *all* reachable next state actions. This pointcut therefore always resolves to a single selection of execution paths within a state machine.

$$pct(S \xrightarrow{i} *) \Rightarrow \{ \hbar \ path(S \xrightarrow{i} *) \} \tag{1}$$

Before advices are located after the trigger. After advices are located before the next state actions.

Definition. The pointcut designator $pct(S \xrightarrow{i} T)$ refers to transitions from state S to state T, triggered by an event i. It defines the set of the largest subtrees of $pct(S \xrightarrow{i} *)$, for which all leaves are next state actions to state T. This constraint can be expressed as follows.

$$pct(S \xrightarrow{i} T) \Rightarrow \{ \hbar \; path(S \xrightarrow{i} *) \} \setminus \{ \hbar \; path(S \xrightarrow{i} NOT(T)) \} \qquad (2)$$

The pointcut defines a set of selections. In the case $\{ \hbar \; path(S \xrightarrow{i} NOT(T)) \}$ is an empty set, it defines only one selection whose root is the trigger i on state S. Otherwise, it defines a set of trees whose roots are *decision actions* and whose leaves are next state actions to T. Before advices are located right after the decision action. After advices are located before the next state actions.

Property. The root of a selection is never contained within a cycle in the state machine graph. A cycle is formed when a jump statement (a goto label statement) refers to one of its ancestors. The jump statement can only be part of the selection if all its reachable states match the pointcut end state. The ancestor is therefore also part of the selection.

4.2 Discussion

This matching method is very expressive because it can localize the important decision points in the execution of a state machine.

Decision points represent conditional statements that have a significant outcome on the state of the system, and on its future behavior. Conditional statements, in general, are hard to match directly, because they can be implemented in different ways, are prone to refactorings, and do not have an identifier. Signature-based matching of conditional statements is therefore not a good idea, and is rarely implemented in AOP languages.

Yet, decision points tend to be important crosscutting points. They are points where different use cases interact. As a result, aspects based on the procedural decomposition need to write complicated pointcuts that essentially attempt to detect those decisions points indirectly, which leads to brittle aspects. We consider the work on Stateful aspects [25] and Trace-Based pointcuts [26] as being proposals that attempt to address this problem at the code level. The transition selection mechanism allows semantically significant decision points to be identified in terms of state machine states and triggers, which are stable elements in the system, and have an intuitive semantic meaning.

The technique has proven particularly useful in practice to log the execution of particular branches of the system and to perform exception handling.

4.3 Quantification over States and Triggers

The definition of a pointcut selection (2) naturally supports quantification. The start state S and the end state T can refer to multistates, or sets of states. Multi states are supported by the UML 2.0 and heavily used in the SDL. Pointcuts can therefore quantify over states, which is easily extended to quantification over triggers and states. Figure 13.a represents the selection $P \xrightarrow{foo} (P1 \ OR \ P2)$ and illustrates matching based on multistates.

Definition. A pointcut $(S \xrightarrow{i} *)$ whose start state S is a multistate defines multiple selections. These selections correspond to all the trace trees that start with a trigger i and matches multistate S. A selection is uniquely defined by the root of the corresponding trace tree.

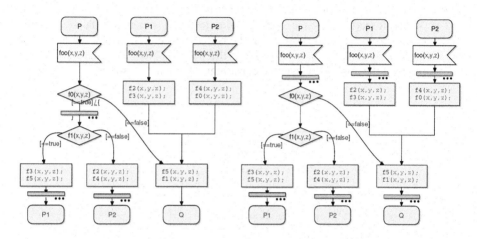

Fig. 13. (a) Selection for $pct(P \xrightarrow{foo} (P1 \ OR \ P2))$. (b) Selections for $pct((P \ OR \ P1 \ OR \ P2) \xrightarrow{foo} *)$.

Figure 13.b represents 3 distinct selections over trigger *foo*: a selection $(P \xrightarrow{foo} *)$, a selection $(P1 \xrightarrow{foo} *)$ and a selection $(P2 \xrightarrow{foo} *)$.

Definition. A pointcut $(S \xrightarrow{i} T)$ whose start state S is a state and whose end state T is a multistate defines multiple selections as defined in (2).

4.4 Pointcut Composition

The definition of a pointcut selection (2) also supports pointcut composition through the logical AND and OR operators. The weaver simply performs the intersection or union of selections. WEAVR pointcut composition in general is discussed in [29].

4.5 Isolation of Selections

The unit on which weaving is performed is a selection of execution paths. It is important to isolate the effects of the weaving between selections because different selections can refer to the same portions of execution paths within a state machine. Advices introduce behavior that is instantiated in the context of each selection matched. An advice might contain reflective calls proper to the next state actions of the selection.

The weaver therefore performs state machine *expansion*. The state machine of Figure 13 contains behavior that is common to all transitions. This behavior is executed whenever a transition ends up in Q. An advice that affects this common behavior should be isolated from transitions that do not match the pointcuts it is bound to.

Figure 14 shows how the common behavior is replicated in order to introduce the after advice correctly. The weaving is performed on the selection, and the woven selection replaces the old one. Paths that did not match the pointcut are not affected.

The WEAVR performs some optimizations to avoid expanding the size of the model too much. In certain cases it might be better to insert a dynamic check around the advice execution rather than expanding the decision tree. This depends on the configuration of the application and the constraints on the model size.

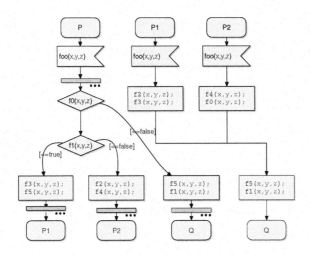

Fig. 14. Isolation of the selection matching $pct(P \xrightarrow{foo} (P1 \; OR \; P2 \; OR \; Q))$. The behavior that is common to paths that do not match the pointcut has been replicated to apply the after advice correctly.

4.6 Ordering of Joinpoints and Control Structures

Advices can introduce new states and new labels into state machines. States and labels can be introduced per State Machine, per Transition or per Joinpoint. In the case of per Joinpoint states or labels, it is possible to refer to states that have been introduced by the advice bound to the previous joinpoint in the transition. This technique enables aspects to construct complex control flow structures. This is illustrated by the Atomicity Aspect of Figure 10. Figure 11 shows the effects of the aspect on the implementation model of Figure 5.a.

The representation of the woven model shows the case where the control structure introduced by the aspect can be determined statically. This is not possible in the general case where the transition decision tree includes forward edges, back edges or cross edges. For example, the implementation of Figure 5.a could contain a loop which invokes resource access multiple times. In these cases the WEAVR maintains a runtime jump table that is ordered according to joinpoint ancestor relationship in the execution trace of the transition.

5 Related Work

We discuss two categories of related work. First, we relate to other approaches to aspect-oriented modeling (AOM). Second, we discuss how this work relates to Stateful aspects and pointcut composition mechanism that capture sequences of events in the trace of the system.

Most approaches to AOM focus on system architecture, design and validation rather than implementation, code generation and verification. In general, AOM approaches can be classified in two main categories [13].

Approaches that emphasize model weaving see AOM as a model transformation technique. Aspects enable crosscutting concerns appearing in models to be modularized and abstracted out. Platform-specific models and code are fully or semi automatically generated. It is therefore beneficial to weave aspects directly at the model level rather than the code level. Typically, these approaches do not aim at generating code-level aspects from models; weaving is fully supported at the modeling level. Examples of model weavers are C-SAW [15] and MDA Query-View-Transformation (QVT) [18] based approaches such as the ATL ModelWeaver [19].

Other approaches propose modeling notations to represent code-level crosscutting concerns at the modeling level. Tool support focuses on analysis tools, code skeleton generators that target AOP languages and round-trip engineering tools to keep model-level aspects and code-level aspects synchronized. The generated code needs to be inspected and manually refined. Behavioral model weaving is therefore not an option; aspects have to maintain their modular structure throughout the development process. Examples of AOM approaches that fall in this category are Theme UML [20] or Jacobson's use case based approach [21]. We think these approaches are more suitable for requirement analysis and early design, rather than Model-Driven Engineering.

Related work concerning the application of AOSD to Harel Statecharts [24] includes the Aspect-Oriented Statechart Framework (AOSF) [22][23]. The AOSF targets early design models and validation using state-oriented state machines, as opposed to system implementation and verification. The AOSF supports the weaving of independent state charts into a composite state chart, where each of the original state charts resides in its own orthogonal region. The joinpoint model proposed is not based on the states of the system, but on individual transition, that are identified by their trigger. Rules specify which transitions trigger crosscutting transitions, in an orthogonal region.

The work on Stateful aspects [25][26] and more advanced control flow pointcut composition operators is also relevant to this work. Stateful aspects can capture a sequence of events in a system. The history of the system is recognized as an important property that should be captured by pointcut designators. Stateful aspects allow important state transitions to be identified through the recognition of a pattern of successive events. We consider the need for such pointcut designators as a symptom that the system implements reactive behavior. As such, the system would be better decomposed using the natural decomposition for reactive systems, state machines.

Finally, the path selection mechanism bears resemblances to the predictive pcflow [5][27]. Again, pcflow is based on a method-based joinpoint model and is expressed in terms of the implementation of the path, rather than in terms of the properties of the path, as it is the case with state transitions.

6 Conclusion

We demonstrate a technique that allow joinpoints located deep inside the implementation of a module to be *inferred* from pointcut descriptors that are entirely defined in terms of behavioral specifications. Traditional interfaces do not provide sufficient information about the runtime behavior of their components. This forces an aspect-oriented programming language to refer directly to the implementation of modules rather than their specification.

We show through some examples that it is possible to define expressive aspects without compromising the modularity of base modules, by taking advantage of the abstraction provided by state machine specifications. We believe that aspect-oriented techniques can achieve a better separation of concerns at the level of state machines compared with code level techniques, especially in the domains of fault tolerance and concurrency. State machine specifications provide more information about the behavior of the modules, which allows aspects to get a better semantic grip on the module. The awareness of the base model with respect to the fault tolerance is implicitly captured by its state machine specification.

Behavioral specifications do not need to be defined with respect to potential aspects. They should appear naturally in the early stages of the software development lifecycle. This approach works particularly well in the context of Model-Driven Engineering because there is a direct mapping from the system specification to its implementation. The particular technique discussed is by no means the only way implementation joinpoints can be inferred from behavioral specifications. Also, the approach could be generalized to programming languages using interface specifications such as Typestates or predicates.

The inference method discussed in the paper is very expressive because it can localize important decision points in the implementation of a state machine. Decision points represent conditional statements that have a significant outcome on the state of the system, and on its future behavior. Conditional statements, in general, are hard to match directly, because they can be implemented in different ways and are prone to refactorings. Signature-based matching of conditional statements is therefore not a good practice, and is rarely implemented in AOP languages.

Yet, decision points tend to be important crosscutting points. They are points where different use cases interact. As a result, aspects based on the procedural decomposition need to write complicated pointcuts that essentially attempt to detect those decisions points indirectly, which leads to brittle aspects. We consider the work on Stateful Aspects as being proposals that attempt to address this problem at the code level. The transition selection mechanism allows semantically significant decision points to be identified in terms of state machine states and triggers, which are stable elements in the system, and have an intuitive semantic meaning.

We also introduce an AOM tool that implements the joinpoint selection mechanism in UML 2.0, the Motorola WEAVR. The tool performs weaving of aspects at the modeling level and is currently being deployed at in production at Motorola, in the network infrastructure business unit.

References

1. Aldrich, J.: Open Modules: Modular Reasoning about Advice. In: Black, A.P. (ed.) ECOOP 2005. LNCS, vol. 3586, pp. 144–168. Springer, Heidelberg (2005)
2. Griswold, W.G., Shonle, M., Sullivan, K., Song, T.N., Cai, Y., Rajan, H.: Modular Software Design with Crosscutting Interfaces. IEEE Software 23(1), 51–60 (2006)
3. Gybels, K., Brichau, J.: Arranging Language Features for More Robust Pattern-Based Crosscuts. In: proceedings of the International Conference on Aspect-Oriented Software Development, Boston, USA, pp. 60–69. ACM Press, New York (2003)
4. Kiczales, G., Mezini, M.: Aspect-Oriented Programming and Modular Reasoning. In: proceedings of the International Conference on Software Engineering, St. Louis, USA, pp. 49–58. ACM Press, New York (2005)
5. Ostermann, K., Mezini, M., Bockisch, C.: Expressive Pointcuts for Increased Modularity. In: Black, A.P. (ed.) ECOOP 2005. LNCS, vol. 3586, pp. 214–240. Springer, Heidelberg (2005)
6. DeLine, R., Fähndrich, M.: Typestates for Objects. In: Odersky, M. (ed.) ECOOP 2004. LNCS, vol. 3086, pp. 465–490. Springer, Heidelberg (2004)
7. Kienzle, J., Gelineau, S.: AO challenge - implementing the ACID properties for transactional objects. In: proceedings of the International Conference on Aspect-Oriented Software Development, Bohn, Germany, pp. 202–213. ACM Press, New York (2006)
8. Mellor, S.J., Balcer, M.J.: Executable UML: A Foundation for Model Driven Architecture. Addison-Wesley, Reading (2002)
9. ITU, Z. 100: Specification and Description Language (SDL), International Telecommunication Union (2000)
10. Telelogic. TAU G2 homepage (2005), http://www.telelogic.com/products/tau/index.cfm
11. Baker, P., Weil, F., Liou, S.: Model-Driven Engineering in a Large Industrial Context. In: Bruel, J.-M. (ed.) MoDELS 2005. LNCS, vol. 3844, pp. 100–109. Springer, Heidelberg (2006)
12. ETSI: Test and Test Conformance Notation, version 3, TTCN-3 Homepage (2005), http://www.ttcn-3.org
13. Cottenier, T., van den Berg, A., Elrad, T.: Modeling Aspect-Oriented Compositions. In: Bruel, J.-M. (ed.) MoDELS 2005. LNCS, vol. 3844, pp. 100–109. Springer, Heidelberg (2006)
14. Cottenier, T., van den Berg, A., Elrad, T.: Model Weaving: Bridging the Divide between Translationists and Elaborationists. In: Nierstrasz, O., Whittle, J., Harel, D., Reggio, G. (eds.) MoDELS 2006. LNCS, vol. 4199, Springer, Heidelberg (2006)
15. Gray, J., Bapty, T., Neema, S., Tuck, J.: Handling crosscutting constraints in domain-specific modeling. Communications of the ACM 44(10), 87–93 (2001)

16. Bast, W., Kleppe, A., Warmer, J.: MDA Explained: The Model Driven Architecture: Practice and Promise. Addison-Wesley, Reading (2003)
17. Frankel, D.S.: Model Driven Architecture: Applying MDA to Enterprise Computing. John Wiley & Sons, Chichester (2003)
18. OMG: MOF QVT Final Adopted Specification, Specification ptc/05-11-01, Object Management Group (2005)
19. Bézivin, J., Jouault, F., Valduriez, P.: First Experiments with a ModelWeaver. In: Workshop on Best Practices for Model Driven Software Development held in conjunction with the 19th Conference on Object-Oriented Programming, Systems, Languages, and Applications, Vancouver, Canada (2004)
20. Clarke, S., Baniassad, E.: Aspect-Oriented Analysis and Design. Addison-Wesley, Reading (2005)
21. Jacobson, I., Ng, P.-W.: Aspect-Oriented Software Development with Use Cases. Addison-Wesley, Reading (2004)
22. Elrad, T., Aldawud, O., Bader, A.: Aspect-Oriented Modeling - Bridging the Gap Between Design and Implementation. In: Batory, D., Consel, C., Taha, W. (eds.) GPCE 2002. LNCS, vol. 2487, pp. 189–201. Springer, Heidelberg (2002)
23. Mahoney, M., Bader, A., Aldawud, O., Elrad, T.: Using Aspects to Abstract and Modularize Statecharts. In: The 5th Internation Workshop on Aspect-Oriented Modeling, in Conjunction with the UML Conference (2004)
24. Harel, D.: Statecharts: A Visual Formalism for Complex Systems. Science of Computer Programming 8, 231–274 (1987)
25. Vanderperren, W., Suvee, D., Cibrán, M.A., De Fraine, B.: Stateful Aspects in JAsCo. In: Gschwind, T., Aßmann, U., Nierstrasz, O. (eds.) SC 2005. LNCS, vol. 3628, pp. 167–181. Springer, Heidelberg (2005)
26. Douence, R., Fradet, P., Sudholt, M.: Composition, Reuse and Interaction Analysis of Stateful Aspects. In: proceedings of the 3rd International Conference on Aspect-Oriented Software Development, Lancaster, UK, pp. 141–150. ACM Press, New York (2004)
27. Kiczales, G.: Keynote talk at the 2d International Conference on Aspect-Oriented Software Development (2003)
28. Cottenier, T., van den Berg, A., Elrad, T.: The Motorola WEAVR: Model Weaving in a Large Industrial Context. In: Proceedings of the Industry Track of the 6th International Conference on Aspect-Oriented Software Development, Vancouver, Canada (2006)
29. Zhang, J., Cottenier, T., van den Berg, A., Gray, J.: Aspect Interference and Composition in the Motorola Aspect-Oriented Modeling Weaver. In: Nierstrasz, O., Whittle, J., Harel, D., Reggio, G. (eds.) MoDELS 2006. LNCS, vol. 4199, Springer, Heidelberg (2006)

A Machine Model
for Aspect-Oriented Programming

Michael Haupt[1] and Hans Schippers[2,*]

[1] Software Architecture Group
Hasso Plattner Institute for Software Systems Engineering
Potsdam, Germany
[2] Formal Techniques in Software Engineering
University of Antwerp, Belgium
michael.haupt@hpi.uni-potsdam.de, hans.schippers@ua.ac.be

Abstract. Aspect-oriented programming languages usually are extensions of object-oriented ones, and their compilation target is usually the (virtual) machine model of the language they extend. While that model elegantly supports core object-oriented language mechanisms such as virtual method dispatch, it provides no direct support for core aspect-oriented language mechanisms such as advice application. Hence, current implementations of aspect-oriented languages bring about insufficient and inelegant solutions. This paper introduces a lightweight, object-based machine model for aspect-oriented languages based on object-oriented ones. It is centered around delegation and relies on a very dynamic notion of join points as loci of late-bound dispatch of functionality. The model is shown to naturally support an important number of aspect-oriented language mechanisms. Additionally, a formal semantics is presented as an extension to the object-based δ calculus.

1 Introduction

The progress of the aspect-oriented programming (AOP) paradigm [43,27] has spawned a wide variety of AOP languages and corresponding implementations [13]. Such languages are usually formulated as extensions of object-oriented "base" programming languages; and they are usually implemented by expressing AOP core mechanisms (such as advice application at join points) [22] in terms of the base language mechanisms.

For example, AspectJ [42,4] is an extension of Java [31,47]. AspectJ compilers generate Java bytecodes. The same holds for other Java-based AOP languages and systems [3,67,52].

In other words, the machine models targeted by compilers for object-oriented and aspect-oriented programs are the same. AOP languages' core mechanisms are *transformed* into a representation using only object-oriented mechanisms, because those are the only ones that the target machine understands. Consequently,

---

* Research Assistant of the Research Foundation, Flanders (FWO).

E. Ernst (Ed.): ECOOP 2007, LNAI 4609, pp. 501–524, 2007.

representations of aspect-oriented core mechanisms tend to be "verbose" in their object-oriented executable representation, as workarounds have to be found for mechanisms that cannot be directly expressed by the target machine.

For instance, regard the application of a before advice at a method execution join point. In AspectJ, it is transformed into two method calls that are inserted at the beginning of each affected method: one call to retrieve an appropriate instance of the aspect, and one to invoke the advice. The latter is implemented as a method in a class representing the aspect [13,35].

The transformation of aspect-oriented code to fit an object-oriented target machine model introduces a semantic gap between the language's expressions and their realisation. It is especially apparent when regarding the target representation of *join points*. Join points are well-defined points in the execution graph of a running application [42,43,27]: points at which functionality defined in aspects is made effective. Transformation of aspect-oriented code to an object-oriented target machine model usually represents them in the form of *join point shadows* [35]: *locations in application code* where join points potentially occur at run-time.

Most AOP language implementations follow an approach centered around this notion, i. e., they regard applications during weaving solely in terms of their static representation in *code*. This contradicts the accepted view on join points as being inherently *dynamic*. In essence, conceptual and technical views on join points and the realisation of attaching advice functionality to them are unnaturally different: dynamic properties are ultimately expressed using static means, such as code locations.

The aforementioned semantic gap has been observed earlier [9] and led to the development of dedicated virtual-machine level support for AOP in the form of the Steamloom VM [9,34,33]. While Steamloom set out to bridge the gap, it has achieved less. On the one hand, several techniques dedicated to offer explicit support for core AOP mechanisms have been devised [33,10,7]. On the other hand, Steamloom operates at bytecode level, still expressing AOP mechanisms targeting an object-oriented machine model. Recent advances in virtual machine-level weaving support [7] still follow this direction.

To effectively bridge the gap, it is required to devise an *aspect-oriented machine model* that can directly be targeted by AOP language compilers. This paper's contribution is a first version of such a model.

As the foundation for the model, we propose the notion of *virtual join points*[1]. The notion of a join point as a point in the execution flow of a program suggests to regard it as a *locus of late binding*. This view has been mentioned several times [42,49,14] but, to the best of our knowledge, not been consequently adopted in implementations so far.

At every join point—seen as a locus of late binding of functionality or value to messages—, dispatch takes place, even though it leads, in most cases, to the execution of the join point's "original" functionality. Dispatch is oriented along multiple dimensions, i. e., relies on one or more different properties from the

---

[1] Some of the core ideas have been formulated in a workshop paper [8].

program state at the time a particular join point is reached. One such dimension is equivalent to virtual method dispatch, where the dynamic type of the object receiving a message send determines the operation to be executed.

In AOP, dispatch dimensions are manifold, and numerous dynamic properties come into question, e.g., the current control flow in case of `cflow`, the current thread, sending/receiving instance, or others. Of course, static properties, such as the message sent in the case of `call` or `execution` join points are also viable candidates.

Viewing join points as loci of late binding yields a consistent point of view, enabling a fresh view on the execution of aspect-oriented programs, and on the implementation of execution environments for aspect-oriented programming languages. If a running application is regarded as a sequence of join points [42], adopting the aforementioned notion suggests to also regard it as a series of late-binding events, of virtual functionality dispatch. In the following, we will elaborate on AOP implementations and how they adhere to the new view on join points mentioned above.

Based on the notion of virtual join points, we propose a machine model for AOP languages called *delegation-based AOP* that faithfully obeys the view on join points as loci of late binding. It is formulated as an extension of a prototype-based object model and uses delegation to achieve late binding.

It is important to note that the proposed model is indeed the core of a *machine model* for AOP; it is *not* a programming language. The model can be thought of as the internal representation of "AOP assembler" in a (virtual) machine with dedicated direct support for AOP mechanisms.

The structure of this paper is as follows. In the next section, we introduce the concept of virtual join points in detail. After that, in Sec. 3, we present the execution model of delegation-based AOP in a purely prototype-based setting, as well as a description of how the model can be extended to support, at the language-implementation level, AOP in class-based languages. An operational semantics is presented as an extension to the δ calculus [2] in Sec. 4. Sec. 5 discusses related work. Finally, Sec. 6 summarises the paper and outlines future work.

2   Virtual Join Points

A join point is an inherently dynamic element of a running application, and it is a locus of late binding. To facilitate late binding at join points, a dispatch mechanism is required; this is similar to virtual methods in object-oriented programming languages. To motivate this claim and further explain it, we shortly describe virtual method dispatch.

Fig. 1(a) shows a program using no procedural abstraction at all: the code of different concerns appears sequentially, possibly several times, in the program. A choice between two concerns—depicted by the "either/or" alternative—is, in such an approach, usually implemented using an `if` statement.

When procedures are introduced into the program, each concern is refactored into one procedure and the original code is replaced by a call to the procedure,

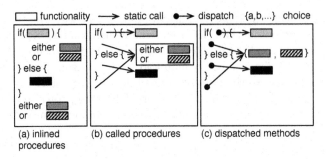

Fig. 1. Sketch of code that uses (a) no procedures, (b) procedures that are early-bound, (c) virtual methods that are late-bound

as seen in part (b). However, the procedure is still statically bound to the call site and there is no variability of which procedure is called at run-time. The concern choice is, in the procedure, also still explicitly represented.

Finally, in part (c), we show the program's shape when virtual methods are used instead of procedures. At each call site, there is a set of potential target methods—which one is executed at run-time is only decided just before the method is called. The explicit implementation of the either/or choice has vanished and is replaced by an implicit process called *dispatching*.

The first programming style's disadvantage is that code is replicated and consequently not well modularised. The second style improves modularity by refactoring replicated code into procedures, while dispatching is still coded in the application. Finally, with virtual methods, the flexibility of late-binding is provided implicitly by the execution environment.

We see a close resemblance between the concepts of procedures and virtual methods on the one hand, and that of join points on the other. In fact, we claim we can seamlessly replace *procedure* and *method* in Fig. 1 with *join point*, in the sense of a semantic action to be executed (we will use the term *join point action* to denote this action). When an advice is bound to a join point, the latter's semantic action consists of the advice execution as well as the original action if it is not omitted, e. g., by an around advice that does not proceed.

From an aspect-oriented point of view, a program looks like in (a) if it is not written in an AOP language: crosscutting concerns are tangled with the application and scattered over it. AOP languages allow to localise these concerns, but current implementations of these languages for the most part *early-bind* advice to join points, sometimes guarded by conditional, so-called *residual* [42] logic. The target code these implementations generate resembles part (b) from the figure. Although conditional logic is generated by the AOP language implementation, it is part of the application code. An implicit dispatch for join points in the target code as in part (c) should be the goal of AOP language implementations.

A logical consequence is to regard every single join point as a locus of late binding, i. e., as a *virtual join point*. An, in this regard, conceptually clean implementation of a run-time environment for aspect-oriented programming languages implicitly represents join points as virtual join point "calls". Each such call is dispatched at run-time and one target is selected according to the current run-time state. The original join point action is, among possibly applicable advice, contained in the set of potential targets. If no advice apply to the join point, there is only one potential target: the default join point action. This is comparable to a virtual method that is not overwritten.

We will now consider how powerful dispatch has to be. In object-oriented programming languages, the standard case is to dispatch a method call only based on the receiver object's type. This can be realised by using a dispatch table. *Multi dispatch* [20], where the receiver and argument types are taken into account, requires extended mapping from multiple types to a method. *Predicate dispatch* [26,50] is the most general notion, attaching an arbitrary predicate to a method: if it evaluates to true, the method is executed.

When a virtual method table is used, only *one* run-time object can influence dispatch, usually the method call receiver. However, AOP languages allow for richer semantics in pointcuts, and pointcut expressions are usually more complex, so that dispatch is oriented along more than one dimension. In the following, we will briefly discuss which dimensions of dispatch are met in existing AOP languages.

AspectJ [42,4] provides dynamic pointcut designators `cflow`, `target`, `this` and `args`, which specify the current control flow, dynamic type of receiver, active or argument objects, respectively. Consequently, dispatch has to regard these.

Other AOP implementations like CaesarJ [3,17], JAsCo [67,66], Association Aspects [60], Steamloom [33,34,9], PROSE [56,57,52,58] or EOS [59] also allow for deploying an aspect, e. g., only in certain threads or for certain objects. As a result, the current thread can be a dimension of dispatch, as well as the active or receiver objects themselves—not only their types.

Even more dimensions are conceivable that hint at the capabilities of upcoming and future AOP languages. If, for example, a pointcut language regards the history of execution [66,1,55] or the interconnections of objects on the heap [55], dispatch dimensions come into scope that are laborious to implement with a purely object-oriented target machine. The generalised concept of virtual join point dispatch, when realised at the core of an execution environment, delivers a more powerful basis on which such languages can be built.

3 Delegation-Based AOP

In this section, we will first introduce the delegation-based AOP machine model in its simplest form, i. e., in a purely prototype-based setting. After that, we will show how the purely prototype-based model can be extended to support class-based languages. A brief discussion and summary close this section.

3.1 Prerequisites

The machine model for AOP proposed here is based on the concepts of *prototypes* and *delegation* [46]. The join point model's granularity is that of *messages*, i. e., each message send constitutes a join point. Both method invocations and member accesses are equally modelled as messages sent to receiver objects. It is this feature by which the model facilitates late binding at all join points: the exact locus of late binding is message reception.

In Fig. 2(a), a single object `obj` is shown. It has three slots responding to the messages `foo`, `bar`, and `baz`. The implementation of the message `bar` sends the message `foo` to `self`, i.e., to the very object that received the `bar` message. The parent of `obj`—parent references are represented as arrows—is some object further up the delegation chain of objects.

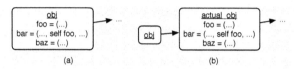

(a)   (b)

Fig. 2. (a) A single object with an unspecified parent, (b) an object and its proxy

In the context of the execution model for AOP proposed herein, an object is not referenced directly, but through a proxy, as shown in Fig. 2(b). The proxy, by default, does not understand any particular messages, but transparently delegates all messages sent to it to the object it stands for. In the figure, `obj` is the proxy object by the name of which the actual object `actual_obj` is known.

Technically, the proxy object determines the actual object's identity at all times: objects might be inserted to or removed from the delegation chain, but since the proxy object will always remain up front, references to it will never need to be updated.

Additionally, as calls are delegated up the delegation chain, `self` will always be bound to the proxy object. For example, when `bar` is sent to `obj`, the call is delegated to `actual_obj`, where the message is understood. Its implementation sends `foo` to `self`. The latter, because `bar` was *delegated* to `actual_obj`, is still bound to `obj`.

3.2   Introducing Aspects

We will now turn to showing how the common mechanism of delegation can be used to late-bind advice to join points. Assume there are two aspects `asp_a` and `asp_b`. Both affect different messages in `obj`: `asp_a` adds a *before* advice to `bar` and an *around* advice to `baz`, `asp_b` adds an *after* advice to both `foo` and `bar`. Both aspects are dynamically deployed at different moments in time while the application is running.

Fig. 3 shows the situation after `asp_a` has been deployed. An additional object, named `asp_a_proxy`, has been inserted in the delegation chain between the proxy and the actual object. This so-called *aspect proxy* understands the two messages augmented by the corresponding aspect, namely `bar` and `baz`.

The effect of this delegation chain modification is that all messages sent to the actual object via its proxy are *first* understood by the aspect proxy, bringing about the application of advice. From here on, the aspect proxy acts as a smart

Fig. 3. The aspect `asp_a` has been deployed

reference (hence our usage of the term *proxy* [30]) to the actual object: it performs actions of its own, as well as possibly addressing `actual_obj`. For example, `bar` is understood in `asp_a_proxy`. The aspect proxy's implementation of the message applies advice functionality before it *resends* the message, i. e., passes on the message while `self` remains bound to the original receiver, `obj`. This means that the original implementation of `bar` in `actual_obj`, when it is eventually executed, correctly sends `foo` to `obj`.

Please note that the figures do not make any assumptions as to where advice functionality is actually implemented; it may be given in-place, i. e., in the aspect proxies themselves, or the latter may call other objects to execute advice.

Next, `asp_b` is deployed as well. The resulting situation is shown in Fig. 4. The aspect proxy for `asp_b` has been inserted in the delegation chain between the aspect proxy for `asp_a` and the actual object.

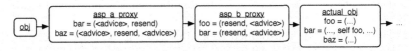

Fig. 4. Both `asp_a` and `asp_b` have been deployed

The situation after the deployment of `asp_b` is especially interesting with regard to the messages `bar` and `foo`. The former is subject to a *before* and an *after* advice introduced by `asp_a` and `asp_b`, respectively. The use of delegation in the machine model facilitates transparent advice application to `foo`: when `bar`'s original implementation sends `foo` to `self`, the message is routed through the proxy `obj` and both aspect proxies, leading to its interception in `asp_b`.

In the example, the aspect proxy of the last-deployed aspect was inserted immediately before the actual object in the delegation chain, which means that the first-deployed aspect applies first. Different orders of advice application are straightforward to achieve by reordering aspect proxies in the delegation chain. Aspect precedence can thus easily be dealt with: it basically is a matter of proxy ordering.

The need for a proxy is now apparent. All modifications due to dynamic weaving affect the delegation chain *leading to* the decorated object. Without the proxy, all references to that object would have to be updated upon dynamic aspect deployment. The proxy ensures a unique reference at all times, making delegation chain modifications between itself and the actual object transparent.

The above examples employ *before*, *after* and *around* advice. In the figures, all advice actions are subsumed under `<advice>`. It is obvious that delegation-based AOP easily facilitates all three types of advice in that it treats before and after advice as special cases of around advice.

A crucial part of all message implementations in aspect proxies is the execution of the decorated join point. In delegation-based AOP, this is achieved by *resending* the respective message to the next object in the delegation chain, during which `self` still remains bound to the original message receiver.

3.3   Adding the Thread Dimension

So far, the description of the model has only shown how late binding is facilitated along two dimensions, namely the identity of the receiver of a message send, and the message itself. We will now show how additional dimensions can be supported, and we will use *thread locality* as the first example for this.

Thread locality can be observed in existing AOP implementations in two forms. On the one hand, aspects can be *scoped* to a single given thread, or a number of threads. That is, their advice apply to join points only when the latter occur in the execution of the respective thread(s). This feature is, for example, directly supported in CaesarJ [3] and Steamloom [33]. On the other hand, thread locality may imply that different (advice or residual [42]) functionality must be executed depending on the thread at hand. For example, the AWED language [51] allows for per-thread aspect instantiation. It also is a core requirement for `cflow` residues to be thread-local, i.e., to maintain control flow information *per thread*.

The *current thread* is thus added as a dimension of dispatch at join points. The delegation-based AOP machine model allows for addressing both forms of thread locality in a uniform way. To that end, the `parent` reference of each object is defined to be a *function of the current thread* rather than a static reference. That way, an object's `parent` can be different, depending on the current thread. Essentially, the delegation chain itself becomes a property of the thread.

For illustration, Fig. 5 shows, again, the sample object `actual_obj` and its proxy, `obj`. This time, two aspects `asp_c` and `asp_d` have been deployed. The former introduces a *before* advice to `foo` that only applies in a thread `T1`, the latter introduces a *before* advice to `bar` that applies globally.

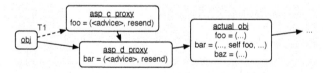

Fig. 5. The aspect `asp_c` is scoped to the thread `T1`, `asp_d` applies globally

In the figure, the dashed line with the annotation "T1" denotes a delegation link that applies in the thread `T1`, while solid lines denote unconditionally effectual links. It can be seen how `asp_c_proxy` delegates to `asp_d_proxy`, effecting the application of `asp_d` in all threads.

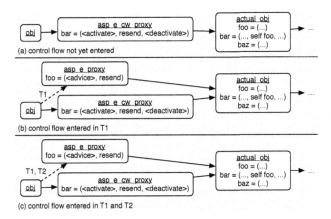

Fig. 6. Dispatch along the control flow dimension through continuous weaving

3.4   Adding the Control Flow Dimension

Next, we will show how the introduced model mechanisms can be used to support yet another dimension of dispatch, namely the current control flow. This basically models the `cflow` construct known from AspectJ [42].

The sample aspect in this case, `asp_e`, applies a before advice to `foo` *only* if this message is sent in the control flow of an execution of `bar`. In the model, this is achieved using *continuous weaving* [32], i. e., the corresponding aspect proxies are dynamically inserted into and removed from the delegation chain as the control flow in question is entered and left. It is important to note that this has to take place *per thread*: when the control flow is entered in T1 but not in T2, only the delegation chain of T1 is to be affected.

Consider Fig. 6 for illustration. In part (a), the situation is shown where `asp_e` is deployed but no thread is currently in the control flow of executing `bar`. Still, `asp_e_cw_proxy`—a *continuous weaving proxy* pertaining to `asp_e`—has been inserted in the delegation chain. It serves the purpose to dynamically deploy the actual aspect proxies whenever a thread enters or leaves the respective control flow. Note that the `<activate>` and `<deactivate>` functionality surrounds the `resend` of the control-flow constituting message like an *around* advice.

Fig. 6(b) shows the situation after `bar` has been sent to `obj` in a thread T1. For that thread, the delegation chain is different now; sends of the `foo` message are understood in `asp_e_proxy`, where advice functionality is applied. Note that the continuous weaving proxy is *not* in the delegation chain for T1, so as to avoid multiple insertions of the aspect proxy due to recursive entries of the control flow.

In Fig. 6(c), another thread, T2, has entered the control flow. The continuous weaving proxy has reacted to this by simply adding T2 to the set of threads for which the "parent function" of `obj` yields the aspect proxy `asp_e_proxy`. That way, advice apply to `foo` in both T1 and T2, but in no other thread.

This approach to handling the actual aspect proxy guarantees that the aspect proxy is inserted into the delegation chain at most once. The model's property of regarding parent references as functions allows for adding and removing particular threads to the set of threads for which the parent function yields the aspect proxy. The aspect proxy is not removed until the last thread leaves the respective control flow. This is taken care of in the continuous weaving proxy.

It is important to stress that no extra features were introduced to the model in order to support the control flow dimension. A continuous weaving proxy is technically identical to any other aspect proxy, or indeed any other object. The only requirement is the capability to dynamically modify an object's delegation chain, while the delegation mechanism handles message flow.

3.5   Supporting Class-Based Languages

The delegation-based AOP machine model is originally based on *prototypes*. We will now show how the model can easily be extended to support class-based languages while retaining all benefits from the prototype-based version, such as instance-local and thread-local aspect deployment.

It is easy to emulate the class-instance relationship known from class-based languages in a prototype-based setting [64,12]: any class is represented by an object defining the class behaviour, while any instance of a class, represented by an object whose parent slot points to the class, only carries its *state*. The instantiation of an object is done by cloning a prototype.

In the extended delegation-based AOP model, objects have references to their classes, and the way methods are invoked along these references can be modified by modifying the path to the class. Fig. 7 shows how the basic principle works: every object (c in the figure), as seen before, is represented by a proxy that references the actual object (`actual_c`). The actual object contains instance-specific attributes, i. e., member fields. The actual object in turn does not directly reference its class, but it does so via another proxy, the so-called *class proxy* (`proxy_C`) whose purpose will be clarified below. Finally, the *class* is represented by an object (C) that defines the messages any instance of the class understands.

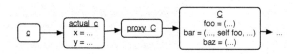

Fig. 7. Objects representing the class C and an instance thereof

If an aspect `asp_f` with a class-wide before advice for the message `C.bar` is inserted, the delegation chain is modified as seen in Fig. 8. An aspect proxy `asp_f_proxy` is inserted in between the class proxy and the class. The proxy understands, exactly in the fashion of the execution model as presented above, the message `bar` and applies advice before resending it.

So, the default class proxy is needed because inserting a class-wide aspect without having this proxy would involve changing the parent links of all currently existing instances of the respective class, as well as those of all instances of the class that are created while the aspect is deployed. Hence, the class proxy exists for the same reasons as the default object proxy introduced above.

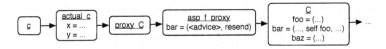

Fig. 8. The aspect `asp_f` introduces a class-wide advice for `C.bar`

There is no interference of the mechanisms for class-wide aspects with those for instance-specific decoration. In fact, class-wide and instance-local decorations can be seamlessly combined. The underlying mechanism is always delegation of messages through proxies. In Fig. 9, there are two instances `c1` and `c2` of the class `C`. Both are connected to their corresponding class object via the default class proxy. However, there is another proxy on the delegation path for `c1`. In fact, this proxy object implements the message `bar` to form aspectual behaviour, but this new behaviour takes effect *only* if `bar` is sent to `c1`. In the same way, the message `foo` is affected by a before advice—but this advice applies to *all* instances of `C` because its place in the delegation chain is *after* the class proxy.

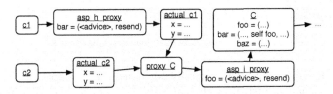

Fig. 9. Two instances of `C`, where one is affected by the aspect `asp_h`, and a class-wide aspect `asp_i`

Proxies for instance decoration are always well isolated from proxies for class decoration, as the latter are inserted between the class proxy and the class, while the former are inserted between the decorated instance and the class proxy. Due to this, instance decorations *always* dominate class decorations.

The concepts relating to extended support for dispatch dimensions introduced earlier also apply in this setting: advice can be restricted to particular threads by making the corresponding parent references functions of the thread. This is illustrated in Fig. 10, where `asp_g` applies only in the thread `T1`.

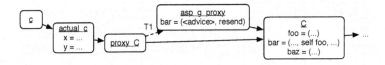

Fig. 10. `asp_g` applies only in the thread `T1`

3.6   Introductions

The delegation-based AOP machine model does not only support *pointcut-and-advice*-flavoured AOP [48]. We will now show how it easily facilitates *introduction* of fields and methods.

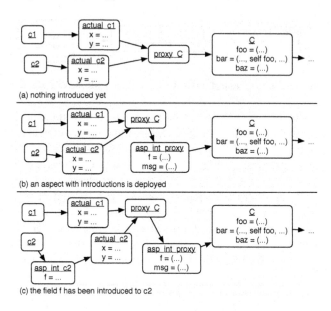

(a) nothing introduced yet

(b) an aspect with introductions is deployed

(c) the field f has been introduced to c2

Fig. 11. Introductions in delegation-based AOP

Assume an aspect `asp_int` introducing a field `f` and message `msg` to the class C. The situation just after the aspect's deployment is shown in Fig. 11(b) (part (a) shows the situation before deployment). An aspect proxy, `asp_int_proxy`, has been inserted in the usual fashion in between the class proxy for C and C itself. The proxy understands two messages, namely `msg` and `f`. No fields have been added yet to either `c1` or `c2`. This is done dynamically, as we will see next.

Above, it was mentioned that `asp_int` introduces a *field* `f`. However, the inserted aspect proxy understands a message of that name which is realised as a *method*. The purpose of this method is to facilitate the dynamic on-demand introduction of fields to objects.

Consider what happens when the field `f` of the object `c2` shall be accessed: the message `f` is delegated until it is understood in `asp_int_proxy`. The implementation of `f` inserts an instance-local aspect proxy for `c2` which solely contains the new field `f`, establishing the situation shown in Fig. 11(c).

`f` is now realised as a *field*, which has no method-like functionality to execute and hence does not proceed, like advice implementations. Thus, whenever the message `f` is sent to `c2` in order to access the field, the message is understood in `asp_int_c2` and not delegated further up the delegation chain.

3.7   Discussion and Summary

The machine model for AOP introduced above is based on the well-known concepts of prototypes and delegation, which have been augmented with the additional property that parent references can actually be functions. In fact, the model allows for such a function to determine its result based on arbitrary parameters, not just the current thread, to realise dispatch along multiple dimensions.

The model, being object-oriented itself, can be used as an execution layer for object-oriented programming languages. As seen in Sec. 3.5, class-based object-oriented languages can easily be supported. We argue that the strengths of the model fully come into play when languages are to be implemented that require extensive use of late binding. Thus, it is especially well suited to support aspect-oriented programming languages.

The model supports the pointcut-and-advice flavour of AOP [48] straightforwardly. Apart from that, the model allows for implementing extended features. Scoping aspect applicability to single instances comes as a natural feature of the model. Yet, other features such as thread-local scoping and per-thread advice—illustrated by the first and second examples, respectively, in Sec. 3.4—are also supported in a unified way: both are done implicitly through parent functions.

Delegation-based AOP also provides very simple mechanisms for realising different aspect precedence strategies. The order of aspect proxies in the delegation chain may depend on several factors, such as the order in which deployment occurs, or explicitly declared precedence. The model also naturally supports dynamic weaving through its reflective capabilities. Proxies can, at all times, be dynamically inserted in and removed from delegation chains.

Set aside the features of pointcut-and-advice AOP, the model also supports *introduction* of fields and methods to existing objects and classes. This is easily achieved simply by exploiting the model's inherent mechanisms. In a nutshell, the delegation-based AOP machine model represents a uniform approach to implementing AOP, based on some simple yet powerful mechanisms.

A proof-of-concept implementation for the delegation-based AOP machine model has been developed as well. Emphasising elegance and simplicity more than efficiency, the relatively young, dynamic Io programming language [37] was used for this purpose. Regarding an efficient implementation, we refer to existing work on efficiently implementing dynamic languages that was achieved in the course of implementing the Self language [65,18,61] and the Strongtalk Smalltalk implementation [63]. In those projects, very efficient compiler technology for dynamic languages has been developed. Adopting their achievements for delegation-based AOP is a core topic of future work.

4   Semantics

We will now introduce the δ [2] calculus, followed by a number of modifications and extensions in order to use it as a formal foundation for our model.

4.1   The δ Calculus

δ is a simple calculus providing a formal foundation for an imperative, object-based system with delegation. It is defined through an operational semantics function $\leadsto_\delta$, which is a finite mapping of expressions and stores onto pairs of addresses and stores:

$$\leadsto_\delta: Exp \times Store \mapsto_{fin} Address \times Store$$

A *store* is basically a lookup table which maps addresses to objects, and stores the *self* pointer:

$$Store = (\{self\} \mapsto Address) \cup (Address \mapsto_{fin} Obj)$$

Finally, an object contains a list of addresses, pointing to its parents (δ indeed allows for multiple parent objects), which are each associated with an identifier, as well as a list of method names with their bodies, and are represented as $o \equiv [\![d_1 = \iota_1 \ldots d_k = \iota_k \| m_1 = b_1 \ldots m_n = b_n]\!]$:

$$Obj = (DelegateID \mapsto_{fin} Address) \cup (MethodID \mapsto_{fin} Exp)$$

A number of operations are defined as well which determine the way expressions are constructed, and of which the following are most relevant in the context of this paper:

$$(Addr) \quad \frac{}{\iota, \sigma \leadsto_\delta \iota, \sigma}$$

$$(Clone) \quad \frac{a, \sigma \leadsto_\delta \iota, \sigma' \quad \iota' \notin dom(\sigma') \quad \sigma'' = \sigma'[\iota' \mapsto \sigma'(\iota)]}{clone(a), \sigma \leadsto_\delta \iota', \sigma''}$$

$$(Select) \quad \frac{a, \sigma \leadsto_\delta \iota, \sigma' \quad Look(\sigma', \iota, m) = \{b\} \quad \sigma'' = \sigma'[self \mapsto \iota] \quad b, \sigma'' \leadsto_\delta \iota', \sigma''' \quad \sigma'''' = \sigma'''[self \mapsto \sigma(self)]}{a.m, \sigma \leadsto_\delta \iota', \sigma''''}$$

(*Addr*) is the basic case, where an address evaluates to itself without modifying the store. (*Clone*) performs a copy-by-value of an object's parents and methods, and stores the result at a new address. Finally, (*Select*) models message sending and makes sure *self* is initialised to point to the message receiver. The *Look* function basically looks up the method body associated with m, either in the receiver object itself, or in one of its parents. It is assumed that only one candidate is found.

The delegation semantics are thus incorporated in the *Look* function, but as the latter will be modified to better fit the context of this paper (cf. Sec. 4.2), its original definition is omitted here.

4.2   Modifications and Extensions for Delegation-Based AOP

For δ to be convenient as a formal foundation for delegation-based AOP, a number of adaptations need to be made. First of all, a simplification can be applied, in that it turns out to be sufficient for each object to have maximally one parent instead of n. This is because (*Select*) will exhibit the same behaviour if a message is sent to an object $[\![d_1 = \iota_a, d_2 = \iota_b \| \ldots]\!]$ as if the same message were sent to $[\![d_1 = \iota_a \| \ldots]\!]$ where $\sigma(\iota_a) = [\![d_1 = \iota_b \| \ldots]\!]$. Indeed, in both cases, lookup will check b's methods only after it failed to find a suitable candidate in a. However, in order to allow an object's parent to vary depending on the context (for example the current thread), a function *Del* is introduced, which associates every object with another function. The latter, in turn, determines the object's parent based on the context. Consequently, parents will no longer appear in an object's representation:

$$Del : Address \mapsto_{fin} (Context \mapsto Address)$$
$$o \equiv [\![m_1 = b_1, m_2 = b_2 \ldots]\!]$$

Note that the *Context* domain is not defined in more detail in order to allow it to be used for any information considered applicable in a particular situation. Furthermore, the notation Del_ι will be used from now on as an abbreviation for $Del(\iota)$ and, in case $Del(\iota)$ is a constant function, even for that constant value. For convenience, Del_ι is assumed to be stored together with the actual object in the store at address ι.

Next, *(Clone)* should be updated to make sure objects are automatically associated with a proxy, and can be referenced through this proxy:

$$(Clone)$$

$$\frac{\begin{array}{l} a, \sigma \leadsto_\delta \iota, \sigma' \\ \iota' \notin dom(\sigma') \\ \sigma'' = \sigma'[\iota' \mapsto \sigma'(\iota)] \\ \iota'' \notin dom(\sigma'') \\ \sigma''' = \sigma''[\iota'' \mapsto ([\![\,]\!]; Del_{\iota''}(context) = \iota')] \end{array}}{clone(a), \sigma \leadsto_\delta \iota'', \sigma'''}$$

Note that $Del_{\iota''}$ is set to be a constant function here. This means that the parent of the proxy object will always be the actual object, regardless of context. Furthermore, the proxy object has got no methods of its own. Thus, all messages sent to it are automatically delegated to its parent.

Also note that the semantics of *(Clone)* as defined here may not be suitable in all cases, for example to create an aspect proxy object which does not need another proxy of its own. For such cases, the old *(Clone)*, or even yet another variant, might be more appropriate. The current version demonstrates what it means for a proxy to be attached to an object, as well as how and when this might be realised.

As stated before, delegation semantics are incorporated in the *Look* function, which is now adapted to take the *Del* function into account. More specifically, it should look for a method m in the object at address ι or any object found by recursively applying the *Del* function, and return its body together with the address of the object where m was eventually encountered:

$$Look(\sigma, \iota, m) = \begin{cases} \{(b, \iota)\} & if\ \sigma(\iota) = [\![\ldots m = b \ldots]\!] \\ Look(\sigma, Del_\iota(context), m) & otherwise \end{cases}$$

Note that $Look(\sigma, \iota, m)$ is undefined if at some point an application of Del_ι is undefined as well. This will happen in case an object has no parent.

At this point, delegation semantics are suitable for delegation-based AOP. The next issue is that there is no *resend* mechanism yet. In order to incorporate this, two new pseudovariables *msg* and *cur* are introduced, which, similarly to *self*, are only relevant during a message send:

$$(Var)$$

$$\frac{}{\begin{array}{l} self, \sigma \rightsquigarrow_\delta \sigma(self), \sigma \\ cur, \sigma \rightsquigarrow_\delta \sigma(cur), \sigma \\ msg, \sigma \rightsquigarrow_\delta \sigma(msg), \sigma \end{array}}$$

Indeed, a *resend* is only possible within the body of a method, and *msg* and *cur* respectively serve to hold the name of the message currently being handled, and the address of the object where the body of this message was found by the *Look* function. Consequently, (*Select*) is now modified to correctly initialise these new variables, and the definition of a *store* is updated as well:

$$(Select)$$

$$\frac{\begin{array}{l} a, \sigma \rightsquigarrow_\delta \iota, \sigma' \\ Look(\sigma', \iota, m) = (b, \iota_d) \\ \sigma'' = \sigma'[self \mapsto \iota][msg \mapsto m][cur \mapsto \iota_d] \\ b, \sigma'' \rightsquigarrow_\delta \iota', \sigma''' \\ \sigma'''' = \sigma'''[self \mapsto \sigma(self)][msg \mapsto \sigma(msg)][cur \mapsto \sigma(cur)] \end{array}}{a.m, \sigma \rightsquigarrow_\delta \iota', \sigma''''}$$

$$Store = \begin{array}{l} (\{self\} \mapsto Address) \cup (\{cur\} \mapsto Address) \cup \\ (\{msg\} \mapsto MethodID) \cup (Address \mapsto_{fin} Obj) \end{array}$$

At this point, (*Resend*) can be modelled to select *msg* on the parent of *cur*, while *self* is not modified, and thus remains bound to the original receiver:

$$(Resend)$$

$$\frac{\begin{array}{l} Look(\sigma, Del_{cur}(context), msg) = (b, \iota_d) \\ \sigma' = \sigma[cur \mapsto \iota_d] \\ b, \sigma' \rightsquigarrow_\delta \iota', \sigma'' \\ \sigma''' = \sigma''[cur \mapsto \sigma(cur)] \end{array}}{resend, \sigma \rightsquigarrow_\delta \iota', \sigma'''}$$

Note that *cur* is updated during (*Resend*). This is necessary to cover the case where the evaluation of the newly found *b* triggers yet another *resend*.

Finally, a couple of dedicated aspect-oriented operations can be defined. It turns out that deploying an aspect is just a matter of rewiring a couple of parents, while aspect undeployment boils down to resetting this rewiring:

$$(Deploy\ Aspect)$$

$$\frac{\begin{array}{l} a, \sigma \rightsquigarrow_\delta \iota, \sigma' \\ asp, \sigma' \rightsquigarrow_\delta \iota', \sigma'' \\ \sigma''' = \sigma''[Del_{\iota'}(context) = Del_\iota] \\ \sigma'''' = \sigma'''[Del_\iota(context) = \iota'] \end{array}}{deploy(asp, a), \sigma \rightsquigarrow_\delta \iota, \sigma''''}$$

$$(Undeploy\ Aspect)$$

$$\frac{\begin{array}{l} a, \sigma \rightsquigarrow_\delta \iota, \sigma' \\ asp, \sigma' \rightsquigarrow_\delta \iota', \sigma'' \\ \sigma''' = \sigma''[Del_\iota(context) = Del_{\iota'}] \end{array}}{undeploy(asp, a), \sigma \rightsquigarrow_\delta \iota, \sigma'''}$$

4.3 Example

As an example, consider the scenario shown in Figs. 2(b) and 3 from Sec. 3. We start out with an object $obj = \sigma(\iota_{obj}) = [\![\,]\!]$ and $Del_{\iota_{obj}} = \iota_{actual\_obj}$ where $\sigma(\iota_{actual\_obj}) = [\![foo = \ldots, bar = [\ldots, self\ foo, \ldots], baz = \ldots]\!]$. Thus, obj is a proxy object with its parent pointing to $actual\_obj$.

Next, $aspA$ is deployed using (*Deploy Aspect*):

$$deploy(\iota_{aspA}, \iota_{obj}), \sigma \rightsquigarrow_{\delta} \iota_{obj}, \sigma'$$

The $Del_{\iota_{obj}}$ function is now set to always evaluate to the constant value ι_{aspA}, but this need not necessarily be the case. The slightly more advanced situation where $aspA$ is applied locally to thread T_1 (cf. Sec. 3.3) is easily covered by a minor change to the (*Deploy Aspect*) operation, where $Del_{\iota_{obj}}$ is set to the following instead (t is the current thread):

$$Del_{\iota_{obj}}(t) = \begin{cases} \iota_{aspA} & if\ t = T_1 \\ Udf & otherwise \end{cases}$$

Of course, in case $t \neq T_1$, the result might just as well be yet another object, rather than undefined. The latter models the case where obj has no parent.

5 Related Work

The discussion of related work is done in two parts. First, we will focus on work that also supports the notion of join points as loci of late binding. We will then turn to presenting implementations or implementation ideas that exploit mechanisms resembling an actual late-binding approach as presented in the preceding sections.

5.1 Join Points as Loci of Late Binding

Join points as loci of late binding have been alluded to in numerous publications presenting formalisms for aspect-oriented programming. A number of these approaches regard join points as *events* [68,15,25,29,28] to which advice essentially *react*. While this can be regarded as a form of late binding, the notions of join points used in the aforementioned publications still differ from our idea in that they assume that *certain* join points are selectively *activated* as events during a weaving step [25], or that additional conditional logic is executed whenever such an event is signalled to determine whether advice are actually applicable [68]. The application is under observation, it is being monitored by some entity pertaining to AOP infrastructure. Conversely, our model regards *all* potential join points as being "active" and thus implicitly as loci of late binding at all times. Moreover, additional conditionals are not required in delegation-based AOP because late binding is done *implicitly* through the appropriate insertion of proxies in the delegation chain.

In the AOSD-Europe project, a generic meta-model for aspect-oriented programming languages has been developed [14]. It explicitly regards join points as points where advice functionality may be late-bound. The model comes with a prototype implementation in the form of an interpreter, which checks for advice applicability at all join points it encounters. This corresponds to an "eager" checking for the applicability of advice. Application of advice is thus less implicit than in delegation-based AOP.

Some formalisms explicitly address *dispatch mechanisms* to model join points and advice application at them [53,45,38]. The FRED language [53] combines concepts from object-oriented and aspect-oriented programming as well as predicate dispatch [26]. This approach is close to delegation-based AOP regarding its derivation. Still, it requires the definition of conditions for dispatch at application level instead of applying dispatch implicitly, like our model.

Lämmel introduces *method call interception* (MCI) as a fundamental language mechanism [45]. MCI allows for superimposing method calls with additional functionality. The MCI model is, however, restricted to method calls only and does not aim at representing a general model for AOP.

The calculus of untyped aspect-oriented programs presented by Jagadeesan et al. [38] is very closely related to the delegation-based AOP model presented in this paper. It models all advice applying at a join point as ordered units of behaviour, each of which is essentially an *around* advice. Such an advice unit closely resembles an aspect proxy in delegation-based AOP. Advice are also implicitly applied at join points. Only method calls, which can be expressed using message sends, are considered as join points in the calculus.

The *parameterised aspect calculus* [19] regards *each* reduction step as a potential join point. Still, the semantics consults a pointcut language element at all reduction steps, leading to eager explicit checking for advice applicability like observed above for the AOSD-Europe meta-model.

The *common aspect semantics base* (CASB) [23] regards every instruction as a potential join point, applying a two-staged function at all instructions. The first function determines whether the current *instruction* may be subject to decoration with advice. If so, the second function is applied to check whether the present *dynamic state* calls for applying advice at the join point at hand. An instruction is hence treated like an AspectJ join point shadow. The view on a running application therefore closely resembles the one found in AspectJ.

In *Pluggable AOP* [44], aspect language mechanisms are modelled as mixins that transform interpreter base mechanisms. Said mixins are represented in the form of proxy objects, and composition with the base interpreter functionality is achieved through proxy insertion in delegation chains that are part of the interpreter's logic. The similarities with the machine model for AOP presented in this paper are of a technical nature. Pluggable AOP augments interpreter base mechanisms by means of proxies and delegation. Conversely, delegation-based AOP has proxies and delegation *as the interpreter's core mechanisms*. In other words, Pluggable AOP transforms the interpreter, whilst delegation-based AOP transforms application structures subject to execution by a never-changing interpreter.

Ossher [54] proposes to represent application objects as "constellation[s] of a number of fragments" that each contribute part of an object's functionality. Fragments delegate to each other in case a piece of desired functionality is not implemented by one. Crosscutting concerns can be dynamically woven in and out by adding fragments to, or removing them from, the delegation chain. His proposal is a suggestion for research directions for virtual machine support for concern composition. The machine model presented herein obviously matches with these ideas.

5.2   Related Implementations

There are several actual AOP language implementations that use techniques related to late binding at join points. None of them is as radical as the model presented in Sec. 3, but certain resemblances exist.

Envelopes as in *envelope-based weaving* [16] wrap potential join point shadows in methods introduced at load-time. They closely resemble virtual join points but are limited in that they basically just map virtual join points to virtual methods. Some AOP implementations utilise a less consequent form of envelopes to realise dynamic weaving. AspectWerkz [5,11] does not replace *all* potential join point shadows with envelopes, but those that are, at class loading time, known to be in the scope of aspects that may be put to use during run-time. Each join point shadow is replaced with a call to a method in a dedicated so-called *join point class*. Dynamic weaving is achieved by replacing said methods using HotSwap [24,41]. AspectWerkz' approach is described in more detail in [13]. JAsCo [67,66], in its run-time weaver [39], follows a similar approach.

One variant of PROSE [57] decorates *each* join point shadow with advice dispatch logic, effectively realising a powerful dispatch mechanism. However, the approach brought about severe performance penalties, as the chosen implementation strategy was nothing like virtual method dispatch. In fact, advice dispatch logic was implemented as an unconditional callback into the AOP framework of PROSE, leading to the execution of costly functionality at all join points.

Implementing AOP languages using *proxies* is an approach chosen by numerous AOP frameworks, of which Spring AOP [40,62] is one of the most popular. Frameworks like Spring AOP create proxies that replace the original application objects and implement the same interface as the latter, but apply advice in their implementations of the respective methods. Proxy-based AOP is technically close to the delegation-based AOP model for yet some more reasons. Aspect precedence is easily expressed by ordering proxies appropriately. Also, proxies can be applied—introduced and withdrawn—dynamically, allowing for dynamic weaving. The main difference between proxy-based and delegation-based AOP lies in the level at which the approaches are realised: proxy-based AOP implementations operate at *application level*. That is, all AOP-related operations are part of the running application, imposing significant performance penalties on join points where advice functionality applies [33]. Conversely, delegation-based AOP is intended to be realised at the level of the run-time environment, promising significantly better performance.

The *composition filters* [6] approach is related to proxies in that filters are applied to messages. Filters may impose additional functionality on message evaluation, thereby effecting advice. Execution of such functionality may also depend on conditions specified in filters. Composition filters relate to delegation-based AOP in the same way proxies do: filtering is specified at language instead of machine level.

Finally, there are implementations that do not affect application *code* as such, but that manipulate meta-level entities to let aspect-related constructs take effect. Systems falling in this category are AspectS [36] and context-oriented programming (COP) [21]. Their relation to delegation-based AOP is apparent: both do modify system-internal dispatch data structures, such as virtual method tables or method dictionaries, to augment functionality at join points. The main difference to delegation-based AOP lies in that they do not explicitly regard *all* join points as loci of late binding—this characteristic is introduced by installing aspects (in AspectS) or activating layers (in COP).

6   Summary and Future Work

Based on the notion of join points as loci of late binding, we have presented a machine model for the implementation of aspect-oriented programming languages called *delegation-based AOP*. The model not only facilitates the implementation of the pointcut-and-advice AOP flavour, but also that of numerous other AOP features, such as aspect scoping (to threads and instances) or introductions. The model is simple and exploits few simple basic concepts—delegation, prototypes, parent reference functions—to achieve all of its goals.

Future work will focus on several issues. An implementation of the model is to be developed in the form of a virtual machine for a high-level aspect-oriented programming language. The machine will support some standard bytecode set (e.g., Java or Smalltalk), but will moreover offer dedicated bytecode instructions supporting the core aspect-oriented features of the machine model. Existing aspect-oriented programming languages are to be mapped to it by means of compilers that target the machine's instruction set. To achieve good performance, existing work on providing efficient run-time environments for dynamic languages is going to be used as a foundation.

Acknowledgements

The authors are grateful for Christoph Bockisch's comments on early versions of this paper. He and Mira Mezini have also contributed to the ideas of this paper during numerous discussions. The authors also thank Klaus Ostermann, Bart Du Bois, Dirk Janssens and Serge Demeyer for their worthwhile suggestions.

The authors thank Joseph Osborn, who has contributed an implementation of delegation-based AOP in Io, elements from which have been used to derive the implementation presented in this paper.

References

1. Allan, C., et al.: Adding Trace Matching with Free Variables to AspectJ. In: Proc. OOPSLA 2005, pp. 345–364. ACM Press, New York (2005)
2. Anderson, C., Drossopoulou, S.: δ - an imperative object based calculus with delegation. In: Proc. USE'02, Malaga (2002)
3. Aracic, I., Gasiunas, V., Mezini, M., Ostermann, K.: Overview of caesarj. In: Rashid, A., Aksit, M. (eds.) Transactions on Aspect-Oriented Software Development I. LNCS, vol. 3880, Springer, Heidelberg (2006)
4. AspectJ Home Page. http://www.eclipse.org/aspectj/
5. AspectWerkz Home Page. http://aspectwerkz.codehaus.org/
6. Bergmans, L., Akşit, M.: Principles and Design Rationale of Composition Filters. In: [27]
7. Bockisch, C., et al.: Adapting VM Techniques for Seamless Aspect Support. In: Proc. OOPSLA 2006, ACM Press, New York (2006)
8. Bockisch, C., Haupt, M., Mezini, M.: Dynamic Virtual Join Point Dispatch. In: Workshop on Software Engineering Properties of Languages and Aspect Technologies (SPLAT '06) (2006)
9. Bockisch, C., Haupt, M., Mezini, M., Ostermann, K.: Virtual Machine Support for Dynamic Join Points. In: Proc. AOSD 2004, ACM Press, New York (2004)
10. Bockisch, C., Kanthak, S., Haupt, M., Arnold, M., Mezini, M.: Efficient Control Flow Quantification. In: Proc. OOPSLA 2006, ACM Press, New York (2006)
11. Bonér, J.: What Are the Key Issues for Commercial AOP Use: how Does AspectWerkz Address Them?. In: Proc. AOSD 2004, pp. 5–6. ACM Press, New York (2004)
12. Borning, A.: Classes versus Prototypes in Object-Oriented Languages. In: Noble, J., Taivalsaari, A., Moore, I. (eds.) Prototype-Based Programming. Concepts, Languages and Applications, Springer, Heidelberg (1999)
13. Brichau, J., et al.: Report Describing Survey of Aspect Languages and Models. Technical Report AOSD-Europe Deliverable D12, AOSD-Europe-VUB-01, Vrije Universiteit Brussel, 17 May, 2005. (2005), http://www.aosd-europe.net/deliverables/d12.pdf
14. Brichau, J., et al.: An Initial Metamodel for Aspect-Oriented Programming Languages. Technical Report AOSD-Europe Deliverable D39, AOSD-Europe-VUB-12, Vrije Universiteit Brussel, 27, 2006. (February 2006), http://www.aosd-europe.net/deliverables/d39.pdf
15. Bruns, G., Jagadeesan, R., Jeffrey, A., Riely, J.: μABC: A Minimal Aspect Calculus. In: Gardner, P., Yoshida, N. (eds.) CONCUR 2004. LNCS, vol. 3170, pp. 209–224. Springer, Heidelberg (2004)
16. Bockisch, C., Haupt, M., Mezini, M., Mitschke, R.: Envelope-based Weaving for Faster Aspect Compilers. In: Proc. NetObjectDays 2005, GI (2005)
17. CaesarJ Home Page, http://caesarj.org/
18. Chambers, C.: The Design and Implementation of the Self Compiler, an Optimizing Compiler for Object-Oriented Programming Languages. PhD thesis, Department of Computer Science, Stanford University (1992)
19. Clifton, C., Leavens, G., Wand, M.: Parameterized Aspect Calculus: a Core Calculus for the Direct Study of Aspect-Oriented Languages (2003), ftp://ftp.ccs.neu.edu/pub/people/wand/papers/clw-03.pdf
20. Clifton, C., Leavens, G.T., Chambers, C., Millstein, T.: MultiJava: Modular Open Classes and Symmetric Multiple Dispatch for Java. In: Proc. OOPSLA'00, pp. 130–145. ACM Press, New York (2000)

21. Costanza, P., Hirschfeld, R.: Language Constructs for Context-oriented Programming: An Overview of ContextL. In: Dynamic Languages Symposium (DLS) '05, co-organised with OOPSLA'05, ACM Press, New York (2005)
22. Dinkelaker, T., et al.: Inventory of Aspect-Oriented Execution Models. Technical Report AOSD-Europe Deliverable D40, AOSD-Europe-TUD-4, Darmstadt University of Technology, 28 February, 2006 (2006), http://www.aosd-europe.net/deliverables/d40.pdf
23. Djoko, S.D., Douence, R., Fradet, P., Le Botlan, D.: CASB: Common Aspect Semantics Base. Technical Report AOSD-Europe Deliverable D41, AOSD-Europe-INRIA-7, INRIA, France, 10 February 2006 (2006)
24. Dmitriev, M.: Towards Flexible and Safe Technology for Runtime Evolution of Java Language Applications. In: Workshop on Engineering Complex Object-Oriented Systems for Evolution, Proceedings (at OOPSLA 2001) (2001)
25. Douence, R., Motelet, O., Südholt, M.: A Formal Definition of Crosscuts. In: Yonezawa, A., Matsuoka, S. (eds.) Metalevel Architectures and Separation of Crosscutting Concerns. LNCS, vol. 2192, pp. 170–184. Springer, Heidelberg (2001)
26. Ernst, E., Kaplan, C., Chambers, C.: Predicate Dispatching: A Unified Theory of Dispatch. In: Jul, E. (ed.) ECOOP 1998. LNCS, vol. 1445, pp. 186–211. Springer, Heidelberg (1998)
27. Filman, R.E., Elrad, T., Clarke, S., Akşit, M.: Aspect-Oriented Software Development. Addison-Wesley, Reading (2005)
28. Filman, R.E., Friedman, D.P.: Aspect-Oriented Programming is Quantification and Obliviousness. Technical Report 01.12, RIACS, May 2001 (2001)
29. Filman, R.E., Havelund, K.: Source-Code Instrumentation and Quantification of Events. In: Leavens, G.T., Cytron, R. (eds.) FOAL 2002 Workshop (at AOSD 2002), pp. 45–49 (2002)
30. Gamma, E., Helm, R., Johnson, R., Vlissides, J.: Design Patterns — Elements of Reusable Object-Oriented Software, pp. 87–95. Addison-Wesley, Reading (1994)
31. Gosling, J., Joy, B., Steele, G.: The Java Language Specification. Addison-Wesley, Reading (1996)
32. Hanenberg, S., Hirschfeld, R., Unland, R.: Morphing Aspects: Incompletely Woven Aspects and Continuous Weaving. In: Proc. AOSD 2004, ACM Press, New York (2004)
33. Haupt, M.: Virtual Machine Support for Aspect-Oriented Programming Languages. PhD thesis, Software Technology Group, Darmstadt University of Technology (2006)
34. Haupt, M., Mezini, M., Bockisch, C., Dinkelaker, T., Eichberg, M., Krebs, M.: An Execution Layer for Aspect-Oriented Programming Languages. In: Proc. VEE 2005, 2005, ACM Press, New York (2005)
35. Hilsdale, E., Hugunin, J.: Advice Weaving in AspectJ. In: Proc. AOSD 2004, ACM Press, New York (2004)
36. Hirschfeld, R.: AspectS - Aspect-Oriented Programming with Squeak. In: Aksit, M., Mezini, M., Unland, R. (eds.) NODe 2002. LNCS, vol. 2591, pp. 216–232. Springer, Heidelberg (2003)
37. Io Home Page, http://www.iolanguage.com/
38. Jagadeesan, R., Jeffrey, A., Riely, J.: A Calculus of Untyped Aspect-Oriented Programs. In: Cardelli, L. (ed.) ECOOP 2003. LNCS, vol. 2743, Springer, Heidelberg (2003)
39. JAsCo Home Page, http://ssel.vub.ac.be/jasco/
40. Johnson, R., Hoeller, J.: Expert One-on-One J2EE Development without EJB. Wiley, Chichester (2004)

41. Java Platform Debugger Architecture Home Page, http://java.sun.com/j2se/1.4.1/docs/guide/jpda/index.html
42. Kiczales, G., Hilsdale, E., Hugunin, J., Kersten, M., Palm, J., Griswold, W.G.: An Overview of AspectJ. In: Knudsen, J.L. (ed.) ECOOP 2001. LNCS, vol. 2072, pp. 327–353. Springer, Heidelberg (2001)
43. Kiczales, G., Lamping, J., Mendhekar, A., Maeda, C., Lopes, C.V., Loingtier, J.-M., Irwin, J.: Aspect-Oriented Programming. In: Aksit, M., Matsuoka, S. (eds.) ECOOP 1997. LNCS, vol. 1241, pp. 220–242. Springer, Heidelberg (1997)
44. Kojarski, S., Lorenz, D.H.: Pluggable aop: Designing aspect mechanisms for third-party composition. In: Proc. OOPSLA '05, pp. 247–263. ACM Press, New York (2005)
45. Lämmel, R.: A semantical approach to method-call interception. In: Proc. AOSD'02, pp. 41–55. ACM Press, New York (2002)
46. Lieberman, H.: Using prototypical objects to implement shared behavior in object-oriented systems. In: Proc. OOPSLA 1986, pp. 214–223. ACM Press, New York (1986)
47. Lindholm, T., Yellin, F.: The Java Virtual Machine Specification, 2nd edn. Addison-Wesley, Reading (1999)
48. Masuhara, H., Kiczales, G.: Modeling Crosscutting Aspect-Oriented Mechanisms. In: Cardelli, L. (ed.) ECOOP 2003. LNCS, vol. 2743, Springer, Heidelberg (2003)
49. Masuhara, H., Kiczales, G., Dutchyn, C.: A Compilation and Optimization Model for Aspect-Oriented Programs. In: Hedin, G. (ed.) CC 2003 and ETAPS 2003. LNCS, vol. 2622, pp. 46–60. Springer, Heidelberg (2003)
50. Millstein, T.: Practical predicate dispatch. In: Proc. OOPSLA'04, ACM Press, New York (2004)
51. Navarro, L.D.B., Südholt, M., Vanderperren, W., De Fraine, B., Suvée, D.: Explicitly distributed aop using awed. In: Proc. AOSD'06, pp. 51–62. ACM Press, New York (2006)
52. Nicoara, A., Alonso, G.: Dynamic AOP with PROSE, http://www.iks.inf.ethz.ch/publications/publications/files/PROSE-ASMEA05.pdf
53. Orleans, D.: Incremental programming with extensible decisions. In: Proc. AOSD'02, pp. 56–64. ACM Press, New York (2002)
54. Ossher, H.: A direction for research on virtual machine support for concern composition. In: Proc. Workshop VMIL '07, ACM Press, New York (2007)
55. Ostermann, K., Mezini, M., Bockisch, C.: Expressive Pointcuts for Increased Modularity. In: Black, A.P. (ed.) ECOOP 2005. LNCS, vol. 3586, Springer, Heidelberg (2005)
56. Popovici, A., Gross, T., Alonso, G.: Dynamic Weaving for Aspect-Oriented Programming. In: Kiczales, G. (ed.) Proc. AOSD 2002, ACM Press, New York (2002)
57. Popovici, A., Gross, T., Alonso, G.: Just-in-Time Aspects. In: Proc. AOSD 2003, ACM Press, New York (2003)
58. PROSE Home Page, http://prose.ethz.ch
59. Rajan, H., Sullivan, K.: Eos: Instance-level aspects for integrated system design. In: ESEC/FSE-11: Proceedings of the 9th European Software Engineering Conference, held jointly with 11th ACM SIGSOFT International Symposium on Foundations of Software Engineering, pp. 297–306. ACM Press, New York (2003)
60. Sakurai, K., Masuhara, H., Ubayashi, N., Matsuura, S., Komiya, S.: Association aspects. In: Proc. AOSD'04, pp. 16–25 (2004)
61. Self Home Page, http://research.sun.com/self/
62. Spring AOP (from the Spring reference documentation), http://www.springframework.org/docs/reference/aop.html

63. Strongtalk Home Page, http://www.strongtalk.org/
64. Ungar, D., Chambers, C., Chang, B.-W., Hölzle, U.: Organizing programs without classes. Lisp Symb. Comput. 4(3) (1991)
65. Ungar, D., Smith, R.B.: Self: The Power of Simplicity. In: OOPSLA '87 Conference Proceedings, pp. 227–241. ACM Press, New York (1987)
66. Vanderperren, W., Suvée, D., Cibrán, M.A., De Fraine, B.: Stateful Aspects in JAsCo. In: Gschwind, T., Aßmann, U., Nierstrasz, O. (eds.) SC 2005. LNCS, vol. 3628, pp. 167–181. Springer, Heidelberg (2005)
67. Vanderperren, W., Suvée, D., Verheecke, B., Cibrán, M.A., Jonckers, V.: Adaptive programming in jasco. In: Proc. AOSD'05, pp. 75–86. ACM Press, New York (2005)
68. Wand, M., Kiczales, G., Dutchyn, C.: A semantics for advice and dynamic join points in aspect-oriented programming. ACM Trans. Program. Lang. Syst. 26(5), 890–910 (2004)

A Staged Static Program Analysis to Improve the Performance of Runtime Monitoring

Eric Bodden[1], Laurie Hendren[1], and Ondřej Lhoták[2]

[1] McGill University, Montréal, Québec, Canada
[2] University of Waterloo, Waterloo, Ontario, Canada

Abstract. In runtime monitoring, a programmer specifies a piece of code to execute when a trace of events occurs during program execution. Our work is based on tracematches, an extension to AspectJ, which allows programmers to specify traces via regular expressions with free variables. In this paper we present a staged static analysis which speeds up trace matching by reducing the required runtime instrumentation.

The first stage is a simple analysis that rules out entire tracematches, just based on the names of symbols. In the second stage, a points-to analysis is used, along with a flow-insensitive analysis that eliminates instrumentation points with inconsistent variable bindings. In the third stage the points-to analysis is combined with a flow-sensitive analysis that also takes into consideration the order in which the symbols may execute.

To examine the effectiveness of each stage, we experimented with a set of nine tracematches applied to the DaCapo benchmark suite. We found that about 25% of the tracematch/benchmark combinations had instrumentation overheads greater than 10%. In these cases the first two stages work well for certain classes of tracematches, often leading to significant performance improvements. Somewhat surprisingly, we found the third, flow-sensitive, stage did not add any improvements.

1 Introduction

Various mechanisms have been proposed for monitoring programs as they run. Aspect-oriented programming (AOP) is one approach where a programmer specifies which events should be intercepted and what actions should be taken at those interception points. More recently, this concept of event matching has been further expanded to include matching of *traces of events* [1, 21, 26, 30]. While this expanded notion of matching on traces is much more powerful, it can also lead to larger runtime overheads since some information about the runtime history must be maintained in order to detect matching traces. Also, instrumentation needs to be put in place in order to update this information at events of interest.

In this paper, we examine the problem of improving runtime performance of *tracematches*. Tracematches are an extension to AspectJ which allows programmers to specify traces via regular expressions of symbols with free variables [1]. Those variables can bind objects at runtime, a crucial feature for reasoning about

E. Ernst (Ed.): ECOOP 2007, LNAI 4609, pp. 525–549, 2007.

object-oriented programs. When a trace is matched by a tracematch, with consistent variable bindings, the action associated with the tracematch executes. Trace matching is implemented via a finite-state-based runtime monitor. Each event of the execution trace that matches a declared symbol in a tracematch causes the runtime monitor to update its internal state. When the monitor finds a consistent match for a trace, it executes its associated action.

There are two complementary approaches to reducing the overhead for this kind of runtime monitoring. The first line of attack is to optimize the monitor itself so that each update to the monitor is as inexpensive as possible and so that unnecessary state history is eliminated. Avgustinov et al. were able to show that these approaches greatly reduce overheads in many cases [5, 6]. However, as our experimental results show, there remain a number of cases where the overhead is still quite large.

Our work is the second line of attack, to be used when significant overheads remain. Our approach is based on analysis of both the tracematch specification and the whole program being monitored. The analysis determines which events do not need to be monitored, i.e. which instrumentation points can be eliminated. In the best case, we can determine that a tracematch never matches and all overhead can be removed. In other cases, our objective is to minimize the number of instrumentation points required, thus reducing the overhead.

In developing our analyses, we decided to take a staged approach, applying a sequence of analyses, starting with the simplest and fastest methods and progressing to more expensive and more precise analyses. An important aspect of our research is to determine if the later stages are worth implementing, or if the earlier stages can achieve most of the benefit. We have developed three stages where each stage adds precision to our abstraction. The first stage, called the *quick check*, is a simple method for ruling out entire tracematches, just using the *names* of symbols. Our second stage uses a demand-driven [24] points-to analysis [11, 15], along with a flow-insensitive analysis of the program, to eliminate instrumentation points with inconsistent *variable bindings*. The third stage combines the points-to analysis with a flow-sensitive analysis that takes into consideration the *order* in which events may occur during runtime.

We have evaluated our approach using the DaCapo benchmark suite [7] and a set of 9 tracematches. We found that even though previous techniques often kept the runtime overhead reasonable, there were a significant number of benchmark/tracematch combinations which led to a runtime overhead greater than 10%. We focused on these cases and found that our first two stages worked well for certain classes of tracematches. We were somewhat surprised to find that our third stage did not add any further accuracy, even though it was the only flow-sensitive analysis, and we provide some discussion of why this is so.

This paper is organized as follows. Section 2 introduces tracematches, explains how they apply to Java programs, and gives some examples of where monitoring instrumentation can statically be shown to be unnecessary. In Section 3 we present our staged static analysis which performs such detection automatically. We carefully evaluate our work in Section 4, showing which problem cases our analysis can handle well, but also which cases might need more work or will probably never be statically analyzable. In Section 5 we discuss related analyses, finally concluding in Section 6. There we also briefly discuss our intended scope for future work on the topic.

2   Background

A tracematch defines a runtime monitor using a declarative specification in the form of a regular expression. The alphabet of this regular expression consists of a set of symbols, where one defines each symbol via an AspectJ pointcut. A *pointcut* is, in general, a predicate over joinpoints, a *joinpoint* in AspectJ being an event in the program execution. Common pointcuts can be used to specify a pattern to match against the name of the currently executing method or against the currently executing type. Special pointcuts also allow one to expose parts of the execution context. For instance, in the original AspectJ language the programmer can bind the caller and callee objects as well as all call arguments for each method call. We however use our own implementation of AspectJ in form of the AspectBench Compiler (abc) [3], which implements tracematches and with respect to context exposure also allows one to access any objects that can be reached or computed from the objects one can bind in plain AspectJ, or from static members [5]. For more details regarding pointcuts in AspectJ, see [2].

An example is shown in Figure 1. This tracematch checks for illegal program executions where a vector is updated while an enumeration is iterating over the same vector. First, in lines 2-5 it defines a plain AspectJ pointcut capturing all possible ways in which a vector could be updated. The actual tracematch follows in lines 7-13. In its header (line 7) it declares that it will bind a Vector v and an Enumeration e. Then, in lines 8-10 it defines the alphabet of its regular expression by stating the symbols create, next and update. The first one, create, is declared to match whenever any enumeration e for v is created, while next matches when the program advances e and update on any modification of v.

Line 12 declares a regular expression that states when the tracematch body (also line 12) should execute. This should be the case whenever an enumeration was created, then possibly advanced multiple times and then at least one update to the vector occurs, lastly followed by another call to Enumeration.nextElement().

The declarative semantics of tracematches state that the tracematch body should be executed for any sub-sequence of the program execution trace that is matched by the regular expression with a consistent variable binding. A variable binding is consistent when at every joinpoint in the sub-sequence each variable is bound to the same object.

Internally, each tracematch is implemented using a finite state machine. Such state machines are similar to state machines that can be used for verification of typestate properties [27]. In such a property, a state machine can be associated with a single object. Whenever certain methods on that object are invoked, this state machine is updated according to its transition table. If during the execution a special error state is reached, the typestate property is violated.

```
1  aspect FailSafeEnum {
2     pointcut vector_update() :
3        call(* Vector.add *(..)) || call(* Vector. clear ()) ||
4        call(* Vector.insertElementAt(..)) || call(* Vector.remove*(..)) ||
5        call(* Vector. retainAll (..)) ||  call(* Vector.set *(..));
6
7     tracematch(Vector v, Enumeration e) {
8        sym create after returning(e) : call(* Vector+.elements()) && target(v);
9        sym next before : call(Object Enumeration.nextElement()) && target(e);
10       sym update after : vector_update() && target(v);
11
12       create next* update+ next { /* handle error */ }
13    }
14 }
```

Fig. 1. Safe enumeration tracematch

Tracematches can be seen as an implementation of checkers for *generalized* typestate properties [18]. While ordinary typestate properties only reason about a single object, the generalized ones allow reasoning about groups of objects. Consequently, the tracematch implementation needs to associate a state not with a single object but rather with a group of objects, stored as mapping from tracematch variables to Java objects. Due to their semantic foundations [1], those mappings are called *disjuncts*. Because multiple such groups of objects can be associated with the same automaton state at the same time, each state of the automaton is associated with a *set* of disjuncts, which we call a *constraint*. (Semantically, as shown in [1], this implementation represents storing object constraints in Disjunctive Normal Form).

When compiling a program that contains a tracematch, the compiler firstly generates program code for the related state machine and secondly instruments the program such that it notifies the state machine about any joinpoint of interest, i.e. any joinpoint that matches any of the declared symbols of the tracematch. When such a notification occurs, the related state machine updates its internal state accordingly, i.e. propagates disjuncts from one state to another, generates possibly new disjuncts or discards disjuncts.

Figure 2 shows the automaton for the safe enumeration tracematch. As one can see, it looks very much like the most intuitive automaton for this pattern but

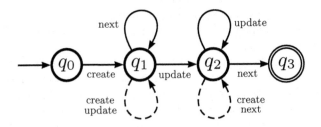

Fig. 2. Finite automaton for safe enumeration tracematch of Figure 1

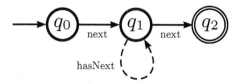

Fig. 3. Finite automaton for tracematch pattern *HasNext*

augmented with additional loops (here dashed) on each non-initial and non-final state. Those loops here appear dashed, because they are of a special kind and have different semantics from usual edges. They are called *skip loops*.

The purpose of skip loops is to discard partial matches. The safe enumeration pattern is unfortunately one of the few where their relevance is somewhat hidden. Hence, in order to explain the purpose of skip loops, consider Figure 3. This figure shows the automaton for the tracematch *HasNext* which uses a pattern "next next" over a symbol alphabet {next,hasNext}.

The intent of this tracematch is to find all cases where there are two calls to Iterator .next(), with no call to hasNext() in between. Since the tracematch alphabet contains both the next and hasNext symbols, matching on the pattern "next next" implies that there was no call to hasNext() between the two next events. This implicit negation is formulated in tracematches by including a symbol in the alphabet but not in the pattern, just like it is done with hasNext here. During runtime, when next() is called on a particular iterator i_1, a disjunct $\{i \mapsto i_1\}$ is generated on state q_1. Now, if another call to hasNext() follows, this binding can be discarded, because at least for the moment for this particular iterator i_1 the requirement is fulfilled. This is exactly what the skip loop on state q_1 achieves. When hasNext() is called on i_1, it *discards* the partial match for i_1 by deleting its disjunct from q_1. (An alternative implementation could move disjuncts back to the initial state, but discarding the disjunct saves memory).

Running example. To get a better feeling for the semantics of tracematches and the implications of our optimization, let us look at the following running example. Assume that we want to evaluate the safe enumeration tracematch over the code shown in Figure 4. The code does not do anything meaningful but it allows us to explain how tracematches work and which cases the different stages of our analysis can handle. In lines 5-10, the program modifies and iterates over the vector, vector, and does so in a safe way. In lines 12-15 it modifies and iterates over another vector, globalVec. It also calls doEvil (..), modifying globalVec while the enumeration is used. This is a case which the tracematch should capture. In lines 17-18 a third vector and an enumeration over this vector are created.

The comments on the right-hand side of the figure label *allocation sites*, i.e. places where vectors or enumerations are allocated. We use those labels to denote objects. An object is labelled with the site at which it was allocated.

In our static analysis, we attempt to remove unnecessary instrumentation points in the base program that trigger the tracematch at a point where it can statically be decided that the particular event can never be part of a complete

```
 1  class Main {
 2     Vector globalVector = new Vector();                                      //v2
 3
 4     void someMethod() {
 5        Vector vector = new Vector();                                         //v1
 6        vector.add("something");
 7        for (Enumeration iter = vector.elements(); iter.hasMoreElements();) {  //e1
 8           Object o = iter.nextElement();
 9           doSomething(o);
10        }
11
12        globalVector.add("something_else");
13        Enumeration it2 = globalVector.elements();                            //e2
14        doEvil(o);
15        it2.nextElement();
16
17        Vector copyVector = new Vector(globalVec);                            //v3
18        Enumeration it3 = copyVector.elements();                              //e3
19     }
20
21     void doSomething(Object o)
22     { /* does not touch globalVector */ }
23
24     void doEvil(Object o)
25     { globalVector.remove(o); }
26  }
```

Fig. 4. An example program

match. Such instrumentation points are commonly called *shadows* in aspect-oriented programming [22, 14], and hence we will also use that term in the remainder of this paper. To see how one could identify unnecessary shadows, let us first manually find such places in the code for our running example.

Shadows occur wherever a tracematch symbol matches a part of the program. In our example, this means that we have shadows at each creation of an enumeration, each update of a vector and each call to Enumeration.nextElement(). However, when looking at the code more carefully, it should become clear that not all of the shadows are necessary for the example program.

In particular, the first sequence of statements in the lines 5-10 is safe in the sense that the pair of vector and enumeration is used correctly and the tracematch will not be triggered. Consequently, no shadows need to be inserted for this part of the program. Lines 12 to 15 and line 25 show an unsafe enumeration that should trigger the tracematch. So generally, shadows here need to stay in place. However, looking at the code more carefully, one can see that actually the shadow at line 12 is also superfluous, because the match that triggers the tracematch does not start before line 13, where the enumeration is actually created. In lines 17 to 18 we have a pair of vector and enumeration where the vector is never even updated. For this piece of code it should be obvious that no shadows are required.

In the next section we describe our static program analyses which automatically identify the unnecessary shadows.

3   Staged Analysis

Our analysis is implemented using the *reweaving* framework [4] in abc. The basic idea is that the compiler first determines all shadows, i.e. all points in the program where instrumentation should be woven. This procedure returns what we call a *weaving plan*. This plan tells the weaver what needs to be woven at which shadows. In order to determine which shadows are unnecessary, a first weaving is done according to the original weaving plan. This results in a woven program on which our proposed staged analyses are performed. The analysis determines which shadows are unnecessary and removes them from the weaving plan. The program is then rewoven according to this new plan, resulting in a more efficient woven program.

The analyses are performed on the Jimple[1] representation of the woven program. In this representation, all instructions corresponding to tracematch shadows are specially marked so that they can be recognized.

An outline of the staged analyses is shown in Figure 5. Each stage uses its own abstract representation of the program and applies an analysis to this representation in order to find unnecessary shadows. After each stage, those shadows are removed so that subsequent stages do not have to consider them any more in their analyses.

The crucial point of this approach is that the earlier stages (on the top of the figure) are more coarse-grained than later ones. Hence they use a more lightweight abstract representation of the program and execute much faster. By applying stages in this order we make sure that at each stage only those shadows remain active which could not be proven unnecessary using an easier approach.

Figure 5 shows the three analysis stages we apply here as boxes. First we apply a quick check that determines if a tracematch can apply to a given program at all, just by looking at shadow counters, which are already computed during the initial weaving process. The second stage uses points-to information in order to find groups of shadows which could during runtime possibly lead to a complete match by possibly referring to a consistent variable binding. The third and final stage is flow-sensitive, meaning that we look at all those groups of shadows and try to determine in which order their shadows could possibly be executed when the program is run. In many cases, all shadows might already be removed in an early stage. When this happens, later stages are not executed at all. In any case, however, the code is eventually rewoven using the updated weaving plan, i.e. weaving only those shadows that have not been disabled before.

As the figure suggests, in general it can make sense to iterate the analysis and reweaving phases. In our experiments for this paper, we used however empty bodies for all tracematches, simply because we were only interested in the cost

---

[1] Jimple is a fully typed three-address code representation of Java bytecode provided by Soot [29], which is an integral part of abc.

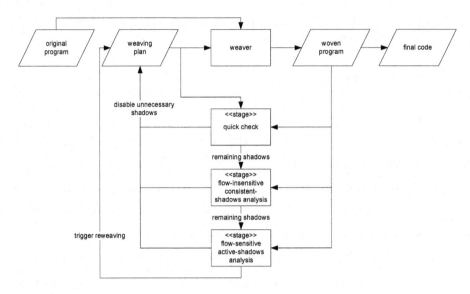

Fig. 5. Outline of the staged analysis

of matching, not executing a tracematch. If all tracematch bodies are empty, the tracematches themselves can trigger no joinpoints and hence their removal does not affect the analysis result in the first iteration.

In the following subsections, we explain all three stages as well as their required program abstractions in more detail.

3.1   Quick Check

One use of tracematches is to specify behavioural constraints for Java interfaces. When developing a library, for example, one could ship it together with a set of tracematches in order to enforce that objects of that library are used in a certain way or in certain combinations. Consequently, it might often be the case that certain tracematches might never match or that only some of their symbols match, simply because the client uses only parts of the library.

For example, imagine a program which uses vectors but no enumerations. In this case, when applying the safe enumeration tracematch, **abc** would normally instrument all locations where a vector is updated, although an analysis of the whole program would show that the tracematch can never match.

The abstract program representation used by the quick check is simply a mapping from tracematch symbols to number of shadows at which the tracematch symbol may match. Those numbers are obtained during the initial weaving phase. For our running example, we would obtain the following mapping because enumerations are created at three places, they are advanced at two places and vectors are updated at three places.

$$\{create \mapsto 3, next \mapsto 2, update \mapsto 3\}$$

We use these counts, plus the tracematch automaton to determine if the tracematch could ever match. The key idea is that if a symbol that is necessary to reach a final state in the automaton has a count of 0 (i.e. no instances in the program under analysis exist), then there is no possibility that the tracematch could match.

We implement this check as follows. For each tracematch, we remove edges from its automaton whose label has a shadow count of 0. Then we check to see if a final state can still be reached. If the final state can't be reached, the entire tracematch is removed and all its associated shadows are disabled.

If the quick check fails for a tracematch, i.e. all necessary symbols were applied at least once, we have to change to a more detailed level of abstraction which leads us to the flow-insensitive analysis.

3.2 Flow-Insensitive Consistent-Shadows Analysis

A tracematch can only match a trace if the trace refers to symbols with *consistent variable bindings*. In the quick check we just used the names of the symbols and did not use any information about variable bindings. In contrast, the flow-insensitive *consistent-shadows analysis* uses points-to analysis results to determine when shadows cannot refer to the same object and thus cannot lead to consistent variable bindings. The analysis is flow-insensitive in the sense that we do not consider the order in which the shadows execute.

Preparation: In order to prepare for this analysis, we first need points-to information for each variable involved in the tracematches. We compute the required points-to information as follows.

First we build a call graph using the Soot/abc internal Spark [19] framework. Spark builds a call graph for the whole program on-the-fly, i.e. by computing points-to information at the same time as discovering new call edges due to new points-to relationships. This first phase results in a complete call graph and context-insensitive points-to information for the whole program.

In our preliminary experiments we found that the context-insensitive points-to analysis was not always precise enough, and so we added a second phase that computes context-sensitive points-to analysis for those variables bound by shadows. For this second phase we use Sridharan and Bodík's demand-driven refinement analysis for points-to sets [24]. This algorithm starts with the call graph and context-insensitive results from the first phase and computes context information for *a given set of variables*, often yielding more precise points-to information for these variables. The advantage of this approach is that we need to perform this rather expensive computation only for variables that are really bound by shadows. In all our benchmarks this was fewer than 5% of the total number of variables. (For exact numbers, see Section 4.)

Our running example illustrates quite clearly why context-sensitive points-to analysis is required. In this case, context information is necessary to distinguish the different enumerations from each other. Since all are created within the factory method elements(), without such context-sensitivity, all enumerations would be modelled as the same abstract object — their common creation site inside

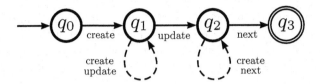

Fig. 6. Automaton from Figure 2 with loops due to Kleene-* sub-expressions removed

the method elements(). Allocation sites e1, e2 and e3 would collapse, and so the analysis would have to assume that all three enumerations might actually be one and the same, penalizing the opportunities for shadow removal.

Building path infos: At runtime, a tracematch matches when a sequence of events is executed which is matched by the given regular expression, however *only* if those events occurred with a *consistent variable binding*. The idea of the flow-insensitive analysis stage is to identify groups of shadows which could potentially lead to such a consistent variable binding at runtime.

At runtime, a final state in the tracematch automaton can be reached from any initial state, generally over multiple paths. A first observation is that edges which originate from symbols within a Kleene-* sub-expression are always optional. For example, in the safe enumeration tracematch (Figure 1), the initial next* *may*, but does not have to, match a joinpoint in order for a sequence to lead to a complete match. Hence, we first generate an automaton using a customized Thompson construction [28] that omits "starred" sub-expressions, modelling them with an ϵ-edges (which are then later on inlined).

Figure 6 shows the fail safe enumeration automaton after this transformation. We call this representation the *reduced* automaton. Note that skip loops are preserved in this representation, however no other strongly-connected components remain. Hence, we can enumerate all paths through this automaton which do not lead through a skip loop.

Then, for each such path we compute a *path info*. A path info consists of two components. The first holds information about which symbols the edges on the path are labelled with. The second records all labels of skip-loops that are attached to states on that path. For the labels of non-skip edges, we will later on also need the information of how often such a label occurs on the path. This yields the following definition.

Definition 1 (Path info). Let *path* be a path from an initial to a final state in the reduced automaton. A path info *info* consists of a set *skip-labels(info)* and a multi-set *labels(info)*, defined as follows. Assume we define for each state q the set *skip-labels*(q) as the set of labels of all skip-loops on q. Then, if *path* = $(p_1, l_1, q_1) \ldots (p_n, l_n, q_n)$, then

$$labels := \biguplus_{1 \leq i \leq n} \{l_i\}$$

$$skip\text{-}labels := \bigcup_{1 \leq i \leq n} \left(skip\text{-}labels(p_i) \cup skip\text{-}labels(q_i) \right)$$

where $\uplus$ denotes the union for multi-sets. (A multi-set or bag is a similar to a set but can hold the same object multiple times.) In the following, we denote multi-sets with square brackets of the form $[a, a, b]$.

For a tracematch tm, we denote the set of all its path infos by $infos(tm)$. It is defined as the set of all path infos for all paths through its reduced automaton.

For the fail safe enumeration tracematch in our example, only one path exists: $(q0, \text{create}, q1), (q1, \text{update}, q2), (q2, \text{next}, q3)$. Hence the set $infos$ has the following form.

$$infos(\text{FailSafeEnum}) =$$
$$\{(\ labels = [\text{create}, \text{update}, \text{next}],\ skip\text{-}labels = \{\text{create}, \text{update}, \text{next}\}\ )\}$$

The reader should not be misled by this example. In general, *labels* and *skip-labels* do not have to coincide. For example, for the automaton in Figure 3, we would have a single path info with *labels* = [next, next] and *skip-labels* = {hasNext}.

Building groups of shadows with possibly consistent binding: With the path infos computed, we have information about what combinations of shadows are *required* for a complete match. In the next step we try to find groups of shadows that fulfil this requirement. This means that we look for groups of shadows which contain the labels of the *labels* field of a path info and, in addition, share a possibly consistent binding. But before we define shadow groups, let us first formally define how a single shadow is modelled.

Definition 2 (Shadow). A shadow s of a tracematch tm is a pair $(lab_s, bind_s)$ where lab_s is the label of a declared symbol of tm and $bind_s$ is a variable binding, modelled as a mapping from variables to points-to sets. In the following we assume that the mapping $bind_s$ is extended to a total function that maps each variable to the full points-to set $\top$ if no other binding is defined:

$$bind_s(v) := \begin{cases} bind_s(v), \text{if } bind_s(v) \text{ explicitly defined} \\ \top, \text{otherwise} \end{cases}$$

Here, $\top$ is defined as the points-to set for which holds that for all points-to sets $s : s \cap \top = s$.

In our running example, the update shadow in line 6 would be denoted by (update, $\{v \mapsto \{v1\}\}$) as the only objects v can point to are objects being created at creation site $v1$.

Definition 3 (Shadow group). A *shadow group* is a pair of a multi-set of shadows called *label-shadows* and a set of shadows called *skip-shadows*. We call a shadow group *complete* if it holds that: (1) its set of labels of *label-shadows* contains all labels of a path info of a given tracematch; and (2) its set of *skip-shadows* contains all shadows which have the label of a skip loop of a state on this path and a points-to set that overlaps with the one of a label shadow.

This definition implies that a complete shadow group has: (1) enough shadows in its *label-shadows* to drive a tracematch state machine into a final state; and (2) that all shadows that could interfere with a match via skip loops are contained in *skip-shadows*.

Definition 4 (Consistent shadow group). A *consistent* shadow group g is a shadow group for which all variable bindings of all shadows in the group have overlapping points-to sets for each variable. More formally, if *vars* is the set of all variables of all shadows in g, then it must hold that:

$$\forall s_1, s_2 \in (label\text{-}shadows \cup skip\text{-}shadows) \; \forall v \in vars : \; bind_{s_1}(v) \cap bind_{s_2}(v) \neq \emptyset$$

Conceptually, a complete and consistent shadow group is the static representation of a possibly complete match at runtime. For such a shadow group, there is a possibility that if the label shadows in this group are executed in a particular order at runtime, the related tracematch could match. Skip shadows in the same group could prevent such a match when executed.

In particular, if a shadow group has a multi-set of label shadows which is *not* consistent this means that no matter in which order those shadows are executed at runtime, this group of shadows can *never* lead to a complete match. Consequently, we can safely disable all shadows which are not part of any consistent shadow group. The complete algorithm for the construction of complete and consistent shadow sets is given in the technical report version of this paper [8].

Based on the consistent shadow groups, flow-insensitive shadow removal is then quite easy. For each shadow that exists in the program, we look up if it is member of at least one consistent shadow group (i.e. it is either a label-shadow or a skip shadow of that group). If this is *not* the case, the shadow can never be part of a complete, consistent match and can safely be removed.

In our running example, this is true for the shadow in line 18. Since for this create-shadow there exists neither an update shadow for the same vector nor a next-shadow for the same enumeration, there can no complete and consistent shadow set be computed that contains the create-shadow.

Here we can also see that context information for points-to sets is important. As noted earlier, without context information, all enumerations would be modelled by the same abstract object. Hence, in this case, the points-to sets for those shadows would overlap and the shadow in line 18 *could* be part of a complete and consistent match, in combination with one of the vectors globalVector or vector.

If after this stage there are still shadows remaining we know that there exist groups of shadows which have a possibly consistent variable binding. This means that if such shadows are executed in a particular order at runtime, the related tracematch could indeed be triggered. Hence, it is only natural that in the next stage we compute information that tells us whether those shadows could can actually be executed in the required order or not. This leads us to the flow-sensitive consistent-shadows analysis stage.

3.3   Flow-Sensitive Active-Shadows Analysis

As input to this stage we expect a set of complete and consistent shadow groups as well as a complete call graph, both of which were already computed earlier. (In the following, when we refer to a shadow group, we always assume it is complete and consistent).

In order to determine in which order shadows could be executed during runtime, we need a flow-sensitive representation of the entire program. It is a challenge to build such a representation efficiently. Since any Java program is potentially multi-threaded, we also have to take into account that shadows could be executed by multiple threads. This makes it more difficult to determine whether a shadow may run before or after another.

A tracematch can be defined to be *per-thread* or *global*. For a per-thread tracematch, a separate automaton is executed for each thread, and only events from that one thread affect the automaton. A global tracematch is implemented using a single automaton which processes events from all threads. Hence, for global tracematches, our analysis must handle multi-threading soundly.

Also, a whole program abstraction may potentially be very large. There might potentially be thousands of shadows spread over hundreds of methods. Hence it is important that we keep our program abstraction concise at all times.

Handling of multi-threading: We handle the first problem of multi-threading conservatively. In the preparation phase for the flow-insensitive analysis stage, we already constructed a complete call graph. In this call graph, call edges that spawn a thread are already specially marked. Using this information, we can easily determine by which threads a given shadow can be executed.

Then, in an initial preprocessing step, we filter the list of all shadow groups in the following way. If a shadow group is associated with a global tracematch and contains shadows which are possibly executed by multiple threads, we "lock" all its shadows (i.e. they will never be removed, not by this stage nor by subsequent stages) and remove the group from the list. The locking makes the analysis conservative with respect to threads. For the resulting list of shadow groups we then know that all shadows contained in a group are only executed by a single thread each. Hence, no additional treatment of multi-threading is necessary.

A flow-sensitive whole-program representation: In the next step, we build a flow-sensitive representation of the whole program. Such a representation naturally has to depend on the static call graph of the program.

Call graph filtering. In order to adhere to our principle of keeping our abstraction as small as possible at all times, we first filter this call graph in the following way. If in the call graph there is an outgoing call edge in whose transitive closure there is never any method of interest reachable (i.e. a method that contains a shadow), this edge and its entire transitive closure is removed.

Per-method state machines. For each method that remains in this filtered call graph, we know that either it is "interesting" because it contains a shadow or

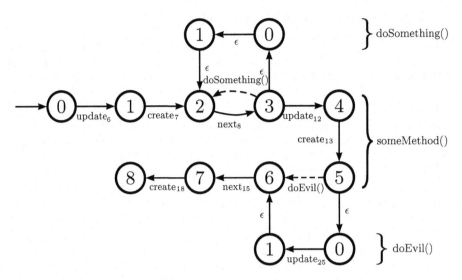

Fig. 7. complete state machine for the running example during construction; for illustrative purposes, the shadow labels are attached with their respective line numbers

it calls another interesting method. For those methods we do need control flow information, i.e. information about the order in which shadows may be executed during runtime and in which other methods may be called.

We encode such flow-information by a finite state machine that represents the abstract transition structure of the whole program. Due to space limitations we cannot give any details about this construction here. We refer the interested reader to the technical report version of this paper [8]. Figure 7 shows the result of this construction for our running example. This state machine consists of per-method state machines for the methods doSomething(), someMethod() and doEvil(). Those then become inter-procedurally combined using ϵ-transitions

Note that this way of combining automata is context-insensitive. In the resulting automaton there exist more paths than are actually realizable at runtime. One could branch out from a call statement c_1 to a possible call target t but then return to another caller c_2 of the same call target. This way of automaton construction is relatively cheap but gives away precision, as Section 4 will show.

Abstract interpretation via fixed point iteration. This whole-program state machine is the input to our actual flow-sensitive analysis. The task of this analysis is to compute if some part of this state machine contains such a path that when executing the program along this path at runtime, the tracematch could match. To us, it appeared that the most sensible way to do so is to perform a complete abstract interpretation of the actual tracematch machinery.

This abstract interpretation evaluates an *abstract counterpart* of the actual tracematch automaton (i.e. the one that is evaluated at runtime) over the whole-program state machine. Since the latter can have cycles, we employ, as is usually done in data-flow analysis [16], a fixed-point iteration.

The only two differences of the abstract interpretation in comparison to the evaluation at runtime are the following. Firstly, wherever the actual implementation binds variables to objects, the abstract interpretation binds them to points-to sets. Consequently, where at runtime, the implementation checks for reference equality, the abstract interpretation checks for overlapping points-to sets. In the case of skip loops, variable bindings are not updated at all (due to the lack of must-alias information, see below).

The other difference is that while during runtime, the implementation exposes no explicit information about where partial matches occurred, the static abstraction needs to determine which shadows were visited on the way to a final state. Hence, in each disjunct, we store an additional *history* component: the set of shadows which this disjunct was propagated through. When such a disjunct reaches a final state, we can inspect its history and so determine which shadows need to be kept active in order to trigger the match for this disjunct at runtime. The history is also updated in case a skip loop is visited.

We start off with an initial tracematch configuration in the unique initial state of this whole-program state machine, which represents the fact that when the program starts, the tracematch is in its initial configuration. In terms of Figure 7, this would associate the following configuration with the initial node of the whole-program state machine.

$$(q_0 \mapsto \textbf{true}, q_1 \mapsto \textbf{false}, q_2 \mapsto \textbf{false}, q_3 \mapsto \textbf{false})\}$$

Here **true** is the constraint $\{(\emptyset, \emptyset)\}$ consisting of a single disjunct with empty variable binding and history while **false** is the empty constraint (modelled by the empty set of disjuncts).

This configuration is then driven through the whole-program state machine until a fixed-point is reached. Whenever a disjunct is propagated, its history component is updated with the shadow that triggered the propagation. Due to internals of the tracematch machinery, this is only the case if a constraint really moves to a new state. For example at node number 1 (of method someMethod()) in Figure 7, the configuration is still same the initial configuration as above. At node number 2, one would get

$$(q_0 \mapsto \textbf{true}, q_1 \mapsto \{(\{v \mapsto v_1, e \mapsto e_1\}, \{create_7\})\}, q_2 \mapsto \textbf{false}, q_3 \mapsto \textbf{false})\}$$

stating that the abstract tracematch automaton has one single partial match in state 1 with a variable mapping of $\{v \mapsto v_1, e \mapsto e_1\}$ which was produced by shadow $create_7$.

At merge-points (here only the same node number 2), configurations are merged by joining their constraints per state, i.e. two constraints with mappings $q_i \mapsto \{d_1, d_2\}$ and $q_i \mapsto \{d_2, d_3\}$ (for disjuncts d_1, d_2, d_3) is merged to a constraint with mapping $q_i \mapsto \{d_1, d_2, d_3\}$.

During the computation of the fixed point, whenever a disjunct reaches a final state of a configuration, we copy its history to a *global set* of *active shadows*. When the fixed point is reached, we know that all shadows in this set may lead to a complete match, with the binding that is stored in the disjunct, and hence have to be retained. All shadows which are never added to this set during the fixed point computation can safely be discarded.

Performance improvements. The aforementioned fixed point computation generally works but it might not be very efficient. Hence, we apply two different performance optimizations, one of which does not sacrifice precision and one of which does. The general idea is that it is sometimes sound not to iterate through certain groups of shadows, given that we "lock" them, i.e. define those shadows as not to be disabled. Refer to [8] for details about these optimizations.

Handling of skip loops. One important issue that has not yet been explained is the handling of skip loops. As explained earlier, the purpose of a skip-loop is to discard partial matches under certain circumstances. In the example we gave in Section 2, this is the case when a disjunct of the form $\{i \mapsto i_1\}$ exists and then hasNext is invoked on the iterator i_1.

At runtime, we can remove this partial match because we know that for the object i_1 the property is currently fulfilled. The automaton can be "reset" to its initial configuration with respect to i_1. At compile time, we are only allowed to apply the same strong update of the automaton constraints if we know for sure that the object referenced by variable i at the hasNext event *must* be the same as the object referenced by i as the previous next event. In other words, we have to know if the references to variable i at both locations in the code *must* be aliased.

As there is currently no must-alias analysis in Soot, we perform a weak update on skip-loops that does not discard partial matches. Unfortunately, this makes it impossible to rule out patterns as the one mentioned above merely by looking at the possible execution order. (Still, we can rule out skip-loops that are only executed on paths that never lead to a final state.) Our next phase of work will investigate the kinds of must-alias analyses we need to handle skip loops more precisely. Fink et al. show in their work [12] what a general solution could look like for the case of typestates, where one only reasons about one object at a time.

4   Benchmarks

In order to evaluate the feasibility and effectiveness of our approach we applied our analysis to a combination of nine different tracematches, applied to version 2006-10 of the DaCapo benchmark suite [7]. The tracematches validate generic safety and liveness properties over common data structures in the Java runtime library. They are briefly described in Table 1. As usual, all our benchmarks are available on http://www.aspectbench.org/, along with a version of abc implementing our optimization. In the near future we also plan to integrate the analysis into the main abc build stream.

The reader should note that we chose some of our tracematches because we knew they would be particularly challenging. For example, the *HashMap* tracematch binds a hash code, which is an integer value. We found it interesting to see

Table 1. description of tracematch patterns

pattern name	description
ASyncIteration	only iterate a synchronized collection c when owning a lock on c
FailSafeEnum	do not update a vector while iterating over it
FailSafeIter	do not update a collection while iterating over it
HashMap	do not change an object's hash code while it is in a hash map
HasNextElem	always call hasNextElem before calling nextElement on an Enumeration
HasNext	always call hasNext before calling next on an Iterator
LeakingSync	only access a synchronized collection using its synchronized wrapper
Reader	don't use a Reader after it's InputStream was closed
Writer	don't use a Writer after it's OutputStream was closed

what effect the presence of a non-pointer variable would have on our pointer-based analyses. The *ASyncIteration* benchmark uses an **if**-pointcut accessing the native method Thread.holdsLock(Object). This is challenging because there is no chance to generally evaluate such a pointcut at compile time. The question is whether this fact generally impedes the analysis or not.

The tracematches *HasNext* and *HasNextElem* specify properties where something *must always* happen in order to avoid a match. After a call to next(), hasNext() must be called before the next call to next(). (In the verification community, such properties are often called *liveness properties* [17].) As mentioned in Section 3.3, the flow-sensitive analysis cannot remove shadows for such properties without using must-alias information. The flow-insensitive analysis would also perform badly on those particular properties, simply because on virtually every iterator hasNext() is called if and only if next() is called. Hence, for those benchmarks we expected a very low shadow removal ratio. Yet, the benchmarks helped us to validate the completeness of our implementation because we knew that in those cases neither the flow-insensitive nor the flow-sensitive stage should remove any shadows.

For our experiments we used the IBM J9 JVM version 1.5.0 SR3 (64bit) with 2GB RAM on a machine with AMD Athlon 64 X2 Dual Core Processor 3800+. We used the -**converge** option of the DaCapo suite which runs each benchmark multiple times to assure that the reported execution times are within a confidence interval of 3%.

Table 2 shows the run times of the benchmarks without our optimizations, but with the optimizations mentioned in [5] already enabled. The leftmost column shows the benchmark name, then follows the raw runtime with no tracematch present (in milliseconds). The other columns show the overheads in percent over this baseline. We marked all cells with values larger than 10% as boldface, values within the confidence interval appear gray. The benchmark *bloat/FailSafeIter* was stopped after around 8 hours of benchmarking time. This benchmark is very hard to handle, dynamically as well as statically, because it makes extraordinarily heavy use of long-lived iterators and collections. We shall return to this benchmark later, when we discuss the precision of our analysis.

Table 2. Runtime overheads of the benchmarks before applying our optimizations

benchmark	no tracematch	ASyncIteration	FailSafeEnum	FailSafeIter	HashMap	HasNextElem	HasNext	LeakingSync	Reader	Writer
antlr	4098	1.42	2.20	0.93	0.44	6.54	-0.15	**25.28**	**966.98**	**108.76**
bloat	9348	**99.17**	0.75	**>8h**	**139.08**	0.58	**3872.66**	**497.35**	-2.95	**92.52**
chart	13646	0.39	0.01	**20.73**	0.15	0.13	0.99	**345.30**	0.32	0.29
eclipse	50003	2.36	1.10	3.44	2.36	0.53	4.81	2.61	0.28	-1.21
fop	3102	-9.96	-8.67	1.06	5.35	-4.13	-9.93	**589.30**	0.71	6.74
hsqldb	12322	0.00	-0.32	0.03	0.19	0.07	-0.16	0.79	0.32	-0.06
jython	11133	1.47	2.04	6.57	1.05	-1.17	2.67	**-11.17**	-0.89	0.50
lucene	17068	1.29	**30.36**	9.57	3.40	**17.17**	2.22	**422.52**	1.78	1.12
pmd	12977	2.96	-0.11	**157.61**	-0.83	-1.85	**158.23**	**31.26**	2.43	-0.21
xalan	13083	1.86	0.20	0.71	1.35	-0.41	2.34	4.20	1.70	0.47

As we can see from the table, some benchmarks expose a significant overhead.[2] In these cases the whole program optimizations presented in this paper are worth applying. In particular, given the sometimes large runtime overhead, the programmer might well want to trade some of this overhead for compile time.

We applied our analysis to all 90 benchmarks, and in Table 3 we report on the improvements for the 18 interesting cases with an overhead of more than 10%. We captured the optimized program after each stage in order to see how many shadows were removed and are still remaining and in order to evaluate the runtime impact of the shadow removal for that stage. The table shows per benchmark five different shadow counts: all shadows, shadows remaining after the quick check, reachable shadows remaining after call graph construction (note that removing unreachable shadows has no impact on the runtime), and finally shadows remaining after the last two analysis stages. The rightmost column shows the last stage that was applied.

The table is split vertically into multiple parts. For the benchmarks in the first part (rows 1-7), the quick check was able to eliminate all shadows. For row 8, the flow-insensitive analysis removed all 294 reachable shadows. In the benchmarks in rows 9-13, the flow-insensitive analysis removed at least some shadows, most often all but a few. In the benchmarks in row 14-16, the flow-insensitive analysis was ineffective. In benchmarks 17 and 18, the analysis failed to complete in a reasonable time or aborted due to insufficient memory.

---

[2] The speedups for fop and jython apparently originate from the fact that those benchmarks are *bistable*. Depending on scheduling order they settle down in one of two different highly predictable states. Additional instrumentation can sometimes affect this order and make the benchmark settle into a more favourable state, i.e. make the benchmark execute faster. This interpretation was suggested by Robin Garner, one of the developers of the DaCapo benchmark suite.

Table 3. Number of active shadows after applying each stage

#	benchmark	all	quick	reachable	flow-ins.	flow-sens.	final stage
1	antlr/LeakingSync	170	0	0	0	0	quick check
2	antlr/Writer	56	0	0	0	0	quick check
3	bloat/ASyncIteration	419	0	0	0	0	quick check
4	bloat/LeakingSync	2145	0	0	0	0	quick check
5	chart/LeakingSync	920	0	0	0	0	quick check
6	fop/LeakingSync	2347	0	0	0	0	quick check
7	pmd/LeakingSync	986	0	0	0	0	quick check
8	lucene/LeakingSync	653	653	294	0	0	flow-ins.
9	antlr/Reader	53	53	46	15	15	flow-sens.
10	bloat/HashMap	57	57	16	2	2	flow-sens.
11	bloat/Writer	206	206	87	8	8	flow-sens.
12	lucene/FailSafeEnum	61	61	41	5	5	flow-sens.
13	pmd/FailSafeIter	529	529	129	90	90	flow-sens.
14	chart/FailSafeIter	469	469	105	105	105	flow-sens.
15	lucene/HasNextElem	22	22	14	14	14	flow-sens.
16	pmd/HasNext	346	346	87	86	86	flow-sens.
17	bloat/FailSafeIter	1500	1500	1015	1015	1015	aborted
18	bloat/HasNext	947	947	639	639	639	aborted

The results show that the quick-check is very effective, removing all shadows in seven benchmarks. The flow-insensitive stage is generally very effective too, reducing the instrumentation and runtime overhead in another seven cases. We wish to point out that even in the case of *bloat/HashMap*, where primitive values are bound, the flow-insensitive analysis can still rule out many shadows by relating those remaining variables which bind objects. In one case (number 8), it is even able to prove the program correct, i.e. that all synchronized collections are only accessed via their synchronized wrapper.

The reader should note that optimizations as we propose here would be hopeless to perform on a a hand-coded monitor in plain AspectJ. Consequently at least in cases 1-8 where we remove all shadows, the optimized benchmark runs faster than it could ever be achieved using not tracematches but AspectJ only.

Looking at the flow-sensitive stage, we were very disappointed to see that it did not manage to remove more instrumentation over the flow-insensitive stage. While in some microbenchmarks which we used for testing, it yielded significant improvements, in the DaCapo benchmark suite it was not even able to remove a single additional shadow. We were able to identify three different factors that lead to this behaviour. We hope that these observations will lead to better analyses which can find further improvements.

Firstly, if a lot of shadows remain after the flow-insensitive analysis, this often indicates that for some reason there is a large overlap between points-to sets. When this is the case, it is however equally hard for the flow-sensitive analysis to tell different objects apart and hence to relate events on those objects temporally.

Table 4. Runtimes of the analysis (left, in m:ss) and runtime overheads of the benchmarks (right, in percent) after applying each stage

#	benchmark	analysis	pre-opt.	quick	flow-ins.	flow-sens.
1	antlr/LeakingSync	< 0:01	25.28	0.15	-0.07	-1.00
2	antlr/Writer	< 0:01	108.76	3.44	4.00	2.76
3	bloat/ASyncIteration	< 0:01	99.17	18.44	18.68	18.59
4	bloat/LeakingSync	< 0:01	497.35	16.69	16.04	16.78
5	chart/LeakingSync	< 0:01	345.30	1.82	1.83	1.60
6	fop/LeakingSync	< 0:01	589.30	-9.16	-7.03	-9.77
7	pmd/LeakingSync	< 0:01	31.26	-0.73	-0.66	-1.09
8	lucene/LeakingSync	2:17	422.52	448.69	-4.04	-4.93
9	antlr/Reader	2:03	966.98	408.93	20.60	20.40
10	bloat/HashMap	7:02	139.08	134.11	2.57	3.61
11	bloat/Writer	7:34	92.52	280.03	4.11	3.59
12	lucene/FailSafeEnum	1:56	30.36	27.84	-1.80	-2.86
13	pmd/FailSafeIter	20:47	157.61	161.27	78.16	79.04
14	chart/FailSafeIter	7:52	20.73	20.52	22.36	20.56
15	lucene/HasNextElem	1:52	17.17	13.18	12.42	11.92
16	pmd/HasNext	4:20	158.23	167.73	169.08	158.13
17	bloat/FailSafeIter	aborted	307987.29	307987.29	n/a	n/a
18	bloat/HasNext	aborted	3872.66	3895.18	4013.53	n/a

As noted in Section 3.3, in such situations we often only perform a lightweight fixed point computation which treats skip shadows conservatively. In cases like *pmd/FailSafeIter* unfortunately, this seems to give away a lot of crucial precision.

Secondly, as we explained in Section 3.3, our whole-program state machine is context-insensitive, meaning that we over-approximate the set of actually realizable paths by not explicitly outgoing with returning call edges. This seems to lose precision in those cases where overlapping points-to sets are actually not the problem.

Thirdly, we handle multi-threading in a very conservative way. In benchmarks like lucene, the program does not trigger the tracematch only because it uses explicit wait/notify. Without analyzing such lock patterns explicitly, there is little hope for any more precision in those cases.

Case 14, *chart/FailSafeIter*, could also not be improved upon because of multi-threading. In addition, points-to sets largely overlapped due to the use of reflection which caused a safe over-approximation of points-to sets.

In the cases of *bloat/FailSafeIter* and *bloat/HasNext*, the analysis ran out of memory. The problem with bloat is[3] that it uses extraordinarily many iterator accesses and modifications of collections. In addition, almost all iterators

---

[3] Just before submitting the final version of this paper, through personal communication with Feng Chen [9] we found out that bloat within DaCapo apparently processes parts of itself as input (bloat is another bytecode transformation package). Hence, it might also be the case that our instrumentation modified bloat's input.

and collections are very long-lived, so that points-to sets vastly overlap. The construction of the whole-program state machine suffers even more from the fact that bloat defines its own collections which delegate to collections of the Java runtime (JRE). Usually, collection classes are defined inside the JRE and thus not weavable and produce no shadows. Hence, due to the call graph abstraction, calls to hasNext() or updates to collections produce no edges in the whole-program state machine. In bloat, all those optimizations fail, making the problem of efficient model construction very hard to solve.

Table 4 shows the runtimes of those 18 optimized benchmarks. As we can observe, there is most often a very direct relation between the number of shadows removed and the speedup gained by the optimization. After applying all three optimization stages, all but the benchmarks in rows 13 and 16-18 execute almost as fast as the un-instrumented program.

Per-thread tracematches. We further analyzed per-thread versions of the trace-matches *HasNext* and *HasNextElem* (in our eyes, the per-thread modifier makes no sense for the other configurations). Unfortunately, this seemed to yield no improvements in terms of precision and shortened the execution time of the analysis only marginally.

4.1 Execution Time of the Analysis

The analysis was run on the same machine configuration as the benchmarks but with a maximal heap space of 3GB. Total runtimes of the analysis are shown on the left hand side of Table 4. The longest successful analysis run we had was pmd/FailSafeIter with a total analysis time of almost 21 minutes. The different stages of this run are distributed as follows (m:ss).

- 0:01 - quick check
- 2:27 - call graph construction, points-to set creation, call graph abstraction
- 0:03 - flow-insensitive analysis
- 0:20 - creation of per-method state machines
- 1:48 - creation of whole-program state machine
- 15:51 - flow-sensitive fixed-point iteration

As we can see, the most expensive phase is the flow-sensitive fixed point iteration, followed by the time spent in the construction of the call graph and points-to sets. The quick-check is so fast that it is always worthwhile. The flow-insensitive analysis, in combination with its preparation phase, still runs in reasonable time. As Table 4 shows, usually the runtime is between 3 and 10 times shorter.

It proved very sensible to make use of the demand-driven refinement-based points-to analysis. For example, in pmd/FailSafeIter, we queried points-to sets for 691 variables only, where a full context-sensitive points-to analysis would have had to compute context-sensitive points-to sets for all 33993 locals in the pmd benchmark.

The flow-sensitive analysis generally adds a large computational burden and our results show that it does not find any improvements over the cheaper flow-insensitive stage. We plan to further refine that phase in future work to see if it is really worthwhile pursuing.

5   Related Work

While a lot of related work has been done in static program analysis and verification (model checking), there has been little previous work on using those techniques to speed up runtime monitoring. We list notable exceptions here.

Typestate properties. Typestate properties [27] have been widely studied in the past. Very recently, Fink et al. presented a static optimization for runtime checking of typestate properties [12]. The analysis they present is in flavour similar to ours. In particular it is also implemented in multiple stages, one of which is flow-sensitive. However typestate properties allow one to express temporal constraints about *one single* object only, making their flow-insensitive and flow-sensitive stages simpler than ours. The authors paid special attention to the handling of strong updates, using must-alias information, which we leave to future work. The analysis Fink et al. present did not address the issue of multi-threading.

   In terms of expressiveness, we believe that tracematches are equivalent to *generalized* typestate properties [18]. While normal typestate properties allow to reason about a single object each, generalized typestate properties allow to reason about multiple objects in combination. The only difference to tracematches seems to be the syntax (state machines vs. regular expressions).

PQL. In [21], Martin et al. present their Program Query Language, PQL. They experimented with a flow-insensitive analysis similar to our consistent-shadows analysis. However, their analysis is still not integrated within the PQL tool, making effective comparisons impossible at the current time. We suspect, that their flow-insensitive analysis performs very similarly to ours since they made similar design decisions. In particular they also do not take must-alias information into account. However, our analysis should in the general case be much faster, because unlike the analysis for PQL ours is staged, employing a very effective quick check first. Also we compute context for points-to sets for certain variables only while they apply this very expensive computation for all program variables.

History based pointcut languages. Various other pointcut languages have been proposed that allow to match on histories of events, both in the aspect-oriented programming [10,23,30] and runtime verification community [9,13,25]. While we believe that for most such languages, depending on their expressiveness, similar analysis could be constructed, one crucial ingredient to the success of such a project is the use of an integrated compiler. For instance, one needs to be able to disable shadows that were proven unnecessary. Without access to an aspect-oriented compiler like abc, this seems almost impossible. Consequently we are not aware of any related work by other research groups on that topic, apart from the ones mentioned above.

6   Discussion and Future Work

In this work we have proposed a staged static analysis for reducing the overhead of finite-state monitors. We have presented three stages including a very coarse-grain and inexpensive quick check based only on shadows matching symbol names, a flow-insensitive consistent-shadows analysis that finds all shadows with consistent points-to sets, and a flow-sensitive active-shadows analysis that also takes into consideration the order in which shadows execute.

As is often the case in program analysis, we were somewhat surprised that the first two simpler stages were the most effective. The quick check analysis is very simple and also quite effective in eliminating tracematches that can never match a base program. We believe that this test will be very useful in situations where whole libraries of tracematches are routinely applied to software as it is developed. For example, libraries can be associated with a collection of tracematches specifying constraints on how the library should be used. In these cases we expect that only some tracematches will actually apply to the program under analysis, and the quick check is a sound and simple way to eliminate those that don't apply. We expect this check to become a standard part of the abc compiler and it will be enabled by default at the -O level of optimization.

The second stage, flow-insensitive analysis to find consistent shadows, was also effective in some cases, and is also not a very complex analysis once one has a good points-to analysis available. We did find that a context-sensitive points-to analysis was necessary and this turned out to be an ideal use case for demand-driven context-sensitive analysis since we were only interested in the points-to information of variables involved in shadows. Based on our results, we think that this consistent-shadows analysis should be available at a higher-level optimization level (-O3), to be used when run-time overheads are high. In many cases we expect the overheads of a program optimized that way to be lower than those of programs using a hand-coded AspectJ monitor which is not analyzable.

Although we expected that the third stage, the flow-sensitive active-shadows analysis, would give us even more improvement, we found that it did not. To implement and test this analysis we developed a lot of machinery to represent the inter-procedural abstraction of the matching automata, and techniques to soundly approximate even in the presence of threads. To our surprise, the end result is that this extra machinery did not lead to more precise shadow removal. However, this exercise did provide an analysis basis and some new insight into the problem and we think that further refinements to this approach are worth further investigations. We plan to work on this by experimenting with new kinds of must and hybrid points-to abstractions and by improving upon the treatment of multi-threading, perhaps by using the *May Happen in Parallel* (MHP) analysis which is currently being integrated into Soot [20].

Acknowledgements. We are very grateful to Manu Sridharan for providing his points-to analysis to us and helping us integrate it into Soot. Steve Blackburn and Robin Garner helped with setting up the DaCapo benchmark suite and interpreting our benchmark results. Stephen Fink helped to clarify our interpretation of his related work. Nomair Naeem contributed with clarifying discussions and by commenting on a draft of this article. We also wish to thank the whole development group of the abc compiler, and in particular the tracematch guys, Pavel Avgustinov and Julian Tibble, for their enduring support and motivation.

References

1. Allan, C., Avgustinov, P., Christensen, A.S., Hendren, L., Kuzins, S., Lhoták, O., de Moor, O., Sereni, D., Sittampalam, G., Tibble, J.: Adding Trace Matching with Free Variables to AspectJ. In: Object-Oriented Programming, Systems, Languages and Applications, pp. 345–364. ACM Press, New York (2005)
2. AspectJ Eclipse Home. The AspectJ home page (2003), http://eclipse.org/aspectj/
3. Avgustinov, P., Christensen, A.S., Hendren, L., Kuzins, S., Lhoták, J., Lhoták, O., de Moor, O., Sereni, D., Sittampalam, G., Tibble, J.: abc: An extensible AspectJ compiler. In: Aspect-Oriented Software Development (AOSD), pp. 87–98. ACM Press, New York (2005)
4. Avgustinov, P., Christensen, A.S., Hendren, L., Kuzins, S., Lhoták, J., Lhoták, O., de Moor, O., Sereni, D., Sittampalam, G., Tibble, J.: Optimising AspectJ. In: Programming Language Design and Implementation (PLDI), pp. 117–128. ACM Press, New York (2005)
5. Avgustinov, P., Tibble, J., Bodden, E., Lhoták, O., Hendren, L., de Moor, O., Ongkingco, N., Sittampalam, G.: Efficient trace monitoring. Technical Report abc-2006-1 03 (2006), http://www.aspectbench.org/
6. Avgustinov, P., Tibble, J., de Moor, O.: Making trace monitors feasible. Technical Report abc-2007-1 03 (2007), http://www.aspectbench.org/
7. Blackburn, S.M., Garner, R., Hoffman, C., Khan, A.M., McKinley, K.S., Bentzur, R., Diwan, A., Feinberg, D., Frampton, D., Guyer, S.Z., Hirzel, M., Hosking, A., Jump, M., Lee, H., Moss, J.E.B., Phansalkar, A., Stefanović, D., VanDrunen, T., von Dincklage, D., Wiedermann, B.: The DaCapo benchmarks: Java benchmarking development and analysis. In: OOPSLA '06: Proceedings of the 21st annual ACM SIGPLAN conference on Object-Oriented Programing, Systems, Languages, and Applications, Portland, OR, USA, October 2006, pp. 169–190. ACM Press, New York (2006)
8. Bodden, E., Hendren, L., Lhoták, O.: A staged static program analysis to improve the performance of runtime monitoring (extended version). Technical Report abc-2007-2 04 (2007), http://www.aspectbench.org/
9. Chen, F., Rosu, G.: Java-MOP: A Monitoring Oriented Programming Environment for Java. In: Halbwachs, N., Zuck, L.D. (eds.) TACAS 2005. LNCS, vol. 3440, pp. 546–550. Springer, Heidelberg (2005)
10. d'Amorim, M., Havelund, K.: Event-based runtime verification of Java programs. In: WODA '05: Proceedings of the third international workshop on Dynamic analysis, St. Louis, Missouri, pp. 1–7. ACM Press, New York, NY, USA (2005)
11. Emami, M., Ghiya, R., Hendren, L.J.: Context-sensitive interprocedural points-to analysis in the presence of function pointers. In: PLDI '94: Proceedings of the ACM SIGPLAN 1994 conference on Programming language design and implementation, Orlando, Florida, United States, pp. 242–256. ACM Press, New York (1994)
12. Fink, S., Yahav, E., Dor, N., Ramalingam, G., Geay, E.: Effective typestate verification in the presence of aliasing. In: ISSTA'06: Proceedings of the 2006 international symposium on Software testing and analysis, Portland, Maine, USA, pp. 133–144. ACM Press, New York (2006)
13. Goldberg, A., Havelund, K.: Automated runtime verification with Eagle. In: Ultes-Nitsche, U., Augusto, J.C., Barjis, J. (eds.) Workshop on Verification and Validation of Enterprise Information Systems (VVEIS), INSTICC Press (2005)

14. Hilsdale, E., Hugunin, J.: Advice weaving in AspectJ. In: AOSD '04: Proceedings of the 3rd international conference on Aspect-oriented software development, Lancaster, UK, pp. 26–35. ACM Press, New York (2004)

15. Hind, M.: Pointer analysis: haven't we solved this problem yet? In: PASTE '01: Proceedings of the 2001 ACM SIGPLAN-SIGSOFT workshop on Program analysis for software tools and engineering, Snowbird, Utah, United States, pp. 54–61. ACM Press, New York (2001)

16. Kam, J.B., Ullman, J.D.: Monotone data flow analysis frameworks. Acta Informatica 7, 305–317 (1977)

17. Kindler, E.: Safety and liveness properties: A survey. Bulletin of the European Association for Theoretical Computer Science 53, 268–272 (1994)

18. Lam, P., Kuncak, V., Rinard, M.: Generalized typestate checking using set interfaces and pluggable analyses. SIGPLAN Not. 39(3), 46–55 (2004)

19. Lhoták, O., Hendren, L.: Scaling Java points-to analysis using Spark. In: Hedin, G. (ed.) CC 2003 and ETAPS 2003. LNCS, vol. 2622, pp. 153–169. Springer, Heidelberg (2003)

20. Li, L., Verbrugge, C.: A Practical MHP Information Analysis for Concurrent Java Programs. In: Eigenmann, R., Li, Z., Midkiff, S.P. (eds.) LCPC 2004. LNCS, vol. 3602, pp. 194–208. Springer, Heidelberg (2005)

21. Martin, M., Livshits, B., Lam, M.S.: Finding application errors using PQL: a program query language. In: Proceedings of the 20th Annual ACM SIGPLAN Conference on Object-Oriented Programming, Systems, Languages and Applications, pp. 365–383. ACM Press, New York (2005)

22. Masuhara, H., Kiczales, G., Dutchyn, C.: A compilation and optimization model for aspect-oriented programs. In: Hedin, G. (ed.) CC 2003 and ETAPS 2003. LNCS, vol. 2622, pp. 46–60. Springer, Heidelberg (2003)

23. Ostermann, K., Mezini, M., Bockisch, C.: Expressive pointcuts for increased modularity. In: Black, A.P. (ed.) ECOOP 2005. LNCS, vol. 3586, pp. 214–240. Springer, Heidelberg (2005)

24. Sridharan, M., Bodík, R.: Refinement-based context-sensitive points-to analysis for Java. In: PLDI '06: Proceedings of the 2006 ACM SIGPLAN conference on Programming language design and implementation, Ottawa, Ontario, Canada, pp. 387–400. ACM Press, New York (2006)

25. Stolz, V.: Temporal assertions with parametrised propositions. In: Seventh Workshop on Runtime Verification, Vancouver, Canada, March 2007, Lecture Notes of Computer Science (To appear)

26. Stolz, V., Bodden, E.: Temporal Assertions using AspectJ. Electronic Notes in Theoretical Computer Science 144(4), 109–124 (2006)

27. Strom, R.E., Yemini, S.: Typestate: A programming language concept for enhancing software reliability. IEEE Transactions on Software Engineering 12(1), 157–171 (1986)

28. Thompson, K.: Programming techniques: Regular expression search algorithm. Communications of the ACM 11(6), 419–422 (1968)

29. Vallée-Rai, R., Co, P., Gagnon, E., Hendren, L., Lam, P., Sundaresan, V.: Soot - a Java bytecode optimization framework. In: CASCON '99: Proceedings of the 1999 conference of the Centre for Advanced Studies on Collaborative research, Mississauga, Ontario, Canada, p. 13. IBM Press (1999)

30. Walker, R., Viggers, K.: Implementing protocols via declarative event patterns. In: ACM Sigsoft International Symposium on Foundations of Software Engineering (FSE-12), pp. 159–169. ACM Press, New York (2004)

Tracking Linear and Affine Resources with Java(X)

Markus Degen, Peter Thiemann, and Stefan Wehr

Institut für Informatik, Universität Freiburg
{degen,thiemann,wehr}@informatik.uni-freiburg.de

Abstract. Java(X) is a framework for type refinement. It extends Java's type language with annotations drawn from an algebra X and structural subtyping in terms of the annotations. Each instantiation of X yields a different refinement type system with guaranteed soundness. The paper presents some applications, formalizes a core language, states a generic type soundness result, and sketches the extensions required for the full Java language (without generics).

The main technical innovation of Java(X) is its concept of activity annotations paired with the notion of droppability. An activity annotation is a capability which can grant exclusive write permission for a field in an object and thus facilitates a typestate change (strong update). Propagation of capabilities is either linear or affine (if they are droppable). Thus, Java(X) can perform protocol checking as well as refinement typing. Aliasing is addressed with a novel splitting relation on types.

1 Introduction

A programming language with a static type system eliminates common programming errors right from the start. For instance, the type system may guarantee that no operation receives an illegal argument. Each type system introduces abstraction to make types statically checkable. Thus, there are always programs that would run without errors but which are nevertheless rejected by the type system.

However, the information provided by the type system is not always sufficient to avoid a run-time error. For example, taking the head of a list may lead to a run-time error if the list is empty but this information is not represented in the list type. While there are refinement type systems capturing such information [15,30], they are not widely used in production programming languages.

A related problem arises with non-trivial object life cycles [24]. Many objects progress through distinct states during their lifetime with state changes caused by method calls. In each state certain methods are disabled and calling them causes a run-time error. A standard type system cannot avoid such run-time errors because it is not aware of the evolving object states. Enhancing a type system to track these state changes is not straightforward because it requires assigning the same variable different types at different places in the program. Such a typestate change causes problems in the presence of aliases that keep

E. Ernst (Ed.): ECOOP 2007, LNAI 4609, pp. 550–574, 2007.

obsolete type assumptions. The main challenge here is to keep track of aliasing to the extent that the change of typing is possible.

A type system with additional structure can supply the information needed for such applications. The first application is a type refinement setting that restricts the semantics of programs by incorporating explicit tests for predicates that refine the underlying types. The type soundness property for the extended system becomes more expressive because it guarantees that these predicates are always satisfied. The second kind requires extending refinement typing with accurate state tracking as provided, *e.g.*, by a linear type system [28]. Unfortunately, most systems do not provide a seamless integration, let alone migration, between standard types and linear types.

Our framework JAVA(X) addresses these issues with a family of annotated type systems and an automatic promotion of standard properties to linear ones. An annotated type system extends the type language of some existing system with value annotations. A value annotation restricts the meaning of the type it is attached to and thus enables the type soundness proof to express additional properties.[1] As refinements are domain specific, they are not hardwired into the system. JAVA(X) is parametrized over a partially ordered set (*poset*) of value annotations X, which a programmer can change and extend them easily.

An alternative approach might rely on pre-/post-conditions and invariants, which are stated as logical formulas, but annotations place less burden on the programmer. For our system, a *refinement designer* chooses a set of predicates on objects and abstracts them to a value annotation poset X. This poset can be tailored to the needs of a particular application domain. Thus, the annotations correspond to domain-specific, shrink-wrapped combinations of predicates that are lightweight and ready to use for the programmer, who has to understand the annotations but does not have to be an expert in logics.

In addition to the value annotations, JAVA(X) has a built-in notion of capabilities that can promote a value annotation to a linear or affine annotation. Capabilities are independent of the chosen annotation poset X. They are attached to individual field references via the *activity annotations* on a type. If a variable has an object type with an *active* capability for a field (and everything reachable from it), then the program may update the field with a new value through this variable.

Active capabilities are propagated in a linear manner, that is, at each time and for each field of a reachable object, there exists one access path (starting with a variable), the type of which has the active capability for this field, through which the field can be updated. Any other access path to the same field may only read the field but not update it. The JAVA(X) type system maintains the invariant that only one access path has the update privilege for an active field.

Beyond the update privilege, an active capability carries the most accurate value annotation for the current contents of the field. Hence, active capabilities are well suited for typestate changes. An update only changes the field type for the access path with the active capability. The types of the other access paths

---

[1] Thus, JAVA(X) performs type-based program analysis [22] in some sense.

(the aliases) do not have to change because they have sufficiently less accurate information.

Thus, active capabilities enable the linear handling of resources such as objects that change their state in reaction to method invocations. However, as described up to now, the system does not seem to allow us to discard such state changing objects because it insists on the invariant that there is always one access path with an active capability for the object. For this reason, JAVA(X) includes the notion of *droppability*. The analysis designer can declare certain states (that is, subsets of annotations) as droppable. If an object is in a droppable state, then its reference can be discarded regardless of its capabilities. In effect, an object in a droppable state is handled in an affine manner: its state is tracked accurately, its active capability cannot be duplicated, but the object may be discarded at any time. An object may switch between droppable and nondroppable states during its life time, just think of a file handle that must not be discarded as long as it is open (see Section 2.2).

Contributions. JAVA(X) is an extension of Java 1.4 with a parametrized annotated type system. Its annotations are drawn from a poset X of value annotations. There is a parametrized type soundness proof for a fully formalized subset MINIJAVA(X). Once a refinement designer supplies a new annotation poset X, a programmer can immediately take advantage of the new invariants guaranteed through it.

We have built a proof-of-concept implementation of a type checker for MINI-JAVA(X).[2] The type checker processes all examples of Section 2.

The main novelty of JAVA(X) is the concept of an activity annotation as a capability for updating a field in an object. Activity annotations enable the promotion of the properties described by X to linear and affine properties, which can be tracked accurately and facilitate typestate change. The main technical innovation is the handling of aliasing via a splitting relation. This relation splits the capability for a resource between different access paths to it on a per-field basis.

Overview. Section 2 introduces JAVA(X) with two examples. Section 3 defines the essential core of the language JAVA(X) and its type system formally. Section 4 sketches the type soundness proof. Section 5 explains the extensions needed for the full Java system, and Section 6 discusses related work. Finally, Section 7 concludes.

2   Examples

We introduce our framework with two examples. The first defines an affine instance of the framework providing a refined typing discipline for an XML-processing library. The second is a linear instance tracking operations on files. We defer the formal definition of an instance of the framework to Section 3.2.

---

[2] http://proglang.informatik.uni-freiburg.de/projects/access-control/

2.1 JDOM Type Analysis

JDOM[3] is a popular Java API for manipulating XML. It views an XML document as a tree composed of nodes of types like `Element` and `Attribute`. Each node (except the root) has a parent field `p` indicating the element that it is attached to. JDOM's `Element` type provides a number of operations for manipulating the tree structure. The method `Element setAttribute(Attribute attr)`, which attaches an attribute node to an element node, serves as a typical example.

JDOM informally imposes a number of invariants on its XML representation. One of them is that "JDOM nodes may not be shared". JDOM enforces this invariant dynamically by checking a *detachment property*: If the attribute node has a non-null parent field then the `setAttribute` method throws an `IllegalAddException`. This exception occurs in the last line of the following example because it attempts to attach the node `attr` a second time.

```
Element p1     = new Element("a");
Element p2     = new Element("a");
Attribute attr = new Attribute("href", "http://www.jdom.org");
p1.setAttribute(attr);           // consumes attr; now attached
p2.setAttribute(attr);           // raises IllegalAddException
```

We now describe an instance of JAVA(X) which statically tracks the detachment property and rejects uses of `setAttribute(attr)` unless it is clear that `attr` is detached. The instance raises a type error for the example just shown.

In earlier work [27], one of the authors has proposed a type system for DOM. While the earlier system covers properties other than detachment, the present system obtains significantly stronger guarantees for detachment (see Section 6).

Detached Nodes. Static checking of the detachment property requires annotations to the `Attribute` type, which abstract over the state of the parent field `p` as in `Attribute{p : ⟨aa, Element⟩}`.[4] The type shows that placing the annotations requires expanding the types to (potentially recursive) record types. The activity annotation aa ranges over the set $\{\triangle(va), \triangledown, \lozenge\}$ where va is drawn from a *value annotation* poset $X_{\texttt{Element}} = (\mathcal{P}(\{\mathbf{N}, \mathbf{D}\}), \subseteq)$ with $\mathcal{P}$ denoting the power set. We abbreviate $\{\mathbf{N}\}$ to $\mathbf{N}$, $\{\mathbf{D}\}$ to $\mathbf{D}$, and $\{\mathbf{N}, \mathbf{D}\}$ to $\mathbf{ND}$. The elements of the poset abstract from the possible states of an `Element` reference. In $X_{\texttt{Element}}$, $\mathbf{N}$ stands for "is null" and $\mathbf{D}$ for "defined" (is not null).

The activity annotation aa provides the access capability. If an `Attribute` reference has its `p` field typed with an *active* annotation $\triangle(va)$, then the parent

---

[3] http://www.jdom.org

[4] In the full type, both the `Attribute` and the `Element` type carry an additional value annotation and there is a record describing the fields of the `Element`, too: $\langle va_A, \texttt{Attribute}\{p : \langle aa, \langle va_E, \texttt{Element}\{\dots\}\rangle\rangle\}\rangle$. In what follows, we concentrate on `Attribute` and generally omit the extra value annotations and the field types of `Element` for readability.

field may be modified through this reference and this modification changes the value annotation va in the type of the reference. If the annotation is *inactive* $\triangledown$, then the field is read-only through this reference and there is no extra value annotation. The *semi-active* annotation $\lozenge$ allows for unrestricted assignment, but does not provide any information through a value annotation. We ignore $\lozenge$ for a moment and come back to it on page 555.

The enclosed value annotation va approximates the status of the attribute's parent reference at run time. It is flow-sensitive and may be different for different uses of the same attribute. Between uses, the system propagates the information whether a node is detached in an affine manner: At most one reference to an attribute may carry definitive, active information about the node's parent field. Any other, aliasing reference must have an inactive type for its parent field.

Writing a signature for a method such as `setAttribute` of class `Element` requires one more ingredient. The signature must specify the effect of the method on the state of the object. This effect change the activity annotations only, the underlying Java type does not change:[5]

$$\texttt{Element setAttribute(Attribute}\{\texttt{p} : \langle \triangle(\mathbf{N} \rightsquigarrow \mathbf{D}), \texttt{Element}\rangle\} \texttt{ attr)}.$$

The $\mathbf{N} \rightsquigarrow \mathbf{D}$ annotation states that the `p` of the `attr` argument must be null ($\mathbf{N}$) before the method call and is not null ($\mathbf{D}$) afterwards. Thus, $\mathbf{N} \rightsquigarrow \mathbf{D}$ describes the effect of a method call like the pre- and post-condition of a specification. Effects only apply to active annotations because modifications are only allowed through active references.

Type checking the example from the beginning of this section with the `setAttribute` signature just given leads to a type error. The typing assumes that `new Attribute(...)` creates an attribute node without a parent, *i.e.*, its `p` field has annotation $\triangle(\mathbf{N})$. The comments indicate the typing after execution of the respective statement.

```
Element p1 = ...;
Element p2 = ...;
Attribute attr = new Attribute(...);  // attr : Attribute{p : ⟨△(N), Element⟩}
p1.setAttribute(attr);  // attr : Attribute{p : ⟨△(D), Element⟩}
p2.setAttribute(attr);  // type error: N required, D given
```

Aliasing. Let us now abstract over the pattern. Suppose there is a method `set2` that accepts two `Attribute`s and attaches each to its own element.

```
void set2 (Element p1, Element p2,
           Attribute{p : ⟨△(N) ⤳ △(D), Element⟩} a1,
           Attribute{p : ⟨△(N) ⤳ △(D), Element⟩} a2)
  { p1.setAttribute(a1); p2.setAttribute(a2); }
```

---

[5] Again, we take the liberty of abbreviating the full syntax, which defines the effect as a change of the type. The full argument type duplicates the whole structure: $\texttt{Attribute}\{\texttt{p} : \langle \triangle(\mathbf{N}), \texttt{Element}\rangle\} \rightsquigarrow \texttt{Attribute}\{\texttt{p} : \langle \triangle(\mathbf{D}), \texttt{Element}\rangle\}$.

It is not possible to invoke `set2` with two aliases of the same attribute:

```
Attribute attr = new Attribute(...);  // attr : Attribute{p : ⟨△(N), Element⟩}
set2(p1, p2, attr, attr);  // type error!
```

The type error occurs because JAVA(X) *splits* the type of `attr` at every point of use such that no active annotation is duplicated. Splitting is driven by a ternary relation $\cdot \succeq \cdot \mid \cdot$ on activity annotations. For the active annotation it holds that $\triangle(va) \succeq \triangle(va) \mid \triangledown$ and $\triangle(va) \succeq \triangledown \mid \triangle(va)$ so that $\triangle$ can only be split into itself and the inactive annotation $\triangledown$; the inactive annotation can only split into itself. Hence, the initial type of `attr` is split into the two types

$$\texttt{Attribute\{p} : \langle\triangle(\mathbf{N}), \texttt{Element}\rangle\} \succeq$$
$$\texttt{Attribute\{p} : \langle\triangle(\mathbf{N}), \texttt{Element}\rangle\} \mid \texttt{Attribute\{p} : \langle\triangledown, \texttt{Element}\rangle\}$$

one of which is assigned to each of the two occurrences of `attr` in the argument list of `set2`. Thus, one occurrence has a suitable argument type for this method, the other one has a mismatch between the required $\triangle(\mathbf{N})$ and the provided $\triangledown$.

JDOM also has API methods that introduce aliasing. For example, the `detach()` method removes an attribute from the element it is attached to (if any) and leaves it in a detached state. The method modifies its receiver object and returns it, too. One possible type signature is

$$\texttt{Attribute\{p} : \langle\triangle(\mathbf{N}), \texttt{Element}\rangle\}$$
$$[\texttt{Attribute\{p} : \langle\triangle(\mathbf{ND}) \rightsquigarrow \triangledown, \texttt{Element}\rangle\}] \ \texttt{detach()}$$

where the type change in the square brackets specifies the effect of a method invocation on the receiver type. Before calling `detach`, the receiver object must have an active parent field in arbitrary state, that is, the receiver may be detached or attached. (We have $\mathbf{N} \subseteq \mathbf{ND}$ and $\mathbf{D} \subseteq \mathbf{ND}$ in our annotation poset $X_{\texttt{Element}}$.) After the call, the receiver's parent field type is inactive. The method returns a detached active reference.

This type is not the only possible choice. We could just as well leave the receiver active and make the return type inactive. Each choice fixes a particular usage pattern, but there is no reason to prefer one over the other. Section 5 introduces annotation polymorphism which allows to defer this choice.

In summary, there are two invariants that guarantee soundness in the presence of aliases. If there is a reference to an object carrying an active annotation for some field, then all aliases have a type with an inactive annotation for this field. Updates are only possible for fields with an active annotation. Such an update also changes the active value annotation of the field.

Unrestricted Assignment. The active and inactive annotations that we have seen so far do not allow a field to be updated through multiple references. As realistic programs contain unrestricted assignments, we need the semi-active annotation $\lozenge$. This annotation neither imposes nor grants access restrictions; like $\triangledown$, it does not track value annotations exactly. Splitting does not affect semi-activity, *i.e.*, $\lozenge \succeq \lozenge \mid \lozenge$. If an alias for an object has a semi-active field, no other alias can have an active annotation for this field. Semi-active fields behave like ordinary instance variables in Java or C#. Hence, semi-active is the default annotation for fields.

Semi-active annotations enable the incremental transition to refined types. For example, the JDOM method `Element setAttribute(Attribute attr)` may initially receive the signature

$$\text{Element setAttribute(Attribute}\{\text{p} : \langle \Diamond, \text{Element}\rangle\} \text{ attr)}.$$

Once we decide to track detachment, we switch to the active annotation discussed in the previous subsection.

2.2 File Access

The detachment property of the preceding section is affine because we can always drop an attribute node. We now give an example of a linear property where only values carrying a distinguished annotation may be dropped.

The problem statement is as follows. Opening a file creates an open file handle on which the program can perform read operations until the file handle is closed. No further operation can be performed on a closed file handle. Furthermore, file handles must not be discarded while they are open.

We use the value annotation poset $X_{\text{FStat}} = \mathcal{P}(\{\mathbf{O}, \mathbf{C}\})$ for the file access example, where $\mathbf{O}$ stands for "open" and $\mathbf{C}$ stands for "closed". As before, we write $\mathbf{O}$, $\mathbf{C}$, and $\mathbf{OC}$ for the evident elements of X_{FStat}. Droppability of files is defined in terms of a droppability predicate, $\rho_{\text{FStat}} \subseteq X_{\text{FStat}}$. Because an open file must not be discarded, we define ρ_{FStat} as $\{\emptyset, \mathbf{C}\}$.

To be able to change the status of a file, we do not attach these value annotations directly to the `File` class but to a private instance field `FStat status`. There are two distinguished `FStat` objects, namely open : $\langle \mathbf{O}, \text{FStat}\{\}\rangle$, and closed : $\langle \mathbf{C}, \text{FStat}\{\}\rangle$. The outermost value annotation of a type, which we have ignored until now, describes a persistent property of the values inhabiting the type. By assigning one of these two values to the `status` field, the implementation of the `File` class communicates its internal status to the outside world. The operations provided by `File` are as follows:

```
File{status : ⟨△(O), FStat⟩}(String name)    // constructor
int  [File{status : ⟨△(O), FStat⟩}]          read()
void [File{status : ⟨△(O) ⤳ △(C), FStat⟩}] close()
```

These method types implement exactly the specification given at the beginning of this subsection: `read()` is only possible in state $\mathbf{O}$ and `close()` changes the state to $\mathbf{C}$. An open file handle cannot be dropped because $\mathbf{O} \notin \rho_{\text{FStat}}$. A closed file handle can be dropped because $\mathbf{C} \in \rho_{\text{FStat}}$.

With these signatures, the following statements result in a type error.

```
File{status : ⟨△(O), FStat⟩} f = new File("/etc/passwd");
f.read();
f.close();   // f now has type File{status : ⟨△(C), FStat⟩}
f.read();    // type error: O expected, C given
```

3   The Language MiniJava(X)

The language MINIJAVA(X) is an object-oriented language with classes and methods but without inheritance, interfaces, casts, and abstract methods. Its formalization is inspired by CLASSICJAVA [13]. Section 5 discusses the extensions needed for all of Java 1.4.

3.1   Syntax

Figure 1 defines the syntax of MINIJAVA(X) and some auxiliary functions for accessing pieces of syntax. The notation $\overline{z_i}$ stands for $z_1, \ldots, z_n$, where z is a syntactic entity. The index i can be omitted if no ambiguity arises. We write $\overline{z_i}^{i \in M}$ and $\overline{z_i}^{i \neq j}$ to constrain the index set.

A program consists of a list of class definitions and a main expression. A class definition contains definitions for fields and methods. A method definition $t \, [t' \rightsquigarrow t''] \, m(\overline{t_i \rightsquigarrow t'_i \, x}) \, \{ e \}$ specifies the type t' of its receiver in the square brackets $[t' \rightsquigarrow t'']$. Calling the method changes the receiver type from t' to t'' and the argument types from t_i to t'_i, respectively. The type change only refers to a change of the annotations, the underlying class type remains unchanged. The type syntax has three levels:

- A *simple type*, u, packages a class name c with a field environment; the field environment records for every field f its field type s and its variance ς, which specifies if the field is only read ($\varsigma = \text{R}$), only written ($\varsigma = \text{W}$), or both ($\varsigma = \text{B}$).

Syntax:

$$P ::= \overline{defn} \ e \qquad\qquad\qquad s ::= \langle aa, t \rangle \qquad \text{(coinductively)}$$
$$defn ::= \textbf{class} \ c \ \{\overline{c \, f}; \ \overline{meth}\} \qquad t ::= \langle va, u \rangle \qquad \text{(coinductively)}$$
$$meth ::= t \, [t \rightsquigarrow t] \, m(\overline{t \rightsquigarrow t \ x}) \, \{ e \} \qquad u ::= c\{\overline{f : s[\varsigma]}\} \qquad \text{(coinductively)}$$
$$v ::= x \mid \textbf{null} \qquad\qquad aa ::= \triangle(va) \mid \Diamond \mid \triangledown$$
$$e ::= v \mid \textbf{new}^{\ell} \, c(\overline{v}) \mid v.m(\overline{v}) \qquad \varsigma ::= \text{R} \mid \text{W} \mid \text{B}$$
$$\quad \mid \ \textbf{let} \ x = v.f \ \textbf{in} \ e \mid \textbf{set} \ v.f = v \ \textbf{in} \ e \qquad A ::= \emptyset \mid A, x : t$$
$$\quad \mid \ \textbf{let} \ x = e \ \textbf{in} \ e \mid \textbf{if} \ e \ \textbf{then} \ e \ \textbf{else} \ e$$
$$\quad \mid \ \textbf{join} \ v = v.f \ \textbf{from} \ e$$

$c \in \textit{ClassName}, f \in \textit{FieldName}, m \in \textit{MethodName}, x \in \textit{VarName}, va \in X_c, \ell \in \textit{Label}$

Lookup functions:

$$\frac{\textbf{class} \ c \ \{\overline{c \, f}; \ \overline{meth}\} \in P}{\textit{fields}_P(c) = \overline{c \, f}}$$

$$\frac{\textbf{class} \ c \ \{\overline{c \, f}; \ \overline{meth}\} \in P \qquad t \, [t_0 \rightsquigarrow t'_0] \, m(\overline{t_i \rightsquigarrow t'_i \ x_i}) \, \{ e \} \in meth}{\textit{mbody}_P(c, m) = \overline{x_i}\{e\}}$$

$$\frac{\textbf{class} \ c \ \{\overline{c \, f}; \ \overline{meth}\} \in P \qquad t \, [t_1 \rightsquigarrow t'_1] \, m(\overline{t_i \rightsquigarrow t'_i \ x_i}^{i \in \{2, \ldots, n\}}) \, \{ e \} \in meth}{\textit{mtype}_P(\langle va, c\{\overline{f : s[\varsigma]}\}\rangle, m) = \overline{t_i \rightsquigarrow t'_i} \to t}$$

Fig. 1. Syntax and lookup functions

- An *annotated type*, t, attaches a value annotation va to a simple type u to describe a persistent property of the objects of type u in a summary approximation. The annotation va is drawn from a type-specific annotation poset $(X_c, \cdot \leq \cdot)$ where c is the class of u. The instantiation of the framework determines X.

- A *field type*, s, attaches an activity annotation aa to an annotated type t. If a reference to an object has the field type $f : s[\varsigma]$ and s carries the active annotation $\triangle(va)$, that is, $s = \langle \triangle(va), va', u \rangle := \langle \triangle(va), \langle va', u \rangle \rangle$, then the field f may be updated *through this reference* and va describes the current field value. The annotation va is at least as precise as the summary approximation va' because assignments change va but leave va' constant. The well-formedness predicate on types (see Figure 3) ensures that $va \leq va'$.

    The activity annotation may also be semi-active $\lozenge$, which allows updates, or inactive $\triangledown$, which indicates that a field is read-only. In both cases, the system maintains only a summary approximation for the field value.

    An activity annotation acts locally on a single field. It does not affect sibling fields nor descendants: their annotations are completely independent. The activity annotation is also reference specific: each alias for the same object may have a different (but compatible) activity annotation on its type. For instance, compatibility enforces that only one alias may have an active annotation for a certain field of an object.

As customary for modeling object types [6], a type may be recursive through its field environment. The syntax does not have explicit operators to introduce or eliminate such recursive types. Instead, the rules of the type grammar have a coinductive interpretation.

A type environment A binds variables x to annotated types t. When writing $A, x : t$ we assume that A does not already bind x.

Expressions e are in a particular restricted form (which resembles A-normal form [12]) to maximize the amount of information that typing can extract and to simplify the soundness proof. In this form, all essential computations only take values v as operands (that is, a variable or **null**) and sequencing is made explicit using **let** (and field access/modification). Any expression in, say, Java syntax can be easily transformed into this form without changing its meaning.

The expression language comprises values, object creation, method invocation, field access, field modification, let expression, a conditional which tests for **null**, and an intermediate join expression $join\,v = v.f\,from\,e$ which does not occur in programs but which arises during execution.

Every **new** expression carries a unique label ℓ, so that the initial value annotation of an object may depend on the place of the **new** expression in the source program.

Field access $let\,x = v.f\,in\,e$ is combined with variable binding to increase the precision of the system. The idea is that the binding of x "lends" capabilities from $v.f$ while evaluating e. Afterwards, the lent capabilities are joined back to $v.f$'s using a join expression.

Field update set $v.f = v'$ in e first sets the field and then evaluates e. It does not return a result because doing so would create an alias for v', which would further complicate its typing rule.

3.2 Instances of MiniJava(X)

An instance of MINIJAVA(X) specifies, for each class c,

- a partially ordered set $(X_c, \leq)$ with least element for the value annotations;
- a non-empty predicate $\rho_c \subseteq X_c$ of droppable annotations such that $b \in \rho_c$ if $a \in \rho_c$ and $b \leq a$ (for all $a, b \in X_c$);
- predicates $R^{\text{new}}_{\ell,c}, R^{\text{null}}_c \subseteq X_c$, for each label ℓ, such that $b \in R^{\text{new}}_{\ell,c}$ ($b \in R^{\text{null}}_c$) if $a \in R^{\text{new}}_{\ell,c}$ ($a \in R^{\text{null}}_c$) and $a \leq b$ (for all $a, b \in X_c$).

We assume that $c \neq c'$ implies $X_c \cap X_{c'} = \emptyset$ and set $\rho := \cup_c \rho_c$.

The predicates R^{null}_c and $R^{\text{new}}_{\ell,c}$ provide the persistent annotations for the null reference and for objects created at program location ℓ, respectively. Indeed, the motivation for including ℓ in the formal presentation at all is the ability to define predicates that depend on the creation location. Otherwise, the system would only be able to capture the nullness property. Several instances of value annotations may easily be combined using the Cartesian product.

Examples. The nullness analysis required for the JDOM detachment property works on the poset $X_{\text{Element}} = (\mathcal{P}(\{\mathbf{N}, \mathbf{D}\}), \subseteq)$ with $\rho_{\text{Element}} = X_{\text{Element}}$ and the two predicates $R^{\text{null}}_{\text{Element}}(va) \Leftrightarrow \{\mathbf{N}\} \leq va$ and $R^{\text{new}}_{\ell,\text{Element}}(va) \Leftrightarrow \{\mathbf{D}\} \leq va$. That is, every object is droppable regardless of whether it has a parent object. Further, the value annotation for null must contain $\mathbf{N}$, and the annotation of a newly created object must contain $\mathbf{D}$.

The file access example uses the poset $X_{\text{FStat}} = (\mathcal{P}(\{\mathbf{O}, \mathbf{C}\}), \subseteq)$ with $\rho_{\text{FStat}} = \{\{\mathbf{C}\}, \emptyset\}$. The two predicates are defined as $R^{\text{null}}_{\text{FStat}}(va) \Leftrightarrow \text{False}$ and $R^{\text{new}}_{\ell,\text{FStat}}(va) \Leftrightarrow (\ell = \ell^o \Rightarrow \{\mathbf{O}\} \leq va) \wedge (\ell = \ell^c \Rightarrow \{\mathbf{C}\} \leq va)$ where ℓ^o and ℓ^c are the program locations where the FStat object open and closed are defined, respectively. That is, a file handle is droppable as long as its status cannot be open. The value annotation of a file status object must contain $\mathbf{O}$ if it was created at location ℓ^o and analogously for C and ℓ^c.

3.3 Dynamic Semantics

Figure 2 defines the dynamic semantics of MINIJAVA(X) as a small-step operational semantics. Its judgment $P \vdash \langle e, \mathcal{S} \rangle \hookrightarrow \langle e', \mathcal{S}' \rangle$ describes a single evaluation step of an expression e under store $\mathcal{S}$ governed by program P. The evaluation step produces a new expression e', and a new store $\mathcal{S}'$.

A store $\mathcal{S}$ is a mapping from locations l to objects $\langle c, \ell, \mathcal{F} \rangle$ where c is the class of the object, ℓ is the place where the object was created, and the field map $\mathcal{F}$ records the values w of its instance fields. The notation $\mathcal{S}, l \mapsto \langle c, \ell, \mathcal{F} \rangle$ assumes that $\mathcal{S}$ does not bind l, whereas $\mathcal{F}[f \mapsto w]$ implies that $\mathcal{F}$ contains a binding for f which is updated to w. The reduction rules for new, let, and if are standard.

Definitions:

$Value \ni w ::= l \mid \texttt{null}$

$\mathcal{E} ::= [\,] \mid \texttt{let } x = \mathcal{E} \texttt{ in } e \mid \texttt{if } \mathcal{E} \texttt{ then } e \texttt{ else } e \mid \texttt{join } w = l.f \texttt{ from } \mathcal{E}$

$l \in Loc \subseteq VarName, \ \mathcal{S} \in Store = Loc \rightarrow ClassName \times Label \times FieldMap,$

$\mathcal{F} \in FieldMap = FieldName \rightarrow Value$

Reduction rules:

$P \vdash \langle \mathcal{E}[\texttt{new}^\ell \ c(\overline{w_i})]; \mathcal{S} \rangle \hookrightarrow \langle \mathcal{E}[l]; \mathcal{S}, l \mapsto \langle c, \ell, \overline{f_i \mapsto w_i} \rangle \rangle$
    $\quad$ if $fields_P(c) = \overline{c_i \ f_i}$

$P \vdash \langle \mathcal{E}[\texttt{let } x = l.f \texttt{ in } e]; \mathcal{S} \rangle \hookrightarrow \langle \mathcal{E}[\texttt{join } w = l.f \texttt{ from } [w/x]e]; \mathcal{S} \rangle$
    $\quad$ if $\mathcal{S}(l) = \langle c, \ell, \mathcal{F} \rangle$ and $\mathcal{F}(f) = w$

$P \vdash \langle \mathcal{E}[\texttt{join } w = l.f \texttt{ from } w']; \mathcal{S} \rangle \hookrightarrow \langle \mathcal{E}[w']; \mathcal{S} \rangle$

$P \vdash \langle \mathcal{E}[\texttt{set } l.f = w \texttt{ in } e]; \mathcal{S}, l \mapsto \langle c, \ell, \mathcal{F} \rangle \rangle \hookrightarrow \langle \mathcal{E}[e]; \mathcal{S}, l \mapsto \langle c, \ell, \mathcal{F}[f \mapsto w] \rangle \rangle$

$P \vdash \langle \mathcal{E}[l.m(\overline{w_i})]; \mathcal{S} \rangle \hookrightarrow \langle \mathcal{E}[\texttt{let } this, \overline{x_i} = l, \overline{w_i} \texttt{ in } e]; \mathcal{S} \rangle$
    $\quad$ if $\mathcal{S}(l) = \langle c, \ell, \mathcal{F} \rangle$ and $mbody_P(c, m) = \overline{x_i}\{e\}$

$P \vdash \langle \mathcal{E}[\texttt{let } x = w \texttt{ in } e]; \mathcal{S} \rangle \hookrightarrow \langle \mathcal{E}[[w/x]e]; \mathcal{S} \rangle$

$P \vdash \langle \mathcal{E}[\texttt{if } l \texttt{ then } e_1 \texttt{ else } e_2]; \mathcal{S} \rangle \hookrightarrow \langle \mathcal{E}[e_1]; \mathcal{S} \rangle$

$P \vdash \langle \mathcal{E}[\texttt{if null then } e_1 \texttt{ else } e_2]; \mathcal{S} \rangle \hookrightarrow \langle \mathcal{E}[e_2]; \mathcal{S} \rangle$

$P \vdash \langle \mathcal{E}[\texttt{let } x = \texttt{null}.f \texttt{ in } e]; \mathcal{S} \rangle \hookrightarrow \langle \text{error: dereferenced null}; \mathcal{S} \rangle$

$P \vdash \langle \mathcal{E}[\texttt{set null}.f = w \texttt{ in } e]; \mathcal{S} \rangle \hookrightarrow \langle \text{error: dereferenced null}; \mathcal{S} \rangle$

$P \vdash \langle \mathcal{E}[\texttt{let } x = \texttt{null}.m(\overline{w}) \texttt{ in } e]; \mathcal{S} \rangle \hookrightarrow \langle \text{error: dereferenced null}; \mathcal{S} \rangle$

Fig. 2. Dynamic semantics

The reductions for $\texttt{let } x = v.f \texttt{ in } e$ and $\texttt{join } w = l.f \texttt{ from } w'$ belong together. They implement the aforementioned lending of the field's capabilities to x. Reducing the $\texttt{let}$ leaves behind a $\texttt{join}$ expression that remembers the lending for the duration of e's evaluation. Once the body of the $\texttt{let}/\texttt{join}$ is reduced to a value, the $\texttt{join}$ reduces. Thus, the join expression has no operational significance, it's just there to make the type system happy.

The reduction for $\texttt{set}$ is standard but it is sequenced with the evaluation of another expression to avoid returning a value from $\texttt{set}$.

A method invocation reduces to the corresponding method body wrapped in $\texttt{let}$ expressions that bind the formal parameters to the actual ones. Operationally, this wrapping is not necessary but it simplifies the soundness proof by separating concerns.

Beyond the explicit errors, an expression becomes stuck if it tries to access a non-existent field of an object or invoke a non-existent method. The latter errors are already captured by the underlying standard type system.

3.4 Static Semantics

This section specifies the static semantics of $\textsc{MiniJava}(\textsc{X})$. Figure 3 defines various relations on types, annotations, and environments. Because types are defined coinductively, all rules involving types have a coinductive interpretation. Figure 4 defines the typing rules for expressions and some auxiliary judgments, Figure 5 lists additional typing rules for intermediate expressions that only arise during the evaluation of a program. Figure 6 contains the remaining rules for programs. Boxed premises in the rules serve as extension points provided by an instance of the framework.

Droppability. A program can only discard a reference if its type is droppable. This policy ensures that the program keeps at least one reference to each "precious" resource, which it recognizes by an active annotation with a non-droppable value annotation. Technically, an object is droppable if all its fields have droppable types. An active field type is droppable if its annotation is. A field which is semi-active or inactive can always be dropped: A semi-active field can only have droppable annotations (by well-formedness of types), and an object is never responsible for the contents of its inactive fields.

Splitting. If a program uses the same variable multiple times, then each use of the variable receives a different type where the activity annotations on the original type of the variable are split among all uses. If field type s splits into s' and s'' ($s \succeq s' \mid s''$), then s, s', and s'' are structurally equivalent and differ only in their activity annotations. So it is sufficient to define splitting on the activity annotations. Splitting of ∇ and $\Diamond$ is trivial. An active annotation splits into one active and one inactive annotation: both $\Delta(va) \succeq \Delta(va) \mid \nabla$ and $\Delta(va) \succeq \nabla \mid \Delta(va)$ are acceptable. Splitting ensures that at most one type for a field reference receives an active annotation.

Well-formedness. The well-formedness relation ensures that the value part of an active annotation of a field type is not weaker then the summary approximation for that field; that a semi-active field type is droppable; that a value annotation is taken from the appropriate annotation poset; and that a field environment is correct with respect to the field declarations of the corresponding class.

Subtyping. Subtyping is structural and derived from the annotation orderings. Moreover, an active field type can be treated as semi-active or inactive if it is droppable. The subtyping of field environments takes the variance ς into account: if a field is only read ($\varsigma = \text{R}$), then it can be treated covariantly; if it is only written ($\varsigma = \text{W}$), then contravariantly; if it is read and written ($\varsigma = \text{B}$), then it must be treated invariantly (Pierce [23, Chapter 15.5] attributes this technique to Reynolds).

Effect application. The effect application relation $\vdash_A A := A' \downarrow \overline{v_i : t_i \rightsquigarrow t'_i}$ is used in the rules for method application and for a restricted version of the `let` expression. Its purpose is to transfer the type state changes from one alias that goes out of scope to another. For example, the expression $\text{let } x = y \text{ in } e$ introduces a new alias x for y. Inside e, the same object may be updated through both x and y which also changes their types. When leaving the scope of x, the type changes to x are lost with the standard `let` rule, but the effect application in the restricted rule merges the final type of x back into y's type.

Technically, the relation defines how type changes $\overline{t_i \rightsquigarrow t'_i}$ for values $\overline{v_i}$ affect an environment A'. If v_j is `null` then nothing happens. If v_j is a variable x, then the new type for x is t defined as $\vdash_t t := A'(x) \downarrow t_j \rightsquigarrow t'_j$. The effect application

Droppability:

$$\dfrac{\boxed{va \in \rho} \quad \vdash_{\scriptscriptstyle t} \rho(t)}{\vdash_{\scriptscriptstyle s} \rho(\langle \Delta(va), t\rangle)} \qquad \vdash_{\scriptscriptstyle s} \rho(\langle \Diamond, t\rangle) \qquad \dfrac{\vdash_{\scriptscriptstyle t} \rho(t)}{\vdash_{\scriptscriptstyle s} \rho(\langle \nabla, t\rangle)} \qquad \dfrac{(\forall i)\ \vdash_{\scriptscriptstyle s} \rho(s_i)}{\vdash_{\scriptscriptstyle t} \rho(\langle va, c\{\overline{f_i : s_i[\varsigma_i]}\}\rangle)}$$

Splitting:

$$\dfrac{\vdash_{\scriptscriptstyle aa} aa \succeq aa' \mid aa''}{\vdash_{\scriptscriptstyle s} \langle aa, va, u\rangle \succeq \langle aa', va, u'\rangle \mid \langle aa'', va, u''\rangle} \qquad \dfrac{\vdash_{\scriptscriptstyle u} u \succeq u' \mid u''}{\vdash_{\scriptscriptstyle u} c\{\overline{f_i : s_i[\varsigma_i]}\} \succeq c\{\overline{f_i : s_i'[\varsigma_i]}\} \mid c\{\overline{f_i : s_i''[\varsigma_i]}\}}$$

$$\vdash_{\scriptscriptstyle aa} \Delta(va) \succeq \Delta(va) \mid \nabla \qquad \vdash_{\scriptscriptstyle aa} \Delta(va) \succeq \nabla \mid \Delta(va) \qquad \vdash_{\scriptscriptstyle aa} \Diamond \succeq \Diamond \mid \Diamond \qquad \vdash_{\scriptscriptstyle aa} \nabla \succeq \nabla \mid \nabla$$

Well-formedness:

$$\dfrac{\boxed{va \le va'} \quad P \vdash_{\scriptscriptstyle t} wf(\langle va', u\rangle)}{P \vdash_{\scriptscriptstyle s} wf(\langle \Delta(va), va', u\rangle)} \qquad \dfrac{\vdash_{\scriptscriptstyle t} \rho(t) \quad P \vdash_{\scriptscriptstyle t} wf(t)}{P \vdash_{\scriptscriptstyle s} wf(\langle \Diamond, t\rangle)} \qquad \dfrac{P \vdash_{\scriptscriptstyle t} wf(t)}{P \vdash_{\scriptscriptstyle s} wf(\langle \nabla, t\rangle)}$$

$$\dfrac{va \in X_c \quad fields_P(c) = \overline{c_i\, f_i} \quad (\forall i)\ s_i = \langle aa_i, va_i, c_i\{\overline{f_{ij} : s_{ij}[\varsigma_{ij}]}\}\rangle \quad P \vdash_{\scriptscriptstyle s} wf(s_i)}{P \vdash_{\scriptscriptstyle t} wf(\langle va, c\{\overline{f_i : s_i[\varsigma_i]}\}\rangle)}$$

Subtyping:

$$\dfrac{\vdash_{\scriptscriptstyle t} t \le t' \quad \boxed{va \le va'}}{\vdash_{\scriptscriptstyle s} \langle \Delta(va), t\rangle \le \langle \Delta(va'), t'\rangle} \qquad \dfrac{aa \in \{\Diamond, \nabla\} \quad \vdash_{\scriptscriptstyle t} \rho(t)}{\vdash_{\scriptscriptstyle s} \langle \Delta(va), t\rangle \le \langle aa, t'\rangle} \qquad \dfrac{\vdash_{\scriptscriptstyle t} t \le t' \quad aa \in \{\Diamond, \nabla\}}{\vdash_{\scriptscriptstyle s} \langle \Diamond, t\rangle \le \langle aa, t'\rangle}$$

$$\dfrac{\vdash_{\scriptscriptstyle t} t \le t'}{\vdash_{\scriptscriptstyle s} \langle \nabla, t\rangle \le \langle \nabla, t'\rangle} \qquad \dfrac{\boxed{va \le va'} \quad (\forall i)\ \varsigma_i' \vdash_{\scriptscriptstyle s} s_i \le s_i' \quad \vdash_{\scriptscriptstyle \varsigma} \varsigma_i \le \varsigma_i'}{\vdash_{\scriptscriptstyle t} \langle va, c\{\overline{f_i : s_i[\varsigma_i]}\}\rangle \le \langle va', c\{\overline{f_i : s_i'[\varsigma_i']}\}\rangle}$$

$$\dfrac{\vdash_{\scriptscriptstyle s} s \le s' \quad \vdash_{\scriptscriptstyle s} s' \le s}{\text{B} \vdash_{\scriptscriptstyle s} s \le s'} \qquad \dfrac{\vdash_{\scriptscriptstyle s} s \le s'}{\text{R} \vdash_{\scriptscriptstyle s} s \le s'} \qquad \dfrac{\vdash_{\scriptscriptstyle s} s' \le s}{\text{W} \vdash_{\scriptscriptstyle s} s \le s'} \qquad \vdash_{\scriptscriptstyle \varsigma} \varsigma \le \varsigma \qquad \vdash_{\scriptscriptstyle \varsigma} \text{B} \le \text{R}$$

$$\vdash_{\scriptscriptstyle \varsigma} \text{B} \le \text{W} \qquad \vdash_{\scriptscriptstyle A} \emptyset \le \emptyset \qquad \dfrac{\vdash_{\scriptscriptstyle A} A \le A' \quad \vdash_{\scriptscriptstyle t} t \le t'}{\vdash_{\scriptscriptstyle A} A, x : t \le A', x : t'}$$

Effect application:

$$\vdash_{\scriptscriptstyle A} A := A \downarrow \overline{\text{null} : t_i \rightsquigarrow t_i'} \qquad \dfrac{v_j = x \quad \vdash_{\scriptscriptstyle t} t := t' \downarrow t_j \rightsquigarrow t_j' \quad \vdash_{\scriptscriptstyle A} A := A', x : t \downarrow \overline{v_i : t_i \rightsquigarrow t_i'}^{\,i \ne j}}{\vdash_{\scriptscriptstyle A} A := A', x : t' \downarrow v_i : t_i \rightsquigarrow t_i'}$$

$$\dfrac{\boxed{va''' \le va} \quad (\forall i)\ \vdash_{\scriptscriptstyle \varsigma} \varsigma_i''' \le \varsigma_i \quad \vdash_{\scriptscriptstyle s} s_i := s_i' \downarrow s_i'' \rightsquigarrow s_i'''}{\vdash_{\scriptscriptstyle t} \langle va, c\{\overline{f_i : s_i[\varsigma_i]}\}\rangle := \langle va', c\{\overline{f_i : s_i'[\varsigma_i']}\}\rangle \downarrow \langle va'', c\{\overline{f_i : s_i''[\varsigma_i'']}\}\rangle \rightsquigarrow \langle va''', c\{\overline{f_i : s_i'''[\varsigma_i''']}\}\rangle}$$

$$\dfrac{\vdash_{\scriptscriptstyle aa} aa := aa' \downarrow aa'' \rightsquigarrow aa''' \quad \vdash_{\scriptscriptstyle t} t := t' \downarrow t'' \rightsquigarrow t'''}{\vdash_{\scriptscriptstyle s} \langle aa, t\rangle := \langle aa', t'\rangle \downarrow \langle aa'', t''\rangle \rightsquigarrow \langle aa''', t'''\rangle}$$

$$\vdash_{\scriptscriptstyle aa} aa := aa' \downarrow \Delta(va) \rightsquigarrow aa \qquad \dfrac{aa' \in \{\Diamond, \nabla\}}{\vdash_{\scriptscriptstyle aa} aa := aa \downarrow aa' \rightsquigarrow aa''}$$

Fig. 3. Relations on types, annotations, and environments. (The rules for types have a coinductive interpretation).

relation on types, $\vdash_t t := t' \downarrow t'' \rightsquigarrow t'''$, changes at most the annotations of t' for which the corresponding annotation of t'' is active but leaves the other annotations of t' intact.

Expressions. The judgment for expressions, $P; A \vdash_e e : t \triangleright A'$, assigns a type t and an updated environment A' (after e's evaluation) to expression e in the context of program P and environment A (see Figures 4 and 5).

- In the variable rule, each use of a variable splits of the properties needed and passes the remaining properties on to subsequent uses.
- The rule for **null** relies on an auxiliary judgment $P \vdash_{\text{null}} t$ which ensures that t is well-formed and carries a suitable annotation.
- The rule for **new** determines an annotation for the newly created object with R^{new}. The judgment $P; A \vdash_{\bar{e}} \bar{v} : \bar{t} \triangleright A'$ types the constructor arguments.
- The rule for accessing field f performs the already mentioned lending of capabilities. The type of the the dereferenced object lends its capabilities at field f through the type access judgment $t_y = t'_y \mid_f t_x$ to the extracted value. After typing the body expression e with the resulting types it merges the final types back into the type of the reference.

    This rule has a number of related rules in Figure 5. They treat the case that the dereferenced object is **null** and the **join** expression that arises from reducing the field access. There is a special rule for a **join** expression where the extracted value is **null**.
- Field assignment **set** $x.f = v$ **in** e changes the type of field f in x's type using the type update judgment $P; u \vdash f \leftarrow t \triangleright u'$ which states that field f of an object with type u can be assigned a value of type t while modifying the object's type to u'. Two rules define this judgment:
    • The first rule allows a strong update of f which may change its type. It requires the old type of f to be *entirely active* (judgment $\triangle \vdash_s s$). If there was a semi-active or inactive field, then the field might be updated through an alias thus invalidating the change in the type.
    • The second rule deals with "ordinary" updates. It requires that the old type of f is semi-active (judgment $\Diamond \vdash_s s$) because overwriting an inactive field would result in an invalid typing assumption about a reference carrying an active annotation for this field.
- The rule for method calls uses the effect application relation to propagate the type changes of the method signature to the resulting type environment.
- There are two rules for **let** expressions. The standard one ensures that the type of the let-bound variable is droppable after evaluating the body of the let expression. The restricted one requires a value in its header, so that a restricted let creates an alias of a variable. In this case, the rule implements lending of capabilities just like described for the field access rule. It uses effect application to merge the changes of the alias back into the type of the original reference.

Expression typing:

$$\frac{\vdash_{\check{\varsigma}} t \succeq t_1 \mid t_2}{P; A, x : t \vdash_e x : t_1 \;\triangleright\; A, x : t_2} \qquad \frac{P \vdash_{\mathtt{null}} t}{P; A \vdash_e \mathbf{null} : t \;\triangleright\; A}$$

$$\frac{P; A \vdash_{\overline{e}} \overline{v_i} : \overline{t_i} \;\triangleright\; A' \qquad \boxed{R_{\ell,c}^{\mathtt{new}}(va)} \qquad t = \langle va, c\{\overline{f_i : \langle aa_i, t_i\rangle[\varsigma_i]}\}\rangle \qquad P \vdash_{\check{\varsigma}} wf(t)}{P; A \vdash_e \mathbf{new}^\ell \, c(\overline{v_i}) : t \;\triangleright\; A'}$$

$$\frac{t_y = t'_y \mid_f t_x \qquad P; A, y : t'_y, x : t_x \vdash_e e : t \;\triangleright\; A', y : t''_y, x : t'_x \qquad t'''_y = t''_y \mid_f t'_x}{P; A, y : t_y \vdash_e \mathbf{let}\, x = y.f \,\mathbf{in}\, e : t \;\triangleright\; A', y : t'''_y}$$

$$\frac{P; A \vdash_e v : t \;\triangleright\; A', x : \langle va, u\rangle \qquad u \vdash f \leftarrow t \;\triangleright\; u' \qquad P; A', x : \langle va, u'\rangle \vdash_e e : t' \;\triangleright\; A''}{P; A \vdash_e \mathbf{set}\, x.f = v \,\mathbf{in}\, e : t' \;\triangleright\; A''}$$

$$\frac{P; A \vdash_{\overline{e}} \overline{v_i} : \overline{t_i} \;\triangleright\; A' \qquad mtype_P(t_1, m) = \overline{t_i \rightsquigarrow t'_i} \to t \qquad \vdash_A A'' := A \downarrow \overline{v_i : t_i \rightsquigarrow t'_i}}{P; A \vdash_e v_1.m(\overline{v_i}^{\,i \in \{2,\dots n\}}) : t \;\triangleright\; A''}$$

$$\frac{P; A \vdash_e e_1 : t_1 \;\triangleright\; A_1 \qquad P; A_1, x : t_1 \vdash_e e_2 : t_2 \;\triangleright\; A_2, x : t'_1 \qquad \vdash_{\check{\varsigma}} \rho(t'_1)}{P; A \vdash_e \mathbf{let}\, x = e_1 \,\mathbf{in}\, e_2 : t_2 \;\triangleright\; A_2}$$

$$\frac{P; A \vdash_e v : t_1 \;\triangleright\; A_1 \qquad P; A_1, x : t_1 \vdash_e e : t \;\triangleright\; A_2, x : t_2 \qquad \vdash_A A_3 := A_2 \downarrow v : t_1 \rightsquigarrow t_2}{P; A \vdash_e \mathbf{let}\, x = v \,\mathbf{in}\, e : t \;\triangleright\; A_3}$$

$$\frac{\begin{array}{c} P; A \vdash_e e_1 : t \;\triangleright\; A' \\ P; A' \vdash_e e_2 : t' \;\triangleright\; A'' \qquad P; A' \vdash_e e_3 : t' \;\triangleright\; A'' \end{array}}{P; A \vdash_e \mathbf{if}\, e_1 \,\mathbf{then}\, e_2 \,\mathbf{else}\, e_3 : t' \;\triangleright\; A''} \qquad \frac{\begin{array}{c} P; A \vdash_e e : t_1 \;\triangleright\; A_1 \\ \vdash_{\check{\varsigma}} t_1 \le t_2 \qquad \vdash_A A_1 \le A_2 \end{array}}{P; A \vdash_e e : t_2 \;\triangleright\; A_2}$$

Type access:

$$\frac{\vdash_{\check{\varsigma}} \varsigma_j \le \mathrm{R} \qquad s_j = \langle aa, t\rangle \qquad \vdash_{\check{\varsigma}} t \succeq t_1 \mid t_2 \qquad s'_j = \langle aa, t_1\rangle}{\langle va, c\{\overline{f_i : s_i[\varsigma_i]}\}\rangle = \langle va, c\{f_j : s'_j[\varsigma_j]; \overline{f_i : s_i[\varsigma_i]}\}\rangle \mid_{f_j} t_2}$$

Type update:

$$\frac{\vdash_{\check{\varsigma}} \varsigma_j \le \mathrm{W} \qquad \begin{array}{c} \Delta \vdash_s s_j \qquad \vdash_{\check{\varsigma}} \rho(\langle va_j, u_j\rangle) \\ s_j = \langle aa_j, va_j, u_j\rangle \qquad s'_j = \langle \Delta(va), va_j, u\rangle \qquad \vdash_s wf(s'_j) \end{array}}{c\{\overline{f_i : s_i[\varsigma_i]}\} \vdash f_j \leftarrow \langle va, u\rangle \;\triangleright\; c\{f_j : s'_j[\varsigma_j]; \overline{f_i : s_i[\varsigma_i]}^{\,i \ne j}\}}$$

$$\frac{\Diamond \vdash_s s_j \qquad s_j = \langle aa, t'\rangle \qquad \vdash_{\check{\varsigma}} t \le t'}{c\{\overline{f_i : s_i[\varsigma_i]}\} \vdash f_j \leftarrow t \;\triangleright\; c\{\overline{f_i : s_i[\varsigma_i]}\}}$$

Fully active types:

$$\frac{(\forall i)\; \Delta \vdash_s s_i}{\Delta \vdash_s \langle \Delta(va), va', c\{\overline{f_i : s_i[\varsigma_i]}\}\rangle} \qquad \frac{(\forall i)\; \Diamond \vdash_s s_i}{\Diamond \vdash_s \langle \Diamond, va, c\{\overline{f_i : s_i[\varsigma_i]}\}\rangle}$$

Auxiliaries:

$$\frac{t = \langle va, c\{\dots\}\rangle \qquad \boxed{R_c^{\mathtt{null}}(va)} \qquad P \vdash_{\check{\varsigma}} wf(t)}{P \vdash_{\mathtt{null}} t} \qquad \frac{(\forall i)\; P; A_{i-1} \vdash_e v_i : t_i \;\triangleright\; A_i}{P; A_0 \vdash_{\overline{e}} \overline{v_i} : \overline{t_i} \;\triangleright\; A_n}$$

Fig. 4. Typing rules for expressions

$$\frac{P;A,x:t_x \vdash_e e:t \rhd A',x:t'_x \qquad P \vdash_t wf(t_x)}{P;A \vdash_e \texttt{let } x = \texttt{null}.f \texttt{ in } e:t \rhd A'}$$

$$\frac{t_y = t'_y \mid_f t_x \qquad t'''_y = t''_y \mid_f t'_x \qquad P;A,y:t'_y,l:t_x \vdash_e e:t \rhd A',y:t''_y,l:t'_x}{P;A,y:t_y \vdash_e \texttt{join } l = y.f \texttt{ from } e:t \rhd A',y:t'''_y}$$

$$\frac{t_y = t'_y \mid_f t_x \qquad t'''_y = t''_y \mid_f t'_x \qquad P;A,y:t'_y \vdash_e e:t \rhd A',y:t''_y}{P;A,y:t_y \vdash_e \texttt{join null} = y.f \texttt{ from } e:t \rhd A',y:t'''_y}$$

$$\frac{P;A \vdash_e v:t' \rhd A' \qquad P;A' \vdash_e e:t \rhd A''}{P;A \vdash_e \texttt{set null}.f = v \texttt{ in } e:t \rhd A''}$$

Fig. 5. Typing rules for intermediate expressions

$$\frac{P = \overline{defn_i}\ e \qquad (\forall i)\ P \vdash defn_i \qquad \text{class names in } \overline{defn_i} \text{ disjoint} \qquad P,\emptyset \vdash_e e:t \rhd \emptyset}{\vdash P}$$

$$\frac{(\forall i)\ \texttt{class } c_i\ \{\overline{c'\ f'};\ \overline{meth'}\} \in P \qquad (\forall j)\ P;c \vdash meth_j}{\text{field names } \overline{f_i} \text{ disjoint} \qquad \text{method names in } \overline{meth_j} \text{ disjoint}}$$
$$P \vdash \texttt{class } c\ \{\overline{c_i\ f_i};\ \overline{meth_j}\}$$

$$t_0 = \langle va, c\{\overline{f:s[\varsigma]}\}\rangle$$
$$\frac{(\forall i \in \{0,\dots,n\})\ P \vdash_t wf(t_i) \qquad P;this:t_0,\overline{x_i:t_i} \vdash_e e:t \rhd this:t'_0,\overline{x_i:t'_i}}{P;c \vdash t\ [t_0 \rightsquigarrow t'_0]\ m(\overline{t_i \rightsquigarrow t'_i\ x_i})\ \{e\}}$$

Fig. 6. Typing rules for programs

4   Soundness

We prove type soundness using the standard syntactic technique [29]. To apply it, we first have to extend typing to configurations $\langle e; \mathcal{S}\rangle$. To this end, we have to introduce an Urtype assumption $\mathcal{A}$. This assumption assigns to each location/object its activity annotated type before it is used in the program. Every activity annotated type of a use of a particular location in the program must be split off the Urtype for the location. The Urtype assumption changes during evaluation to reflect changes of the field values of an object with active fields. The most important point about the Urtype assumption is that it guarantees consistent use and distribution of the activity annotations throughout the uses of the locations in the program.

We start by introducing a function $R_{L,\mathcal{S}} \in \mathcal{P}(Loc) \to \mathcal{P}(Loc)$ so that its smallest fixed point $\mu R_{L,\mathcal{S}}$ is the set of locations reachable from $L \subseteq Loc$ through $\mathcal{S}$. The predicate $drop\text{-}ok(e, A, \mathcal{S})$ indicates whether all locations with a non-droppable type are reachable from e.

$$R_{L,S}(M) = (L \cup \bigcup \{ran(\mathcal{F}) \mid l' \in M, \mathcal{S}(l') = \langle c, \ell, \mathcal{F} \rangle\}) \cap dom(\mathcal{S})$$
$$drop\text{-}ok(e, A, \mathcal{S}) = \forall l \in dom(\mathcal{S}). \ \text{↳} \ \rho(A(l)) \vee l \in \mu R_{fv(e),S}$$

Let *Path* range over finite access paths $\overline{f}$ of field names. The notation $f \oplus \overline{f'}$ attaches f to the front of path $\overline{f'}$. The predicate

$$aliases\text{-}ok(l, \mathcal{A}, A, \mathcal{S}) \Leftrightarrow A(l), \mathcal{S}(l) \precsim \{A(l_i).\overline{f_i} \mid \mathcal{S}(l_i).\overline{f_i}\}$$

relates all type assumptions about a single location l with an Urtype assumption $\mathcal{A}$. Every active annotation in the typing must be sanctioned by an active annotation in the Urtype assumption. The Urtype assumption for a location is responsible (1) for the local activity annotation of fields that refer to defined locations and (2) for the full type of fields that contain null. The definition collects relevant types in a multiset (indicated by $\{\dots\}$) because each occurrence of a type contributes to the activity. Thus, the *aliases-ok* predicate ensures that there is at most one active annotation in all type assumptions about l.

Some auxiliary notation is needed to define the action of access paths on types and stores:

$$t.\varepsilon = t \qquad \frac{t = \langle va, c\{\overline{f_i : s_i[\varsigma_i]}\} \rangle \qquad s_j = \langle aa, t_j \rangle}{t.(f_j \oplus \overline{f_{j_i}}) = t_j.\overline{f_{j_i}}}$$

$$\mathcal{S}(w).\varepsilon = w \qquad \frac{\mathcal{S}(l) = \langle c, \ell, \overline{f_i \mapsto w_i} \rangle}{\mathcal{S}(l).(f_j \oplus \overline{f_{j_i}}) = \mathcal{S}(l_j).\overline{f_{j_i}}}$$

It remains to define the "sanctions" relation between an entry in an Urtype assumption (an annotated type), an entry in a store, and a multiset of annotated types. Its first stage projects out, for each field, the corresponding field type, the stored value, and the multiset of field types.

$$\frac{(\forall i) \ s_i, w_i \precsim \{s_i^\iota \mid \iota \in J\}}{\langle va, c\{\overline{f_i : s_i[\varsigma_i]}\} \rangle, \langle c, \ell, \overline{f_i \mapsto w_i} \rangle \precsim \{\langle va^\iota, c\{\overline{f_i : s_i^\iota[\varsigma_i^\iota]}\} \rangle \mid \iota \in J\}}$$

Its second stage states that the annotation from the Urtype assumption splits into the multiset of the activity annotations. For each null value, the multiset of types is also split from the type in the Urtype assumption.

$$\frac{aa \succeq \{aa^\iota \mid \iota \in J\} \qquad w = \texttt{null} \Rightarrow t \succeq \{t^\iota \mid \iota \in J\}}{\langle aa, t \rangle, w \precsim \{\langle aa^\iota, t^\iota \rangle \mid \iota \in J\}}$$

The typing judgment $P; \mathcal{A}; A \vdash_c \langle e; L; \mathcal{S} \rangle : t \triangleright A'$ for configurations $\langle e; \mathcal{S} \rangle$ in context L (a multiset of locations) formalizes the main invariant of the preservation lemma. It holds if the store is consistently typed, the expression is well typed, the program is well-formed, the locations occurring in the expression are all defined in the store, every location which is not reachable from L and the locations in the expression must have a droppable type, the locations in L are all typed and use up enough capabilities of the final assumptions A' so that all types in the remaining assumption A'' are droppable.

$$\frac{\begin{array}{ccc} P; A \vdash_S S : A & P; A \vdash_e e : t \rhd A' & \vdash P \quad fv(e) \subseteq dom(S) \\ drop\text{-}ok(fv(e) + L, A, S) & L \subseteq dom(A') & P; A' \vdash_{\overline{e}} L : \overline{t} \rhd A'' \quad \rho(A'') \end{array}}{P; A; A \vdash_c \langle e; L; S \rangle : t \rhd A'}$$

$$\frac{\begin{array}{cc} & dom(S) \subseteq dom(A) \\ dom(A) = dom(A) & (\forall l \in dom(S))\ P; A; A; S \vdash_\eta l : A(l) \end{array}}{P; A \vdash_S S : A}$$

$$\frac{\begin{array}{ccc} S(l) = \langle c, \ell, \mathcal{F} \rangle & \boxed{R^{\texttt{new}}_{\ell,c}(va)} & ran(\mathcal{F}) \subseteq dom(S) \cup \{\texttt{null}\} \\ (\forall i)\ \mathcal{F}(f_i) = \texttt{null} \Rightarrow P \vdash_{\texttt{null}} s_i & (\forall i)\ P \vdash_s wf(s_i) & aliases\text{-}ok(l, A, A, S) \end{array}}{P; A; A; S \vdash_\eta l : \langle va, c\{\overline{f_i : s_i[\varsigma_i]}\} \rangle}$$

The judgment $\vdash_S$, which states the consistency of the assumptions about the store, has a standard inductive reading despite the presence of cyclic structures in the store. All potentially cyclic references are broken by the explicit use of the type environment A.

The preservation lemma uses an extension relation $\precsim$ between Urtype assumptions, which holds between successive configurations. It basically states that active capabilities cannot be created from nothing.

$$\frac{dom A_1 \subseteq dom A_2 \quad (\forall l \in dom A_1)\ A_1(l) \precsim A_2(l)}{A_1 \precsim A_2}$$

$$\frac{(\forall i)\ s_i \precsim s_i'}{\langle va, c\{\overline{f_i : s_i[\varsigma_i]}\} \rangle \precsim \langle va', c\{\overline{f_i : s_i'[\varsigma_i]}\} \rangle} \qquad \frac{(aa = \Delta(va) \vee aa = aa')\quad t \precsim t'}{\langle aa, t \rangle \precsim \langle aa', t' \rangle}$$

The type preservation lemma states that reducing an expression does not change its type. The notation $A{\restriction}_M$ denotes the environment obtained by restricting A to the variables in M.

Lemma 1 (Preservation). *Suppose* $P; A_1; A_1 \vdash_c \langle e_1; L; S_1 \rangle : t \rhd A_1'$ *and* $P \vdash \langle e_1; S_1 \rangle \hookrightarrow \langle e_2; S_2 \rangle$. *Then there exist* A_2, A_2, *and* A_2' *with* $A_1 \precsim A_2$, $dom(A_1') \subseteq dom(A_2')$, *and* $\vdash_A A_2'{\restriction}_{dom(A_1')} \leq A_1'$ *such that* $P; A_2; A_2 \vdash_c \langle e_2; L; S_2 \rangle : t \rhd A_2'$.

Proof. By induction on the definition of $\hookrightarrow$.

The progress lemma ensures that a well-typed expression is not stuck.

Lemma 2 (Progress). *Suppose* $P; A; A \vdash_c \langle e; L; S \rangle : t \rhd A'$. *Then either* e *is a value, or there exists* $\langle e'; S' \rangle$ *such that* $P \vdash \langle e; S \rangle \hookrightarrow \langle e'; S' \rangle$, *or* $P \vdash \langle e; S \rangle \hookrightarrow \langle \text{error: dereferenced null}, S \rangle$.

Proof. By structural induction on e.

5   From MiniJava(X) to Java(X)

The formalization of MINIJAVA(X) covers the core expression language of Java
1.4 and imperative field update. This section discusses the extensions necessary
for the full system JAVA(X) with inheritance, subtyping, and with constrained
parametric polymorphism over annotations in the style of HM(X) [21].

We have refrained from formally specifying the extensions in this paper because they add technical complication and obscure the simplicity of the approach
by cluttering the presentation.

5.1   Polymorphism

The extension to polymorphism essentially adds annotation variables to the type
language and allows constrained abstraction over them. The splitting, droppability, and subtyping relations become constraints, which can be abstracted over. In
fact, the addition of polymorphism to a monomorphic type-based program analysis is a schematic, but tedious effort. Our extension is modeled after the HM(X)
framework [21] which provides a parameterized extension of Hindley-Milner typing (including type inference) by suitable constraint theories and subtyping.

The resulting constrained polymorphism adds technical complication, but it
greatly increases the expressiveness. As an example, we revisit the typing of the
detach() method of the JDOM API. In Section 2.1, we had to decide on one
particular usage pattern for detach(). Either the typing made the method return
the active reference or it modified the active receiver object. With annotation
polymorphism, the system can postpone the decision by abstracting over the
annotations and making the required splitting into a constraint. Here is the
resulting type abstracting over the activity annotation variables ψ' and ψ'':

$$\forall \psi' \psi''. \ \triangle(\mathbf{N}) \succeq \psi' \mid \psi'' \Rightarrow$$
$$\texttt{Attribute}\{\texttt{p} : \langle \psi'', \texttt{Element} \rangle\}$$
$$[\texttt{Attribute}\{\texttt{p} : \langle \triangle(\mathbf{ND}) \rightsquigarrow \psi', \texttt{Element} \rangle\}] \ \texttt{detach}()$$

The splitting constraint $\triangle(\mathbf{N}) \succeq \psi' \mid \psi''$ fixes the relationship between ψ' and
ψ''. The two type signatures for detach() suggested in Section 2.1 are the only
instances of the above parameterized type.

5.2   Inheritance

Inheritance and interfaces can be treated with a minor—but important—
extension as in RAJA [16]. In MINIJAVA(X), the type of an object includes
only the descriptions of the fields belonging to the object's class. In JAVA(X),
with subtyping and a cast operation, the type of an object includes descriptions
of all fields of all classes and a cast changes the class type but leaves the field
environment untouched. Figure 7 contains the rule for a cast; the subsumption
rule changes so that it can also raise the class type (as well as the annotations
as shown in Figure 4). Interface types can be treated in the same way. Their
addition just affects Java's subtyping relation.

$$\frac{P; A \vdash_e e : \langle va, c'\{\overline{f : s[\varsigma]}\}\rangle \,\triangleright\, A'}{P; A \vdash_e (c)e : \langle va, c\{\overline{f : s[\varsigma]}\}\rangle \,\triangleright\, A'}$$

Fig. 7. Type cast rule for JAVA(X)

The expanded class type is required for type checking cast operations in a meaningful way. Suppose that class A is a subclass of class B:

```
class B {}
class A extends B {
  Object mystate;
  public A (Object state) {...}
}
```

and the following use of an A object:

```
B b = new A (init);
A a = (A) b;
```

Suppose the newly created A object has type A{mystate : $\langle \triangle(\text{init}), \dots \rangle$}. If each class type only had the fields of its own class, then the subsumption to B would strip away the information about the mystate field. This information would be lost forever and the subsequent upcast back to A would have to invent some information about mystate.

With our choice, a cast or subsumption never changes the field map but only changes the static class name associated with it. Thus, information is neither lost nor reinvented.

Another issue is method consistency. If a subclass overrides a method of a superclass, then the annotated type in the superclass must subsume the one in the subclass as in method specialization [19].

6   Related Work

There are two closely related lines of work in type systems: refinement and ownership. Refinement types add extra information to an existing type system to check additional properties at compile time. Ownership types enforce access restrictions by providing extra structure on reference types.

Freeman and Pfenning [15] have proposed refinement types as an extension to ML with union and intersection types. Their approach attaches a property lattice to each type as we do, but they do not distinguish linear and non-linear resources. Their ideas have been further refined in various directions. For example, indexed types can express invariants of data types [30]. Type state checking [26,25] is a precursor of refinement typing using similar techniques but for a more restricted first-order imperative language.

Another direction is the development of a logical system to model properties on top of the type system, as in the work of Mandelbaum et al. [18]. They graft a fragment of intuitionistic linear logic on top of the ML type system adapted for use with the monadic metalanguage. While this approach is highly expressive, it requires a lot of program modifications. Our work encodes the logical properties in annotations and has a built-in mechanism (activity annotations) to transform standard properties to linear properties.

Type qualifications are similar to type annotations. A typical work on type qualifications is the paper by Foster et al. [14] which enables the flow-sensitive checking of atomic properties that refine standard types. They present an efficient inference algorithm for their system. The goal of their work is similar to ours, however, our work combines flow-sensitive and flow-insensitive aspects.

Semantic type qualifiers [7] share some concerns with our work. They allow the specification of a type qualifier together with a logical formula defining its meaning in terms of the program state. They automatically discharge the resulting proof obligation and thus obtain a correct system automatically. However, their properties only correspond to our value annotations and they do not support the notion of strong update.

A number of works solve specific problems with ad-hoc constructed type systems and may be viewed as specializations of one of the above frameworks, in particular exploiting flow-sensitivity. Examples are the work on atomicity and race detection [10,11], the work on Vault [8], and many others.

JavaCOP [1] is a tool for implementing certain annotated type systems for Java. It provides a language for defining predicates on typed abstract syntax trees for Java. JavaCOP is integrated with a Java compiler that checks the defined predicates before generating code. While JavaCOP provides a flexible and convenient framework for implementing such systems, it is a purely syntactic tool: it neither provides any soundness guarantees nor does it have a notion of flow dependency which would be necessary to track linear resource use. $\textrm{JAVA}(X)$ provides both. Both JavaCOP and $\textrm{JAVA}(X)$ make the important distinction between analysis designers (who define predicate/design annotation posets) and programmer (who work in terms of annotations).

The Fugue system [9] implements typestate assertions and checking for C♯. It structures the state of an object in different frames corresponding to the nesting of subclasses. For each frame, the programmer can state formulae in first-order predicate logic. In comparison to $\textrm{JAVA}(X)$, Fugue has a different approach of handling aliases, it introduces extra program constructs to expose typestate, it requires the programmer to writer formulae instead of predefined abstract values, and there is no soundness proof.

Another related system is the Hob system [17]. It basically allows the specification of pre- and postconditions using an abstract specification language based on sets. However, the underlying interpretation of this language is configurable to different logical systems and there is an aspect-oriented mechanism to simplify authoring of specifications. $\textrm{JAVA}(X)$ manages abstraction the other way round.

An analysis designer carves out domain-specific abstract values from predicates, thus hiding some complexity from the programmer.

The goal of an ownership type system is to improve modularity by partitioning the state of a system in a hierarchical manner. Such a system restricts inter-object accesses to those that are compatible with the hierarchy. Although Java(X) was not conceived with ownership in mind, it turns out that notions like unique and borrowed references are closely related to our notion of active and inactive references.

There is a lot of work on ownership types and related notions [2,31,20] but we focus only on the most closely related work by Boyland and others. In a series of articles culminating in 2005 [5], Boyland and others have established a notion of permissions which are attached to an object type along with an effect system to abstract the state dependencies of a method call. The permissions govern whether a reference is readable or writable. In earlier work, Boyland [3] has proposed splitting of permissions in fractions where only the full permission "1" allows full read/write access and proper fractions only allow read access. This kind of permission seems to be related to our notions of active, inactive, and semi-active. Effects are also present in our system, albeit in the form of explicit state transitions on the argument and receiver types of a method.

It is also instructive to compare the notions of active, semi-active, and inactive with similar notions in the realm of ownership type systems as categorized by Boyland and others [4]. Their categorization includes the permissions R (read), W (write), $\bar{R}$ (exclusive read), and $\bar{W}$ (exclusive write: no other alias may write)[6]. Active corresponds to $RW\bar{W}$ (read, write, and exclusive write permission), semi-active to RW, and inactive to R (transposed to a per-field setting; their original work categorizes variables).

In previous work [27], we have proposed an annotated type system for a Java subset without inheritance that provides improved types for the DOM interface. The previous work has inspired the example in Section 2.1 but it is limited in several respects: It is tied to one particular amalgamation of annotation and activity, it can only keep track of one affine state of a resource (either the resource is in this state or nothing is known about it; there is no notion of droppability), it does not support type state change, and it does not treat inheritance. The present work overcomes all these weaknesses.

Hofmann and Jost [16] have defined a type-based analysis to predict the consumption of heap space by Java methods. Their system RAJA is inspired by amortized complexity analysis. The underlying design ideas of their type system are similar to ours, however, the details are different and our work has been developed independently. For example, splitting works very differently and Java(X)'s annotations of arguments may change through method calls whereas RAJA's annotations are simply used up because they denote a potential passed to a method invocation through the parameters.

---

[6] Their remaining permissions O, I, and $\bar{I}$ are not important here.

7 Conclusion

JAVA(X) extends the type system of Java 1.4 with an annotation framework for tracking value-based properties as well as affine and linear properties. A transient property of an object is always tied to the value of a particular field of the object. The system only requires the specification of posets for the properties of field values and adds the tracking of linear and affine uses of references in a generic way. Linear and affine uses of references improve the accuracy of the properties because they are subject to type state change.

Our first experiences with the type checker are encouraging. Future work includes extending the type checker to full JAVA(X) and implementing some form of type inference. We also would like to connect some notion of semantics to our purely syntactic annotations and to investigate further variations of the activity annotations.

Acknowledgments. We thank Martin Hofmann for extensive discussions and the anonymous reviewers for their helpful comments.

References

1. Andreae, C., Noble, J., Markstrum, S., Millstein, T.: A framework for implementing pluggable type systems. In: Proc. 21th ACM Conf. OOPSLA, Portland, OR, USA, pp. 57–74. ACM Press, Portland (2006)
2. Boyapati, C., Liskov, B., Shrira, L.: Ownership types for object encapsulation. In: Morrisett, G. (ed.) Proc. 30th ACM Symp. POPL, New Orleans, LA, USA, January 2003, (ACM SIGPLAN Notices (38)1) pp. 213–223. ACM Press, New York (2003)
3. Boyland, J.: Checking interference with fractional permissions. In: Cousot, R. (ed.) SAS 2003. LNCS, vol. 2694, pp. 55–72. Springer, Heidelberg (2003)
4. Boyland, J., Noble, J., Retert, W.: Capabilities for sharing: A generalisation of uniqueness and read-only. In: Knudsen, J.L. (ed.) ECOOP 2001. LNCS, vol. 2072, pp. 2–27. Springer, Heidelberg (2001)
5. Boyland, J.T., Retert, W.: Connecting effects and uniqueness with adoption. In: Abadi, M. (ed.) Proc. 32nd ACM Symp. POPL, January 2005, pp. 283–295. ACM Press, New York (2005)
6. Cardelli, L.: A semantics of multiple inheritance. Information and Computation 76(2/3), 138–164 (1988)
7. Chin, B., Markstrum, S., Millstein, T.: Semantic type qualifiers. In: Proc. 2005 ACM Conf. PLDI, pp. 85–95. ACM Press, New York (2005)
8. DeLine, R., Fähndrich, M.: Enforcing high-level protocols in low-level software. In: Proc. 2001 PLDI, Snowbird, UT, United States, June 2001, pp. 59–69. ACM Press, New York, USA (2001)
9. DeLine, R., Fähndrich, M.: Typestates for objects. In M. Odersky, editor, *18th ECOOP*. In: Odersky, M. (ed.) ECOOP 2004. LNCS, vol. 3086, pp. 465–490. Springer, Heidelberg (2004)

10. Flanagan, C., Freund, S.N.: Type-based race detection for Java. In: Proceedings of the 2000 ACM SIGPLAN Conference on Programming Language Design and Implementation (PLDI) (SIGPLAN Notices), Vancouver, British Columbia, Canada, June 2000, vol. 35(5), pp. 219–232. ACM Press, New York (2000)
11. Flanagan, C., Qadeer, S.: A type and effect system for atomicity. In: Proc. 2003 PLDI, pp. 338–349. ACM Press, New York (2003)
12. Flanagan, C., Sabry, A., Duba, B.F., Felleisen, M.: The essence of compiling with continuations. In: Proc. 1993 PLDI, pp. 237–247, Albuquerque, New Mexico (June 1993)
13. Flatt, M., Krishnamurthi, S., Felleisen, M.: A programmer's reduction semantics for classes and mixins. In: Alves-Foss, J. (ed.) Formal Syntax and Semantics of Java. LNCS, vol. 1523, pp. 241–269. Springer, Heidelberg (1999)
14. Foster, J.S., Terauchi, T., Aiken, A.: Flow-sensitive type qualifiers. In: Proc. 2002 PLDI, Berlin, Germany, June 2002, pp. 1–12. ACM Press, New York (2002)
15. Freeman, T., Pfenning, F.: Refinement types for ML. In: Proc. PLDI '91, Toronto, Canada, June 1991, pp. 268–277. ACM Press, New York (1991)
16. Hofmann, M., Jost, S.: Type-based amortised heap-space analysis. In: Sestoft, P. (ed.) ESOP 2006 and ETAPS 2006. LNCS, vol. 3924, Springer, Heidelberg (2006)
17. Lam, P., Kuncak, V., Rinard, M.: Crosscutting techniques in program specification and analysis. In: AOSD '05: Proceedings of the 4th international conference on Aspect-oriented software development, pp. 169–180. ACM Press, New York (2005)
18. Mandelbaum, Y., Walker, D., Harper, R.: An effective theory of type refinements. In: Shivers, O. (ed.) Proc. Intl. Conf. Functional Programming 2003, Uppsala, Sweden, August 2003, pp. 213–225. ACM Press, New York (2003)
19. Mitchell, J.C.: Toward a typed foundation for method specialization and inheritance. In: Proc. 17th ACM Symp. POPL, January 1990, pp. 109–124. ACM Press, San Francisco, CA (1990)
20. Noble, J., Vitek, J., Potter, J.: Flexible alias protection. In: Jul, E. (ed.) ECOOP 1998. LNCS, vol. 1445, pp. 158–185. Springer, Heidelberg (1998)
21. Odersky, M., Sulzmann, M., Wehr, M.: Type inference with constrained types. Theory and Practice of Object Systems 5(1), 35–55 (1999)
22. Palsberg, J.: Type-based analysis and applications. In: ACM. (ed.) ACM SIGPLAN – SIGSOFT Workshop on Program Analysis for Software Tools and Engineering: PASTE'01, June 09, pp. 20–27. ACM Press, New York (2001)
23. Pierce, B.C.: Types and Programming Languages. MIT Press, Cambridge (2002)
24. Schrefl, M., Stumptner, M.: Behavior-consistent specialization of object life cycles. ACM Trans. Software Engineering and Methodology 11(1), 92–148 (2002)
25. Strom, R.E., Yellin, D.M.: Extending typestate checking using conditional liveness analysis. IEEE Trans. Softw. Eng. 19(5), 478–485 (1993)
26. Strom, R.E., Yemini, S.: Typestate: A programming language concept for enhancing software reliability. IEEE Trans. Softw. Eng. 12(1), 157–171 (1986)
27. Thiemann, P.: A type safe DOM API. In: Bierman, G., Koch, C. (eds.) DBPL 2005. LNCS, vol. 3774, Springer, Heidelberg (2005)
28. Walker, D.: Substructural type systems. In: Pierce, B.C. (ed.) Advanced Topics in Types and Programming Languages. chapter 1, MIT Press, Cambridge (2005)
29. Wright, A., Felleisen, M.: A syntactic approach to type soundness. Information and Computation 115(1), 38–94 (1994)

30. Xi, H., Pfenning, F.: Dependent types in practical programming. In: Aiken, A. (ed.) Proc. 26th ACM Symp. POPL, January 1999, pp. 214–227. ACM Press, New York (1999)
31. Zhao, T., Palsberg, J., Vitek, J.: Lightweight confinement for Featherweight Java. In: Proc. 18th ACM Conf. OOPSLA, Anaheim, CA, USA, 2003, pp. 135–148. ACM Press, New York (2003)

Attribute Grammar-Based Language Extensions for Java*

Eric Van Wyk, Lijesh Krishnan, Derek Bodin, and August Schwerdfeger

Department of Computer Science and Engineering
University of Minnesota
Minneapolis, MN 55455, USA
{evw,krishnan,bodin,schwerdf}@cs.umn.edu

Abstract. This paper describes the ableJ extensible language framework, a tool that allows one to create new domain-adapted languages
by importing domain-specific language extensions into an extensible implementation of Java 1.4. Language extensions may define the syntax,
semantic analysis, and optimizations of new language constructs. Java
and the language extensions are specified as higher-order attribute grammars.

We describe several language extensions and their implementation in
the framework. For example, one extension embeds the SQL database
query language into Java and statically checks for syntax and type errors in SQL queries. The tool supports the modular specification of
composable language extensions so that programmers can import into
Java the unique set of extensions that they desire. When extensions follow certain restrictions, they can be composed without requiring any
implementation-level knowledge of the language extensions. The tools
automatically compose the selected extensions and the Java host language specification.

1 Introduction

One impediment in developing software is the wide semantic gap between the
programmer's high-level (often domain specific) understanding of a problem's
solution and the relatively low-level language in which the solution must be
encoded. General purpose languages provide features such as classes, gener-
ics/parametric polymorphism, and higher-order functions that programmers can
use to specify abstractions for a given problem or problem domain, but these
provide only the functionality of the desired abstractions. Domain-specific languages (DSLs) can be employed to provide this functionality, but they can also
provide domain-specific language constructs (new syntax) for the abstractions.
These constructs raise the level of abstraction of the language to that of the
specific domain and thus help to reduce the semantic gap. As importantly, domain specific languages also provide domain-specific optimizations and analyses

---

* This work is partially funded by NSF CAREER Award #0347860, NSF CCF Award
#0429640, and the McKnight Foundation.

E. Ernst (Ed.): ECOOP 2007, LNAI 4609, pp. 575–599, 2007.

that are either impossible or quite difficult to specify for programs written in general purpose languages. But problems often cross multiple domains and no language will contain all of the general-purpose and domain-specific features needed to address all of the problem's aspects, thus the fundamental problem remains — programmers cannot "say what they mean" but must encode their solution ideas as programming idioms at a lower level of abstraction. This process is time-consuming and can be the source of errors.

ableJ is a language processing tool that addresses this fundamental problem. It supports the creation of extended, domain-adapted variants of Java by adding domain-specific language extensions to an extensible implementation of Java 1.4. An extended language defined by this process has features that raise the level of abstraction to that of a particular problem. These features may be new language constructs, semantic analyses, or optimizing program transformations, and are packaged as *modular language extensions*. Language extensions can be as simple as the Java 1.5 enhanced-for loop or the more sophisticated set of SQL language constructs that statically check for syntax and type errors in SQL queries. We have also developed domain-specific extensions to support the development of efficient and robust computational geometry programs and extensions that introduce condition tables (useful for understanding complex boolean expressions) from the modeling language $RSML^{-e}$ [22]. Extensions can also be general purpose in nature; we have defined extensions that add algebraic datatypes and pattern matching from Pizza [18], add concrete syntax for lists, and others that add the automatic boxing and unboxing of Java primitive types.

ableJ is an attribute grammar-based extensible language framework in which an extensible host language is specified as a complete attribute grammar (AG) and the language extensions are specified as attribute grammar fragments. These are written in Silver [25], an attribute grammar specification language developed to support this process. The attribute grammars define semantics of the host language and the language extensions. Silver also supports the specification of concrete syntax that is utilized by parser and scanner generators. The Silver extensible compiler tools combine the AG specifications of the host language and the programmer selected language extension to create an AG specification for the custom extended language desired by the programmer. An attribute grammar evaluator for this grammar implements the compiler for the extended language. Concrete syntax specifications are similarly composed.

It is important that constructs implemented as language extensions have the same "look-and-feel" of host language constructs. That is, their syntax should fit naturally with the host language, error messages should be reported in terms of the extension constructs used by the programmer, not in terms of their translations to some implementation as is the case with macros. Also, extension constructs should be efficient and thus generate efficient translations. Forwarding [26], an extension to higher-order AGs [32], facilitates the modular definition of languages and supports the implementation of constructs that satisfy this look-and-feel criteria. One can implicitly specify the semantics of new constructs by translation to semantically equivalent constructs in the host Java 1.4

language. For example, an SQL query translates to calls to the JDBC library. But it also allows the explicit specification of semantics since attributes can be defined on productions defining language constructs to, for example, check for errors at the extension level, as is done with the SQL extension.

In Silver, attribute grammars are packaged as modules defining either a host language or an extension to the host language. Module names, like Java packages, are based on Internet domains to avoid name clashes. The module `edu:umn:cs:melt:java14` defines Java 1.4 and defines the concrete syntax of the language, the abstract syntax, and the semantic analyses required to do most type checking analyses and to do package/type/expression name disambiguation. The grammar defines most aspects of a Java compiler but it does not specify byte-code generation. Language extensions add new constructs and their translation to Java 1.4 code; a traditional Java compiler then converts this to byte-code for execution. Thus, ableJ is a preprocessor that performs type checking and other semantic analysis. The static analysis we perform supports the analysis of extensions to ensure that any statically detectable errors (such as type errors and access violations) in the extended Java language can be caught so that erroneous code is not generated. Programmers should not be expected to look at the generated Java code; errors should be reported on the code that they write.

Of particular interest are language extensions designed to be *composable* with other extensions, possibly developed by different parties. Such extensions may be imported by a programmer into Java without requiring any implementation level knowledge of the extensions. Thus, we make a distinction between two activities: (*i*) implementing a language extension, which is performed by a domain-expert feature designer and (*ii*) selecting the language extensions that will be imported into an extensible language specification in order to create an extended language. When extensions are composable, this activity can be performed by a programmer. This distinction is analogous to the distinction between library writers and library users. Thus a programmer, facing a geometric problem in which the geometric data is stored in a relational database may import into Java both the SQL extension and the computational geometry extension to create a unique domain-adapted version of Java that has features to support both of these aspects of his or her problem.

The goal of composability does restrict the kind of features that can be added to a language in a composable language extension. The primary determinant is the type of transformations (global or local) that are used to translate the high-level extension constructs into the implementation language of Java 1.4. If global transformations are required in translating to the host language then the order in which these reductions are made may matter and selecting this ordering would require that the programmer have some implementation level knowledge of the implementation of the extensions being imported. Thus, composable extensions (which include those listed above) use primarily local transformations.

Contributions. The paper shows how general purpose languages, in this case Java 1.4, can be implemented in such a way that rich domain-specific and general purpose language features can be imported to create new extended languages adapted to particular problems and domains. Two key characteristics of the extensions presented here are that they perform semantic analysis at the language extension level and that they are composable. Thus, it is feasible that programmers, with no implementation-level knowledge of the extensions, can import the set of extensions that address a particular problem. Note however that ableJ can also be used to define non-composable extensions that introduce features that require fundamental alteration or replacement of host language constructs. The rest of the paper is structured as follows: Section 2 shows several sample language extensions; Section 3 describes the attribute grammar based implementation of Java 1.4 and some selected extensions to illustrate how the semantic analyses of the host and extensions can be combined. Section 4 shows how extensions are composed and discusses analyses of extension specifications. Although the composition of AG based semantic analyses is the focus of this paper, Section 4 also briefly describes an integrated parser/scanner that supports composition of concrete syntax specifications. Section 5 describes related and future work and concludes.

2   Sample Language Extensions

Several composable extensions have been specified and implemented for the host Java 1.4 language; we describe several of them here. Sample uses and their translations to the host language are given, as well as short descriptions of the unique characteristics of each extension. Others are described during the description of the Java 1.4 host language specification in Section 3.

SQL: Our first extension embeds the database query language SQL into Java, allowing queries to be written in a natural syntax. The extension also statically detects syntax and type errors in embedded queries. A previous workshop paper [24] reports the details of this language extension; we discuss it here and in Section 3.3 to describe how it interacts with and extends the environment (symbol-table) defined in the Java attribute grammar. Figure 1 shows an example of code written using the SQL extension to Java 1.4. The `import table` construct defines the table `person` and its columns along with their types. For example, the column `person_id` has SQL type `INTEGER`. This information is used to statically type check the SQL query in the `using ... query` construct. Thus, if the column `age` had type `VARCHAR` (an SQL string type) instead of `INTEGER` the extension would report the appropriate type error on the `>` expression at compile time instead of at run-time as is done in the JDBC library-based approach. The extension translates SQL constructs to pure Java 1.4 constructs that use the JDBC library as shown in Figure 2. Here the SQL query is passed as a Java `String` to the database server for execution. When queries are written this way, statically checking for syntax or type errors requires extracting queries from the Java strings and reconstructing them. This is much more difficult than when the query constructs can be examined directly as is possible in the SQL extension.

```
public class Demo {
  public static void main(String args) {
    import table person [ person_id INTEGER, first_name VARCHAR,
                          last_name VARCHAR, age INTEGER ] ;
    int limit = 25 ;
    connection c = "jdbc:/db/testdb;";
    ResultSet rs = using c query
                {SELECT last_name FROM person WHERE age > limit } ;  } }
```

Fig. 1. Code using the SQL extension to Java 1.4

```
public class Demo {
  public static void main(String args) {
    int limit = 25 ;
    Connection c = DriverManager.getConnection("jdbc:/db/testdb;");
    ResultSet rs = c.createStatement().executeQuery((
        "SELECT "+" last_name "+" FROM "+" person "+" WHERE "+" age "+
        " > " + (limit) )) ;      } }
```

Fig. 2. Equivalent code in Java 1.4

Complex Numbers: This extension adds complex numbers as a new primitive type to Java 1.4. This extension specifies the new type, means for writing complex number literals, and subtype relations with existing host language types (e.g., that the new type is a super-type of the host language `double` type.) It also specifies productions to coerce `double`-typed values into the new type. Thus, in the code fragment `double d; complex c; d = 1.4; c = d + 1.7; c = complex(1.2,2.3);` written in a version of Java extended with the complex number type the first assignment to c first translates to `c = complex(d + 1.7,0.0);` after which the complex literal translates to calls to constructors for the Java class `Complex` constructor that implements the complex number type. Finally, this extension also overloads the arithmetic operators, such as `+` and `*`. It is further described in Section 3.2.

C++ allows operator overloading as well. But in the attribute grammar-based extensible language approach proposed here, there are mechanisms for optimizing new numeric types that do not exist in C++. Thus, the production for complex addition may optimize the operands before performing the addition.

Computational Geometry: More interesting opportunities for optimization are prevalent in the domain of computational geometry; we have specified numerical types for unbound-precision integers in a language extension [27] for this domain. This extension was developed for a small C-like language and takes advantage of domain knowledge that is unavailable in general purpose languages and library-based implementations. It uses this information to perform optimizations that generate C language code that is 3 to 20 times faster than the equivalent code utilizing the CGAL geometric library - typically regarded as the best C++ template library for the domain.

Algebraic Datatypes: ableJ can also be used to specify general purpose language extensions. We have written an extension that extends Java 1.4 with Pizza-style [18] algebraic datatypes. Figure 3 shows code in this extended version of Java inspired by the examples in [18]. The extension translates this to pure Java 1.4 code that includes new `Nil` and `Cons` subclasses of `List`. The subclasses have a tag field used to identify them as nil or cons objects. There are fields on `Cons` for the `char` and `List` parameters to the `Cons` constructor as shown in Figure 3. The translation of the pattern matching `switch` statement is a nested

```
algebraic class List {
  case Nil;
  case Cons (char, List);
  public List append (List ys) {
    switch (this) {
      case Nil:
        return ys;
      case Cons (x, xs):
        return new Cons (x,
                  xs.append (ys));
    }
    return null;    }
}
```

Fig. 3. Code using a version of Java extended with Pizza-style algebraic datatypes

`if-then -else` construct that uses the tag field to determine the constructor in place of pattern matching.

3   Extensible Java and Java Extension Specifications

In this section we describe the Silver AG specifications that define the host language Java 1.4 and describe several composable language extensions. We have simplified some minor features of the grammar to aid presentation and to focus on aspects that are important while specifying extensions. For example, the interaction of the extensions with the type checking and environment (symbol-table) specifications are highlighted.

Silver [25] supports higher-order attributes [32], forwarding [26], collection attributes [3], various general-purpose constructs such as pattern matching and type-safe polymorphic lists, as well as the traditional AG constructs introduced by Knuth [15]. Silver also has mechanisms for specifying the concrete syntax of language constructs. These specifications are used to generate a parser and scanner for the specified language. Language extensions are specified as AG fragments, also written in Silver. New productions define new language constructs, new attributes and their definitions on productions define semantic analyses such as type checking and the construction of optimized translations of constructs (using higher-order attributes). Silver's module system combines the specifications of the host language and the selected language extensions to create the AG specification defining the new extended language. This process is described in Section 4.1. A Silver module names a directory, not a file, and the module consists of all Silver files (with extension .sv) in that directory. The scope of a declaration includes all files in the module.

Section 3.1 describes part of the Java 1.4 host language AG specification. Section 3.2 describes how extensions interact with the typing and subtyping information collected and processed by the host language AG. Section 3.3 shows how extensions interact with and extend the environment (symbol-table) defined by the host language AG. Due to space considerations, these specifications are necessarily brief and have been simplified so that the main concepts are not obscured by the intricacies of building real languages. All specifications are available online at www.melt.cs.umn.edu.

3.1 Java Attribute Grammar Specification

A simplified portion of the Java 1.4 host-language AG specification is shown in Figure 4. A Silver file consists of the grammar name, grammar import statements (there are none here) and an unordered sequence of AG declarations. The specification first defines a collection of non-terminal symbols; the non-terminal CompilationUnit is the start symbol of the grammar and represents a .java file. Nonterminals Stmt, Expr, and Type represent Java statements, expressions, and type expressions respectively. Other nonterminals are declared (but not shown) for class and member declarations. The nonterminal TypeRep is used by abstract productions to represent types. Next is the declaration for the terminal symbol Id that matches identifiers with an associated regular expression. Mechanisms to give lexical precedence to keywords over identifiers are provided in Silver but are left out here. The terminal declaration for the while-loop keyword follows and provides the fixed string that it matches (indicated by single quotes).

Concrete productions and the incident nonterminals and terminals are used to generate a parser and scanner. The parser/scanner system is further discussed in Section 4.3. In the specification here, attribute evaluation is done on the concrete syntax as this simplifies the presentation. In the actual AG the concrete syntax productions are used only to generate the abstract syntax trees over which attribute evaluation is actually performed. Aspect productions, which are used later, allow new attribute definitions to be added to existing concrete or abstract productions from a different file or grammar module.

Several synthesized attributes are also defined. A pretty-print String attribute pp decorates (occurs on) the nonterminals Expr, Stmt, and others. The errors attribute is a list of Strings and occurs on nearly all nonterminals. The typerep attribute is the representation of the type used internally for type-checking. It is a data structure (implemented as a tree) of type TypeRep and decorates Type and Expr nonterminals. For each nonterminal NT in the host language there is a synthesized attribute hostNT of type NT. On a node of type NT it holds that node's translation to the host language. These attributes are used to extract the host language Java 1.4 tree from the tree of an extended Java program. This is discussed further in the context of extensions below.

Following these are two productions, one defining the while loop, the other defining local variable declarations. The environment attributes defs and env

```
grammar edu:umn:cs:melt:java14;

start nonterminal CompilationUnit ;
nonterminal Expr, Stmt, Type, TypeRep ;
terminal Id / [a-zA-Z][a-zA-Z0-9_]* / ;
terminal While_t 'while' ;

synthesized attribute pp :: String occurs on Expr, Stmt, Type ...;
synthesized attribute errors :: [ String ] occurs on Expr, ... ;
synthesized attribute typerep :: TypeRep occurs on Type, Expr ;
synthesized attribute hostStmt :: Stmt occurs on Stmt ;
synthesized attribute hostExpr :: Expr occurs on Expr ;
synthesized attribute hostType :: Type occurs on Type ;

concrete production while
s::Stmt ::= 'while' '(' cond::Expr ')' body::Stmt
{ s.pp = "while (" ++ cond.pp ++ ") \n" ++ body.pp ;
  cond.env = s.env ;    body.env = s.env ;
  s.errors = case cond.typerep of
                booleanTypeRep() => [ ]
              | _ => [ "Error: condition must be boolean"]
              end  ++ cond.errors ++ body.errors ;
  s.hostStmt = while(cond.hostExpr,body.hostStmt);    }

concrete production local_var_dcl  s::Stmt ::= t::Type id::Id ';'
{ s.pp = t.pp ++ " " ++ id.lexeme ++ ";"
  s.defs = [ varBinding (id.lexeme, t.typerep) ] ;
  s.hostStmt = local_var_dcl(t.hostType,id); }

concrete production idRef  e::Expr ::= id::Id
{ e.typerep = ... extacted from e.env ... ;
  e.errors = ... ;    e.hostExpr = idRef(id); }

synthesized attribute superTypes :: [ SubTypeRes ] collect with ++ ;
attribute superTypes occurs on TypeRep ;

concrete production doubleType  dt::Type ::= 'double' ;
{ dt.pp = "double";  dt.typerep = doubleTypeRep() ;    }

abstract production doubleTypeRep   dtr::TypeRep ::=
{ tr.name = "double"  ; tr.superTypes := [ ] ;      }

abstract production arrayTypeRep   atr::TypeRep ::= elem::TypeRep
{ tr.name = "array"  ; tr.superTypes := [ ] ; }
```

Fig. 4. Simplified Java host language Silver specification

implement a symbol table and are described further in Section 3.3. Silver productions name the left hand side nonterminal and right hand side parameters (terminals, nonterminals, or other types) and borrow the Haskell "has type" syntax : : to specify, for example, that the third parameter to the while production is named `cond` and is a tree of type nonterminal `Expr`. Attribute definitions (between curly braces) follow the production's signature. For the while loop the definition of the `errors` attribute uses pattern matching to check that condition is of type `Boolean`. Pattern matching in Silver is similar to pattern matching in ML and Haskell. In Silver, nonterminals play the role of algebraic types and productions play the role of value constructors.

Type representations (trees of type `TypeRep`) are constructed by the productions `doubleTypeRep` and `arrayTypeRep` and used to create type representations on `Type` nodes, as in `doubleType`. One attribute on a typerep is `superTypes`, which is a list of supertypes of that particular type along with the means for converting to the supertype if runtime conversion is required. This attribute is a *collection* attribute (similar to those defined by Boyland [3]). It allows aspect productions to contribute additional elements to the attribute value. In the `doubleTypeRep` production, the `superTypes` attribute is given an initial value (using the distinct assignment operator :=) of the empty list since it has no super types in Java 1.4. The complex number extension will specify an aspect production on `doubleTypeRep` and contribute to this list of super types to indicate that the complex number type is a super type of double. This is described in Section 3.2. We have omitted some details here since the manner in which type representations are implemented is not as important as how extensions can interact with the Java AG to define new types.

3.2   Types and Subtyping in Java AG and Its Extensions

Types and subtyping are important aspects of Java and therefore of extensions to Java. Thus the host language specification must provide the mechanisms for examining the types of expressions, defining new types, specifying new subtype relationships, and checking if one type is the subtype of another. For example, if a new type for complex number is specified in an extension how can this new type interact with existing host language types? How can we specify that the Java `double` type is a subtype of the new complex number type? How can this be done in a composable manner? This section shows the Java AG for examining and creating types through the specification of two composable extensions: the enhanced-for loop in Java 1.5 and a complex number type.

Enhanced-for Loop Extension: Here, we show how to add the enhanced-for loop from Java 1.5 as a composable extension to the Java 1.4 AG specification. This extension is quite simple and not very compelling since the construct now exists in Java 1.5. However, we discuss it because its semantics are well understood and it illustrates several concepts in writing extensions and using parts of the type checking infrastructure of the Java AG. The construct allows the programmer to specify loops that iterate over the members of any array or

```
ArrayList herd = ... ;              ArrayList herd = ... ;
for (Cow c: herd) {                 for (Iterator _it_0 = herd.iterator();
  c.milk ();                           _it_0.hasNext();)  {
}                                     Cow c = (Cow) _it_0.next();  c.milk();     }

          (a)                                      (b)
```

Fig. 5. Use of enhanced-for statement (a), and its translation to Java 1.4 (b)

expression of type `Collection`[1] that implements the `iterator`, `hasNext` and `next` methods. Figure 5(a) shows a fragment of code that uses the enhanced-for construct. It uses forwarding to translate this code into the Java 1.4 code in Figure 5(b) that makes explicit calls to methods in the `Collection` interface.

The grammar module `edu:umn:cs:melt:java14:exts:foreach` contains the specification of the enhanced-for extension and defines a new production and attribute definitions. Figure 6 shows part of the specification. This grammar imports the host Java language grammar since it utilizes constructs and attributes defined in that grammar. The concrete production `enhanced_for` defines the concrete syntax of the new construct and provides explicit definitions for the `pp` and `errors` attributes. The extension does not declare any new terminals, non-terminals or attributes but uses those defined in the host language. The definition of the `pp` attribute is straightforward and is used in the generated error message if a type-error exists. This occurs if the type of the expression `coll` is not a subtype of the `Collection` interface or is not an array type. This check is realized by examining the node (stored in local attribute `st_res` of type `SubTypeRes`) returned by the `subTypeCheck` function and pattern matching the type against the `arrayTypeRep(_)` tree. The `SubTypeRes` node is decorated with a boolean attribute `isSubType` that specifies if `coll.typerep` is a subtype of the `TypeRep` for Java Collection interface returned by the helper function `getTypeRep`.

The `subTypeCheck` function, the `SubTypeRes` nonterminal, and productions for building trees of this type are part of the Java host language AG framework that extension writers use to access the typing information maintained by the host language. This use of semantic information at the language extension level distinguishes AG based extensions that use forwarding from macros.

The `enhanced_for` production also uses *forwarding* [26], an enhancement to higher-order AGs, to specify the Java 1.4 tree that the node constructed by the `enhanced_for` production translates to. Pattern matching and `st_res` are used again here in determining whether the enhanced-for translates to a `for` loop with iterators (stored in the local attribute `for_with_iterators`) or a `for` loop that increments an integer index to march across an array (stored in the attribute `for_over_array`). The definitions of these attributes are omitted here but use host language productions and the trees t, id, coll, and body to construct the appropriate tree as expected. The value of `for_with_iterators` for the enhanced-for in Figure 5(a) can be seen in Figure 5(b).

---

[1] Java 1.5 introduces the `Iterable` type for use in the enhanced-for loop. Since `Collection` is the similar type in Java 1.4, we use it here.

```
grammar edu:umn:cs:melt:java14:exts:foreach;
import edu:umn:cs:melt:java14;

concrete production enhanced_for
f::Stmt ::= 'for' '(' t::Type id::Id ':' coll::Expr ')' body::Stmt {
 f.pp = ...
 f.errors=if st_res.isSubType||match(e.typerep,arrayTypeRep(_)) then [ ]
 else["Enhanced-for "++f.pp++" must iterate over Collections or arrays."];
 forwards to if st_res.isSubType then for_with_iterators
             else case e.typerep of
                     arrayTypeRep(_) => for_over_array
                   | _               => skip()        end ;
 local attribute st_res :: SubTypeRes ;
 st_res = subtypeCheck(coll.typerep, getTypeRep("Collection" ) ;
 local attribute for_with_iterators :: Stmt ;
 for_with_iterators = ... ;
 local attribute for_over_array :: Stmt ;
 for_over_array = ... ;                                        }
```

Fig. 6. Silver code that implements the enhanced-for statement

Forwarding provides an implicit definition for all synthesized attributes not explicitly defined by the production. When an enhanced-for node is queried for its hostStmt attribute (its representation as a host language construct) it forwards that query to the pure Java 1.4 construct defined in the forwards to clause. That tree then returns its translation. The Java 1.4 tree does not simply return a copy of itself since its children, body for example, may contain instances of extension constructs that must be "translated away" in a similar fashion. Some optional features present in the Java 1.5 enhanced-for loop, namely variable modifiers and statement labels, have been omitted here for reasons of clarity and space. These are easily handled; the extra concrete syntax specification that parses the labels and passes them to the enhanced-for abstract production is the only real complication. The complete specification may be accessed at www.melt.cs.umn.edu.

Complex Numbers. Adding a new complex number type as a language extension requires specifying new type expressions and adding new subtype relationships – in this case, specifying that the Java double type is a subtype of the introduced complex type. So that complex numbers types can be present in, for example, local variable declarations, the complex number extension grammar defines the terminal symbol Complex_t which matches the single string "complex" and the production complexType seen in Figure 7. The complex type constructs are translated via forwarding to references to a Java class Complex that implements complex numbers. This is packaged with the language extension. The type representation typerep of complex numbers is constructed by the production complexTypeRep. The production complexLiteral specifies complex number literals. It defines such expressions to have the type (typerep) of

```
grammar edu:umn:cs:melt:java14:exts:complex ;
import   edu:umn:cs:melt:java14;
terminal Complex_t 'complex' ;
concrete production complexType  t::Type ::= 'complex'
 { t.typerep = complexTypeRep();  forwards to ''Complex number class'' }
concrete production complex_literal
c::Expr ::= 'complex' '(' r::Expr ',' i::Expr ')'
 { c.pp = "complex (" ++ r.pp ++ "," ++ i.pp ++ ")" ;
   c.errors = ... check that r and i have type double ... ;
   forwards to ''new Complex( r, i)'' ;     }

abstract production complexTypeRep  tr::TypeRep ::=
 { d.superTypes := [ mkComplexToComplex() ] ;  }
aspect production doubleTypeRep    d::TypeRep ::=
 { d.superTypes <- [ mkDoubleToComplex() ] ;  }
abstract production mkDoubleToComplex  t::SubTypeRes ::=
 { t.isSubType = true ;   t.supertype = complexTypeRep() ;
   t.converted = complex_literal(''complex'', ''('', t.toConvert,
                            '','', ''0.0'', '')''); }
```

Fig. 7. Portion of complex number language extension specification

Complex numbers (complexTypeRep()) and checks that r and i have the correct type. The definition of the **errors** attribute is omitted here but it uses pattern matching as was done earlier in the **while** loop in Figure 4.

Adding New Subtype Relationships: To achieve a natural, close integration of the extension and the host language, the host language AG provides mechanisms for specifying new subtype relations and means for run-time conversion. Host language productions like the assignment production utilize this information to implement the complex number translation steps illustrated in Section 2.

The aspect production doubleTypeRep in Figure 7 adds a new super type to Java doubles. This is realized by contributing a new *super type* element (of type SubTypeRes, constructed by production mkDoubleToComplex) to the collection attribute superTypes that decorates TypeReps. The information in each *super type* in doubleTypeRep's superTypes is used by the Java AG function subTypeCheck to determine if doubleTypeRep is a subtype of another specified type. If so, the function returns the super type (SubTypeRes) tree, which includes functionality for run-time conversion, if needed. The mkDoubleToComplex production builds a tree that sets the isSubType attribute to *true* and the supertype attributes to the complex number TypeRep. It plays the role of a function that creates the Expr tree that performs the run-time conversion of a yet-to-be-specified input double-typed Expr. The inherited attribute toConvert plays the role of the function input and the synthesized attribute converted plays the role of the output. It is set to the complex literal constructed from the input double expression and the literal 0.0. The terminal symbols and literal 0.0 are shown as strings in the stylized definition of converted. In the actual specification they need to be properly typed terminals and Expr nonterminals.

```
grammar edu:umn:cs:melt:java14 ;
nonterminal SubTypeRes ;
synthesized attribute superType :: TypeRep ;
synthesized attribute converted :: Expr ;
inherited attribute toConvert :: Expr ;

concrete production assign
a::StmtExpr ::= lhs::Expr '=' rhs::Expr ';'  {
 a.pp = lhs.pp ++ " = " ++ rhs.pp ++ ";"  ;
 local attribute res :: SubTypeRes ;
 res = subTypeCheck(lhs.typerep,rhs.typerep);
 res.toConvert = rhs ;

 a.errors = if length(transformed) == 1 then [ ]
      else if length(transformed) == 0 then [...type error...]
      else [... internal error, multiple translations ....];
 production attribute transformed :: [ StmtExpr ] collect with ++ ;
 transformed := if ! res.isSubType  then [ ]
               else [ converted_assign(lhs, res.converted) ] ;
 forwards to if length (transformed) != 1 then skip()
            else head (transformed) ;                        }
abstract production converted_assign  a::StmtExpr::=l::Expr r::Expr {...}
```

Fig. 8. Portion of Java host language specification

To see how this information is used, consider the host language assignment production `assign` specified in Figure 8. It calls `subTypeCheck` to check if the type of the expression on the right hand side (`rhs.typerep`) is a subtype of the type of the left hand side expression (`lhs.typerep`). The synthesized attribute `converted` and inherited attribute `toConvert`, both of type `Expr` act as the function described above that creates the expression tree whose type is `lhs.typerep` and performs any run-time conversion on the `rhs` to give it the type of `lhs`. For Java 1.4 classes, `res.converted` is the same tree as `res.toConvert` since no source-level conversion are needed. This provides the extension point or "hook" that language extensions that introduce new types will use.

The `assign` production forwards to an assignment in which the run-time conversion is applied to the `rhs` tree. This forwarded-to assignment is created by the `converted_assign` production. The production attribute `transformed` is a collection that holds the trees to which the initial assignment `assign` will forward. If `lhs` is a subtype of `rhs` then the new assignment is added to the list, otherwise it is initially empty. If `transformed` has exactly one element, then no errors are generated. If it is empty, then the `lhs` and `rhs` are not compatible. It is possible for aspect productions on `assign` to add new elements to `transformed` (as the autoboxing/unboxing extension does below) so that if there is more than one element, then an error is raised since a decision cannot be made as to which one to forward to. If `transformed` has exactly one element, then that is what

```
aspect production assign  a::StmtExpr ::= lhs::Expr '=' rhs::Expr ';'
{ transformed <- if match(lhs.typerep, getTypeRep("Integer")) &&
                  match (rhs.typerep, intTypeRep())
  then [converted_assign ( 1, ''new Integer ( rhs )'')] else [ ]; }
```

Fig. 9. Portion of the autoboxing/unboxing extension specification

`assign` forwards to – otherwise an error will have been raised and it forwards to the `skip` statement. Similar productions for other "copy" operations (parameter passing) exist in the Java AG and can be similarly extended.

The definition of the host language assignment is not trivial - but the complexity arises because it is designed to be extended later and we want the definitions of the extensions to be the simpler ones to write. If there is no discipline in adding new elements to the subtype relationship, then extension composition could introduce non-trivial circular subtype relations. This can be avoided if extension writers adhere to the guideline of not adding a set of subtype relations in which a host type is both the subtype and the supertype.

Autoboxing/Unboxing. Java 1.5 automatic boxing and unboxing can also be added as an extension to the Java 1.4 host language. This is done by adding to the **transformed** collection attribute on the **assign** production in Figure 8. The aspect production in Figure 9 adds the boxing of primitive type **int** to class **Integer** by checking that **lhs** and **rhs** have the appropriate types. When they do, the **transformed** attribute in **assign** will contain only the assignment constructed by the **converted_assign** production and the use of the **Integer** class constructor shown in the contribution to the attribute. (The <- operator adds the value of the following expression to the collection attribute, folding up all such values using the specified **collect with** operator, ++ in the case of **transformed**.) Note that this production is not adding to the subtype relationship, but simply overloading the assignment operator when **lhs** and **rhs** have the specified types. Overloading of other operators is accomplished similarly.

3.3   Using and Extending the Java Environment

Semantic analysis performed on a node in the syntax tree often requires information from another node. For example type-checking a variable expression requires information from the syntax tree node where the variable was declared. Similarly, access to an object might depend on its permission level, again set on its declaration. Attribute grammars pass such information around the abstract syntax tree using a combination of synthesized and inherited attributes.

In ableJ, declarations for the environment are collected using the synthesized attribute **defs** which is a list of environment items (**EnvItem**). These are passed up the tree up to a production that defines a new local scope, such as the enhanced-for production in Figure 6. It adds the definitions to the inherited environment attribute **env** that is passed down the tree for use by, for

```
nonterminal EnvItem ;
synthesized attribute env_items :: [ EnvItem ];
nonterminal Scope with scope_type, env_items;
synthesized attribute defs :: [ EnvItem ] ;
inherited attribute env :: [ Scope ];
abstract production varBinding
e::EnvItem ::= name::String  dcl::TypeRep {...}

function addLocalScope
[Scope] ::= items::[EnvItem] enclosing_env::[Scope] {...}

-- lookUp returns typereps of name from nearest matching enclosing scope
function lookUpVar [ TypeRep ] ::= name::String env::[ Scope ] {...}
```

Fig. 10. The API of the ableJ environment

example, variable references. In the enhanced-for production, the following attribute definition performs this task:

```
body.env=addLocalScope([varBinding(id.lexeme,t.typerep)], f.env);
```

The varBinding production is used to create the data-structure binding the
name of the identifier to its type representation. (In practice, more information
than just the identifier's type is needed, but we have omitted those details here.)
Figure 10 contains a partial specification of the nonterminals, productions, and
functions used to pass declaration information to the parts of the syntax tree
where it is used. It is important that language extensions, such as the enhanced-
for, can contribute to this process.

The env attribute is a list of scopes; each stores bindings of various kinds for
a particular scope in the object program as a list of EnvItems in the attribute
env_items, as seen in Figure 10. These bindings are represented by trees created
by different productions, varBinding being one example. The environment contains scopes for top level declarations in the current file, declarations from other
files in the same package, single-type named imports, and on-demand imports.
Other scopes may be created and added to when needed, for example within
methods and inner class definitions.

While the enhanced-for loop only uses existing host language constructs for
manipulating the environment, other extensions may want to add new kinds of
information to the environment. The SQL extension extends the environment to
contain the type representations of the tables and columns defined in the import
table constructs shown above. As the environment is defined, the specifications
in the enhanced-for loop and the SQL extension work together so that an SQL
query enclosed in an enhanced-for loop can extract from the environment the
definitions added by any import table constructs.

Figure 11 shows a small portion of the Silver specification of the SQL language
extension. Of interest is that the import-table construct adds to the environment
(via defs) a variable binding with a new kind of TypeRep tree constructed by the

```
grammar edu:umn:cs:melt:java14:exts:sql ;
import   edu:umn:cs:melt:java14 ;

concrete production sqlImport
s::Stmt ::= 'import' 'table' t::Id '[' columns::SqlColTypes ']' ';' {
 s.defs = [ varBinding (t.lexeme, tableTypeRep (columns.defs)) ];   }

abstract production tableTypeRep  tr::TypeRep ::= col::[EnvItem]  { ... }
inherited attribute sql_env :: [EnvItem];
concrete production sqlQuery
e::Expr ::= 'using' c::Conn 'query' '{' q::SqlQuery '}' { ... }

concrete production sqlSelect
q::SqlQuery::='SELECT' flds::SqlExprs 'FROM' t::Id 'WHERE' cond::SqlExpr{
 local attribute result :: [ TypeRep ] ;
 result = lookUp (table.lexeme, q.env);
 q.errors = flds.errors ++ cond.errors ++
 ...ensure that result has length 1 indicating precisely 1 decl for t...;
 columns = if length(result) == 1
           then case (head(result)).typerep of
                tableTypeRep (cols) => cols
                | _                  => [ ]; -- error raised above.
           else [ ] ;
 flds.sql_env = columns;    cond.sql_env = columns;
 cond.env = q.env;          }
```

Fig. 11. Portion of Silver specification of the SQL extension

the production tableTypeRep defined in the SQL grammar. This information propagates up the syntax tree through host language defined productions to an enclosing scope-defining production that adds this information to an inherited env attribute. From here, it flows down the tree, through the sqlQuery construct to a sqlSelect construct which uses the lookUpVar function to get the list of type representations bound to t in the nearest enclosing scope that binds t. This list should have length 1, otherwise an error is generated and columns will be the empty list. The local attribute columns is a simplified SQL environment sql_env built as a list of EnvItems that are passed to the fields flds and condition cond.

The SQL extension uses pattern matching to extract the value for columns from the TypeRep bound to t. The use of the production name tableTypeRep which is defined in this grammar and is not visible to other extensions ensures that the value extracted is what the SQL extension added in the sqlImport production. Although other extensions may inappropriately remove bindings from an environment they may not subtly alter its contents in a manner that is undetected by the SQL extension. Similarly, since the production tableTypeRep is unknown to other extensions, any information contained in the type representation is not accessible to other extensions. This ensures that values added to the environment by one extension construct (SQL import-table) are passed correctly to another construct (SQL query) even if they pass through constructs defined in a different extension (enhanced-for). Extensions may incorrectly remove elements from the environment, but this type of mistake is dramatic and tends to arise in all uses of the offending extensions.

4   Composition of Language Extensions

4.1   Composing Host Language and Extension Specifications

The declarative syntax and specifications in Silver are easily composed to form the specification of a new extended language. Figure 12 contains the Silver specification for Java extended with the SQL and the computational geometry extension that implements the randomized linear perturbation (rlp) scheme for handling data degeneracies in geometric algorithms. The details of the features provided by the rlp extension are not of interest here. This composed extended language has features to support both the domains of relational database queries and computational geometry. The import statements import the grammar specifications of the named Silver module. The with syntax clauses import the concrete syntax specifications from the named modules to build the parser for the extended language. The main production is similar in intent to the C main function; here it delegates to the main production java_main in the java14 host specification. The parse value passed to java_main is the parser constructed from the concrete syntax specifications imported into the module. This is a boiler-plate Silver specification that can easily enough be generated from the names of the extension grammar modules which are to be imported into the Java 1.4 host language.

```
grammar edu:umn:cs:melt:composed:java_sql_cg ;
import core ;
import edu:umn:cs:melt:java14 with syntax ;
import edu:umn:cs:melt:java14:exts:sql with syntax ;
import edu:umn:cs:melt:java14:exts:rlp with syntax ;

abstract production main top::Main ::= args::String
{ forwards to java_main(args, parse) ;   }
```

Fig. 12. Composed language Silver specification

4.2   Issues in Composition

Even though the process of composing language specifications, for both concrete syntax and AG-based semantics, is a straightforward union of the components and can be performed automatically, there may be no guarantee that the resulting language specification is well-defined. For example, an undisciplined composition of concrete syntax productions may lead to ambiguous grammars or may introduce conflicts (shift-reduce or reduce-reduce) into the parse tables for LR-style parsers. In terms of semantics, combining AG specifications may result in circular AGs in which an attribute instance may be defined such that its value depends on itself. If programmers are going to compose extended languages from the composable, modular language extensions proposed here, then detecting or better yet preventing these sorts of problems becomes critical. There are some analyses that can be performed at different times that provide some assurance that the composed language is well-defined.

The table in Figure 13 identifies tools and techniques that perform some analysis and points in time in which they are performed. The first two analyses listed along the top relate to syntax specifications, the last two to semantics. Analysis can be performed by the extension designer during development, it can be performed when the extensions are composed (perhaps by a programmer) with the host language specification, or it can be performed dynamically – during parsing or AG evaluation. (We do not consider analysis during execution of a program written in an extended language.) These analyses may differ for different tools and techniques and are thus not precisely the same (or even applicable) for all approaches. The table is meant to provide a framework for comparing approaches and understanding the goal of composability in extensible languages.

If an analysis can be performed when the extension designer is implementing an extension (at design time), then information from that analysis may be used by the designer to fix any discovered problems. Alternatively, an analysis can be performed when the set of extensions is composed with the host language. These analyses may prevent a programmer from using an ill-defined language, but this analysis may be done too late as the person directing the composition of the extension may not be the extension designer and may not be able to make use of the information to fix the problem.

analyses → points in time ↓	lexical determinism	syntactic determinism	AG non-circularity	termination of tree construction
Ext. design	Copper	Copper		
Ext. composition		Yacc	Knuth [15], Vogt [32]	
Parse/ AG Eval.	GLR	GLR	JastAddII	

Fig. 13. Analyses and points in time for analysis

A language recognizer, traditionally a scanner, exhibits *lexical determinism* if for non-erroneous input it returns exactly one token. A recognizer, traditionally a parser, is *syntactically deterministic* if for non-erroneous input it returns exactly one syntax tree [15,32]. An AG specification is *non-circular* if for any syntactically valid syntax tree, no attribute instance has a circular definition. Similar analyses exist for AGs with forwarding [26]. A general termination analysis may ensure that a finite number of trees are created (via forwarding or in higher-order attributes in AG systems, or in term rewriting systems).

Visser's scannerless generalized LR (GLR) parsers [30] do not have a separate scanner but parse down to the character level. For any context free grammar (including ambiguous ones) a GLR parser can be created that will parse any valid phrase in the language of the grammar and return all syntax trees corresponding to the phrase – for ambiguous grammars more than one tree may be returned for some phrases. Thus, one does not know until parse time if a single tree will be generated for a correct input phrase. Disambiguation filters [23] can be written to filter out undesired trees on ambiguous parses but there is no static guarantee for the grammar designer that the specified filters ensure syntactic determinism. Yacc [13] is deterministic and an analysis at composition time exists, but LALR(1) parsers are somewhat brittle in that seemingly innocuous additions to a grammar may cause conflicts. This problem is exacerbated when multiple extensions that add new syntax are combined. Thus, Yacc-like tools may not be suitable for extensible languages. In Section 4.3 we describe an integrated parsing and scanning system (called Copper) that places some restrictions on the type of concrete syntax that extension designers can specify. These ensure at extension design time that no conflicts are created when the host language syntax and syntax from other extensions observing the restrictions are composed.

For attribute evaluation, circularity/definedness tests are known for standard AGs [15], higher-order AGs [32], and AGs with forwarding [26]. These can be performed when grammars are composed, but are in essence whole-program analyses that require examining the entire grammar. JastAddII [7] is a Java-based AG system that employs reference attributes [11]. These can be thought of as attributes that contain pointers (references) to other nodes in the syntax tree and have been shown to be especially useful in linking a variable reference node to its declaration. There is no static analysis to ensure that such grammars are not circular however and thus JastAddII uses a dynamic check. This system has also been used to build an extensible Java 1.4 compiler. The lack of a static check may be less critical than in the case of parsing. Adding new constructs/productions tend to not add new types of attribute dependencies and thus AGs are much less "brittle" and more easily extended than LALR(1) grammars.

Also of interest are analyses that ensure that a finite number of trees are constructed via forwarding or as higher-order attributes. We are investigating approaches which extract rewrite rules from the attribute grammar specification in such a way that if the rewrite rules can be shown to terminate, then forwarding will terminate. The approach then determines orderings on term constructors (productions in AGs) to show that the extracted rules terminate. Such an analysis combined with the circularity/definedness analysis provides a guarantee of termination during attribute evaluation.

4.3   Parser-Context Based Lexical Disambiguation

Our integrated parser/scanner system (called Copper) uses a standard LR parsing algorithm that is slightly modified in the manner in which it calls the scanner: it passes to the scanner the set of terminal symbols that are "valid lookahead" for the current state of the parser, *viz.*, those that have non-error entries (shift, reduce, or accept) in the parse table for the current parser state. Simply put, the parser passes out what it *can* match and gets back what *does* match. The scanner's use of the parser state for disambiguation allows the parser to determine what terminal a certain string matches based on the context.

Crafting the concrete syntax specification of an extension that when combined with the concrete syntax specification of the host language results in a deterministic LR specification is not trivial but can be accomplished by the extension designer. Our goal, during composition of several extensions with the host language, is to *maintain* the deterministic nature of the grammar. This characteristic is maintained by restricting the type of syntax that can be added in the extension and depends on the integrated nature of the parser and scanner. The parser-context based lexical disambiguation is key to the process.

The analysis that an extension, say E_1, will not introduce shift-reduce or reduce-reduce conflicts in the parse table of a language composed from the host and extensions E_1 and others, say $E_2, ..., E_n$, is based on an examination of the parser table of the host language and the parse table of the host composed just with E_1. The details of this analysis will appear in a technical report [29], but the essence of the analysis is that the extension E_1 is allowed to (i) add new states in the parser table that are used solely in parsing extension constructs and (ii) add a restricted set of items to existing host states that only allow a shift-action to a new extension-added state. The *critical characteristic* of the composed parse table is that the states are partitioned so that every state is associated with exactly one grammar: either the host or one of the extensions.

Each production introduced by extension E that has a host nonterminal, say H, on the left side must have a right hand side that begins with what is called a "marking token" for that extension. The marking tokens are used to obtain the partitioning of the parser states as described above. These are not to be referenced elsewhere in the extension. For example, in the SQL extension the concrete production sqlQuery with signature Expr ::= 'using' Conn 'query' '{' SqlQuery '}' the marking token is 'using'. These productions provide the shift-action, based on the marking token, mentioned above that take the parser from a "host state" to an "extension state".

Additionally, restrictions are made on "back references" to host language nonterminals on the right hand side of extension productions. If these restrictions are not followed, the analysis is likely to fail. Each extension production with a host nonterminal H on the right-hand side should adhere to one of these two forms:

- $E \rightarrow \mu^L H \mu^R$, where μ^L is a host or extension terminal such that E does not derive $\mu^L X$ for any $X \neq H \mu^R$, and μ^R is a host terminal, preferably one that would be commonly found after an H-expression, such as a right parenthesis after a math expression.
- $E \rightarrow \mu^L H$, where μ^L is under the same restrictions as before, and the H is when derived invariably at the end of the extension expression — *e.g.*, the loop body in an extension defining the enhanced-for loop.

The goal of these restrictions is to limit the ways that extensions can affect the host language parse table so that conflicts are not introduced. Because ableJ provides mechanisms for overloading the operator symbols, the syntax specifications of most extensions (such as the SQL extension) meet these restrictions.

But due to the partitioning of the LALR(1) DFA described above, in a context-filtered system, most extension terminals will not show up in the same context as a host terminal; for example, in our SQL extension, as only host states have Java identifiers in their valid lookahead and only SQL extension states have the keyword `select`, the two tokens are never together in the valid lookahead set of any parser state. Hence, no disambiguation is needed between `select` and Java identifiers. Thus, "select" can still be used as a variable name in the Java code (but not as a column name in the SQL query.)

It is worth noting that even if extensions do not pass these tests, the integrated parser/scanner approach has, in our experience, been much less brittle than standard LALR(1) approaches since it avoids many of the lexical ambiguities that would exist in traditional disjoint approaches. In fact the set of grammars that are deterministic in the integrated approach is strictly larger than those that are classified as LALR(1). Thus, performing the deterministic check at composition time is more likely to succeed. The enhanced-for loop production shown in Figure 6 does not meet the above restrictions because it does not introduce an extension defined marking token but instead reuses the host language defined `'for'` terminal. Yet in composing several different extensions this production has not introduced any conflicts into the parser table. Additional details are available in the technical report [29].

The key to checking for lexical determinism is the partitioning of parser states into states associated with the host or a single extension grammar. This restricts the type of lexical conflicts (terminals with overlapping defining regular expressions) to one of two types. The first type is a conflict between an extension defined terminal and a host language defined terminal or another terminal defined in the same extension. In this case, the extension writer can use several techniques to resolve the ambiguity. Copper provides several precedence setting constructs and a means for writing Silver expressions to perform the disambiguation at parse time. We will not go into these details here; the key point is that the extension writer can be made aware of the ambiguity at extension design time and fix it. This disambiguation is then maintained during composition.

The second possible type of conflict is between the marking tokens of two different extensions. These are unavoidable and must be resolved "on the fly" by the programmer. We introduce the notion of *transparent prefixes* to enable the programmer to do this without knowledge of the language grammars. Transparent prefixes allow a disambiguating prefix (typically based on the name of the extension) to precede the actual lexeme of tokens in the program, without being visible to the parser. This prefix then directs the scanner to recognize the following lexeme as coming from that grammar. This approach is motivated by the use of fully qualified names in Java in which classes with the same name from different packages are distinguished by specifying the package name.

5   Discussion

There have been many efforts to build tools for extensible compilers for Java and other languages. Some of these, like ableJ, are attribute grammar-based. Others are based on traditional rewrite systems or pass-based processors.

Attribute Grammar Based Tools: Much previous work has investigated the use of attribute grammars as framework for the modular specifications of languages [9,14,8,1,20]. There are also several well-developed AG-based language specification tools: such as LRC [16], JastAddII [7], and Eli [10]. These systems implement transformations in different ways, some are functional while others are object-oriented. They do not support forwarding and thus the modularity and ease-of-composition of language features specified as AG fragments is achieved by writing attribute definitions that "glue" new fragments into the host language AG. JastAddII and Eli do not have the general purpose features of pattern matching and polymorphic lists in Silver and instead use a "back-door" to their implementation languages (Java and C) for general-purpose computations.

JastAddII [7] is based on rewritable reference attribute grammars and has been used to develop an extensible Java 1.5 compiler [6]. To the best of our knowledge Silver and JastAddII are the only AG systems that allow for the implicit specification of semantics by translation to a host language. JastAddII does so by the application of (destructive) rewrite rules. But since rewriting of a subtree takes place before attributes may be accessed from the that tree, one cannot both explicitly and implicitly specify a construct's semantics. For example, consider the enhanced-for loop extension described in Section 3.2. With JastAddII, any semantic analysis is performed only after rewriting is done and the equivalent host language for-loop is generated. Thus all semantics are implicit (except for the attributes that are computed during rewriting that may be used to guide rewriting). With forwarding, rewriting is non-destructive. Extensions and forwards-to trees exist side-by-side allowing some semantics to be specified explicitly by the extension while others are specified implicitly via forwarding. On the other hand, the rewrite rules in JastAddII are more general than forwarding and can be used in a wider of variety of language processing applications, such as using rewrite rules to implement optimizing transformations. In Silver, such transformations must be encoded as definitions of higher-order attributes.

Other Approaches to Extensibility: Embedded domain-specific languages [12] and macro systems (traditional syntactic, hygienic and programmable [33]) allow the addition of new constructs to a language but lack an effective way to specify semantic analysis and report domain specific error messages. However, some modern macro systems have more advanced error-reporting facilities, e.g. [2]. Traditional pass-based approaches such as Polyglot [17] require an explicit specification of the order in which analysis and translation passes are performed on the syntax tree. Requiring this level of implementation level detail to compose extensions is what we hope to avoid.

JavaBorg is an extensible Java tool that uses MetaBorg [4], an embedding tool that allows one to extend a host language by adding concrete syntax for objects. It is based on the Stratego/XT rewriting system [31] that allows for the specification of conditional abstract syntax tree rewriting rules to process programs. In addition, it allows for the specification of composable rewrite strategies that allow the user to program the manner in which the rewrites are performed. These rewrites can be used to perform generative as well as optimizing transformations – both general purpose and domain-specific. Rules and strategies may be bundled into libraries and composed. MetaBorg is well-suited for performing transformative optimizations since its rewrites are destructive and performed in-place. However, specifying semantic analyses like error checking, even when using dynamically generated rules and annotations [19], is less straightforward than using attributes. Although these can perform the same functions as synthesized and inherited attributes, there is no static analysis to ensure type-safety and termination (circularity/definedness [26] analysis) as there is with attribute grammars. It is also not clear that different extensions can be so easily combined. MetaBorg uses scannerless GLR parsers [30].

Intentional Programming originated in Microsoft Research and proposed forwarding in a non-attribute grammar setting. The original and more recent work [21] uses a highly-developed structure editor for program input since traditional LR parsing of extensible languages was not seen as viable. But our integrated parsing/scanning approach [29] suggests that deterministic LR-parsing methods are viable. Similarly, other work [5] based on meta-object protocols for language extension uses the GUI facilities in Eclipse for program input.

6 Ongoing Work and Conclusions

The ableJ framework aims to report all errors that a traditional Java compiler would report. As of this writing there are two types of errors that are not yet reported. The first is definite assignment errors, which may be handled by an an extension to Silver that constructs control flow graphs for imperative programs and performs data flow analysis by model checking these graphs [28]. Second, a relatively few productions in the Java AG specification propagate the **errors** attribute up the syntax tree but do not add their own errors. These are being completed. We are building a version of Java 1.5, in which most new constructs (other than generics) [2] are specified as modular language extensions to Java 1.4.

One reason that libraries are a successful means for introducing new abstractions in functional languages, is that the programmer can freely import the set of libraries that address his or her particular problem at hand. It is our belief that for language extension techniques (either those proposed here or others described in Section 5) to have real-world impact they must be composable in a manner that is similar to libraries. In this paper we have shown that it is possible to implement languages and *composable* language extensions so that new,

---

[2] While nearly all of Java 1.5 generics can be translated to Java 1.4 by type-erasure, methods with type parameters in the return type are an exception and must be either translated to bytecode or to incorrect Java 1.4 code (with method-overloading errors) from which it may be possible to generate executable bytecode.

customized, domain-adapted languages can be created from the host language and selected language extensions with no implementation level knowledge of the extension.

An important area of future work centers on means for ensuring, either by analysis of specifications or by restricting the types of extensions that can be described, that language extensions that have the look-and-feel of the host language can be easily composed by the programmer.

References

1. Adams, S.R.: Modular Grammars for Programming Language Prototyping. PhD thesis, University of Southampton, Department of Elec. and Comp. Sci. UK (1993)
2. Batory, D., Lofaso, D., Smaragdakis, Y.: JTS: tools for implementing domain-specific languages. In: Proc. 5th Intl. Conf. on Software Reuse, pp. 2–5. IEEE Computer Society Press, Los Alamitos (1998)
3. Boyland, J.T.: Remote attribute grammars. J. ACM 52(4), 627–687 (2005)
4. Bravenboer, M., Visser, E.: Concrete syntax for objects: domain-specific language embedding and assimilation without restrictions. In: Proc. of OOPSLA '04 Conf. pp. 365–383 (2004)
5. Eisenberg, A.D., Kiczales, G.: Expressive programs through presentation extension. In: AOSD '07: Proc. of the 6th Intl. Conf. on Aspect-oriented Software Development, pp. 73–84 (2007)
6. Ekman, T.: Extensible Compiler Construction. PhD thesis, Lund University, Lund, Sweden (2006)
7. Ekman, T., Hedin, G.: Rewritable reference attributed grammars. In: Odersky, M. (ed.) ECOOP 2004. LNCS, vol. 3086, pp. 144–169. Springer, Heidelberg (2004)
8. Farrow, R., Marlowe, T.J., Yellin, D.M.: Composable attribute grammars. In: 19th ACM Symp. on Prin. of Prog. Lang. pp. 223–234. ACM Press, New York (1992)
9. Ganzinger, H.: Increasing modularity and language-independency in automatically generated compilers. Science of Computer Programing 3(3), 223–278 (1983)
10. Gray, R.W., Heuring, V.P., Levi, S.P., Sloane, A.M., Waite, W.M.: Eli: A complete, flexible compiler construction system. CACM 35, 121–131 (1992)
11. Hedin, G.: Reference attribute grammars. Informatica 24(3), 301–317 (2000)
12. Hudak, P.: Building domain-specific embedded languages. ACM Computing Surveys, 28(4es) (1996)
13. Johnson, S.: Yacc - yet another compiler compiler. Technical Report 32, Bell Laboratories (July 1975)
14. Kastens, U., Waite, W.M.: Modularity and reusability in attribute grammars. Acta Informatica 31, 601–627 (1994)
15. Knuth, D.E.: Semantics of context-free languages. Mathematical Systems Theory, 2(2) 127–145 (1968) Corrections in 5, 95–96 (1971)
16. Kuiper, M., J., S.: LRC — a generator for incremental language-oriented tools. In: Koskimies, K. (ed.) CC 1998 and ETAPS 1998. LNCS, vol. 1383, pp. 298–301. Springer, Heidelberg (1998)
17. Nystrom, N., Clarkson, M.R., Myer, A.C.: Polyglot: An extensible compiler framework for Java. In: Hedin, G. (ed.) CC 2003 and ETAPS 2003. LNCS, vol. 2622, pp. 138–152. Springer, Heidelberg (2003)
18. Odersky, M., Wadler, P.: Pizza into Java: translating theory into practice. In: Proceedings of the 24th ACM SIGPLAN-SIGACT symposium on Principles of programming languages, pp. 146–159. ACM Press, New York (1997)

19. Olmos, K., Visser, E.: Composing source-to-source data-flow transformations with rewriting strategies and dependent dynamic rewrite rules. In: Bodik, R. (ed.) CC 2005. LNCS, vol. 3443, pp. 204–220. Springer, Heidelberg (2005)
20. Saraiva, J., Swierstra, D.: Generic Attribute Grammars. In: 2nd Workshop on Attribute Grammars and their Applications, pp. 185–204 (1999)
21. Simonyi, C., Christerson, M., Clifford, S.: Intentional software. SIGPLAN Not. 41(10), 451–464 (2006)
22. Thompson, J.M., Heimdahl, M.P., Miller, S.P.: Specification based prototyping for embedded systems. In: Nierstrasz, O., Lemoine, M. (eds.) Software Engineering - ESEC/FSE '99. LNCS, vol. 1687, Springer, Heidelberg (1999)
23. van den Brand, M., Scheerder, J., Vinju, J., Visser, E.: Disambiguation filters for scannerless generalized LR parsers. In: Horspool, R.N. (ed.) CC 2002 and ETAPS 2002. LNCS, vol. 2304, pp. 143–158. Springer, Heidelberg (2002)
24. Van Wyk, E., Bodin, D., Huntington, P.: Adding syntax and static analysis to libraries via extensible compilers and language extensions. In: Proc. of LCSD 2006, Library-Centric Software Design (2006)
25. Van Wyk, E., Bodin, D., Krishnan, L., Gao, J.: Silver: an extensible attribute grammar system. In: Proc. of LDTA 2007, 7th Workshop on Language Descriptions, Tools, and Analysis (2007)
26. Van Wyk, E., de Moor, O., Backhouse, K., Kwiatkowski, P.: Forwarding in attribute grammars for modular language design. In: Horspool, R.N. (ed.) CC 2002 and ETAPS 2002. LNCS, vol. 2304, pp. 128–142. Springer, Heidelberg (2002)
27. Van Wyk, E., Johnson, E.: Composable language extensions for computational geometry: a case study. In: Proc. 40th Hawaii Intl' Conf. on System Sciences (2007)
28. Van Wyk, E., Krishnan, L.: Using verified data-flow analysis-based optimizations in attribute grammars. In: Proc. Intl. Workshop on Compiler Optimization Meets Compiler Verification (COCV) (April 2006)
29. Van Wyk, E., Schwerdfeger, A.: Context-aware scanning: Specification, implementation, and applications. Technical Report 07-012, Univ. of Minnesota (April 2007), Available at http://www.cs.umn.edu
30. Visser, E.: Syntax Definition for Language Prototyping. PhD thesis, University of Amsterdam (1997)
31. Visser, E.: Program transformation with Stratego/XT: Rules, strategies, tools, and systems in Stratego/XT-0.9. In: Lengauer, C., Batory, D., Consel, C., Odersky, M. (eds.) Domain-Specific Program Generation. LNCS, vol. 3016, pp. 216–238. Springer, Heidelberg (2004)
32. Vogt, H., Swierstra, S.D., Kuiper, M.F.: Higher-order attribute grammars. In: ACM PLDI Conf, pp. 131–145. ACM Press, New York (1990)
33. Weise, D., Crew, R.: Programmable syntax macros. ACM SIGPLAN Notices 28(6) (1993)

Metamodel Adaptation and Model Co-adaptation

Guido Wachsmuth

Humboldt-Universität zu Berlin
Unter den Linden 6
D-10099 Berlin, Germany
guwac@gk-metrik.de

Abstract. Like other software artefacts, metamodels evolve over time. We propose a transformational approach to assist metamodel evolution by stepwise adaptation. In the first part of the paper, we adopt ideas from grammar engineering to define several semantics- and instance-preservation properties in terms of metamodel relations. This part is not restricted to any metamodel formalism. In the second part, we present a library of QVT Relations for the stepwise adaptation of MOF compliant metamodels. Transformations from this library separate preservation properties. We distinguish three kinds of adaptation according to these properties; namely refactoring, construction, and destruction. Co-adaptation of models is discussed with respect to instance-preservation. In most cases, co-adaptation is achieved automatically. Finally, we point out applications in the areas of metamodel design, implementation, refinement, maintenance, and recovery.

1 Introduction

Metamodel Evolution. In Model-Driven Architecture (MDA) [1], metamodels are a fundamental building block. Models occurring in a MDA process comply to metamodels, constraints are expressed at the meta-level, and model transformations are based on source and target metamodels. Like other software artefacts, metamodels evolve over time [2] due to several reasons: During design, alternative metamodel versions are developed and well-known solutions are customised for new applications. During implementation, metamodels are adapted to a concrete metamodel formalism supported by a tool. During maintenance, errors in a metamodel are corrected. Furthermore, parts of the metamodel are redesigned due to a better understanding or to facilitate reuse.

Example 1 (Petri net metamodel evolution). Fig. 1 illustrates the evolution of a metamodel for Petri nets. A Petri net consists of any number of places and transitions. Each transition has at least one input and one output place. The initial metamodel μ_0 captures these facts. Since a Petri net without any places and transitions is of no avail, we restrict Net to comprise at least one place and one transition. This results in a new metamodel μ_1. In a next step, we make arcs

E. Ernst (Ed.): ECOOP 2007, LNAI 4609, pp. 600–624, 2007.

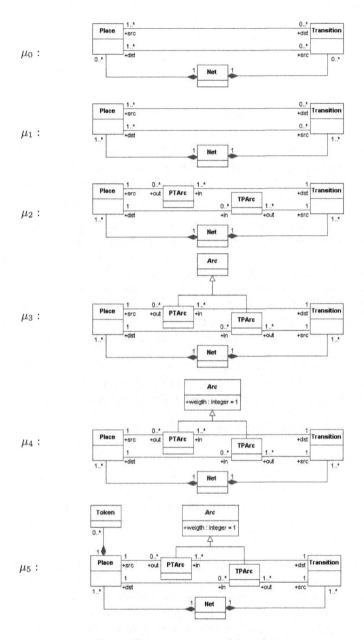

Fig. 1. Petri net metamodel evolution

between places and transitions explicit. The extraction of PTArc and TPArc yields μ_2. This step might be useful if we want to annotate metaclasses with means for graphical or textual description in order to assist automatic tool generation. As PTArc and TPArc both represent arcs, we state this in μ_3 with a generalisation

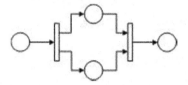

Fig. 2. Simple Petri net

Arc. In an extended Petri net formalism, arcs might be annotated with weights. We can easily reproduce this extension by introducing a new attribute `weight` in μ_4. Until now, we cover only static aspects of Petri nets. To model dynamic aspects, places need to be marked with tokens as captured in μ_5.

Metamodel evolution is usually performed manually by stepwise adaptation. In this paper, we provide a theoretical basis to study the effects of metamodel evolution in terms of metamodel relations. We employ well-defined evolutionary steps for metamodels compliant to OMG's Meta Object Facility (MOF) [3]. The steps are implemented as transformations in QVT Relations, the relational part of OMG's Query-View-Transformation language [4]. Each step forms a *metamodel adaptation* and is classified according to its semantics- and instance-preservation properties. This work is mainly inspired by the ideas of object-oriented refactoring [5,6,7] and grammar adaptation [8,9].

Co-evolution. Models need to co-evolve in order to remain compliant with the metamodel [2]. Without co-evolution, these artefacts become invalid.

Example 2 (Petri net model co-evolution). Fig. 2 contains a simple example of a Petri net. Models of this Petri net compliant to metamodels introduced in Example 1 are given in Figure 3. These models co-evolve with their metamodels. While the first model ι_0 is compliant to μ_0 and μ_1, new metaclasses in μ_2 enforce new instance objects in ι_1, which complies with μ_3, too. The introduction of `weight` in μ_4 necessitates the introduction of default values in the corresponding model ι_2. This model is also an instance of μ_5 because it provides an empty marking.

Like metamodel evolution, co-evolution is typically performed manually. This is an error-prone task leading to inconsistencies between the metamodel and related artefacts. From the fields of software architecture and language definition, we learnt that these inconsistencies usually lead to irremediable erosion where artefacts are not longer updated [2]. In this paper, we aim at automatic co-evolution steps deduced from well-defined evolution steps [10]. This *co-adaptation* prevents inconsistencies and metamodel erosion.

Transformational Approach. In this paper, we propose a transformational approach to assist metamodel evolution by stepwise adaptation. Transformational metamodel adaptation has several advantages over manual ad hoc adaptation. First, changes become explicit. Thus, transformations provide documentation and traceability. Second, we state several preservation properties of

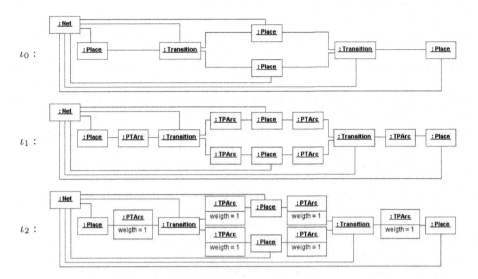

Fig. 3. Petri net instance co-evolution

transformations. This allows one to qualify an adaptation according to semantics-or instance-preservation. The co-adaptation of models is achieved automatically by co-transformations. Finally, adaptation scripts are pieces of software on their own. They can be reused in similar adaptation scenarios or be modified to alter adaptation decisions. Generalisations of those scripts define new transformations.

Structure of the Paper. In Section 2, the origins of our work, i.e. object-oriented refactoring and language engineering, are discussed. In Section 3, we present a set of binary metamodel relations. Based on these relations, we define several forms of semantics- and instance-preservation properties for metamodel transformations. In Section 4, we develop a set of QVT Relations that assist the evolution of MOF 2.0 compliant metamodels. In Section 5, we address co-evolution of models. In Section 6, we discuss the benefits of a transformational approach in the context of metamodel design, metamodel implementation, metamodel maintenance, and metamodel recovery. The paper is concluded in Section 7.

2   Background

In this section, we discuss the origins of our work. These are the refactoring of object-oriented software and the adaptation of context-free grammars.

2.1   Object-Oriented Refactoring

Refactoring Object-Oriented Code. Nowadays, software refactoring [11] is a common practice. It forms a central concept for agile development processes, e.g.

eXtreme Programming [12] and Rational Unified Process [13]. As the first author, Opdyke formalised refactorings for object-oriented frameworks concerned with behaviour preservation [5]. Roberts carried on these ideas and designed the Refactoring Browser for Smalltalk programs [6]. In another thesis, Bravo developed a method for automatic detection of design flaws in object-oriented software [14]. These *bad smells* advise refactorings between which a user can choose. Fowler et al. captured these ideas and common refactorings in a practical guide to improve the design of object-oriented code [7].

The refactoring of an object-oriented program might result in the evolution of the schema for persistent data. Thus, persistent data needs to co-evolve. The problem of schema evolution was tackled for object-oriented database management systems [15,16] as well as for object-oriented programs [17,18].

Refactoring UML Class Diagrams. Most examples in the book by Fowler et al. are illustrated by UML class diagrams. Boger et al. extended the idea of refactoring to UML models and developed a refactoring browser for UML diagrams [19]. Sunye et al. presented behaviour preserving refactorings for UML class and interaction diagrams [20]. Then, Markovic took OCL annotations in UML class diagrams into account [21]. He presented a set of QVT Relations for the refactoring of OCL annotated class diagrams. All these works address software development. Before, refactoring techniques dealt mainly with implementation code. Now, refactoring can be applied in the design of object oriented software, too. In the tradition of code refactoring, UML diagram refactoring is concerned with behaviour preservation.

MOF compliant metamodels are closely related to UML class diagrams. Since metamodels describe the structure of models, behaviour-preservation properties do not characterise metamodel refactoring accordingly. In this paper, we discuss semantics-preservation for such structural descriptions. We define semantics-preservation properties in terms of modelling concepts of a metamodel and its set of possible instances. Instance-preservation properties are useful to characterise co-evolution problems. Moreover, pure refactoring is insufficient to assist metamodel evolution. We extend structural metamodel refactoring with construction and destruction operators. Thereby, we rely on ideas from grammar engineering. These are discussed next.

2.2   Grammar Engineering

Grammar Adaptation. In their efforts to establish an engineering discipline for grammarware [22], Klint et al. suppose a transformational setting for stepwise grammar adaptation as a central concept. In his works, Lämmel gives a formalisation for this approach [8]. He develops several relations between grammars to characterise a framework of grammar transformations by its preservation properties. The framework proved to be valuable for the semi-formal recovery of a VS-Cobol-II grammar [23,9]. Besides work on generic refactorings [24,25], Lämmel suggests the approach to be applicable to any structure description formalism, e.g. algebraic type declarations or UML class diagrams. In this paper, we follow this suggestion and adopt these ideas for metamodels. We combine these ideas with object-oriented refactoring techniques to provide a transformation library for stepwise metamodel adaptation.

Co-adaptation. Co-adaptation is a well-known problem in grammar engineering. In format evolution, documents need to co-evolve with evolving structure descriptions [26]. Grammar transformation rules need to be migrated after grammar extension [27]. Lämmel stated the problem of coupled transformations in a more general context [10].

2.3 Metamodel Evolution

Metamodel evolution and coupled co-evolution of other software artefacts like constraints, transformation rules, and models are well-known problems in model-driven software development [2,28]. Hößler et al. propose a generic instance model to handle evolution on all meta levels [29]. Other approaches suppose difference models as a solution to handle co-evolution [30,31]. Metamodels are changed manually. Then, the difference to the last version is calculated. This difference model is used to derive automatic transformations for instance co-evolution.

In contrast to these approaches, we envision a transformational setting for stepwise metamodel adaptation. Each transformation implements a typical adaptation step typically performed manually. We classify these transformations according to preservation properties. Thus, the effect of each adaptation step is made explicit. Differences between metamodels are traceable without calculation. For each transformation, we provide corresponding co-transformations. Thereby, we provide instant co-adaptation of models. At each step these models conform to the actual metamodel version.

3 Preservation Properties

We are interested in preservation properties of metamodel transformations. We generalise ideas from grammar engineering [8] and define various metamodel relations starting from equivalence. In a next step, we employ these relations to define miscellaneous forms of semantics- and instance-preservation. Finally, we point out the correlation between semantics- and instance-preservation.

3.1 Metamodels

Though we deal particularly with MOF 2.0 metamodels in this paper, we do not rely on a concrete metamodel formalism in this section. Generally, the set of all metamodels conforming to a given metamodel formalism M is denoted as:

$$\mathcal{M}_M := \{\mu \models M\}$$

We use $\mathcal{C}_M(\mu)$ to denote the *concepts* defined by a metamodel $\mu \in \mathcal{M}_M$. For MOF 2.0 [3], we treat qualified names of non-abstract metaclasses as those concepts:

Definition 1 (MOF 2.0 concepts). *The set of* concepts $C_{MOF}(\mu)$ *defined by a MOF 2.0 compliant metamodel* $\mu \in \mathcal{M}_{MOF}$ *is the result of the OCL query*

```
Class.allInstances() ->
    reject(c | c.isAbstract) ->
      collect(c | c.qualifiedName)
```

The set of all *metamodel instances* conforming to a metamodel μ is denoted as:

$$\mathcal{I}(\mu) := \{\iota \models \mu\}$$

This set might be restricted to those instances relying only on a given set of concepts $\mathcal{C}$:

$$\mathcal{I}_\mathcal{C}(\mu) \subseteq \mathcal{I}(\mu)$$

Example 3 (Instance set restriction). In Figure 1, it holds

$$\mathcal{C}_{MOF}(\mu_4) = \{\texttt{Net}, \texttt{Place}, \texttt{Transition}, \texttt{PTArc}, \texttt{TPArc}\}$$
$$\mathcal{C}_{MOF}(\mu_5) = \mathcal{C}_{MOF}(\mu_4) \cup \{\texttt{Token}\}$$

The restriction of $\mathcal{I}(\mu_5)$ to instances only relying on concepts in $\mathcal{C}_{MOF}(\mu_4)$ yields all models not instantiating $\texttt{Token}$. These are exactly the instances of μ_4, i.e. it holds

$$\mathcal{I}_{\mathcal{C}_{MOF}(\mu_4)}(\mu_5) = \mathcal{I}(\mu_4)$$

Note that the suggested notion can be applied to a wider range of metamodel formalisms. For example, $\mathcal{M}_G$ might be the set of context-free grammars with $\mathcal{C}_G(\gamma)$ yielding the nonterminals occurring in a grammar γ.

3.2   Metamodel Relations

We now define some relations between metamodels. The metamodels presented in Figure 1 (cf. Example 1) exemplify these relations.

Definition 2 (Equivalence ($\equiv$)). $\mu_1 \in \mathcal{M}$ *and* $\mu_2 \in \mathcal{M}$ *are equivalent* ($\mu_1 \equiv \mu_2$) *iff:*

1. $\mathcal{I}(\mu_1) = \mathcal{I}(\mu_2)$.

In Figure 1, it holds $\mu_2 \equiv \mu_3$, since the abstract generalisation does not affect the set of instances. A less strict definition of equivalence can be obtained by claiming a bijective mapping between instance sets instead of equality.

Definition 3 (Variation relation ($\equiv_\varphi$)). $\mu_1 \in \mathcal{M}$ *and* $\mu_2 \in \mathcal{M}$ *are variants modulo* φ ($\mu_1 \equiv_\varphi \mu_2$) *iff:*

1. $\varphi : \mathcal{I}(\mu_1) \to \mathcal{I}(\mu_2)$ *is a bijective function.*

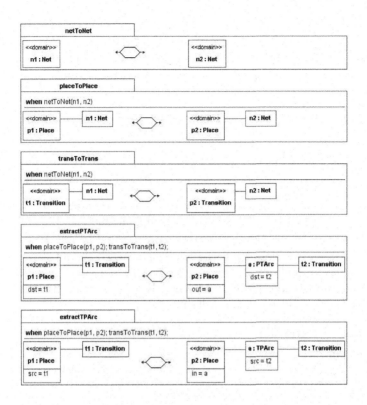

Fig. 4. Bidirectional transformation between model instances of μ_1 and μ_2

Variation is useful to characterise extraction and inlining of properties. For example, $\mu_1 \equiv_\varphi \mu_2$ applies to Figure 1 where φ is presented in Figure 4 as a set of QVT Relations. Equivalence and variation both relate metamodels with isomorphic sets of instances. This is often too restrictive to characterise related metamodels. We now define some relations between metamodels with non-isomorphic instance sets.

Definition 4 (Sub-metamodel relation ($\overset{\leq}{\equiv}$)). $\mu_1 \in \mathcal{M}$ *is a sub-metamodel of* $\mu_2 \in \mathcal{M}$ ($\mu_1 \overset{\leq}{\equiv} \mu_2$) *iff:*

1. $\mathcal{C}(\mu_1) \subseteq \mathcal{C}(\mu_2)$,
2. $\mathcal{I}(\mu_1) = \mathcal{I}_{\mathcal{C}(\mu_1)}(\mu_2)$.

A sub-metamodel offers only some of the concepts of its super-metamodel. The instance set of the super-metamodel is restricted to those instances, only instantiating concepts offered by the sub-metamodel. A sub-metamodel lacks only instances of its super-metamodel because of the lack of concepts. For example, in Figure 1, it holds $\mu_4 \overset{\leq}{\equiv} \mu_5$. A new metaclass **Token** is defined in μ_5. Instances of μ_5 instantiating this metaclass cannot be instances of μ_4. On the other hand, all instances of μ_5 not instantiating the new metaclass are instances of μ_4.

A super-metamodel allows for more instances by providing more concepts. In contrast, enrichment and extension are concerned with metamodels that provide the same concepts.

Definition 5 (Enrichment relation ($\stackrel{\subseteq}{\equiv}$)). $\mu_2 \in \mathcal{M}$ *is richer than* $\mu_1 \in \mathcal{M}$ $(\mu_1 \stackrel{\subseteq}{\equiv} \mu_2)$ *iff:*

1. $\mathcal{C}(\mu_1) = \mathcal{C}(\mu_2)$,
2. $\mathcal{I}(\mu_1) \subseteq \mathcal{I}(\mu_2)$.

A metamodel is richer than another one, if it has at least the same instance set and the same set of concepts. For MOF compliant metamodels, this is useful to characterise generalisation and restriction of properties. In Figure 1, it holds $\mu_1 \stackrel{\subseteq}{\equiv} \mu_0$. Both metamodels define the same metaclasses and all Petri net models conforming to μ_1 conform also to μ_0. Because μ_0 allows to model a Petri net without any transition or place, μ_0 is richer than μ_1 which restricts its instances to have at least one place and transition.

Definition 6 (Extension relation ($\stackrel{\subseteq}{\equiv}_\varphi$)). $\mu_2 \in \mathcal{M}$ *extends* $\mu_1 \in \mathcal{M}$ *by* φ $(\mu_1 \stackrel{\subseteq}{\equiv}_\varphi \mu_2)$ *iff:*

1. $\mathcal{C}(\mu_1) = \mathcal{C}(\mu_2)$,
2. $\varphi : \mathcal{I}(\mu_1) \to \mathcal{I}(\mu_2)$ *is an injective function.*

Extension does for enrichment what variation does for equivalence. The instances of the extended metamodel are not instances of the extension (as for enrichment), but they are mapped into the new instance set by an injection φ. In Figure 1, it holds $\mu_3 \stackrel{\subseteq}{\equiv}_\varphi \mu_4$. Instances of μ_3 are no longer instances of μ_4 because they do not provide the new mandatory weight for arcs. Nevertheless, those instances can be easily mapped into the new instance set by providing a default weight.

The relations presented so far are useful to characterise metamodel adaptation. To characterise co-adaptation, only the instance sets of two metamodels have to be considered. Therefore, we define two more metamodel relations.

Definition 7 (Instance-preservation relation ($\stackrel{\subseteq}{\equiv}$)). $\mu_2 \in \mathcal{M}$ *preserves instances of* $\mu_1 \in \mathcal{M}$ $(\mu_1 \stackrel{\subseteq}{\equiv} \mu_2)$ *iff:*

1. $\mathcal{I}(\mu_1) \subseteq \mathcal{I}(\mu_2)$.

Definition 8 (Instance-variation relation ($\stackrel{\subseteq}{\equiv}_\varphi$)). $\mu_2 \in \mathcal{M}$ *varies instances of* $\mu_1 \in \mathcal{M}$ *by* φ $(\mu_1 \stackrel{\subseteq}{\equiv}_\varphi \mu_2)$ *iff:*

1. $\varphi : \mathcal{I}(\mu_1) \to \mathcal{I}(\mu_2)$ *is an injective function.*

Again, we distinguish strict preservation and injection. The metamodel relations discussed so far correlate with both of these new relations.

Theorem 1 (Correlation of metamodel relations)

1. $\equiv \, \subset \, \overset{\sqsubset}{\equiv}$,
2. $\overset{\leq}{\equiv} \, \subset \, \overset{\sqsubset}{\equiv}$,
3. $\overset{\sqsubseteq}{\equiv} \, \subset \, \overset{\sqsubset}{\equiv}$,
4. $\equiv_\varphi \, \subset \, \overset{\sqsubset}{\equiv}_\varphi$,
5. $\overset{\sqsubseteq}{\equiv}_\varphi \, \subset \, \overset{\sqsubset}{\equiv}_\varphi$.

These correlations result directly from the definitions given in this section. For example, it holds $\mathcal{I}(\mu_1) = \mathcal{I}_{\mathcal{C}(\mu_1)}(\mu_2)$ for $\mu_1 \overset{\leq}{\equiv} \mu_2$ accordingly to Definition 4. This implies $\mathcal{I}(\mu_1) \subseteq \mathcal{I}(\mu_2)$ since a restriction of an instance set subsets the complete instance set (ref. Section 3.1). Thus, it follows $\mu_1 \overset{\sqsubset}{\equiv} \mu_2$ accordingly to Definition 7. Other correlations stated in Theorem 1 can be proven in a similar way.

3.3 Semantics-Preservation

We can now employ the metamodel relations defined so far in this section to define properties concerning semantics-preservation for metamodel transformations. We model a metamodel transformation as a relation between metamodels.

Definition 9 (Semantics-preservation properties). *A metamodel relation* $R \subset \mathcal{M} \times \mathcal{M}$ *is*

1. strictly semantics-preserving *iff* $R \subseteq \equiv$,
2. semantics-preserving modulo variation φ *iff* $R \subseteq \equiv_\varphi$,
3. introducing *iff* $R \subseteq \overset{\leq}{\equiv}$,
4. eliminating *iff* $R \subseteq \overset{\leq}{\equiv}^{-1}$,
5. increasing *iff* $R \subseteq \overset{\sqsubseteq}{\equiv}$,
6. decreasing *iff* $R \subseteq \overset{\sqsubseteq}{\equiv}^{-1}$,
7. increasing modulo variation φ *iff* $R \subseteq \overset{\sqsubseteq}{\equiv}_\varphi$,
8. decreasing modulo variation φ *iff* $R \subseteq \overset{\sqsubseteq}{\equiv}_{\varphi^{-1}}^{-1}$.

A metamodel transformation is *strictly semantics-preserving* iff it results always in an equivalent metamodel. It is *semantics-preserving modulo variation* iff it results always in a variant of the original metamodel. A transformation is *introducing* (respectively *eliminating*) iff it results always in a super-metamodel (respectively sub-metamodel) of its input. It is *increasing* (respectively *decreasing*) iff its result is always richer (respectively less rich) than its input metamodel. The transformation is *introducing modulo variation* iff its result is always an extension of the original metamodel. Respectively, it is *eliminating modulo variation* iff the original metamodel is always an extension of the result.

In the next section of the paper, we present a library of transformations between MOF compliant metamodels which separate these preservation properties.

3.4   Instance-Preservation

Semantics-preservation properties characterise metamodel transformations accordingly to the offered modelling concepts and possible instances. With respect to the need for co-adaptation, we need to characterise the preservation of existing instances. We now define some properties concerning instance-preservation.

Definition 10 (Instance-preservation properties). *A metamodel relation* $R \subset \mathcal{M} \times \mathcal{M}$ *is*

1. strictly instance-preserving *iff* $R \subseteq \overset{\sqsubset}{\equiv}$,
2. partially instance-preserving *iff* $R \subseteq \overset{\sqsubset}{\equiv}^{-1}$,
3. instance-preserving modulo variation φ *iff* $R \subseteq \overset{\sqsubset}{\equiv}_{\varphi}$,
4. partially instance-preserving modulo variation φ *iff* $R \subseteq \overset{\sqsubset}{\equiv}_{\varphi^{-1}}^{-1}$,

A transformation is *strictly instance-preserving* iff its result preserves always the instances of the original metamodel. It is *partially instance-preserving* iff all instances of the resulting metamodel are always preserved instances of the input metamodel. The transformation is *instance-preserving modulo variation* iff its result always varies the instances of the original metamodel. It is *partially instance-preserving modulo variation* iff all instances of the resulting metamodel are always varied instances of the input metamodel.

Due to Theorem 1, semantics-preservation properties imply a certain instance-preservation property.

Theorem 2 (Correlation of preservation properties). *A metamodel relation* $R \subset \mathcal{M} \times \mathcal{M}$ *is*

1. strictly instance-preserving *if it is* strictly semantics-preserving, introducing, *or* increasing;
2. partially instance-preserving *if it is* eliminating, *or* decreasing;
3. instance-preserving modulo variation φ *if it is* semantics-preserving modulo variation φ, *or* increasing modulo variation φ;
4. partially instance-preserving modulo variation φ *if it is* decreasing modulo variation φ.

In the remainder of the paper, we will use instance-preservation properties to identify co-adaptation scenarios. There are two cases where co-adaptation is necessary. First, a variation φ hints a co-adaptation. Second, partial instance-preservation might be extended to complete instance-preservation.

4   Transformational Adaptation of MOF Compliant Metamodels

4.1   Overview

In this section, we present a transformation library for the stepwise adaptation of MOF compliant metamodels. The transformations separate

Table 1. Semantics-preservation properties of presented transformations

Adaptation	Semantics-preservation	Inverse
Refactoring		
rename element	preserving modulo variation	rename element
move property	preserving modulo variation	move property
extract class	preserving modulo variation	inline class
inline class	preserving modulo variation	extract class
association to class	preserving modulo variation	class to association
class to association	preserving modulo variation	association to class
Construction		
introduce class	introducing	eliminate class
introduce property	increasing modulo variation	eliminate property
generalise property	increasing	restrict property
pull property	increasing modulo variation	push property
extract superclass	introducing	flatten hierarchy
Destruction		
eliminate class	eliminating	introduce class
eliminate property	decreasing modulo variation	introduce property
restrict property	decreasing	generalise property
push property	decreasing modulo variation	pull property
flatten hierarchy	eliminating	extract superclass

semantics-preservation properties introduced in the last section. Thereby, we can distinguish three kinds of transformations. First, we identify transformations for semantics-preserving (by variation) refactoring. Second, introducing and increasing transformations assist metamodel construction. Finally, eliminating and decreasing transformations allow for metamodel destruction. Table 1 groups the transformations presented in this section by this classification. It also gives semantics-preservation properties and inverse transformations.

We give the transformations as QVT Relations [4]. Thereby, we use its graphical notation. In the remainder of this section, we discuss each transformation in detail. We start with constructors and accordant destructors. Since most transformations for refactoring rely on construction and destruction, they are presented subsequently.

4.2 Construction and Destruction

Introduce/Eliminate Class. Introducing a new metaclass into a package is a common step in metamodel construction [5]. Figure 5 shows an implementation of this adaptation. As a precondition, elements in the package must be distinguishable and the package must not own the metaclass already. Afterwards, the package owns the metaclass while elements in the package must stay distinguishable.

In general, this adaptation is *introducing*. The new metaclass offers a new concept and allows thereby for new instances. Instances of other metaclasses are not affected. If the new metaclass is abstract, the adaptation is *strictly semantics-preserving* since the set of instances persists.

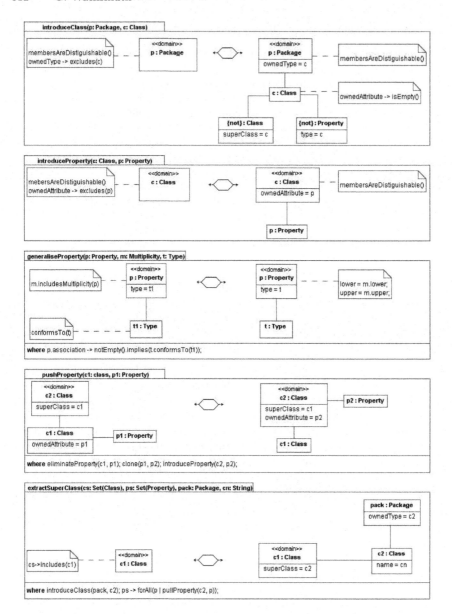

Fig. 5. QVT Relations implementing metamodel construction and destruction

The QVT Relation presented in Figure 5 can also be applied right-to-left. This way, a metaclass is eliminated from a package. Afterwards, elements in the package are still distinguishable and the package does not own the metaclass anymore. As a precondition, the metaclass must not have any subclasses and it must not be referred by other classes. This ensures the elimination is reversible by introducing the metaclass. Thus, the adaptation is *strictly semantics-preserving* particularly for abstract metaclasses and *eliminating* in general.

Introduce/Eliminate Property. Introducing a new property into a metaclass is another common metamodel construction [5]. Its implementation as shown in Figure 5 is quite similar to the one for introducing a new metaclass. As a pre- and postcondition, elements from the namespace defined by the metaclass must be distinguishable. Thus, the new property is distinguishable from other properties owned by the metaclass itself or its superclasses.

Only for the particular case of an abstract metaclass without non-abstract subclasses, this adaptation is *strictly semantics-preserving*. In general, it is *increasing modulo variation* since the concerned metaclass and its subclasses allow for new instances. Only instances of the concerned metaclass and its subclasses are affected. Variation is needed if the property introduced is obligatory. This can be achieved by providing a default value for the property introduced.

Again, the relation can be applied right-to-left eliminating a property from a metaclass. Once more, *strict semantics-preservation* holds only for an abstract metaclass without non-abstract subclasses. The destruction is generally *decreasing modulo variation*. Variation can be performed by eliminating all slots of the property.

Generalise/Restrict Property. Property generalisation and restriction are two adaptations we adopt from grammar adaptation [8]. A property can be generalised or restricted in terms of its multiplicity and its type. As the implementation in Figure 5 states, types of association ends must not be generalised since this would affect both association ends.

Generalising a property is an *increasing* adaptation. Without offering new concepts, it allows for new instances. Old instances are not affected, so co-adaptation is not needed. Contrarily, restricting a property is *decreasing*. Some of the old instances will meet the restriction. Other instances need to be co-adapted. Restricting the upper bound of the multiplicity requires a selection of certain values. This can be achieved automatically. Restricting the lower bound requires new values for the property usually provided manually. Restricting the type of a property requires type conversion for each value.

Pull/Push Property. Pushing a property into subclasses respectively pulling a property into a subclass are well known object-oriented refactorings [5,7]. An implementation realising both of them is given in Figure 5. To push a property into subclasses, the property is eliminated in the superclass[1] and a clone of it is introduced in each subclass.

Combining decreasing elimination and increasing introduction, this adaptation is generally *decreasing modulo variation*. Only for abstract superclasses, it is *strictly semantics-preserving*. Otherwise, instances of the superclass are affected by elimination. Instances of subclasses are not affected. Co-adaptation can be performed as for property elimination.

---

[1] Here, `eliminateProperty` refers a right-to-left execution of `introduceProperty`.

As the inverse adaptation, pulling a property into the superclass can be performed by right-to-left execution. Thereby, the property is introduced into the superclass and its clones in the subclasses are eliminated.

For non-abstract superclasses, the adaptation is *increasing modulo variation*. In this general case, the superclass allows for new instances. Co-adaptation is needed only for old instances of the superclass. As for property introduction, this can be done by providing a default value.

Extract Superclass/Flatten Hierarchy. Superclass extraction and its counterpart of hierarchy flattening are other well-known object-oriented refactorings [5,7]. Figure 5 gives an implementation for superclass extraction. The transformation extracts a set of properties common to a set of classes into a new superclass. This metaclass is introduced into a specified package. Then, each property is pulled into the new superclass. In another implementation the new superclass might be integrated into the class hierarchy.

This adaptation would be *strictly semantics-preserving* for an abstract superclass. However, to use the implementation right-to-left to flatten hierarchy we abstain from this restriction. Thus, preservation properties can be derived from class introduction. The adaptation is *introducing* since the superclass offers a new concept. Since instances of the subclasses are not affected, no co-adaptation is needed. On the other hand, flatten hierarchy by eliminating a superclass and pushing all its properties into the subclasses is an *eliminating* adaptation. Instances of the subclasses are preserved.

4.3 Refactoring

Rename Element. Element renaming is a very simple and common refactoring [5,7]. In Figure 6, we present a QVT implementation. As a precondition, elements in each namespace of the element to rename need to be distinguishable. As a postcondition, this still holds after renaming.

The adaptation is *semantics-preserving modulo variation*. Co-adaptation is achieved automatically by a simple mapping from the old element to the renamed one.

Move Property. Moving a property is another simple refactoring. In contrast to the refactoring presented by Fowler et al. [7], we follow Opdyke [5] by moving a property along a one-to-one association as shown in Figure 6. The implementation simply eliminates the property from the source metaclass and introduces it in the target metaclass.

This adaptation is *semantics-preserving modulo variation*. Instances of the affected metaclass can be automatically co-adapted by moving property values along the link between instances of source and target metaclasses.

Extract/Inline Class. Extraction and inlining are generic refactorings [24]. In object-oriented refactoring, properties are extracted along generalisation or delegation. We already mentioned extraction along generalisation as superclass extraction. Extraction along delegation is often referred to as class extraction [5,7].

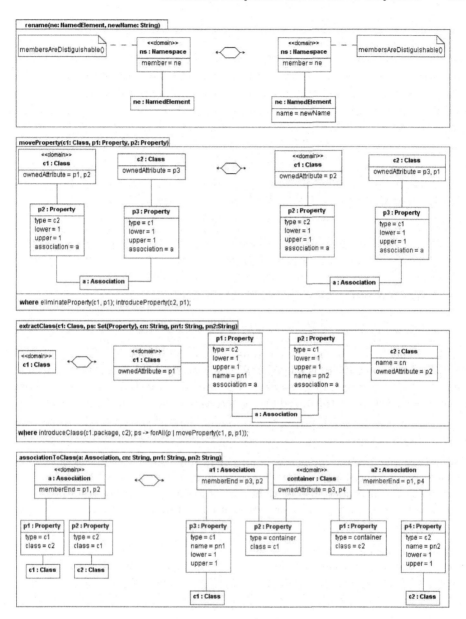

Fig. 6. QVT Relations implementing metamodel refactoring

An implementation is given in Figure 6. To extract a set of properties, a new metaclass is introduced. Then, a one-to-one association between this container class and the affected metaclass is established. Finally, the properties are moved along this association into the new class. Extraction of an association between two classes into a new class is a similar refactoring. An implementation is also given in Figure 6.

Both extractions are *semantics-preserving modulo variation*. Instances of the affected metaclasses can be automatically co-adapted by instantiating the container class, linking the affected instances with this new instance, and moving property values into the container instance.

As the inverse transformations, class inlining is achieved by right-to-left execution. Both adaptations are *semantics-preserving modulo variation* as well. Co-adaptation is performed as right-to-left extraction co-adaptation.

5   Co-adaptation of Models

In the last section, we presented metamodel transformations for stepwise metamodel adaptation. Thereby, we touched already on co-adaptation of models. We now discuss co-adaptation of models in detail.

5.1   Transformation Patterns

Like metamodel adaptation, we exploit transformations to describe model co-adaptation. A co-transformation depends on its triggering metamodel transformation. Therefore, we describe co-transformations by transformation patterns. A transformation pattern is a QVT Relation with parameters for metamodel elements, e.g. metaclasses or properties. A metamodel transformation instantiates a co-transformation pattern to derive a corresponding co-transformation.

Example 4 (Transformation pattern). It its left part, Figure 7 shows a co-transformation pattern for property introduction. It contains three parameters: C for the affected metaclass, P for the introduced property, and Query for a OCL query specifying a value. These parameters are instantiated by a concrete property introduction. The right part of Figure 7 shows the resulting QVT Relation for introducing a property age into a metaclass Person.

5.2   Co-construction

Introduce property and *pull property* are the only constructors concerned with co-adaptation. Instances of the affected metaclass become invalid if a

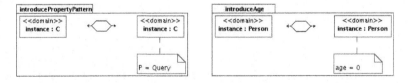

Fig. 7. Co-transformation pattern for property introduction

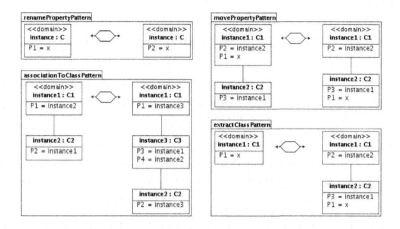

Fig. 8. Transformation patterns for model co-refactoring

mandatory property is introduced. Therefore, co-adaptation needs to introduce a value for the new property into each instance of the metaclass. The according co-transformation pattern was given in Figure 7. The corresponding metamodel transformation can instantiate the pattern with the affected metaclass and the introduced property. Furthermore, the user has to specify an OCL query providing a value for the introduced property.

Due to Theorem 2, all other constructors are *strictly instance-preserving*. Thus, co-adaptation is needless.

5.3 Co-refactoring

All refactoring transformations are *semantics-preserving modulo variation* and thereby *instance-preserving modulo variation*. We present co-transformation patterns for each transformation in Figure 8. For *rename element*, we give an implementation for property renaming. Implementations for the renaming of other elements are quite similar. To preserve the instances of the metamodel, instances of the renamed element are mapped onto instances of the the new named element.

Co-adaptation for *move property* preserves instances by moving values of the property along a link that instantiates the association from the adaptation. For *extract class*, an instance of the container class is created additionally. The same co-adaptation can be used right-to-left for *inline class*. Co-adaptation for *association to class* and its inverse is similar to this.

5.4 Co-destruction

Eliminate class and *flatten hierarchy* are *partially instance-preserving* destructors. Thus, some metamodel instances are preserved. These are all those metamodel instances that do not contain instances of the eliminated class. Co-adaptation for the remaining metamodel instances is achieved by removing instances of the class from these models. We deal with *eliminate property* and *push property* in a similar way. Both destructors are *partially instance-preserving by variation*. To co-adapt metamodel instances, slots of the eliminated property are removed from objects occurring in a model.

Automatic co-adaptation for the *instance-preserving* destructor *restrict property* is somewhat more difficult. If the upper bound of the property is restricted, metamodel instances containing objects that exceed this bound need to be co-adapted. This can be done automatically by removing elements until the upper bound is met. The user might assist this by an OCL query specifying preserved elements. For lower bound restrictions, new values are needed to co-adapt models containing objects that fall short of this bound. As for *introduce property*, new values are specified by an OCL query given by the user. Considering type restriction, things get even more complicated. A pragmatic approach is to remove all mistyped elements from objects in a co-adapted model. This might introduce lower bound shortfalls. New values might overcome this problem. Again, these values are specified by the user in terms of an OCL query. This query can take the mistyped elements into account. Thus, these elements might be casted to the restricted type in a user defined way. In a somehow simpler approach, co-adaptation is completely deferred to the user. In this case, the user specifies in an OCL query new elements for affected slots in terms of old elements.

6   Applications

6.1   Metamodel Design

The transformational approach facilitates a well-defined stepwise metamodel design. Starting from basic features, new features are introduced by construction. Exhaustive usage of this principle leads to an agile process. Refactoring enables generalisation of metamodel features. This way, common concepts become explicit. Construction allows to reuse these concepts by specialisation. Generalisation and specialisation permit a pattern-based metamodel design [32]. Furthermore, scripts of consecutive adaptation steps document design decisions. By changing particular steps, metamodel designers can alternate designs.

6.2   Metamodel Implementation

Metamodel-dependent model processors, e.g. editors, compilers, simulators, debuggers, code generators, documentation generators, or pretty-printers, should be generated semi-automatically. This ensures conformance between tools and metamodels. Metamodel erosion is avoided [2]. Grammar-based tool generators are well known for specification languages relying on restricted grammar formalisms, e.g. by prohibiting left recursion. To use such generators, language engineers need to develop compliant versions of their grammars. The same phenomenon is observable for metamodel-based tool generators and metamodelling tools in general. The MOF specification [3] itself provides two different metametamodels, i.e. Essential MOF (EMOF) as a minimal specification and

Complete MOF (CMOF) as an extension to the former one. Several metamodelling tools rely on their own metametamodels, e.g. the Eclipse Modeling Framework on Ecore [33], Kermeta on the Kermeta language [34], and the ATLAS Transformation Language on KM3 [35]. To use these tools, metamodels need to comply to these metametamodels. Refactoring ensures equivalence to original versions. According to the tool, one can switch between metamodel variations. Co-adaptation ensures preservation of models.

6.3 Metamodel Refinement

In [36], Staikopoulos and Bordbar propose a method called *One Step Refinement* for bridging technical spaces or domains. The authors suggest a successive refinement of the target metamodel to meet a richer source metamodel. In each step, the target model is extended by a new concept which is constructed out of old concepts. The process is repeated until an extension is created, such that all concepts of the source metamodel can be easily mapped into concepts of the extended target metamodel. As a side effect, an overall transformation from the source metamodel to the original target metamodel is derived.

The transformational setting presented in this paper assist this approach. The target metamodel is extended by introducing new concepts while the overall transformation can be derived from co-transformations.

6.4 Metamodel Maintenance

Like other software, metamodels are subject to maintenance. This includes remedying defects, reengineering to improve design, and meeting changes in requirements. Metamodel maintenance also benefits from a transformational setting. Erroneous features can be corrected by construction and destruction. Due to the local character of transformations, other features stay unchanged. Refactoring provides for reengineering a metamodel design without introducing defects. Scripts of adaptation steps can be adapted and reused in a similar context. Generalisation of those scripts leads to definitions for new transformations. This can be used to implement common redesigns, e.g. subsequent introduction of patterns [32]. Construction and destruction assist adjustment to changing requirements.

6.5 Metamodel Recovery

Often, language knowledge resides only in language-dependent tools or semiformal language references. Language recovery is concerned with the derivation of a formal language specification from such sources. This comprises both, grammar recovery [23] and metamodel recovery [2]. For grammar recovery, a transformational approach already proved to be valuable [8]. In a similar way, the presented transformational setting assists metamodel recovery.

7   Conclusion

Contribution. In this paper, we combined ideas from object-oriented refactoring and grammar adaptation to provide a basis for automatic metamodel evolution. We defined several relations between metamodels to characterise metamodel evolution. These were employed to deduce properties for semantics- and instance-preservation of metamodel transformations. We do not restrict metamodel relations and preservation properties to object-oriented, e.g. MOF compliant, metamodels. The notions presented are useful for other structural descriptions, e.g. grammars, as well. Furthermore, we presented a set of QVT Relations to assist automatic metamodel evolution by stepwise adaptation. The transformations were classified in three groups accordingly to their preservation properties, namely refactoring, construction, and destruction. Implementation and preservation properties were discussed for each transformation. The problem of co-evolution was stated. It was shown how automatic co-adaptation can solve this problem for metamodel instances.

To prove the relevance of our work, we proposed applications in metamodel design, metamodel implementation, metamodel refinement, and metamodel recovery.

Future Work. From a theoretical point of view, we will focus our ongoing research on the evolution and co-evolution of constraints and transformation rules. Another interesting topic will be the question when a metamodel needs to be adapted. In our practical work, we concentrate on two prototypical implementations. Furthermore, we employ our transformational approach for metamodel-based development of domain-specific languages. In a practical setting, we need to deal with several versions of metamodels and models. This is another interesting research topic. We will now discuss each of the topics mentioned more in detail.

Evolution of Constraints and Transformations. In this paper, we were concerned with co-adaptation of models. Constraints and transformation rules also co-evolve triggered by metamodel evolution. Furthermore, constraints and transformation rules evolve on their own. Constraints might be adapted to be more or less restrictive. Transformation patterns might be adapted to match more or less instances. Again, a library supporting automatic stepwise adaptation while guaranteeing certain preservation properties will be valuable. For metamodel adaptation, it would be interesting to express co-adaptation in terms of this library.

The Smell of Structure. As stated in the subtitle of the book by Fowler et al. [7], one of the main goals in object-oriented refactoring is to improve the design of existing code. Often, a refactoring is indicated by a bad smell [14], e.g. duplicate code, long methods, or message chains. These smells are almost all code-centric. For metamodel evolution, we are concerned with the question if structure can indicate an adaptation. How does structure smell? Works on object-oriented metrics [37,38,39] might be a good starting point for further research.

Tool Support. Our first attempts to provide a prototypical implementation relying on ModelMorf [40] failed due to missing support for in-place transformations. We are now working with an implementation of QVT's relational part provided by ikv [41], an industrial partner of our research group. The implementation was applied in a project between ikv and the biggest consumer electronic vendor in Korea in the area of embedded systems for in-place model to model transformations. The implementation was ported by ikv to the Eclipse Modeling Framework (EMF) [33]. This enables us to make metamodel adaptation available for EMF.

Furthermore, we started a prototypical implementation providing metamodel adaptation for CMOF. This tool is implemented as an Eclipse plugin in Java. It is built upon a Java implementation of CMOF [42] and the Eclipse Language Toolkit.

For both tools, we envision four editing modes for metamodels: First, a *free mode* allows for arbitrary manual changes. Second, an *adaptation mode* allows only for transformational adaptation. Third, a *construction mode* restricts the user to construction and refactoring. Finally, a *refactoring mode* is even more restrictive and allows only for refactoring.

DSL Development. We started to employ an adaptive development process for domain-specific languages based on metamodels. In our work, we are concerned with languages from the domain of disaster management [43]. We are working on two case studies. The first study is concerned with the development of a new language. Metamodel adaptation is used to develop alternative designs, to meet requirement changes, and to maintain the language. The second study is concerned with language recovery. Metamodel adaptation is used to capture implicit language knowledge explicitly in a metamodel.

Versioning. In a practical setting, one has to deal with several metamodel versions. For each metamodel version different model versions need to be taken into account. Co-adaptation might affect all these model versions. On the other hand, only few versions of a model might indicate a metamodel adaptation leading to a new metamodel version. Finally, co-adaptation might join different model versions. Thus, further research is needed to integrate metamodel adaptation with versioning approaches [44].

Acknowledgement. This work is supported by grants from the DFG (German Research Foundation, Graduiertenkolleg METRIK). I am grateful to Eckardt Holz, Ralf Lämmel, Daniel Sadilek, and Markus Scheidgen for encouraging discussion, and for helpful suggestions. I am also thankful to Dirk Fahland, Lena Karg, and Falko Theisselmann for comments on earlier versions of this paper.

References

1. Object Management Group: MDA Guide Version 1.0.1 (2003)
2. Favre, J.M.: Meta-model and model co-evolution within the 3D software space. In: ELISA'03: Proceedings of the International Workshop on Evolution of Large-scale Industrial Software Applications, Amsterdam, The Netherlands, pp. 98–109 (2003)

3. Object Management Group: Meta Object Facility Core Specification, version 2.0 (2006)
4. Object Management Group: MOF QVT Final Adopted Specification (2005)
5. Opdyke, W.F.: Refactoring Object-Oriented Frameworks. PhD thesis, University of Illinois at Urbana-Champaign, Champaign, IL, USA (1992)
6. Roberts, D.B.: Practical Analysis for Refactoring. PhD thesis, University of Illinois at Urbana-Champaign, Champaign, IL, USA (1999)
7. Fowler, M., Beck, K., Brant, J., Opdyke, W.F., Roberts, D.B.: Refactoring: Improving the Design of Existing Code. Addison-Wesley Professional, Redwood City,CA, USA (1999)
8. Lämmel, R.: Grammar adaptation. In: Oliveira, J.N., Zave, P. (eds.) FME 2001. LNCS, vol. 2021, pp. 550–570. Springer, Heidelberg (2001)
9. Lämmel, R., Wachsmuth, G.: Transformation of SDF syntax definitions in the ASF+SDF Meta-Environment. Electronical Notes in Theoretical Computer Science 44 (2001)
10. Lämmel, R.: Coupled software transformations (extended abstract). In: SET '04: 1st International Workshop on Software Evolution Transformations, Proceedings, pp. 31–35 (2004)
11. Mens, T., Tourwé, T.: A survey of software refactoring. IEEE Trans. Software Eng. 30 (2004)
12. Beck, K.: Extreme Programming Explained: Embrace Change. Addison-Wesley, London, UK (2000)
13. Kruchten, P.: The Rational Unified Process: An Introduction. Addison-Wesley, London, UK (2004)
14. Bravo, F.M.: A Logic Meta-Programming Framework for Supporting the Refactoring Process. PhD thesis, Vrije Universiteit Brussel, Belgium (2003)
15. Banerjee, J., Kim, W., Kim, H.J., Korth, H.F.: Semantics and implementation of schema evolution in object-oriented databases. SIGMOD Rec. 16, 311–322 (1987)
16. Nguyen, G.T., Rieu, D.: Schema evolution in object-oriented database systems. Data Knowl. Eng. 4, 43–67 (1989)
17. Dmitriev, M.: Safe Class and Data Evolution in Large and Long-Lived Java Applications. PhD thesis, University of Glasgow (2001)
18. Meyer, B.: Schema evolution: Concepts, terminology, and solutions. Computer 29, 119–121 (1996)
19. Boger, M., Sturm, T., Fragemann, P.: Refactoring browser for UML. In: Aksit, M., Mezini, M., Unland, R. (eds.) NODe 2002. LNCS, vol. 2591, pp. 336–377. Springer, Heidelberg (2003)
20. Sunye, G., Pollet, D., Traon, Y.L., Jezequel, J.M.: Refactoring UML models. In: Gogolla, M., Kobryn, C. (eds.) UML 2001 – The Unified Modeling Language. Modeling Languages, Concepts, and Tools. LNCS, vol. 2185, pp. 134–148. Springer, Heidelberg (2001)
21. Markovic, S., Baar, T.: Refactoring OCL annotated UML class diagrams. In: Briand, L.C., Williams, C. (eds.) MoDELS 2005. LNCS, vol. 3713, pp. 280–294. Springer, Heidelberg (2005)
22. Klint, P., Lämmel, R., Verhoef, C.: Toward an engineering discipline for grammarware. ACM Transactions on Software Engineering and Methodology (TOSEM) 14, 331–380 (2005)
23. Lämmel, R., Verhoef, C.: Semi-automatic grammar recovery. Softw. Pract. Exper. 31, 1395–1438 (2001)

24. Lämmel, R.: Towards generic refactoring. In: RULE '02: Proceedings of the 2002 ACM SIGPLAN workshop on Rule-based programming, pp. 15–28. ACM Press, New York (2002)
25. Heering, J., Lämmel, R.: Generic software transformations (extended abstract). In: Proceedings of the Software Transformation Systems Workshop (2004)
26. Lämmel, R., Lohmann, W.: Format evolution. In: Kouloumdjian, J., Mayr, H.C., Erkollar, A. (eds.) RETIS '01: 7th International Conference on Re-Technologies for Information Systems, Proceedings. vol. 155 of books@ocg.at. OCG, 2001, pp. 113–134 (2001)
27. Lohmann, W., Riedewald, G.: Towards automatical migration of transformation rules after grammar extension. In: CSMR '03: 7th European Conference on Software Maintenance and Reengineering, Benevento, Italy, Proceedings, pp. 30–39. IEEE Computer Society Press, Los Alamitos (2003)
28. Deng, G., Lenz, G., Schmidt, D.C.: Addressing domain evolution challenges in software product lines. In: Bruel, J.-M. (ed.) MoDELS 2005. LNCS, vol. 3844, pp. 247–261. Springer, Heidelberg (2006)
29. Hößler, J., Soden, M., Eichler, H.: Coevolution of models, metamodels and transformations. In: Bab, S., Gulden, J., Noll, T., Wieczorek, T. (eds.) Models and Human Reasoning, pp. 129–154. Wissenschaft und Technik Verlag, Berlin (2005)
30. Hearnden, D.: Software evolution with the model driven architecture (PhD Confirmation report)
31. Gruschko, B.: Towards structured revisions of metamodels and semi-automatic model migration. In: Position Paper for the Eclipse Modeling Symposium (2006)
32. France, R., Ghosh, S., Song, E., Kim, D.K.: A metamodeling approach to pattern-based model refactoring. IEEE Software 20, 52–58 (2003)
33. Budinsky, F., Merks, E., Steinberg, D.: Eclipse Modeling Framework, 2nd edn. Addison-Wesley, London, UK (2006)
34. Fleurey, F., Drey, Z., Vojtisek, D., Faucher, C.: Kermeta language (2006)
35. Jouault, F., Bézivin, J.: KM3: A DSL for metamodel specification. In: Gorrieri, R., Wehrheim, H. (eds.) FMOODS 2006. LNCS, vol. 4037, pp. 171–185. Springer, Heidelberg (2006)
36. Staikopoulos, A., Bordbar, B.: Bridging technical spaces with a metamodel refinement approach. A BPEL to PN case study. Electronical Notes in Theoretical Computer Science (2006)
37. Lorenz, M., Kidd, J. (eds.): Object-oriented software metrics: a practical guide. Object-Oriented Series. Prentice-Hall, Upper Saddle River, NJ, USA (1994)
38. Henderson-Sellers, B.: Object-Oriented Metrics: Measures of Complexity. Object-Oriented Series. Prentice-Hall, Upper Saddle River, NJ, USA (1995)
39. Lanza, M., Marinescu, R.: Object-Oriented Metrics in Practice: Using Software Metrics to Characterize, Evaluate, and Improve the Design of Object-Oriented Systems. Springer, Heidelberg (2006)
40. TATA Research Development and Design Centre: ModelMorf: A model transformer (available at http://www.tcs-trddc.com/ModelMorf/)
41. ikv: Company home page. ⟨http://www.ikv.de⟩
42. Scheidgen, M.: CMOF-model semantics and language mapping for MOF 2.0 implementation. In: Machado, R.J., Fernandes, J.M., Riebisch, M., Schätz, B. (eds.) Joint Meeting of the 4th Workshop on Model-Based Development of Computer Based Systems (MBD) and 3rd International Workshop on Model-based Methodologies for Pervasive and Embedded Software (MOMPES), 13th Annual IEEE International Conference and Workshop on the Engineering of Computer Based Systems (ECBS), Proceedings, IEEE Computer Society, Los Alamitos (2006)

43. Sadilek, D., Theisselmann, F., Wachsmuth, G.: Challenges for model-driven development of self-organising disaster management information systems. In: Happe, J., Koziolek, H., Rohr, M., Storm, C., Warns, T. (eds.) IRTGW'06: Proceedings of the International Research Training Groups Workshop, Dagstuhl, Germany. vol. 3 of Trustworthy Software Systems. Berlin, pp. 24–26 (2006)
44. Object Management Group: MOF 2.0 Versioning Final Adopted Specification (2005)

Author Index

Lecture Notes in Computer Science

For information about Vols. 1–4525

please contact your bookseller or Springer